Walkin' Lawton

Chiles on the Walk, 1970. Courtesy of Florida Photographic Collection, State Archives & Library of Florida.

John Dos Passos Coggin

WALKIN' LAWTON

Cover design concept by Chris Brotemarkle

ISBN 10: 1-886104-58-1
ISBN 13: 978-1-886104-58-7

The Florida Historical Society Press
435 Brevard Avenue
Cocoa, FL 32922
www.myfloridahistory.org/fhspress

P•R•E•S•S

This book is dedicated to my maternal grandfather, John Dos Passos.

Table of Contents

Publisher's Note

Lawton Chiles was one of the most inspirational and influential politicians to come from Florida. His unique campaign style and passion for improving people's lives established a legacy that deserves recognition today. John Dos Passos Coggin conducted more than one hundred interviews with the family, friends, and co-workers of Lawton Chiles to create this definitive biography. Coggin's insightful writing based on extensive research illuminates both the political career and personal life of the fascinating Lawton Chiles. The Florida Historical Society Press is proud to publish this important new work.

The state of Florida changed radically during Lawton Chiles' lifetime, growing from the thirty-fifth most populous state to the fourth largest. This influx of new residents significantly increased Florida's political influence. Today, Florida is one of a handful of "swing states" that determine the outcome of our country's presidential elections. During his four decade political career in the Florida House of Representatives, the Florida State Senate, the United States Senate, and as a two-term Governor of the state, Lawton Chiles helped Florida deal with the many problems that accompany sudden growth and shaped national policies.

Lawton Chiles' efforts to reform health care sparked a national debate that continues raging today. The successful "Truth" campaign that discourages teen smoking is the result of Chiles' litigation against the tobacco industry. He championed transparency in government resulting in important legislation. His very frugal campaigns, which were always successful, are models for backers of campaign finance reform. It is interesting to note that many of the areas where Lawton Chiles made great progress during the last half of the twentieth century remain issues not fully resolved by our nation's political leaders. Chiles' life and career, as carefully chronicled by John Dos Passos Coggin, are an inspiration for both politicians and voters today.

John Dos Passos Coggin is a writer and political strategist who graduated from Yale University and completed his graduate studies at the University of Maryland College Park. His articles have appeared in the *Tampa Bay Times,* the *Baltimore Sun,* and the *Florida Times-Union.* He is the maternal grandson of John Dos Passos, the acclaimed novelist best known for his *U.S.A.* trilogy. With *Walkin' Lawton,* Coggin has created a work that serves as both a scholarly study of an exceptional political career and the personal story of a unique individual who was the product of his Florida roots.

Dr. Ben Brotemarkle
Executive Director
Florida Historical Society
October 2012

Preface

My path to this biography of Lawton Chiles began in Orlando, Florida, in the summer of 2004. There I learned of the Florida politician's famous 1,000-mile walk across his state. I learned that his boots from "The Walk" were on display in the Florida State Capitol.

The legend of "Walkin' Lawton" stayed with me through college and after. The song of his populism was thrilling and original.

"People are people everywhere," Chiles concluded, having walked halfway across Florida for his 1970 U.S. Senate campaign. "They like to talk politics; they like a politician who will listen to their ideas and concerns. They like the walk."

In his walking campaign newsletters,[1] Chiles told of meeting Floridians old and young, rich and poor, black and white. It was Chiles' mission on the campaign trail to record their stories—the human capital that was key to victory.

"This walking-talking effort," he observed soon after beginning on foot, "may be the hardest way to campaign, but I'm convinced it's the best way for me to get to know the people and their problems and for them to get to know me. When I complete this walk, I'll have a gut-knowledge about this state that no other candidate for any office can possibly have."[2]

One of the most significant impacts of the Walk was a shift in the candidate's position on the Vietnam War. While walking near Live Oak, Chiles reported that he had always considered himself a hawk before the campaign, but he'd come to believe the United States should pull out of Vietnam: "President Nixon has now said that we are not seeking a military victory. If we are not going to seek to win, then I think we should get our troops out as soon as possible."

Chiles, I discovered during my research, was a political and cultural treasure—his life story deserved to be told. As a state legislator, governor, and U.S. senator during a forty-year career in public service, he was an evolutionary figure in Florida history.

Chiles was born at a time when alligators outnumbered people in Florida. His hometown of Lakeland, an isolated block of neighborhoods in an isolated state, shaped his boyhood beliefs. At the age of ten, he fell in love with politics in the town square. Hunting trips and fish camps developed his affection and respect for nature. Stories of Florida's pioneers, told around the campfire, lifted his spirits. He wanted to sustain the strong oral traditions of his forbears.

He knew, however, that the Lakeland of his youth—a tiny bastion of phosphate miners, citrus growers, and Ku Klux Klan chieftains—had limited his worldview on race, foreign policy and other issues crucial for a modern statesman.

His 1970 campaign for the U.S. Senate first signaled his desire for true evolution. Outmatched in terms of money and endorsements by his Democratic primary opponents, Lawton Chiles and his wife, Rhea, settled on a novel campaign strategy. The candidate would walk the entire state to canvass voters, starting at the Panhandle town of Century on the Alabama border, crisscrossing the heartland, and ending at Key Largo.

Rhea Chiles understood and supported the risks inherent in this and future campaigns. "He was innately courageous, but he was not a continual warrior," she recalls. "When the occasion arose, he could seize something from within himself, and he showed up. That to me was always a mystery. I never quite understood it. It was a little bit dangerous to me; I never knew quite where we were going. It's a spiritual quality. It's something that was not easy to characterize."

By the end of the 1,003-mile journey, Chiles had met more than 40,000 people. Each day taught lessons on agricultural policy, the Vietnam War, and the environmental movement—transmitted directly from farmers, soldiers, and student advocates. Nine notebooks preserved his observations.

On the road, Chiles earned the nickname "Walkin' Lawton" and a place in American political legend. He witnessed lifestyles and livelihoods far from his own. He learned and reflected.

During Chiles' public career, as Florida gained millions of new, diverse residents, his commitment to self-education and self-improvement was his best asset. He won every election he contested. He was restless by nature, always moving from one adventure to another without a moment of sentimental ponderance. Adaptation was inevitable. He thrived on diversity.

Chiles' sense of humor, especially his infamous "gotcha" jokes, helped break down cultural barriers in a growing, multicultural state.

Perhaps no one testified better to Governor Chiles' diverse cultural appetite than Florida's chefs. The governor hungered for every treat on the menu: the most savory Cuban sandwiches, the smallest but sweetest barbecue pits, the heartiest cups of frijoles negros, and the most delectable sushi plates.

His voluntary limits on campaign contributions, set at $10 per person in 1976 and at $100 per person in each subsequent election, helped keep his ear tuned to all Floridians' changing concerns.

Chiles believed in popular sovereignty and popular wisdom. He would listen for hours while a farmer from the smallest county in Florida leaned on his tractor and discussed crop prices. His downhome speech and countenance especially endeared him to the rural people of north Florida. A resident of the lumber town of Milton, Russell Sloan, met Chiles in 1970 and later recalled of the politician, "He was a common old farm boy. He treated the poor just as good as the rich. He never had no big head."[3]

Chiles respected well-published urban intellectuals and rural folk equally. The political oratory of Czech playwright and President Vaclav Havel inspired him. Chiles was an avid reader of American essayist Ralph Waldo Emerson. And he used David Osborne and Ted Gaebler's *Reinventing Government* as a playbook for his first gubernatorial term.

Yet, for all his evolution, Chiles stayed true to himself. His "country Zen"— learned in the woodlands of Polk County, Florida, and honed in the woodlands of the Panhandle—was his signature voice. Some of his expressions were part of Florida pioneers' oral tradition; others were his own concoctions. One of his most colorful sayings is recalled by U.S. Senate staffer Bob Harris:

> [Senator Chiles] told this one guy one time, "I've asked y'all to do this over and over and over. And I guess I'm just gonna have to give you unshirted hell about this. . . ."
>
> He went on, and the guy came up to me afterward and said, "What is unshirted hell?"
>
> I said, "That's a beatin' without your clothes on, buddy. That's not good."

"You never know when they will come out," Chiles said of his eccentric phrases. "You don't write these down. They come out of your skin. Like splinters."

In the final hours of Chiles' last and toughest race, his 1994 gubernatorial reelection bid against Republican Jeb Bush, the governor delivered perhaps his most enduring and inscrutable line: "The old He-Coon walks just before the light of day."

For Chiles, political theater was not superficial. It was a means of bringing new voters into the political process—it made politics fun. Many political opponents, fixated on a Southern caricature, underestimated Chiles. "You think he's this country lawyer," the *Tallahassee Democrat's* Bill Cotterell said, "and he can follow you in a revolving door and come out first. And you don't notice it until he's done it to you."

For certain, we celebrate his good work as a public servant on governmental transparency, infant mortality, and tobacco litigation. His "Government in the Sunshine" legislation set a new standard for open government, and his self-imposed campaigned spending limits restored public trust in politicians. Florida's case against Big Tobacco cemented Chiles' national profile and inspired the successful national "Truth" campaign against youth cigarette use.

The Chiles agenda enriched the lives of children most of all by expanding health insurance access, lowering infant mortality rates, and reducing teen smoking. "The fragile cry of his young grandson . . . born several months premature, inspired him as Senator and Governor to want to give every child a healthy start in life—the chance to make the most of their God-given talent," President Bill Clinton recalled at a memorial service for the Florida governor.[4]

Chiles was the first national elected official to envision early childhood health care as the key to reducing crime, improving education, and ultimately balancing the budget. "First base is our children," he said. "The answer to all of our pressing problems begins with the child."

"He was determined that this was the way to get to these intractable social conditions," explains his wife, Rhea, who collaborated with Governor Chiles on many children's initiatives, "that there was no other way, but this was the one string to pull out of the snarl. If you got to children soon enough, early enough . . . you could eventually improve the crop. If you prepare the seed crop, you [can] eventually grow a better product."

A small front-end investment in children, according to the Chiles philosophy, would pay dividends down the line in lower crime, better education, high incomes, and a balanced budget.

Chiles was adamant that once children became teenagers and young adults, the opportunity for government to facilitate their development was gone. The first five years of a child's development, in his estimation, were the most crucial. "At birth," the governor said, "the brain has about 100 billion neurons. By age one, that figure explodes to 1,000 trillion. Talking to children, showing them games, even playing classical music to them during these first years can make a difference of twenty IQ points—an astounding implication for the state as it struggles to provide good childcare for mothers who are leaving welfare for work."

Chiles' signature children's initiatives, especially Healthy Kids and Healthy Start, paid quick dividends. His policies reduced Florida's infant mortality rate, expanded health insurance access, and raised the children's immunization rate.

We also celebrate Chiles for his wit, vulnerability, and soul. The conduct of the U.S. Senate in the 1980s tested his Christian faith. The escalation of the federal budget deficit frustrated him. His genuine request for budget discipline isolated him in a chamber full of the sanctimonious. "I was never so disappointed with a group of people in my whole life," Chiles said when he decided to retire from the U.S. Senate in 1987. "I just couldn't get over it."

Time, medicine, and inspiration alleviated his depression, but not his political bug. He returned to politics in 1990 as Florida's governor, more popular than ever. His final turn in politics as Florida's governor was his greatest. In his home state, close to his favorite turkey hunting fields and favorite people, Chiles found a "second life." He considered the governorship a better job than the presidency.

In his long career, Chiles knew political failure as well as success. On Capitol Hill and in Tallahassee, he lost major bids for tax reform, deficit reduction, and universal health insurance. Sometimes, he aggravated the situation by letting poor staff work go unpunished. He accepted friends completely, even false ones.

Chiles preferred to push personnel management away from his desk, to maximize his time for crafting a vision of government. This practice left his true allies little recourse but resentment. They rightfully viewed it as a blind spot that hurt his agenda.

But Chiles' fidelity to his friends defined him. "Lawton was always Lawton," law school classmate Dexter Douglass recalls. "He was the type of guy you were willing to forgive, and he very rarely ever did anything that would give you cause to shoot him."

Considering his whole character, good and bad, Chiles deserves a stronger place in history. He belongs in Florida's political pantheon with LeRoy Collins, Bob Graham, and Reubin Askew. He deserves national acclaim, too. His magnanimous contribution to American political legend recalls Huey Long's, though Chiles was as honest as Long was crooked.

Soon after I finished this book, I took in a Buckwheat Zydeco concert that inspired many revisions. Mr. Buckwheat's overflowing spirit in his musical performance reminded me of Lawton Chiles. "We come to party witcha, if you don't mind," the band leader said to start the show. Before most songs, Mr. Buckwheat reminisced about his Louisiana musical roots and teased the audience with Creole phrases. Few understood the fast chatter except his frequent chime: "It can be dat way sometimes." But they clapped and cheered anyway. Mr. Buckwheat ambled from one side of the stage to another with his accordion, wearing a giant grin on his face. When he stopped and hovered over the crowd, the folks below bunched together and whistled and shouted. Then he shuffled to another corner of the stage and shared his muse anew with a small group or returned to center stage and played a duet with the rub board player. The number of applause lines for the maestro's every jibe reminded me of a State of the Union address. The audience joined the refrain of "peace, love, and happiness" as Mr. Buckwheat closed the show.

The next day, my thoughts returned to writing and to Florida, and how music might relate. Both Mr. Buckwheat and Governor Chiles, I thought, brought their homebrewed spirit on the road as cultural ambassadors. It was President Bill Clinton who, in memoriam, likened Governor Chiles to a wandering minstrel for America. Mr. Buckwheat had even played a hit song, "Walkin' to New Orleans," which seemed to be a tip of the hat to "Walkin' Lawton."

Walkin' Lawton is a compilation of Chiles' greatest political hits—full of blues, rhythm, and catchy choruses. It is a record of an American life lived with gusto. At the end of his story, it's not hard to imagine Chiles still on the road, somewhere in north Florida, stopping only to pat a lost hunting dog on the head or to shake hands with a couple farmers and ask for their votes.

John Dos Passos Coggin
Annapolis, MD
January 2012

Acknowledgements

The people of Florida foremost deserve my thanks for introducing me to the Lawton Chiles story.

The Chiles family is Florida's finest. I am grateful for their hospitality, trust, and friendship during this journey. They knew Lawton Chiles' golden heart before Florida did, and this biography tells their story.

The financial support of the Lawton Chiles Foundation, which is administered by the Chiles family, made my research possible. The logistical support provided by the Chiles family ensured that my research, including interviews, was comprehensive. I hope *Walkin' Lawton* has rewarded the family's faith in my industry and honored the Lawton Chiles legacy.

Special thanks to Senator Sam Nunn for writing the introduction to *Walkin' Lawton*. Nunn knew the head and heart of Lawton Chiles. He campaigned with him, played tennis with him, and prayed with him. Nunn's contribution is a source of spiritual and intellectual guidance for this biography.

Gratitude and thanks are in order for Professor Christopher H. Foreman at University of Maryland School of Public Policy. Long before the first chapter had been written, Foreman believed in this project. He has been a strong stakeholder at every stage of its development.

Thanks to historian Douglas Brinkley for reading the manuscript and endorsing its quality. "Get the manuscript between covers," Brinkley said. His support has helped make that happen.

Thanks to Governor Howard Dean for recognizing the value of the Chiles legacy. It's a privilege to have "People-Powered Howard" give his endorsement to this biography. Dean knows a genuine populist and public policy innovator when he sees one.

I interviewed more than one hundred people during my research. They contributed their oral histories, often with grace and wit, to my manuscript. Their words were the beams and bricks that built this book:

Jamie Adams, Julie Anbender, DeLane Anderson, Cindy Aplin, Reubin Askew, Dubose Ausley, Dennis Beal, Juanita Black, Steve Bousquet, Faye Boyd, Jim Boyd, Colin Bradford, Bob Bradley, Rick Brandon, Bobby Brochin, Lonnie Brown, Carol Browner, Bob Butterworth, Dominic Calabro, Art Carlson, Randy Chastain, Alfred Chiles Jr., Bud and Kitty Chiles, Ed Chiles, Joe W. Chiles Jr., Lawton Chiles IV, Rhea Chiles, Rhea Gay Chiles, Tandy Chiles, Bob Coakley, Doug Cook, Jim Cordero, Bill Cotterell, Ted Covington,

Acknowledgements

Bragg Crane, Jim Daughton, Dexter Douglass, Jim Eaton, Rob Evans, Rick Farrell, Tom Fiedler, David Fonvielle, Steve Freedman, Mary Jane Gallagher, W.C. Gentry, Rae Grad, Kay Hagan, Michael Hall, Bob Harris, Tom Herndon, Wayne Hogan, Sonny Holtzman, Mallory Horne, Bruce Hunt, Charles Intriago, Dee Jeffers, Toni Jennings, Bennett Johnston, Burke Kibler, Deborah Kilmer, Frank Koutnik, Jim Krog, Jenny Lee, Jack Levine, Bentley Lipscomb, Buddy MacKay, Sarah MacKay, Charles Mahan, Mike Maher, Snow Martin Jr., Margaret Maruschak, Dave Mica, Ann and Jimmy Miller, Jon Beth Mills, Peter Mitchell, Jon Moyle Sr., Tim Nickens, Sam Nunn, David Osborne, Joe Pena, Jared Perez, Ken Plante, Jack Pollack, Jack Pridgen, Brian Proctor, Bill Rufty, Greg Ruthven Sr., Joe L. Ruthven, Joe P. Ruthven, Ron Sachs, Charles Salem, April Salter, Dean Saunders, Christina Scelsi, Mark Schlakman, Linda Shelley, Mark Silva, Damon Smith, Tom Staed, Dan Stengle, Janet Studley, Robin Swan, Adelaide Clement Sweat, Parker Thompson, Steve Uhlfelder, John Van Gieson, Wayne Watters, Jamey Westbrook, T.K. Wetherell, Phil Wise, Chuck Wolfe, and Willie Wolfson.

Special thanks to Dr. Mike Denham for sharing some of the prized transcriptions of oral history housed at Florida Southern College's Center for Florida History in Lakeland, Florida.

Thanks also to Ron Sachs Communications for sharing their archive of interviews conducted for their 2003 DVD production, *Lawton Chiles: A Great Floridian*. Thanks to Art Carlson for conducting the interviews.

I thank Tanya and Kenneth Rachfal for allowing me the use of their basement as a temporary writing studio.

No book is without its literary inspirations. I acknowledge the literature that sustained my optimism for a writing career of my own, and inspired the style of *Walkin' Lawton*.

The concise, often satirical biographies in John Dos Passos' *U.S.A.* were templates for my own. Richard Feynman's *"Surely You're Joking, Mr. Feynman!"*, an assigned text from my high school days, taught me that even a subject as complex as physics can be fun in the hands of the right storyteller. George Stephanopoulos' *All Too Human: A Political Education* gave me an appreciation for well-scripted dialogue as a tool for political history. Political memoir, I learned, could read like a great screenplay.

My gratitude to friends and family who read my manuscript and conveyed thoughtful criticism: Kathryn Au, Lara Dos Passos Coggin, Lucy Dos Passos Coggin, Tom Crane, Bill Jongeward, Steve Leopoldo, Diane Martinez, Dan McDermott, Nathan Taylor, and Sean Williamson.

Thanks to the public policy experts and public interest champions who served Lawton Chiles as staff, read my manuscript, and contributed their wisdom to it: Colin Bradford, Doug Cook, Rick Farrell, and Dan Stengle.

Finally, I offer my gratitude to my publisher, Florida Historical Society Press. Dr. Ben Brotemarkle, Director of the FHS Press, has a keen ear for powerful oral history. The FHS Press copyeditor, Kirsten Russell, has an equally keen eye for the mechanics of a manuscript. Their labor has given the Lawton Chiles story—an essential chapter in Florida's history—another chance to inspire.

Introduction
by Former U.S. Senator Sam Nunn

"Do not go where the path may lead," Emerson wrote, "go where there is no path and leave a trail."

The public service of my friend and colleague Lawton Chiles is well represented by this admonition from one of his favorite authors. I first came to know of Lawton as many did in 1970, when he walked the state of Florida in his run for the United States Senate.

In my view at that time, "the Walk" seemed inspired, unique, and a bit of a long shot. It came over time to define the man and his service. But it didn't start out that way. As he told me later, the Walk itself was the idea of his Muse—his wife, Rhea, who prompted him to do it only after he and his advisors came to the conclusion that the traditional political path before him, which required extensive fund raising, was not practicable or even possible. Creativity is a great Rhea Chiles talent, and the Walk was a poor man's "gold mine."

So Lawton walked and listened and learned, and over hundreds of miles the experience challenged and molded him. He had always seen himself as a bit of a populist, but he began to expect more of himself. He began to feel a deeper responsibility to the people he hoped to represent. His greatest lesson from the Walk, he would say, was that the way you ran was the way you governed.

Lawton preceded me in the Senate by two years. He introduced himself to me in a call shortly after I won my election in 1972. Even that introduction had his unique and straightforward stamp on it. He told me I must be good because I had defeated a good man, Senator David Gambrell. As we worked together and I got to know Lawton, I came to understand that I had found a friend with whom I shared values, vision, and convictions.

Lawton was one of the early sponsors of public financing for elections. He understood the corrupting influence of large donations in politics. Lawton was appropriately humble about the experience of the Walk. He felt he had been blessed, but he understood that experiences like his were nearly impossible to duplicate. Lawton strongly believed that public financing of elections could level the playing field and help dilute the corrosive effect of big money.

Throughout our Senate careers, we worked together on governmental reforms, national security, and the national budget. Although Lawton's almost instinctive common sense and problem-solving made him difficult to classify, I would say he was a "tight hawk" on national security. He was a staunch anti-communist who sponsored funding for the Contras. He also supported the post-Vietnam defense build ups initiated in the Carter Administration and greatly expanded in the Reagan Administration.

He was also, however, a deficit hawk. By 1984, his concerns over the emerging deficits "as far as the eye can see" caused him to begin to question whether we were balancing our needs to invest domestically and on national security with our need for fiscal responsibility. This was a difficult time. Also by 1984, the Reagan Administration's leading budget balancer, OMB Director David Stockman, had given up on his quest, and the Administration was requesting another significant increase in defense spending.

Lawton stepped into the breach. It was a thankless task. To his left, he had our fellow Democrats advocating for domestic and entitlement spending. To his right, he found our Republican brethren with their demands for increased defense spending and more tax cuts. Fortunately for our nation, he was well suited to the task. Lawton was an active listener. He believed there was power in giving a colleague the opportunity to speak his piece. "Sometimes," he joked, "if I give them enough time, they will talk themselves out of a hardened position." At worst, he felt he might better understand how and where he might meet them halfway.

Lawton was a natural for elective office because he loved being a politician, he loved people, he loved Florida, and he loved America. He had great respect for the political insights and skills of former Speaker Sam Rayburn, and he tried to legislate with the Speaker's famous reminder, "Any jackass can kick a barn down, but it takes a carpenter to build one." He was a good Democrat. His friends included not only our fellow southerners and contemporaries Senators Lloyd Bentsen, J. Bennett Johnston, and Howell Heflin, but also Senators Ted Kennedy, George Mitchell, Chris Dodd, Paul Tsongas, Joe Biden, Carl Levin, Pat Moynihan, and Congressman John Dingell.

But he was not partisan. He had great affection for Senators Mark Hatfield, Pete Domenici, Dick Lugar, John Warner, and Congressman Henry Hyde. He was a leader in the Senate Prayer Breakfast and was admired and even loved by his Republican as well as Democratic friends. He believed that at their best, our Republican colleagues represented and fought for time-honored traditions, free enterprise, and fiscal responsibility. The work he did with Senators Pete Domenici, Warren Rudman, and Fritz Hollings laid the foundation for both the Bush and Clinton budget agreements. Lawton respected and liked his colleagues, and they returned the favor.

But the last few years in the Senate were hard on Lawton. The failure of our institutions to make hard choices frustrated him greatly, and it turned out that the trouble ran deeper. It wasn't until he announced he was running for Governor of Florida in the spring of 1990 that I learned he had suffered from clinical depression. By that time the whole world knew. In answer to a reporter's seemingly unfriendly question, he responded forthrightly, and millions of Americans learned what Prozac was and that their illnesses could be effectively treated. William Styron, the writer of *Sophie's Choice,* thanked him. We should not have been surprised by Lawton's honesty and candor. It was a habit he never broke, and his constituents knew it. His polls bounced up.

Lawton believed that the good Lord gives us the opportunity to perform our duties in such a way that we are able to apply the experiences and skills we have developed over a lifetime on a meaningful mission. I know he saw himself as a very blessed man. He loved being Governor of Florida. He had grown ever closer to his God and the love of his life, Rhea, his children and his grandchildren. He was doing his duty—helping his people and his state.

I'm not much of a turkey hunter, but Lawton made it fun. At Jim Baker's ranch in Texas, Lawton spent hours calling two gobblers and let me have the shots—the only two I've ever killed. He loved the outdoors and particularly the woods. Lawton was one of those rare friends who is never really gone, because my memories are so vivid.

When I see Lawton in my mind's eye, I see him in the woods in the early morning hours, watching the forest awake. When the good Lord calls me home and I walk through the light, I hope one of the trails Lawton has left will lead me to the tree in the woods where he sits, and he will call a turkey and get me another shot.

A Map of "The Walk"

Century
DeFuniak Springs
Tallahassee
Madison
Live Oak
Gainesville
Ocala
Sanford
Orlando
Lakeland
St. Petersburg
Ft. Myers
West Palm Beach
Key Largo

Munn Park

Munn Park was Lawton Chiles' boyhood playground in his hometown of Lakeland, Florida. Located downtown beside a railroad station, the park's simple setup of lawn, paths, and benches drew crowds young and old.

At Munn Park, Chiles fell in love with politics. Politicians running for statewide office visited Lakeland via train and delivered speeches from the park bandstand. Before television became a mainstream middle-class commodity, politics in the park was evening entertainment.

By age ten, Chiles knew public office was his calling. Florida politician Spessard Holland, the boy had decided, was his role model. Like Chiles, Holland was a Democrat from Polk County; he hailed from Bartow, a small town near Lakeland. All the men in the Chiles family were for Holland—especially Lawton's Uncle Olin, whose employment depended on political patronage. If Holland lost, Olin would lose his beverage control job.[5]

Holland frequented Munn Park. As a state senator representing Polk County, Holland ran for governor in 1940.[6] The evening of April 25 that year, Lakeland's Munn Park hosted one of his finest political rallies.[7]

Ten-year-old Lawton Chiles probably attended that night's rally. Holland delivered the fighting populist, Southern oratory that Chiles loved to memorize and rehash like movie lines.

Holland climbed the stage at about eight o'clock and gave the capacity hometown crowd of 4,000 a once-over, smiling at the faces of kin whose lineages he could recite back to the days when Florida flew a Spanish flag, kids whose fathers he had struck out in pick-up baseball games, and old-timers his mother had taught at Summerlin Institute.[8]

Everyone there knew Holland's biography. He had been a star pitcher at Summerlin Institute and Emory College. As a fellow at University of Florida his command on the mound in an exhibition game against the Philadelphia Athletics had impressed the team owner so much that he was offered a major league contract.[9] After graduating law school in 1916, Holland qualified for a Rhodes Scholarship, but passed it up to volunteer for service in World War I. Once overseas, he transferred from desk duty to field service as an aerial observer. He and his pilot shot down two planes before crashing.[10] Holland entered politics upon his return to Florida.[11]

The closest parking spots had filled up by morning. Folks returning from lunch had sat on their cars awaiting the rally. Some sat on orange carts. A few probably clopped in on horse-drawn buggies, but turned back when they saw the traffic gridlock.[12]

Audience members swatted at mosquitoes with Panama hats, hoping to kill a hat-full before the speaker's opening salvo. Some hummed the Holland campaign song, "Ahead with Holland," set to the jazz tune, "Hot Time in the Old Town Tonight."[13]

Once the Summerlin Institute band finished their last number, a hush descended. Without television, Lakelanders wanted to see and hear the candidate up close. They craved the theater provided by Huey Long and other great Southern orators.

Holland's Polk County tours often moved him to reminisce about Old Florida on the stump. These tales of Florida's pioneers excited young Lawton Chiles. Holland would harken back to the day when his father showed him the "old grandpa" of the alligators in Peace River. Holland's "Grandfather Gandy" had killed it and hauled the carcass to the Bartow town square for exhibition. Holland summoned memories of the Fourth of July when Bartow celebrated its first clay street, running from the depot to the Polk County National Bank, and the town's first automobile. He honored the hometown boys sent to the Spanish-American War and Bartow's survival of the big freeze of 1894-95.[14]

This night, however, for his final speech in Lakeland before the May 7 primary, Holland skipped the homecoming address and threw strikes from the first.[15] He responded to rumors spread by opponents saying he believed workers deserved no more than one dollar a day, and that he wanted citrus employees exempt from recent workmen's compensation laws.[16]

"I am for—the men and women who work with their hands," Holland began, pounding a clenched fist into his open hand.

"I have been a Democrat all my life," he testified, "and I have fought some hard fights for my party. In 1932, I went to bat for Roosevelt when he was campaigning for the forgotten man, for the rights of the common man. You have always found me fighting for human values.

"And so I find it particularly contemptible that some persons have come here and tried to betray, not me, but those who know of my efforts in behalf of labor and who have worked with me to advance the interests of laboring people."[17]

He read a 1935 letter written by the president of the Florida State Federation of Labor and a bulletin published by a committee of railroaders—both affirming his pro-worker credentials.

"Why should anyone go out of his way to state such a malicious falsehood?" he asked to a round of applause. "Because they know that Spessard Holland is out in front in this race."[18]

When Holland announced for governor the first of January, 1940, Florida's editorial boards from Polk County to Dade County to Liberty County rushed to print the first coronation. "He is as young as the junior class of war veterans," the *Fort Myers News-Press* noted, "young enough to be nimble and old enough to know that a lot of things won't work." Although he shied away from yelling "'yoo-hoo' at voters across the street" and "going around slapping voters on the back," he "knows plenty of first names." The *Winter Haven Herald* proclaimed Holland "an ideal candidate, equally at home with the wool hat boys on a fish fry, on his feet in strenuous debate, arguing in a court of law or addressing a woman's club." The *Plant City Courier* trumpeted the "one candidate whose name, in every county, stands for honesty, integrity, capability and strength of character." Holland had pledged a government that is "wholly non-sectional" during his campaign for governor.[19] "I know that's the way you would have me, above all things," he affirmed.[20]

Holland would face straw man opposition from the Republican Party in November. Since the Democrats enjoyed one-party rule in Florida and a run-off followed if no candidate won a majority in the first May primary, every shaver with filing money and an FDR button campaigned for a shot at round two as if playing the lottery.

Holland already planned a long family vacation in Highlands, North Carolina after beating ten also-rans for the nomination.[21]

But Holland liked to play to hometown crowds most of all—the theater continued until he knew he had roused every loyal heart.

Senator Holland shook as he closed the speech with his clean government pitch. "If I thought the governorship were for sale, I wouldn't be interested." The crowd stood up to clap. "I am leaving my case in your hands—my neighbors and my friends—and I believe I am leaving my case in safe hands."[22]

Munn Park political rallies were a tradition for the Chiles men. Lawton Chiles bonded with his father and three uncles at these events. He listened to their every political jibe. The Chiles men differed in political beliefs, but all were avid observers of the sport.

Uncle Olin espoused atheist socialism while Uncle Alfred and Uncle Herbert were anti-union, anti-FDR, conservative Democrats. "Uncle Olin was so opinionated," Joe W. Chiles, Uncle Alfred's son, recalls."I mean, you've gotta understand he was never wrong about anything in his life." Olin Chiles voted for Progressive Party candidate Henry Wallace, a liberal firebrand, in 1948.

Lawton Chiles' father and namesake, Lawton Chiles Sr., supported traditional, pro-union and pro-New Deal Democratic values. The Party addressed his economic concerns; he had lost his job as a conductor for the Atlantic Coast Railroad during the Great Depression.[23]

"Big Lawton," as he was sometimes known, spoke up about his political beliefs to his family. His easygoing, gracious manner earned him a respectful audience for these convictions. "He knew what he was doing," nephew Joe W. Chiles later recalled, "and was very comfortable with himself." According to Chiles classmate Bill Ellsworth, "Lawton Sr. always seemed to have a smile and could work a smile into his countenance."

Polk County needed every stimulus that the New Deal provided. During the 1938-1939 season a bumper orange crop had sold at a budget-busting low price.[24] County officials cut a month off the 1939 school year.[25] The town of Auburndale had filed for bankruptcy protection in summer of 1939.[26] Winter 1940, a five-day freeze killed groves across the state; thermometers fell to eight degrees.[27]

Bone Valley's phosphate miners worried, too. If Congress declared war on Germany, Florida's biggest buyer, lines to Lakeland High School's soup kitchen would lengthen.[28]

The county's recent spike in bootlegging, gambling, robberies, and murders concerned everyone. In March 1935 Florida Southern College President Ludd Spivey called for a county-wide conference to address the occurrence of "more murders in Polk County during the past 18 months than in all of Great Britain."[29] E.E. Callaway, a 1936 Lakeland gubernatorial candidate, called Polk the worst "Hell Hole" in America. "Lakeland," he continued, "and the entire county is a cesspool of dives, joints, bars, gambling dens etc. and any officer who does not know this is blind and dumb."[30] One grand jury in the county juggled nine murder cases at once in 1938.[31]

Lawton Chiles Sr., like most Floridians and most Southerners of his time, probably voted Democrat down the ticket for regional reasons as well as economic and social ones.

Southern Democrats identified with an anti-Northern Civil War legacy. Through the New Deal, they voted to stick it to the Radical Republicans in Washington who had freed the slaves during the Civil War and then ordered federal troops to their state capitals, barred ex-Confederates from the polls, and welcomed new black political leadership to the U.S. Congress during Reconstruction. When the federal occupation ended in 1877, Florida restored the conservative Democratic super majority from county commissioner to governor.

These mostly Protestant "Yellow Dog Democrats," concentrated within fifty miles of the Georgia border, cracked that they would sooner cast a ballot for a lost yellow dog than a carpetbagger Republican. They heralded the 1885 Constitution, which split executive power between the governor and six elected officers, as redemption for the Yankee invaders' abuses. Yellow Dogs passed a poll tax in 1889 and denied Florida's minority black community membership in the Democratic Party in 1902, and broke their leash only in the 1928 presidential race to support Republican Herbert Hoover over Catholic Democrat Al Smith. President Franklin Roosevelt's New Deal called them home to the Democratic Party.

Sunday evenings, Lawton Sr. and his brothers gathered at his house after dinner for political talk—especially after a big rally at Munn Park. The conversation mesmerized young Lawton Chiles Jr. "Lawton was a sponge," childhood friend Burke Kibler recalls. "Sometimes you'd think he would be daydreaming," then "he would run home and spit out all he heard."

In Munn Park, Chiles also learned the vastness of Southern political lore. "I would sit there and listen," Joe W. Chiles related, "I know that Lawton [Jr.] was there sort of sitting at their feet, evaluating—much too young for any of us to participate."

Lakeland's phosphate mining executives, bankers, citrus growers, cattle ranchers, and railroad managers told fantastic stories of the first Southern demagogues.[32] For these political characters who spun speeches on the stump before television or radio, their careers depended on colorful oratory.

Before Louisiana Governor and U.S. Senator Huey Long gave Southern political orators a national brand, there were South Carolina Governor "Pitchfork Ben" Tillman and U.S. Senator "Cotton Ed" Smith.

In his 1898 bid for the U.S. Senate, "Pitchfork Ben" attacked President Grover Cleveland: "When Judas betrayed Christ, his heart was not blacker than this scoundrel, Cleveland. . . . He is an old bag of beef and I am going to Washington with a pitchfork [to] prod him in his old fat ribs."[33]

Tillman developed a reputation for shouting down hecklers. At one lecture, he snapped: "Oh, shut your mouth. You don't know the A, B, C of this thing; I have forgotten fifty years ago more than you ever knew."[34]

In Omaha, Nebraska, Tillman stuck one of his own supporters with his rhetorical pitchfork: "I'd like to know—honestly I would—I'd like to know what mental process led you to applaud that."[35] One Iowa paper commented, "He swung his pitchfork and prodded his helpless victims until the tines ran blood. Then he would withdraw the instrument from the quivering wound, hold it up to display for a moment and then jab it in again."[36]

Ed Smith, self-proclaimed cotton farmer's champion of the early twentieth-century U.S. Senate, called South Carolina politics a "monkey circus."[37] "Cotton Ed" and his supporters campaigned with cotton bolls as boutonnieres; the candidate rode to speaking engagements atop a cotton baled wagon. He called the crop "my sweetheart, my old sweetheart."[38]

Smith spoke at the National Cotton Convention in 1904. "New England beat us once with the bullets," he said. "They have just beaten us again with the ballots: now, for God's sake, let's try and beat them with the bolls!"[39]

At the 1905 Southern Interstate Cotton Convention in New Orleans, Smith was introduced as "The Gatling Gun of South Carolina," to which he responded, "Gentleman, if I am a Gatling Gun, I am loaded for bear!"[40]

Chiles almost certainly heard the infamous "Catholics for Huey Long" story from Louisiana:

> At a campaign stop in Acadia, a local politico advised Huey Long, "Huey, you ought to remember one thing in your speeches today. You're from north Louisiana, but now you're in south Louisiana. And we got a lot of Catholics voters down here."
>
> "I know," Long replied. "When I was a boy," he would tell Catholic crowds, "I would get up at six o'clock in the morning on Sunday and I would hitch our hold horse up to the buggy and I would take my Catholic grandparents to mass. I would bring them home, and at ten

o'clock I would hitch up the old horse again, and I would take my Baptist grandparents to church."

The boss later commented to Long, "Why Huey, you've been holding out on us. I didn't know you had any Catholic grandparents."

"Don't be a damned fool," Long said. "We didn't even have a horse."[41]

From the graybeards at Munn Park, Lawton surely heard the tale of Jacob Summerlin, "King of the Crackers." The colonial-era white pioneers of Florida, also known sometimes as "Crackers," spoke with special vocabulary and cadence. Though these Crackers were cowboys, not politicians, their speech patterns—tied to the land and its wildlife—appealed to Chiles as much as the best rhetoric at politics in the park.

Many Crackers, like Summerlin, were cowboys. Legend told that the Alachua County native Summerlin was the first child born in Florida territory after Spain ceded the land to America in 1819. Jake, they said, handled a bullwhip and rode a horse by age seven; as a teenager he lit out for central Florida's Peace River Valley with a few of his father's calves.[42] He and his cowhands drove Spanish cattle across the palmetto savannah with eighteen-foot buckskin whips that cracked over a steer's head like thunder. "Crackers," folks called them.[43] A network of almost six hundred lakes did the work of cowboys in holding herds in place so ranchers could keep an eye out for black bear and wild boar.[44] By the Civil War, Summerlin had raised a cattle herd of 20,000.[45] After the war, he provided 120 acres for a courthouse, school, and Methodist and Baptist churches for a new Polk County seat to be called Bartow.[46] "When this was announced to the public, everybody thought that Uncle Jake was the greatest man in all South Florida," Benjamin Blount later remembered.[47]

Summerlin, who was probably Florida's richest man when he died in 1893, rejected imperial trappings:

I don't try to ape quality. I ain't wore a coat in twenty years; I ain't setting up to be a fine gentleman, my old blue trousers and my check shirt suits me, and a good pair of stout galluses. Rain or shine, I don't want any more. My boys can dress up in store clothes if it suits them, go to college, talk big. I'm going on this way until I drop in my tracks. I'm going to work when I please, play when I please—nothing under the sun but a native-born, sun-baked Florida Cracker.[48]

Summerlin and other Crackers like Francis Asbury "Berry" Hendry inspired a legion of sayings from those trying to mimic their take on common sense. If in a tight spot, pioneers would moan, "This place is so small you couldn't cuss a cat without getting fur in your mouth."[49] When luck smiled on a cattleman, his wife might quip, ""Even a blind hog will root out an acorn every once in a while."[50]

Chiles especially loved the story about cowmen who put burlap bags around their horses' heads at night so the mosquitoes wouldn't drive them crazy.[51] Bugs swarmed so thick "a man could swing a pint cup and catch a quart" of them. Another of Chiles' favorite tales was about prairie parties over chicken perleu.[52] The typical chicken perleu feast involved boiling dozens of birds over an open fire, serving them with rice and coffee, and singing till sunup.[53]

Cracker tales reminded Lawton of his own pioneer ancestry. His paternal great-grandfather, Seaborn Chiles, worked as a circuit-riding Methodist preacher in the 1840s and 1850s, and settled in Fort White, the first in the family to make his home on Florida soil. Family lore told that he was a good pastor to his church members but a mediocre preacher.[54] Seaborn's son, Joseph Chiles, fought for the Confederacy as a teenager until Union forces took him prisoner at Jacksonville. After the war, he walked from the Delaware prison down to Fort White in north Florida. After his first wife died, Joseph remarried in his early fifties and fathered a family of five children: Olin, Herbert, Lawton, Alfred and Nina. As boys, the brothers hitched the train to Lakeland when they wanted to cut a rug. Their father would wire the police chief in advance and ask him to keep them out of trouble.

Joseph's family moved to Lakeland in 1916, to a property on Boone Court, west of Lake Hollingsworth and south of Bartow Road, part of the town's first suburb, Dixieland. Olin and Herbert served in World War I in the Army; Alfred enlisted in the Navy after the war.[55] Joseph opened a general store with his sons. Lawton M. Chiles Sr., a railroad man, and Margaret Patterson met and married in the 1920s.

Lawton Chiles Jr.'s maternal great-grandfather was Dr. John Patterson, a surgeon in the Confederate Army. He came to Auburndale in 1881 from Tennessee, and named Lake Juliana after his wife, Julia Ann Lyttle Patterson. The Pattersons moved from Auburndale to Lakeland in 1914.

In 1939, Lawton Jr. and his sister Jeanette, three years his elder, moved from Dixieland to a five-bedroom frame house on Lake Morton, first built by

Grandpa Chiles on his acreage in 1919.[56] It was at 91 Lake Morton Drive and Chiles Street, across from Lake Morton Elementary School.[57]

Munn Park also functioned as a play pen for Lawton Chiles and other Lakeland children. Before Chiles' time, kids had played war in the park with a French 75 mm cannon from World War I anchored on the grounds. They cranked it up and down and back and forth, and tried to open the breech block.

When the state trade expo came to town in 1925, Main Street closed down for a week and vendors set up booths with red, white, and blue bunting. A gaggle of kids snitched boxes of paperback book matches from the booths. The Saturday night after the expo ended, they carried 1,000 packs of matches to the park, tore the cardboard off, and stuffed the cannon from muzzle to breech. A hot second after the matches lit, a million sparks boomed into the sky. The fireworks brought police and fire trucks and Monday morning a crew arrived to fill the cannon with cement.

As a boy, Chiles and his friends found many similar amusements in Munn Park. They climbed the marble Confederate monument in the park center.[58] They rode bikes to the park and paid a dime to see a serial picture or a magic show at the Polk, the county's first air-conditioned theater. Inside, under the painted stars on a royal blue ceiling, they imagined a twinkling night sky.[59]

Beyond Munn Park, the measure of Florida and the scope and diversity of the rest of the United States were unknown to young Lawton Chiles.

Between 1920 and 1940, Florida's population almost doubled, creating more than a dozen new counties. At the turn of the twentieth century, Jacksonville was Florida's largest city; by 1940, Miami matched it in population at more than 170,000. By 1912, thirty trains rumbled by Lakeland's Union Station daily.

But Lakeland had progressed little from its pioneer roots. It was a town bent on survival, not enlightenment or diversification. If national news did not pertain to orange groves or phosphate mines, Lakelanders took little notice.

As a boy, Chiles lived happily in isolation, ignorant of his own town's physical and social boundaries. Lakeland claimed about 20,000 souls in 1940, but the middle-class homes clustered around Lake Morton and Lake Hollingsworth were his world.

Segregation reigned in Lakeland at this time; middle-class and upper-class whites lived on the south end of town. According to Bill Ellsworth, "Even poor families, if they could afford it, would have a maid come in at times to clean up, wash, and what have you."[60] A typical newspaper ad for a house-cleaning company read, "Wanted: five colored women, experienced in laundry work, bring referral cards."[61] Whites referred to the black section as "the Quarters" or "colored town."[62] Pine Street, just north of the railroad tracks, they called "Dodge City." Whites crossed over to attend Lakeland High School, go to church, or go the hardware store. "North side was the wrong side of the tracks" by 1940, according to resident and Lawton Chiles' childhood friend Burke Kibler. Bill Ellsworth recalls one of the few black-white interactions in his time, between black yardmen and white homeowners—and their kids:

> I never will forget my father used a lawn man, Ike, for years after I somehow got out of doing the lawn and he had two little boys who came there. I remember the kids, and I was older. They would come there, y'know, when he'd do it and help pick up the brush. My father answered the doorbell when he was retired, and here is a colored young man who's about six feet six inches both ways, asking for Mr. Ellsworth. Well, to make a long story short, that was one of the children who had grown up and he was a professional wrestler with a professional wrestling team. But he remembered my father. He comes back to see him. My father was saying, "Holy cow, who is this?" and "What are you doing here?" He was certainly a little apprehensive until [the man] introduced himself.[63]

As soon as they could, young white professionals moved to Success Avenue and other streets south of Chiles Street, between Lake Morton and Lake Hollingsworth. The town's richest homes clustered around Lakeland Yacht and Country Club on Lake Hollingsworth. The woods bordered the new homes along these lakes; a Boy Scout clubhouse was sited between Lake Morton and Florida Avenue. To a white Lakeland boy, "Lake Hollingsworth was the end of the world," Bill Ellsworth notes.[64]

The north end of Lakeland sheltered its well-established black community. After the Civil War, free blacks had migrated to Polk County in droves to cut woods and lay track.[65] Hundreds served in World War I.[66] The survivors raised families in two sections north of the Lakeland railroad tracks or bordering them, Teaspoon Hill and Moorehead.[67] Moorehead School and Rochelle taught black youth.[68] Since the Civil War, when Bartow-area slaves began worshiping in open fields apart from whites, blacks founded religious enclaves in the county.[69] The Mount Pleasant African Methodist Episcopal Church arrived in Lakeland by 1903.[70] Men labored in citrus, strawberries, phosphate, and railroads; women worked mainly as domestics. Doctor David J. Simpson and Dr. Alfonso William Blake provided medical care and led the professional class.[71] Visiting family in Bartow, Winter Haven, or Fort Meade, they traveled in separate train compartments. Black railroaders organized separate unions unprotected by federal labor laws.[72] "We always had to be aware, even as children, of the status of blacks in society," Lemuel Geathers of Winter Haven later remembered. "It was something you questioned but had to accept."[73] The 1896 U.S. Supreme Court ruling *Plessy v. Ferguson* had upheld "Jim Crow" tradition. James Henry Ammons Jr., also of Winter Haven, would recall that "the only time we saw or interacted with white people was when we went to the shopping center or when we went to work for them."[74]

Young Lawton Chiles saw little of activist black Lakeland or the Ku Klux Klan. He probably accepted the town's apartheid as tradition since time immemorial. But these opposing underground cultures shaped Chiles' generation in Polk County. The backlash against new black power began soon after the Civil War. From the turn of the century till Lawton's birth, Florida led the nation in lynching. Mulberry, a phosphate boomtown ten miles south of Lakeland, led Polk County in violence. From the Civil War through the turn of the century, mobs hung countless victims at its namesake tree.[75] "The tradition goes that the tree, out of shame and disgrace, sickened, lost its greenery, and soon dwindled away to a mere post, after several years of this sort of crime," local historian Robert Lee Thompson reports.[76] The Ku Klux Klan returned after World War I. In May 1920, a white flagman on the Atlantic Coast Line Railroad accused porter Henry Scott of "annoying" a young white woman on a train. Soon a "mob riddled the negro's body with bullets."[77] By 1921 Abraham Lincoln Klan # 5 operated at Lakeland; the town Klan was Florida's first klavern with its own meeting hall.[78] The Klan's Polk membership peaked around 1925 or 1926, but the threats continued, against unionized blacks especially.[79] One night in 1934, three men showed up at the door of United Citrus Worker officer Frank Norman's Lakeland home. They introduced themselves as sheriff's deputies sent to investigate a lynching in nearby Haines City; they had found a card with Norman's name on it in the dead man's pocket. Norman agreed to help them identify the corpse. No one found Norman's body, but two years later rumors appeared in the press that

Klan members had once dumped a dozen union officials in flooded phosphate mines.[80]

During Chiles' boyhood, the Klan made a home in Lakeland for their values and their membership. One night in August, two hundred robed and masked Klansmen bearing American flags paraded through Lakeland's Moorehead section and burned a large cross at a public rally. *Life* magazine ran photographs of the burning, prompting public outcry for Governor Cone to punish the KKK.[81] Lawton Jr.'s Uncle Alfred briefly belonged to the Klan, recounted Joe W. Chiles:

[Daddy] spoke of marching in Lakeland out in colored town once. And how all the curtains would come down, or the shades would, and then when [Klansmen] marched by, [the curtains or shades would] be cracked by somebody looking out. And I don't know that he was in it long, but he said he got out when he saw that it was so extreme and so radical that he didn't want to have any part of it, further. But it was originally sort of like a fraternity, or a secret society, and I don't know how long Daddy was a part of it, it might have been just a few months, he might have only marched once, but there was that sense of intimidation that [the Klan] could get to put people in their place.

Chiles had a schoolmate, Jimmy Miller, whose father belonged to the Klan. Vigilante justice reinforced black fellowship. "Cooperation is the keynote of the era," remarked one black Lakelander. "We must hang together or hang separately."[82]

In south Lakeland, surrounded by live oaks, shallow lakes, and watermelon patches, Chiles enjoyed a Tom Sawyer existence. Kids fished for bass in Lake Morton, near Chiles' home, or fished in a phosphate pit in town. "That was when you could catch little turtles out of Lake Morton," Ann Miller recalls. "And you still had snail eggs and cat's tail growing on your bank. The water, it wasn't polluted, so your fish in there—we ate 'em."

Few needed to drive as far as Polk County's Green Swamp to hunt; phosphate companies south of Lakeland allowed ten-year-olds with their first .22 rifle to take aim at ducks and other fowl.

"Hunting was a guy thing in high school," Joe W. Chiles explains. "Lawton, as sociable as he was, would have had these other guys, other fellows."

Classmate Larry Richardson would remember Lawton Jr. as a self-taught hunter; Lawton Sr. was a "sit on the porch kind of guy" according to classmate Ann Miller. Lawton and high school classmates often hunted in Groveland.

Like all Lakeland kids, Lawton stole oranges and watermelon from local fields or markets. "I hate to say this," Ann Miller related, "but I'll bet in our neck of the woods there were very few people who had not ever stolen a watermelon. Just like oranges. People stole oranges. But they thought it was your privilege to pick."

Other kids at Lake Morton Elementary flew airplanes around the building for fun. Lawton Jr., taking after his father, introduced himself through pranks and practical jokes.

Ann Miller recalls: "Lawton and his dad had that same . . . way they could smile. It was never a smirk. But it was, you didn't know really what was gonna happen. I can still see it."

Lawton's sister Jeannette, nicknamed "J. J.," brought home a boyfriend from University of South Carolina to meet the family in Lakeland in Lawton's junior or senior year of high school. Joe Ruthven, a Carolina farm boy, had never seen Florida before. The day he arrived he found Lawton playing on Lake Morton. "He always had a group of friends," Ruthven added. "There was always somebody at the house visiting with him." The lake's clear water and surrounding neighborhood struck Ruthven as "absolutely gorgeous." You could "swim the lake, perfectly safe, nobody ever locked the doors."[83] Ruthven introduced himself and then Lawton asked him if he would be good enough to drive down to the grocery and get a loaf of bread. The moment Joe closed his car door, Lawton hurled a smoke bomb. Lawton's friends on the street corner giggled as the car filled with smoke. He "didn't run me off," Ruthven recalls of Lawton.[84] On later visits, Joe and Jeannette cheered on the trickster at football games.[85]

At Lakeland High School, on a dare, Chiles once splashed into Lake Wire behind the school and treaded water for several hours.[86] Lawton joined the varsity track team sophomore year and ran the 880-yard relay and the 220-yard sprint through senior year.[87] Bill Ellsworth ran the 330-yard sprint, to Lawton's continual delight. "It was always told to me by Chiles that the guy behind me was almost always about to catch me," Ellsworth recollected, "Lawton would terrorize me." Sometimes "I'm sure it was true, but most of the time he made it up, I'm sure to get me to run faster."[88] "Growing up then was not very complicated," recollected classmate David Lyons. "We were all jokesters. We had a common bond growing up in a time that was relatively prosperous and care-free." Ann Miller concurred: "We all got into a little trouble every now and then. We were all guilty of turning benches over on Lake Morton on Halloween. And we all did that. It was before they were concrete."

Schoolmate Betty Cox Richardson found "a good sense of humor and a kind soul" in Lawton.[89] Lawton "was always involved with somebody or trying to be, or trying to get over breaking up, like any teenager," Bill Ellsworth related. "I think perhaps looking back on most of the girls he was serious with, if you can be serious in high school, they were quality people that may have affected his life, shall we say, for the better."[90]

A few blocks from Munn Park, Chiles attended elementary, middle, and high school. There he found his first fraternity of friends.

While Lawton attended sixth grade at Lake Morton Elementary, he found a second-grader named Snow Martin Jr. hiding under a lakeside oak, frightened of his first day at a new school.[91] Snow had just moved to Lakeland from Bartow and knew no one. His father had unsuccessfully run for the state senate seat that Holland vacated to become governor. "There I was," Martin recalls, "this brand-new kid on the block, scared to death just standing there." Chiles "took me under his wing and we became friends from that day until the day he died." Martin and other friends often saw Lawton on his bicycle working a newspaper route, washing his dog in Lake Morton, or just fooling around. "Ten-year-old, twelve-year-old kids rode bicycles downtown and watched movies with no fear of safety," Martin explains. One day, though, a car hit Lawton on his bike, sending him sky high and breaking one of his legs. Locals liked to say that the impact catapulted his pants onto the telephone lines.[92]

Ann Miller and Lawton met in sixth grade, when his family moved to Lake Morton. Her father also worked for the Atlantic railroad and she had known Lawton's family for years prior to the move. Ann enjoyed Lawton's sense of humor:

> Lawton broke his leg. We were in the sixth grade. And Lake Morton's Auditorium was on the third floor, and he sat on the front row because he had to keep his leg—he was in a cast. So Lovie Mae Oxford was our sixth grade teacher but she also directed the music . . . and she always led it real funny, you know it was not just doing this whatever. She was leading and not paying attention and she tripped over Lawton's foot. She out of embarrassment pitched one fit. I still see

Lawton hoppin', going that way down the stairs and she was chasing him, accusing. But he did not, he did not trip her.

Bill Ellsworth knew him by name before Lawton moved from Dixieland and they began attending Lake Morton Elementary together. "I think he became very well known before classes opened," he speculated, "because being the new boy in the neighborhood, when someone is mysteriously breaking out all of the windows on the north side of the school immediately brought him into a position of notoriety since all the other kids in the neighborhood didn't do it and knew who did." Ellsworth found the newcomer's name "catchy" and they shared the same age. His first recollection of meeting Lawton was at a touch football game on the banks of Lake Morton soon after the war began. Ellsworth joined the game and "of course, on the team, or the leader of the team, or the leader of the pack, whatever, was Lawton Chiles."[93]

Lawton's debut as center on the Lakeland High's junior varsity football team introduced him to the whole town. In the tenth grade, Lawton was put on the front line to receive a kickoff as a packed Bryant Stadium watched. Bill Ellsworth recounts:

> They kick the ball to him; I don't even think it was supposed to be an onside kick. He reaches down to get the ball and he kicks it back to the opposing team. The stands became violent. First great chance, and they all knew his name quickly, "who is that idiot!?" and they started screaming. I was in the stands; I wasn't privileged to even sit on the bench. And it's true. He clumsily kicked the ball back. So that was his entrée into athletics. And of course, if he did it on purpose, it added to his name recognition; obviously, in this community it certainly did. And he did end up playing center and he ended up playing first string.[94]

Senior year the varsity football team, the Dreadnaughts, lost every game but a six-to-six tie in Plant City.[95] Some of Lawton's discouraged teammates quit to become cheerleaders. "One of my very close friends, Fisk Tolle," Bill Ellsworth recalls, "has the distinction, and he often says that he lettered in his senior year in cheerleading and football."[96]

Through high school, few social events took Lawton Chiles more than a few miles from Munn Park.

"Social life usually meant going to a high-school ball game on Friday, the Polk Theater on Saturday and church on Sunday," according to Lakeland's Neva Jane Langley. "All of the teenagers had favorite seats [at the Polk Theater], where they would always sit to be near their friends." A big night on the town ended with a visit to the ice cream parlor after the picture show.[97] Kids only saw television at the Florida State Fair, if at all. Young couples planned dates at the Lakeland teen center, called the Hi Spot, where they danced, played cards, and shot pool.[98] Generally, local teens dated in groups.

Teens with cars gathered for a summertime swim at Kissengen Springs, between Bartow and Fort Meade.[99] The *Lakeland Ledger* describes Kissengen as a "grassroots place where people could put aside all pretense and be informal and have a general good time just relaxing and being sociable."[100] Visitors rented lockers with baskets at the bath house for ten cents. Boy Scouts camped at the springs. "It was fabulous," Ann Miller recalls, "you know it was sulfur water but it was fresh." The springs were popular until phosphate mining ruined the spring and it vanished into the Peace River. "On the way back from the Springs," related Bartow's Ira Sullivan Reese, "everybody gathered at John's Drive-in out on Highway 17 for hamburgers" smothered in John's special hot slaw.[101]

As older brothers marched off to war, some never to return, Chiles' generation watched the home front from their classrooms. When Japan attacked Pearl Harbor, Dyas Gregg was in Lakeland's Polk Theater with her sister and grandmother. "When we stepped outside," Gregg recollected, "everyone was talking about war and the Japanese bombing us, and I couldn't figure out what was going on."[102] Three days afterward, Governor Holland announced a clamp-down on non-essential state expenditures. He worked with the White House to secure federal funds for Florida and rationing boards assembled to address tire and other material shortages.[103] Florida's National Guard mobilized, including Polk's 116th Field Artillery Regiment at Bartow, Lakeland, and Winter Haven.[104] The Army Corps of Engineers secretly tested chemical weapons in the Green Swamp, a popular hunting ground.[105] Upward surging U.S. demand for phosphorus bombs, oils and smoke screens revived the phosphate industry; Polk farmers supplied U.S. and British troops with unprecedented amounts of Vitamin C-rich orange juice.[106] A common ad for war bonds in the *Lakeland Ledger* shrieked, ""Suppose every man, woman and child in this town should be killed!" It depicted the grim reaper charging out of the shadows, brandishing a stone sword. "This is a typical American small town, with a population of about 3000," the ad continued, "Well, 3,283 Americans were struck dead in a single day not so long ago—on just one of the many battlefronts on which we're fighting."[107] Lakeland homes displayed gold stars on their windows in memory of fallen family heroes. Bill Ellsworth reflected on boyhood in a wartime economy:

It was great excitement, somewhat, because the entire area was covered up with service people because of our air bases and training camps and everything in Florida. In some respects, you felt like you were part of the war with troop trains coming through, and Food Machinery [Corporation] out here on Lake Bonny manufacturing amphibian track assault vehicles, and they were testing them at Lake Parker and Lake Bonny and always running aground, just like we'd see in the movies. But we didn't have to go to the movies; they were testing them there every day. And of course they had Lodwick Field, which was built before the war to train British boys to fly, and that was extended after the war, I suppose. And then we had Dranefield set up, and they just didn't stay out there. You'd look up and they'd be bivouacked. I can remember going around all the time on the west side of Lake Bonny and there was a bivouac. They were out cooking breakfast. You'd go as a kid and they'd serve you breakfast. They were just kids, but we didn't know they were kids; they were just a little older than us. So you were in a war atmosphere, and counting the trains going by carrying things back and forth, and up in the sky was nothing but planes all the time. We'd count the number of planes and formations and things of that nature. . . . So, who was thinking about leadership? I mean, we were living the part and eagerly probably waiting to go.[108]

Lawton, Ellsworth, and another friend George Carr joined the Boy Scouts, where they played war by building pill boxes, ditches and obstacle courses. Chiles stuck to Carr and Ellsworth socially. Carr, a year older, also had attended Lake Morton School. "He always said," Ann Miller recalls of Carr, "he swam across the Lake to go home every day. But George was one of those young men that forever was the absolute gentleman . . . very highly respected, long drawn out Southern drawl." Both played as centers on the football team. When George graduated, Lawton took over as starter. Lucky boys on vacation on Anna Maria Island saw a Navy PT boat motor from the pier and scan the horizon for Japanese submarines, or watched bombs explode on Passage Key's artillery range, sending colonies of terns into the air.[109]

For his part, Lawton Sr. introduced ducks to Lake Morton. Rationing boards controlled sugar, meat and other goods, but no regulation governed wild game. "Whether it was true or not," Snow Martin Jr. later recounted, "I have always understood that he instituted the ducks on the lake for the purpose of providing food." Lawton Sr. brought mallards, and eventually the well-fed birds stopped returning North.[110] From time to time Lawton Jr. was accused of shooting ducks on the lakes. No one, however, actually hurt the ducks. "We didn't eat the ducks," Ann Miller explains. "We only fed the ducks, and the swan." Lawton Sr. "probably would have taken a BB gun and sat out there on the front porch if they started eating his ducks."

Chiles dallied with a secret society called the Sphinx that met monthly off-campus for "no purpose other than to raise Cain."

Through high school political activism, Chiles finally began to explore the rest of Florida and the greater South.

Junior year, teachers nominated he and Bill Ellsworth for a Boys' State convention in Tallahassee. At the convention, Lawton supported the gubernatorial candidacy of a new friend, Edmond "Eddie" Gong of Miami.[111] Jack Pridgen, a class behind Lawton at Lakeland High, recalls that Lawton "was on the football team, so I knew of Lawton Chiles. I knew that he was a so-called 'big man on campus' type and a big achiever."[112] Lawton rose to the international vice presidency of Key Club, a leadership and civil organization, in his junior year. The club planned high school dances, parties, and other extracurricular activities, and those tapped by seniors to join considered it a plum post. Lawton and Bill Ellsworth had ridden the train to Macon, Georgia, for a National Key Club Convention, where Lawton won the position. "To the extent of how he served or what he did, I don't know; it's suspect," Ellsworth has said. "But that would be, as I recall, my first true inclination that he had aspirations."[113] His family applauded the accomplishment.

As seniors, Lawton, Ellsworth, and about twenty other students took a week off school to attend the national Key Club convention in Memphis, Tennessee. The group threw money in a pot for the person who arrived at the event first. Lawton and Ellsworth decided they would hitchhike to save time and money while the others took the train. They discovered that a friend's father owned a citrus packing plant in Plant City that shipped fruit out day and night, and figured they would hitch a ride on a fruit truck before sunup and win the jackpot. Ellsworth embellished the adventure:

> So anyway, we got in this, and it didn't even have a sleeper cab, in this fruit truck. I'm in the middle of course and we go on up there, so much so that the trucker, I kept falling asleep supposedly and bothering the trucker because I was leaning on him . . . [the trucker] had to deviate because there were floods in Georgia, so he had to go out of our way and we end up, the next night as I recall, anyway, in the wee hours of the morning somewhere up the line, three o'clock in the morning, it was the next day, I'm sure, he decides he's going one way and we're going the other and he stops the truck in a little two-bit town and puts us out at the city park. It was either Georgia or Tennessee. It may have been as far as Tennessee. And here we are. We didn't know where we were! We didn't have any idea, you know. Anyway it was fun. There was an older man shooting rats in the park with a .22. . . . And we watched him do that and at about five-thirty in the morning, in the café across the street, lights go on. Naturally we go over there because there is no traffic. You couldn't hitchhike. . . . The lady had opened the café up for breakfast obviously, so we eat breakfast; we had a little money and ate breakfast. . . . So all that delay and running through Georgia and everything, we naturally ended up coming to Memphis, we did not win the pot. And as I remember, most of my time was spent in Memphis in a real hustling pool hall right out of the movies, watching these sharks take on each other. It was right out of the movies.[114]

After a day politicking as international vice president in Memphis, Lawton and Ellsworth toured the town with dates. Ellsworth recalls a girl who sat with Lawton on the bus ride back:. "Lawton ate hamburgers and hot dogs and candy bars all the way, at every truck stop; she was paying." Ellsworth and friends sat in the back. "Now and then, he'd give us a nibble."

Lawton aspired to the student body presidency that year, too, but lacked the grades to qualify. Bill Ellsworth won the post instead. "From Lawton's standpoint, he was a quick-take too and he didn't do okay sometimes because he didn't give himself enough time for the quick-take," Ellsworth explains.[115] "So he became president of the senior class and in some respects, that's probably more important."[116] When the high school seniors staged a "city government for a day," Lawton served as police chief. The senior yearbook praised Lawton, also known as "Uncle Bud," for his "sharp mind and extraordinary leadership ability."[117] "He was always a go-getter," classmate Frances Brown remembers.[118]

Bill Ellsworth expounds on his and the student body's kinship with Lawton:

> He also seemed to have an intuitiveness, as far as who might be important and who might not be. He never, ever would shun anybody if they might not be, but he might be able to, particularly among older people, understand that some people were maybe movers or shakers with more potential or what not. If he gravitated to them, it was because of a likeness but, in that regard, he never refused or didn't want to gravitate to everybody. He gravitated to everybody. . . .
>
> So it was always there, and somewhat recognized, I'm sure, by everybody that knew him, after his football game when he was in the tenth grade. I mean that carried through in college and whatever, and in politics, I'm sure. It was just his general character and personality makeup. He wasn't out there trying to be the friendliest guy or the most jovial guy, or tell the loudest jokes or the best jokes or be the leader of the pack; he was there, always there, always constant, and always a friendly person, so much so that people valued his friendship.[119]

The 1948 senior class president also "knew that he should be something" according to Ellsworth. He "had much more insight than most of us about that, which I would assume pointed to a future that he had in mind."[120]

His mother, local president of the United Daughters of the Confederacy and granddaughter of a Civil War surgeon, wanted him to become a doctor. "Mom," Lawton would say, "I'd make a better lawyer."[121] His mother responded, "You'd better be a good one then."

Joe W. Chiles recognized his cousin's convictions around the dinner table one night at the Lawton Chiles household when talk turned to scandal-plagued Governor Fuller Warren. Joe W. spoke up from the card table set for the kids: "Oh I remember how you all supported Fuller Warren. Fuller Warren was just the greatest. And you all really thought Fuller Warren was so terrific. And now, look at him now, what do you think now?" The conversation probably referred to the 1951 murder of civil rights activist Harry T.

Moore in nearby Brevard County. Governor Warren's approval rating had suffered due to this and other bombings during the "Florida Terror."

Lawton Jr., sitting across the table, put his tableware down, and angrily stared down his cousin, younger by four years. "Here I am in his house," Joe W. related, "and I'm feeling very intimidated. I shut up and said nothing more on the subject."

Eighteen-year-old Lawton Chiles' political views in 1948 resembled those of every other graduate of the Munn Park political school. He loved Florida orange juice, "Imperial" Polk County, and Spessard Holland.

Legend told that at age sixteen, Lawton Chiles drove the U.S. Senator-elect Spessard Holland around central Florida on his thank-you tour.[122] Pundits had praised Holland for becoming, in the state's 113-year history, the second governor and the first native Floridian to serve as both governor and senator.[123] Joe W. Chiles later recalled Governor Holland's visit to Lakeland High School: "Everybody walked out onto the stage, all the students, teachers, and everybody stood up out of deference to the man." To his driver, though, Holland had joined the most exclusive club in the world—a fraternity of statesmen.

Wouldn't it be a heckuva note, Lawton mused, if he took Senator Holland's seat one day? "He had the ambition even then to be a U.S. senator," classmate Dexter Douglass explains. "I think it was something he wanted since he was ten."[124]

Holland had never lost an election. Other politicos thought of crowds as wild animals to be tamed; they bragged about coaxing the worst of rabbles into "eating out of their hands." But Holland considered politics a gentleman's sport, a ritual of soaring rhetoric and Christian metaphor.

Only the most extreme elements of Polk County opposed Holland. These ex-Confederates ambled in from the scrub, leaned on their canes, and spun yarns about the scorched cotton bales and dead hogs that marked General Sherman's "March to the Sea" and nighttime Union retreats through Florida's gator-infested swamps during the "War Between the States." They saw themselves as the unconquered, whose Tallahassee brethren had raised the Rebel flag every morning from the attack on Fort Sumter to the surrender at Appomattox. Despite silver-haired Holland's self-proclaimed status as a "hopeless reactionary," they cringed at his co-sponsorship of the 1937 law repealing the poll tax with Miami Senator Ernest Graham, which had earned him the respect of blacks as well as most poor whites.[125] They repudiated Holland's Confederate family legacy: Holland's father and paternal grandfather had defended Atlanta against General Sherman's invasion. His mother's father fought with General J.E.B. Stuart in Virginia.[126] These veterans had witnessed the first of a series of reforms that led African-American novelist and folklorist Zora Neale Hurston to eventually call Holland "my ideal of a southern statesman."[127]

Though born into a Florida far removed from Zora Neale Hurston's, Chiles had reached the same conclusion about Holland. He had never met his equal as a gentleman, politician, and Southerner. He probably doubted he ever would find a better political mentor than Holland, or a better political classroom than Munn Park.

Raised on one side of a small town in an isolated state, Chiles knew all the richness of Southern folklore—and none of its defects.

A Personality for Politics

"She's the most important thing that ever happened to me," Lawton Chiles said of his wife, Rhea. "I don't know how to explain it any other way. We have been partners in all the races and in all the offices."[128]

Born in Pittsburgh, Pennsylvania, Rhea Grafton moved to Florida with her family at the age of six or seven. She attended Ponce de Leon High School in Coral Gables. Her mother was a homemaker; her father delivered bread.

Rhea first saw Lawton Chiles in high school, at a state Key Club convention at St. Petersburg Beach in 1947. The all-male Key Club elected girls for sponsors, and Rhea attended as one of four sponsors. Lawton, running for international vice president of the Key Club at the time, delivered a speech and handed Rhea a campaign card.

The couple first dated at University of Florida. Years later, as Governor and Mrs. Chiles, they recalled their courtship. Rhea had found Lawton "very physically attractive," though he "seemed like a challenge." He "sure danced differently." Lawton had also considered himself a challenge. "Did he ever!" Rhea added. But, "as it turns out," Governor Chiles retorted, "I was not."[129]

During their courtship, Rhea supported Lawton's interest in politics. Politics "was part of his software," she later recalled. "It was going to come out along the way," but "he had to get his ducks in the row."

The couple married on January 27, 1951, at Miami Beach. They had grown up in distinct social worlds but fallen in love anyway.

When Lawton entered University of Florida in 1948, his home of Polk County still resisted modernity. The area's public schools were chronically underfunded and poor in quality. Polk County refuged some of the state's most active Ku Klux Klan. In summer 1949, Klan night riders fired into several homes in Polk City. They then burned a cross on the grounds of a blacks-only school.

The county's largest towns sprawled outward after World War II without the services to meet new demand from Florida tourists. Winter Haven, one of the largest municipalities, "consisted mostly of woods and little swamp areas along the lake shore"[130] according to one vistor. The "big excitement was the doctor who lived on the lake and had a seaplane. We'd get to watch him take off." Lakeland life likewise ambled along. The town's Silver Moon Drive-In Theatre welcomed its first moviegoers in 1948. Downtown measured only a few blocks. Most social life occupied the lakes, ponds, and woods—fishing, boating, and hunting.

Rhea's hometown of Coral Gables, in contrast, symbolized cosmopolitan order and design. Built in 1914, the town was planned as a paragon of the Mediterranean Revival architectural style—meant to evoke the Spanish Riviera. Inspired by landscape architect Frederick Law Olmstead, who designed New York City's Central Park, planners for Coral Gables constructed broad avenues, impressive buildings, plazas, and fountains. Green space abounded. The original planners reserved acreage for tennis courts, country clubs, and golf courses. Perhaps the first distinguishing design evident to town visitors would be its roofs, tiled with terracotta, ochre, and sienna colors. To complete the look of paradise, this pastel roof-scape elegantly balanced the greens of palm trees and blues of swimming pools.

Mutual friend Bill Ellsworth considered Lawton and Rhea a strange match:

> [Rhea's] brother [Ed] was a very bright guy. He was an architect. He was older. Same old thing, veteran, got out, got older, I mean; he was just chagrined to death as she was running around with this guy from Polk County, from Hicksville. I mean, she's a Coral Gables chick and Coral Gables at that time, and still is to a certain extent, is "the place" down there. . . . And then she's running around with this guy. And nobody could figure it out. In fact, she'll tell you the story, I mean – 'Get rid of him! He's never going to amount to a hill of beans! What a hayseed. Come home! What are you doing talking to him?' And then sometimes opposites attract, and of course that always happened.[131]

Lawton Chiles resembled most of the other boys on the political prowl at University of Florida. "No, I can't say that he was outstandingly different from other boys," Rhea says of her husband.

At college, Lawton pursued a traditional career path minted by the prior generation of rising male lawyers, judges, and politicians. The social world of Gainesville barely outsized Lakeland's.

Florida's young white college-bound men preferred Gainesville's University of Florida over Tallahassee's Florida State University in 1948. FSU and UF both became co-ed in 1947, but the latter had traditionally admitted men only and in Chiles' time, social inertia and casual discrimination still favored men.

In Gainesville, future governors, State Supreme Court justices, and legislators—almost exclusively men—played each other in pickup football games on the green, dated the same sorority sisters, and would remember where they were when World War II ended.

University of Florida's small size and extensive career network guaranteed an outlet for Lawton's ambition. The UF student body totaled about 9,000, including about 1,000 seniors. Students felt community kinship. Gainesville's nickname was "Hog Town." UF classmate and Chiles buddy Bill Ellsworth describes a college community that was comforting, if homogenous:

> It's easy to get around and know somebody. It's easy to hitchhike and stay with somebody, overnight or a week. . . . People hitchhiked. People took rides. Going home from the weekends, people bummed rides. People picked up people. God knows how you got a ride home and back. . . . Right, and they'd go down the road on the way back to Gainesville and there'd be guys hitchhiking and you could pile them in until you couldn't take them. And you made friends that way, believe me.[132]

The tiny galaxy of rising political stars eyeing a seat in the state legislature after graduation could meet, greet, and befriend rivals and assemble allies. They knew last names and parents and grandparents of all the greater Gators.[133] An enterprising student could reconnoiter the majority of Florida's future luminaries of science, medicine, politics, and business in four years at Gainesville. UF "Gators" cordoned off career paths for friends from their favorite cliques, fraternity members, and old college sweethearts. Rich,

31

brilliant Floridians might travel to Harvard or Princeton for college, but risk returning home jobless.

Lawton Chiles participated in campus politics, but so did hundreds of others, including dozens of budding scholars, star athletes, and aspiring statesmen. Campus campaign platforms, according to Chiles, dealt with small campus issues, like "where you were going to sit in the football stadium." Lawton worked as campus chairman for the Billy Matthews for Congress campaign. Rallies occurred all across his district and Chiles stumped as a surrogate for Matthews one night in Waldo, Florida.[134] Chiles entered the University of Florida Hall of Fame in his senior year. "Bud . . . a familiar figure in the political pow-wows," read a caption accompanying Chiles' picture in the Hall of Fame section of the 1952 UF yearbook, *The Seminole*.[135]

Part of a generation that included future Governors Reubin Askew and Bob Graham; citrus magnate Ben Hill Griffin; legal mastermind, founder of the Holland & Knight law firm, and future president of the American Bar Association, Chesterfield Smith; U.S. Senator Bill Nelson; State Supreme Court Justice and UF President Stephen C. O'Connell, State Supreme Court Justice Stephen H. Grimes; and State Supreme Court Justice Charles T. Wells, Chiles excelled as a networker and tinkerer in the process, and worked among superlative classmates.

Chiles, Askew, and these distinguished compatriots won coveted openings in UF's elite leadership society, Florida Blue Key. The society, founded in 1923 as an organization committee for homecoming, by Chiles' time was a social club for the super students—a farm team for the Florida Democratic party. The Blue Key homecoming, the parade, banquet and Gator Growl show, drew the entire campus, as well as state Senator William Shands, U.S. Senator Claude Pepper, U.S. Senator George Smathers, and the rest of the state's political class. Chiles' pal Dexter Douglass, tapped in 1950, says of Blue Key, "It taught you one thing: You make your friends before you need them." Chiles "did not distinguish himself with flashes of brilliance," grade-school pal Snow Martin Jr. recalls, "but with a constancy, a consistent method."[136] "When it came time to tend to business, he did," according to Stephen H. Grimes.

"He was a good student, well above average," Dexter Douglass says of Chiles. "If he didn't graduate with honors, he was very close."[137] Many classmates, however, expected Douglass to rise faster than Chiles politically. Douglass was vice president of Blue Key, president of the Phi Delta Phi legal fraternity, and president of Scabbard and Blade, a military honorary organization.

Rhea was political coordinator for her sorority, Alpha Delta Pi. She describes the UF campus party system as an "incubator" for Florida's future political leadership. Lawton led the varsity party in the campus party system. At one point, Rhea withdrew her sorority from a student political party "in total outrage that they weren't promising women enough high posts in the student government." Lawton came to her house to persuade her to reconsider, but she refused. "Oh yeah, we tooth and nailed it," Rhea recalls.[138]

But during the post-World War II economic boom, fraternity antics and hunting stunts marked the groom in UF's institutional memory as much as his political acumen. Lawton and his classmates recollected joyfully their college years at the barstool and in the bird field.

Lawton rushed the fraternity Alpha Tau Omega (ATO), a social enclave for Lakelanders. Stephen Grimes, future chief justice of the Florida Supreme Court, presided over the Alpha Tau Omega fraternity when Chiles entered UF as a freshman in 1948. "I recall very well we really wanted to get him to join ATO," Grimes says. "He was the kind of fellow everybody liked, and we felt he'd be a real asset to the fraternity. . . . He was always a leader, and had a low-key, magnetic personality."[139] Bill Ellsworth joined ATO with Lawton. By the time Snow Martin Jr. rushed ATO in 1951, Lawton supervised the process—especially for his hometown. "I became an ATO pledge because of Lawton," Martin Jr. recalls. "Bud," as he was known around campus, "was a good guy to be friends with."[140] Martin Jr. summarizes the Greek scene:

> Well, you know there were probably a dozen fraternities that, in retrospect, were essentially equivalent. Fraternities then tended to draw from specific geographic areas, and ATO was very, very strong in Lakeland and in part of Tampa, we were heavy in Orlando and oddly enough in Jax Beach. The SAEs for example were heavy in Tallahassee and Orlando. The Phi Delts tended to be heavy, or KAs would tend to be heavy in South Tampa, the Plant High School crowd. The ATOs drew the Hillsborough crowd. I think most of the Jesuit-type guys were probably either ATOs, SAEs or Phi Delts. But truthfully, there were no real distinctions between them; they were all real good houses, really.[141]

Snow Martin Jr. recalls Chiles' affinity for bars:

There was a bar in Gainesville called The Kit Kat Club and the front door was two doors, side by side, and both of them had a circular glass in the middle of them, so you could see through and wouldn't pull the door open in the face of somebody. It was a circle that probably had about a twelve-inch diameter, and Chiles knew how to break it with one punch by hitting it and withdrawing real quick. And after coming under the influence of alcohol, he would demonstrate this. I can recall twice he showed me how to do it.[142]

Chiles and Martin Jr. as undergrads joined a campus group called L'Apache, which comprised nine members from the nine big fraternities and organized dances and parties. The initiation ceremony involved drinking a pint of whiskey and walking around a circle of the members so each could hit the pledge with a two-handed paddle. And thereafter, the pledge wore a black shirt with a red dagger to school dance functions. "Most of my recollections of Undergraduate School have to do with raising hell, frankly," Snow says.[143] "[Chiles] drank, but never to the point of losing control."[144]

"He had a great time," Dexter Douglass recalls. "We didn't miss any parties."[145] In the Fall Frolics of 1951, Merv Griffin, long before he became a billionaire entertainment mogul, sang with the Freddy Martin Orchestra. The following February, Vaughn Moore and the Moodmaids were featured in the "Leap Year Valentine's Day," dance on campus. Chiles probably attended both.[146] Bill Ellsworth recalls Gator frat life:

Now it's the rage, but back then people had them, the cycle crowd was in high school and it was cheap transportation then, compared to cars, and people did a lot of wild things. I can remember the administration building, and I don't know if it's still there or not, they'd drive the motorcycles up the steps and inside and all that kind of stuff. . . . I had a roommate that never went in and out of the door when I was a freshman. He kept his motorcycle out the window and he went in and out the window.[147] ...

We had hazing. We had paddling. We had all of the road trips. We had all of the stuff that fraternities have which probably are all outlawed and banned now. And you know you go through those things and it's sort of like "can you make it?" "will you make it?" and all that kind of stuff. So [you join] a pledge class together. You're tortured constantly. You have to go through all these rituals. In fact, in those days at the University of Florida, every freshman had to wear what they called a "rat cap," which was a little cap with a bill, which identified you as actually what you are.[148]

On the other hand, Ellsworth recalls, "We had great times, great experiences, very few fatalities and very few bad injuries." The television set had not yet supplanted books, hunting, and swimming as college pastimes. UF students traveled down water-rutted dirt roads to the Ichetucknee River. There they would picnic, swing of trees, inner tube down the river, camp, and build fires. Ellsworth would join Lawton at his grandparent's place in north Florida:

See, [Lawton's] parents had, or his mother's family had a place, an old shack, on the Suwannee River, near the mouth of it. We would go there sometimes. It's one of these places where the bedrooms were half partitioned because they had to get the airflow across the ceiling. They didn't have ceiling fans. Maybe the two feet from the top where the bedroom wall would hit the ceiling was wide open. Shall we say it wasn't the most private place in the world?[149]

ATO buddies often joked that Lawton would rather hunt than politick. "My only recollection of all that," Snow Martin Jr. told, "is one day in the back end of the ATO House, they were cleaning the dove they had shot, and they would clean 'em by first ripping the head off, and I had never been much of a hunter, but that absolutely solidified it forever, watching those dove have their heads ripped off." Chiles and four or five ATO brothers would shoot game on a regular basis. "But no, and I know Chiles hunted frequently, I just never could bring myself to fire a gun at something that was alive."[150]

Chiles continued a traditional path to public office in law school. Lawton Chiles graduated University Florida in 1952 as a business major and immediately entered law school at the same institution.

He interrupted his legal education to serve as an Army artillery officer in Korea.[151] "He didn't write letters—well, he did back from Korea," Rhea recalls. "He loved to get a card to me that made me laugh. There was one that said, 'You have everything it takes, baby, to have a great love affair.' It opens up and says, 'Me.'"[152]

35

When Lawton returned safely from Korea, he and Rhea moved into Flavette Village apartments in Gainesville and he started law school in earnest.[153] Rhea observed little if any trauma in Lawton from his Korean War experience:

> Lawton wasn't in combat. . . . He was out there, on the edge, but I don't think he ever saw combat. . . . And Lawton was an outdoorsman. . . . He got along fine out in the boondocks. But I never noticed any vestige of emotional trauma from the war at all [in him]. In fact, he talked about it with [a Korean nicknamed Froggy, who] was sort of his boy. He loved Froggy, and had a lot of fun with Froggy. That's the way [Lawton] talked about it, was the adventure.

The military service benefited the newlyweds by expanding Lawton's social and political network, according to Bill Ellsworth: "He lucked out even more 'cause he goes away and then he comes back and he meets more people as they come back, a whole bevy of people younger than we are accelerated up and they're in law school, and he makes a wide range of friends with those people, who became very prominent."[154]

At law school, Lawton drew friends from a smaller pool of the state's aspirant political elite, including Julian Clarkson, Gene Spellman, Dexter Douglass, Bob Montgomery, Jimmy Kynes, and Worley Brown. Chiles met Clarkson in Phi Delta Phi; Clarkson was president of the legal fraternity when Chiles joined. Snow Martin Jr. added, "then of course when Lawton came back [from Korea], you know, he had a wife and kids and this and that and you know. He was like an adult and didn't pal around with the college kids as much."[155]

At Bryan Hall, then the home of the law school, Chiles worked in the library, earning seventy-five cents an hour in the circulation department. Mandell Glicksberg, an assistant professor and law librarian, hired him as a student assistant in the law library, and taught him constitutional law as well. "He never seemed to feel that he was above anybody," Glicksberg recalls. "He was the sort of person it was easy to talk to. It was very comfortable to be around him." Classmate Betty Taylor concurs: "He certainly was a person who could meet everybody. I was impressed by him. He was very friendly, and genuine in his interest in people." Future Governor Reubin Askew met Chiles in law school; they shared their plans to run for the state legislature. Askew:

Lawton and I were in Law School together, so I met him in Law School and liked him—had no reason not to like him. I think Lawton was a pretty likeable guy. He finished a little bit ahead of me in Law School as I recall, but I met him in Law School and we worked together on some projects. We worked together on a Blue Key project on what would be the slogan for homecoming at the University of Florida, 1955. It was a slogan contest and we finally came up with "Relax a While Gator Style," which I thought was beautiful.[156]

Before law school ended in 1955, Lawton and Rhea planned to move to his beloved "Imperial Polk County" to raise their children: a daughter Tandy, born in 1952; followed by a son, Bud, in 1953, and a second son, Ed, in 1955.

Back in Lakeland, Lawton could ask his parents for help in giving his children a smart start. Family gatherings circumscribed Lawton and Rhea's social schedule.[157] When they moved into their own place, they and their children visited "Big Lawton" and Margaret Chiles for Thanksgiving dinner. "My grandmother, I called her the Groove, was the archetype," Bud Chiles, Lawton and Rhea's eldest son, recalls. "No matter what was going on inside her, when you asked how she was, the most you were going to get out of the Groove is 'Fine, and you?' Expressing feelings and emotion is not in our genes."

Margaret Chiles occasionally invited the grandchildren to play hearts and eat homemade pound cake. For church potluck at Lakeland's First Presbyterian, she brought popular dishes such as green beans, turnip greens, and icebox cookies. Mrs. Chiles had begun her long membership at the church in 1916. She graduated from Lakeland Senior High School in 1919 and then attended Florida State College for Women and Stetson University.

Mrs. Chiles was "a stitch," family friend Ann Miller recalls, "feisty." Everyone loved her fried corn, fried chicken, rice and gravy. According to Ann, for one of Mrs. Chiles' signature dishes, "you fried bacon, then you fried the corn in the bacon drippings, and then you crumbled the bacon back in the corn." Margaret was also active in the United Daughters of the Confederacy, the Lakeland Garden Club, the Daughters of the American Revolution, and the Polk County Pioneers.

Bud recalls how he and his siblings visited his father's parents at their place on the Suwannee River in north Florida. Lawton Sr. and Margaret commuted to this and another home in Gainesville via Cadillac. The couple bought a new Caddy every year, Bud relates, with money made from commercial real estate development. At dinner with the grandchildren, Lawton Sr. would hide silver dollars under the kids' plates. Sometimes, at dinner's end, Lawton Sr. would say, "It's time to go to [Fanning Springs]." Then, once the kids got excited, Big Lawton would add, "Goin' to the bedsprings." That meant it was time to go to bed.

Joe P. Ruthven, Lawton Jr.'s brother-in-law, recalls that "after [Big Lawton's] heart attack, he wasn't able to do much, but he was very sociable."[158] For Christmas, Lawton and Rhea would visit the Ruthvens—who joined the Chiles family when Lawton's sister Jeanette married businessman Joe P. Ruthven. Lawton, not to be outshined by his father's charisma, dressed up as Santa, and Rhea cooked special bread.

In Lakeland, Lawton Chiles began to leverage his Gator network to begin the legal career that by American tradition presaged elected office.

High school buddies Bill Ellsworth, George Carr, and Lawton Chiles graduated from law school about the same time. In their hometown, personal favors mattered more than merit. Lakeland circa 1955 had modernized superficially, like many small towns beset by television and suburban values. The Polk Theater had lost business to television; so had Munn Park. Phosphate, orange groves, cattle ranches, and railroads still ruled the chamber of commerce; doctors, lawyers, small businessmen, and other tradesmen comprised the middle class.

Lakeland boasted four or five major lawyers.[159] Chiles found work for one of Lakeland's richest and most formidable, former U.S. Rep. J. Hardin Peterson Sr. Known by locals as "Mr. Pete," Peterson Sr. shared personality traits and political heritage with U.S. Senator Spessard Holland.[160] Bill Ellsworth describes Mr. Pete:

> Jay Hardin Petersen, Sr., defeated Herbert Drane. That goes back to the 1920s and 1930s. He was a wonderful man, Mr. Petersen; he knew everybody in the south and who your family was. That was in his blood. And in those days, the country, it's gotten bigger, but from the pre-Civil War everybody knows everybody. In the Civil War, if you've studied history, you all know everybody and are related, and if they don't know you, they know who you know. Mr. Petersen was that way still. [If] you would say, "My name is Ellsworth," [he would say,] "Well, I know Ellsworth, are you kin to so-and-so?" He was one

of those people who knew family histories, not necessarily in the south, [but] all over.[161]

After a short stint at Mr. Pete's office, Chiles started his own firm with George Carr and Bill Ellsworth, locating in the basement of the Thelma Hotel on the corner of Kentucky and Lemon. Lawton's brother-in-law Joe P. Ruthven gave his legal business to Chiles' firm. Rhea, who briefly worked as a secretary for the firm, describes the inception of Chiles, Carr, and Ellsworth:

Child custody [cases]. People who were being gassed by the mining companies. Crazies, come falling down the—we were underground, we were down below the hotel. Lawton says whatever falls down the stairs we'll take! And so we did. It was a lot of fun.

Some clients did not pay, to Ellsworth's aggravation. When Ellsworth sued such clients, Chiles would try to calm him down, saying "you just go get more."[162]

Lawton, for his part, excelled at settling with insurance companies, and the firm would celebrate when they anticipated settlements.[163] He also worked for Florida Southern College as a business law instructor to supplement his income, from to 1955 to 1958:

My clientele wasn't growing much, and I was about to starve. Hearing that there might be an opening for a part-time business law teacher at Florida Southern College, I went to the campus for an interview with President [Ludd] Spivey. Just before entering the president's office, Dean [Jean A.] Battle warned me that Dr. Spivey would ask me if I had used alcoholic beverages and that I should be very careful how I answered. Because of my financial straits at the time, I was hardly able to afford to eat, let alone purchase alcoholic beverages. Therefore, in answer to Dr. Spivey's anticipated question, I was able to answer that I had no liquor in my house. That answer, along with the fact that I was willing to accept the small salary Dr. Spivey offered, got me the job, and I began moonlighting as an instructor of business law.[164]

For the first two years in Lakeland, Lawton focused on family and friends as he built his legal reputation and financial war chest.

His third year as a Lakeland lawyer, twenty-seven-year-old Lawton Chiles felt ambition tug at his collar as he toiled in the Thelma Hotel's basement. Chiles again leveraged his Gator network, legal partner Bill Ellsworth explains, to play a bit of state politics:

> I know he utilized that all the time because I would meet with him at times and he was always telling me about people and keeping me abreast of people we knew through all these years, even in high school, and he runs across and knew them and this and that and all. I never saw them again, but he maybe significantly saw them and kept in contact with them. That didn't make the man, but that certainly helped along the way I would think, before everything became wire and everything became TV and everything became publicity and newspapers and all that.[165]

Chiles served as Farris Bryant's campaign treasurer for Polk County during Bryant's first unsuccessful bid for governor in 1956. Lawton's law school classmate Jimmy Kynes, himself state co-chair of the Bryant gubernatorial campaign, encouraged him to participate.

Far from signs, speeches, and sunshine, Chiles grew to hate lawyering. He worked across from Munn Park, the site of his biggest boyhood joys. He must have wondered how many more years he could spend as a political spectator—no different than a hayseed on an orange cart in the park, waiting for the world to come to Lakeland. Bud Chiles reflected:

> My dad was just a young lawyer working the basement of the Thelma Hotel in downtown Lakeland. I guess he must have hated practicing law pretty bad to take such a gamble rather than waiting for a more opportune time to run for office. I remember asking my dad, when I was very young, about a Colt .45 pistol I found in a drawer at his office. He told me that he and his . . . other law partners passed the gun around depending on who had the toughest divorce or child-custody case. That story helped me understand why he favored politics over the law.

Lawton still revered Florida's senior senator, Spessard Holland; he considered him "adroit" and "graceful," a model of Southern manners. Bud Chiles says of his father, "He always had this idea of what a senator should be."

Lawton Chiles decided to run for the state legislature, a public body where he could learn the artistry of power before finding a place beside Holland in the U.S. Senate.

Of his cohorts at UF law school, Dexter Douglass did not figure Lawton as the next governor or U.S. senator. Even if Lawton reached one of those posts, he would be the stereotypical big fish in a small pond. On the 1958 American political landscape, Ohio, New York, Virginia, and Massachusetts commanded the clout. They sired presidents, secretaries of state, and U.S. senators, and produced the ideas that shaped national debate, from the Monroe Doctrine to the Fourteen Points to the New Deal. Florida, considered the stepchild of the South, fought for exposure in the newsreels alongside the likes of Mississippi, Alabama, and Rhode Island.

The Sunshine State's everlasting coastal flats only served military needs for runways and barracks. American vacation-seekers enjoyed the Jersey Shore, Cape Cod, and the Outer Banks, and left Florida's wild to the snakes and mosquitoes. California's Disneyland was still on the drawing board, Disney World still a dream. Jacksonville still exceeded Miami in population size; both claimed 100,000 residents. North Florida, more a suburb of Georgia than a unique cultural center, dominated state business and politics.

Perhaps what distinguished Chiles most from other politically ambitious Gator lawyers was his creative partnership with Rhea.

Rhea relished the life of the creative mind. In Lakeland, she discovered the arts scene at the Little Theater. Home design, indoor and outdoor, enthralled her. Like her brother Ed, Rhea enjoyed a sensibility for architecture. She remade every home her family occupied in Lakeland. Her redesign of their house on Coventry Avenue won her a *Better Homes and Gardens* magazine contest.

She studied painting under William Pachner, George Burrous, and Marilyn Bendell. At one point she co-owned the Paradigm Art Gallery. And she helped found and direct the Polk Museum of Art in Lakeland. Her paintings, especially her portraits of friends and family, won plaudits from everyone who saw them. One of her signature works, a map of Old Florida, attest to her strong command of color and texture.

"I was lookin' it over," she says of her new family's first years in Lakeland, "and tryin' to figure it out, and where I fit in and who I wanted to run around

41

with, and where Lawton was going. It was that time of your life where your eyes are darting everywhere and your ears are open to everything."

Rhea's artistry enhanced and energized all of Lawton's earliest household discussions of political life. She believed in his political vision. She could imagine how his wildest ideas might take shape on the campaign trail.

She helped compensate for her husband's few political blind spots, according to mutual friend and lawyer Dexter Douglass: "Rhea is a very, very unappreciated person. Everybody knows she's got a lot of talent. But she's got a lot of talent that people don't know she really has. And one of 'em was being an excellent gauge, a political gauge of people, and what was going on. To some extent, I thought she had a better sense of deciding whether somebody would be good or not."

Lawton believed loyalty was sacrosanct, and practiced the principle to a fault. Adelaide Clement Sweat joined Chiles, Carr, and Ellsworth as a typist. Sweat remembers Lawton's difficulty in firing one of the other secretaries. She saw a writing tablet with Lawton's signature that read, "She is good, she is good, she is good." Chiles had discovered his distaste for hiring, firing, and other human resources obligations in private practice.

And then there was Lawton's dynamo personality, the ideal ingredient for public office. His Lakeland neighbors have remembered this quality foremost. Burke Kibler had known him since grade school, but he befriended Lawton anew when they joined the military reserve in Lakeland, a unit called the 414th Strategic Intelligence Detachment. They worked there side by side three or four years.[166] Kibler was impressed with Lawton's love of film, especially on the day Lawton called him after seeing *Around the World in 80 Days*.

According to Kibler, his buddy was a "great believer" in hurricane parties. Chiles would join Kibler's gatherings to enjoy good drinks, TV, and radio. "When the hurricane would change direction and go away," Kibler recalls, "you were almost disappointed."

Lawton and Rhea met Robert and Nitzi Waters soon after moving to Lakeland. The Waters and Chiles families went camping at Ocala National Forest. Bob and Lawton hunted. The Waters hosted a Halloween party for neighborhood kids one year. Mrs. Waters called Lawton to tell him about it:

> We didn't call him to do anything, y'know. He just said, "What can we do to help?" I said, "Well, I don't know, we've pretty well got it lined up" at that point. But all of a sudden, that night, they appeared and said, "What can we do to help?" Lawton was dressed up like a mummy or something, so I said, "You come down in the basement

with me," because I was doing that witch thing, y'know, and passing the grapes. . . .

So the kids came down this long hall and we had a big trunk-looking box that Debbie was in, my daughter. [As they climbed] over the logs and through all of the moss we had hanging with the spiders and everything, Debbie would open the trunk and grab their legs. Well, of course they'd scream, but there were more kids coming so they had to keep going. And they'd get down to me where [we] had that spooky music playing . . . and we had dummies stuffed around, scary things. So the whole time I went through my spiel, Lawton's over in the corner [holding a flashlight, and] then I would say, "Now as you leave, be very careful, my brother is out in the lawn, and he will be looking for juicy little children." [Then] Lawton would put his flashlight under [his face] and turn around and go, "Raaaah." Well, those kids would practically kill one another climbing to get out.[167]

Lawton and Rhea befriended the Wolfsons, Willie and Elaine, one of a number of Jewish families in the area. Willie thought "the rapport between Lawton's family and our family was just absolutely beautiful."

Lawton's walking style, Willie recalls, was "nice and easygoing"; he "strolled." Willie expected Lawton to run for president and thought he could win.

Many friends and enemies of Louisiana political legend Huey Long noticed his peculiar gait. "No one who describes him ever says that Huey walked up," T. Harry Williams said in his famous biography of Long. "The usual expression is something like 'Huey came running up.' As he walked, or ran, he threw out his legs to the side in an odd movement. . . . If he was walking with a group, he scurried ahead of the pack."[168]

Neighbor Juanita Black describes Lawton's as a Will Rogers sense of humor. To her, Lawton "could have been a jester." He "could make light of serious situations and not be offensive and some people can't do that." Even "in his jest there was a seriousness about whatever he was saying." Lawton "never trafficked on what he could do, nor did he try to cover up what he couldn't do." Instead, "he just had a way of turning it around."

"He just had an air about him that you felt confident with," law school classmate Dexter Douglass recalls. "And I think it spilled over a lot. It made up for a lot of, maybe, errors. He was the type of guy you were willing to forgive, and he very rarely ever did anything that would give you cause to shoot him."

3

The First Campaign

When Lawton Chiles decided to run for state representative in March 1958, his wife Rhea told their three children, "This is Daddy's time; we're going to help him. Your time will come."[169]

The campaign targeted State Rep. Roy Surles, a ten-year incumbent and chair of the Finance and Taxation Committee, representing Polk County in Tallahassee. "I was very much for his running for political office," Rhea said. "I thought that was the route to my happiness. Because I knew it was what he needed to do."

The two Democratic primaries would occur on September 9 and 30, followed by the general election on November 4. The Democratic primary mattered most in a one-party county like Polk. Few Republicans dared challenge Democratic hegemony in Florida and the rest of the South. Insightful Republicans fled to the North, where they could win elections. "Republicans were sort of like gnats on a horse's back," future Lieutenant Governor Toni Jennings would recall later. When future Governor Buddy MacKay served in the U.S. Air Force from 1955 to 1958, he registered to vote as a Democrat, as he recalls:

> I wrote the supervisor of elections, Miss Fan Pasteur, asking her for the document one needed to register as a Republican. What I received in the mail was the paperwork to register as a Democrat. I telephoned Miss Pasteur and informed her of the mistake. She said,

"That wasn't a mistake. If you register Republican you will embarrass your family." This is the true story of how I became a Democrat.[170]

Joe P. Ruthven would remember first hearing about Chiles' campaign at a Lakeland High football game. "Well, we were at a football game and he sat behind us. [Lawton] told us he was getting ready to throw his hat in the ring, and I didn't really know what he was talking about. Then he started telling us about his plans to run for the House."[171]

High school friend and supporter Sarah MacKay later commented on Lawton's campaign, "We thought it was great. Didn't think he had a chance, but we thought it was great."

Jack Pridgen, a friend from University of Florida, joined Chiles' campaign as his sole staffer, but also advised against the run. The citrus industry was backing Surles's reelection, as did the phosphate and cattle industries. Pridgen's boss, the Director of Public Relations at Florida Citrus Mutual, tried to talk Pridgen out of it. Pridgen didn't know of anyone who thought Chiles could win.[172] Lawton Chiles aimed to overpower Roy Surles with charisma, according to Jack Pridgen:

> In fact, I remember Lawton telling me—not at that first meeting where he told me he wanted to run, but after we got into the campaign—that one of the reasons he felt Surles was vulnerable and could be beat was because he didn't relate to people. I never knew how Surles originally got elected to the legislature, what sort of campaign or what got him there. . . . He would go to the legislature and come back and go into his law office and do his law practice and legislative business, but he didn't get out among the people.[173]

Chiles' one-time legal partner and high school friend Bill Ellsworth describes Roy Surles:

> He was a very difficult person to deal with. It was like he had a sour countenance, a sour outlook. I don't mean to be disparaging to the man, he never did anything bad to me. He knew my father. He spoke to me because of my father, who was in the title business and all. But Roy was not a jokester or prankster. He was withdrawn . . . aloof. If anything, it was like he was upset about something all the time. Maybe he had ulcers.[174]

Long-time friend and attorney Snow Martin Jr. concurs:

In retrospect, he was properly named, because he was very surly. It was difficult to warm up to him. He was a little bit righteous, holier than thou. Chiles kickin' his ass was good for the community, very frankly. Oh, he served well, I don't mean to be too critical of him, but he wasn't the sort of person you'd warm up to.[175]

Chiles' high school friend Ann Miller recalls Roy Surles: "You always wondered how Roy ever got elected. You wanted to light a firecracker under him."

Lawton would also compete with Surles by campaigning in the black community—a rare tactic for a white Florida politician in the 1950s. Lawton's younger son, Ed Chiles, comments, "In Polk County you didn't step out and be liberal on race issues."

Florida disgraced the nation with 4.5 lynchings for every 100,000 blacks from 1900 to 1930, a rate twice as high as that of Mississippi.[176] Florida's most recent lynching had occurred in 1945; a mob kidnapped Jesse James Payne, a sharecropper accused of sexual molestation of a child, from the Madison County jail, and filled him with buckshot.[177] By the time Chiles ran for the state legislature, national broadcast news and wire reports disseminated Florida's worst displays of bigotry across the country. No longer did word of lynching and mutilations spread merely by whisper campaigns at church.

As developers drained swamps to build the first suburbs and luxury hotels from Miami to St. Petersburg, businessmen recoiled at the potential economic damage done by intolerance. Governor LeRoy Collins warned Florida's business roundtable that social stability was necessary for tourism, and won concessions on civil rights that were unprecedented in the Deep South.

But in Lakeland, far from the beaches and the rest of the tourism economy, bigotry thrived. The county focused on phosphate mines and agriculture. In a 1958 editorial entitled "Polk Back-Country," *The Ledger* mused bucolic:

Polk is one of Florida's largest counties and there is still much expanse of back-country acreage in Polk. Much of it is as quiet, rustic and primitive as it was back in the middle of the eighteenth century when the Indians were still roaming the woods. There is, for instance, the vast stretch north of Polk City, between the Lakeland-Groveland highway and the Lakeland-Dade City highway. Except for a few hundred yards at the east end, the seventeen-mile stretch of road between those two main highways is dirt road that winds through swamp and pasture land, and only about half a dozen houses are seen, all but one of them built long ago.

It is the road that leads through the Polk communities of Green Pond and Rockledge, about which many Polk Countians hear only at election time every two years when returns are listed. Except for the roar of a plane now and then, an occasional blast from a train whistle or an inquisitive city slicker driving through on a Sunday afternoon for some refreshing exploration, it is a serene rural expanse. Many Polk hunters know the area well, of course. For decades it has been known as an area in which coons, possums, turkeys, wildcats, deer and even bears roamed.[178]

Future Chiles staffer Bob Harris, a black Lakelander, recalls his hometown: "The only time I personally even *saw* white people was when I went downtown shopping or something like that—nothing casual, nothing social. I could go literally days in Lakeland and never really see a white person except them driving by in a car or something." *Brown V. Board of Education* did not impact Lakeland until 1969 or 1970, according to Harris. "The [black] people who had the most interaction, I think, in white communities, were maids."

Northwest Lakeland, a five or six square mile area, remained the black ghetto. Instigated by advances in black political power, the Ku Klux Klan and its political representatives orchestrated repressive tactics targeting black progress. One media report tallied state KKK membership at 30,000 in 1957. A 91st anniversary parade through Lakeland and Plant City in June 1957 attracted 300.[179] A May 1958 article in the Lakeland *Ledger* complained of conditions at the town's school for black retarded children. The school, housed in two former army barracks, employed three teachers and served forty-five students. One building lacked screens, a doorknob, a bathroom, or a water fountain.[180]

"My father's was the first generation that straddled that and turned from [racial bigotry in politics]," says his younger son, Ed Chiles. "He raised us in a way to respect people." The New Deal had converted Florida's black community from Lincoln Republicans to FDR Democrats and by 1950, blacks constituted nearly a quarter of Polk County's 37,000 registered voters. Lawton Chiles sought the votes of the black community, according to Bob Harris:

Back then, the Democratic Primary was the race. Republican opposition didn't exist. So Chiles decided to take [Roy Surles] on. The climate in Lakeland, in the black community, was most blacks voted Democrat. Probably all. But Surles didn't campaign in the black community; he just took that vote for granted. Chiles, when he decided to run, did [campaign in the black community].

Chiles met Harris' father, a pastor at First Baptist Institutional on Memorial Boulevard in Lakeland. The first-time candidate learned tactics:

Since Chiles wasn't a minister, the pastor and his colleagues ruled that he couldn't speak to the group from the pulpit. So Chiles met the minister of the church and other local black ministers in the basement; the group was called the ministerial alliance. Chiles went in and he said, "I'm runnin' against Surles, and I intend to campaign vigorously in this community, and I want you boys to help me." And a voice from the back of the room said, "we're gonna help you, Lawton. The first thing we're gonna do is improve your vocabulary. Ain't no boys in this room!"

Lawton Chiles' campaign in every community in Polk County would feature a novel strategy that capitalized on his charisma: the door-to-door canvass. Typical campaigns in the county circulated through barber shops, beauty parlors, civic clubs, and fish fries. Some candidates frequented a popular ice cream place called Gill's on South Florida Avenue. A July homecoming for Senator Spessard Holland at Peace River Park in Bartow hosted 2,000 for a fish fry, a water ski show, concert, and fireworks.[181] Lawton covered the traditional circuit. Democratic candidates for public office in Polk agreed to seven rallies in Polk County before the Sept. 9 primary. At the first Polk Democratic rally in the town of Kathleen, Lawton Chiles spoke: "I'm going to right the bigness of government. I'm not going to be Mr. Chiles when I'm elected. I'm going to be your humble servant."[182] At the sixth Polk Democratic rally in Bartow, Lawton Chiles said he would not "sit here" in the house "for ten years. I may ask you to give me a higher job."[183]

Lawton also partnered with Rhea to knock doors across Polk County to achieve maximum voter contact and edge out Roy Surles. Campaign director Jack Pridgen observed that "it became the talk of the county. 'Yeah, I saw Lawton and Rhea Chiles,' so-and-so says. 'Yeah, me, too, I saw them over at' such-and-such." Lawton hit one side of every street while Rhea covered the other.

Later, Rhea spoke with *The Ledger* about the race: "I saw parts of Polk County I had never seen before. . . . There was a joy to it," although several dogs bit her. "It was all right during the first five weeks. I had always been a dog lover and I had no trouble. Then, in one of the new subdivisions outside of Lakeland, a little dog bit me on the back of my leg. . . . I believe in the adage that dogs bite people who are afraid, because after that I was bitten by three dogs right quick." Rhea started carrying dog biscuits in her pocketbook to neutralize aggressive pooches. Lawton enjoyed jabbing her about it, but one day a German Shepherd and a pointer cornered Lawton. "Finally, I had to holler across the street to Rhea, 'Dog biscuit!'" he related later. "Wife-like, she's never let me forget that."[184]

Rhea once stuck a pair of shoes in a freshly tarred road. "We were in [the town of] Frostproof," she recalls, "[and] we were eating lunch across the street from the bank when it was robbed. Then I almost got stuck in some tar. They had just paved a road and my shoes got stuck. I almost left them there, and I finally had to throw them away." [185]

Lawton ate salt tablets to replace electrolytes as he pounded the pavement. "At the end of the day I could take off my shirt, throw it in the corner, and it would stand up," he later recalled. "No one else seemed to realize it, but Rhea and I would go home at night, look at each other and say, 'It's there. We're going to win.'"[186]

While knocking on doors, Lawton encountered his toughest sale yet, a watermelon farmer he had stolen from as a boy. The farmer had shot at young Lawton with either bird shot or shotgun shells loaded with rock salt, and had hit him in the rear end, but ultimately voted for the candidate.[187]

Rhea later recalled sometimes hitting 350 doors a day.[188] Estimates of the total number of doors knocked during the entire campaign vary. One tallies it at 12,000. Another totals 13,000. Another puts it at 14,500 doorbells.[189] Lawton claimed that he visited more than 13,500 homes.[190] Rhea and Lawton depended on the family maid Ruby to watch the children while they canvassed from eight in the morning to six in the evening. Five-year-old Bud Chiles sometimes would answer telephone calls for his parents. Bud would say,

"They're out champagning." Rhea: "It was a bit disconcerting." Tandy, who campaigned throughout the neighborhood, posted a flyer on her own family's door. The flyer read: "Please vote for my Daddy."[191]

The walking campaign lasted nine weeks and 9,000 miles. It was on the dirt driveways and back streets of Polk County that Lawton Chiles discovered his natural affinity for retail politics. Like a traveling salesmen, he pitched and pitched to strangers, fine-tuning his script and mannerisms for old and young, rich and poor, Republican and Democrat. To veterans of door-to-door canvass, whether politically or commercially driven, the tales of the best and worst days on the street commit to one's long-term memory, to be related like war stories years after. The campaign experience can bind together strangers.

At doors, Lawton learned to gauge the precise moments when, by the thinness of their smile or fold of their arms, voters betrayed their decision before vocalizing it. Hundreds of doors later, he commanded an encyclopedic knowledge of the mundane, like doorknob types and screen door frames, and the essential, like thunderstorm clouds. Some storm clouds portended a quick downfall; others would kill the day's activities. He learned to walk off the failures, like slammed doors, insults, or threats, and celebrate the occasional household that offered free cookies or lemonade. Young Lawton, like Huey Long before him, must have discovered his calling as a natural-born politician by going door to door.

Lawton, Rhea, and campaign manager Jack Pridgen devised a strategy for get-out-the-vote, leveraging Lawton's connections with the Jaycees. Lawton once ran for the presidency of the Jaycees but lost. The Jaycees was a social haven for young veterans of World War II and the Korean War. Many supported reforms toward clean and efficient government.[192] Pridgen explains,:

> He had been active in the Jaycees and every town of any magnitude had a Jaycee organization. So we started exploring the possibility of enlisting the aid of Jaycees around the county who would be willing to get up before daybreak and get out on the road and put a flyer with the newspaper or the milk bottle, believe me there were milk bottles at the doors at that time, and just blanket their communities with these flyers. It was a real challenge when you think about getting enough people to commit themselves to do that sort of thing when they've got to go to work in the morning and all that kind of stuff, but we brought that off. I produced a flyer that was so basic it said, "Good morning. Today is your day to vote for good government. Vote for Lawton Chiles." It had this photo, a mug shot as I recall, and it was

an 8½-by-11 sheet of paper flyer. The logistics of getting those things carted all over the county and distributed to people who were going to distribute them to the doors was something. What I always did on election day, later, and Lawton did on election day, was go out and just wander around the precincts on election morning particularly to test the winds to see what people are talking about and how they're reacting and so forth, and that flyer just took the county by storm. Everybody wanted to know how in the world could that have been accomplished 'cause everybody they saw had one, and how in the world could they have accomplished this feat. So he won.[193]

Pridgen recalls that he and the campaign volunteers put the flyer under the newspaper at homes and with the milk bottle, so it wouldn't blow away. Some tucked the fliers in between the door handle and the door. About a hundred volunteers worked get-out-the-vote.

Lawton Chiles, who turned twenty-eight during the campaign, defeated Rep. Roy Surles in the Democratic Primary by 1,326 votes.[194] A high school and college classmate, attorney Bill Ellsworth, credited Chiles' personality with victory.

I think what Lawton loved, and he was so good at, were interactions with people on their level. He could go from the high to the low. And they felt comfortable with him. He would listen. He was a truly sincere observer of people in many walks of life. He liked people and maybe he could do something for them or help them out, and they always felt that he could and he was going to give them a square shot. He wasn't in it for himself. He was a representative of the people. I often thought, How do you describe Chiles? Chiles was the kind of person that, let's say you have a game of basketball, the kids in the neighborhood. Here was a guy that didn't look like he could dribble and probably couldn't and he was standing on the sidelines. Most kids like that are shy, but Lawton had a demeanor about him. He'd smile and the next thing you knew, "Here, come on in!" He was that type of person without saying anything. His presence and demeanor attracted people to him and they'd just say, "Hey, you want to take a shot?" and "Yeah, sure," whatever. He had that easy way about him and made people comfortable.[195]

So did Chiles' brother-in-law Joe P. Ruthven:

Well, if you talked to anybody, anybody you talked to didn't give him a chance, because there was just no way he was going to beat Roy Surles. I remember we did a lot of business with automobile dealers back in those days with the tire business and I don't know of any automobile dealer that I went to calling on to sell tires that thought he'd win. But as the campaign developed, about midway through it, it was very obvious he was the most popular person there. And I think, I distinctly remember Roy Surles being there one day with Red Holcomb, and I think Roy realized at that time that all the attention was on Lawton, not on him, but by then it was too late to do anything.[196]

High school friend Sarah MacKay commented on the campaign, "Nobody before Lawton and Rhea had walked the county; they were alone out there." *Lakeland Ledger* reporter Lonnie Brown also believed Chiles' 1958 campaign to be the first in Polk County history involve a door-to-door effort. The contest had been generational, according to Bill Ellsworth.

I don't even remember the score, but it was significant. It was significant. And of course it was electrifying for us. It was wonderful. Of course he was in a state of shock. And of course all of the crowd, all of our friends just loved it. It was like "we did it to them, those people— all those older people in all our lives we've had to put up with," you know, "we did it to them, we've taken over."[197]

Lawton once estimated the total cost of the campaign at $1,200.[198] On another occasion he quoted the figure at $3,500.[199] *The Tampa Tribune* trumpeted Chiles' victory:

Young, plucky Lawton M. Chiles Jr., a Lakeland attorney, bowled over legislative veteran Roy Surles to win a two-year term to the Florida house. Chiles, a twenty-eight-year-old, upset the forty-four-year-old incumbent, via a campaign in which he or his wife knocked on more than 13,500 doors in the county. Surles, one of the most powerful men in the Florida legislature, was seeking his sixth straight term, but conceded defeat to the youthful lawyer shortly before nine o'clock tonight.[200]

The editorial called the campaign "virtually devoid of issues."[201] *The Ledger,* which had endorsed Surles for re-election, interpreted the upset:

Chiles got out and shook hands all over the county, giving everybody a warm smile and asking everybody to vote for him. Voters like such attention. It is a human factor that comes ahead of everything else in politics. Each voter, no matter what his station in life, likes to feel important, and is important, especially on election day. It simply is not Surles' nature to loosen up and shake hands all around in the spontaneous manner of an extrovert, as he and all his friends have long recognized. He had amply proved himself over the years as an able and thorough lawyer and legislator but the people wanted personal attention during the campaign season, and so Surles' accumulation of 10 years of seniority in the Legislature was erased by a neophyte in politics who had the valuable knack of communicating himself to the voters in a personal way. It is a personality factor that can carry Chiles far in politics and it undoubtedly will—if his spectacular victory of yesterday is an accurate indication, and it surely is. We congratulate him heartily on his victory and wish him much success as he moves into the area of public service in an official capacity.[202]

Friends credited Rhea with the victory as much as Lawton. Jack Pridgen: "The ultimate decisions were always made by him and his wife. He had the final say of course, but he put humongous stock in her thinking, her judgment, her intuition and advice, her guidance." Snow Martin Jr.: "Lawton early on recognized quicker than a lot of men do that their wives are smarter than they are." Snow Martin Jr. summed up Rhea's role in the race against Surles:

The day of the election, we had a crowd [and] we went to every house in Polk County that was in our District, and we stuck a flyer in their door. "Today is the Day to Vote for Good Government." This was all her doings. And he busted Roy Surles' butt. Yeah, he enjoyed doing it, but without her direction and sense of how to do things, Chiles just would have been another one of us lawyers, truthfully.[203]

Rhea said, "I don't think Lawton ever talked about losing . . . or not becoming what he had in mind of what he wanted to be . . . what he intended to do."[204]

The End of the Pork Chop Gang

Chiles began his career in state politics on a mournful note. His father died of a heart attack in September 1960, while fishing at his cottage in Chiefland on the Suwannee River.

Lawton Sr. had lived though to see his only son graduate college, law school, join the state legislature, and begin a political life riven with issues unknown to most Lakeland boys.

Civil rights was the top concern of the Legislature when Chiles joined its membership. College students in Tallahassee boycotted the city bus system, the Woolworth's lunch counter, and the "whites only" Florida Movie Theater. The capital's red clay canopy roads meandering through quail coveys and cotton plantations resembled south Georgia more than central Florida. Tallahassee taxi companies, municipal swimming pools, and golf courses honored Jim Crow.

The young legislator, however, had never experienced a strong friendship with a person of color. Segregation had probably removed the persecution of blacks from his world view.

Eager to establish the same sense of fraternity that enriched his university and law school experience, Chiles made friends on all sides of the issue. He voted as his cohorts expected from a Lakeland boy with a mind to rise fast; he supported the status quo on civil rights.

Among the state's political class, only Governor LeRoy Collins avowedly supported civil rights reform; he acted as a broker between business moderates and violent anti-black elements. When Governor Farris Bryant took office in 1961, reform had no political support.

Future Chiles Senate staffer Bob Harris, then a student at Florida A&M University (FAMU), fumed about the state legislature's idleness:

> I was at FAMU from '60 to '64. . . . We were still doing sit-ins, and still being attacked for marching down the street, so to speak. One of the discussions that he and I had was, I really did feel very strongly, I was also editor of the school paper, so I wrote a lot of stuff about the movement in Tallahassee. . . . The absence of any statement by anybody in the state legislature. It was just a deafening silence over there, and they all ceded everything to [Governor Farris Bryant]. And the governor was totally reactionary. He was George Wallace without getting any of the notoriety, which was fairly interesting to us, because he was doing exactly the same thing. We got beat up in the street. And one march, I'm trying to remember the summer, I think it was the summer of '61, and I got a swollen ankle out of it . . . and all we were doing was marching in front of the Woolworth lunch counter in accordance to the rules that the court has established. They didn't stop us from marching; they just put limits on how many people could do it. The cops came and started beating us up, like we were robbing the banks or something.

When Lawton Chiles chose the issue for his first big political play, legislative apportionment, he was embracing a topic with rich racial ramifications. It would require an insurgency against the dominant political bloc in Tallahassee—called "the Pork Chop Gang." As he began his lobbying for reform, however, Chiles appealed to fairness rather than race.

Chiles and his legislative allies believed in the equitable apportionment of legislative seats based on population, and used race-neutral rhetoric to exert political pressure on the Pork Chop majority. The Pork Chop Gang, a cadre of mostly north Florida politicos, partied like fraternity brothers and believed the only part of Florida that mattered was north of Ocala. They wanted to freeze the apportionment process, so that north Florida and other rural regions ruled the state legislature, population growth be damned. Their ideal system would ensure that regardless of population, every county sent a minimum of one House member to Tallahassee, and large counties sent a maximum of three. Members used this unfair system to preserve their preferred political order: segregation, low taxes, light corporate regulation, and plentiful pet projects for north Florida. From 1945 to 1965, malapportionment granted the small county group fifty seats and the urban counties about twenty five. Governor LeRoy Collins introduced a bill for reapportionment every legislation session during his six years in office from 1955 to 1961 and it failed every time.

Lawton Chiles and Reubin Askew were elected the same year, 1958. Askew served in the House four years and the Senate eight years—the reverse of Lawton. Askew describes one encounter with the Pork Choppers. From time to time, the Pork Chop gang would caucus to decide if they would vote as a bloc on an issue:

> All the rest would just sit around until finally I went over to Lawton and I said, "You know, we need to appear like we're doing something." He said, "I agree." So we sat down and decided that we'd go back in this big committee room at that time behind the chamber and, if we didn't tell anything but jokes and stories, to be able to show, you know, that there was a little cohesiveness. Interestingly enough, it really bothered all the small county group all of a sudden while we were doing our thing, but it was Lawton's and my way of trying to organize a minority as opposed to just having miscellaneous other people in it besides that small county group.[205]

Senior reform legislators overshadowed and influenced Chiles. State Senator Verle Pope, nicknamed the "Lion of St. Johns" for his impassioned oratory, led the ideological opposition to the Pork Chop Gang. "Verle Pope was bigger than life, sure 'nuff, and a talker," according to fellow state legislator Mallory Horne, "and he was a great reader, so he could talk about anything. And he was a sportsman and he chewed tobacco." State Senator Ed Price describes Pope's rhetorical routine:

> The Press Corps sat right above us in the Senate in those days, with a little glass enclosure up there, and when Verle got ready to make his speech that he gave every year. . . . [Verle Pope] would go up to the water cooler by the well of the Senate, turn around and look to be sure the press was all in place up there, and then he'd get up and give this speech. He'd talk about the terrible lobbyists for the loan sharks with their "teeth of diamonds" and "veins of gold" that would come

up and try to drain the gold and every piece of change out of all these little people of Florida. He'd just give a tremendous array. He was a great orator, really was. And oratory was still a business in those days. And he'd point up in the gallery up there to 'em so there was a great battle that went on between some senators and lobbyists, and that type of thing.[206]

Chiles himself could recruit members to a cause, long-time friend Mallory Horne recalls. The two first met in the legislature. Horne paid him no heed at first. "We were well into our first session before I knew who he was. He was quiet and non-assuming."

Horne describes his confrontation with Lawton over reapportionment:

Lawton just jumped in the front [of] it. I was torn by reapportion-ment. I had just gotten elected from Leon County. Anyway, I had indicated that I was gonna go with the overwhelming majority. It was an easy vote at the time. [In] my first confrontation with Lawton—we'd been to parties together, and we knew each other, but it was remote—I sat down in front of him on the aisle, and we were about to get into some of the skirmishes on reapportionment. He walks down with one of these statute books open to the constitution. "Horne, how many ways can you read this?" And I sorta turned my head, and he read it to me, like I was a damn child. "The legislature shall be appor-tioned as nearly according to population as is practicable." And he really pissed me off because he wouldn't leave it. "How many ways, as a lawyer, can you read that?" [Lawton said,] and he took it and went on back. Well, it was the worst political mistake I ever made. But I read it one way.

Ours was the most unfairly apportioned legislature in the nation.

The point of this story is that Lawton could have attracted state-wide attention to himself by trapping me with an eloquent oration on this most fundamental of issues. But he didn't! He gained a vote on the proposition and a friend for life.

In addition to addressing principles of fairness, Chiles and his allies sought to rewrite the social and professional code set by the Pork Chop Gang. Cartoonists and journalists looking to caricature the Pork Chop Gang used State Senator L. K. Edwards as a template. Edwards's favorite drink was "half and half," a quart of whole milk mixed with chocolate milk, downed in one long take. Mallory Horne reflects,

> L. K. Edwards was like—he always wore white suits, he had a black driver and a long black limousine driving up to the Capitol. . . . But L. K. made a lot of money, carried a lot of money, spent a lot of money, and ate like a horse. We'd go to breakfast, and he might eat a dozen eggs and then a chocolate sundae. But he was jolly, and the extent of his debate was something that would kinda catch on, like when they were both on appropriations, he'd just erupt: "Wait a minute, senators! Y'all been passin' out these turkeys, and I ain't been turkeyed yet!"

Ed Chiles, Lawton's younger son, recalls filling L. K.'s plate with oysters at his father's parties.[207] Republican State Senator Ken Plante describes L. K. Edwards as a buttermilk drinker:

> We always had to keep quarts of buttermilk back in the refrigerator in the Senate lounge. I have seen those young pages bring out that quart; it was always in a glass jar, and he would pop the top on that thing and just drink that quart straight down without taking it away from his lips.

Dexter Douglass recalls Edwards: "You had to like him. Great huge guy in his white suit. He was something else. He was a big Gator man, I'll tell ya." According to Mallory Horne, "[Lawton] liked [The Pork Chop Gang] personally. . . . Who couldn't like L. K.?"

Chiles and his allies worked to tighten legislative ethics rules. Senator Ed Price describes the lobbyist corps in Tallahassee under Pork Chop control:

> Many of the lobbyists and a large number of legislators lived at the Cherokee Hotel. Many of them had hotel rooms there and had free breakfasts, all they wanted to attend. And the lobbyists, most of the legislators, most of the senators, both the "pork choppers" and the rest of us, were sort of independent in this period. I didn't accept anything from a lobbyist when I went to Tallahassee. The lobbyists provided free booze, free boat rides, and trips to New York and many other places. I can recall when I got up there to the house that I had

rented for my family; there was a case of whiskey on my back door. I found out where it came from and sent it back. I got a rotisserie from a man that was in the racetrack business from Fort Lauderdale. I sent it back and wrote him a letter and told him I just made it a habit not to accept anything of that nature, insulted him but that's the way I wanted it. And I never did [accept things]. So I didn't go to a lot of those things.[208]

The lobbyist for Winn Dixie grocery wielded considerable influence in the legislature. In 1967, State Senators Reubin Askew and Lawton Chiles sponsored the successful passage of a "Government in the Sunshine" law aimed at increasing transparency and public access to government.[209]

Chiles, Pope, Askew, and allies enforced a code of respect for their fellow legislators, regardless of party. Mallory Horne discovered this as a freshman:

One night out at Joe's Spaghetti House, there sat Verle Pope at another table. A lobbyist walked in, seeking to aggrandize himself with Verle Pope, and said, "I ran into that sorry, crooked, son-of-a-bitch Charley Johns," loud enough so everybody could hear it. And Verle, [Charley's] enemy on the floor for as long I can remember, jumped up and grabbed that guy and shook him, saying, "He's a senator, don't do that now." Which didn't fit at all to me, and gradually I adjusted to that.

The professional courtesy extended to the governor. Tandy Chiles learned this lesson from her father Lawton:

I remember vividly, we said something about [Republican Florida Governor] Claude Kirk and we were mouthin' off on him. [Lawton] said, "Don't you ever let me hear you talk [that way] about anyone in public office. You may not respect that person, but you respect the office they hold." That was about the quickest way to really get in trouble. He meant business, too.

By 1967, the Pork Chop Gang disbanded. Years of fighting rebels like Chiles, Askew, and Pope had splintered the Gang, and a federal district court ruling in Miami enforced "one man, one vote" in Florida unequivocally. State political power shifted from north to south, from Democratic conservatives to liberals.

After they disrupted the last of the Pork Chop Gang, Chiles and his reform caucus adopted a new cause—killing Governor Haydon Burns' 1965 road bond initiative. For this fight, Chiles enlisted new friends and colleagues.

Edmond "Eddie" Gong entered the legislature in 1963 and soon joined Chiles' posse. Eddie Gong once joined Lawton and Wilbur for a weekend at a fish camp in Florida's Big Bend. Gong recalls that Chiles once got out of the shower shaking a box of Arm & Hammer baking soda into his arm pits. Chiles described it as a Cracker technique for keeping dry.[210] "[Eddie] used to come over and ride my horses," Rhea Chiles remembers, "and the kids called him Papa Gong Cassidy."

Senator Wilbur Boyd of Bradenton allied with Lawton Chiles. Rhea describes the bond between her husband and Wilbur, perhaps his closest friend:

> They were simpatico. I think they were elected the same time, and at the same age; they could have been brothers. They kind of looked enough alike. The two of them, I think they saw themselves or acted as though they saw themselves as the beginning of maybe a critical mass where they could become politically aware in a way they wanted to be, and then attract other people to it. And they sharpened their claws in the Burns road bond boondoggle. Claude Kirk was just fodder for the guns. They would run at him every chance they had. They were like young lion cubs, practicing the art.

Senator Julian Bennett of Panama City and Senator Reubin Askew also joined Chiles in opposition to the road bond.

In May 1966, the state legislature passed a plan by Democratic Governor Haydon Burns of Jacksonville to issue $300 million in bonds to widen roads to four lanes across the state. Chiles and other opponents viewed the plan as graft to ensure Burns' reelection in 1966, and resolved to fight the bond at the ballot box that November when Florida voters could weigh in on the issue. "Lawton called [me]," Senator Bennett recollected, "and said, 'Get in your car. We're going to take this to the people.'" Chiles, Bennett, Ed Price, Wilbur Boyd, Reubin Askew, and their allies barnstormed the state stoking opposition to the bond, ridiculing the bond as a reward to Burns's cronies.

"That was such a Quixote kind of quest," Chiles later recalled. "Part of it was that you had watched this fellow [Burns], who as so adroit, put together and buy everybody. And I think we sort of sat around and told each other how bad it was for a long time, and then I had to go out and do something about it."[211] That November, Floridians rejected the road bond and Burns lost the governor's race.

Chiles challenged other corporate lobbies, such as the powerful whisky lobby, according to Jack Peeples, an aide to Governor Collins and long-time friend to Chiles.

One year the whiskey lobby pushed lawmakers to introduce a price-fixing bill that would ban the publication of liquor prices in newspaper ads. A legislator allied with the industry walked the floor of the legislature with a newspaper liquor ad and a pair of scissors.

According to Peeples, the lawmaker "showed the ad to the legislators and said, 'Isn't that terrible? Some man will be enticed to take his kids' milk money and buy whiskey with it.' And he took the scissors and cut out the price, leaving a hole in the ad. 'There,' he said. 'That's better.'"

So Chiles approached the legislator and asked to borrow his scissors and newspaper. He cut out the entire liquor ad and said, "Now that's better." Then Chiles called on his colleagues to sign his amendment banning liquor advertising outright. Peeples called the operation Chiles' "Elmer Gantry speech."

Lawton Chiles, elected to the State Senate in 1966, considered himself ready for higher office in all ways except financial. In an October 1969 interview with the *Orlando-Sentinel*, Chiles coveted his perch:

> Nature just decreed that I would be born in Polk County and fortunately for me it is neutral ground. Well look at it this way. In Dade County, I am not a north Florida guy. In Jacksonville I am not a Dade County man. I can go to west Florida, and I come from Senator Holland's county. That is enough for their conservative way of thinking. And in central Florida, which is the breadbasket of the state, I am one of their own. Again, Polk County is agriculturally oriented to the extent that your small counties do not think of the county as an urban center, as they do of anyone from Tampa. But yet I come from Lakeland and certainly Lakeland is not pork chop country nor do I have a pork chop record.[212]

His family supported him and enjoyed the rush of politics. Lawton's younger son, Ed, describes Tallahassee during the legislative session as an "incredible sandbox to grow up in." Ed added: "I don't have many memories without politics." Lawton and Rhea rented the nineteenth century Boone Plantation House during session. Rhea kept her horses in the stables out back. There was a big water tower. Lawton built a swing hanging from the biggest oak at the Mansion. The kids called it "kamikaze" because all of them fell off it. After school, the kids would go to the FSU circus and roller-skate in the Capitol halls. Ed worked as a page for the legislature for $56 a week in the House and $70 a week in the Senate. Ed, Bud, and Tandy made friends with other legislators' kids. Lawton and Rhea hosted parties for the legislature at the Boone Mansion; they served frog legs, raw and fried oysters, and corn. Rhea Chiles painted many legislators' wives in the Florida legislature. "I never charged for any of those," Rhea explains, "I think what I found interesting was the fact that when I looked at what I had done, I had captured something. . . . That was the fun of it." Family friend Homer Hooks describes Rhea's role in her husband's political career:

> I don't recall any specifics except that at every rally I attended she was there and this was not true of most candidates. In those days the ladies showed up some times and smiled and looked with awestruck eyes at their husbands like somebody said Nancy Reagan used to. Rhea was an active politician. She knew people. She knew how to call them up and get votes. She was not above going house to house. She was a right hand supporter.[213]

The kids knew Election Day as well as Christmas on their calendar. Ed Chiles recalls helping his dad and his allies at political rallies across Polk County. Ed, Tandy, Bud and their cousins Greg, Joe Lawton, and Kay got signs, bumper stickers, and literature out of the truck for local campaign events. They slathered goo on the signs of opponents, slapped bumper stickers on cars, and listened to colorful political speech and slogans like "get on the right track with Jack." They would make balls out of rolled up bumper stickers and lapel stickers and throw them.

Lawton's family relished their leisure hours. After supper in Lakeland the kids would play outside and the parents would sit out on the curb. Lawton and Rhea played bridge, gin rummy, and checkers. Ed had a spider monkey he named King Kong. When it escaped, the local newspaper reported that

"King Kong is on the loose." The family also kept rabbits, cats, and dogs. The family had two dogs; Winky and then Buck. Winky would join Bud on his paper route until the dog got killed in traffic.

Lawton loved dressing as Santa Claus. On alternate years, Lawton and Rhea Chiles and Joe P. and Jeanette Ruthven would host the holiday. Christmas Eve, Lawton's mother served dinner. One Christmas in the mid or late 1960s, after Lawton and Rhea visited San Francisco, Lawton baked sourdough bread. Rhea made gift baskets for the loaves, which were given as presents. Lawton cooked dove Christmas morning, along with ambrosia, grits, and eggs. Bud Chiles recalls:

> He would dress up as Santa. . . . When we were kids he did it too. . . . In the house on Coventry . . . he would go out in the neighborhood or the kids would come by on Christmas Eve and we would have a thing . . . would do caroling, kids would come sit in his lap. He had a big old Santa suit. . . . It was a social thing on Christmas Eve; families in the neighborhood would come by. . . . My Mom would always make Christmas bread, for days she would make this Christmas bread; that was a big tradition, too, taking this Christmas bread all around town to all the friends and relatives—everyone would get a loaf.

Lawton's niece Kay Ruthven recalls, "Aunt Rhea would always make this great Christmas bread. And she's a talented baker. And she would even put little holly and red berries on it—I don't know if it was candy, or what it was. I always wanted to be able to do that." The maid Ruby would bake blackberry cobbler for breakfast in Tallahassee, using fresh berries picked by the children. Tandy recounted: "When we sat down to eat, we all sat down, and the rule was, he who cooked it didn't have to clean it up. So the rest of us, if you ate and you didn't cook, you cleaned up. You just got up out of your chair and you just jolly well got in there and did it." Bud Chiles:

> On Christmas Day he would often be pulling a fast one on somebody. . . . I'll never forget one Christmas that my brother got a new rifle, a .22 magnum; so he was gonna get this. . . . [Dad] was like, "I'm getting this for Ed, you've got a shot gun." . . . I'm like sittin' on the couch. . . . I wanted that .22 magnum really bad. . . . He would always

do that stuff, hide something . . . and you're literally like in tears and then he'd go reach under the couch and say "what is this?"

His children recollected Lawton's pranks and his parenting. Greg, Joe Lawton and Kay Ruthven sometimes visited their Uncle Lawton and Aunt Rhea at their Lakeland home overnight. The kids, playing upstairs, heard a cherry bomb explode outside. Lawton ran upstairs, "I better not hear any more cherry bombs." About fifteen minutes later, another cherry bomb ignited. Greg and his siblings agreed that Jerry Black down the street had been throwing the bombs. The next morning, the maid Ruby cooked pancakes. On the kitchen counter, the kids found two or three cherry bombs. Lawton had been chucking them out all along.

One day a cop brought Ed Chiles home in Lakeland after catching him throwing oranges at cars; one fruit hit his squad car. Ed recalls, "I thought I was in for the whipping of my life." Lawton told his youngest son, "I don't think you are ever going to do that again, are you? I got in trouble when I was your age. I was throwing rocks at cars."[214] Lawton once caught Tandy sneaking out in the family car with a friend. Lawton told Tandy: "I know you have a big lump in your throat. I know you're ashamed. I'm not gonna punish you, but you've really disappointed me."

In 1966, Lawton and Rhea adopted a daughter, Rhea Gay, at a few weeks old. It was Rhea's idea. She had a void in her life because Lawton was so busy and they were empty nesters at this point. She and Rhea Gay were constantly together, whether in Washington or Florida.

Rhea Gay once adopted a cat she found in the back yard, to her mother's dismay. Rhea Gay looked up at her mother ruefully, "But Mommy, it's mine, I adopted it." Rhea Gay called the new pet "udder cat," since they already had one. Rhea exclaimed, "Thank God it wasn't a snake or an elephant." Rhea Gay reflects:

> I was kind of a wild child, running around the back yard barefoot most of the time, climbing trees, getting in trouble. I lived in the ocean, they could not get me out of that water. And so my dad came up with this crazy story that I had to come out of the ocean by sunset because when you see the sun go down in the ocean, for one second the whole ocean boils, and you'll be boiled alive like lobster. And I'd be like, really, I don't wanna chance that one.

Lawton taught the boys how to hunt, and he asked them to clean and eat anything they killed. In the offseason, Lawton took the boys to shoot skeet. Bud Chiles recalls:

> I got pretty good at hitting skeet after years of practice. I remember vividly how my dad challenged me one day on the skeet course. I could routinely break twenty-five clay pigeons in a row. That comprises a round. Breaking fifty in a row was a holy grail for me and for a lot of other shooters. I was almost sixteen as I completed a perfect round, began the second round flawlessly and I was only two stations, four shots away from the magic fifty. My dad turned to me and said these fateful words, "If you make fifty I'm going to buy you a car for your birthday." Well, that was it, folks. I didn't cut another feather that day. My dad was a pretty good judge of character, I guess.

Lawton taught them how to hunt turkey. Bud Chiles remembers the first turkey he ever killed:

> "I was only carrying a shotgun to make my dad feel better. I fully intended to hunt squirrels all morning with my .22 caliber. But a weird thing happened. After I had hunted a few hours and shot a bag of squirrels, I fell asleep. When I woke up there were about twenty turkeys all around me feeding. I was in shock. But I managed to load the shotgun and blasted into the flock killing one and probably wounding several others. I took that turkey along with the squirrels down to my dad's truck and put them all on the hood together. Then I waited for him to come out of the woods. I was hiding to watch his reaction. I remember the curious look on his face as he saw the squirrels and turkey together.

One Saturday when Bud was eleven, he and his father returned from a dove shoot in northern Polk County. His father suggested that they stop at a turkey shoot north of Lakeland. The shoot featured a barbecue and a drawing for a new model 1100 Remington shotgun. Bud Chiles remembers that day:

Literally the smoke was still hanging in the air along the dirt road we drove in on as the drawing commenced. My dad quickly bought a single ticket for a dollar just before the selection was made. He then did something that shocked me, and as I have retold this story it shocks even people who are not eleven years old. He said, "Son, hold that ticket in your right hand and hold your left nut with your other hand." I was speechless, but sure he was pulling one over one me once again. I held tight to the ticket with my right hand, but that's as far as I was willing to take it. My dad gave me the look that [meant] he was not kidding. "Hold your left nut tightly with your other hand, we need to win this gun," he added. What was I supposed to do? It was the craziest order he had given me in my short and innocent life. With great reluctance and deeply embarrassed I shoved my hand down my pants and felt around for the little item in question. He looked down and said, "Grab it and we'll win." Just when my hands found its target they called my number as the winning number.

Bud looks back on growing up: "I scarcely remember a time when my dad would hug me or tell me that he loved me. Oh, I knew he did. I knew it when he was proud of me, but he had a really hard time expressing it."

Lawton Chiles' allies in the state legislature, especially Senator Wilbur Boyd, agreed to support a bid for the U.S. Senate. The Chiles and Boyd families vacationed together on Anna Maria Island near Bradenton; Wilbur and Chiles hunted together often. Rhea Chiles later recalled Wilbur and Lawton's adventures:

There was a time when they—these two got into such trouble all the time. They backed up a boat, a john boat, into a hornet's nest, that was hanging down from a limb. And they were fishing, and they backed the boat up under this overhanging bough, and this disturbed this hornet's nest. And they ended up rippin' off their clothes and jumpin' in the water, and they came out of the water and were standin' on the side of the bank, buck naked. And this car drove up, and I don't know who was in it. . . . They were always gettin' into something like that.

According to Faye Boyd, when Wilbur and Lawton were together, Wilbur would "laugh at 'im and it was funny. But he wasn't the practical joker that

Lawton was. He'd go along with it and help him out." The Boyd and Chiles families would share summers on Florida's Anna Maria Island on the Gulf of Mexico.

State Senator Reubin Askew, respected across-the-aisle for his integrity, admired Chiles.

> He was good, very bright, and very able, and—you can check the record on this—he was, as I recall, the main sponsor of the creation of what became the Department of Environmental Protection. It started off as something like an Air and Water Pollution Control Department . . . which was I believe our first major piece of environmental legislation.
>
> Lawton could sometimes say witty things that could kill a bill without having to talk about the substance. He just had a talent for it.
>
> I think Lawton got along with his colleagues a little bit better than I did. Lawton was sort of "one of the boys" and I never was. You know, I don't drink and so much of the socialization in the legislature is around the bottle. Of course, Lawton never had a drinking problem at all, you know, but he was able to socialize. Even more than that, he was a hunter and I wasn't. . . . I wasn't a great outdoorsman, didn't profess to be. Lawton just naturally got along with his peers, I think, better than I did. Plus, people respected Lawton. You could disagree with Lawton, but in the end you knew when he made a decision it was his decision. His closest friend could have thought something else. Lawton just had enormous integrity and in his own way was so folksy.[215]

Even GOP state legislator Tom Slade called Chiles "a very, very sophisticated person who is able to present a Li'l Abner, 'aw shucks' demeanor."[216]

Lawton Chiles finally secured the financial foundation necessary to risk a U.S. Senate bid, thanks to an upstart restaurant chain called Red Lobster. Using his own money and borrowed funds, Chiles invested in the restaurant's founding real estate.

The first Red Lobster opened in Lakeland in 1968; Chiles and high school classmate Bill Ellsworth had bought the land near Lake Parker for it and owned the restaurant building. Chiles later recalled that the building and land cost $200,000. He invested only $1,500 of his own dollars; the rest he borrowed from an uncle and his maid, Ruby.

The seafood restaurant's quick success allowed Chiles and Ellsworth to construct three more restaurants in Tampa, Daytona Beach, and St. Petersburg. They continued to rent the buildings that housed the restaurants at these four locations, receiving a base fee and a percentage of the sales.

The rental income from the restaurants built Chiles a campaign war chest for higher office. Lakeland friend and attorney Snow Martin Jr. explains Lawton's role in Red Lobster:

> Well, that was all Ellsworth's doings. He built the first one for them and leased it to them, fixed rent, percent of gross. Ellsworth told me one time that every meal there, he made a quarter, and he and Lawton were partners in it. Lawton's participation was nominal only; Ellsworth did it all. . . . Bill Ellsworth's financial activities on behalf of them enabled Lawton to afford to be in politics.[217]

Soon, Lawton was able to repay Ruby at 10 percent interest for her $1,500 loan, far above the 4 percent rate prevailing at the time. By 1993, Chiles' shares in the restaurants were valued at $1.3 million.

The same year as the Red Lobster boom, Chiles had hired an aide, Charles E. Canady, a school vice principal from Lakeland. "The good Lord did not make Lawton an executive with the feeling for minute details," Canady said. "It is just not in his nature to tend to the tiny details, but hand him a legislative agenda and he will cross bridges, bring lawmakers together and get things done."[218] Charlie Canady became Lawton's first full-time chief of staff and campaign manager.

"I can remember sitting in the drugstore one day," Chiles family friend Snow Martin Jr. recalls, "and something was said about a car. [Rhea] said, 'No one needs that until they are in the United States Senate.' [Clearly], in her mind, [the U.S. Senate] was the next step in the progression."[219]

Rhea once said that if her husband had liked money as much as politics he could have owned the Empire State Building.[220] Nonetheless, in the summer of 1969, she and Lawton agreed to convene their first U.S. Senate campaign meeting. Florida's senior senator and Lawton's mentor, seventy-seven-year-old Senator Spessard Holland, was contemplating retirement. Two possible Democratic candidates for Senator Holland's seat had already made the papers: State Senator Bob Haverfield from Dade County and House Speaker Fred Schultz from Duval County. Chiles and his allies knew more legislators would file before Holland declared his intentions officially.

Former Governor Farris Bryant, "Florida's LBJ," loomed largest. A May primary would decide the Democratic nominee if someone won a majority; otherwise, a runoff would follow. Republican Congressman Bill Cramer would likely oppose the Democrat in the general election. If Holland stepped down, Chiles would run.

A new problem threatened to end the nascent campaign though. Despite twelve years in the state legislature and chairmanship of the Senate Ways and Means Committee, no one outside Polk County knew Lawton Chiles' name. The television, print, and radio advertising necessary to build Chiles' name recognition would require another financial windfall like Red Lobster. Former Pasco County State Senator DeCarr Covington tried to lighten the mood. "Personally," Covington told Lawton, "I'd get started talking about more basic things. If I were you I'd get myself a haircut."

When former Governor Farris Bryant reconsidered and entered the Senate race in spring 1970, the well-funded campaigner strained Chiles' campaign account to the brink of bankruptcy. Republican Ed Gurney's 1968 Senate victory had cost $757,000, about 77 percent of which paid for media.[221] Chiles estimated his own net worth at $200,000 to $300,000.[222] He detested fundraising.[223] He had borrowed money from his mother already to pay office costs. His brother-in-law, Joe P. Ruthven, had fundraised but conceded that "he could have done better selling peanuts on the corner." Joe W. Chiles and his brother and father gave 2 percent of the total money spent on the first primary campaign—about $5,000. Legend held that Joe W.'s check reached campaign headquarters just in time to stop the telephone company from cutting off service.

Walkin' Lawton

Thursday, March 12, 1970, Chiles called together his inner circle to his Lakeland home on Lake Hollingsworth. A recent poll showed that only 4 percent of Florida voters had heard of him. How could the campaign vault its candidate into the imagination of 2.7 million voters with a two-person staff and an empty bank account? The group kicked around ideas all afternoon. Then Rhea returned to an idea proposed in 1966 when Lawton had contemplated running for governor.[224] He could canvass the state on foot, county by county, town by town. The candidate said, "I've either got to give up, sell out to somebody, or go on the walk."[225] Rhea, adamant that the campaign finish debt-free, worried for Lawton's safety on the highway, but smiled at the walk's serendipity.

Friend and future American Bar Associate President Chesterfield Smith called the plan "the most damn fool idea I ever heard of." College buddy Bill Skipper agreed.[226] Bill Henry, another college classmate, advised against it: "How are you going to capture the imaginations of Floridians by putting on an old pair of boots and looking like a country hick?"[227] Burke Kibler thought it was "one of the dumbest things I ever heard of." Homer Hooks counseled that "it would produce zero votes if any, or fewer than zero, that he could spend his time more effectively in going to the cities and doing some house-to-house and door-to-door, of course, but what good would it be to walk from Clewiston to Bonifay Springs and see eight people, to put it in stark terms."[228] Most of his friends, Dexter Douglass recalls, "thought it was stupid . . . and told him so!"[229]

By nightfall, Chiles had resolved to lace up his walking boots. He would walk for economy and face-to-face conversation; to introduce himself to Florida one person at time, and leave the million-dollar chase to the competition. His message would reach voters on Florida's dirt driveways and tractor trails as well as its TV and radio airwaves. Outside shacks and in back alleys, he would give the penniless as long a hearing as the Rotary Club. Each day would teach him solutions to agricultural policy, the Vietnam War, and pollution—all transmitted directly from farmers, soldiers, and student advocates. The media events earned walking, whether watching cattle cross the road or finding a stash of snakeskins, would enchant reporters more than the champagne-and-caviar circuit. Rhea envisioned brass bands and confetti advancing this campaign asking voters to "Walk a Few Miles with Chiles." Chesterfield Smith called Spessard Holland to relate the news. After a long pause, Smith asked, "Do you hear me?" Silence followed. Then Holland murmured, "You know, it just might work."[230]

Chiles asked his staffer Jim Boyd, a cousin of campaign chairman and friend Senator Wilbur Boyd, to pull out a map and looked for a starting point:

> They were gonna walk the state and they wanted me to go up to Florida, north Florida, and find a place to start, and then let them know, and schedule the Walk from there. So I went home that afternoon and packed up, and left that afternoon and drove up toward the Panhandle. I'm not sure I got all the way to the Panhandle. But the next day I was in Pensacola, and I began to look around. I had a map, and began to look for towns and logical places where we could start. And so, I saw this town up toward the Alabama border, it was north of Pensacola. And it was called "Century," and I figured "Century" had a ring to it. And so I went up and looked around Century, and there really wasn't much there, and figured out a place where we could start, and then what the route would be across north Florida to get to Tallahassee by the opening of the legislative session and not before.

Chiles felt like a "fella who got in a poker game and had enough money to play one hand."[231] A "handful of 'howdy' and mouthful of 'much obliged' wouldn't be enough" anymore, his son Ed recalls. Florida's previous campaign stunts had launched the careers of cartoonists and columnists, but not of politicians. Bernarr Macfadden, a fitness guru and national magazine publisher, ran for the U.S. Senate in 1940 by helicopter. Undaunted by defeat, he took to the skies again eight years later to promote "physical culture" and political reform—this time in a campaign for governor. He won less than 5,000 votes statewide. Gubernatorial candidate Frederick Van Roy fared worse in 1940. Van Roy spread his campaign message via postcards proposing a 1945 Centennial World's Fair at Crystal River, the home of his real estate business. His single-issue venture received 2,716 votes.[232]

The walk from Century to the Keys would test Chiles' ambition and his shoe leather. As the crow flies, the distance from Miami to Pensacola equals the mileage from Atlanta to Washington, Indianapolis to Lincoln, Nebraska, or San Francisco to Portland, Oregon. The Tallahassee to Key West leg compares with Montgomery, Alabama, to Springfield, Missouri. The commute from Miami to Tampa resembles that of New York to Boston.[233] Political scientist V.O. Key observed that organizing Florida's far-flung population centers in Pensacola, Tampa, Jacksonville, St. Petersburg, and Miami around a single campaign platform "becomes in terms of geography something like that of rallying for common action the citizenry of Lansing, Michigan; Dubuque, Iowa; Muncie, Indiana; and Huntington, West Virginia.[234] Previous gubernatorial and Senate candidates cut high-priced TV and radio ads to speak to Florida, the South's largest state since 1960.[235] In the central office at Lakeland headquarters, Charles Canady posted behind his desk a big map titled "40% of Florida's Registered Democrats are within 100 miles of Imperial Polk County." The free media earned by the walking campaign would have to reach the other 60 percent.

Lawton telephoned his friends to announce he was bound for Century. Rhea knew his enterprise would shake up the establishment as much as their household:

> He was innately courageous, but he was not a continual warrior. When the occasion arose, he could seize something from within himself, and he showed up. That, to me, was always a mystery. I never quite understood it. It was a little bit dangerous to me. I never knew quite where we were going. It's a spiritual quality. It's something that was not easy to characterize.

In hindsight, Burke Kibler considered the decision vintage Chiles: "Lawton was very independent. He'd listen quite well. He wouldn't ever tell you what he was going to do. I don't think he told anybody, except Rhea."[236] Julian Clarkson worried that "people who didn't know him would think Chiles was some kind of nut." The news spread quickly. Tom Slade, a Republican state senator and candidate for state treasurer, "didn't think [Chiles] had a snowball's chance in hell. He didn't have any money. He didn't have any organization. It was a total Mission Impossible."[237] Democratic State Rep. Bob Graham of Miami thought Lawton's walk had to be "one of the dumbest ideas that I had ever heard of."[238]

Wendell Gerard, a Farris Bryant supporter, called Democratic Senator Reubin Askew of Pensacola, advising him that Bryant didn't "want to see Lawton hurt" by this walk. "Well, Wendell," Askew replied, "I don't think you ought to worry about Lawton. He's a tough cookie." Wendell insisted that Askew call Lawton and beg him off the campaign. "Not on your life," Askew retorted. "I couldn't do that. Besides, Farris told him he wasn't going to run to begin with, which I'm sure you're aware of."[239]

Lonnie Brown, a young reporter at the *Lakeland Ledger*, called Chiles to confirm the rumors, thinking of him as just another Polk County rube. "I've been told that you're going to walk from one end of Florida to the other to draw attention to the campaign," Brown began the conversation. Chiles said, "That's the plan." Brown asked what he had done to prepare. Chiles replied, "I've thought about it a lot." Brown snickered. Then Chiles explained how his door-to-door Polk County walkabout had won him a state representative seat in 1958.[240]

Monday, March 16, campaign press secretary Jack Pridgen fielded questions from the press. "He wants to get down to earth," Pridgen said, "in touch with people of the state, to learn from them what they are concerned about and to give them his ideas on the issues facing the country and the state." Chiles would walk six days a week and rest the seventh, averaging 10 miles a day.[241] He would sleep nights in a camper driven by an aide and arrive in Tallahassee on April 7. After the sixty-day legislative session, he would resume walking to Key Largo in time to finish just before the September primary.[242] The camper would carry voters who had walked with him a while back to their cars.[243]

An aide drove the camper up and Chiles flew to Century, a town of about 240 people.[244] Since its founding at the turn of the twentieth century, it smelt of the Panhandle's oldest industry—the pine sawmill. The company town settled by freed slaves once cut more lumber than any on the East coast.[245] Now, the sawmill's new ownership faced old problems.[246] Century lacked a bank, fast-food restaurant, motel, or library. Many workers used outhouses behind their shacks.[247] A steam-engine mill with generators provided electricity.[248] Century and the rest of Escambia County had seen few Republicans in office or at the voting booth since Reconstruction; Spessard Holland had claimed their uncontested votes for decades.[249]

Chiles woke at dawn Tuesday, March 17, for breakfast at Granny Hattie's Southern diner. He dressed to walk: white shirt and tie, slacks, and a pair of Army boots.[250] A green leaflet stuck out of his shirt pocket that read: "I'm Lawton Chiles, the Walking Senator."[251] The campaign camper read: "Senator Lawton Chiles Camper." Everyone thought Lawton's surname was "Camper."

The first fellow he saw he had to talk down from a telephone pole. Chiles gave him an earful about his walking-talking campaign. Finally the lineman broke in to say he would like to help, but he hailed from Alabama. Chiles said he would appreciate it if he told his neighbors about him. He figured he had walked far enough West and could turn around.[252]

He shook hands with the sawmill's first shift. One woman walked up to Chiles and introduced herself as Rosemary Emmett, an insurance agent. "I have a darn walking insurance policy," she said, "if you're interested." It would cost him fifty cents a week; he took a business card.[253]

Dozens of well-wishers watched him leave Century on State Road 4. If he could climb Jay Hill he could coast to the Keys, they said. Just over the Escambia River he spotted it. Tall longleaf pines blossomed silver-white as far as he could see. A light breeze shed their pollen. At the summit, he found a resting spot in the grass. His pocket pedometer stopped clicking.[254] A highway patrolman pulled up and asked his business. You're only halfway up the hill, he advised; another sandy ridge awaited him around the bend. A middle-aged woman approached from her nearby home. She introduced herself as Ruth Godwin and asked if he wanted company. Together, they climbed the other half of the hill.[255]

Farmers broke the red soil for crops. A dust cloud whirled across the highway and gritted his cheeks, hair, and eyebrows.[256] In Jay, a town of 6,000, he met John Pittman, a former legislator, at the electric co-op and lunched at his farm.[257] He ate collard greens, fried chicken, and rice; for dessert, apple popovers and another piece of chicken.[258]

Back on the road, Chiles took cover from the rain at a livestock auction. At a break in the auction of high-priced cattle and hogs, he took the microphone and announced his candidacy. Dozens of farmers massed around him, decrying low wheat and soybean prices, oppressive interest rates, and proposing a cooperative farming venture to cut out the middleman and guarantee a decent return. One told him he made two-and-a-half cents on a loaf of bread. Subtracting fertilizer and fuel costs, he barely broke even. "The row farmer," Chiles noted on a pad, "is the one who's really having a tough time of it."[259]

In the evening, Chiles found a telephone in a general store. He gave reporters a recap of the eight-mile journey:

> I got a real good feeling walking along the road and doing my thing. Everyone told me if I made it up the hill to Jay on Highway 4, I'd make it all the way to the Keys. I made it up the hill.[260]
>
> Instead of spending money on airplane tickets to fly over the voters, I purchased four pairs of shoes, which will carry me directly to the voters. This is no gimmick.[261]
>
> This is part of my economy campaign, as I don't intend to compete with other candidates in seeing how much money can be raised. [Walking also allows me] to personally meet the voters, who have a right to expect they can talk to the people who want to represent them.[262]

Reporters talked to locals. "Heck, I wouldn't vote for a man like that," declared one patron at McCurdy's Dairy Bar. "Why, he can't even afford a car."[263]

"He'll take too long to get things done," another cautioned.[264]

"He was very personable, a very casual, down home likeable person," Jay City Clerk Linda Carden later recalled. "It was impressive that he was doing it."[265]

Chiles checked his pedometer: one mile. Flustered, he pitched it in the woods with all his might.[266] He slept in his camper on the outskirts of town. His aide tied a ribbon around a tree so he knew where to resume walking the next day.[267]

Next morning, Chiles dictated a report on the previous day's activities to his campaign headquarters, where his reports became newsletters for supporters.[268] Jack Pridgen would edit the transcripts for clarity and length before they reached the public. "It's great to have my feet on the ground," he related, "and to be with good Florida people, to learn from them and tell them of my ideas. This day has certainly confirmed my belief that there is a crying need to bring more of our government back closer to home and to the people it is intended to serve."[269] He set out from Jay for Munson at about eight o'clock. He figured he was walking about three miles an hour. Some Santa Rosa County commissioners met him and chatted. Soon he reached the intersection of State Road 4 and county road 191, what the locals called the "Crossroads." He met a couple of mechanics there. One told Chiles he was paying $3,000 in income taxes, and he thought much of it was being doled out by the federal government in hand-outs. He complained that the rich paid too little in taxes, and some people these days just didn't want to work at all. A local bus driver had almost lost his job because he had tried to stop kids from firing screws with a sling-shot. Neither man had seen a Washington politician before.[270]

A few people stopped to offer Chiles a ride. One of them persuaded him to take a Coke for the road. As he got close to Pittman's Grocery, two fourteen-year-old girls, Brenda Ellis and Alicia Simmons—walked up to him. They had seen him on television the previous night and asked Alicia's father if they could walk with Chiles awhile. They followed him until he got to Pittman's.

When Chiles stopped for lunch, he felt his legs get "kinda stove up like the old race horse." He took some time to loosen up and air out the two blisters on each foot. He walked alone, at half his normal speed of four miles an hour; the moon lit the last mile to Munson. Jim Boyd had taken the camper ahead and parked it beside a pool in Blackwater River State Forest. The noise sent a fox squirrel scurrying up a tree. Chiles recorded the day for a newsletter and fell asleep to the tree frog's bark.

They got up Thursday morning about six o'clock and Chiles noticed the pool for the first time. Swallowtail kites circled above a longleaf pine and turkey oak canopy. Florida flame azalea blossomed orange in wiregrass underbrush. Not a soul around. He dared Boyd to skinny-dip. The cold swim loosened up his leg muscles and when the sun rose, they dried off and hit the road.

Chiles visited the state forest nursery near Munson and inspected its pine seedlings. A brisk headwind on the road added an hour, he guessed, to his travel time. The Blackwater River marked the state forest's eastern boundary. Its clear, soft water flowed over a sandy bottom. Atlantic white cedars shadowed the sandbars.

Two women, one from Bagdad and one from Crestview, joined him. They had read about him in the paper and wanted to chat. *The Tampa Tribune* commented on his campaign that day. "A million dollars is considered the bare minimum for a campaign for Senator or Governor," it decreed, "and that kind of money is not be had entirely from people whose sole interest is good government." If the Chiles campaign succeeded, it might "help bring political campaigning out of the skies and down to earth."[271] *Tampa Times* columnist Charlie Robins offered campaign tips for Chiles' competitors: bike the state with the slogan "Sprocket to Me"; float around the state, "making a raft from an old campaign platform"; or campaign by balloon, since "the advantages of hot air as a motivating force during a political campaign are too obvious to belabor."[272]

Chiles also met a Mr. Perry Nixon on the road. Nixon promised his support at the polls; Chiles chuckled at the man's presidential surname and thanked him.

He stopped in Baker. Blueberry fields grew and cattle pastured where longleaf pine forest once flourished. A brick general store, built in 1908 on the site of a cattle pen, dominated the main intersection.[273] An ad on the store's west side declared in red type "Coke Is It!"[274]

He left Baker Friday morning about eight o'clock, hoping to make the nine miles to Crestview by noon. A rain shower sent him back to the camper for fresh clothes, but soon he turned from State Road 4 onto US 90, a Spanish colonial trail paved over.[275] The highway crossed the Panhandle to Tallahassee and continued to Jacksonville, CSX railroad track paralleling much of the way.[276] Traffic picked up quickly. Radio newscasts promoting his visit attracted a crowd; in cars and pickup trucks along the highway and dirt crossroads, they had waited.[277]

Eglin Air Force Base, a nearly half million acre facility billed as "the largest air base in the Free World," employed the town, county, and neighboring jurisdictions.[278] Air Force and Army employees and retirees bemoaned pollution in nearby rivers and streams. On a high gravel ridge between the Yellow and Shoal Rivers, Crestview boasted some of the state's best bass fishing and turkey and deer hunting. Bald eagles nested in the crowns of its tallest pines. The region demanded conservation. Chiles reaffirmed his plan for a "NASA-type team with management skills, technological know-how, venturesome spirit and sufficient funds" to tackle national environmental policy. In a month, the country would use its first Earth Day to push for further federal involvement beyond the Council on Environmental Quality created in January. The Clean Air Act, the Safe Drinking Water Act, and the Clean

Water Act remained in planning stages; so did the Environmental Protection Agency.[279]

Many cursed the delay in construction of Interstate-10, which would replace US 90 as the Panhandle's main artery to central and south Florida. Chiles agreed, promising he would do everything he could to finish it. Some heard about his blisters on the news and pushed their home remedies on him. One told him to soak his feet in Clorox; another gave him foot powder. Neal Cobb, Crestview police chief, took him to Hudson Hardware and bought him a new pair of shoes. "Lawton," Cobb said, "you've got to walk, you ain't hardly got no money."[280]

Downtown, a couple dozen businessmen organized a luncheon for Chiles. James Lee, a former road board member, invited him to dinner. He ended the day nursing his feet, watching Jacksonville University defeat St. Bonaventure in a national basketball championship. "This walking-talking effort," he wrote that night, "may be the hardest way to campaign, but I'm convinced it's the best way for me to get to know the people and their problems and for them to get to know me. When I complete this walk, I'll have a gut-knowledge about this state that no other candidate for any office can possibly have."[281]

Word came that House Speaker and Senate candidate Fred Shultz had grounded his campaign plane and begun to tour the state by motor home.[282] Chiles' hometown paper had published his first progress report on March 20, 1970.

Cecil Anchors, Clerk of the Circuit Court in Okaloosa County, kept him company the Saturday morning on the way to Mossy Head. Anchors, a quail hunter, walked a "hunter's pace." Chiles walked an even quicker step to keep up. About noon he spotted a shelter erected up the road and welcomed the chance to catch his breath. Turned out Cecil's wife and four other couples from Crestview had arranged a picnic lunch for him: fried chicken, potato salad, baked beans, French fries, angel food cake and iced tea. He soon hiked with a full belly that reacted to every step. A recent University of West Florida graduate from DeFuniak Springs, Charles Barefield, walked up. He told Chiles everyone at his school was buzzing about his campaign and he would try to catch up with him again in his hometown. A school teacher, Bill Griffin, had scanned the highway for Chiles for hours until finding him. Griffin, aged thirty, and his wife, were going back to college, even with four young children.

It rained three times over the course of the day and he changed shirts a couple times. He cleared the fifteen miles to Mossy Head at about two o'clock. Senator Wilbur Boyd arrived to accompany him a couple days. "Traffic sure moves faster on US 90 than it did on State Hwy. 4," Chiles reported. "I can vouch for the fact that a lot of cattle and hogs are shipped through here. I don't know how many of these vans went by, but every time one did, it would blow my hat off and I could always tell by the smell that it contained livestock and had come from a good distance."[283]

Sunday, Chiles attended church at First Presbyterian in DeFuniak Springs, a nineteenth century railroad boomtown.[284] The church, Greek revival white petronite dating to 1923, fronted Lake DeFuniak.[285] When the service ended, nearly everyone approached him. "The kindness and generosity of the people in this part of Florida has completely overwhelmed me," he noted. A mile of Victorian homes with gingerbread trim, bay windows, and turrets rimmed the circular spring-fed lake. Three years after the railroad came to DeFuniak in 1882, the national Chautauqua educational movement chose the lake as the venue for its month-long winter meetings. The trainloads of scholars built a two-story, domed "Hall of Brotherhood" on its banks; their coffers paid for libraries, homes, and churches.[286]

Mrs. Catherine Claussen invited him to lunch at her restaurant in the Greyhound bus station on US 90. She had followed him in the news since Century. Chiles wolfed down fried chicken, turnip greens, black-eyed peas, rice, gravy, cornbread, and chocolate cake. He gabbed with the black dish-washers and cooks.

He talked about dogs with a couple locals. One claimed he could stop a charging dog by pointing his finger. The other, a postman, shared a story he'd once heard.[287] If a dog cornered you, he said, you should "pull your pants pockets out and then kinda bow over and make a loud noise." The gesture would confuse the dog so much that it would keep away. They all laughed.[288]

As he walked out of town Wednesday morning, a dog growled at him on the street. He figured it mastiff or pit bull and ignored it. Over his shoulder, he saw it start to charge. He turned and pointed his finger, until it almost had him. Remembering yesterday's conversation, he turned his pockets out, bent over and yelled. "You would have thought a snake bit that dog," it fell back so far.[289] Chiles sat down and chuckled at the picture of him and the yelping mutt, wondering if any voters had watched.

80

On courthouse grounds facing US 90, Walton County honored Confederate veterans with the state's first such monument.[290] Chiles trudged up and down eleven miles of piney sand hills into Holmes County. The uplands extended north to Alabama, reaching heights of more than three hundred feet. Nothing marked the way but turkey scratch.

Associated Press writer John Van Gieson accompanied Chiles to Ponce De Leon Springs; he was the first reporter to walk with the candidate. "It was hard keeping up with him," Van Gieson recalls. He tried writing on a pad while walking and talking but ultimately gave up and focused on listening to Chiles.

A big semi whooshed past. "You always know when it's a cattle truck or pigs," Chiles said as he retrieved his hat. "They just drench you." He picked up a broken car antenna on the roadside. "That's the second walking whip I've found." Senator Boyd pulled up, and Chiles snickered at the story he had ready to spring on him. "There was this old drunk sitting in his broken-down car. I say, 'I'm Lawton Chiles and I'm running for U.S. Senate.' He looks at me and says, 'Who you running from?'" Boyd and Chiles both laughed. Chiles soon found another car aerial and gave it to Boyd. "Good thing there's no magic in these," Chiles said, "or I just might put a curse on those trucks."[291]

Near the city limits, campaign workers drove up with cold Cokes. Chiles chugged his and crammed it in his pocket. "I would never be a litterbug," he said. "I carried a Coke can ten miles in my pocket one day." They crossed the highway to the Ponce de Leon Restaurant. Jo Ann Le Moyne, working inside, gave Chiles a glass of iced tea. He grinned, and she said, "If everybody could give a smile now and then, it would be something, wouldn't it?" Chiles asked for her vote, but she explained her British citizenship. "Gosh," he said, "I need to get you naturalized so you can vote for me." Van Gieson filed his report with the title "That Speck on the Horizon: It's Walkin' Lawton Chiles."[292] Based on this article, he has the best claim to coining the term "Walkin' Lawton"—a rich contribution to Florida folklore.

Chiles and Senator Boyd covered the twelve miles to Ponce de Leon in about three hours, arriving around noon. They met the town's mayor and one of its councilmen at the outskirts and sat down for a fish fry at a roadside park, courtesy of some new friends from Crestview.

They toured the proposed site for a state park at Ponce de Leon Springs. According to legend, Spanish explorer Ponce de Leon called its cool bubbling waters the "fountain of youth." More than ten million gallons gushed daily into a cement-walled pool flowing into the Choctawhatchee River. The park would include the springs, its cypress groves, hollies, and magnolias. Chiles looked forward to its purchase.[293] He catalogued the litter and vandalism he found in roadside parks. "The aluminum can," he remarked, "looks like it's going to be with us forever." He saw broken lights, stolen barbecue grills, and wrenched faucets. He promised himself he would stiffen the penalties for those crimes.

Senator Boyd jotted down some notes from his time walking. "I must admit," he reflected, "I was concerned that people might think Lawton Chiles is maybe a little bit off his rocker or something." But "the thing that just amazed me and excited me was the look in people's eyes which said they really just wanted to talk."[294] *The St. Petersburg Times* marked the occasion. "What worries me," columnist Dick Bothwell wrote, "is how he is going to communicate with people along Florida 4 and U.S. 90. If they are anything like the ones on U.S. 19 and Interstate 4, the senator has got a problem right there. How can you tell a guy going seventy miles an hour your views on the issues?" "Let's hope," Bothwell added, "the people who stop to offer him a ride and are refused don't get sore and vote against him."[295]

Thursday morning, a man stopped him to ask about busing and school integration. Chiles said he believed the "the purpose of the educational system is to educate children, not to achieve a mathematical formula for mixing of races." He argued that it had been wrong, over the years, to bus black children to maintain segregation, and "it is wrong now to bus black and white children against their will and disrupt the entire school system." He emphasized the need to get back to the school system as an instrument to teach children, rather than as "an instrument of social change."[296]

Soon after that encounter, his eighteen-year-old daughter, Tandy, and his seventeen-year-old son, Bud, drove up to visit.[297] Tandy later reflected,

> When he was on the Walk, he didn't come to my high school graduation, because it was farther down the route than he had said he would walk, and he had made that commitment. So he was not gonna back down from it. And I was disappointed, but he wrote me a beautiful letter and he gave me a pocketbook, a beautiful square pocketbook. And I knew he had picked it out.

A shoe salesman stopped him as he hiked double time to Westville to meet some voters waiting for him. He had heard about Chiles' foot problems and had waited by the roadside all morning for him. He measured his feet.[298] He displayed a catalogue. Chiles agreed to buy some immediately, but received a half-hour clinic on the mail-order shoes' comfortable padded soles anyhow. The shoemaker insisted he didn't need money up front, or an address. "I'll find you," he said. "In fact, what I'd like to have is a letter from the walking Senator about how good my shoes are." Chiles agreed to do it if the shoes fit.[299]

In the meantime, he bought a new pair of shoes when he got to Bonifay— not as high-topped as the previous ones, but still heavy. Breaking them in would take a few more blisters, he knew. He inspected the town's forestry department facility, then turned in. "Today was a special day," he wrote. "I walked past the halfway mark between Century and Tallahassee. It's a great feeling."[300]

Aide Jim Boyd experienced Bonifay differently: "I remember two of those nights, one of the first nights, we stayed in the Bonifay city dump 'cause we couldn't find another place to park the camper." After the group spent the night in the dump, they "got up next day [and] started back where we left off."

Lawton made for Chipley, the last of the three towns founded along the railroad track laid by Confederate Colonel William Chipley soon after the Civil War.[301] On the way, Chiles met Senator Dempsey Barron, who trotted up on horseback, leading another horse. Senator Barron tried to persuade him to give his feet a break. Farther along, a delegation from the Florida Library Association lobbied him about an hour on a bill that would increase state funding of library services. Holmes County, home to Chipley, would receive double the usual amount if it passed. He complimented the bookmobile service, which he had used to check a book out while on the highway a while back. Dempsey wrote a note about the adventure for a Chiles campaign newsletter: "We were having a conference down at my law office in Panama City today, and it was voted by members of my firm what we probably should establish a Pony Express to move Senator Chiles along a little faster. So I brought the horses up and thought I'd tempt Lawton to join me in a ride but as always he was a man of his word and continued to hoof it across Florida."[302]

Chiles left Chipley the next day. All the bus drivers honked their horns and waved at him. Tandy, out of school for the holidays, walked with him and got a kick out of watching the buses go by and honk for her dad. Rhea had sent

Bud up to walk for a week since he was getting in trouble at high school.[303] Bud couldn't understand why his dad insisted on walking in the rain.[304]

Saturday night, the gang returned to Chipley for a possum and sweet potatoes supper prepared by the Sportsman Club. The tables brimmed with wild game: raccoon, rabbit, duck, turkey, deer, and moose. The club's hospitality obliged Lawton to try possum for the first time. Congressman Bob Sikes, the self-proclaimed "He-Coon" of the Panhandle, gave the keynote address. Introducing Sikes, Sam Mitchell, an old football coach in Washington County, described the Great Depression. His dad, Mitchell remembered, had taken him outside one day, showed him some animal tracks, and said, "Son, on the other end of that track is your next meal. You'd better get going."[305]

Next day Chiles visited Marianna, antebellum cotton market near the Chipola River.[306] He toured its correctional school for boys and talked to some residents who had been to the school two or three times before settling into a new program that split them into group sessions. The kids, Chiles noted, "get together with anything that's bothering them or any problems that they're having between each other. It gives them an identity, it really gives something that they can attach to and it makes them realize, I think, that someone does care."[307]

In the rain, four of five people stopped in their cars to talk. Chiles crossed the Apalachicola River into Gadsden County around nightfall. South of Victory Bridge, the river cut hundred foot-deep ravines. Florida yew, stinking cedar, and Ashe magnolia blanketed the bluff.[308] Foot-long magnolia leaves surrounded cream flowers with a purple center.[309] Less than a mile north, Jim Woodruff hydroelectric dam lit the river's headwaters at Lake Seminole. He turned his watch to the Eastern Time Zone and climbed Chattahoochee bluff. Finding no one to talk to but barred owls, he parked the camper near the dam, several hundred yards inside Georgia.[310]

Next morning, he visited Chattahoochee's Florida State Hospital for the mentally ill for several hours. Before the railroad, the town's port had harbored dozens of steamboats carrying cotton from Georgia to the port of Apalachicola on the Gulf of Mexico.[311] It marked the eastern boundary of Florida's Cotton Belt, which stretched to the Suwannee River. The hospital, first built as a federal arms depot during the second war against the Seminoles, now employed Chattahoochee. The patient-doctor ratio worried Chiles, as did its nursing shortage, especially in the largest such facility in the state with over 5,000 patients. Half the hospital lacked air conditioning. "The thing about the hospital that alarmed me more than anything else," he reported, "is that over 10 percent of the patients—584 of them—have criminal charges pending against them, yet there are only twenty beds under security. So there are all kinds of patients in here charged with rape, murder, assault with intent to commit murder and other serious offenses without proper security measures. The present situation cannot be allowed to continue."[312]

From Chattahoochee bluff, US 90 sloped down gently to the river's pine floodplain.[313] At dusk he walked Gretna, a mostly black village. He met an aunt who watched over teenage girls in the community, dispensing advice on family planning and child care. He talked to farmers transplanting young shade tobacco in the iron-rich red clay just south of town. They described the high risk in growing the light-brown, silky leaf used to wrap cigars under the shade of treated yellow cloth. Tobacco companies contracted with them to buy their crop in return for meeting their production cost. But tobacco companies had just cut their contracts by 40 percent across the board. Their grandparents planted brightleaf tobacco for their owners' pipes; now, they wondered how long they could plant shade and whether to leave the county.[314] Thousands from Florida's blackest jurisdiction had already moved in the last decade; the Gadsden County economy ranked last among Florida's counties.[315] Black voters felt shut out of the political world, too. Gadsden County's blacks outnumbered whites two to one, but whites controlled local government. The county counted 6,852 white Democrats and 4,797 blacks on its voter rolls. On the Republican side, there were 306 whites and 103 blacks.[316] Chiles asked the farmers if the new restrictions on cigarette packaging and television advertising had hurt them. If anything, the farmers replied, the restrictions had helped, since they had boosted demand for cigars.[317]

He camped just outside Quincy. Wednesday's walk to Quincy convinced him summer had arrived. He cooled off in City Hall, where the city commission was meeting to count votes from the recent municipal election. Tom Cumbie, a druggist, invited him to go turkey hunting the next morning. "It's great to be in Quincy," he wrote, "looking down hill to Tallahassee!"

They woke about five-thirty Thursday morning to listen for turkey gobbles on the wind. A half hour later, Chiles had bagged a fifteen-pound tom and headed for town square. The sun rose over the county courthouse's two-story tan brick and brown cupola and white Ionic columns. Magnolia, live oak, and a Confederate war memorial shaded the grounds. There he regaled Sheriff Bob Martin and County Judge H. Y. Reynolds with the story of the hunt. They quipped that since he came from out-of-town, maybe they would lock him up a couple days for questioning. Chiles agreed to leave the turkey with them and they let him go for good behavior.

He got word that folks expected him in Havana and turned north onto State Road 12. The brown-and-green marquee of Quincy's Leaf Theater marked the tobacco trail's start. Eleven miles of fields and aromatic curing barns led to downtown Havana's brick warehouses. Their stores supplied Cuba's cigar industry until Fidel Castro took power.[318] A local invited him over for a catfish stew lunch, but he declined and hastened back to the main road. He spent the night in Midway, a black hamlet near the Leon County line.

The *Milton Press Gazette*'s Malcolm Johnson weighed in on his progress. "Chiles hasn't attracted much statewide attention in his walk so far from the Alabama line north of Pensacola into Chipley this week," Johnson reported, "but he is undoubtedly making time with the local weekly newspapers in the West Florida towns he passes. That's important for a fellow from 'way down south in Polk County; and an affinity once developed out there along the hog and hominy trail is one it's hard to shake off."[319]

Friday, April 3, his fortieth birthday, Chiles left at daybreak for Tallahassee. He walked the first of the red Appalachian foothills that led to the capitol.[320] Michael Wright, a *Tallahassee Democrat* reporter, joined him early. As Chiles waved to honking cars, he told Wright:

It's easy to become insulated from the people and the real issues. But, you know, getting out and listening to the people you learn what the real issues are. When you're campaigning and flying from city to city, you don't always have time to listen. Out on the road like this, you have the time. One of the most important things I've learned since I've been on the road is that the people don't feel represented in Congress. State and local government are disappearing and losing their effectiveness.[321]

Less than a mile up the road, they approached an I-10 construction site. Chiles grabbed a hard hat and climbed a ladder to talk to the workmen. While he was up there, he looked down and remembered that he had "never been very partial to heights." He teetered at a gust of breeze. A photographer neared, and he descended as quickly as he could. Capitol press corps television newscasters surrounded him, requesting interviews on the way into town. One man wanted to shoot his entry into the capital for a Mobile, Alabama, television station.[322]

Lakeland Ledger writer Tom Henderson interviewed Chiles as he walked the last few miles into the Capital. "The people have been tremendous all along the way," Chiles told Henderson. "The news seemed to go ahead of us and there would be someone to greet us in almost every little town along the way. They knew that all they had to do was jump in their car and I'd be down the road. Many of the people I have met see themselves as stepchildren of the government."[323]

Chiles liked the Panhandle diet so much he gained weight on the trail. "But now," he claimed, "I'm watching it and have lost most of that weight I picked up."[324]

As he entered Tallahassee, Chiles commented, "I wonder all the time what the response will be from the people in the other parts of the state to my walking campaign."[325] As much as north Florida's folkways warmed to him, its 1.5 million residents comprised only a quarter of the state's population.[326]

A car stopped beside him. The driver introduced herself as Mrs. Dorothy Cavanah, en route to Jackson, Mississippi, from Jacksonville. "We heard you were walking through here and we just wanted to stop, say hello, and wish you the best of luck," Mrs. Cavanah said.[327]

He toured a Volkswagen dealership on the edge of town. The salespeople crowded around him asking questions: "You must be the walking senator." ... "How are your feet?" ... "How's the trip been?" ... "How do you feel now?" In the afternoon, a busload from Lakeland pulled up at the Varsity Theater.[328] Rhea, his mother Margaret, an aunt, and about thirty friends joined him for the last miles to the Capitol. Margaret, almost seventy, walked uphill. Michael Wright asked her about the campaign. "We're gaining ground every day," she replied. "The only way to learn about state affairs is to get out and walk like this."[329] Another newsman offered Margaret Chiles a ride. "I walked him when he was a baby," she said. "I can walk him now." Rhea concurred with Margaret. "I think it's great," she offered, "he's doing it like it ought to be done. He's listening to people rather than telling them what they want to hear."[330]

A crowd of supporters and reporters had gathered around three or four birthday cakes when he arrived at Gray Park next to the capitol building. They raised their homemade signs high. "Peace be with Lawton Chiles as he walks 1,000," one sign read. "Happy Birthday to the Walking Senator," read the inscription on a birthday cake. An outline of a person walking was drawn in icing on the cake. On another cake, from a group of Senate secretaries, there appeared a small toy camper, toy shoes, and a picture of a turkey. "These Shoes Are Made for Walking," read the inscription. Chiles stuck an arrowhead in the cake to top it off; he had found the artifact near Victory Bridge. To the audience's delight, he claimed the arrow was "pointing toward Washington." They sang "Happy Birthday." He admitted aloud, "There were times that I wondered if I'd done the right thing in taking this walk."[331] He added in a newsletter, "No matter how much you can spend on television, and even if you reach a million people at once that way, you can only listen to one person at a time."[332]

Chiles took a break from the walking trek and began the sixty-day legislative session in Tallahassee. He lived a half mile away from Leon High School; to stay fit, every morning he walked to the school track and ran a mile and a half.[333] During the session, a pair of boots arrived in the mail from the shoemaker he met near Westville, and he threw off his old ones.[334] Representative Joe Kreshaw showed him how to rub his feet with Vaseline. The trick, Kreshaw explained, was to soften, not harden his soles.

During the session, Chiles organized a campaign strategy meeting in Tampa. Rhea, Charlie Canady, Jack Pridgen, and Senator Wilbur Boyd mapped out the miles ahead in a hotel meeting room decorated with campaign news clippings. "I could walk thousands of miles and it wouldn't do me any good," Senator Boyd admitted, "but this thing has gotten their attention and when they look they see an outstanding man. They figured at the current pace the walk would hit the Keys about August 20; they would save up enough money for a media and barnstorming blitz in the final hours."[335]

Most days on the trail, the Chiles team found themselves the only show in town. Bryant let his name recognition work for him, and Schultz campaigned via TV ads and a newsletter, "Flying with Fred." But voters identified more with the idea of the walking campaign than anyone named "Lawton Chiles." One dear supporter in Citrus County had confessed to a Chiles campaign volunteer, "I'd just do anything for you, Johnny, but I'm gonna vote for that walkin' fella." Voters knew everything about the walking man except his name. Rhea began telling voters, "Just remember, Chiles rhymes with miles."[336]

The last morning in Tallahassee, Friday June 5, friends organized a farewell breakfast for him that drew two hundred. Twenty-two state senators and some city policemen agreed to walk with him. After adjournment at about five o'clock, Chiles led his caravan out the Senate chamber. Ken Plante, a Republican senator, pinned a sign on his back that read "slow moving vehicle." They paraded up Monroe Street and turned right onto US 90. One by one folks peeled off till just Chiles and his new driver, Harp Robson, climbed the hundred-foot hills. Robson, behind the wheel of a new red camper, invited people by loudspeaker to come see "the walking senator." Some friends drove up and invited him to their home-grown peach stand on the roadside. "They gave me some of the most succulent peaches I've ever eaten," he noted. Arbor vitae and palms lined US 90; rows of crape myrtle bloomed pink-red.[337] Split rail fenced cow pasture and pecan orchards fronted the road, too. Around 10 o' clock, Chiles stopped to eat dinner and rest his legs, which had seized up again. He wished he had run a few more times around the track.

Saturday morning, he hit the pavement early. He passed a dirt and gravel crossroad running south from plantations between Tallahassee and Lake Miccosukee. Before railroads, mules had hauled wagon loads of cotton under its live oak and Spanish moss canopy to Port Magnolia on the St. Marks River. Growers shipped by rail until the boll weevil came.[338] Now, if rain hadn't turned it to red mush, pickup trucks of quail hunters kicked up dust on Old Magnolia road.[339]

Chiles crossed a bridge over Lake Miccosukee's cypress-kneed edge into Jefferson County. He met a black grocery store owner just outside Monticello named Frank Mosely. Mosely had grown up in the area but had moved to New York and survived the sinking of his Merchant Marine ship in World War II. His wife had worked as a manager at Central Life Insurance Agency in Tallahassee since 1934. He said everything he got he worked for. Chiles commented in his newsletter, "I really feel our time and efforts should be spent seeing that everybody has an opportunity to get to the point that they can do for themselves. We simply can't do everything for everybody." He concluded, "It did my heart good to talk to his man, to see the kind of business he's doing there, and to listen to his philosophy."[340]

He saw the hilltop Jefferson County courthouse from a distance, beyond Jefferson High School's white Doric columns. Local slaves had built the two-story brick Colonial Revival school. Magnolias and cabbage palms shaded the courthouse, a tribute to Thomas Jefferson's home. Nineteenth-century Greek and Romanesque Revival lined the traffic circle around it: the Perkins Opera House, two story brick with corbelled cornice, cast iron and stained glass first floor storefronts; Simmons Drug Store; and Register's Barber

Shop, framed soon after the Civil War. "Walking into Monticello," Chiles reported, "made me think of Jefferson's home at Monticello that I had visited with my family some time ago."[341]

Chiles met the mayor of Monticello, Ike Anderson. Local Bill Scruggs, an old friend of Spessard Holland's, gave him a tour of historic downtown. Dexter Douglass came over from Tallahassee to show him around. "Some of the people [in little towns] that I talked to," Douglass later recounted, "called back and said, 'Man, he was the best thing they'd ever met.'"[342]

In the afternoon, he visited a greyhound race at the track north of town, which had drawn the whole county. On the way he passed tractor trailers loading up ripe watermelons in fields. One of the track managers offered to announce him to the crowd over the loudspeaker. He trumpeted the "walking senator" on his way to the Keys and wished him well.

He stayed the night at Scrugg's place in town. "My legs have performed well today," he reported, "but I've accumulated a few blisters—one real big one on my heel that I know is going to give me some trouble." His boxers caused trouble, too. "I'd walked a couple steps and tug them down, walk a couple steps and tug them down." He gave up. "Now I'm sort of like the braless generation. I'm shorts-less because there just wasn't anything I could stand to wear today."[343]

Chiles attended church at Monticello's First Baptist with Bill Scruggs. After lunch, he made for Greenville. The next day he walked by a house with a yard full of cars and a crowd gathered on the front porch. He waved as he passed. They started laughing, saying "You must be the walking senator." They introduce themselves as the Kinsey family: Jeff Kinsey, some of his sons, and his eighty-four-year-old father who walked up to meet Chiles with the help of a cane. Chiles sat on the front porch and talked Vietnam War politics with them over dinner. One of the grandsons had finished a tour of duty. The Kinseys complained they felt shut out of government and thanked him for stopping by.

Farmers harvested shade tobacco in old cotton fields. Driveways wound through mossy live oak groves to antebellum manors. A car passing another one almost hit Chiles and a boy walking with him so he started walking farther from the road. About halfway between Greenville and Madison, he met a storeowner named Mrs. Yarborough who warned him to watch out for roadside rattlesnakes. She had spotted four in the tall grass in the last couple days. He reassured her that he had only seen snake skins on the way and he told himself that folks must be throwing snake skins out their car windows.

He walked with one eye on the road and one on the grass all the way to Madison.

At Madison High School, teachers, students, and parents from both county high schools, white and black, had gathered to plan for Madison High's court-ordered integration in September. They discussed spring training when he arrived. Athletes from Madison High and the black school would train together and the black high school's coach would join Madison High as an assistant coach.

Word reached Chiles that Farris Bryant had formally announced his bid for the U.S. Senate. Bryant's entry added a fifth competitor to the Democratic primary that now included Fort Lauderdale attorney Alcee Hastings and peace candidate Joel Daves, an attorney and former legislator from West Palm Beach. "It really comes as a relief," Chiles reported. "Certainly, I'm disappointed he decided to run against me; if I had my druthers, I'd druther he hadn't." Nevertheless, "the confidence that I've gained from my walking-talking campaign is solid and I'm going all the way." Chiles had resigned his State Senate seat; there was no turning back now. "Bryant is a fine man but he's of another era. His was the era in which he fathered the Cross Florida Barge Canal without too much worry about the rape and destruction of the Ocklawaha River and in which he was so proud of luring an Aerojet facility to Florida that he didn't worry about the fact that he put it adjacent to Everglades National Park." Chiles recalled a man telling him that Bryant would stumble when he tried reach out to working people, young people, teachers, conservation-minded people, and South Floridians "because he didn't build any roads down there during his administration." Despite those liabilities, the man claimed, Bryant would win votes. Chiles chuckled; the man had "just named off a healthy portion of what makes up our voters today."[344]

In Live Oak, Chiles walked comfortably in a green pair of silk undershorts given to him by Senator Beaufort from Jacksonville. A man took a break from cutting grass to shake his hand and introduce himself as O.T. Watley. Chiles asked Mr. Watley what had happened to his hands. Seven thousand five hundred volts of electricity, he said, had gnarled his hands and feet. The doctor warned him not to work, but he started his lawn service business anyway. "What a wonderful example this man is," Chiles commented, "and what a contrast he is with people who refuse to even try to get a job but rather want someone to hand it all to them on a platter."[345]

He toured the Boy's Ranch, an orphanage and general child care facility for boys from broken homes. Jim Strayer and his wife Betty—a classmate of Chiles' from Lakeland High—showed him around the 1,000-acre plot. He left impressed at the life the boys led in the cottage-style red brick homes, gym, and stables—all on the Suwannee River.

In Lake City, he spoke to supportive crowds at the Kiwanis Club and the Lions Club. He stayed a night at Senator Bishop's house, where he sampled what the locals called leftovers: conch peas, corn bread, country-fried ham, and roasted corn.

He picked up a folk tale on the road. In the old days, Cracker families gathered on the banks of the Suwannee River for a country fun day. The men would climb down the limestone outcroppings, fill their wooden skiffs with sticks of dynamite and half-inch fuses and paddle to their best fishing hole. They returned with enough beer-bellied catfish and bass for their wives to cook chowder in their wash pots. Columbia County boasted the best wash pot chowder in the state—and the most one-armed men.[346]

Vietnam questions dogged Chiles. He found himself in opposition for the first time. His stance had changed from hawk to dove during the campaign. Now that President Nixon had ruled out military victory as a mission, Chiles pushed for a quick troop withdrawal. "We must be firmly committed to getting out," he stated in his newsletter, "and I don't think we should get involved in any more land wars in Asia."[347]

He ventured south off US 90 toward Lake Butler, the western gateway to Florida's "Iron Triangle." Since 1913, Raiford's State Prison Farm had powered the local economy from Lake Butler north to Lawtey and east to Starke. The maximum security facility housed Death Row and the state's electric chair.[348] On the way out of Lake Butler, Chiles met up with the *Jacksonville Journal's* George Harmon. As they talked, they ran into a Sergeant Collins, head of the local Florida Highway Patrol division. Sgt. Collins wanted to talk taxes. He had scratched out some equations that predicted taxes should rise as demand for services rose. Chiles described Florida's growth explosion and the high cost of capital infrastructure like schools, sewers, prisons, and libraries to service new neighborhoods. He proposed that the federal government share revenue with high-growth states. Sgt. Collins condemned the growth in bureaucracy he witnessed. Government, he claimed, "is kind of like we're going to help the old lady across the street whether she wants to be helped or not."[349]

At the Alachua County line, a Gainesville delegation met him: Clyde Martin, a banker who used to live in Lakeland; Senator Bob Saunders; Bill Cross from University of Florida and faculty advisor to Blue Key; John Dotson, treasurer of the UF student body; and other UF students and professors. Chiles and Senator Saunders walked through Waldo, doubled back to Starke in Bradford County for a Rotary event, and then returned to see all of Waldo's downtown with the police chief and the ex-mayor.

Next morning, Chiles made for Gainesville. Gregory Favre, editor of the *Palm Beach Post*, drove from West Palm Beach to join him for the walk into town. Senator Saunders and Chiles canvassed the county courthouse, city hall, banks, drug stores, service stations, breakfasts, parties, two watermelon festivals and "just about everywhere else where people moved."[350]

Chiles spoke at a Jaycee dinner in town. Folks asked him his view on the draft. "I know a lot of people would like to get rid of the draft and so would I," he answered, "but if we have a volunteer army, we're really going to have a professional army, and this scares me. Those who worry about an industrial-military complex or a military establishment would really have something to worry about. This would be the largest lobbying force that we could have. It would become a tremendous political force, something that our country should not have." He added, "I would rather stick with the draft and see that we get it working fairly." The overflow crowd gave him a standing ovation.[351]

Friday afternoon, he left Gainesville on US 441 south and entered Payne's Prairie. For eight miles, the highway snaked through thousands of acres of wet prairie draining into vast limestone sinkholes. Red-head sandhill cranes waded in the shallows. Piled gators sunbathed, their jaws cocked open, on islands of palmetto and sedge. A man stopped him and asked, "Do you know it is one hundred degrees out here?" Chiles thought he was pulling his leg, but soon it felt a whole lot hotter. He let the rain wash his sweat-soaked clothes. He counted forty-two dead snakes or snake skins on the roadside and figured himself strong stock to have survived.

L.K. and Marge Edwards invited him over for dinner at their century-old white-frame house in Irvine. They fed him a home-cooked meal: country ham, creamed corn, English peas, deviled eggs, rich orange-colored home-made butter, and beef. Chiles finished the feast with ice cream with nuts, and homemade coconut and lemon cake. Senator Edwards—"The Sage of Irvine"—entertained after dinner. He played a record about a "former distinguished senator from Kentucky, Marcus Cassius Clay, who was a third cousin of Henry Clay." Clay, an abolitionist Republican in the "Solid Demo-cratic South," killed five or six men in self-defense. Once, when running for the U.S. Senate, Clay walked into a town that had threatened him with death upon his arrival. He took to the bandstand: "For those of you who believe in the law of God, I brought this." He placed a Bible on the stand. "For those of you who do not believe in the law of man, I brought this." He pulled out a copy of the U.S. Constitution. "For those of who don't believe in either one of those laws, I brought these." Clay brandished two Colt dragoons and a Bowie knife. He gave his stump speech and left town untouched.[352]

Chiles turned the story over in his mind as he approached Ocala, Farris Bryant's hometown, Monday morning. At the city limits, supporters wel-come him. He began the day with a half-hour live radio talk show, then a walkthrough of four shopping centers, city hall, the county commission building, and speeches to the Kiwanis club and the Young Democrats. "I'm convinced Marion County is wide open," he reported in his newsletter, "and that Bryant, having left here for Jacksonville after being governor and pay-ing few visits prior to becoming interested in the U.S. Senate race, may be surprised here."[353]

East of Ocala, he took a boat ride on the Ocklawaha River to tour the site of the proposed Cross-Florida Barge Canal for the first time. "I had a real sick feeling leaving Silver Springs and Silver River," Chiles told the *Lakeland Ledger,* "fearing that the beautiful area may be destroyed. But now, it looks like the greatest damage already occurred and is in the northern area (Rod-man Dam)."[354] Ross Allen, originator of the Silver Springs tourist attraction nearby, wondered what the rationale was for the canal. Oscar Rawles from the U.S. Corps of Engineers and reporters from the *Lakeland Ledger, Palm Beach Post-Times*, and Channel 2 TV accompanied Chiles. Rawles said one third of the canal was complete at a cost of about $50 million; completion would cost another $50 million.[355] Chiles witnessed the tree crusher nick-named "the monster" which the Corps used to clear logs for a dam, and sur-veyed environmental damage along the riverbanks. He canvassed fisherman along the way, asking how the catch was. Some fish in the impoundment res-ervoirs created to raise the river water level were not fit to eat, some were damaged.[356] He met a young Corps ecologist on the boat named Dave Bow-man. A graduate of University Florida with a degree in wildlife ecology, Bow-man said he and the three or four others in his specialization found job offers to be "scarcer than bald eagles." His friends joined the military; he had already served. "I'm afraid," Chiles concluded of the experience, "this is another case like you see in government too often where somebody's grandiose idea just didn't pan out, and the taxpayer pays."[357]

He took side trips to stops in Pasco County: Zephyrhills, Dade City, and a big retirement center in New Port Richey. Then DeLand, Daytona Beach, and New Smyrna Beach in Volusia County.[358] In Volusia, a young lawyer accompanied him for two days. At the end of the second day, he turned to Chiles and said: "You know I've been walking with you for two days in my county and I suddenly realized you haven't bought anything all the time you've been here. You're worse than Sherman the way you live off the land!"[359] Chiles savored the walk on Daytona Beach. "It suddenly occurred to me," he wrote afterward, "that this was as close to a vacation as I would get this summer."[360]

Lake County supporters schooled him about the pollution sources ruining Lake Harris, Lake Eustis, Lake Griffin, and Lake Dora. In Lake Griffin especially, nutrient loads from sewage and artificial fertilizer had bloomed forests of green algae, killing fish. Chiles reaffirmed the need for high technology to save the environment. "We really should be attacking this," he stated in his newsletter, "the same way we attacked the project of going to the moon—an advanced team made up of people from universities, government, and industry. I believe that everyone—certainly government agencies that are putting projects where it's possible to destroy some of our natural resources—should have ecologists working with them to see that we keep nature's life balance as constant as we possibly can."[361]

Walking into Sanford on Sunday, he hit the halfway mark to the Keys. He attended the ground-breaking of the Good Samaritan Rest Home, the project of Mother Ruby Wilson, a black community activist. During the ceremony, the large crowd gathered sang a spiritual that struck Chiles as a "politician's hymn." "When I have done the best I can," they sang, "and then some of my friends don't understand, stand by me, Lord." Chiles remarked, "It seems a shame that Mother Ruby Wilson's life should be hidden in Sanford rather than being an influence all over the state."[362]

At a Sanford coffee event Monday, he chatted with a teacher named Dorothy Bethel. She taught a remedial reading class sponsored by the federal government for several years but stopped when the funding dried up. The course taught kids at the tenth grade level, but many of the black and white boys in the classes—limited to twelve students each—read at a fifth grade level. After the class, she said, kids swelled with pride and wanted to stay in school. "It really frustrates me," Chiles reported, "to see an important program like this—one that helps people help themselves—curtailed while at the same time millions and millions of dollars are wasted by the federal government. This is one of the reasons I'm in this race."363

Leaving Sanford at seven o'clock, Chiles made Maitland by lunchtime. As he strolled past the city limits, someone approached with a bottle in his hand. He introduced himself as Martin Peden, a Borden's milkman from Orlando, and handed him a carton of cold milk. Peden had seen him walking and thought he might need a thirst-quencher. He had followed the walking senator in newspapers and on TV and delighted to meet him.

Chiles walked through Casselberry with city councilman Bill Brier, then shook hands at an art exhibition on Abraham Lincoln in Fern Park. In his newsletter, Chiles celebrated progress:

> In the early stages of this walking-talking and listening campaign, a lot of people commented (some predicted) that I'd get a real good reception in north and west Florida because people there are more grass-roots oriented in their politics, but that in the central and southern part of the state I wouldn't get the same reaction. I'm really finding out that that's wrong. People are people everywhere. They like to talk politics, they like a politician who will listen to their ideas and concerns. They like the walk.364

Lawton's son Bud, a teenager, joined part of the walking campaign. On the road, he took notes for a poem about his dad's journey across Florida:

The Walking Senator

7:30, a hot summer morning. The sun
approaches adolescence.
a sleepy, quiet town struggles wordlessly
to wake itself.

an old farmer strains his eyes,
his omnipresent collie's ears prick
up in strict attention.

in the distance a lone figure steps
off brisk, long paces—beckoned

96

by the sleepy town, and the winding
concrete path he travels.

hands clasp, years of difference
but equal respect. unquestioning
eyes and a familiar title assure
the young man that his feat has
preceded him.

the farmer squints his eyes; now
in an opposite direction. pride
flows through the old veins—he
shook the hand.

now, once again in the distance,
the lone figure quickens his pace:

heart pounding with anticipation;
twelve miles and a thousand hand-
shakes before the sun reaches
maturity.

—Lawton "Bud" Chiles III, 1970

6

The Burden of Victory

At the Orlando city limits, television, radio, and TV newscasters met him with a big pan of water with dry ice in it. It bubbled and smoked, but a brick at the bottom, they promised, would shield his feet from the dry ice. They urged him to cool his feet off. His feet found the dry ice in a hurry and he fumbled to get it off and put his boots back on.

Chiles arrived in Kissimmee Saturday morning just in time for a Fourth of July Silver Spurs Rodeo parade. He looked around and noticed that all the other public officials had gotten in cars. Only he and the horses walked. The crowd applauded him for sharing a road with so many horses in front of him, leaving so much behind for him to step in.[365]

He read in the news that the Nixon Administration had reported an increase in the unemployment rate to 4.7 percent, but excused it with a reminder that it rose even higher under President Kennedy. It reminded him of Francis Kershlis, a skilled "tool and die" worker at Orlando's Martin-Marietta aerospace plant he had met earlier. By the early 1960s, the plant employed more than 10,000 workers, making it the state's largest factory.[366] The company still employed her and her husband, but big layoffs had hit recently, leaving many to pick fruit in the fields. Raised on welfare in a housing project along with her nine siblings, Mrs. Kershlis owned her own home now, and urged that federal government spend more efficiently on the good social programs they administered.

At the Polk County line Sunday afternoon, July 5, about twenty supporters, reporters, and family welcomed him with lemonade, water, and Cokes. Right after he crossed, he jumped back from a nipping dog. "Wouldn't it be a heck-uva note if I got bit by a dog in my own county," he thought, "after walking 550 miles through Florida undamaged?"[367]

Cars sped along U.S. 17-92, Chiles waving and drivers waving back. Campaign workers had set up yellow and black signs ahead and behind the Senator to notify drivers. Chiles' wife and two daughters greeted him, followed by Chiles' sister Jeanette and her husband, Joe P. Ruthven. Chiles picked up his four-year-old daughter, Rhea Gay, and carried her for a while. At a filling station, he learned a group of friends had organized dinner in Davenport for him. "That's what's so great about this," Chiles enthused, chugging a bottle of Gatorade. "They just happened. They're nice surprises." Rhea told *Lakeland Ledger* reporters, "I'm going to keep walking as long as I can. They might have to scrape me up, but I'll keep at it."[368]

In Haines City Monday, Chiles met the mayor at the city limits, dunked his feet in a water tub filled by some kids, and walked into town for a coffee and a luncheon with local businessmen. In the afternoon in Lake Alfred, he met the city commissioners and manager. He returned to Haines City for a downtown walk and a football field rally.

After a day in Winter Haven he drove to Tallahassee for a one-day special session. He officially filed for the U.S. Senate while in town, reporting $77,000 in expenditures since November. House Speaker Fred Schultz had spent $230,000—mostly his own money.[369]

He toured Auburndale Thursday morning. All day, the camper played "Walk with Me, and Talk with Me Awhile, Mr. Sun." Nearly every car honked at him. "I feel great," Chiles told *Lakeland Ledger* reporter Lonnie Brown. "I can eat anything. I can sleep anywhere."[370] Chiles and then Brown climbed a ladder leaned against a General Telephone building in Auburndale, so they could meet workers tarring the roof. The candidate talked to them about ten minutes then edged down in baby steps. "I have to make myself do that," Chiles told Brown. "I don't like ladders. Sometimes I dream about falling off of them at night."[371]

After Chiles finished lunch, campaign staffer Jack Pollock and *Ledger* reporter Lonnie Brown rejoined the candidate. "'Bout time to leave for Lakeland," Pollock told Chiles. "You wanna ride up to 92? The car's right over there." "Naw," Chiles said. "I'll walk. Come on." Chiles left for Lakeland with Brown at his side.[372] The sun scorched them. A dark blue car pulled off U.S. 92 and a young man in Army fatigues got out and approached. "I know you must be thirsty," Ray Justice said, opening a bag, "So I brought you these."

He handed them three Cokes in paper cups. Justice would ship off to Vietnam in a few weeks and wanted to meet the candidate before he left. Chiles inquired about his views on the war. Justice wasn't sure, but he had his orders and he would go. Chiles thanked Justice for the drink and his thoughts. "He must have a lot on his mind," the candidate said as he gulped the Coke, "yet he stopped to bring me a Coke."[373] Chiles reiterated his opposition to the Vietnam War to Brown: "I don't know where a hawk lives anymore. The President says he doesn't want a military victory over there, so I say let's get out." The candidate sent the empty cup back to the camper. "There's so much litter along the highway," Chiles added, "I hear companies are paying to get throw-away cans back, and even at a penny a piece, I could finance a fantastic campaign if I picked up everyone I saw."

He had worn out three pairs of shoes, Chiles told Brown. "I have talked to a lot of people," he said. "But I've listened to a lot more. And that is the important thing, I think. I've filled five notebooks, and I feel that it would be a shame to lose the election now after I know so much about the voters of this state."[374] He noticed planes flying overhead. "Sometimes I wonder if Claude Kirk or Fred Schultz is up in them, checking on me to make sure I'm walking," Chiles cracked.[375]

About halfway to Lakeland on US 92, the clouds turned black and dumped buckets. Lightning flashed and Chiles signaled to the motor home, driven by 19-year-old Randy Chastain, to come pick them up. They drove down the road a quarter mile and pulled into a vacant lot. Chiles removed his shoes and pulled off two layers of socks, splotched yellow with Vaseline. He changed into dry clothes and chatted about folks he'd met along the way. Chiles described the slow-working poison of big-money politics. When the rain stopped, Chiles motioned to resume. Chastain cranked up the camper and backtracked to where the candidate had stopped. "I get the impression that you start back from where you left off every time something like this happens, is that right?" Brown asked Chiles. "Well, yes. It'd be cheatin' otherwise," Chiles replied. "I'd have given you a couple hundred feet," Brown told Chiles. "Nobody'd notice. Nobody'd know." Chiles grinned. "It'd still be cheatin'. If you weren't here, somebody else could find out." Just as Chiles found his gait again a passing car sprayed him with water.[376]

At Lakeland's outskirts, traffic picked up and car horns blared. About a dozen people joined, then a couple hundred once he got to Lake Parker, including Mayor Marvin Henderson. He had covered fifty miles in Polk County since Sunday. The caravan continued a couple miles until they filed into Lodwick Hanger for chicken perleu. A crowd of more than 2,000 packed the venue. A country band struck up "I'm Walking the Floor Over You" when Chiles approached. Some presented the candidate with good luck charms for the rest of the walk: a small umbrella, a portable toilet, a bathing suit, a pair of shoes, a pair of crutches, and a huge ball of twine to unwind as he walked so he could find his way back home. Ben Hill Griffin gave him orange seeds to plant along the road. "I feel like we are going to win," Chiles reported at Lodwick. "The Walk is working. It is overtaking me."[377]

"The crowd response was so great and so warm that it really got to me and I could barely talk," he wrote. "I'm getting another feeling like I had in 1958." The Walk, he felt, assured victory. "A team of plow mules couldn't get me to stop."[378]

At the Hillsborough County line, he met Senator Louis de la Parte and Senator Ray Knopke for a walk into Plant City. At the edge of town more joined in: newsmen from Channel 8 and Channel 13 TV, and the publisher of the *Plant City Courier*. In a tour of Plant City Steel, he hurt his right foot jumping off a beam. Concerned he sprained an arch; he showed his sore foot to a doctor. "I could see myself," he thought, "having to use that pair of crutches that were given to me at Lodwick to complete the walk." But he had only bruised a tendon.

Saturday, he walked the eighteen miles to Tampa so he could rest Sunday. Sunday, July 12, Lonnie Brown recorded his twenty-mile walk with Chiles through Polk County. In a *Ledger* diary entitled "Walk Now A Commitment for Lawton Chiles," he wrote that "it is not just a walk any more. It is The Walk. . . . Chiles and The Walk are as one now," he decreed.

Senators Knopke and de la Parte walked Chiles around Tampa Monday morning. They visited American Can Co. then walked from the Spanish Park Restaurant to the Columbia Restaurant. A stranger holding a check poked his head out of one of the restaurants. "I think your walking campaign is great and I want to participate," he said. Chiles looked at the check: Bill Hyder, one hundred dollars and zero cents. With a spring in his step, he walked into the Columbia for warm Cuban bread dunked in coffee.

In the afternoon, Chiles toured the Model Cities office. The biracial staff, he noted, had gone to work "organizing block clubs in the neighborhoods to get people to have pride in their neighborhoods, to develop community spirit and to help them learn to communicate what they think their needs, interests, and frustrations are." The office also collected information on the police department, recreation department, and other local agencies for quality control. The people he met worked for "one of the best federal programs I've seen." After dinner, he attended a boxing match that featured Sonny Frazier's song-and-dance act. Someone asked him how he liked it. "Big as he is," he quipped, "when he sings, I smile!" The announcer introduced Chiles as "the walking senator."

Wednesday morning early, he walked Bayshore Boulevard to Sandy Ridge. Two students at Tampa University, Ron Black and Bob Lastra, told him about their new environmental club on campus. Ron proposed a volunteer army to replace the draft. When Chiles cautioned him that a professional army would become a powerful new lobby in Washington, he seemed to reconsider. Bob noted that his brother, an Army serviceman with eighteen years experience, feared a standing army. The career soldier would become a "hired Hessian." At the Pinellas County line, campaign volunteers and reporters greeted Chiles.

Mike Richardson of the *St. Petersburg Times* joined him for a twenty-mile trek across the county the next day. Chiles toured the mayor's office, the new state office building and the courthouse, and struck up conversations at filling stations and roadside stores. Gordon Mather and his wife invited him over for dinner—after a hot shower. They surprised him with a cake with his name on it and a comfortable chair labeled, "This chair is reserved for the next U.S. Senator, Lawton Chiles." The response "in this so-called Republican territory," Chiles remarked, is outstanding. "I can't tell the difference from Polk and Hillsborough County."

The next week he marched south along US 41: Bradenton, Sarasota, Venice, Port Charlotte, Punta Gorda, and Englewood. He rallied the Punta Gorda-Port Charlotte Kiwanis to support expanding Route 41 to four lanes all the way to Miami. To speed up construction, he urged that all candidates for governor and U.S. senator walk the highway and see the traffic jams.

In Osprey, a retiree named Webster Chapman invited him over for breakfast. As Chiles canvassed the town, Chapman heralded him in his big New York-plated Cadillac. From front porches, general stores, and gas stations, they came to meet "the walking senator." A motel owner outside Venice heard the announcement and approached Chiles to offer him a free room.

Chiles yelled up to Bill Vasbinder, an Englewood electrician at work on a power pole, to tell him he was running for the U.S Senate. You'll have a better shot at my vote, Vasbinder replied, if you threw me up that piece of equipment I dropped. Chiles tossed it up with some muscle, almost knocking the lineman off his pole. "After that I wasn't sure if I had his vote," he thought, "but he got me a little eager when he said he might vote for me if I threw the equipment up to him."

He met Bob Wolff, a Fort Myers contractor who built aluminum screen porches and rooms. When Wolff left the states to serve in Vietnam, windows cost $12. When he returned a year and a half later, the same window cost $24. Wolff and his business partner borrowed money every three months to pay their three salaried employees' withholding tax. He worked long hours to bring home $100 a week for himself. Government, he claimed, only served big business. When he requested a loan from the Small Business Administration, they asked him how many millions were needed. Chiles asked him his opinion on how to fight inflation. First, he would "find out what's causing it, then pull out the cause by the roots like a poison plant, not merely chop away at the stalk."

Back on US 41, he met a Mrs. Godown and daughter Jan, who had tracked his progress since Century. Every night they had prayed for his safety. "Lots of people have asked me if I feel alone out on the highway," Chiles reported. "Now I really know why I haven't felt alone. I have people like the Godowns looking after me like that." He recorded his thoughts on Fred Schultz's first blitz of TV ads: "Although I haven't had a chance to see one yet, it seems a little late to start. . . . My commercial starts every morning about seven, and it goes on till about dark. People can see it any time they come by the section of the road that we are walking on, and I think we're getting excellent coverage."[379]

After a Spanish bean soup and fresh-boiled shrimp picnic at the Lee County line on a road shoulder, Saturday July 25, organized by his campaign committee, Chiles made for Ft. Myers.[380] In town, TV commentator Vern Lundquist asked him to justify the walk. Chiles replied that voters would rather read about treating his feet with Vaseline than some grand policy pronouncement.[381] Julian Clarkson invited Chiles over for dinner. "You remember I campaigned against the Burns road bond issue in November of 1965," Chiles told Clarkson. "When the road bonds were rejected at the polls, I knew Burns would not be re-elected in 1966. I wanted to run against him for governor. Although I got talked out of making that race, it was then I formed the idea of a walk through the state. I had made my start in politics by walking in Polk County, and I felt like I could do the same thing in a statewide race."[382]

Tuesday morning he began the 140-mile trip to West Palm Beach. He ate Dismal Key Fish Chowder at the home of a cousin, Floyd Ellis. He begged for the family recipe to no avail.

On State Road 80 out of Fort Myers, he met an old-timer named James Wightman. As a young man, Wightman walked behind six mules seventeen miles a day, harrowing wheat in Washington State. He harrowed such a straight line with four horses and two mules that he broke the state record by finishing a quarter section in three days. Government, he argued, needed more common sense and guts. "He looked fifty," Chiles reckoned, "but is seventy-two, and he is still running sixty-five cows on seventy-five acres and working mighty hard!"

He detoured north to Arcadia, a cattle and citrus capital on the Peace River. Folks there compared Chiles to the legendary "Acre-foot" Johnson who carried mail in the nineteenth century on foot between Fort Meade and Fort Myers. According to legend, Johnson wore a size 20 shoe and passed horse carriages when he got to walking. One afternoon, someone asked him to call a square dance in Arcadia. He walked to Fort Myers to buy shoes and returned in time for the dance. But he quit delivering mail when the post office refused to let him strap a chair on his back for passengers. "I'm sure glad I'm not walking against him for the U.S. Senate," Chiles mused.[383]

Outside La Belle, Chiles met Art Carlson, a rising senior at University of South Florida working at an outpost of the Florida Methodist Youth Camp. He had gone to Fort Myers on a supply run. On the way back he noticed a camper pulled off to the roadside. He had read about Chiles enough to know it was probably "Walkin' Lawton." He didn't know much other than the moniker, and out of curiosity he stopped to say hello. They chatted for fifteen or twenty minutes. Carlson left impressed with his sincerity and interest; Chiles had asked for suggestions for his campaign. As Carlson pulled away he turned to his buddy and exclaimed: "What an amazing guy. What an intelligent guy. Too bad he doesn't have a snowball's chance in hell of winning."

A crowd had gathered around his camper when Chiles arrived at La Belle, known since 1933 for Flora and Ella's homemade pies. After meat and three vegetables, the town's diner served coconut, peanut butter, and chocolate meringue and pecan pies to the blue collar community.[384]

Dr. Elizabeth Baldwin at the local public health clinic turned his attention to their problems communicating with the federal government. The feds required her to set up a night clinic for migrant workers, but she argued that they only came for treatment during the day. She had to take her staff off day shift to fill the night shift, leaving her short-handed in the daytime. Every time she protested, the feds pushed back. When Chiles arrived in the day-time, the clinic buzzed with patients, mostly Mexican-American and black. He was glad to see doctors handing out contraceptives and birth control advice.[385]

Wednesday afternoon, he lunched with his wife and Rhea Gay in Avon Park. He got fresh clothes and supplies, and told Rhea as many road stories as time would allow. "I think he thought," she later recalled, "no matter what the pundits are going to say, no matter what the newspapers say, I know the people are out there receiving the message—they're getting it and they're responding to it." He would "snicker about that and say, 'I know something, you know, that they don't know.'"[386]

In hindsight, Bud recognized the period was tough for his mother. Rhea ran the household, paying bills; the teenage children missed their father. "We were just wild," Bud Chiles recounts.

Thursday, Chiles trekked thirty-one miles from La Belle to Clewiston, the "Sweetest Town in America." He walked Lake Okeechobee's sugarcane coun-try. Since the 1920s, Clewiston sheltered the U.S. Sugar Corporation, the country's largest and oldest sugarcane producer.[387] Farther on Route 80 he found Belle Glade, known as "Muck City" for its black humus, nitrogen rich soil suited for sugarcane. Cracker settlers once held "cane grinds" in the fall during the harvest. For a day, they would chew cane, drink hot cane juice, tell stories and sing. They sopped up cane syrup with a biscuit and brewed beer from the syrup, topped with sticky "polecat" froth.[388] By the 1930s, local black labor worked the fields on the Lake Okeechobee floodplain for giant corporations.

Ten years prior to the Walk, CBS news aired Edward R. Murrow's exposé on Belle Glade agricultural practices. "The question posed by thoughtful men," Murrow argued, "is, must the two or three million migrants who help feed their fellow Americans, work, travel, and live under conditions that wrong the dignity of men?"[389] Now, U.S. Sugar and other firms planted 180,000 acres in Everglades sugarcane. Jamaicans, Barbadians, Domini-cans, and Haitians worked the fields with machetes.[390]

Chiles observed the public housing shortage for migrant workers. Only two projects in town handled about 3,200. He talked to Harvey Poole, a black man managing one of the projects; Dr. John Grady, a doctor and mayor of Belle Glade; a rep from one of the sugar companies; and a man from the

State Health Department. "The problem," he surmised, "is tremendously complex and anyone who seeks to oversimplify it does a disservice to the situation and the people involved." The area needed more vocational education to advance beyond day labor and education for workers on proper diet, he believed. "Another thing," he continued, "is that many of the migrant workers appear satisfied with the way they are living." They "don't want to work regularly, don't want a residence to be responsible for, don't want to be tied down to any place." Many had condemned the "Big House" owned by grower George Wedgeworth, Chiles observed. But he claimed the 120-room complex housed people better than most lodgings in the area. Wedgeworth provided it rent free to some seventy to eighty residents. Joe Collins, the black man who manages the house, explains that only about twelve or fifteen of them actually worked for the grower. Wedgeworth paid for the maintenance, lights, water, and electricity—over $14,000 a year. Chiles thought Belle Glade ideal for a Model Cities program to build on progress already made due to federal intervention.

Monday morning, he arrived at the West Palm Beach city limits and met supporters at a Publix grocery. "The long trek from Ft. Myers to the sea is now ended," he noted, "and I realize that I will be knee-deep in people down the east coast walking through Palm Beach, Broward, and Dade Counties."

Chiles visited the RCA plant that employed about 2,000 workers on one shift. He spoke to the Palm Beach and West Palm Beach Kiwanis Club. In Boca Raton, he visited Florida Atlantic University and talked to students and professors. "Boca Raton is really growing," he reported. "There are a tremendous number of condominiums, apartments and housing developments being built in the area."

A.J. Ryan, former legislator colleague, Emmet McTigue, a college buddy, and other supporters welcomed him at the Broward County line. He walked into Pampano Beach with them, visiting a brand-new shopping center and mall. "The people in Broward," he observed, "are more frustrated and hostile than [in] about any place I've been. I can remember about ten years ago when people were saying, 'Why would anyone live in Dade County when they could just move across the line and live in Broward?' Well, it looks like too many did move." Schools, hospitals, and water and sewer facilities had not met demand. Developers incorporated little towns with their own building codes and zoning regulations, then picked up and moved when infrastructure problems began. "I don't know who the hell is supposed to be representing me," one man told him, "but whoever it is has sure not done anything for me."

Walking from Pampano Beach to Ft. Lauderdale, Chiles made more progress than the vehicle traffic on U.S. 1. It rained that day, leading to six accidents along his path. He spent Monday in Ft. Lauderdale. In the morning he visited Florida Power and Light and other plants; in the afternoon he walked to Dania. Tuesday he arrived in Hollywood and that afternoon, he skipped ahead to attend a candidates' forum at Tiger Bay Club in Miami. Next morning, he returned to Broward and walked into Dade County, touring North Miami Beach, Hialeah, Miami Springs, Palm Springs Mile Shopping Center, and Miami Beach.

In Miami, Chiles began to despair about his chances and wondered whether to push on to Key Largo. His son Bud recalls:

> By the time my dad had reached Miami, he was losing hope. He was out of money, last in the polls, tired from all the brutal days in heat, dust and traffic. He was ready to give up when I came down to spend a few days with him. I said to him, "What about your faith, your belief, your beliefs, your convictions that this was going to work if you saw it all the way home?" I challenged him and then God did a miracle. All of the sudden, in Miami, the honk and wave started.

With a campaign sign and a smile, the candidate spread word of the walk across the city, intersection by intersection and car by car. Drivers honked at Chiles, he waved to them, and then more drivers honked. The "honk and wave" was born—a staple of modern American campaigning. Chiles' ears rung from the horns as he returned to the camper at night. Lawton's uncle Alfred Chiles remarked, "I just wonder if Lawton is really just down the drain with this Senate campaign. He's out standing on corners waving at people."

Carol Browner, who later served on Chiles' staff, remembers her mother describing Walkin' Lawton's visit to Miami. "I remember my mother coming home—she was at University of Miami—during the 1970 election. And he must have walked through part of the campus. She meets him. . . . I remember [my mother] coming home and talking about what a great man he is, because his thinking has changed." (He'd changed from hawk to dove in his views on the Vietnam War.)

Friday morning, Chiles toured the Justice Building. In the afternoon, he visited the *Miami Beach Daily Sun*. A retiree named Harry Reichenthal awaited his arrival, holding a sign whose cut-out letters read, "Welcome to Miami Beach, Lawton Chiles, the walking senator, the man that will represent the people and is campaigning without spending money." After the *Daily Sun*, they walked together toward Lincoln Mall. In a thick New York Jewish accent, Reichenthal heralded Chiles' approach. "He's coming," he cried, "he's coming! The walking senator is coming! Come out and see the walking senator." He told Chiles that if he did not campaign for him, he would have nothing to do. "We need something for these retired people to do," Chiles observed. "They have much to contribute and they want to play a valuable part in society, so we must help them find a way to put their experience to work."[391]

Saturday, he walked Liberty City, a black neighborhood in northwest Miami. A storefront had burned down in a recent riot. "It was obvious," he noted, "that the same zoning codes and road repairs were not used here that were applied to other portions of the city." He talked to a twenty-four-year-old man who had quit college after two years working toward a sociology degree. The dropout had been drinking beer all morning and his face lit up when Chiles asked him how things were going. He wondered why "we can't have human rights where people want to help each other rather than just civil rights, where someone was made to do something by the law." He and his neighbors thanked Chiles for stopping.

In the afternoon, he walked Little Havana. Locals in busy coffee shops grilled him on Fidel Castro and the trade embargo with Cuba. "I have the strongest feeling that the clock is running out on us in Latin America," Chiles reported, "and Latin America is more important than Europe to us. We've got to keep Latin America from becoming Communistic." He added, "I hope to become an expert on Latin American affairs for two reasons: 1) because I think Florida is the Gateway to there; and 2) because the United States Senate has no real expert on this vital problem."[392]

Saturday night he handed out campaign brochures at the gates to a Miami Dolphins football game. During halftime, someone recognized him and asked him about the Walk. Others in nearby rows overheard and chimed in. Fifteen minutes later, he returned to his seat.

Chiles walked into John Pennekamp Coral Reef State Park in Key Largo on Wednesday, August 19.[393] The last mile, *Miami Herald* political journalist

John McDermott walked with him. Chiles wrote his last progress report for his newsletter:

> Well, it's over! There were times when I dreamed I was an old man and I was still walking, like maybe this was going to go on forever. . . . What has the walk accomplished? Unquestionably, it has given media exposure I could never have had otherwise. It helped me prove my concern about overspending in political campaigns. And I have to admit that I may never be as healthy physically again. . . . I'm delighted I've been able to meet and talk with over 40,000 people all over the state. . . . Whewwwww . . . can it really be over?[394]

With five pairs of boots, he covered 1,003 miles in ninety-two days.[395] He cut twelve pounds and three inches off his waist.[396] Nine notebooks preserved his observations.[397] With two weeks left until the Primary Day on September 8, he hugged his wife and youngest daughter at the finish line and then resumed work. "Now I wonder what I'm going to do tomorrow," Chiles told the *Miami Herald*.[398]

Soon after the walk ended, Fred Schultz called Julian Clarkson to inform him that he expected to place second behind Bryant, and he looked forward to Chiles' endorsement.[399] A Schultz campaign poll showed them leading Chiles by ten points, but the Walk had created momentum.[400] The Bryant camp believed that Chiles ran fourth behind Bryant, Schultz, and Hastings, in that order.[401] On August 23, the *Miami Herald* published campaign spending reports filed August 17. Schultz had spent almost half a million, more than the total Senate salary earned in a six-year term, and won the endorsement of the *St. Petersburg Times*; Bryant had spent little more than $100,000 and won the endorsement of the *Miami Herald*.[402] Chiles had spent little more than $90,000. Forty percent of Bryant's contributors gave $500 or more; 44 percent of Schultz's gave more than $550. Fifty-two percent of Chiles' 530 contributors gave less than $100; only twenty-five percent amounted to $1,000 or more. Ben Hill Griffin, Burke Kibler, Chesterfield Smith, Bill Ellsworth, Julian Bennett and his mother ranked among this biggest contributors. The largest single contribution, $2,000, came from Polk County Judge Richard Bronson.[403] His biggest block of money came from seven workers at the OK Tire firm in Lakeland, Joe P. Ruthven's business, who combined to give $6,900.[404] The Chiles campaign only found two journalists predicting they would qualify for the run-off with

Bryant: Roland Manteiga of *La Gaceta*, a Latin periodical in Tampa, and John McDermott at the *Miami Herald*.

On Primary Night, about 150 friends and volunteers waited for results at Chiles for Senate headquarters in Lakeland. The candidate stood alone in the main room when TV news announced the first state totals. He clapped and cheered as the early returns showed him running neck-and-neck with Bryant, far ahead of Schultz. Charles Canady called his campaign chairman in Dade County, chatted briefly and then turned to Chiles. "Dade County is going for L.C. and Bryant," he said. The candidate stared in disbelief and Canady repeated: "What's the matter? I said Dade County is going for L.C. and Bryant." "Thank God," Chiles sighed. "I thought you said Dade County is going for Alcee and Bryant."

Around midnight, Chiles began shaking hands, thanking volunteers, and bucking up staff for round two. Rhea Gay had gone to sleep but Lawton's wife and three teenage children stayed up until almost three in the morning. Wednesday morning newspapers gave Bryant about 233,000, Chiles 183,000, and Schultz 171,000.[405] Phones at headquarters rung off the hook with calls from former staff cut loose by the Schultz, Daves, and Hastings campaigns. In the final tally, about 13,000 votes separated Chiles from Schultz.[406]

Farris Bryant opened the three-week run-off campaign advertising his experience. His campaign slogan read; "Bryant Now . . . Because there's no time for on-the-job training."[407] "My opponent says he walked one thousand miles," Bryant proclaimed. "I built most of the roads he walked on."[408] Chiles toured the state in a uniform that had become a second skin: boots, khaki pants, and powder blue short-sleeved shirt and tie.[409] Although Chiles now campaigned mostly by car, a Bryant aide repeatedly condemned the Walk as a sham. If he really covered that much ground, the aide argued, Chiles would have had to have walked thirty miles an hour.[410]

On Run-Off Night, September 29, about two hundred people filled Chiles for Senate headquarters.[411] Less than two hours after polls closed at seven o'clock, Chiles had won. "He ran an honorable race and an imaginative one," Bryant told the press during his concession speech. "I offered him my support in any way he wants to use it."[412] A congratulatory call from Spessard Holland followed soon after. "Well, yes, let the President come down [and campaign for Cramer] and let him bring the vice president, but as long as I have you behind me, I will be happy," Chiles told Holland. "I had one citizen in Florida who I wanted to have help me, and I'm glad you said yes."[413]

As Chiles prepared for his victory speech, the crowd's cheering reached deafening levels. Lawton, Rhea, and Ed climbed chairs so everyone could see. Rhea held Lawton's arm up in the air and photographers snapped shots of the winning team. "I have always believed," Chiles said, "that a majority of the people, properly informed, will not be wrong." Then, grinning, "Today they sure voted right." He had won the run-off by almost a two-to-one margin over Bryant, who carried only Orange and Lake Counties. Since last September, the Chiles campaign had spent $163,000, and only $41,000 on newspaper, radio, and television advertising. "This is the moment we've been waiting for," Chiles concluded. "There's only Bill Cramer left, and he's all mine. I can't wait."[414]

In a contested Republican Senate primary, President Richard Nixon had picked Cramer as a rising star. The supposed harbinger of a two-party system in Florida, pundits christened him "Mr. Republican."[415] In 1968, Nixon carried the Sunshine state by denouncing the civil rights movement, Democratic tax hikes, and the welfare state.[416] He ran strong in St. Petersburg and Sarasota, thanks to new Republican voters from the Midwest. George Wallace's bigotry drew record crowds in north Florida, pulling conservative Democrats into his camp and leaving liberal Democrat Hubert Humphrey with barely enough big-city south Florida support for second place.[417] The split ensured GOP Senator Ed Gurney's historic victory that year. "They gather around one man," Gurney observed of the Democrats, "and they suffer this terrible schizophrenia between liberals and conservative."[418] Since President Lyndon Johnson signed the 1964 Civil Rights Act, conservative "Yellow Dog" Democrats nationwide had protested by the hundreds of thousands in key races. Some re-registered as Republicans; others too lazy to break their leash punished liberal Democrats in primaries.

Now, against Chiles, the Nixon White House staked its time, money, and prestige on this "Southern strategy." Florida topped the list of victory prospects in the closely divided U.S. Senate. Cramer's crusade against sixties counter culture would target first the state's "Cracker corridor," from Century west to Starke to as far south as Ocala, and expand the beachheads opened by Nixon and Gurney. The Democratic Party still held an almost three-to-one edge in Florida's voter registration, but Pinellas County—Cramer's home—had joined Sarasota to become the second majority-Republican county in the state.[419] Cramer would ignore black voters, who after decades of oppression constituted only 10 percent of Florida's electorate and rarely registered Republican.[420] As Barry Goldwater told fellow Republicans before his 1964 presidential campaign, "We're not going to get the Negro vote as a bloc . . . so we ought to go hunting where the ducks are."[421] Cramer's campaign charged the adjective "liberal" with the intensity of a curse word from day one. National Republican strategist Lee Atwater refined the technique in later elections:

> You start out in 1954 saying "Nigger, nigger, nigger." By 1968 you can't say "nigger"—that hurts you. Backfires. So you say stuff like forced busing, states' rights, and all that stuff. You're getting so abstract now you're talking about cutting taxes, and all these things you're talking about are totally economic things and a byproduct of them is blacks get hurt worse than whites. And subconsciously maybe that is part of it. I'm not saying that. But I'm saying that if it is getting that abstract, and that coded, that we are doing away with the racial problem one way or the other. You follow me—because obviously sitting around saying, "we want to cut this," is much more abstract than even the busing thing *and* a hell of a lot more abstract than "Nigger, nigger."[422]

Cramer began the verbal assault early Wednesday: "We need to change the ultra-liberal leadership of the Senate. Voting for Cramer means changing the Senate. Voting for Chiles means more of the same."[423] When asked by the *Miami Herald* how his boss planned to address Chiles' walking campaign, a Cramer aide shot back: "He didn't really walk from one end of the state to the other." Once Cramer demolished the myth, he said, the Chiles campaign would collapse.[424]

At a press breakfast Wednesday, Chiles said, "I think we will hear the word ultra-liberal used in the campaign. Cramer will try to connect us with the liberal, radical, Democratic image."[425] The afternoon of October 1, the Chiles campaign met at Tampa's International Inn. About thirty key supporters plus staff sat around a conference table. Somebody asked if the candidate would keep his "working man" uniform or switch to a suit for the general election. Ben Hill Griffin leapt to his feet. "If you haven't got a suit," Griffin said, "why, you just go downtown and get one and charge it to me." Chiles started to ask the full group to consider a change of tactics before Gainesville's Jim Quincey interrupted. "Lawton, there's not a one of us in this room who would have told you to go to Century and start walking," he objected. "Suppose you tell us what you have in mind." The campaign agreed to stick with what worked. They set a budget of $200,000 for the five weeks before the general election.[426] To fight the liberal label, Chiles would refuse donations from national labor or national Democratic officials.[427] He would drive and fly to campaign stops and then tour on foot, in uniform. His Polk County roots, they hoped, would connect to Miami as much as north Florida's Cracker circuit. A populist pitch, blessed by conservative icon Spessard Holland, might call the Yellow Dog Democrats home.

The Associated Press declared in mid-October "the difference between the U.S. Senate campaigns of Bill Cramer and Lawton Chiles is champagne and oysters Rockefeller at $1,000 a couple, and fried chicken and cole slaw at $1 a head." The Chiles team had thrown a block party at Dante Fascell Park in south Dade County the same night Cramer held a closed-door fundraiser at Miami Beach's Fontainebleau Hotel.[428] Chiles decided less than a week beforehand to stage the rival rally.[429] For $1,000 a couple, the Republicans featured Attorney General John Mitchell and his wife, Martha at a cocktail party. Waiters served champagne and beluga caviar to about 125 guests mingling among ice swans.[430] More than a thousand paid $100 per couple for dinner afterward. The two events raised about $145,000 for the Cramer campaign.[431] "The sixties was the permissive decade," Cramer promised the VIPs, "but now with President Nixon and Spiro Agnew and John Mitchell and, of course, Martha Mitchell, the age of permissiveness is at an end."[432] "I've never heard of Bill Cramer's opponent before," Attorney General Mitchell told guests, "and I hope I never do again."[433]

Seventeen miles away, the Chiles campaign offered their candidate, country music and State Senator Eddie Gong. The dinner committee passed out 1,576 boxes of chicken. Another two hundred people bought one-dollar tickets and skipped the chow. The event raised $1,776, minus the cost of the chicken. National and local reporters shut out of the Cramer event lined up for plastic plates in Fascell Park. The next day, the national media touted Chiles' "working people's reception," and televised Cramer's response: "I eat chicken, too."[434] The *Miami News* called the election "caviar against Pepsi."[435] A week later, Jack Barrett, *St. Petersburg Times* cartoonist, parodied the White House's obsession with claiming Florida for the Republican Party in November. Entitled "Operation Overkill," Barrett's cartoon depicted caricatures of President Nixon, Pat Nixon, Vice President Spiro Agnew, Secretary of Transportation John Volpe, Attorney General Mitchell, Martha Mitchell and Cramer riding atop a tank—its cannon targeting Walkin' Lawton.

By the end of October, Chiles had visited nearly every county in Florida, his speeches promoting crime control, a crash federal anti-pollution program, withdrawal from Vietnam, opposition to the Cross-Florida Barge Canal, and closure of tax loopholes for the wealthy. Cramer called Chiles "Liberal Lawton" and "the busing Senator." Chiles countered with press releases castigating "Oil Spill Bill" for failure to prevent an oil spill in Tampa Bay through federal regulation. Cramer adopted the hard hat as the symbol of his anti-crime campaign, often wearing one at campaign events. Chiles, he asserted, was "soft" on "the hippies, the yippies, the bombers, the burners."[436] Cramer once told reporters anyone to the right of him would fall off the earth.[437] Chiles described himself as a "progressive conservative." When asked what that label meant, he said, "I don't know."[438] Chiles found a rhetorical theme for the campaign on TV and at events, capitalizing on the strength of fellow Democrat Reubin Askew's gubernatorial campaign against Republican Governor Claude Kirk. "There's an AC current running strong through the whole state of Florida," he claimed. "It stands for Askew and Chiles." The "AC" current would overcome the "DC" current of Washington "tourists" stumping for Cramer.

An October 15-19 poll published in the *Miami Herald* on October 25 showed Chiles leading Cramer, 60 percent to 37 percent, 3 percent undecided. That same Sunday most of Florida's newspapers endorsed Chiles.[439] These included the *Miami Herald* and Cramer's hometown paper, the *St. Petersburg Times,* which the Republican denounced as "ultra-liberal."[440] "Our reasons are fundamental," the *Times* editorial read. "Cramer is an intelligent man. But during sixteen global years, holding a safe House seat, he has not grown. Narrowly provincial, devoted first to self interest, Cramer has proved himself incapable of expanding in mind and spirit. . . . In contrast, we—like so many others—have been impressed with Lawton Chiles' rugged integrity. Although Chiles needs campaign money he has refused tainted political contributions."[441] A few days later the *Miami Herald* dismissed Cramer's "Liberal Lawton" fixation, branding Chiles an "old corn cob" like Spessard Holland.[442]

Washington Post columnist Philip Carter wrote a fictional letter as one media consultant to another, giving up on Chiles as a prospective buyer of TV ads and radio spots:

Chiles comes on like a forty-year-old Tom Sawyer: the boots, the khaki pants, the short-sleeve blue shirt, the cowlick, the shoulders, the accent, the smile. He will be hard to replicate. He calls himself a "progressive conservative." He says he's against busing, but he gives rednecks hell for saying "nigger," and he gets away with it. He's against pollution. He's for Social Security and Medicare. He's against big government. People here say he's a populist, but whatever it is, they like it. . . . I consider this my resignation. I hear Chiles has road maps now of all the highways to San Francisco. I'm looking for a job selling shoes.

Carter had observed Chiles and his opponent at the Florida Forest Festival in Perry the previous week. Surrounded by anti-busing, church-going farmers in bib overalls and pulp mill workers, proud of their Dixie heritage and suspicious of fast-talking Miami liberals, Cramer could incite a rebellion against the Democrat Party in Taylor County. The congressman took the stump and pledged to "fight the bombers and the burners and the rioters, the people who want to destroy our country" and "put the Bernadine Dorhns and the Rap Browns and the Stokley Carmichaels out of business." A few people clapped. Along the parade route folks had yelled at Chiles: "There's the Walkin' Senator. He's still a-walkin'. Keep on a-walkin', Senator." Taylor County applauded when Chiles spoke: "I've had a great adventure in this walk. Some people have a chance to climb a mountain or explore someplace new. But I had a chance to walk across Florida."[443]

In the final week of campaigning, President Nixon announced he would stump for the Republican underdog at four Florida venues—West Palm Beach and Miami on October 27, and St. Petersburg and Tallahassee two days later. Lawton Chiles' wife Rhea, son Ed, and friends gathered in front of the TV at the Lake Hollingsworth house to watch the St. Petersburg afternoon rally, which drew thousands. The Miami Beach Convention Hall had packed in almost 10,000 for the president.[444] Rhea sighed, "well, that's it, we can't beat that." Ed ran down to a South Florida Avenue payphone, crying as he dialed his Dad. When he heard his son's concerns, Lawton whooped: "They're just a bunch of turkeys, we've got 'em where we want 'em." To the press the next day, Chiles stated, "The fact he is endorsing all Republican candidates, not just my opponent, rather dilutes the importance of the visit."[445] President Nixon flew to a get-out-the-vote GOP rally the next day in San Jose, California, where about 1,000 anti-Vietnam protesters pelted his limousine with rocks, eggs, and bottles.[446] Bill Cramer reiterated his support of recent federal crime-legislation signed by President Nixon—laws against rioting, bombing, and cop-killing. "On Tuesday," Cramer claimed, "the people will react [to 1960s social hysteria] with a clean four-letter word—V-O-T-E."[447]

Chiles voted at 7:30 a.m. Election Day, Tuesday, November 3, and shook hands at the Florida Tile Co. and Lindner Industrials in Lakeland before visiting Ybor City, Tampa's Latin quarter. The Ybor visit was part of a ritual Chiles developed with his friend, Senator Louis De la Parte, in primary elections. They stopped at Cuervo's Café for Cuban toast and coffee.[448] By early afternoon, Chiles had returned home. As polls closed, Charles Canady pulled open a drawer from his desk at headquarters to show a paper with the campaign's final predictions: Vote turnout, 1.7 million; Chiles 952,000 (56 percent). At 7:20 p.m., Canady made his first call to his campaign chairs around the state. "Miami Beach is going for us three-to-one and better," he reported. Chiles made no forecasts; "I'm just nervous," he told Senator Wilbur Boyd. At 7:32 p.m., Walter Cronkite appeared on the TV screen as CBS flashed the message "Chiles Wins In Florida." "This is the first of the senatorial races to be decided," Cronkite intoned. Chiles still fixed onto the returns, which showed him gradually pulling away from Cramer. At 7:58 p.m., Canady commanded everyone to hush up. "Palm Beach is having a record vote," he explained, "over 100,000, and we've got a big lead." Cheers erupted. But the next state total, announced during WTVT Channel 13's 8:00 p.m. tally, brought Cramer to his closest margin since the early returns, a narrow Chiles lead of about 141,000 to 135,000. Photographers and cameramen moved in on the candidate to capture his reaction. An hour later, Chiles had maintained his strength in north Florida, while racking up a big margin in Dade County (122,000 to 74,000). At 9:40, another channel reported figures from 70 percent of Florida's precincts, Chiles leading now by 84,000, his total at 678,000 to Cramer's 594,000. At 10:02, NBC's David Brinkley gave Florida to Chiles.

The U.S. senator-elect declared victory to the press. "I guess maybe I'm a little numb at the feeling of it because of the trying time and the long road it's taken," Chiles told about thirty newsmen, holding hands with Rhea.[449] "It was Rhea here who told me back in the dark days before I made the decision, that I should make the walk," he mused aloud. "When I had started the first day, my heart started to sing and I felt even then that win or lose this was the beginning of a dream fulfilled."[450] "I can hardly believe it," his wife cheered. The U.S. senator-elect described an encounter the previous Saturday with a fiddle player at a Lake Butler rally. "The man gave me a crumpled five-dollar bill and said he had been praying for me every night, said I was his only hope," Chiles began. "That is the kind of cross you start worrying about—how to fulfill." He worried that "an awful lot of people see me as something I'm not."[451]

Floridians had asked him ad nauseam, are you really different? Are you gonna go up there and forget about us? Chiles sensed acutely a burden of expectations unprecedented in his career. He sensed the creation of a new, unwritten contract with Florida for good government. His campaign had set a national standard for populist outreach in the modern media age. The Walk, the honk and wave, and his campaign newsletter, avant-garde in 1970, became conventional campaign wisdom over the next four decades. The Chiles campaign also popularized the side-by-side "common man versus rich man" media event, a model for future populists. The breakdown of voters by associations and interest groups also influenced election strategy since. Cattlemen for Chiles, seniors for Chiles, and Dade County for Chiles members all received distinct messages, a tactic forerunning the modern "micro targeting" sensationalized by Republican strategist Karl Rove.

While no politician since has replicated the Walk's distance and genuine spirit of fellowship, its emphasis on systematic, personalized voter contact, known by campaign pros as "field," has entered the political mainstream of both major parties. Successful modern campaigns aspire to monitor numbers of doors knocked, phone messages left, and volunteers recruited. They emulate the scope of the largest national field effort, the U.S. postal service. Campaign managers expect field directors as much as the campaign message to tilt the balance of tight elections. Local candidates for delegate, sheriff, or county council especially like to stage honk and wave rallies at popular intersections; losing candidates often base their campaigns on little else. Campaigns from city council to U.S. Senate distributed serialized campaign newsletters like Chiles' progress reports during the Walk; his style resembles the chatty, short blurbs of today's internet blogs.

Chiles waited nearly an hour for Cramer to concede. The Chiles victory margin exceeded 100,000 in the final tally: 902,438 to 772,817. By now the headquarters crowd numbered over six hundred and spilled into the outside parking lot. U.S. Senator-elect Chiles climbed up on a car with his family and thanked Canady, Pridgen, and the volunteer army before stepping down for a victory lap through the crowd. "We never knew that the Walk was going to work," Rhea later recounted, "I think we felt that all of the sudden, win or lose, we had achieved what we had set out to do; victory was sweet nothings on the top of a very nice cake." Asked to retell how the idea for the Walk developed, she said: "one evening, it just occurred to me we couldn't knock on all the doors, but we could in some way symbolize that intent." But she cautioned, "you couldn't just put any persona out there on the road. You had to have a Lawton Chiles."[452]

In the days following, congratulations poured into Chiles headquarters. On Canady's desk, telegrams spread out. One of the first arrived from Waterville, Maine at 9:01 a.m. "Heartiest congratulations on your victory. I look forward to working with you in the Congress," wrote Senator Ed Muskie of Maine, frontrunner for the Democratic presidential nomination in two years. Rumors already circulated that Senator Muskie might ask Chiles to join the ticket to provide regional balance.[453] "What you did in Florida is to me perhaps the greatest single political inspiration of 1970," read a letter from Senator George McGovern.[454] "I want to again express to you my congratulations, and to tell you how pleased I am with your impressive victory," wrote Senator Ted Kennedy.[455] Friends and strangers looking for souvenirs cleared the office walls of press clippings of the Walk.[456]

The entire Chiles for Senate campaign, including two primaries and a general election, cost $404,000 and ended in the black.[457] Yet, the Cramer general election campaign alone cost more than half a million.[458]

U.S. Senator-elect Chiles waved to passing drivers at the intersection of Central Avenue and 34th street in St. Petersburg for an hour Friday as part of his statewide "thank you" tour. A chilly wind off the Gulf whipped him as he stood on the median holding a campaign sign "Lawton Chiles for U.S. Senate" with the "for" crossed out. "Congratulations, you earned it," yelled one passerby, recognizing his walking boots. "Come back and see us . . . still at it huh?" others commented. One hollered, "Give 'em hell, boy!"[459]

Government in the Sunshine

Soon after his inauguration as a U.S. senator, Lawton Chiles leaned back in his chair, propped his penny loafers up on his desk, and exclaimed, "this is the greatest job in the world. You can legislate 365 days a year."[460]

Senator Chiles knew and revered the U.S. Senate's two-century heritage. The great triumvirate of orators, Daniel Webster, Henry Clay, and John C. Calhoun, had given the Senate its antebellum "Golden Age." Months before the Civil War, Mississippi Democratic Senator Jefferson Davis had led the Southern delegation out of the chamber with a message to the North: "It remains for me to bid you a final adieu."[461] At the turn of the twentieth century, Senator Albert J. Beveridge had delivered his famous imperialist oratory, toasting to a hundred years of American dominance in world affairs. At the end of World War I, Senator Henry Cabot Lodge Jr. (R-MA) urged forbearance from the League of Nations. Senator Robert "Fighting Bob" La Follette Sr. (R-WI) led the Progressive Era's push for fair wages, abolition of child labor, and women's suffrage. Senator Robert Wagner (D-NY), a member of Franklin Delano Roosevelt' Brain Trust, wrote much of the New Deal's labor legislation. The South's filibuster of the Civil Rights Act of 1964 had given the deliberative chamber's tactics and rules national recognition. The U.S. Senate had just sent two of its members, Senator John F. Kennedy (D-MA) and Senator Lyndon Johnson (D-TX), to the White House. Above all, Chiles had won the seat of his political hero, Senator Spessard Holland.

Senator Chiles "thought that compromise was eloquent," staffer Doug Cook explains. "He was of that old school that loved the Senate because it was a compromise body. It was a body where the blood got cold."

Senator Chiles' first hires worried about their office's ties to their predecessor Spessard Holland, especially on social issues. When Senator Holland announced his retirement, *The Washington Post* eulogized: "Holland's crowning legislative achievement was his successful sponsorship of a constitutional amendment that outlaws the poll tax in federal elections." Holland had signed the Southern Manifesto against *Brown v. Board of* Education in 1954, but ten years later, his leadership ensured the 24th amendment's passage. "I'm as much of a Southerner as anyone, but this is a moderate proposal," Holland called the amendment. "It seems to me the South can help its own cause by taking an affirmative position on this."[462] "That leaves the 'Holland mantle' most likely to State Senator Lawton Chiles of Lakeland," suggested the *Tallahassee Democrat*.[463]

Senator-elect Chiles deliberated over how to honor the Holland legacy and transcend it. The Florida Democratic party circa 1970 leaned right compared to the national party platform; yet, Chiles legislative aides Bob Harris and Rick Farrell regarded the Holland legacy as ultraconservative and antique. Senator Chiles Senate staff had started as just three full-time people: Jack Pridgen press secretary, Charles Canady administrative assistant, and George Patten Jr. as legislative assistant. To their relief, Senator Chiles soon replaced all the Holland holdovers with new, young staff tuned to an agenda for modern Florida. Elemental government reform led Chiles' agenda: transparency, ethics, and efficiency. Months after arriving in Washington, Senator Chiles disclosed his financial assets to the Congressional Record and announced that his office would receive no honorariums for speeches.

In a private meeting in Bartow, Senator Spessard Holland counseled his successor that it took him eight years to win a seat on the Appropriations Committee.[464] The congressional seniority system had allowed advocates of the Southern way of life to hold onto their committee gavels until they died. By 1940, the 76th Congress, the average age of senators had increased to sixty. By the 92nd Congress, which began in 1971, seventy-three-year-old Senator Richard Russell set the upper limit.[465] Seniority decided where senators sat at committee tables, the sequence of who could question witnesses, as well as committee and subcommittee chairmanships. On a new senator's first day on the job, he or she waited for senior members to choose their favorite office suite, their desk on the Senate floor, and their parking space in the Senate garage. Elders advised freshmen to listen to floor debate at least a month before joining the fray. Seniority on the Senate committees separated the mere "bomb-throwers" from the powerful "cardinals" who killed or recommended bills at their leisure. None of Senator Chiles' peers considered changing the tradition. "The longer I stay in Washington," Senator Leverett Saltonstall of Massachusetts once said, "the more sympathetic to [the seniority rule] I become."[466]

"I tried to say during my first race for the Legislature that I didn't purport to know much about state government, but I wanted to learn," Chiles acknowledged. "I felt the same way about the Senate race."[467]

A *St. Petersburg Times* reporter asked Chiles what committees he looked forward to joining. "Well, naturally, I'd like appropriations," he began, "that's where the action is. . . . And Florida with the space program should have a man there . . . then there's finance and foreign relations and . . . " He paused for a moment, and then beamed. "I'm ready for 'em all."[468]

"I'm a great admirer of Senator Holland," Chiles told the *Miami Herald*, "but I don't think I'm going to be an imitator of him."[469]

Bud Chiles commented on his father's affinity for elder statesmen: "He always talked about that sort of older Senator, he had a book in him to write about an older Senator and a younger senator and a guy who ends up running for president; he never did it but he talked to me about it a lot . . . the older senator mentoring the younger."

The other freshman senators elected in 1970 had previously served in the House or as governors—except for U.S. Senator-elect James Buckley of New York. But since the empire state exceeded Florida in size, the Rules Committee awarded Buckley seniority and relegated Chiles to last place.[470] Florida's 37 percent rate of population growth in the 1960s led the nation, but it was still the ninth-largest state in 1970.[471] Senator Chiles, however, began his first year with gusto. During his "thank you" tour of Florida, the Lake Wales Chamber of Commerce presented the U.S. Senator-elect with a "100" pin to remind him of his freshman status in the chamber. "At least I can't backslide," he quipped.[472]

His first months in the Senate humbled him more than the "100" pin; Washington knew little of "Walkin' Lawton." Late for a big vote one day, Senator Chiles bolted for the "Senators Only" elevator before it closed. "I guess I looked too young and un-senatorial because the policeman blocked me," Chiles later recalled.

"Who the hell do you think you are?" the officer demanded.

"I'm the junior U.S. senator from Florida," the senator snapped. "Who the hell do you think you are?"

The officer stammered, "I'm just an old policeman who used to work around here."

During the 1971 May Day celebration, the biggest demonstration day in D.C., tens of thousands of Vietnam protesters laid siege to the capital, shutting down the streets, intending to close down the federal government. Thousands were arrested. Students for a Democratic Society pulled up by the busload. Lawton walked to work from his townhouse in Georgetown to the Capitol. He saw a policeman hit a fellow over the head with a nightstick and push him into a paddy wagon. Chiles exclaimed, "you don't have the right to do that," and the officer grabbed him and shoved him into the wagon. Chiles informed him, "I just want you to know you're throwing the United States Senator from Florida in the wagon." The policeman pulled him out quickly.

The Senator and his team soon adopted a rhythm typical of freshman outfits, where first-time Washington firecrackers shared the boss's jubilation at experimentation with the levers of power, but their execution seldom equaled their idealism. Senior staff soon spent as much time with Senator Chiles as his family, crafting his daily schedule and interacting with other offices on the Senator's behalf. Although the White House had seen technical advance and expansion since the Franklin Delano Roosevelt years, the U.S. Senate in the 1970s resembled a state legislature more than the seat of government for a global superpower, according to Chiles staffer Rick Farrell:

It was a big deal when they got typewriters that you could go back and correct over something, off the page. It was amazingly antiquated in the sense that everything was typed with five carbons, and we had a system where there was a pink carbon, a blue carbon—the Lakeland office got the pink carbons and the Miami office got the blue. It was a very different time. The potentials for communications, for research, and all that, were quite different. That was the nature of it. And I think the Senate was—because it's just a traditional place—it was probably fairly slow to take advantage of even the new developments. I can remember it was a really big deal when we got a fax machine—amazing. . . . We eventually had computers at our desk and we used them as word processors, that's all. They were not for communications, they were not for research—they were just basically, glorified typewriters.

Chiles' freshman term work never achieved national recognition. The mainstream media habitually delineated three informal categories: horse race, human interest, and process; reporters buried most Chiles stories as boring, technical process issues. Senator Chiles mustered the skill and alliances to accomplish a few governmental reforms of enduring significance to American democracy and popular sovereignty.

Chiles' prime legislative directive was to replace Washington's oldest traditions with one of Florida's newest: the "Government in the Sunshine" law. Whether they sought refuge at closed-door hotel fundraisers or committee hearings, he believed, politicians defending secrecy had something to hide.

A closed door, "executive session" meeting of the Agriculture Committee inspired Chiles to pursue transparency on a federal level. "What did we discuss?" questioned Chiles rhetorically. "The most boring topic in the world, no state secrets, nothing confidential, nothing other than it was just kind of the way it was done. To me, it was what do those people think when they come up there and see that sign. What do they think goes on behind that closed door?"

To bind himself to the cause of Government in the Sunshine, Chiles would return to Florida at least one week a month and walk with the state's ever-changing electorate.[473] Florida had expanded the franchise since Chiles' halcyon days at Munn Park. From 1940 to 1960, Florida transformed from the smallest to largest state in the South. From 1945 to 1960, Florida grew by an average of 558 people per day.[474] An average of 1.8 million people settled in Florida each decade from 1940 to 1990; most settled in south Florida. More and more, Florida south of Ocala dominated politics.[475] The introduction of mosquito control during the 1940s, as well as World War II's massive military base construction, brought ample work and better quality of life. The advent of air conditioning in the 1950s enhanced quality of life.[476] The pair of boots cobbled by the Panhandle shoe salesman he met on the Walk, now decorating his Senate office, reminded him of his pledge to return regularly to the state.[477] So did his new administrative assistant, Charles Canady, and press secretary, Jack Pridgen, who led a staff of fifteen.

Self-education complimented his quest for greater transparency. Senator Chiles pored through hundreds of pages of briefing material on every political issue each night. His keen listening ability, honed on the Walk, aided his intellectual evolution, according to staffer Margaret Maruschak:

> Lawton Chiles had an almost ethereal way of being so present to the situation. Today you'd say it was kind of a Zen thing, where he would look like he was almost zoning out, but he was listening so hard. Aside from being an extremely appealing quality in a person . . . it's very affirming to talk to somebody that you sense is really listening to you.

Senator Chiles took to heart the humility advised by his mentors, according to Senator Sam Nunn:

> Lawton reminds me of when I first got to the Senate. . . . I had a meeting, Senator Stennis asked me to come to his office, and he'd been one of my long-time heroes. And he sat me down at a desk that was formerly the desk of Senator Russell, and Senator Russell's former office. And we talked a long time but he sort of closed out by saying, "Sam, some senators come here and they really grow as a senator, and some come here and they only swell."

To enhance his understanding of Latin American issues, he hired a tutor to teach him conversational Spanish daily; a graduate student visited his house daily at seven in the morning.[478] He learned enough to get "frustrated as hell" with the language, his son Ed recalls. Staffer Jim Boyd traveled with Lawton on an official visit to Lima, Peru:

> And we had dinner one night in this restaurant, and they brought us out oysters, and there was an oyster the size of almost a dinner plate that came out. And Lawton, he just saw that oyster, and he realized that this had the possibility of being a great joke. So he made me carry that oyster down from that restaurant that night and back to my hotel room. And I had to carry it through customs all through Latin America. And when I brought it back, I had to take it out and clean it and then give it to him. And it was lucky I wasn't arrested, I mean seriously, because it wouldn't have looked good for me to be arrested, nor for Lawton to be involved in bringing something like that into the country. But anyway, we managed to do it. And he took

that oyster shell back up to some of his friends in Tallahassee, who had oysters—Apalachicola oysters and all this other. And he said, "I've somethin' to show ya." And he pulled out this oyster shell, and he said, "I know where these beds are." It was really crazy. He would do things like that all the time.

Staffer Colin Bradford started working for Chiles in 1973, signing on as a legislative assistant for foreign affairs and economic matters. Bradford advised Chiles on Latin America. He recalls Chiles' humor as well was his curiosity about Latin affairs. One day, Bradford brought his daughter Kristen to work:

> She would have been seven years old, she's with me and I go in to see the senator about something, and he says hello to her, and for some reason I leave the room. And she stays in the room and I walk back in the room; she's sitting on his lap, and she's saying "ninety-six, ninety-seven, ninety-eight, ninety-nine, one hundred." And Chiles says, "isn't that wonderful, you can count to one hundred!" That's just the guy in a nutshell.

Bradford added, "Oh, we tell that story all the time, 'cause it's so emblematic of his humanity, his warmth, his balance."

One of Senator Chiles' first hires, a Polk County school teacher named Bob Harris, helped foremost in building his office's reputation as a watchdog for fraud, waste, and other abuses in government procurement. Senator Chiles sponsored the Federal Procurement Act of 1974, a law to establish a central federal office to streamline procurement.

Harris, one of the few black staffers on Capitol Hill, also started an informal dialogue with the Senator on a host of racial concerns. Harris, a former Auburndale school teacher and co-founder of northwest Lakeland's Neighborhood Service Center, joined Chiles' staff in summer of 1973. Senator Chiles had become chair of the Procurement Subcommittee; Harris was tasked with assembling a staff as chief clerk of the subcommittee. Once Harris completed the administrative set-up, he began conducting investigations. In addition to legislative assistant duties, Chiles tasked Harris with the job of listening to his speeches and hallway chatter to make sure they respected all races equally. Rick Farrell explains his perception of Harris' role:

Bob sort of was a person who could say look, that's now how you would wanna approach this, this is really what the concern is, and that was not only in speech and all that but even on issues, what's really important? Because when you are a senator from a state like Florida, on racial issues you're walking a bit of a thin line. What issues are really important to the black community in Florida as opposed to what might be the priority for black voters nationally? So Bob sort of acted as his point of reference on a lot of these things. And you know that was back when, Bob was brought on early. There really weren't very many black staffers to begin with and very few working for southern senators, so he was sort of out there on that, getting ahead of the game. Later on everybody had some black staffers but initially on the Hill that was not the case, there weren't that many.

"Inherently, people who lived in that era in the South have it in their DNA," Rhea explains. "[Senator Chiles] knew it; he wished it were not there." When Senator Chiles stepped out of bounds, he asked Harris to sit him down and say, "You shouldn't have said that" or "You're being whitey here."

"He knew where he was weak," agreed Chiles' younger son Ed. Especially after the Walk, "he knew he had to be a different guy; any of that old thing in him that wanted to play it the old way was going to be dangerous." The Walk campaign had "captured him." Harris remarked that in the 1973, the black staff working in the offices of the U.S. Senate could have "held a meeting in a phone booth, and still had elbow room. There were like seven people."

Harris introduced to Senator Chiles the history of the infamous Rosewood, Florida massacre. The senator did not know that in 1923, a mob of angry whites had burned the majority-black town in Levy County.

Harris lent his boss the book *Roots* by Alex Haley. After reading it, Senator Chiles said, "I don't understand how I could have missed all of this." Harris continued:

He called me to the office one day . . . and he said, "I just got off the phone with this guy who is a troop leader down in Tampa for . . . the cubs scouts. His troop was going to some little island out of Tampa on a little ferry, and they had a black kid in the troop, and the guy on the ferry wouldn't take him." [The troop leader] called Chiles, [who said], "I can't do anything about that. But, who in the heck would do this to a kid!"

I said, "There's been worse done to kids."

He said, "Gosh, Bob, when that happened, all I could see was Roger's face [Bob's son]. And I thought: you can't do that to a kid."

I said, "Yeah, you can. This is what I've [been] trying to tell you, there's nothing rational about racism. It doesn't fit a rational discussion."

Harris added: "So from that [racial] standpoint, he almost had a little naiveté. . . . I do not perceive it to be a weakness, to be inquisitive about your sense of where you are, and where you ought to be." Senator Chiles and Bob Harris would play tennis before work sometimes. Sometimes observers would confuse Harris for the senator's bodyguard. Bob Harris:

We were playing at the country club there in Virginia, and it was really hot. It had to be a Friday 'cause there was no Senate in session. So the woman in the clubhouse brought out a glass of orange juice and gave it to Chiles, and he gave it to me. And he looked at her and said, "Can I get one for myself?" So she went back and got another glass for him.

We're sweatin' like heck, we're between sets. She comes out with one towel and hands it to him. He hands it to me, and says, "Can I get one for me?" So she comes out and brings [a towel] to me.

So we're standing there. He said, "Don't say it." And I said, "But you think—" He said, "Don't say it, Robert." I said, "Okay." So in the car as we're going back to his house to change clothes to go on into work, he finally says, "You'd think she would have learned after [my first request]."

Harris recalls, "We discussed, many times, stuff ... like that. Chiles had this ... tremendous tug-of-war going on between what was political and what was right. And when they clashed, he almost always went with what was right." It helped that Chiles was a keen listener.

"He was really, really good on memory recall," Harris relates. "We used to have a saying that he was an ear person. You could tell him everything. It might pop out at the strangest times, but it was back there somewhere."

Senator Chiles first introduced the bill for the Government in the Sunshine Act in 1972. Senator Chiles and Governor Reubin Askew worked on the Government in the Sunshine Law in the Senate. Chiles asked Governor Askew to come up to Washington and testify on the federal bill:

> I go up there to testify, and he's the only one there at this big table. I sit at the witness table and I'm the only witness. We have a row of press that's very interested in opening up all of government and this whole huge number of television cameras behind me. ... Frankly, I had to restrain myself from laughing. ... There was a little hamburger place across from Law School. Lawton and I would go over there and have hamburgers and a cup of coffee. I thought to myself, Here are these two guys that not too long ago [were] just quietly having a cup of coffee across the street from the Law School without any attention, and [now we have] all this attention and it's just him and it's just me.[479]

The bill was initially tabled. Mindful that national sunshine legislation might require long-term strategy, Senator Chiles attacked smaller, "good government" reforms. Senator Sam Nunn recalls:

> I think Lawton took a lot of joy in the legislative process. He hadn't been a governor when he got there, but he had been a legislator and he knew how to get things done—he knew it took patience, he knew you didn't just wave a wand and it happened, so he was a great legislator. He knew how to work with people—people trusted him and he made a lot of friends, so I think the legislative process was a joy.[480]

His was the first Senate office to move the administrative, constituent service, casework side of his workload to his home state. Senator Chiles set up a constituent service office in Lakeland, directed by Charles Canady, to handle administrative casework; it opened in September 1971.[481] Rick Farrell joined the Chiles Senate staff in summer 1972, worked for him in Lakeland for about a year, then moved to the Washington office as a legislative assistant and then legislative director. Farrell describes the Lakeland office run by Charles Canady:

It was a very tightly run ship. He was one of the first senators to make that kind of investment in terms of putting that many staff people in the state office as opposed to having them locate in Washington. And so when I worked there, there were about six or seven of us who were young, out of college—for many of us it was our first job. Because we were in Lakeland there wasn't that much else to do. We basically worked round the clock, we worked Saturdays we worked Sundays—all we did was work. . . . I think it really helped him with his identity in the state, helped him build his political base. . . . Particularly in the early years you really can't make much of a mark legislatively anyway, there's not a lot you can do. And so I think his excellent constituent service and case work, and getting involved in local projects, was really an important factor in his first re-election.

Chiles first two years' committee assignments, on Agriculture and Forestry, Government Operations, and Joint Committee on Congressional Operations, limited his reach.

As chairman of the Governmental Affairs Subcommittee on Intergovernmental Relations, however, Chiles could actually write original legislation. He turned what many dismissed as a dead-end committee assignment into an asset.

Senator Chiles exposed abuses in military meat-buying and in federal furniture purchase, achieving more than 150 convictions.[482]

Senator Chiles discovered that the federal government was wasting $200 million a year on new office furniture. According to his calculation, the used furniture in storage could fill a room 10 feet wide and 201 miles long, but the General Services Administration continued to buy new shipments of chairs and tables.[483] His investigation produced 135 indictments and saved taxpayers approximately $230 million. In 1980, Congress placed a moratorium on all GSA furniture purchases.

Senator Chiles joined the Senate Special Committee on Aging in 1972.[484] His work there, relevant to Florida's large population of seniors, garnered him attention from senior senators. Senator Chiles on Special Committee on Aging agenda:

Our treatment [of senior citizens in America] has been similar to the ancient Eskimo practice of putting their old people on an ice-flow and pushing them off to sea. Not only have we failed to realize that no particular birthday causes people to stop having feelings, hopes, aspirations, desires and needs, but we are also squandering vast amounts of knowledge, wisdom and energy that we desperately need in trying to cope with society's problems.[485]

Deborah Kilmer met Senator Chiles while she worked on the Senate Special Committee on Aging; Senator Chiles was a junior member. Kilmer worked for the committee until 1980; from then on she worked on his personal staff as a legislative assistant until Senator Chiles' retirement.

Social Security was a big issue on the Special Committee on Aging. Kilmer: "I can remember Ted Kennedy standing in the hall saying, 'Lawton, why don't you just jump off the building!' He proposed cutting Social Security; it was part of an overall budget." Kilmer added, "He was always looking for ways to not only sustain Social Security, but control it as far as budget [was concerned]."

Senator Chiles sought the fellowship of Democrats and Republicans, searching for the collegiality he had enjoyed in the Florida Senate. He sought open, agile minds. When asked who his favorite senator was, Chiles often said, "Well, my friends are generally Southerners, but my favorite senator is Hubert Humphrey."

As Senator Richard Russell (D-GA) and his Southern lieutenants died over the next two years, Senator Chiles welcomed their replacements' new perspective on civil rights, deficit reduction, and governmental reform. In 1949, when Lyndon Johnson arrived at the Senate, Southerners chaired the three most powerful Senate committees: Appropriations, Foreign Relations, and Finance. Russell of Georgia had embodied the old guard. His champions called him "the South's greatest general since Robert E. Lee" for his mastery of the legislative maneuvering necessary to stall twenty-five years of civil rights reform.[486] Chiles himself took Russell's seat on the Senate Democratic Steering Committee.

His party controlled both houses of Congress; Democratic leader Mike Mansfield bypassed senior senators to name Chiles to the Senate Democratic Steering Committee, which controlled committee assignments. Senator Bennett Johnston describes the 1970s Senate culture:

As far as the political culture [is concerned], the Senate has changed vastly since Lawton came in, in 1970, and I was elected in

1972. At that time there was relatively little partisanship. The Senate Democrats rarely had a caucus. They'd have one at the start of the year to ratify the committee appointments. But we just didn't have those caucuses to plot out strategy. Political strategy was basically done by the committee chairman, and the ranking minority member. We had at that time a huge Democratic advantage as I recall, like sixty-seven or sixty-eight Democrats, a lot of southern Democrats. And we had good friends across the aisle and sought votes across the aisle.

Chiles staffer Rick Farrell added:

I think those senators from the southern and western states, the Lloyd Bentsens and all of that, they found common ground among themselves as they thought through how they would be dealing with issues that had a particular significance from a southern perspective as [Senator Chiles] moved away from that Old South perspective to some new place, which was much more progressive on racial issues and much more moderate middle-of-the-road position on a whole range of issues, but did not appear to basically be turning its back on the South. There was a carefulness there.

In 1975, Senator Chiles joined a majority of southern Democrats in support of a second five-year extension of the Voting Rights act. New friends and allies Sam Nunn of Georgia, Lloyd Bentsen of Texas, and Ernest "Fritz" Hollings of South Carolina voted with him.[487] Senator Chiles extended social invitations to Republican colleagues too, like Mark Hatfield of Oregon and Ted Stevens of Alaska, and eventually, Pete Domenici of New Mexico. Senator Sam Nunn bonded with Senator Chiles from the first:

Lawton called me shortly after I got elected, probably a week after the election, and said, "When are you going to be in Washington?" and I said, "I'm coming in a week or so," and he said, "Well, I don't know you, but you've got to be a good man because you beat a good man. . . . You beat David Ghambreal, and David was a good senator and a good friend of mine."

[Lawton added], "Let's get together with our wives," and so we did that and I felt that was a rather unusual kind of introduction by telling me the fellow I'd just run against was a good senator, which he really was, but Lawton was that way—he was candid and absolutely honest from the day one. I knew as soon as he got off the phone, I said to Colleen, "Let's get with them soon, because I'm going to like that guy."[488]

"They were alter egos," Chiles staffer Bob Coakley says of the Chiles-Nunn bond. "The staff really couldn't get in the middle."

Senator Chiles had also found common ground with Senator Nunn on federal budget policy. Both supported vigorous enforcement of the 1974 Budget Act, creating the first congressional Budget Committee. They were the junior rebels standing up to the Southern Old Guard.

The law's purpose was to control and discipline the federal budget approval process in both chambers, via the budget committees. These new committees would propose overall spending limits at the start of each budget cycle, which if approved by a majority vote of both chambers, would theoretically constrain the appropriations committees from spending. They would try to impose rationality and predictability on the budget process. Rhea Chiles noticed how the day-to-day frustrations of budget negotiation distracted her husband:

He saw how the debt service on that and how deficits were eating our lunch, our infrastructure. . . . You couldn't pay for education and all that. . . . This went on for a long, long time. But I think the accumulation of trying to dig that ditch, of trying to get that done was finally just . . . he couldn't let it go, he just worked at it too hard.[489]

Senator Ed Muskie (D-ME) mentored Senator Chiles on budget issues, but Senator Sam Nunn related to Walkin' Lawton best. "[Senator] Muskie was not the kind of guy you wanted to go out and have a beer with," Chiles staffer Rick Farrell explains.

"I would have told Lawton my deepest, darkest secret," Senator Nunn said, "and trusted him . . . not only [to] not repeat it—if it was, indeed, something confidential—but also to think about it and, if it was a problem, to reflect on it and be a help."[490]

Senator Chiles bonded with Senator Nunn, Senator Bentsen, and other colleagues on the tennis court, according to Rhea Chiles. "[Lawton] was never really very good," she recalls. "I wasn't either, but we had a lot of fun."

The Chiles family played tennis more frequently once they built a tennis court in their own back yard. Lawton and Rhea paid for it with insurance money earned after a major burglary. The "highway robber" of the beltway had stolen jewelry and silver. "I built a tennis court and I said, 'Well, let's see 'em try and take that.'"

As her husband laid the foundation for passing Government in the Sunshine, Rhea Chiles built a political network for her own project called Florida House—a sort of embassy for the Sunshine State in Washington.

Rhea devised the idea for Florida House on a family visit to Washington, D.C. in 1963. As the family drove down Embassy Row, the children asked to see Florida's embassy. "We explained to them that the different states don't have embassies," Rhea says. "They thought that was short shrift." When Lawton became a U.S. senator, Rhea found a boarded up 112-year-old townhouse between the Supreme Court and the Library of Congress. "This was the era of the fires and the riots and it was not a safe place," Rhea said. She put up $5,000 and raised another $120,000 to buy the townhouse in 1973. Floridians donated art and antiques for the interior design. The mission was to create a beautiful meeting place for politicians, tourists, and businessmen to meet and discover and re-discover Florida while in Washington. The institution would rely strictly on private donations. The Victorian home, close to the Capitol and U.S. Supreme Court, cost $125,000 to buy and $240,000 to renovate.

"The biggest hurdle we had was with the congressional delegation," Mrs. Chiles said. "They looked at us with a jaundiced eye because it meant fundraising. I think they thought, 'We have enough trouble raising money on our own. We don't want to get into this,' and they didn't think it would fly at all."[491] By 1973, Florida House was established. Rhea reflected: "It was a rather substantial project when you look back on it. It was rather unusual. People would say, what is it? What are you doing? What is that? What is Florida House?" She leveraged her husband's contacts for fundraising for Florida House:

> It was sort of a thing that had a lot of things going for it. It had a lot of momentum and everybody wanted it to succeed and they liked it. I think the thing that helped it the most was that I was able to bring people from Florida up to Washington and engage in social activities with Florida House and get on the board. And I nursed those board members. I saw to it that they had transportation, I saw that they

went to the places that we could have entrée to that they would never have seen . . . rare gem collection at the Smithsonian. . . . We had a wonderful board, still do.

Senator Chiles: "that's probably a more tangible sort of accomplishment than anything that happened. . . . [Florida House] was [Rhea's] baby, her project."[492]

In art, Rhea found a world apart from the rush of Washington power games:

When you're living it, it's very hard. It's hard for me to look back. . . . It was all happening. There was so much coming at me, so much involvement—which was what we chose, so I'm not complaining. It's hard to sort out anything that's monumental because it was all monumental and it was all going so fast and so furiously. Look at this! Look at that! Then there's so and so! And look at there, there's the Taj Mahal!

Rhea painted for fun:

Well, there was never a time when I did serious artwork—I dabbled all my life. But I was always happy for the involvement, because it was something I could jump into. I could get out of the car, and change the clothes, run down to Sarasota and take lessons. Or be just with the group, just jump right into the group and paint—and that was great fun.

Senator Chiles did not share her aesthetic sensibility, according to their daughter-in-law Kitty Chiles:

Lawton had terrible taste in clothes. . . . He had this Navy blue tux that he just wore for years and it was really just, it was just not good. . . . Finally Rhea called Bud and said you need to come we've gotta go, we have to dress him, this has gotta be over. . . . He would wear plaids and stripes. . . . His hair was awful. . . . She started actually cutting his hair herself and got a good style for him.

Senator Chiles preferred to escape Washington in a bird field. He scoured Maryland and Virginia for the best turkey roosts. Dubose Ausley hunted with Senator Chiles when he returned South:

I've got a farm north of town, part in Florida and part in Georgia and they got a lot of turkeys. And we'd hunt off of horseback, hunt quail off of horseback. And I think he enjoyed being with me 'cause I never talked to him about politics. He was a kind of interesting guy. He had a strange personality in the sense that he'd get in one of those moods and he wouldn't talk. He just wouldn't say anything. And then every now and then sometime we'd be huntin' and he'd be very talkative and he would ask me about things. When he asked me, I would tell him. And I think he respected my input 'cause I never tried to have any input, unless he asked me.

He "prided himself on a gobbler that he called up," Burke Kibler observed. "The killing of the gobbler didn't matter to him nearly as much as the fact that he would get the gobbler to come up so that he could see him, and I think sometimes he deliberately would not shoot him because he did not want to clean the turkey."[493] Chiles hunted with Lloyd Bentsen in Florida; he took trips to Alaska and Canada. He loved exploring new spots with Wilbur Boyd. In Washington, he would collect his wooden turkey calls and drive in the dark an hour and half to Virginia woodland, arrive at four-thirty or five, and listen for gobbles at dawn. He would return in time for the ten o'clock Senate session. This routine recurred two or three times a week during turkey season. Burke Kibler recalls that "he loved being alone with the turkey, the quietness, seeing the world awakening, the fascination of seeing the turkey come up; hunting enriched his soul." Chiles loved the dog work, too. Senator Nunn hunted with Lawton:

I remember Lawton, he had a great sense of humor. And he was always kidding, and Rhea was the same way and still is. But anytime he shot a bird, a bird would get up, and he'd shoot the gun and the bird would fall. And Lawton would always say, "Did you shoot?" as if he had hit the bird every time.

Chiles claimed to have once watched a turkey turn its head around 360 degrees. Chiles buddy Jack Watson sometimes cut off beards of bagged turkeys and sent them to Chiles' Senate office.[494] Rick Farrell: "Oh yeah, he'd go out to some place in the foothills of Virginia, out towards the mountains, at three or four in the morning. He'd come in, he'd be in the office by 9:30 a.m. I remember once he came in with a turkey."

Having ended his private law practice, Senator Chiles returned to Lakeland during Senate recess for turkey hunts. Senator Chiles hunted in Polk County's Green Swamp. "We'd take the kids 'cause the kids were young," Robert Waters recalls. "We'd take the kids camping, and then Lawton and I would go hunting." They hunted deer, turkey, and "little wild pigs." Often, private landowners in the county invited Chiles up to take shots at fowl. One such time, his hosts "were working hard to get a deer to run by Lawton so he could kill him, which they did." According to Waters, "Nobody had any action but Lawton, because most of the people that invited him up there made sure that a deer would run by Lawton." From the big ranchers that owned the best hunting preserves, "Lawton had an open invitation and a key to the gate."[495] Rhea Chiles appreciated how the outdoors balanced her husband's Washington schedule: "I was so bothered [by stress], and to live with someone who wasn't, was great therapy all the time."

Both Lawton and Rhea played tennis. One day, they invited old friends, Nitzi and Robert Waters, out to a tennis match at a private club and spa near Tarpon Springs. "I told [my husband] we'd better dress," Nitzi said. "We don't want to embarrass Lawton and Rhea. I mean here he was a Senator going over there." So they wore white pants and navy blazers and drove over to pick up their hosts. When they arrived about ten o'clock in the morning, Lawton and Rhea were not ready. Lawton came out of his room in his pajamas and hollered, "Who has seen my white shorts?" He and Rhea had just gotten tennis clothes for Christmas. His son Ed explained he had worn them the day before and thrown them in the hamper. Lawton yelled, "Well, get 'em outta there!" At the spa, they pulled up in the car. Lawton had called in advance and the doorman ran out to get their bags. The doorman walked up and welcomed Robert Waters to the facility, addressing him as "Senator Chiles." "I'm not the Senator, that's the Senator," Waters said. The doorman looked at Chiles' rumpled shorts and sport coat and exclaimed, "What!?" Waters repeated, "That's the Senator!" The gang broke into laughter as the guy finally ushered Lawton into the spa.[496]

The Chiles family bonded over food. One day at the townhouse, Rhea found a package of Margaret Patterson Chiles' icebox cookies in the mail. She had labored her "entire married life" to replicate Margaret's recipe, but

Lawton would always taste them and comment, "They're good, but maybe you could change this around." This time she would fix him, she thought. She put on her apron and dirtied the kitchen with flour, snickering all the while. When Senator Chiles arrived home, she announced, "Well I've tried once more and this time I did it and made them right." Lawton glanced at the cookies on a plate and went into the other room to take his jacket off. Then he chewed a morsel and complimented them curtly. In his shirt pocket he pulled out a piece of paper and handed it to Rhea. It read: "I can always smell a trap, and these ARE my mother's cookies." ("I was good at this, I had thought about this, I was licking my chops," Rhea relates, but "you never had him.") One occasion in Washington, Bud, Ed, and Lawton cooked dinner by themselves. Bud distinctly recalls that "we thought we were going to have to sell the house, because there was no way we could clean up the mess we made in the kitchen that day."

Senator and Rhea Chiles doted on their adopted daughter Rhea Gay. The girl, five years old when her father became a U.S. senator, recounted her Washington, D.C., childhood fondly. She recalls visiting the Kennedy Center with her parents and social events with other U.S. senators. Rhea Gay: "I was the only kid at all these events half the time. It was really a unique growing-up experience. I really think I had an incredible childhood, one-of-a-kind. The only drawback was we moved a lot." One Christmas, Rhea Gay sat on the lap of President Nixon [dressed as Santa Claus] at the White House and asked him for presents. Senator Chiles took Rhea Gay to see musicals such as *Annie* or *The Sound of Music*. Rhea Gay remembers playing a game, "Murder," at her parents' frequent parties:

> Everybody would sit in a circle. Each person got one card, and who-ever got the queen of spades was the killer. The object was you'd sit in the circle, and that was back in the days with people drinkin' and smokin'. And you'd go around and you'd wink, and that's how you'd kill somebody. And so that's how I got to be a good winker. They used to let me play all the time, it was fun.

She remembers her parents watching British TV shows in their pajamas, with tea. "There were times when he'd get on the phone . . . but most of the time, he would come home and boom, it was family time." Chiles enjoyed his family when he had the time. He would come home from work and shout to his youngest daughter, "Let's footride!" Then he walked around the house as

Rhea Gay rode on his feet. At bedtime, Chiles transformed into Uncle Remus to spin yarns of Br'er Rabbit escaping Br'er Fox. "I have vivid memories of every single Uncle Remus character," Rhea Gay claims, "all the voices, the bear, the fox, the rabbit."[497]

By the fifth year of his first term, the excitement of realizing his childhood dream still animated Senator Chiles. The social compact with Florida promulgated by the Walk commanded his conscience. The Walk had impacted national politics.

In 1972, multiple copycats ran for elected office. Dan Walker ran successfully for governor of Illinois by walking across the state, crediting Chiles with the idea. Richard Clark walked across Iowa and won a Senate seat. Senator William Proxmire began a 1,200-mile walk across Wisconsin.[498] Sam Nunn reflected on the Walk's legacy in Georgia:

> We had twelve Democrats running, and I was running against the incumbent Senator David Gambrell—as well as former Governor Vandiver, state treasurer by the name of Bill Burson, and others. Bill Burson had worked for Senator Talmadge, was well known in Georgia and was given a real chance of getting in a run-off, which would have finished me off. Bill made the fateful decision to pattern his campaign after Walkin' Lawton—but he didn't have Rhea's guidance and common sense. Burson didn't realize Lawton had walked in highly populated areas and that he left his walk frequently for appearances and television interviews along the way. So—in the spring of 1972, Bill Burson started walking among the pine trees in deep South Georgia—he couldn't be reached for months for radio or television interviews—there was one picture of him walking down a deserted road and he was never heard from again. So thank you Rhea for getting both Lawton and me elected to the U.S. Senate.[499]

But Senator Chiles did not want to enter the history books for just campaigning. He yearned for more time to successfully orchestrate passage of Government in the Sunshine legislation. Rhea wished to slow down, too:

> When we went to Washington, it was like a kid going into a circus. There were so many rings to watch. . . . I wish that it had come at a slower pace, because so much happened in all those years, those early years.

Rhea wanted more out of her role as a Senate wife than was allowed by Washington tradition. Most wives attended social functions while their husbands managed affairs of state. As Executive Assistant to Senator Chiles in Washington, Margaret Maruschak noticed Rhea's conflict and tried to include her in as much substantive office activity as possible.

Maruschak joined Chiles' staff in 1971 as a part-time typist. She then moved to legislative research and correspondence duties for three years. When Dale Marler, the Executive Assistant for the Washington office, left for Florida, Maruschak replaced him. In the 1970s, it was unusual for a southern senator to hire a woman from the North. "He was one of the most unusual people I've ever met," Maruschak says of Senator Chiles.

In her work with the senator, Maruschek recalls, she made sure Rhea knew of upcoming events and could choose to attend them:

> In my position, some people work for the senator, and they kinda leave the wife out. I made a strategic decision based on some advice I'd gotten from a good friend, and it was one of the best decisions in my life. . . . I think Mrs. Chiles interpreted me, she read me that I was going to do everything I [could] to support their relationship.

Rhea Chiles has interpreted her role in her husband's political career:

> Lawton was a convener. He could pass legislation because he was a wonderful listener. He knew what the right needed and what the left needed and what the middle ground was. For me to presume that I could tell him how to make a vote would be like telling a high-wire artist to hang on or to step to the left or to the right. He hardly needed my advice. Certainly, he was interested in my opinions. I never felt like I didn't have his complete ear if I wanted to bang on it about something.[500]

Maruschak explains her work with Rhea:

> [Senator Chiles] had very high ideals, and I thought I know that he'll be happier, she'll be happier, the office will run more smoothly, if I do everything I can to keep them on the same page. I'm not in the middle of their private conversations but I can, even in my tone of

voice, in the way I share information, I can make it seem as though Mrs. Chiles is not a bother to me, but that it's important that she be on board in order that everything here run smoothly. And there were ups and downs in that over the years, obviously, and I just set it as one of my must-dos all the time, make sure that that's a priority, and I told her that I would do that, and I think I did it.

Finally, as he planned re-election, Senator Chiles won his first big legislative victory. Congress enacted Government in the Sunshine legislation in September 1976. Senator Chiles reflected, "When I first came here I wanted to be a generalist. I had walked the state and had a bushel basket of bills I wanted to introduce, but I found out you have to learn your subject area so people have confidence in you and follow your lead. . . . For instance, I talked about sunshine in government so much that people started calling me the Sunshine Kid."

President Gerald Ford signed the bill at a White House Rose Garden ceremony. The sunshine bill required about fifty federal agencies outside the Cabinet offices to open their meetings to the public, including the Securities and Exchange Commission, Federal Reserve Board, Federal Election Commission, and Federal Trade Commission. It also opened up Senate and House committee meetings to public scrutiny, barring national security and other compelling exceptions. During debate on the bill, Senator Chiles remarked:

> When we read the polls and find that Congress ranks behind used car dealers with regard to the respect that the public holds for them, then I do not think we can believe that the public believes that what we are doing is correct. They do not trust us, and one reason why they do not trust is the number of closed doors we have here.[501]

Government Affairs Committee staffer Bob Harris recalls:

> The great fear on the role of the senators, [was] we're not gonna be able to speak candidly, number one, in the mark-ups, and number two, we're gonna have to know what we're talking about. Now that these meetings are gonna be open. So there weren't a lot of people who were real pleased with him, about proposing this great sunshine amendment.

Senators had sometimes mocked Senator Chiles' quixotic battle for transparency. One of his exemplary moves toward transparency was Senator Chiles' aversion toward proxy voting; he voted in person always. Appropriations Committee staffer for Senator Chiles, Michael Hall:

> If you're chairman of an appropriations subcommittee in a markup, people will tell you, "Hey, I can't come, but you have my proxy to vote on anything that comes up," or "Here's my proxy, just for issue A. If that comes up, I want you to vote no for me." He wouldn't do that. Consequently, he'd get beat. He would get beaten often on issues. He said, in the long run he thought he'd be ahead because people respect the way he did it.

The press as an institution did not support the cause of sunshine as ardently as advocates expected, either. Individual reporters with their own confidential sources preferred to bypass the legislative fight.

Watergate raised the profile of transparency as a political issue, and marked a turning point in the debate on sunshine legislation. The loyalty of Senator Chiles' committee staff was essential. Whatever regrets and discontents Senator Chiles harbored, they were a mystery to his staff. Staff sometimes found Senator Chiles inscrutable. Aging Committee staffer Deborah Kilmer: "It wasn't always easy. He gave this kind of laid-back, slow, quiet demeanor at first. And you had to sometimes pull things out of him. . . . It wasn't shyness, he was just quiet, kind of aloof at first. . . . Also, he was a renaissance man, people didn't appreciate that at first." Kilmer: "He would sleep through his hearing. . . . He would sit there half-asleep during the hearing, and then it would be his turn for questioning and he would sit up and ask some of the best questions and follow-up, not just sit and read the questions but follow-up and ask something." Bentley Lipscomb, a staffer on the Special Committee on Aging, recalls his boss's spongy memory:

> He had incredible memory. I saw him sit in a staff meeting one day, and we a bunch of interns and young staffers that were in there. Farrell was conducting the meeting. Chiles was sitting up behind his desk. . . . He had his eyes shut. And I thought "Jesus, he's just gone to sleep." And then about two weeks later, we were in another meeting,

and he quoted almost verbatim what was being said when I thought he was asleep. So, lesson learned.

Debbie Kilmer: "For a while we had no turnover. The stability, sustainability of working for him, which only made him more effective because we had such institutional memory, such knowledge, and we had such a good team that worked together."

Although Senator Chiles' warmth, humor, and Cracker drawl impressed company at barbecues, hunting jaunts, and tennis matches, he reserved a quiet demeanor for interactions with Senate staff. He never asked staff to call him "Lawton," nor did he expect familiarity. Senator Chiles maintained a professional distance from staff, according to Chief of Staff Rick Farrell:

> Chiles, no one would ever use that kind of language in front of him. He always maintained a certain reserve, a certain distance from everybody who was a staff person. And I think it was deliberate and I think it was smart. And I think I was as close to him as anyone. I never called him Lawton. Never, ever once. People did, and he didn't like it. His attitude was: I worked hard to get elected senator, elected governor, and that's the title that should be used. So I think he always understood that because of the office he held, and because of the need, and he was smart about the need, he wanted staff to always remember that they were talking to a U.S. senator, that they were talking to a governor, and that he may be friendly with them and they may have dinner together and they may do a lot of things together, but they were not on the same plane. And not that he saw himself being better, but because of the office . . . there was always a difference.

Jack Pridgen was the only staff that called him, "Lawton." Staff on Capitol Hill showed deference, inquiring about the Senator's mood and schedule before addressing him personally. Despite Senator Chiles' distaste for pomp and artifice in elected office, and his inclination to clown around, at the office he steered a middle course of sobriety. Staff quickly recognized the office as a place of industry and discretion; they briefed Senator Chiles on issues, debated issues, and usually respected their boss's words as final. He let his office handle scheduling. Personnel matters he enjoyed leaving to Charles Canady, Rick Farrell, and other senior staff. "He found it hard to say,

'Don't you do that anymore,'" Rhea observed. "He would just ignore it or say it'll be better or leave early and go out to the country."

Chiles' faith fortified him, too, in his fight for Government in the Sunshine, according to his daughter-in-law Kitty Chiles:

> He became a man that was developing this relationship with God. That became clear when he would pray. When we would be together over the holidays if we were all down at the beach, pretty much every morning they would be in their room and a lot of times we would go in there. They would have their Bibles and he would talk with them. I'd never done anything like that. . . . It was so informal, there was nothing organized about Lawton's faith.

Chiles senior staffer Rick Farrell reflected on the legacy of the sunshine law:

> And now everybody takes it for granted that you can watch the FEC, and FCC, and all these groups, meet, and make their decisions, and it all works fine, it's not any problem, but back then they were acting like it was the end of the world and this kind of young senator from Florida just didn't get it.

Chiles staffer Dave Mica also commented:

> To this day, the full effects of that are just getting felt. . . . When you operate on a board or commission or elected office or something like that the tendencies to hate it are so huge, or to want an exemption, are so huge, it is unbelievable . . . and I was like that. . . . I used to talk to the boss. . . . He'd say, "We can get it done; there's nothing to hide."

Margaret Maruschak recalls waiting anxiously up until the last minute to hear if she had an invitation to go to the Rose Garden for the signing of the Government in the Sunshine Act. "And I remember," she said, "distinctly the senator calling me on a particular morning, and I just said, 'This is Margaret,' and he started singing a song that was popular at that time, 'I Never Promised You a Rose Garden.'" Maruschak would attend.

145

Lawton IV

"The question was," Senator Chiles concluded at the end of his freshman term, "'how could I run again and still be the person that they thought they'd voted for?'"[502] The Walk had influenced Florida campaign strategy and inspired national copycats. Florida Governor Bob Graham harnessed some of the spirit of the Walk for his own "workdays" during his successful 1978 and 1982 bids for governor. For the workdays, Graham visited Florida workplaces of all kinds and joined the staff for one day. He worked as a bellhop, garbage collector, and citrus packer. Graham compared the Walk and the workday:

> It was seven years after his Walk that we sat down with a small group of people and said, "We really want to understand why Lawton's Walk was so effective," and then, "What can we do to capture those same characteristics?"—not being a copycat by doing the walk. That led us to the idea of doing one hundred workdays throughout the campaign. I believe, immodestly, that it did pick up on many of the things that made Lawton's Walk so effective.[503]

Search began for an idea as innovative as the Walk that would renew the people's trust. According to Rhea Chiles, the Walk was where her husband "fell in love with the people. He really loved to tell the stories about the people he met and I think that's when he . . . began to trust their ability."[504]

Hundreds of thousands of newly settled Floridians, moreover, had never heard of Walkin' Lawton. Many of the new voting bloc, "vacation voters," had moved to the state explicitly to escape high tax rates and live in communities dedicated to sunny, secure retirement. They eschewed obligations to local school systems, health care clinics, and public transit. Some originally visited for vacation and decided to stay. Disney World's grand opening in fall 1971 was, after advances in pest control and air conditioning, the last reform that guaranteed Florida's supremacy in American tourism. The subsequent construction of Florida's Turnpike and Interstate 4 linked Orlando—the state's amusement epicenter—to the state's major airports and beaches. I-4 also linked Florida to the Eastern seaboard via Interstate 95.

Senator Chiles ultimately decided to maintain Florida's trust by imposing a limit of $10 per person on his 1976 re-election campaign contributions. His campaign also banned PAC money contributions and capped total campaign spending at $400,000—the amount spent in 1970. After Watergate, a handful of national politicians, such as Senator Mac Mathias of Maryland, had set contribution limits.[505] In his 1974 re-election bid, Florida Governor Reubin Askew had limited campaign contributions to $100. In 1974, Florida law held that individuals or corporations could contribute a maximum of $3,000. Askew won with 60 percent of the vote. The contribution limit would serve Senator Chiles convenience and his conviction. "I'm not a fundraiser," the Senator told an interviewer, "I just hate to go to a man and ask him for money. I've had some friend come to me and say, 'So-and-so wants to give you some money, if you'll just go and see him.' So I'd go and he'd give me a hundred dollars, and I'd go back and tell my friend and he'd say, 'But he was going to give you *five* hundred.'"[506]

Whether out of personal timidity or respect for Chiles' hard-charging campaign personality, Senate colleagues like Bennett Johnston of Louisiana saw the contribution limit as a unique extension of Chiles' character:

> It very well suited Lawton Chiles. And it certainly took away both appearance and the evil of money, which has gotten to be just terrible, I think, in the Senate. Almost nobody else could do that but Lawton.

Senator Sam Nunn:

I think Lawton's limit of ten dollars in his campaign was unique; it was novel, it was refreshing, it was exciting for a lot of young people. And I think it put a real spotlight on the fundraising excesses that have become even more and more prevalent ever since. It wasn't something many people could do 'cause they didn't have the personality to go with it. And they didn't have the knack of being able to generate a lot of free publicity.

Senator William Proxmire supported Chiles' campaign limits. Some senators saw it as "holier than thou" posturing. Chiles' former colleague in the Florida legislature, Republican State Senator Ken Plante, called the campaign finance limits "a tad of a gimmick," but a credo "that to a great degree he also believed."

Friends, family, and staff reacted first with shock and frustration but gradually gave way to the idea. Senate staffer Bob Harris told his wife, "I'm so sorry, I really screwed up. There's no way. This guy is nuts!" Chief of staff Rick Farrell tried to lift the contribution cap:

I understood where it was coming from, and admired him for his feeling that not taking money gave him an independence and an ability to deal with everybody on an absolutely equal footing. But from a practical standpoint, one saw, Florida is a big state; it takes money to run there, every aspect of doing a ten-dollar thing was very daunting. And in fact, [he] probably was putting in place something that might have interfered with his re-election when there was really nothing else to interfere with his re-election. He was popular, and there as not anybody on the horizon that looked like somebody.

Old friend Burke Kibler:

Ten dollars—now, I used to tell him, "Lawton, you're making people be duplicitous and hypocritical and you know damn well there's no way you can do that." I bet I wrote a thousand letters for Lawton to people and friends—I probably didn't write that many, but I wrote a bunch of them asking to send ten dollars . . . but the cost of doing it, the time you took—you know, I doubt you would break even. Getting enough money that way was just a terrible thing.[507]

Son Ed Chiles recalls the night at Pier 66 in Fort Lauderdale when his father told him and his brother and sister, Bud and Tandy, the news about the campaign contribution limit. Tandy said, "That's great; wonderful." Ed and Bud remarked, "Shit, this is awful." Bud Chiles ultimately acquiesced to his father's rationale:

> Dad was serious about getting big money out of politics. He hated the feeling he got when he felt someone owned a piece of him. He wanted to be free to vote his conscience and to pursue the agenda that was on his heart, not carry the water for fat cat contributors. He described it as "having a hook in you."

Rhea recalls the decision: "[Lawton] decided to take home the girl he came with." Senator Chiles "did not have any confidence in polls or in bringing somebody in from anywhere else to run a campaign in Florida; he didn't want any part of it. He trusted his gut and he trusted his experience as a Floridian." Senator Chiles liked to think of himself as a riverboat gambler.

Once committed to the contribution cap, Senator Chiles' children sold the strategy across the state. Bud Chiles and his new wife Katherine "Kitty" Orr traveled the state for 18 months setting up fish fries, barbecues, and phone banks to raise money. In January they were off and running, two or three weeks per city. Kitty remembers telling Lawton "after about six months of events that he could stop introducing me as his brand-new daughter-in-law."

Tom Staed, nicknamed "Inspector Clouseau" by the Senator, chaired the 1976 campaign. "We never, ever had a problem" with the fundraising, Staed recalls. "In fact, it was a great, great gimmick. The campaign was the most fun I've ever had on any kind of campaign, anywhere, before or since. It was just hilarious." Each ten-dollar donor received a ticket stub thanking the contributor for "one equal share" in the campaign.[508] Rhea Chiles, as before, helped hone the campaign, according to Senator Sam Nunn:

> A lot of Lawton's great ideas were stimulated by Rhea and probably a number of them created by Rhea and all of them were encouraged and supported by Rhea, so Rhea was just a fundamental part of that political team. . . . If you were running against one you were running against both of them![509]

150

Charlie Canady Sr. enforced discipline as campaign manager. Working at the Lakeland headquarters alongside Charlie Canady Sr., Kitty and Bud Chiles once lost a trash bag full of $800 in ten-dollar checks. Someone had confused the bag of checks for actual trash and thrown it in the dumpster outside the office. In the scorching days of summer, the dumpster reeked. Charlie Canady exclaimed, "we're not leaving here until we find this money." Bud, Kitty, and Charlie climbed into the dumpster and sloshed around until they found the money bag.

Charlie Canady judged whether a campaign event exceeded the budget. Kitty would report to Charlie with a plan, and he would reply, "Nope, too expensive!" Sometimes Bud and Kitty would stay in towns for three weeks, guests of a campaign supporter. Kitty relates, "I knew nothing about politics, had no interest in it, didn't even know this man [Lawton]. I wasn't even sure what to call him. Nobody really helped me out with that."

Bud recalls going to Ocala, Jacksonville, Sarasota, Miami, Fort Lauderdale, West Palm Beach, Orlando, Gainesville, and Tallahassee. Bud and Kitty got as much food donated as possible. Everything was focused on an event two or three weeks down the road, a fundraiser where Lawton would deliver short remarks. "We got so good," Bud remembers, "we could serve a plate to a supporter for about a dollar."[510] Bud Chiles and his father vacationed in the Florida Keys during the campaign:

> We were returning from a diving trip in the Keys. We brought back a trunk-full of Florida lobster. We immediately proceeded to a campaign event in Ft. Lauderdale, but we forgot about the lobsters. We threw the lobsters out, but the smell would not go away. It was 95 [degrees], and by the next day, when we got in the rental car for the return trip to the Miami Airport, the smell was so bad we all had to put our heads all the way out of the window as we drove down I-95. The whole time I [was] thinking, What is he going to do to get out of this one?!
>
> When we got to the rental place, [Dad] called the clerk over and asked him in a very annoyed tone, "Come over here and smell my car. Have you ever smelled a car this good? How could you rent me a car that smells so God awful?" The clerk was speechless.

Senator Chiles and Tom Staed called the campaign team The Gang Who Couldn't Shoot Straight, inspired by the eponymous 1969 Jimmy Breslin novel and 1971 Robert De Niro film.[511]

The victorious 1976 re-election campaign racked up a historic 40,000 contributors. The tally more than quadrupled the record number of donors set by Governor Reubin Askew's 1974 re-election campaign.[512] Senator Chiles won the general election with 60 percent of the vote.[513]

Returning to Washington for a second term, he redoubled his attacks on waste, fraud and abuse in federal bureaucracy. Senator Chiles' frugal campaign style informed his watchdog mentality, according to Senate budget staffer Rick Brandon:

> In 1979, [Senator] Chiles and [Rick] Brandon had been asked to come to a meeting to discuss issues close to big bankers. They sat at a long conference table, surrounded by fifteen banking CEOs and their lobbyist. During the meeting, Chiles seemed distracted and disinterested. Finally, the lobbyist leaned over and told Chiles, "I'm not sure you understand the sum of wealth and power sitting around this table today." Chiles looked around the table, then said, "The way I count it, it's $150," referencing his $10-a-person contribution limit. The meeting was over.[514]

The Paperwork Reduction Act of 1980 was the culmination of Senator Chiles' efforts to build on Government in the Sunshine and spread efficiency and accountability to other sectors of the federal government. Chiles persuaded both Senators Barry Goldwater and Ted Kennedy to support the bill, which attempted to force the government to trim its current burden of paperwork and justify new forms created for the American public. The law required a 25 percent drop in the "paperwork burden" over three years.

"Have you ever looked at a federal form or looked at a federal regulation on your record-keeping requirements?" asked Bob Coakley, the staffer who worked with Senator Chiles on paperwork issues. "There is always this little statement that says we estimate that it takes so much time to do that—and if you'd like to comment on whether you agree or have any suggestions, please file comments to either the agency or OMB . . . well, that's Lawton Chiles. And during the course of a year I would say over 200-to-250 million people see that. They don't know that it's Lawton Chiles."

Janet Studley worked for Senator Chiles as chief counsel to his Subcommittee on Federal Spending Practices and Open Government, which at the time was part of the Governmental Affairs Committee. The subcommittee, which Chiles chaired from 1974 to 1998, had jurisdiction over the Government in the Sunshine Act, among other policies. She worked in his office from 1977 to 1981.

"At the time," Studley says, "as you can imagine, it was post-Watergate. So, the climate was right for good government, open government, transparency in government types of initiatives, because we had gone through such a bad time during the latter part of the Nixon administration." Senator Chiles thrived on office debate, according to Studley:

> Of course the Senate has changed a lot since I worked there, and since Chiles was a senator. Even then, there weren't that many senators, or staff, that had the kind of access to the senator they worked for, as we did. He would call us in on an issue we were handling, and want to hear everyone's view. I'd send him memos, and he'd send them back with a note and a smiley face. But he saw them, there wasn't this sense of having a gatekeeper, the way a lot of offices have.

Staffer Bob Harris also recalls the office as a haven for open discussion:

> [Senator Chiles] was very interesting, because he supported major legislation. He would try to amend it if it didn't suit him completely. . . . If he failed to do it, he didn't vote against a bill, which is what a lot of people were used to southerners doing: "I can't weaken the bill so I'm gonna vote against it." He didn't do that. He treated the staff the same way. "You got an open voice, make your argument, but once I make the decision, then the argument is over." And we clearly understood that. "I don't wanna give you the impression that I won a lot of 'em. I lost a lot."

Some senators balked at the proposal; Bob Harris and Studley briefed Senator Chiles on the issue while other staffers looked on.

Janet Studley, Dennis Beal, and Bob Harris formed the liberal faction in the office.

Rarely did Senator Chiles let emotional appeals control the intraoffice debate. On one occasion, a legislative proposal was made to set up a process for employment discrimination claims for Senate staff; the bill came through his Government Affairs Committee. Senator Chiles mused aloud to his staff that voters could punish discriminatory officeholders at the ballot box, in lieu of legislation. "At one point," Studley recalls, "I looked up and said, 'Well, Senator, is what you're saying, that if your constituents are bigots, it's okay for you to be a bigot?'" Senator Chiles said, "This meeting is over."

Senator Chiles expected staff to bring him at least as many solutions as problems. Staffer Debbie Kilmer, for example, would brief him on a confounding matter of public policy, and he would reply, "Then make lemonade." Kilmer would explain the issue further, and Senator Chiles would repeat, "Then just make lemonade." She would sometimes walk out of such encounters thinking, "Make lemonade? What does that mean?" But, ultimately, she appreciated this approach as instructive and empowering.

Bob Coakley, who worked for Chiles on the Government Affairs Committee, encountered similar situations. "You'd come to him with an idea," Coakley recalls, "and he'd say, 'Now, what is the light at the end of this tunnel?' And if there was no light at the end of the tunnel, you were in trouble. You don't bring him ideas unless there is light at the end of the tunnel." Chiles would also tell staff, "Put the wood in front of me and I'll chop it." This was probably his way of indicating that it was his job to give voice to an argument on the national stage, once supporting evidence had been gathered by staff.

One of the most controversial votes of his second term was far from Senator Chiles' good government agenda: ratification of the Panama Canal Treaty. "The air is strange in there," Senator Chiles said of the Senate chamber just before the 68-32 vote in support of the treaty. A large majority of the 70,000 constituent letters received by his office were in opposition.

President Jimmy Carter signed the Treaty in September 1977 and Floridians sent vitriolic letters and phone calls to the Chiles office. Given its proximity to South America, Florida reacted to the Panama Canal vote more than most states. The popular opposition to the Canal Treaty rallied passionately to the side of their senators and congressmen; the supporters stayed home. Florida's high veteran population especially galvanized against it. *Miami Herald* reporter Tom Fiedler first met Lawton Chiles at a tennis tournament; they played against one another in the mid 1970s. Fiedler claimed that the opposition suffered from a "misplaced sense of patriotism." Senator Chiles sometimes talked to himself and read the Bible as he prepared to cast his vote. "The happiest time in a politician's life is when conscience and convenience cross," Senator Chiles said. "Here they did not."

Just before the vote, Senator John Stennis (D-MS), one of the chamber's most respected senior members, leaned over to Senator Chiles and advised, "Lawton, sometimes you just gotta give a vote for the country." Senator Chiles liked to retell the story to emphasize the political sacrifice entailed. Chiles Staffer Dean Saunders heard the story when he asked his boss about the Panama vote after the fact:

> Well, I'll tell ya, Dean. I did that for a couple reasons. Number one, we didn't really control the canal anyway. The Panamanians controlled the water, and as a result, they could shut that canal off whenever they wanted. And there was growing dissent in Panama, and we were the object of a lot of that dissent. And so I ultimately supported giving the canal back to them for those reasons. You know, occasionally, in politics, you have to cast a vote for the country.

Senator Chiles also fought to bring rationality and order to the federal budget process, working his way up to the chairmanship of the Budget Committee. He had worked in his freshman term with Senator Ed Muskie (D-ME) to pass the Budget and Impoundment Control Act of 1974, or Budget Act. Now he had the seniority to raise his own profile on the issue, and he viewed displacing Senator Robert Byrd (D-WV) as Democratic leader as imperative to his goals for budget reform, governmental transparency, and ethics. When Senator Chiles rejoined the U.S. Senate for a second term in January 1977, Senator Mike Mansfield was no longer Senate majority leader; Senator Robert Byrd had replaced him. Chiles' chief of staff Rick Farrell:

> Mansfield ran the Senate with what would seem—particularly in comparison to say a Lyndon Johnson—with a gentle hand, but I think he was held in such esteem by senators, that they were very reluctant not to cooperate with him, because he was more of an intellectual, thoughtful guy, not one to badger and threaten senators like other majority leaders might have done perhaps. ... Mansfield was somebody who had been there a good while, and I think he led by example, he led by suggestion. Some would say not as much got done, it wasn't done as quickly as it should have been, but I think once again he fostered the kind of collegial type of atmosphere that I think Chiles really liked. ... He was very responsive to Mansfield. Not that he agreed with Mansfield all of the time, but I think he

appreciated the style of leadership. And Mansfield used to be criticized sometimes, because he was not perhaps strong enough to take the White House on, and he wasn't an assertive personality. But he had tremendous reservoirs of respect, I think from most senators, from both sides of the aisle.

Senator Byrd's leadership of the Senate Democratic Caucus upset the Mansfield model, starting with the budget process, which the West Virginian liked to keep loose, interminable, and expensive. To senators who played the appropriations process to enrich their fundraisers, Senator Chiles and other budget reformers appeared severe. Overarching budget targets, budget rationality, data-driven decision-making—these were talking points for most U.S. senators, not the basis of actual policy. Budget reformers fighting Senator Byrd, burdened by their deficit charts and fastidious rules, were as popular and ineffectual as high school hall monitors.

Senator Chiles blamed Senator Byrd for the unraveling of the budget process and other Senate trends. The Budget Act had aimed to balance presidential and legislative budgetary powers in the aftermath of Watergate. The 1973 War Powers Resolution, new House Democratic organizational rules, and the Budget Act all fortified the legislative branch. Congressional staff expanded and junior members grabbed more power from seniors via subcommittee chairmanships. The dispersion of power, however, led to unexpected gridlock and feelings of alienation in Congress. The sense of fraternity fragmented. Liberal, conservationist Congressman Morris "Mo" Udall (D-AZ) opined:

> It used to be that my brother, who held the seat before I did, would drive his car or take a train, which meant that if you were from west of the Mississippi, you were stuck in Washington for five, six months while the session ground on. You'd have a party and invite all your committee members and their wives, or the Eighty-seventh Congress Club would have an annual get-together. But now, I would venture that the average member does not know, could not identify half of his colleagues.[515]

The new power structure diffused Senate power in such a way that every senator felt like a leader, and with the right marketing, a "super-senator." The twenty-four-hour news cycle, largely due to the advent in 1980 of Ted

Turner's Cable News Network (CNN), created overnight media sensations. Even principled budget rationalists like Senator Chiles chafed at the proliferation of rules, committees, subcommittees, and filibusters necessary to pass a federal budget. Senator David Pryor, one of Senator Chiles' friends, compared the Senate experience to "getting stuck in an airport and having all your flights canceled."[516] Self-important, pork-barrell politicians like Senator Robert Byrd used the hysterics over process as excuse to ram still more pet projects through the appropriations committee and mock the Budget Committee. The ease of the enterprise encouraged more denigration of the Budget Committee.

The premature birth of his namesake grandson, Lawton Chiles IV, in fall 1981, inspired Senator Chiles' budget work. As a state legislator, Chiles had supported appropriations for Women and Infant Children (WIC) and other children's health programs. As a U.S senator, he fought to muster every federal resource to the cause. Healthy mothers and babies, Senator Chiles believed, would improve public health and save public funds. Staffer Dave Mica explains, "Words can't describe the profound nature of the impact when the little one was in neo-natal clinic. The gravity of that didn't escape him a single day. And he put his energies into making it better for others. . . . He directed the staff hard." Jack Levine, director of the Center for Florida's Children, said, "It didn't begin with Lawton the IV, but it was fueled by him: It became personal."[517] Rick Farrell:

> It evolved over time. . . . It was interesting how something would come to his attention like that—it was the same with biotechnology. He was like, "I want to get in the middle of biotechnology," and I was like, "You don't even know what that is." . . . That was one of the fun things about being on his staff. If something came your way that was of interest, and if he got interested, then he would do things.

Senator Chiles discovered that poor children's health and educational services made difficult social problems like poverty and welfare and crime intractable. Rick Farrell: "I think he became convinced that in many respects there is no issue more important than this, because it has so many implications in so many areas." Senator Chiles leveraged his position as chairman of health and labor appropriations subcommittee to increase funding for early childhood development programs. Senator Chiles searched his faith for answers to his grandson's illness. Senator Sam Nunn:

Lawton also had a deep faith. He didn't discuss it that much publicly—at least around me he didn't—but he had a deep and abiding
spiritual faith and he had close bonds with people who had a similar
faith and he was open.[518]

On October 20, 1981, Lawton Chiles IV was born to Kitty and Bud Chiles
very prematurely at one pound, nine ounces. American medicine knew much
less about premature birth complications than it did in subsequent decades.

Today, the American Pregnancy Assocation defines babies born before the
thirty-seventh week of gestation as premature. The risk of complications
increases, the more premature the birth. One of the largest concerns is for
the development of a premature baby's lungs, but the entire body can be
affected. Possible complications include respiratory distress syndrome,
pneumonia, apnea, and bradycardia. Doctors prepare for these problems
and treat them with state-of-the-art technology in the neonatal intensive
care unit (NICU).

When Lawton IV was born, doctors gave him a 2 percent chance of survival, and would not allow Senator Chiles to see him at Shands hospital in
Gainesville, due to medical complications for three to four weeks after his
birth.

Bud Chiles recalls:

When they finally allowed him to visit, he had just come through a
miraculous surgery where Lawton [IV] amazingly recovered after
Kitty and I went in to say our final goodbye. I tried to prepare Dad for
what he would see. My dad was fortifying himself by telling me how
many Vietnam hospitals he had visited with mangled and horribly
injured men. When my dad finally peered in over the isolette at the
NICU in Gainesville and saw Lawton for the first time, he rocked
back on his heels. He was visibly moved and shocked. From that time
forward he was never the same—he put children and their interests
on the front burner. He said at the time, "If we can afford fifteen
nuclear aircraft carriers, we can afford to take care of our children."

Kitty recalls, "[Lawton IV] just was bones basically, like a little sick bird,
with all these things hooked up to him."

Doctors had smothered Bud and Kitty in bad news and bad expectations for their first child for a month. "They go through the whole litany: there's gonna be brain damage, lung damage, heart damage, gut damage, he'll be blind," Bud relates. Kitty adds, "Cerebral palsy, probably institutionalized for life." Family, friends, and doctors worried for Kitty's health.

"And then the baby is born and you have a whole different feeling," Bud says. "This baby is fighting for life, it's got a personality."

Senator Chiles counseled his son and daughter-in-law, "You just see him walking in the woods with you, picture him that way. Picture flying a kite together, laughing and running—and don't listen to all that stuff. Get that mental image and just hold onto it."

Lawton IV stayed at the hospital four months; word of the family crisis spread across Florida and to Washington, D.C. Senator Chiles visited often. "People came up and started talking to him and telling him stories about their grandchild or their child or this situation over here," Kitty recalls, "and he began to learn more about things like prenatal care and the whole issue began to sort of swirl around him."

Senator Chiles discussed the issue on TV, sometimes blaming premature on irresponsible prenatal care. He studied the science more and more.

"For Bud's parents, for [Senator Chiles]," Kitty says, "I think there was something very special about Lawton IV; plus, it was his namesake. I actually thought he was gonna die, and so they kept coming into my room first day, second day, third day, 'You have to name the baby.' . . . I'm like, 'No, I'm not naming this baby.' Bud and I talked and said we would not name our child Lawton Chiles IV. Three Lawtons was enough." Kitty gave the baby the name thinking it would never be used.

"It was such a huge faith issue, I remember [Senator Chiles] saying when he came to see me," Kitty relates. "I think it was the second visit, not the first one, when he came to the hospital, and I'm showing him this machinery that Lawton is hooked up to, here's the heart rate, here's the breathing machine, this is the blood-oxygen level, and I'm telling him how bad things are. He's like, 'You've gotta stop looking at those machines, you've gotta get your eyes on God. You cannot let this dictate what you're thinking about.'" The survival rate for one-pound babies was extremely low in the early 1980s.

Senator Chiles knew that staffer Bob Harris had been born premature. When Lawton IV was born prematurely, Senator Chiles called Harris, who remembers their conversation:

[Senator Chiles] told me that his grandson was premature. I told him the story of my being born premature, and I said, "It's so much better now, 'cause now they got incubators." When I was born, we didn't have incubators. ... We were on a farm in Knight's Station, and when the farm animals were born premature, my grandmother knew what to do. She kept their lungs clear and kept them warm. So she stayed up with me in front of the oven, and made sure that I stayed warm and that fluid didn't build up in my lungs [so] I wouldn't choke to death. [I told Senator Chiles], "That's what saved my life."

I said, "I think God understands and he replaces whatever physical shortcomings you have with a tremendous determination, 'cause I ran track at FAMU on the fastest relay team in the world, and yet had a doctor tell me that my lung capacity would never allow me to participate in athletics. So, he was wrong." ... And that's what I told Lawton. "Whatever they say about your grandson, they're probably wrong. And he can fill that void with determination."

Harris recalls of Chiles, "I always felt that when we would talk candidly about race, I could be absolutely more candid with him than I could with almost any other white person I knew."

Senator Chiles tried to scale up his famous face-to-face politicking skills to communicate the issue of early childhood care to the nation. He excelled at small group or one-on-one discussions with Floridians. "Chiles one-on-one is devastating" staffer Bob Harris said. To open conversations with constituents, Senator Chiles liked to retell an abridged version of Noah S. "Soggy" Sweat's "if by whisky" speech. Its moral: there are always at least two sides to an issue. Mississippi politico Sweat copyrighted the speech in 1952 because so many office-seekers added it to their stump without attribution. In an anthology of American oratory, political commentator William Safire once described the speech as "written to satirize the fine art of fence straddling, and should be delivered with a straight face above a firm jaw."[519] Sweat:

My friends, I had not intended to discuss this controversial subject at this particular time. However, I want you to know that I do not shun controversy. On the contrary, I will take a stand on any issue at any time, regardless of how fraught with controversy it might be. You have asked me how I feel about whisky. All right, here is how I feel about whisky.

If when you say "whisky" you mean the devil's brew, the poison scourge, the blood monster that defiles innocence, dethrones reason, destroys the home, creates misery and poverty, yea, literally takes the bread from the mouths of little children; if you mean the evil drink that topples the Christian man and woman from the pinnacle of righteous, gracious living into the bottomless pit of degradation, and despair, and shame, and helplessness, and hopelessness—then certainly I am against it.

But, if when you say "whisky" you mean the oil of conservation, the philosophic wine, the ale that is consumed when good fellows get together, that puts a song in their hearts and laughter on their lips, and the warm glow of contentment in their eyes; if you mean Christmas cheer; if you mean the stimulating drink that puts the spring into the old gentleman's step on a frosty, crispy morning; if you mean the drink that enables a man to magnify his joy, and his happiness, and to forget, if only for a little while, life's great tragedies, and heartaches, and sorrows; if you mean that drink the sale of which pours into our treasuries untold millions of dollars, which are used to provide tender care for our little crippled children, our blind, our deaf, our dumb, our pitiful aged and infirm; to build highways and hospitals and schools—then certainly I am for it.

This is my stand. I will not retreat from it. I will not compromise.[520]

Senator Chiles loved the well-told Southern tale. He also enjoyed a quick country quip. "Let that ox stay in the ditch," was one of his favorite expressions. Like the phrase "Let sleeping dogs lie," it meant that some political problems are best left alone. If Senator Chiles wanted to convey a sense of urgency about an issue to his staff, often he would warn them, "The cat's on the roof." More concisely than a fact sheet or memo, the phrase indicated that a crisis was at hand.

Florida constituents and staff saw Walkin' Lawton do his best politicking at campgrounds and barbecues. Soon after reelection to a second term, Senator Chiles and two aides had camped in a cabin on the Everglades. As they bedded down for the night, a rat ran through the cabin. One of the aides, raised in Fort Lauderdale, worried about the rodent. Legend holds that Senator Chiles told the aide not to fret, since the rats only wanted to nibble the wax out of his ears. Rats loved earwax, Senator Chiles explained, and stuffing one's ears with tissue would keep them out. So the three slept. The next morning, the Fort Lauderdale boy awoke refreshed, unmolested by rats. He removed the tissue from his ears and thanked Senator Chiles for the tip.[521]

Senator Chiles frequented central Florida's sweetest, spiciest, and most soulful barbecue joints. There he would talk football with fellow Gator fans. Dave Mica joined Senator Chiles' staff as central Florida district assistant, charged with organizing constituent support and casework for that region. He would work out of Lakeland from 1979 to 1984. Mica drove his boss when he visited central Florida, at the wheel of a Ford Pinto. The senator provided no reimbursement for mileage. "He was a fiscal conservative, some would say cheap." Mica: "We'd listen to it on the radio with as big an intent as the biggest redneck football fan on the planet." It was legal to contact a recruit, and Senator Chiles kept in touch with the Gator coaching staff and wrote letters and called to help them land the finest for football. Senator Chiles knew the central Florida back roads well. Once in a while he'd tell his driver, "go here, it's a shortcut." Dave Mica recounted standing in line with the senator one night at King's Taste Barbecue in Tavares, the Lake County seat. They got barbecue takeout. Mica: "it was so damn good. . . . We got a couple boxes of that and he chowed on that in the Pinto and we worked on that from there all the way back to Holmes Beach where the condo was." Senator Chiles took Dave Mica hunting: "He'd take me huntin' and he taught me how to basically hold a gun. . . . I was never anti-gun I was a city boy though. . . . I remember we went into a dove field once . . . he basically showed me how to do that, it was pretty funny they'd about land on my gun and I'd miss 'em."

Senator Chiles loved to visit Carl Allen's Cracker restaurant in Auburndale, near the senator's hometown. In a 1976 survey by the Florida Bicentennial Commission, the state voted Allen Florida's number one Cracker. His restaurant served, on tables that were once sowing machines, an array of traditional fare: rattlesnake, fried rabbit, armadillo, mullet, turtle, and catfish. "Most people don't know how to eat rattlesnake," Allen once said. "Got lots of bones, almost like a fish. Have to kind of pull the meat back off 'em. Good, though. Really good."[522]

The Senator would stop at Lakeland's Reececliff restaurant for homemade pie, or leave central Florida to visit the "Tampa Mafia" at the Tropicana Restaurant in Ybor City. There he'd drink Cuban coffee with the owner or watch the Bucanneer festival. As a Senate staffer, Debbie Kilmer sometimes acted as an advance person, locating eateries for the senator. Senator Chiles loved to ask her: "Ms. Debbie, what culinary delights do you have planned for me while we're here?" The Senator often had black beans from Versailles restaurant in Miami shipped up to him.

Senator Chiles also liked Peebles Barbecue of Auburndale, supposedly the best barbecue in Polk County. The joint only opened a few days a week and shut down during summer. It served the featured dish on paper plates in a screened building without air conditioning. "Enough of the staff had been there with him," Dave Mica said, "that whenever he was down there and we went to Peebles Barbecue I was under orders to get barbecue sauce to send back to staff in Washington."

Staffer Bob Harris drove his boss around Florida, too. "[Senator Chiles] was unabashedly the worst driver. He was totally oblivious to the fact. . . . I saw death about sixteen times." Harris did an impression of Claude Pepper, sometimes they would be riding in the car and Senator Chiles would say, "Do Pepper." Bob Harris drove Senator Chiles through Florida's Panhandle in the late 1970s. They often attended all-white social events; Harris called then, for unexplained reasons, "popcorn parties." One was a fish fry outside Fort Walton Beach, Harris recalls:

> The guy that drove us out there went in a pickup truck, the three of us in the front seat. Chiles was serving the food, as they did at the big fish fry. He and all the local politicians were behind the counter serving the people coming through, and they were shaking his hand. So we get back in the truck, and Chiles asked the guy that was driving us, "A lot of these people were giving me a funny handshake. They were slippin' their little finger between like this." The guy said, "Yeah, Lawton." So Chiles says, "At first I was just shaking their hand regularly, but then so many of them were doing it. I started doing it, too." The guy looked at me and said, "Ah, Lawton, that's the Klan handshake. They think you're a Klansman." And Chiles says, "Well, that oughta be worth a few votes in this area." He was totally unflappable, he was never flustered about anything.

Senator Chiles and Bob Harris noticed the dearth of black folks at Florida town hall meetings; so the office started scheduling meetings in the evening to make sure working class folks could attend. Bob Harris recalls another incident in north Florida while traveling with the senator:

We went to, I think it was Monticello, I'm not sure, it might have been Bay County. Lawton was famous for forgetting stuff. You had to make double copies of everything. So, we get ready, we are on the schedule that Charlie Canady has us on. And we had a breakfast, I believe it was the Rotary Club I'm not sure, in Monticello. Monticello is this little tiny town. So, what they did basically, was, at this restaurant, they pulled the curtain across the thing and everything that way was the Rotary Club meeting. So he forgot his comments. . . . I had no intentions of attending this thing 'cause I knew it was gonna be a popcorn party. So, I grab [the speech], run down to the place. And I'm walking in, and this guy steps in and he says, "You can't come in here." And I said, "I don't really want to come in here, but I have to deliver something." And he said, "Well, you go around to the back." And I said, "Okay."

I go around to the back, and Chiles sees me, from across the room where he's shaking hands and stuff—the program hasn't started. In about four steps, he's there. And he's between me and this guy, and he says, "Come on in, Robert," and he grabbed my elbow. And I said, "I don't wanna come in. This guy has told me I can't come in. So I just brought your comments over." Chiles says, "I want you to come in." And I said, "I don't want to come in." So, by this time the president of the organization splits for the door, too, and he says, "Lawton, do I know this gentleman?" And Chiles says, "Yeah, this is Robert Harris, he works for me." He said, "Well, come on in." And I said, "No, I can't come in. That guy said I can't come in." So the guy says, "I didn't know he worked for you, senator." So I told Chiles, "I'd rather not come in." Chiles says, "Well, I want you to come in," you know, real low. "Okay, fine."

So he pushes me, I make a left turn and go right to the kitchen. And I go in the kitchen where the black people are. And I said, "How are y'all doing? I'm Bob Harris, I work for Senator Chiles." And this one guy said, "Bob Harris, didn't you run track at Florida A&M?" I said, "Yeah." So we shake hands. And pretty soon Chiles walks in, he follows me in. He says, "I'm Senator Chiles." And he starts shaking hands. Pretty soon the Rotary Club president comes in, and we're darn near holdin' the meetin' in the kitchen. He just took all the steam out of the whole thing. It was great.

Staffer Damon Smith remembers well his first day working for Senator Chiles on the road in south Florida. Smith worked as south Florida district assistant from 1978 through the 1982 reelection campaign.

[Senator Chiles] was always tryin' to play these games and make you feel like he gotcha. I'll never forget, it was the first day workin' with him, and I picked him up at the Fort Lauderdale airport. And I had these instructions that we were to go up to West Palm Beach, and we were gonna have dinner with a friend of his. . . . We were to get up the next morning. [Chiles was going to deliver a speech to the Boca Raton Chamber of Commerce that morning.] I was obviously rather nervous—the first day on the job. And we got to the event fifteen minutes early, so he could meet and greet all these people. . . . Probably about five minutes before the breakfast was to begin, which was pretty early—I think it started at seven. He looks at me and he says, "Where's my speech?" And I said, "What speech?" He said, "The speech you're supposed to have for me. I'm supposed to give these people a speech." And I said, "Senator, nobody gave me a speech to bring for you, and I don't have it." He looks at me and says, "Well, you've got your yellow pad there. Why don't you write down some of the things you think these people would be interested in hearing, and put 'em down for me so I'll know what so say."

So I'm scramblin', I'm sittin' there and I'm nervous wreck and it's just not going well and I'm writin' these things down, and ballin' up these pieces of paper, startin' over again, and doin' all that stuff. Finally, he walks up to the podium and I'm sittin' on the front row and I'm still tryin' to scratch out the stuff and he looks over at me and he winks, and he stands up and he says, "Ladies and gentlemen, I purposely didn't bring a speech today because I wanted to hear what y'all had to say." Starts it out with a Q and A.

Anyway, he got me on the first day.

At constituent meetings in Florida, Senator Chiles leveraged his charisma and Cracker culture more than his policy platform. He knew that his children's advocacy, measured in additional funding, would antagonize the Panhandle and the rest of rural Florida.

When Senator Chiles spoke to larger crowds, he fidgeted sometimes. Staffer Dave Mica: "I tried to break him of it; I don't know that I ever succeeded. . . . .When he was in a big group sometimes he would put his hand in his pocket—he never carried much money he always asked you for that, and then he carried either an American Express or Diner's Club and most of the time nobody took that, but he also had change in there and he'd jingle the change when he'd be talkin'." South Florida district assistant Damon Smith concurred with Dave Mica: "We often said that on a one-on-one, there was probably nobody better than he. But put him in front of a crowd of a thousand people to make a speech, and a lot of times he'd bomb."

As early as 1979, Senator Chiles doubted the purpose of a third Senate term. Even after the Government in the Sunshine Law mandated a transparent committee process, the U.S. Senate preferred to build a federal budget ad hoc, project by project and senator by senator. Senator Chiles felt alone in the fight for budget discipline, but he knew it was the key to freeing funds for children's health care and preserving Social Security and Medicare. During the Carter administration gas shortage, old friend Florida State Senator Ken Plante traveled to D.C. to meet the Florida congressional delegation:

> We talked and [Senator Chiles] began to tell me what a terrible shape the federal government was in financially. And that it was out of control. And he did not know how to get it under control. And that he truly felt that as radical as this sounds, that it almost would take the government collapsing and enough conservatives like himself, both Democratic and Republican around, to take it and bring it back together again. . . . That was very frightening, if Lawton felt that strongly. And I'm sure that he didn't really mean for the government to collapse, but out of frustration he did not know what else to do.

Senator Chiles chafed at reporters' attempts to label him as liberal, conservative, or independent. He described his style as "one of a journeyman. You put a brick today, another one the next day, and soon you have a wall. I think it's important that you work on something every day. . . . When I've been successful, that's how it has been done."

Since January 1981, the senator had introduced 27 bills and cosponsored 196 more. Of the 27 homegrown bills, 3 passed the Senate. According to Chiles, his proudest, most accomplished legislation was a series of amendments patched onto other bills. "When I first came here I wanted to be a gen-

166

eralist." He said. "I had walked the state and had a bushel basket of bills I wanted to introduce, but I found you have to learn your subject area so people have confidence in you and follow your lead. . . . For instance, I talked about sunshine (openness) in government so much that people started calling me the Sunshine Kid."

Once he resolved to run again, Senator Chiles searched for the means to recast the spell of the Walk on Florida. At first, Senator Chiles wanted to run his second re-election campaign without any contributions.[523] He contemplated whether to raise his $10 limit on contributions to $100 or even $200.

A reporter once asked Senator Chiles if he had decided yet on a limit. The politician responded first by rubbing his belly. "I have this friend," Senator Chiles said, patting his gut. "When I listen to it, I do better than when I don't. I haven't heard from it. I've called it a couple of times, and it said, 'Don't call me, I'll call you.'"

Bud and Ed pushed their father to raise the limit higher. Lawton settled on $100. Senator Sam Nunn:"When pressured by well-meaning friends to lift his self-imposed limit on contributions, Lawton quietly replied, 'I've learned from Samson and Delilah. I can't let you cut off my hair.'"[524] Even with a $100-per-person cap, finances were tight. Dave Mica recalls working for the 1982 U.S. Senate Chiles campaign for about $12,000 a year. Damon Smith put the figure at $16,000. To cut costs, Charlie Canady used campaign volunteers to run presses and print and deliver 100,000 yard signs. Dave Mica:

> So, I'll never forget this—I had to find some volunteers to do it. We set up strategic drop points all over the state. I managed to get Charlie to allow me to rent a truck, whoever we got to drive it. . . . You can't imagine non-printers working at a print shop doing silk screen. . . . It took us weeks and weeks to get 'em done. . . . The damn kid who was driving the truck told me afterwards they shifted one time in the truck and they shifted over and almost flipped the truck. He said, "I was up on two wheels, I was in Bonifay, I knew I would be dead and the boss would lose all his signs, and somehow God made it come back down and it bounced up on the other side!"

Damon Smith recalls the 1982 federal campaign contribution limit as $1,000 per person. Smith comments on bundling: "There might have been some bundling that went on. But nobody ever violated any federal law. It was no more bundling than if somebody had three children and a wife, and they ended up giving $500 in $100 [parts] instead of $1,000. I don't think that anybody ever got to the point where it was of any significance."

Chiles announced at the end of a two-week, twenty-four-county campaign trip in August 1981, "I always run scared. I'm scared to death."[525] To leverage his small money politics, Senator Chiles replicated the feast for the common man he first showcased in the 1970 campaign outside Miami's Fontainebleau Hotel. In late October 1982, the Chiles for Senate campaign held a dollar-a-box chicken feast at Miami's Grapeland Heights Park less than a mile from the Marriot Hotel where Republicans held a $500-a-couple fundraiser for Van Poole, hosted by Vice President George H. W. Bush. At the park, Senator Chiles commented before a bank of three TV crews and seven newspaper reporters, "I can't believe that they're doing it again." Walter Atkinson, retired Eastern Air Lines mechanic, munched a box of chicken in the park. "I guess it was the smartest move he pulled in that campaign," Atkinson said. "I thought [Chiles' 1970 general election opponent, GOP Congressman] Cramer had it; a lot of people thought that Cramer had it. It was such a great gimmick."[526]

Senator Chiles compared his Republican opponent Van Poole's predicament to that of a husband and wife dressed as the rear and front of a cow for a costume party, who spook a grazing bull on their way to the event. The husband wonders aloud what to do about the approaching bull, and his wife says, "I don't know what you're going to do, sweetie. I'm gonna eat grass. Maybe you'd better brace yourself." Chiles added, "I want to say to Mr. Poole, 'Hitch up, Van, and brace yourself, because I think it's going to be an interesting race.'"[527]

Before the campaign's victorious end though, in August 1982, Lawton's sister Jeanette Chiles Ruthven died of a stroke at the age of fifty-five. She had suffered a stroke three and a half years earlier that had partially paralyzed her. Joe P. Ruthven: "the doctors said she wasn't supposed to ever get out of bed again. But she had a lot of courage and determination, and had gotten to the point where she could drive a car again."[528] Kay Hagan: "The Ruthvens called Uncle Bud, 'Uncle Bud.' Bud, Tandy, etc., would call my mother Aunt J. J." Jeanette was visiting Kay in Bedford, Virginia in March of 1979 or 1980 when she suffered her first stroke. Kay Hagan describes Lawton and Jeanette's relationship:

> I can remember Uncle Bud—after my immediate family—was one the first people I got up with. And I don't remember if I got up with

him or if Joe Lawton did, but he and Aunt Rhea both came to the hospital, I think, the very next day. And I think there was this huge discussion because he was missing a very important vote here, and he chose to miss that vote and come by. I can remember him being at the bedside. At that point we had no idea what her outcome was.

Lawton's sister Jeanette suffered a stroke. Ann Miller recalls Jeanette and Lawton relating "very well." Ann does not recall ever seeing Jeanette smoke. People knew Jeanette as "J.J." Jeannette Chiles was born February 18, 1927, and died of heart disease August 20, 1982.[529] Chiles Senate staffer Debbie Kilmer's father suffered a stroke:

My father had a stroke when we were working in the Senate, and was quite bad off, in Idaho . . . just his sensitivity in coaching me, because his sister had gone through a stroke. Both he and Rhea. . . . Both of them are very interested in medicine. . . . When it came to that stroke, it was amazing how the two of them taught me about the brain, and which side was affected and all this.

Kitty Chiles: "When J.J. died, Jeanette, that was huge. She was so young. And [she and Senator Chiles] were so close. She was such a part of the family."

Senator Chiles told the press at his victory party at a Lakeland country club that he and his wife were headed for "the deep woods" before they returned to Washington.[530] He had thinking to do.

9

A Walk Unfinished

On a typical day in the middle his third term, U.S. Senator Lawton Chiles awoke at 6:00 a.m., dressed and showered, and left for work at 6:45 a.m. Senator Rick Brandon, staff director of the Budget Committee, called at 7:05 a.m. to run down the agenda for the White House budget summit. At an 8:00 a.m. budget summit, Senator Chiles joined a bloc of other senators on the Budget Committee to hear White House Chief of Staff Jim Baker lecture them on the president's defense spending priorities. President Ronald Reagan appeared at the end to speak briefly.

At his personal office, Senator Chiles met with chief of staff Rick Farrell to discuss the day's agenda. The senator settled on the last item on the blue schedule card that Farrell handed him, a 5:00 p.m. departure from Dulles Airport for Tampa, Florida. "Where is *my* agenda?" he asked Farrell, holding a blue card that listed his appointments hour by hour, including lunch. Senator Chiles reasserted, "Here are all the things that you want me to do, but where is there space on here for what Lawton wants to do?"[531] They both shrugged and continued hashing out the day's Capitol Hill activities. Another aide interrupted them to remind Senator Chiles of his floor speech on budget restraint. Senator Chiles got up, waited for an aide to hand him his speech, and head out for a ten-minute speech on the need for adherence to federal budget targets in spite of Reagan Administration defense spending imperatives and Social Security costs.

After the speech, Senator Chiles met with Budget Committee staff to discuss the White House summit. Then he called Jim Baker to discuss the summit and an upcoming turkey hunt in Texas. Aside from a chance encounter with Senator Sam Nunn in the hallway, Senator Chiles counted the rest of the day's minutes until a car picked him up to take him to Dulles Airport. Senator Chiles dozed the moment he climbed into the car. His driver smiled. Staffer and sometime driver Dave Mica recalls, "To this day Lawton Chiles was the only guy who could get on a helicopter and when he needed some rest he could fall asleep in a helicopter. It was unbelievable." Senator Chiles slept to escape the current day, not to prepare for the next. Or, he tried to sleep and failed.

Senator Chiles worked frenetic hours to amplify the tremendous official power at his disposal since becoming ranking member on the Senate Budget Committee at the start of his third term. "It's kind of like jumping on the back of a tiger," Senator Chiles said of the promotion. He hoped for a "bipartisan approach" to the Budget Committee process. Under Senate rules, the new position gave Chiles control of the fifteen-member Minority Committee staff. "For the first time, I'll now have the ability to hire an expert on foreign policy, hire an expert in defense spending, and have people of my own who can answer my questions," Chiles said.[532] Colleague and friend Senator Pete Domenici (R-NM) describes Senator Chiles as "front and center when it came to controlling our spending." Senator Domenici adds, "He knew the deficit could not continue to add to the debt in the proportions that it was. But Congress was not ready to come to grips with it."[533] Social Security, Medicare, and Senator Chiles' ambitions for children's health care depended on federal budget discipline—especially deficit reduction. "'I characterize the deficit as a Pacman," Senator Chiles said, referring to the video game. "It's eating everything else. . . . But nobody seems to appreciate that, least of all the president."[534] Chiles' colleague Senator David Durenburger (R-MN) explains the pressure on senators:

> You are important if you are in demand. You work hard to prove how valuable you are. It's a volume-oriented kind of operation: the more hands you shake, the more letters you write, the more times you appear on TV, the more hearings you hold, the more valuable you are. Somehow quality is subsumed by quantity.[535]

Still, the federal budget thwarted Senator Chiles' every attempt at reform, according to his staffer Bob Harris:

He told a story on the Senate floor. This is typical Chiles. His budget proposal was being hammered by the liberals and the conservatives. He said, "This reminds me of the boy who is given the job to go clean out the outhouse. And then when he comes in to dinner, nobody wants to sit next to him."

Senators Domenici, Sam Nunn (D-GA), Mark Hatfield (R-OR), and Dewey Bartlett (R-OK), as well as U.S. Congressman Buddy MacKay (D-FL), were Chiles allies. Representative MacKay, although a freshman, knew the frustrations of budget reform:

One of the first lessons I learned in Congress was how to count. The incident that led to his insight is still fresh in my mind. In early March 1983, my chief of staff, Greg Farmer, my colleague, Congressman Tim Penny, and I had undertaken to host an organizational meetings of the Class of '82 Budget Group. To assure a good crowd, I had agreed to provide pizza and beer. Between us, we had personally contacted all fifty-two Democrats in our class. The response had been enthusiastic. "I'll try to come," "I'll put it on the schedule," and "I'm glad you're doing this" were the most common responses. Encouraged, we had decided we would probably have at least forty in attendance. That translated into 120 cans of beer and twenty pizzas, paid for out of my own pocket. At the appointed time, Tim, Greg, and I found ourselves alone in the room, with the exception of one colleague, Jim Moody, a member of Congress from Wisconsin. Jim said he didn't think our ideas for budget reform were realistic. He had come for the pizza, beer, and fellowship.[536]

Senator Chiles responded to the initial losses in the budget debates by recommitment and escalation. He won national recognition for his first-ever filibuster in summer 1984, when he stalled a vote on federal agriculture spending for a week. The farm bill's appropriations were passing under the waivers of the 1974 Budget Act, in violation of the spirit of the deficit control law. "We're seeing restraint go out the window," Senator Chiles said. "There would be no reason to be chairman of the committee if the budget were waived every week."

"I'm really enjoying it," he said in autumn 1984, despite Reagan's landslide re-election. "I'm happier in the Senate than I've ever been."[537] That December, he challenged his chief Democratic opponent on budget policy, Senator Robert Byrd (D-WV), for the post of minority leader, and lost grandly. He announced his campaign against Senator Byrd one week before the secret ballot caucus on the issue. "You can only circle your wagons so long," Senator Chiles said. "At some point you have to say you're going to hitch up the team and move out. What I'm saying is now is the time."[538] But Senator Byrd threatened to retaliate from his post on the Senate Appropriations Committee and trounced his challenger thirty-six to eleven.[539] Although most acknowledged that Senator Chiles had poorly planned the campaign, staffer Bob Harris claimed regardless that "the merits didn't count" in the race. Rep. Buddy MacKay recalls the animosity between Senator Chiles and Senator Byrd:

Lawton told me at one time, that he had something of importance in his freshman term, perhaps early in his freshman term, and Byrd put a hold on it—didn't even tell him he'd done it. And so when he found out, instead of confronting Byrd, he found something that Byrd wanted and put a hold on that. And Byrd was astounded that a freshman would stand up to him. So anyway, it didn't start off well.

Rhea Chiles said the Democratic caucus "were like kids, the senators were, behind [Senator Byrd's] back, passing notes, laughing and carrying on." Colleagues mocked Senator Byrd's fixation on the finest of parliamentary procedures. To his face, however, Democratic senators hung on his every word—especially as it related to money. "They just knew that he was the kind of guy that never forgot, never forgave, and he was in a position to retaliate, which he did," Senator Chiles' eldest son, Bud, explains. Senator Byrd maintained files detailing daily quid pro quo, according to Chiles' chief of staff Rick Farrell. "[Senator] Robert Byrd kept score. He knew everything he did for every senator. He kept little blue cards, and when he wanted something, he'd almost pull them out and remind [a senator, for instance,] 'You know, Lawton, when you needed more office space we took care of you' . . . even the little stuff."

Senator Chiles, however, had no appetite for political retribution. Chiles staffer Carol Browner observed that Senator Byrd "could tell you every person who ever voted against him on something. That's not Chiles."

"All you've got is your reputation," Senator Chiles would tell his staff. He preferred honey to vinegar in negotiations with fellow members, mindful that his opponent today might be his ally tomorrow. While Senator Byrd won the day through Machiavellian tactics, Senator Chiles preferred the works of American philosopher Ralph Waldo Emerson as templates for political ethics. The senator especially favored the Emerson essay "Circles," which proclaims that "there is no end in nature, but every end is a beginning." Nature, Emerson suggests, is comprised of concentric circles and shares the properties of circles. In a political context, Senator Chiles interpreted this ethic as a form of karma—a comforting maxim of justice. Every failure on the floor of the legislature, according to "Circles," contained elements of the next success.

The magnitude of Senator Chiles' December 1984 defeat proved the practical limations of an Emersonian ethic. Senator Chiles' only solace may have been the knowledge that his bout against Senator Byrd had loosened the West Virginian's grip on power. When Senator Byrd ran for Senate majority leader in 1988 he lost to Maine Senate George J. Mitchell.

At the White House, Senator Chiles met the same intransigence as he did in Congress. Chief of Staff Jim Baker and the rest of the presidential budget staff tacitly agreed to budget targets but ignored them in practice. Senator Chiles questioned President Ronald Reagan's qualifications and his budget, according to staffer Damon Smith:

> I'll never forget, we were in Miami and Lawton was in the Senate, in Washington, and walked out of a committee meeting. . . . We invaded Granada, I don't know, three or four months after the Marines had been blown up in Lebanon, and we'd lost that—that was the first car bombing. And Lawton had this microphone shoved in his face: "What's your take on the invasion of Granada?" And, regrettably so, he quipped back, "I guess Reagan's finally found a war he can win." Which immediately became just incendiary across the state, amongst the veteran's populations and everybody else. And we were in the ditch in a big way because it didn't take twenty-four hours for us to see these editorials just shaming that whole process.

Rob Evans, a Chiles activist in Orlando, later recalled a conversation with Senator Chiles about Vice President George H. W. Bush:

> One time I asked him about how well he knew George Bush. He said, "Well, Rob, George Bush is a very proper person." I said, "What

do you mean, proper?" He thought for a minute, and he said, "Well, he's sorta the kind o' guy that would step out of the shower to urinate." And I thought that was kinda funny.

Less than a year after losing the race for minority leader, Senator Chiles lost his most faithful political champion—his mother. Margaret Patterson Chiles died in August 1985 of a heart attack at the age of 84.

Senator Chiles released a public statement: "She was a great lady, a very strong, independent person. She just wanted her individual freedom, wanted to live in her own house."

Like his mother, Senator Chiles valued the privacy of his emotional life. Lawton's daughter-in-law Kitty Chiles speculated that icebox cookies and other Southern cuisine was the "love language" between the mother and son. Staffer Dave Mica recalled visiting Margaret frequently during Senator Chiles' central Florida field trips:

> He loved spending time with his mom. I remember Election Day of his last election, we stopped by and he was gonna spend a little time with his mom. . . . I was waiting outside . . . making notes . . . playing around with a little pepper plant that he had out back, and I touched my eyes. And he wanted to know why I was crying. . . . He ragged me the whole afternoon about that.

Kay Ruthven, Lawton's niece, recalls Margaret's delight in advertising Lawton's political career, even abroad:

> When I graduated from undergraduate school at Florida State, and before I went to law school, grandmother Chiles and I went to Europe together. She had never been to Europe; she was seventy years old. And I had been to school in London, and I thought grandmother would love to go travel Europe. So the two of us, just the two of us, went over there, and we spent a lot of time by train. And she had this "Lawton Chiles for U.S. Senate" button, which was not your typical campaign button. It was five inches, six inches, and her routine was that, no matter who we were sitting next to, that button would accidentally fall out of her pocket book and she would pick it up—and there's no way you can miss it. Then she would proceed to tell whomever we were sitting next to, that her son was a U.S. sena-

tor. And I bet I heard her tell that story, if not ten times a day, three times a day, as we were traveling throughout Europe. So she was very proud.

At Margaret's private graveside service, Rhea told the children that "they've got lots of Margaret in their genes." Rhea recalled the departed's "tremendous energy, high idle," and suspected "that's where Lawton got his dash, his rash commitment to 'let's do it.'" This dynamo, Rhea added, "could be used for good or bad."

Margaret Chiles always said she admired politicians with stalwart values: "I don't expect a politician to vote the way I want all the time. I don't think anybody really expects that. Just don't straddle the fence. If you're scared, you're through. It's like getting in the car with somebody who goes the wrong way around Lake Mirror and then makes a couple other mistakes. You're through . . . you won't ride with that person again."

Still mourning his mother's death, Senator Chiles underwent heart bypass surgery in December 1985 at a hospital in Lakeland, Florida. That May, he had complained of chest tightness while carrying suitcases up two flights of stairs at Hilton Head, South Carolina.[540] He seemed to recovery quickly from surgery. "I was surprised," related friend and attorney Burke Kibler, "I went up to the room and he was sitting in a chair . . . less than twenty-four hours after surgery."[541] Tandy Chiles remembers the first thing her father said post-surgery:"They didn't put any Seminole [mascot of Florida State University, chief rival of University of Florida's Gators] blood in me, did they?" Senator Ted Kennedy sent his colleague a leather-bound volume of hunting stories.

Within a few weeks, Senator Chiles was hunting again. Doctors advised him to adhere to a low-cholesterol, low-salt diet and heed his family history of heart disease. Eldest son Bud Chiles recognized the danger in his father's Southern diet: "fried mullet, fried oysters, fried shrimp, fried chicken, and barbecue." Tandy Chiles recounted the doctors telling him "not to eat anything with a face or a tail." Senator Chiles began walking several miles a day and drinking wine in moderation. "You have to take the bitter with the sweet," he told reporters.[542] Burke Kibler: "My sense is that [the surgery] made a great impact on Lawton and Lawton's feelings about his Maker."

The depression that afflicted Senator Chiles post-surgery surprised him and his family. Kitty Chiles: "I don't think anybody [expected it]. They sure didn't tell him that. In hindsight he said he never would have done it, but I think he [still] would have [knowing the possibility of complications afterward]." In January 1986, Senator Chiles complained he had lost his appetite for food and for sleep. Tandy discussed her father's post-surgery blues:

> He didn't know it was gonna happen. If they did talk to him about it, he didn't hear 'em. . . . It left him feeling very vulnerable. . . . Once he got over the raggedness of it, the raw emotions of it, then he was able to use it. . . . It threw him, it took time to go through. He didn't wanna spend the time, and he didn't wanna spend the effort doing it, but he realized once he did, he got stronger for it.

Senator Chiles sought fellowship in a Senate prayer group, which met every Wednesday and included Senator Sam Nunn, Senator Pete Domenici, Senator Mark Hatfield, Senator Dewey Bartlett, and the Senate Chaplain, Dick Halvor. Senator Nunn describes the group:

> It was a remarkable hour: we'd talk about family, we'd talk about faith, we'd talk about the Senate challenges, we'd talk about things happening back in our state, and we'd share our frustrations with how much partisan politics there was. . . . We had faith in each other, and we shared things in complete openness with each other that we had total confidence were not gonna go beyond the room. . . . So it was quite unusual, very quiet, nobody knew about it. . . . We weren't trying to a keep it great secret, we just operated that way.

Senator Chiles also opened up emotionally to his family like never before, according to eldest son Bud Chiles:

> I remember the letters and notes he would write us. This totally blew our minds when he started writing down his feelings about his family and his friends. He started hugging and he even kissed us when we saw him. He began to talk about what he was feeling and going through.

Senator Chiles wrote Bud and his wife Kitty a three-page letter describing his search for God, the longest letter Bud ever received from his father. "It was him sharing his faith, which was very sincere and very heartfelt," Kitty related, "It had a big effect on both of us."

Senator Chiles reached the pinnacle of Senate budget leadership in November 1986 when the Democrats retook the U.S. Senate and he became chairman of the Senate Budget Committee. He had kicked his post-surgery blues and attacked the job with vigor, guile and joy. On Election Day 1986, reporter Bill Rufty saw Senator Chiles in top form—he was Walkin' Lawton again. Senator Chiles and Rufty ran into famous Florida Cracker Carl Allen outside the *Lakeland Ledger* building after an editorial board meeting. Rufty watched how Senator Chiles seemed to transform as he chatted with Allen. His shoulders drooped, he put his hands in his pockets, and he looked bow-legged like a Cracker caricature.[543]

Staffer Dean Saunders remembers that Senator Chiles would say, "It's a sorry frog that won't croak in his own pond." The expression meant, according to Saunders, "If you've got an idea, share it with me, and don't hold back."[544] Saunders travelled with his boss around central Florida:

I can remember we'd be going from point A to point B, and I'd be taking him home or something and he'd say, "Hey, pull in here, this sporting goods store, I gotta get some shotgun shells." And invariably, I can remember, we'd get up to the counter, he'd kinda look at you, and he'd sorta put his hands on his pocket, and he'd say, "I don't have my wallet. Hey, can you float me a loan?"

Saunders learned what he called the "Seven P's" from his boss:

My first traveling assignment with him, I'll never forget. We were going to [*Q-Zoo in the Morning,* a radio show]. Now, *Q-Zoo in the Morning* was a rather, at the time, edgy, funny sort of talk kinda deal. But it was on a very popular radio station and *Q-Zoo in the Morning* had a lot of following in the Tampa market. . . . So that was my first assignment. I was gonna go pick him up at Louis de la Parte's house. Now, Louis de la Parte was a former state senator he was staying with. So I had my route all mapped out. And Charlie Canady is going with us. I think he's meeting us at Louis's house or something.

So I pick the Senator up, and I've got my route mapped out . . . going 275. The Senator says, "Dean, don't you think it'd be faster to go down Mabry?" Which terrifies me . . . I didn't know all the back roads and stuff, and didn't know Tampa like I knew Orlando. . . . Charlie is an extremely type-A, control freak personality. . . . The road dead-ends at the interstate ... so the radio station is on the other side. ... We're probably about ten minutes late, that's my job, for him never to be late. ...

Somewhere in the conversation [the Senator] says, "Dean, did I ever tell you the story about my captain in the Army?"

"No, Senator, what's that?"

"He used to tell me about the seven P's. Prior proper planning prevents piss-poor performance."

"[Yes], sir, I got it."

That's all he said, he never fussed. From then on, I knew, you call ... you plan for all those contingencies. ... So, that didn't happen again. But it was funny, 'cause I would say to the younger guys, "You gotten the seven P's yet?"

Dean Saunders admired Senator Chiles' ability to smoothly defuse tense situations with humor.

Senator Chiles attended the second White House budget summit convened by President Reagan. The White House, however, again ignored Senator Chiles' call for budget discipline. Chiles Budget Committee staffer Rick Brandon: "There was a sense that President Reagan was out of touch, depended totally on his advisors, and didn't know what was going on, and didn't care enough to find out." Brandon added: "When senators would raise substantive points to him, he would tell them anecdotes or read prepared points off his three-by-five cards that weren't really to the point." Chiles chief of staff Rick Farrell:

The Reagan Administration was just trying to funnel ungodly amounts of money in defense spending, so they were all for violating the budget when it came to that. To them it was useful when it came to health care spending or helping poor people, then they'd be like "Oh my god, the budget doesn't provide for that." When it came to what they wanted, they had no adherence to it at all.

Fellow Democrats in Congress scoffed at Senator Chiles' passion for deficit reduction. "Well, [Senator Chiles] was dedicated and conscientious," Senator Sam Nunn said, "and with most other people, or a large number of people, it was all a game."[545] The bullwhip of the Budget Committee was to be the budget resolution, which set spending levels for the biggest priorities like military, health care, and education. The budget resolution was supposedly the Congress' first defense against deficits. Senator Chiles called the Budget Committee the "best poker game in town" because of its theoretical focus on bipartisan, face-to-face negotiation. "That man could listen to what was going on in a room with seven senses," Budget Committee staff director Rick Brandon says of Senator Chiles' skill bargaining. "He could just sniff out where other people were coming from."[546] Senator Chiles proposed compromises that combined tax hikes with cuts in defense and Social Security.

Senators circumvented the budget resolutions though. Continuing resolutions, once anomalies, became the norm. The powerful Senate hierarchy that Senator Chiles once respected, led by the likes of Lyndon Johnson and Mike Mansfield, had devolved into a loose, diffuse mess. Senators no longer pursued areas of expertise; instead, they pursued media celebrity as the key to policy influence. Bud Chiles:

> And the Senate had gone from the Mike Mansfields to the independent stars that were all like the NBA. Everybody had their own little media circus that they ran, and the money. It would come with the money. And so the Senate went from a place where issues really got debated and done like we saw with Muskie and the Clean Air and Clean Water bill in '72, to a place where not much got done really.

Greg Ruthven Sr., Lawton's nephew, remembers his uncle's amazement at the "elasticity" of the federal budget. In 1985, Congress passed the Balanced Budget and Emergency Deficit Control Act, which built a roadmap for deficit control. Two years later, however, Congress extended the deadline for the deficit cap. "He thought he was just chicken little," Bud Chiles says of his father. "The sky is falling, the sky is falling and nobody is listening." Senator Chiles' personal staff and Budget Committee staff clashed, dimming reform prospects further. "[Senator Chiles] just wanted it to be over," chief of staff Rick Farrell said. "And he knew it was a failing on his part. He didn't like doing [personnel management] and wasn't very good at it."

At the mercy of Congress and the White House, Senator Chiles noticed that he was ending and beginning his days depressed and exhausted. He felt wounded and raw. Senator Chiles compared federal budget deliberations to churning butter: "the harder you churn, the harder it gets."[547] He found himself disgusted with Washington, D.C. Staffer Bob Harris sympathized:

D.C. was like a stage. And when you did get forced to go to some of these things, people walked up to you and said, what do you do? And I'd say, Bob Harris, my name is Bob Harris. They didn't care about your name, they wanted to know what you do before they asked you your name.

Anxiety ultimately drained every hour of his day. Senator Chiles, according to wife Rhea, "broke his pick" while battling the deficit. He "used up what he had and went bare rim on the highway."

"[My depression] would always start with an inability to sleep at night," Senator Chiles said. "After a couple of nights, I'd start worrying about not being able to get any rest, then I would spiral down from there."[548] His stressed stomach would reject food. He would fight the budget fight on the Senate floor, return home, and continue to work the issue in his mind. Guilt wracked his conscience. "Small things that bothered you before become very, very large. You begin to wonder what you've done wrong. It becomes a more constant thing."[549]

Neither family nor staff could pinpoint exactly when this depression began. "Belatedly I found out that he was having trouble sleeping, he was having stomach [problems]," press secretary Jack Pridgen later recalled. Pridgen said of his boss, "He's a pretty even-tempered kind of guy. His innards aren't readily identifiable."[550]

Senator Chiles hid personal issues from staff, according to chief of staff Rick Farrell:

> He would convey unhappiness or displeasure mostly with silence or a look, rarely dress somebody down. When he did, it was done in a very quiet sort of way; people would come out of his office in tears, and you're like "What did he say?" and they'd say, "Well, he didn't really say anything, but I could tell he was really, really mad and unhappy with what I did." He [would] get over it—he wouldn't hold a grudge. . . . It was years before I felt comfortable talking to him about anything but strictly Senate business, and he didn't particularly encourage [off-the-cuff conversation]. It was like, "We're here to work."

The Senator's eldest son Bud noticed something amiss before the staff did:

This struggle heated up inside him by the mid-eighties and led to what he called "the blacks," a struggle with depression. The Senate was not what he dreamed it would be. The more powerful he became, the more disillusioned he grew. He started in the U.S. senate at the very bottom rung of seniority, number 100. He had a staff of about twenty souls. By the time he left Washington he chaired the Budget Committee, he chaired the largest and most important sub-committee on Appropriations, and he had about 300 people working for him. He was one of the Cardinals who ran the Senate. But he wanted the Senate to do something about budget deficits and trade imbalances, and to spend more and focus more on early childhood development. He was greatly frustrated by the Reagan military spending juggernaut. And the lack of will on the part of the White House and Congress to bring spending under control.

Senator Chiles still worked a full day while depressed. "In retrospect," ranking Budget Committee member Senator Pete Domenici said, "he would come to meetings a little more at the last minute and then say he would have to leave very, very quickly. I thought he had too much to do. But it could very well have been some kind of malaise setting in."[551] Budget Committee Staff Director Rick Brandon later recalled that "his level of disengagement, or his lower level of engagement, was clear to me." In hindsight, chief of staff Rick Farrell remarked that "he just didn't seem himself; he didn't seem the normal kind of person he'd been over the years." But most staffers kept to their work and ignored the senator's mood. Senator Chiles hid the worst of his anxieties from colleagues and staff. "They all knew I was frustrated," he reflected afterward. "You think, maybe they're as bad off as I am. Who am I to cry to them?'"

Senator Chiles recalled his policy predicament in the Senate. "Here I was, chairman of the Senate Budget Committee with oversight of a $1 trillion budget, here I was with eighteen years of seniority and friends in high places—and I was standing before the National Press Club pleading for someone—anyone—to take on the infant mortality issue and find a way to come up with $1 billion to provide universal access to health care for pregnant mothers. You'd think that all I [would have] to do was go on the Senate floor, hold up the report that says that 40,000 infants are dying and that if you spend [a] $1 billion budget you can slow down this fast track to the morgue. You'd think there would have been a stampede to pass the Healthy Birth Act."

Rhea believed her husband wanted to quit politics, but "didn't want to pull the trigger." Senator Chiles decided to take the question to the people. He began walking across Florida again during autumn of 1987, starting in the Panhandle. Son Ed Chiles, who joined his father for some of the walk, called the process "tough to watch." Bud Chiles concurred:

> He'd gone out on the Walk and he went out to west Florida trying to relight the candle. And it basically didn't do it for him. And he was just cooked. He was just stunned. He was in bad shape. . . . I saw him some on that trip when he was out in west Florida. He didn't look good, didn't feel good.

Senator Chiles noted during the walk, "It began to dawn on me that something was wrong inside me. What I sensed was for the first time I wasn't enjoying talking to people."[552]

"It's the will that's missing," Senator Chiles said, announcing his retirement in December 1987. "We keep thinking that we can come up with a process that will supplement the will. It hasn't happened. Nothing supplements the will, and we have not been able, collectively, the president and the Congress, to supply the will."[553] He called the previous year "horrendous."[554] Son Bud Chiles and other family members welcomed the decision. "I admired him for quitting the Senate," Bud said. "It is hard to walk away from all that power and all that celebrity." Staff reacted with a mix of shock, understanding, and bitterness, according to chief of staff Rick Farrell:

> I think everybody was shocked, because there was nothing, nothing on the surface. We were actively working on a re-election campaign, we were doing things, and we were planning. I was going to meetings of the Democratic Senatorial Campaign Committee. I was involved in a lot of things for the re-election, so to be told over the weekend, "Oh, by the way, I'm not running" . . . was very upsetting. . . . There are people's jobs at stake, for one thing, but more than that, a lot of people had been with him a long time. All this depression stuff didn't come out till later, so . . . it didn't make sense. Why? [He was] a relatively young man and there was no reason to think he wouldn't be re-elected. It might be a tough race, but his numbers were good, he was

popular. He was coming into his own as a senator in terms of seniority. We talk about him being chairman of the Budget Committee, which is a significant post, but he was also chairman of the Labor HHS Appropriations Subcommittee, which funds health for the government. He was a powerful senator. Why would you walk away from that?

Future Florida House Speaker T.K. Wetherell, a Florida House member at the time of Senator Chiles' retirement, reflected on the decision:

> There were some people that were pretty upset with Lawton. Basically, he just found his inner voice and said, "I'm leavin'." He was one of the most powerful politicians in the world. He controlled all the damn money. And if you wanted something, you had to go see Lawton Chiles. I don't care whether it was a military base or a bucket o' sand.

Dr. Charles Mahan, one of Senator Chiles' allies on children's health care, recalls his colleague's fatigue with Washington:

> He had gotten everything squared away with the budget. He got everybody on the committee to promise not to put any turkeys in the budget, earmarks. . . . At the last minute, when it got on the floor, they all started doing it. And he said, "I was never so disappointed with a group of people in my whole life. I just couldn't get over it."

10

This Time the People Won

"I have no burning desire to do anything," Lawton Chiles said in 1988, just before retiring to Tallahassee, Florida. "But at the same time I don't know why I should be called upon to say I ain't never going to run for anything again."555

The political class in Washington and Florida expected no more campaigns from Chiles. The October 1988 death of his good friend from law school, former Florida attorney Jimmy Kynes, was the final milestone in a dark year.

Far from Washington, Chiles' stress level plummeted, but depression still dogged him. Doug Cook, a longtime friend and staffer, explains:

> His depression . . . was not simply caused by a chemical imbalance, but [was caused] by a frustration and disappointment with himself and his times. He wanted to be a better husband, a better father, a better friend, and a better public servant leader. He loved Native American folklore and he would often state that a great chief would "stake himself out and challenge his adversary to come to him."

"It was scary for him," eldest son Bud Chiles says of his father's mental illness, "and scary for me to watch him go through it."

Bud devised stratagems to try to reanimate his father. Friend and Lakeland attorney Burke Kibler tried to persuade Lawton to join him at his law firm Holland & Knight.556 The Chiles family invited Rick Farrell, former chief of staff of his Senate personal office, to come down to Florida for what was ostensibly a business meeting about children's health care. Farrell describes the reality:

As it turned out, that was just a cover story, because we get down there and [Rhea has] arranged a sailing trip and we're like, "What do you mean? Why would we be going sailing?" Anyway . . . she was trying to have us . . . entertain him and try to get him engaged, because he looked terrible and he was just not engaged. He was not with the program. . . . He was friendly and all, but he was . . . not interested in anything. And she was just trying to cheer him up.

After we left, I said, "What was that all about?" And we talked about it . . . but even then, we didn't know. I thought he was . . . physically sick, because he looked awful. Very thin. He looked old. He looked like he had aged a lot. . . . I thought, My God, there is something wrong with him physically. But I didn't know what his mental state was.

Depressed, red-eyed from insomnia, and nursing a sore stomach, Lawton was anxious to feel normal again. He visited his family doctor in December 1989. "It wasn't gonna be something that was gonna work itself out," his eldest daughter Tandy says of the decision. "And that's when he sought help." The doctor diagnosed him with clinical depression and prescribed Prozac. "I don't remember when I've felt better," Lawton Chiles, sixty, said soon after beginning the drug. "It's the kind of thing I want other people to know about."[557] His appetite and sleep improved, and he resumed hunting and fishing. "He started to have that twinkle in his blue eyes," elder son Bud recalls. Former Senate staffer Doug Cook remembers his old boss's recovery:

In December of '89 I was down in Key West when Chiles called me and said, "I'm gonna fly out to Arizona or New Mexico or something to get treatment for this depression. I've researched this and I've gotta do something about it." And it was apparent, we had one good day and three bad days and another good day and three more bad days, and so two days later he called me back and he said, "Nope. I ain't doing that. I'm gonna go in and see [my personal physician]." Six weeks after that, shit, it's like pre-1986 Chiles; I mean he's great, he's terrific, and every day he gets better and then we don't have any bad days.

Sometimes, Lawton credited Prozac so much with his improvement that he "wanted to scream it from the mountaintops," according to his younger son Ed. Other times, he wanted to quit Prozac and live well without pills. Lawton, Rhea, and the rest of the family had just begun learning about depression's roots in chemical imbalance.

Healthy and happy in the spring of 1990, Lawton resumed heavy work on one of his key planks in the Senate, children's health care, from his post as chair of the National Commission to Prevent Infant Mortality. The Commission, legislated into existence in 1986, had given Chiles a bully pulpit as powerful as the Budget Committee chairmanship. Commission staff provided their chair insight into the latest research in infant mortality, school nutrition, and prenatal care. Dr. Rae Grad, former head of the southern regional project on infant mortality for the Southern Governors Association, led the Commission staff as executive director. "He was a very active participant," Dr. Grad says of Senator Chiles. "He did not phone it in, he took this issue very, very, very seriously, and put in his political muscle was well as his personal muscle. He had skin in the game in this." She recalls a Commission hearing at a high-crime housing project in Chicago:

> It was just one of the scariest places. And Senator Chiles said we're gonna have a hearing there. So we had a hearing . . . he's facing the audience and I'm facing him so I can see beyond him out the window. And I'm watching out the window and I'm watching some thugs come and take the wheels off a car.

From his chairmanship on the National Commission to Prevent Infant Mortality, Chiles advocated greater funding and access for prenatal care. "There's nothing wrong with our medicine," he said. "We're just applying it at the wrong time—after the crisis occurs." He had become aware of the paltry U.S. statistics on infant mortality during his tenure on the Senate Appropriations Committee's Subcommittee on Labor, Health and Human Services, and Education. "Japan's infant-mortality rate is half of ours—5.2 deaths per 1,000 children under age one, while ours is over 10. The interesting thing is that, thirty years ago, their figures were worse than ours—the worst in the industrialized world. What has happened since then is that they have made children a national priority. They give early and comprehensive care to all their pregnant women, and it has made a dramatic difference."

The Commission produced innovative publications like "Eat to Learn, Learn to Eat," to support improved nutrition in public schools. Dr. Grad recalls investigating the nutrition problem with Senator Chiles at a Detroit public school:

> There was a math class about ten o'clock in the morning, and the teacher opened the class by saying, "Okay, store's open." I thought, What does he mean, store's open? And so the students would go up and in his drawer he had mounds and mounds of candy bars, and they would give him a quarter or a dime and he would give them a candy bar. And afterwards we said, "What was that about?" And he said, "None of them eat breakfast, the best I can hope for in this math class is a little bit of a sugar rush. I sell them candy bars."

Through the Commission, Chiles met experts like Dr. Charles Mahan, an obstetrician and former chief state health officer. Chiles held hearings for the Commission nationwide. Dr. Mahan joined the Senator at a hearing Florida:

> It was in the county commission chambers in [Miami] Dade County and it was to be a hearing—they usually picked topics—this one was on teen pregnancy. And they had three really young black girls there that had had babies. So the commission chambers were typical, where the commissioners would sit up on a raised platform and look down on the masses, and then there was a table in front where people testifying would be, and the three girls were seated at the table, and they were just scared to death . . . and Lawton looked down and he saw how scared they were, and he started asking them some questions and they couldn't even speak . . . so he walked down across the table from them . . . pulled up a chair and then leaned way across the table . . . and he said, "I know it's really scary being here, with all these lights and all these people. But just forget all these other people and just talk to me about what it was like for you." And they just looked at him like a grandfather and they just opened up. It was pretty neat. And he'd do that anywhere with kids, he'd always get down to their level.

The Commission's chief priority was reducing infant mortality nationwide. Dr. Rae Grad explains, "We would train women from housing projects to go back into housing projects and say to women, 'I'll help you go to your prenatal care visit.' Very powerful, but not rocket science. This is classic Lawton Chiles, how he would think."

Once he retired from the Senate and treated his depression, Chiles could devote himself fully to the Commission. "I decided that problems aren't solved in Washington," he asserted, "but on the grass-roots level, in places like Gretna, Quincy, [and] Havana." In these small towns in north Florida's Gadsden County, he investigated the causes of the state's extremely high infant mortality rate. Florida's only county with a majority-black population, Gadsden suffered a high poverty rate and high unemployment rate. Once a tobacco agriculture center, the county depended on nearby state jobs in Tallahassee to pay bills. Its elaborate courthouses, antebellum mansions, and red clay fields resembled south Georgia. Finally, Gadsden led the state in infant mortality; the number of infant deaths there doubled the national average. Every facet of the region fascinated Chiles.

"I started thinking that if here, in the county I reside in, is the worst rate of infant mortality, I have to do something," Chiles said. He lobbied the Florida legislature to provide $150,000 for a new nonprofit called Gadsden Citizens for Healthy Babies. The group trained and paid older women in the community to serve as "resource mothers" for young mothers, many of them teens without access to prenatal care. In March 1990, Chiles attended the graduation of the first nine resource mothers from the training. "Golly, here they were in their white dresses, and they had a rose and flowers and they were so proud, it made me proud for them," he said.[558] Rev. George Madry, head of Gadsden Citizens for Healthy Babies, called Chiles "our savior, our guiding light."

Florida children's advocate Jack Levine worked with Chiles on children's health policy in Gadsden County and understood the county's symbolism for Chiles:

> The proximity of Gadsden County, our neighbor to the West, to the capital city, always became this glowing example of disparity and while the geographic distance was minimal, the amazing difference was so great. What happened there was another example of Chiles' receptivity to people from another class and from another background. Chiles was 85 percent country, and the 15 percent that was

city was really almost a fascination for him but really never a comfort zone. So when we look at a rural, semi-rural, mostly agricultural and impoverished population in need, that country boy I think started showing itself in a very, very open and honest way. Hereto his comfort with the ministers, looking at infant health and family services as a spiritual connection was very real in the Gadsden work, and really almost became a laboratory for how the experiment of how to get a community to embrace the needs of a pregnant girl or a pregnant woman, that was very real.

Levine believed that Chiles' method of inquiry in Gadsden and elsewhere was "solely conversational":

There are some who have truly questioned his interest and/or ability to read much. Now, I'm not implying anything as in terms of disability or anything like that. But given his preference, his learning style was absolutely auditory. And he processed what people said in the whole package. It was the messenger as much as the message, which is a significant, significant skill that he honed over his entire career as far as I can perceive. And then he translated this amazing ability to listen clearly and carefully into this almost uncanny communications style, which oftentimes appeared to the first observer as kind of scattered or almost too informal, some would say kinda herky-jerky. But I'll tell ya, when it came down to the reality of what he needed to say when he needed to say it, he was a fine craftsman when it came to clarity and precision.

Chiles seized opportunities to follow up on issues personally, according to Levine:

One that flashes to mind was in St. Petersburg at a teen-mom program, and it was early afternoon, and he got very intrigued by this one sixteen or seventeen-year-old mom's story of what she was doing to both help herself and help her little son. And as the story went, I was not on site, but it was told to me, almost minute-by-minute by the program director, a good friend of mine, it was getting on time for her to be leaving with the little boy—I think a toddler's child, maybe a year and a half or two. And [Lawton] asked how she was getting home. And she said: well, my mom doesn't get off work until after four so usually we wait here until she comes and picks us up. And when two of his assistants were listening to this, they got all nervous about what he was gonna say, 'cause that was way into his next meeting appointment. But sure enough, he said, I'd like to meet your mom, do you mind if I stay on here and wait for her to come and pick you up? Now, not that he offered to take her, 'cause he didn't want to intervene. But he wanted to be there to get another piece of the puzzle. That's what Lawton Chiles did, is he measured his relationships by trying to get the whole picture. And he just plain wanted to meet the grandma, and did.

In addition to duties at the Commission and Gadsden Citizens for Healthy Babies, Chiles took a post as director of the LeRoy Collins Center for Public Policy in Tallahassee. He taught classes at University of Florida. "It's great to see a bunch of bright young people who are interested," he said of the experience. "For the first day, we got by. No one jumped up and said, 'This guy's a fraud.'"

As a newly minted professor, Chiles connected with children's policy experts such as Dr. Steve Freedman, founder and director of the Institute for Child Health Policy at University of Florida in Gainesville. Chiles and Dr. Freedman discussed children's health insurance, according to the latter:

> That was when really we got kind of close, because we would just sit and talk for hours on end about general government things but primarily kids' health care and how we had moved from a view of kids as basically possessions of their parents to the dignity of having an independent value in society and this whole business of insuring kids separately from their parents, if their parents really couldn't afford to insure them or the opportunity to insure them wasn't there, was just kind of compelling to him.

Political consultants, peer politicians, and pundits assumed that like most supposedly retired officeholders, Lawton Chiles had chosen to continue policy work as a platform for another political bid.

For a time, while Lawton taught classes elsewhere, Rhea moved into the couple's condominium in Holmes Beach. "I had some months where I could just do my own thing and live with myself as a person rather than as a wife or a mother or somebody doing something in another role." Rhea resumed painting regularly, emulating the style of Georgia O'Keefe. "Color and organization of space have always been very interesting to me," she said. "I'm very apt to go into a room and push a chair around or move something on a table, because my mind just goes to shapes and colors and how things are arranged."

Soon both Lawton and Rhea were in Tallahassee. They attended church at Calvary Presbyterian Church downtown, near their home on 6th Street and the capital political community.

In spring 1990, Democratic party insiders began a pilgrimage to Chiles to persuade him to run for governor against Republican incumbent Bob Martinez.

Vaclav Havel, Czech playwright and politician, succeeded where Democratic activists failed. Havel, Czechoslovakia's tenth and final president and the Czech Republic's first president, delivered an address in February 1990 to a joint session of the U.S. Congress. The speech describes the ideas that inspired his country's transition from communism to democracy. Its passage on moral responsibility inspired Chiles:

> We still don't know how to put morality ahead of politics, science and economy. We are still incapable of understanding that the only genuine backbone of all our actions, if they are to be moral, is responsibility—responsibility to something higher than my family, my country, my company, my success.
>
> If I subordinate my political behavior to this imperative, mediated to me by my conscience, I can't go far wrong. . . . This is why I ultimately decided, after resisting for a long time, to accept the burden of political responsibility.

"That speech had a tremendous impact on [Governor Chiles]," former Senate staffer Doug Cook said. "I don't know that I had ever seen him so excited." The speech spoke directly to Chiles' moral method of justifying political involvement.

Chiles had begun studying and emulating Havel's political values as early as fall 1989. The University of Chicago Law School invited the former U.S. senator to deliver a speech on public service. In his address, Chiles hinted at a political future for himself:

When I held public office, I used to try to listen to my inner voice—my heart, my gut, my soul. Now that I have been out in the countryside, I am hearing America's inner voice, and it is saying, "I want honest and courageous leaders. I want someone to ask me to sacrifice today and to look at the long haul and to call on me to serve when I can be of help." . . . I left the Senate less than a year ago, frustrated, and I stand before you today renewed.[559]

Havel's 1990 address, though, pushed Chiles from ideation to action. In Havel, Chiles had found another political actor who responded to a powerful "inner voice"—the conscience.

Miami Herald's Tom Fiedler, who frequently covered Chiles in the Senate, explains the impact of Havel on Chiles:

He was so inspired, having heard Vaclav Havel talk about the importance of democracy and the human spirit. ... In many ways, I think [the talk] lifted this cloud that had come to envelop him, and prompted him once again to re-engage in public life and in politics, and then to go forward, also knowing that he was confronting all the concerns people had about electing someone to office, to significant office, who had what was seen by many people as a "mental illness."

Chiles' first choice for Florida governor was not himself though. His next move was to persuade Bob Crawford, the current state senate president, to answer his nation's call for courage and run for governor.

Crawford, bent on running for agriculture commissioner, suggested that Chiles run instead. Former Democratic Congressman Buddy MacKay from Ocala, Florida, an ally of Chiles' on federal budget reform, concurred with Crawford. Lawton shrugged off the suggestion until MacKay visited him at home in March 1990. "I think that was the beginning of the beginning," Rhea Chiles later recalled.[560] MacKay, reeling from a narrow loss in his 1988 Senate race, but burning with ambition, told Lawton he wanted to reenter politics. He had noticed a poll for the 1990 governor's race that indicated strong support for a Chiles-MacKay ticket.

The Chiles-MacKay campaign thus began, the product of a host of instigators. Rhea Chiles compared her husband's gradual return to politics to "pulling on an outboard motor. It takes a lot of tugs but finally it kicks into life."

Former Florida Governor Reubin Askew was one of the first to hear the news in April 1990 that Lawton Chiles had decided to enter the race for governor with Buddy MacKay as his running mate. Askew and Chiles, at that point both teaching politics to university students, had arranged to teach each other's classes. At a class break, they saw each other in the men's room. "I'm going to announce for governor tomorrow," Lawton told Reubin. Surprised by the decision, Askew replied, "Well, wonderful!"[561]

Eldest son Bud Chiles interpreted his father's turnaround:

As he began to feel better, the old juices started to flow. The interest in issues and politics increased. We talked less and less about spiritual things and more and more about politics. Later, after my dad decided to run for Governor, [Senator] Sam Nunn summed it all up so well, "you were almost cured, Lawton." I thought how right that comment was.

Lawton's brother-in-law Joe P. Ruthven said, "I think he was lost not being in the public office, so I was glad when he decided to run for governor."[562] "What kicked me off was the feeling that Bush and other leaders weren't listening [to the revolution in Eastern Europe]," Lawton Chiles said of his decision to reenter politics. "The world's never going to be the same. These people marching, walking into the square willing to risk their lives, and I was still sitting on the sidelines. No longer could I just say, "Look, I've done my part, I've spent thirty years, and I don't owe anything else."[563] Chiles family friend and attorney Burke Kibler added: "Lawton just was someone that didn't just want to hibernate."[564]

Chiles family members and former staff rejoiced in seeing their favorite candidate on the campaign trail. "When he then decided that he was going to run for governor," *Miami Herald*'s Tom Fielder said, "it was almost like the rebirth of Lawton Chiles." Lawton "wanted to go kill something again," according to son Ed. Elder son Bud Chiles agreed:

Part of me was greatly relieved. I was mentally and spiritually and physically exhausted from the months of this battle with the "blacks." It was great to see him smile and talk like the old days. On a beautiful day in the piney woods of North Florida, hunting quail on horseback, he would say, "Bud, it's a great day to be alive."

"I'm thinking to myself, God is in heaven," exclaimed former Senate staffer Doug Cook.

Campaign staffer Bentley Lipscomb claimed that a "supernatural" aura protected Chiles-MacKay. Monetary contributions started arriving before they opened a bank account. Before they formally announced their campaign, the *Tallahassee Democrat* and *Palm Beach Post* endorsed Chiles-MacKay for the Democratic nomination. The *Tallahassee Democrat* called the duo "Butch Cassidy and the Sundance Kid."

Donations came from new and old friends. The 1990 Chiles campaign and all preceding ones received money from Frank R. Hunt Jr., who had roomed with Chiles at the ATO fraternity house at the University of Florida. Hunt, a lifelong Republican and president and owner of Hunt Truck Sales in Tampa, would mail his old pal a campaign check for $10 with a note that said, "You know I'm voting for the other guy." Bruce Hunt recounts that his father had "tremendous respect for Governor Chiles (despite their conflicting views)."

Environmental groups and other traditional Democratic bastions supported the campaign. The League of Conservation Voters pointed to a record of green achievement: as a U.S. Senator, Chiles had sponsored legislation creating the Big Cypress National Preserve in 1974 and expanded it in 1988; he fought offshore oil drilling; he opposed the Cross-Florida Barge Canal; and he passed legislation in 1983 that banned phosphate minimg in Osceola National Forest.

Chiles and MacKay agreed to limit campaign contributions to $100 per person, inspiring tens of thousands of small donors. The day Chiles formally announced for governor, April 15, 1990, *St. Petersburg Times* reporter Lucy Morgan called the candidate for comment on a rumor that he had sought depression therapy at a clinic in Arizona. Chiles corrected the story for Morgan. "It wasn't Arizona, it was Nevada. It wasn't 1989, it was 1987," he said. "It wasn't depression; it was a sex-change operation."[565]

"I think that that's a heckuva exciting race," Lawton Chiles said of the fledgling campaign for governor, "It reminds me of the time when I got my dime to go to the picture show. I got a chance to watch the guys in the white hats fight the guys in the black hats."[566] For Rhea Chiles, "getting used to the idea [of returning to politics] wasn't an overnight thing. When you get older you don't jump as quick."[567] But she acknowledged that "he's the right man with the right background at the right time to do the right thing. Are you going to shake your fist at God and say no?"[568] She began helping the campaign process its fundraising checks by computer. "I won't go with him when the only requirement is that Lawton Chiles appear," she said. "I'm an appendage at that point."[569] Lawton confessed that only months before the campaign began, "my main challenge was to keep from pulling a gun on myself while I shaved." He also affirmed, however, "I don't think I'll ever be out of politics, unless they bury me face down."[570]

Depression claimed Lawton intermittently as he campaigned. Buoyed by better moods, the candidate had quit Prozac soon after the campaign began in April. Some stressful days "would send him waffling," Rhea said. "I started waking up some at night," Lawton said. "I would not be as peppy as I had been. I could just start seeing some of the signs."

Their eldest son, Bud, recalls "qualifying day," when the campaign filed officially with the board of elections. Traditionally an emotional highlight of statewide campaigns, qualifying day was one of Chiles' worst moments:

> I'll never forget it I was standing there in the closet with him, and he really couldn't get dressed. He said, "I don't know." I was like, "You've gotta go do this now, you've come too far. You can't pull out now, there's nobody left. It'll be chaos. You're gonna feel better." He really did; he came out of it. He was fine.

Other occasions Lawton would sit at home and stare out the window until Bud urged him, "Dad, you've gotta get ready to go to this editorial board meeting." Campaign staffer Mary Jane Gallagher recalls another recurrence of depression at an airport tarmac full of supporters:

> [Lawton Chiles] said, "I'm not gettin' out." I said, "Yes sir, you are." He goes, "Oh, you can take care of this." I said, "No, you're not. I know you're havin' a bad day." I said, "Come on, get your briefcase, let's go."

Soon after restarting Prozac in early August 1990, Chiles recovered and campaigned full stride.

Throughout his own ordeal, Chiles continued to inquire after others sick or in need. Tim Nickens, a reporter at *The Miami Herald* during the campaign, first met Chiles in April 1990. Nonetheless, when Nickens fell sick with pneumonia while covering the campaign, Chiles called him and asked, "When are you gonna get back out here?" Chiles continued to monitor the reporter's life milestones, calling him after his first daughter was born in

February 1991 to say, "Hello, Papa"; calling him when his father-in-law died and when his father died that same year, and sending flowers. "He had that touch," Nickens says of Chiles. "He wasn't looking for favorable coverage—I didn't think. It was on a human basis."

The Chiles-MacKay campaign opened up to reporters about depression, aiming to resolve the issue politically. Mental illness had killed previous campaigns, although by 1990, approximately 15 million American suffered from depression. In 1972, Democratic presidential nominee Senator George McGovern (D-SD) dropped running mate Senator Thomas Eagleton (D-MO) from the ticket after revelations that Eagleton had received electro-shock therapy for depression.[571] "A lot of people have depression, off and on," Lawton Chiles said. "Certainly Lincoln talked about the black dog that hounded him. The amazing thing is how many people have depression at one time in their lives, and we really don't know much about it."[572] Abraham Lincoln once confided to a friend: "I am the most miserable man living. If what I feel were equally distributed to the whole human family, there would be not one cheerful face on earth. . . . To remain as I am is impossible; I must die or be better." Chiles added, "I'm in good company. Nobody is going to argue that it affected [Lincoln's] performance in office."[573]

Lawton Chiles' rival for the Democratic gubernatorial nomination, veteran U.S. House member Bill Nelson from Florida's Space Coast, attacked Chiles' health when policy debate failed to move polls. Many Democratic activists, eager to back an established name, had already moved to the Chiles camp since April, giving Chiles an early lead. Nelson promoted his relative youth and the athleticism that allowed him to be an astronaut, while criticizing the "burnout" that led to Chiles' retirement from the U.S. Senate. Nelson came within about ten points of Chiles in the polls at his campaign's peak.

Nelson's advance stalled, though, when his running mate, House Speaker Tom Gustafson, said, "I don't want to have a suicide during [Chiles'] term of office or during the election." Bill Nelson repudiated the comment. Buddy MacKay called it an example of "instability on Tom Gustafson's part."[574]

Chiles angsted for a fight, but on public policy not personal health issues. He disclosed his medical records to the public two weeks before the Democratic primary and wrested the issue away from Nelson. "He often told me," former Senate aide Dennis Beal said, "the reason he likes politics [is] it's sorta like the old gunslinger in the Old West. It all boils down to high noon."[575] Chiles-MacKay campaign manager Jim Krog:

Nelson was having a press conference and Chiles actually went to the press conference and broke in on the press conference, scared Nelson to death. And at that point, the press corps loves it. And in the end I don't know that it helped us or hurt us. It made us feel better anyway.

Lawton's eldest daughter Tandy Chiles managed field operations for the campaign in the key central Florida counties of Orange, Osceola, and Seminole, and supported her father's transparency on health matters:

He was able to come out and say it in a way that people understood, because there was the humility about it. . . . What it did was, it gave people that were on it, it made them feel like their stigma, that I think he really, really helped change the stigma about taking chemicals for a chemical imbalance. And the fact that he was able to do that tickled him.

Senator Sam Nunn (D-GA), stumping for Chiles on the campaign trail, ridiculed accusations that his old Senate colleague was too old and tired to govern. "He can't beat me at tennis, but then he never could," Senator Nunn said. "That's because he never let me leave the court until he won a game," Chiles retorted. "Anyone who didn't get depressed [in Congress] was out of touch with reality," Senator Nunn added. "[Chiles] had no president to help him, and congressional leadership didn't help. I have no doubt about his energy and ability to lead this state."[576]
American author William Styron, who received a National Magazine Award for his description of his own clinical depression, endorsed the Chiles campaign in his acceptance speech. "Unfortunately, there is still a stigma attached to people who have suffered from depression," Styron wrote in a statement. "In the Florida gubernatorial campaign, [former U.S.] Senator Lawton Chiles' opponents are using this issue to smear him. I can only hope that the attention and notice the essay has received will contribute to a change in the public's attitude towards mental health problems."[577] Chiles-MacKay, fueled by wild popular nostalgia for the top of the ticket, shellacked the Nelson campaign, garnering almost 70 percent of the Democratic primary vote.

Jim Cooper, a Gadsden County commissioner and Chiles supporter, summed up the views of many in his party. He preferred a "good man with a little health problem as governor than a healthy crook."

Campaign staff expected stiffer odds for Chiles-MacKay in the general election. On the plus side, the emergence of Jim Krog, a lobbyist for a Miami law firm, as campaign manager had focused the operation. From 1976 to 1980, Krog worked as a legislative aide to Governor Reubin Askew. "Before Jim came in," Tallahassee lobbyist John French said, "the Chiles campaign was akin to a sixties kind of movement—it had a lot of good people but was really just a well-intentioned mob." Chiles and MacKay still resisted formal hierarchy, preferring a loose ship even with Krog as skipper. Krog's actual title was "campaign coordinator."

But Chiles had not run for office in eight years when he declared for governor in 1990. During the interim tens of thousands of new Floridians had joined the voter rolls. Incumbent GOP Governor Bob Martinez benefited, too, from other demographic trends. The grandson of Spanish immigrants, former mayor of Tampa and a recent convert to the Republican Party, Governor Martinez symbolized rising Hispanic and GOP power in Florida. Waves of Mexican, Nicaraguan, Puerto Rican and Cuban migration had hit south Florida. Even in rural north Florida, Latin grocery stores popped up between bait and tackle shops and dollar stores. Miami sheltered 60 percent of America's Cubans, and half the city's residents spoke English as a second language. Between 1970 and 1990, the state's Hispanic population quadrupled from 400,000 to 1.6 million.

Chiles-MacKay nevertheless sideswiped the Martinez campaign. The poor national economy in 1990 hurt incumbents across the country. Governor Martinez's shape-shifting policy on taxing Florida's service sector had ruined his job approval rating. The governor "got the worst of both ends on it," Chiles supporter and Lakeland attorney Burke Kibler said. Voters hated him for proposing and signing the tax initially, and hated him for changing his mind and pushing the legislature to repeal the tax.[578] Chiles, moreover, had a "love affair going on with the people" and the press, according to campaign staffer Dean Saunders. Rhea Chiles told her husband at the campaign kickoff, "What you need to do is just keep your mouth shut. All you can do is lose votes now." Looking at poll after poll, MacKay adviser Greg Farmer told Chiles' running mate Buddy MacKay: "I don't know what you're doing, but it's working. For goodness sake, don't start campaigning, or you'll screw everything up!"[579]

The Martinez campaign stirred up minor controversy about possible campaign finance chicanery. They accused the Chiles-MacKay campaign of "bundling," or grouping of multiple small contributions into one package delivered to the campaign by a rich organization—like grocer Winn-Dixie. Campaign staffer Dean Saunders later recalled problems with enforcing the $100-per-head contribution limit at an organization that ultimately processed about 75,000 donations.

> I can remember getting a particular group of checks for five thousand dollars. I went back and traced it all, and of course, you could give corporate contributions. ... There were twenty-five different corporations that had written checks for a hundred dollars. ... I went back and traced them all and they all came from the same family. ... I said, "Governor, I think we need to send these back." He said, "Absolutely." So I did. It kinda smacked of stuff, so I sent 'em back.

When Chiles campaign staffer Bentley Lipscomb hired Jimmy Buffett to perform at an official campaign concert, he worried he may have tempted the press corps one time too many. During the Buffett song, "Let's All Get Drunk and Screw," Chiles got up on stage and lip-synched with the band. Lipscomb recalls:

> They knew that he wasn't doin' it maliciously. The press, who lived with him, literally, for the last four or five months of the campaign, knew that he had no idea what he was singin'. I was standin' in the back of the damn auditorium down there, sayin' oh God, I can see the headlines tomorrow, "Let's all get drunk and screw," but it never happened.

But odes to Walkin' Lawton, the people's champion, far outnumbered critical analyses of the Chiles campaign in the major newspapers. "We'd just beat the dog out of [Governor Martinez] every day about the money he was taking," Chiles campaign manager Jim Krog explains, "and [Governor Martinez] tried to come back at us and couldn't do it."

Reporters adored the Chiles-MacKay populist style. Chiles had presented himself and Buddy MacKay to Florida as the state's "dream team" for the general election. Their uniform: madras shirts and khaki pants. Their slogan: "This time the people win!"[580] The Chiles-MacKay campaign headquarters invited comparisons to the folk heroics of the 1970 Walk.

The campaign had moved into a partially vacated Chevy dealership in Tallahassee.[581] Buddy MacKay recalls:

> We were sharing a building with a used-car dealership and sharing the phone system. The phone would ring and it would [be for either] Chiles-MacKay or Thomas Chevrolet. So I said, "Lawton, how in the world are we gonna straighten that out?"
>
> He said, "Well, I think Thomas guys would be better at political issues than our guys would be at selling Chevrolets, so don't worry."

Young volunteers gave the campaign practical ideas for publicity, campaign manager Jim Krog recalls:

> We had more volunteers than you could shake a stick at. At any one time we could put together four or five hundred volunteers in Tallahassee to do anything. So we get 'em in there, we're playin' through on this thing, we put up a sign in the window, and people started honkin'. . . .
>
> This kid says, "Well, let's put a sign up here, I've just been down to MacDonald's down the street, you know the ten millionth hamburger. Let's put a sign up that says, 'Be one of the proud [contributors to Chiles-MacKay],' and then we leave the number blank and we change the number of contributors every day." . . .
>
> We put that sign up and we changed it every day and people started writing about [it] and talkin' about it. That was the deal. And then one of the kids took another thing, it says, "Honk if you're a contributor," and nailed it to the bottom. And we'd be in there late at night and you'd hear people going by, "Honk! Honk! Honk!" at all of the stop signs at this intersection.

During a campaign visit to Jay, Florida in the Panhandle, Chiles stopped at a high school. Speaking before a sophomore biology class, the candidate sensed their apathy. He found a jar containing a large pickled snake. The *St. Petersburg Times* photographer covering the event snapped photos of Chiles with the jar, remarking, "That guy knows just what to do for the camera."[582]

Every major Florida newspaper endorsed Chiles for governor. The campaign took advantage of his strong press relations to broadcast the driest details of its policy agenda. In addition to campaign finance and ethics reform, the madras duo promised a new standard for government efficiency and accountability. They envisioned an agile bureaucracy propelled by data-driven decision-making, customer service, privatization, agency mergers, and civil service reform. They based much of their platform on government guru David Osborne's first book, *Laboratories of Democracy,* and his forthcoming and more celebrated sequel, *Reinventing Government.* "I encouraged them to plagiarize me," Osborne said.[583] The "reinvention" of government along these lines would supposedly build public trust for progressive tax reform down the road. Their tax plan called for investments in education and health care and a stable revenue stream to secure the state's long-term finances. "We've got to convince people we're going to spend their money in a proper, efficiency way before we start talking about how we'll raise revenue," Lawton Chiles said.[584] This meant painful budget cuts at the outset of their administration to trim fat and close the deficit. The candidate hoped also that the enormity of the 1990 recession presented a policy window for reform. Florida showed all the telltales of economic downturn: low condo prices, poor ticket sales for amusement parks, airline layoffs, savings and loan bailouts, bank closures, and retail inventory buildup.

The Chiles campaign held town meetings across the state to discuss their ideas with the public. "What we're doing is what I get the energy from, you know," Chiles told a reporter about the meetings. "I think where I got off the track awhile is when I quit doing that in the primary. I began to go back to the old thing of airport press conferences. It's a bore, and you're not learning anything, you're not doing anything."[585] The Chiles-MacKay campaign aired its bureaucratic reform agenda until it bored the press. One reporter opined to the campaign: "This campaign is about as boring as a two horse apocalypse. If you want any press coverage at all, you'll have to come up with a totally different plan."[586]

Lawton Chiles defeated Governor Martinez with 56 percent of the vote, despite being outspent two to one during the campaign. The incumbent even lost by over 50,000 votes in his home county. "I'm always hearing voices," the governor-elect said on election night. "Then I started hearing the word 'Camelot.' Camelot is a state of mind. If you have it and I have it, we can start bringing Camelot back."[587] Governor-elect Chiles planned to invite more than 50,000 to his free inaugural celebration in Tallahassee. Neither invitations nor tuxedos were required to attend "Florida Jubilee 1991." Chiles-MacKay likewise limited contributions to $100 for the inaugural fund. "We've got so many people who really want to join us in the opening of the administration," Chiles said. "We're saying, 'Y'all come.'"[588]

Reporters suggested that the governor-elect wear a tuxedo with a madras cummerbund to the Jubilee.[589] He may have disappointed them on that count, but he endeared himself to the press once more with one of his first acts as governor. Governor Chiles changed the start time of the Cabinet meetings to 9:30 a.m. to accommodate an extra half hour of turkey hunting.

Photo Gallery

Munn Park, 1911: the venue hosted many political rallies and was a classroom for Lawton Chiles.
Postcard courtesy of Lakeland Public Library, Special Collections, Lakeland, Florida.

Rhea Grafton and Lawton Chiles, married January 27, 1951, at Miami Beach. Photo courtesy of Chiles family collection.

Lakelanders gather around the gazebo in Munn Park to hear political oratory, 1938.
Photo courtesy of Lakeland Public Library, Special Collections, Lakeland, Florida.

Lawton Chiles as a high school football player-center. Photo courtesy of Chiles family collection.

Florida Senator Spessard Holland, Lawton Chiles' political mentor. Photo courtesy of Senator Sam J. Ervin Jr. Library and Museum.

Army Lieutenant Lawton Chiles and friends in Japan. Photo courtesy of Florida Photographic Collection, State Archives & Library of Florida.

Family portrait taken for Lawton Chiles' first political campaign, 1958 (clockwise from left): Rhea, Zippy the cat, Tandy, Lawton, Bud, and Ed. Photo courtesy of Chiles family collection.

Rhea Chiles in the 1960s with one of her best-known paintings, a map of "Old Florida." Photo courtesy of Chiles family collection.

Senator L.K. Edwards of Irvine served in the Florida Legislature along with Chiles in the 1960s. Edwards, a fan of white suits, long limousines, and chocolate sundaes, epitomized the legislative caucus known as "The Porkchop Gang." Photo courtesy of Florida Photographic Collection, State Library & Archives of Florida.

Senator Wilbur H. Boyd, one of Chiles' best friends and colleagues in the Florida Legislature, 1966. Photo courtesy of Florida Photographic Collection, State Library & Archives of Florida.

Chiles meeting voters during his 1970 Walk across Florida. Photo courtesy of Lawton Chiles Legal Information Center, University of Florida Levin College of Law.

Chiles during the 1970 Walk across Florida. Photo courtesy of Lawton Chiles Legal Information Center, University of Florida College of Law.

Chiles on the 1970 Walk across Florida. Photo courtesy of Florida Photographic Collection, State Archives & Library of Florida.

Florida U.S. Senator-Elect Lawton Chiles and his family move to Washington, D.C. Photo courtesy of George A. Smathers Libraries, University of Florida.

Senator Chiles on the tennis court, where he enjoyed games with staff, family, and friends. Photo courtesy of Chiles family collection.

Wilbur Boyd and Lawton Chiles sharing good times in Florida. Photo courtesy of Chiles family collection.

To my good friend Lawton — a great Senator and a terrific Brother!

Sam

Senator Chiles and Senator Sam Nunn (D-Georgia) worked together, played tennis together, and prayed together. They were like brothers. Photo courtesy of Chiles family collection.

Senator Chiles and son Ed with their turkeys. Photo courtesy of Chiles family collection.

Senator Chiles camping at an unknown location and date, probably in north Florida circa mid-1980s. Photo courtesy of Brian Proctor.

Lawton Chiles campaigns in 1990 for the Florida governorship with running mate Buddy Mackay. Chiles defeated incumbent Republican Bob Martinez 56 percent to 43 percent. Photo courtesy of Chiles family collection.

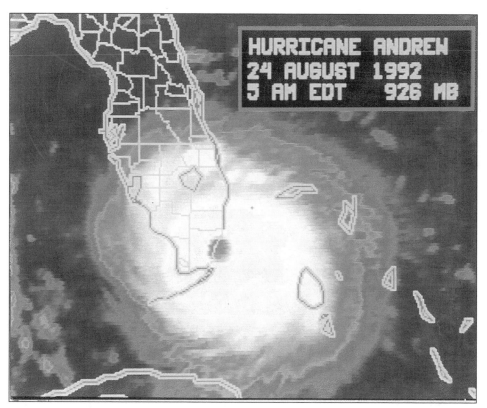

Infrared image of Hurricane Andrew over Dade County, August 24, 1992. Photo courtesy of National Hurricane Center.

Hurricane Andrew, ultimately ranked as a Category 5 storm, approaches Florida. Photo courtesy of NOAA.

Hurricane Andrew flattened many neighborhoods southwest of Miami. Dade County had a strong building code, but it often went unenforced. Photo courtesy of FEMA.

Governor Chiles excelled at political theater, and used his charisma to raise money for Hurricane Andrew relief. Photo courtesy of Chiles family collection.

Governor Chiles, the self-proclaimed "He-Coon" of Florida, celebrates his 1994 re-election with Lieutenant Governor Buddy MacKay. Photo courtesy of Lawton Chiles Legal Information Center, University of Florida Levin College of Law.

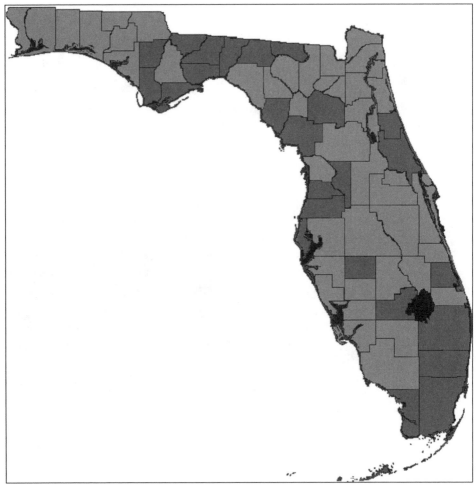

Governor Chiles won re-election in 1994 by a narrow margin in terms of vote percentage, but he carried counties (shaded darker) from every region in Florida, from the Panhandle to the Keys. Map in public domain.

Governor Chiles revels in coonskin regalia at the Tallahassee street festival following his 1995 inauguration. Photo courtesy of Florida Photographic Collection, State Archives. & Library of Florida.

President Bill Clinton and Governor Chiles promote Florida's community colleges. The two Southern politicans found considerable common ground on matters of style and substance. Photo courtesy of Lawton Chiles Legal Information Center, University of Florida Levin College of Law.

Governor Chiles enjoys a quiet moment away from politics at his "Cook Shack," his hunting cabin just outside Tallahassee. Photo courtesy of April Salter.

Governor Chiles visits the Lillie C. Evans Elementary School in Miami, Florida, February 1997. Photo courtesy of April Salter.

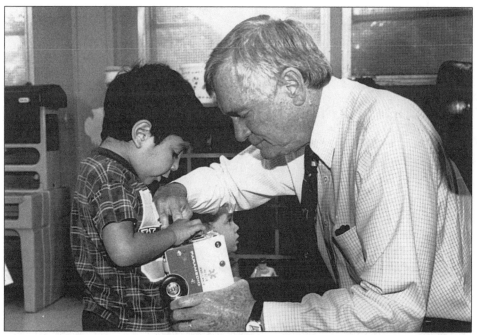

Governor Chiles visits the Fun Time Nursery in Naples, Florida, January 1996. Photo courtesy of April Salter.

Governor Chiles writes the 1994 State of the State as Giddy, the family dog, looks on. Photo courtesy of Chiles family collection.

Governor Chiles announces a multibillion dollar settlement with Big Tobacco signed on August 25, 1997. Photo courtesy of April Salter.

Governor Chiles playing with one of the many dogs in his life in 1998. Photo courtesy of Florida Photographic Collection, State Archives & Library of Florida.

Governor and Rhea Chiles. Photo courtesy of Lawton Chiles Legal Information Center, University of Florida Levin College of Law.

Lake Hollingsworth in Lakeland, Florida, a popular spot for water sports near Chiles' boyhood home, 2007. Photo by John Dos Passos Coggin.

Lower Suwannee River National Wildlife Refuge in 2007. The river was a favorite fishing hole for Lawton Chiles' father. Photo by John Dos Passos Coggin.

Senator Chiles explains the hydrology of a creek in Osceola National Forest. Photo courtesy of George A. Smathers Libraries, University of Florida.

Soon after Governor Chiles' death, the Florida Legislature passed legislation to mark the path that he took for his 1970 Walk across Florida, the "Lawton Chiles Trail." Photo by John Dos Passos Coggin.

Chiles began his 1970 Walk across Florida in the Panhandle, near the Alabama border. He traversed small towns like Jay, whose surrounding cotton fields are pictured above in 2007. The Panhandle differed markedly from the rest of the state. Photo by John Dos Passos Coggin.

The Chaos Theory of Government

As a U.S. senator, Lawton Chiles felt "locked in by a system." On return visits to Washington, he cringed at how little the culture had changed. His colleagues lived "by Pavlovian bells and quorum calls. It's like I stepped out of Alice's glass."[590] Never had he contemplated the governorship, sequestered from the deals, alliances, and debate of the legislature. But placing his hand on his cowhide family Bible to take the oath of office, sixty-year-old Governor Chiles enjoyed the idealism most first-time chief executives feel in their forties. Governor Chiles called his years as chief executive the "don't give a damn phase of my life."

Soon after moving into the Governor's Mansion, he gushed, "I feel like one of those helium balloons. Now our job is to winnow our desires down to realistic endeavors, so we can concentrate and expend our power wisely."[591] In a January 1991 interview with *St. Petersburg Times*, the governor stated, "One of the things we learned in Kentucky [at a National Governors Conference], when we heard governor after governor say, 'Whatever it is you want to do,' divide that in half, and divide that in half, and then you probably have too much to do."[592]

Yet, like most gubernatorial administrations, Chiles-MacKay jittered with campaign mania in its first hundred days, as staff caught up on sleep and ate their first regular meals in months. Governor Chiles had originally planned to deliver an inaugural address based on David Osborne's ideas for "reinventing government." The incoming Republican governor of Massachusetts, William Weld, beat him to it though, according to Osborne.

[Governor Chiles] was gonna give a speech about "steering, not rowing"—that was gonna be the theme. If you the people of Florida will do X, I'll do Y. If you'll row in this direction, I'll steer in this direction. State government can't do everything. . . . State government can steer. . . . It was all about that and it was straight from out of my stuff. At the same time that this had all happened in Florida, there was a new Republican in Massachusetts where I lived, named Bill Weld, who got elected in that same election in 1990. . . . Bill Weld got elected. Somebody gave him, right after the election, a copy of *Laboratories of Democracy*. He read it . . . and then he asked to meet with me. And I went in and met with him. . . . I had the introduction and two chapters of *Reinventing Government* written. And so I said sure, you can see that. . . . And I was just shocked when he gave an inaugural speech right out of my stuff. He just used all the terms. It was incredible. And what happened in Tallahassee, somebody told me, is they got an article off the wire service on this speech Weld had just given. Somebody ran down the hall with it and said, "Look, Bill Weld just gave your speech." And they had to change their speech.

Caffeine-addicted campaign staff skilled in volunteer recruitment and event planning gave way to policy professionals from previous administrations, think tanks, and academia. Staff in the executive office of the governor angled for access to their boss, like voters in a parade pushing closer to their candidate.

Governor Chiles renounced the responsibility of personnel management, resulting in office chaos. The first chief of staff, Jim Krog, former campaign manager and lobbyist, explains the governor's theory of "controlled chaos":

[Governor Chiles] liked nothing more than to watch a good argument. He liked that. He liked what I call the "chaos theory of the office" where you get two or three people and they would argue it out. 'Cause he got a sense for what the argument was and what the answer was and how he could get to where the answer was.

One of the two legislative affairs directors, Wayne Watters, describes the method:

There were battles over the direction that policy was going to go into, and they were encouraged—they were encouraged. 'Cause if he didn't want it to happen, it wouldn't have happened. I had come from two years in the Senate president's office, where we would bat around ideas and we'd come to a conclusion and that was it, we're done [snaps fingers]. That's how we're gonna do it, right? These discussions would go on for days and weeks, probably months.

Governor Chiles' experience in the U.S. Senate, where Florida office chief Charles Canady Sr. ruled staff, encouraged him to experiment with a new management style. Former Senate staffer Dave Mica reflected on Canady's approach:

We used to work so hard on the staff stuff in Lakeland. Canady was such a slave driver. I had one colleague who came in one day and said, "I can't take it any more, I'm going to Colorado and I'm taking [one of the secretaries]." . . . They got married and moved to Colorado. He's been out there since.

Canady ultimately clashed with Rhea Chiles in his quest for absolutism, and thereby lost all his influence in the office, according to former Senate staffer Dean Saunders:

Charlie [Canady] gave a mandate [to Senator Lawton Chiles], "It's me or your wife." That was stupid. You can't come between a man and his wife; you can't make those kinds of demands. That's stupid. It was tragic; really, it was a shame that that happened.

Chiles never fired Canady, but he never invited him to Tallahassee, either. In Jim Krog, Governor Chiles found an easygoing personality to replace Canady's command-and-control ethic in the director's chair. Chiles family like brother-in-law and former Lakeland mayor Joe P. Ruthven respected the governor's allegiance but applauded his decision to part with Canady, calling it long overdue. Former Senate chief of staff Rick Farrell concurred:

And we used to always joke—of course, thank God, [Chiles is] not governor, he's a senator, he doesn't have to run anything, because that's not his strong point. He would keep people as staff longer than he should have gotten rid of. And I don't know that he fired any-body—I had to fire people.

According to former Senate staff Dennis Beal, Governor Chiles once told him about hiring and firing, "Why the hell do it yourself when you got people to do it for you?" Krog envisioned himself a campaign brawler who lived to win and loved to schmooze—not a policy professional or bureaucratic man-ager. Toward the end of the Chiles-MacKay campaign, Krog had kept a man-nequin with the face of Governor Martinez campaign manager J.M. "Mac" Stipanovich propped up in his office. In the mannequin's coat pocket was a picture of Governor Martinez.[593] And Governor Chiles liked the tone that Krog set in the office: loose, confrontational, and loud. Krog argued with the other two senior staffers who aspired to lead the office, communications director Mary Jane Gallagher, a veteran of Chiles' federal infant mortality policy shop, and budget director Doug Cook, a veteran of Chiles' Senate staff.

Governor Chiles imported old friends to the executive office, gave them vague titles, placed them in the room with Cook, Gallagher, and Krog, and hoped the resulting ego explosion would advance his agenda. Wayne Wat-ters from legislative affairs describe the scene:

> I used to tell people in the legislature, "our fights with the legisla-ture don't even compare to the internal fights we have. Our internal fights are just so much more intense than when we come up here and try to get something done."

The original trio resented the encroachment of these strange power bro-kers, and Washington insiders resented Tallahassee natives. Staff reacted with a mix of awe and alienation when the governor appointed Jack Peeples, as head of the Chiles-MacKay transition team. L. Grant "Jack" Peeples, a Miami lawyer, restaurant owner, and former aide to Governor LeRoy Col-lins, had known Chiles personally since the 1950s and attended high school with Rhea. *Miami Herald* reporter Mark Silva called Peeples a "walking encyclopedia" for his forty years of state institutional memory going back to the Collins gubernatorial administration. But staff from Chiles' Senate years criticized Peeple's sudden prominence in the governor's policy shop. Bentley Lipscomb, former Chiles Senate staff and '90 campaign staff, recalls meeting Peeples at the Tallahassee campaign headquarters:

> One day [Peeples] walked in with a black suit on, with a starched white button-down shirt. I thought, Jesus Christ, who is this guy? It was like 104 outside. He had on all these formal-looking clothes.

Mallory Horne, former Speaker of the Florida House and President of the Florida Senate, a Chiles ally since the sixties, advised Governor Chiles regularly on policy, as did Dexter Douglass, Tallahassee lawyer and law school classmate. Governor Chiles' wife and children offered advice in an unofficial capacity. Governor Chiles valued his wife's counsel:

> I've called her the keeper of the flame. She's the person who continually says, "Well, now, that doesn't sound like what you were talking about when you said you were going to run for the job, the vision that you talked to people about. How does that equate with that?" She always comes back to the touchstone, what I should be about.[594]

Governor Chiles despised nepotism, though. After the 1990 campaign, Tandy Chiles angled for a job with the new administration:

> [My father] not only would not help you, he would hurt you. I wanted to have a job after I'd done the campaign. He would hurt me, hurt me. He would go out of his way to say, "See, I didn't get anything from anybody." So it wouldn't be your advantage sometimes to be a kid, 'cause he didn't want it to smack of anything like that.

If he sensed anything going "crosswise," Governor Chiles shut it down.

A second, larger cadre of unofficial advisers arrived at the governor's office with benevolent loyalty. This class of friends advised Governor Chiles on personal matters more than policy: Sonny Holtzman, a Coral Gables lawyer, helped deliver money in Dade County since the 1970 campaign. John "Jack" Watson III, Miami lawyer and Chiles hunting and fishing buddy, knew Chiles since ATO at University of Florida. Jack knew Rhea since they attended Ponce de Leon High School in Coral Gables. Watson said of Governor Chiles, "I guess you could say he's my best friend." Steven Alan Anderson, a Tampa real estate and commercial lawyer, raised money for Chiles. He was a member of "The Gang That Couldn't Shoot Straight." Louis de la Parte Jr. of Tampa, former president of the Florida Senate, knew Chiles since their Florida legislature days. De la Parte was also a former law school classmate.

Lawton Chiles and Wilbur Boyd both met in 1958 as freshman legislators. They soon started sharing rooms while the Legislature was in session. Ed Chiles commented: "I don't know anybody who's as close to my father as Wilbur is. They're almost like brothers." When Chiles began as governor in 1991, Boyd was president of Employee Service, Inc., in Bradenton. David Burke Kibler III of Lakeland, chairman of Holland & Knight, and his partners Chesterfield H. Smith and Julian D. Clarkson assisted Chiles. Lawyer Jon Cameron Moyle Sr. of West Palm Beach helped.[595] Some friends from grade school, such as Eddie Gong, found Governor Chiles a tough client. "As a Chinese-American, I must say that Chiles is the most inscrutable Westerner I've ever met," Gong said.

Finally, innumerable acquaintances appeared at the governor's door asking for personal favors, exploiting Governor Chiles' easygoing demeanor. Other well-intentioned friends stopped by just to see if the Walkin' Lawton they knew from the newspapers matched their memory. Governor Chiles kept his walkin' boots in his office, beside a "special interest" notebook enumerating his 75,000 1990 campaign donors.[596] They proved tempting for a governor with a constitutional inability to say "No." The crush of attention stalled office traffic, according to chief of staff Jim Krog:

> I can remember when he first became governor, the euphoria of everybody because everybody believed. They knew him when he walked, they knew him when he [ran], they'd given him a hundred dollars . . . they knew him, he was theirs. They owned a piece of him, and he believed they owned a piece of him, that he was them. And so when somebody called up, it could be some old fishin' buddy from such and such, who said I've just gotta see the governor, well he didn't have time to see every fishin' buddy in the world—and he wanted to. So he'd come in and I'd go in, and I'd say, "These five guys showed up on the doorstep. What do you wanna do?' And he'd say, "Well, you can't bring 'em in here, 'cause once they get in my office I'll never get 'em out.'

The persistent found a way through:

> So what we do is I would take my office was right there, his office, the big ceremonial office, is here, and we had the little office there, so I'd get 'em, take 'em through my office 'cause it had a door, and I'd

take 'em into the big office and I'd sit 'em down. I'd say, "Listen, I'm gonna go get the governor. He's in the middle of a meeting, but I know he wants to talk to you for a few minutes, because you're here." . . . We knew who were his friends. . . . He'd come in and sit down in the chair with 'em, and he'd be stretched out like he's gonna spend the next two hours with 'em. And I'd leave him in there for about five minutes, and I'd pop in the door and say, "Listen, Governor, I'm sorry, they're screamin' back in there." He'd turn to me and say, "Well, can you spend a few more minutes with these guys? Figure out how you can help 'em." And he'd leave. So I'd figure out if they really needed something, thank 'em and then go.

These small-time political parasites exacerbated the already intense infighting in the executive office. Office skirmishes spilled over into the legislature, threatening the governor's long-term agenda.

The Chiles administration handicapped itself at the outset with a disastrous State of the State address in March 1991. The governor worked for twelve hours on the speech in his Mansion bedroom the night before the address, writing every word longhand on a yellow legal pad. He stopped only twice for a haircut and dinner. At midnight, he came downstairs to review the draft with staff. The editorial meeting broke up an hour later. "He loves the adrenaline rush, the last-minute-before-college-examination kind of feel," communications director Mary Jane Gallagher said.[597]

The next morning, the legislature interrupted the State of the State for applause just five times. Governor Chiles concluded the speech by holding up a three-legged milking stool as a symbol of separation of powers and checks and balances in state government—the governor, House, and Senate. "Look at this stool," he said. "It's got three legs. If you pull one out, it won't stand." Instead of interpreting the gesture as a metaphor, the press corps dismissed it as a non sequitur. State Rep. Dan Webster (R-Orlando) quipped, "Maybe we're the bench."[598]

The Chiles administration recovered and met some of its campaign finance and ethics reform priorities. The legislature passed a bill limiting contributions to state and local offices to $500 and creating a public financing pot for viable statewide candidates. Liberal Democrat State Rep. Ron Saunders (D-Key West) helped the governor secure votes on the bill. "If you've got one of the greatest living politicians suggesting something, as a politician myself, I've got to listen," Saunders said. "I mean, the guy is a living legend." Senate minority floor leader Rich Crotty (R-Orlando) explained the success: "[Governor Chiles] has an uncanny ability to replace substance with symbolism. And make it work."[599]

One of the Chiles administration's first bills on ethics reform had already taken effect that January, aiming to end lobbyist traditions like the "beer fairy." In 1976, State Senator Jack Gordon (D-Miami Beach) listed a $105 gift from the "beer fairy," when he found ten cases of beer on his doorstep. A year later, after having sponsored a tax increase on booze, he had to pay for his own. Since then, Florida legislators accepted the beer fairy as routine, and editorial pages acclaimed the governor's stand against the practice.[600]

The governor even seemed to master the politics of his most important policy document—his first budget—despite hard times. Before the Chiles administration acted on its plans to reform the tax code and reinvent government, it had to fill the state's budget shortfall. The Cook-Gallagher-Krog power trio negotiated the first administration budget in the midst of national economic recession. "People think we're at each other's throats," communications director Mary Jane Gallagher said, "but we're having some of the best debates in the world."[601] The prior year's 1990 state budget, passed in June, totaled $27 billion. In December 1990, Doug Cook, Chiles' budget coordinator for the transition stated, "We have walked in during the third act of a tragedy. We have significant revenue shortfalls that far exceed what we had originally estimated. The situation is much worse than expected." The Gulf War exacerbated uncertainty about the recession. Florida's constitution required a balanced budget.[602] Doug Cook on the first year's budget:

> The first year we inherited a horrible budget, terrible, terrible mess. And we had to whack the hell out of it, and Chiles hated it. Because he'd come in, he had an idea I'm gonna reform government blah, blah, blah, blah; actually his second day in office he had to cut the budget $250 million. And had we been smarter, we would have submitted it to the legislature and just let the legislature handle it, but he was so exasperated by Reagan's lack of leadership on a lot of these issues, and so filled with this, "I've gotta do something about it," that we whacked the budget.

In fall 1990, Texas faced a $3.8 million budget gap, California and Connecticut faced $2 billion budget gaps.[603] In Chiles' transition period 1990-1991, he asked state agencies to cut budgets by 5 percent, allowing agency heads to choose programs for elimination instead of an across-the-board axe.[604]

In Governor Chiles' first week in office, he cut the general revenue budget by 5 percent. He cut the Martinez 1990-1991 budget four times before July 1, 1991, removing $1 billion from a $30 billion Florida budget. Nine months into office, Chiles-MacKay had cut the budget more than any administration in Florida history, a total of $1.6 billion. That nine months also saw a quarter million new residents move to the Sunshine State, including 100,000 children.[605] Governor Chiles addressed the state on television on the opening night of the 1991 legislative session to discuss the economy and build a case for shrinking government, cutting $163 million from the budget and combating the $1.4 billion budget deficit.[606]

According to chief of staff Jim Krog, the budget battle brought out the political prizefighter in his boss. The budget deficit totaled $1.4 billion, and the governor wanted to terminate every "turkey," or pork project, in the document. Rep. Sam Mitchell, a Panhandle Democrat, instituted one of the most infamous turkeys: to exempt ostrich feed from the sales tax. Representative Mitchell lived about two miles from the state's largest ostrich breeder.[607] Florida TaxWatch estimated in 1990 that about $100-to-$200 million of turkeys are tallied in the budget every year.[608] Governor Chiles targeted the turkeys as the quickest source of savings in a recessionary budget year. Jim Krog describes the 1991 planning process for the first "turkey-less" budget:

> So we put our legislative people on it. . . . We literally looked for every turkey that went in the budget. . . . All these lobbyist friends of mine, I told them "I wouldn't put it in. If you've got it you've better bury it so damn deep so we can never find it."

At public meetings with the president of the Senate and Speaker of the House, both Democrats, Governor Chiles pressed for boldness, according to Krog:

> And so we'd sit in the conference room and invite 'em all over, and they would all puff up and tell me when I'd go up and see 'em, "We're gonna tell him, you just can't do this." I said, "Wrong answer, guys. Won't work. He wants this and he wants it badly." So we sit down and we're going through the budget thing, the turkeys, and all this

stuff. .... There's five senators here and five house members here, and he looked at them and said, "Nope, if that's the case we're gonna have a real problem. You guys probably can win the first round; you will never win the subsequent rounds. Because I can be out of this office and on an airplane and in every TV market in this state. I think that I've got enough political juice to pull this off. I think you guys are in a bubble; you need to get out of the bubble. And you need to be a little bit braver. And you need to take a little more risk, and you need to stop worrying about this, and let's all get together and do this." ... And pretty soon, they'll come back with five different ways to compromise.

The governor had successfully secured passage of most of his budget requests, killed myriad turkeys, and balanced the budget. But his senior staff had spoiled his relationship with the legislature for the rest of the term.

After budget negotiations, Governor Chiles recharged spiritually on hunting trips with his best friends. "If he went into the woods with his mind tied in knots," the governor's son Ed Chiles said, "the time there untied it." Chief of Staff Jim Krog reflected on the balance between work and leisure:

> Once you're governor, you're governor twenty-four hours a day, seven days a week. He liked to hunt, he liked to go out, and he liked to go to movies. He liked to have a life. He liked to drive his own car; he didn't want a lot of security. We had to cut the security detail back, which made FDLE anxious. But we did it. He said, "I don't need nine guys rolling around there with me at night. A couple people—they're not coming after me." He was a very normal elected official; he didn't have an ego that was bigger than the sky.

The governor hunted with former U.S. Secretary of State Jim Baker, former President George H. W. Bush, and Texas energy executive T. Boone Pickens, in locales as diverse as Virginia, New Mexico, South Dakota, Alabama, and Georgia. Florida Speaker of the House T.K. Wetherell and Governor Chiles hunted turkey together often.

Governor Chiles hunted with then-Governor Ben Nelson of Nebraska. Florida or Florida State usually played football against Nebraska late in the season. The governor had a standing bet going—the governor whose state school lost would host the winner on a spring turkey hunt in his state.

Governor Chiles wanted to be the first governor to get a "grand slam" in turkey hunting—a successful hunt for all four major North American species of the great bird. He was upset when Governor Nelson beat him to it. Governor Chiles hunted with Rob Keck, who served as CEO of the National Wild Turkey Federation for thirty years:

> He'd get me on the phone sometimes just to have me hear a new turkey call he was trying out and wanted to know what I thought of it. Lawton would come to our big annual NWTF convention and show up wearing a camo jacket and a weathered hunting hat that made him look like Jed Clampett. He'd just wander around the booths talking to hunters and call manufacturers, and loving every minute being around turkey hunters with his same passion for the sport.

"I don't think anyone epitomized the passion and love for turkey hunting better than Lawton Chiles," added Keck. "He showed that turkey hunting was a common element that cut through all politics, race and the hustle and bustle of modern living."[609]

One of the Florida Department of Law Enforcement agents who formed the governor's security detail once tried to join a hunt, but Governor Chiles told him, "We got a new governor, and you're not going hunting with me."[610] Dubose Ausley, a friend of the governor's from their days working in the state legislature, called Governor Chiles' office during turkey season. "I'd have people come by here and say, 'Nobody in the governor's office is returning my call. I can't get anybody,'" Ausley recalls. "I said, 'Watch this.' I'd call in, and [Governor Chiles] would come to the phone."

Ausley reflects on his friendship with the governor:

> We'd ride [horseback] an hour and a half and he'd never say a word. It'd be one of those days where he just didn't feel like talking. I always honored that and I think [it's] another reason he and I were friends, because I didn't infringe on those inner voices that may have been talking to him . . . while he was thinking.[611]

FDLE agents often lost track of their protectee on hunting days, T.K. Wetherell explains. "[Governor Chiles would] come out to the farm, and we'd hunt. God, it was so funny. FDLE would call, 'Is he there?' 'Well, I don't really know,' [I would tell them]. He asked for the code to the gate last night.

I saw a car come in, about daylight. And I got a feeling he probably is, but haven't been back to check anyplace." On one occasion, according to Virginia Wetherell (T.K.'s wife), Governor Chiles found a lost hunting dog on the Wetherell property:

> He walked back to the house one morning before T.K. got back, and he wanted me to call a number. He found someone's hunting dog had gotten caught in Ted Turner's fence. We share boundary line with Ted Turner, and the dog's collar was caught in the fence, and he was afraid that the dog would die if he ripped the leg off, or might bite him. He could see his collar with a name on it, so I called the number and I said, "Governor Chiles is here and he has found your dog in the woods caught in a fence." And they said, "Oh, sure!" They didn't believe me.[612]

When Governor Chiles returned to the fence to check on the dog, it had ripped his paw off and bled to death.

Governor Chiles asked the Mansion chef to prepare wild game from his hunt, or shared a range of other culinary favorites with family, friends, and staff. Mansion chef Jenny Heerema regularly prepared fresh quail, venison, and turkey, as well as black beans. For dessert, the governor enjoyed chocolate crepes with yogurt cheese, or icebox cookies prepared with heart-healthy ingredients. Governor Chiles brought bags of his favorite cookies on road trips. Eldest son Bud Chiles reminisced about his father's evolved tastes:

> My dad loved to eat. He loved just about everything from sushi to collared greens. But he loved to eat game the best. His freezer at the Governor's Mansion was always filled with venison, elk, quail, turkey, ducks, dove, as well as grouper, tuna, and bass. He taught the Mansion chef to cook game. How to smoke a turkey, how to prepare the choice cuts of venison, and how to pan sautéed quail. But he was the master chef when it came to preparing game. He learned how to make the sauces that were a reduction of the essences that the game produced as it cooks. We would enjoy feasts of game and we would wear ourselves out trying to determine what was the best.

Younger son Ed Chiles, himself a restaurateur, cooked game with father at the Mansion. The governor loved eating at restaurants on the road, too, according to chief of staff Jim Krog:

> And he loved to eat particularly when Rhea wasn't with him, 'cause Rhea always was trying to make sure that he ate good. Loved spicy food but shouldn't eat it. Loved sushi. Loved Cuban food. So we'd go somewhere, and meet him somewhere and he'd say, "Oh we gotta go to this place. Pull in here for sushi," or "Pull in here for seafood," or "Pull in here, I gotta have some oysters 'cause I know this little place around here." So you're out of the way, now you're late, you're calling ahead. That was his way of sayin' "I've been to these places for twenty years, and if they heard I was in town and I really didn't go in there and eat, what the hell am I doin'?"

When the legislature recessed, Governor Chiles and staff often lunched at a Cajun joint in Tallahassee called Goodtime Charlie's. "I don't think it could pass inspection by the health department," legislative affairs staffer Wayne Watters said. "It was rough. But he just loved that place." Debbie Kilmer, director of Federal Relations for the Chiles administration, recalls the governor's taste for sushi. One night while she stayed at the Mansion as a guest, Kilmer left a container of takeout sushi on the step going up to the governor's residence. At breakfast the next morning, Rhea said, "Debbie, he got in real late, and you know what, he ate it." Debbie replied, "I left that there as a joke."

However his agenda fared, the political press still celebrated the governor's populism and sense of humor. Unlike prior governors who worked at the ornate desk in the Executive Office of the Governor, Governor Chiles preferred a side office nicknamed the "hunt club." The governor met with legislators and lobbyists around a couch in the hunt club, and used the big desk only for signing ceremonies. On official trips, Governor Chiles always sat shotgun while an FDLE agent drove the state car. He only sat in the back taxi-style when traveling with Rhea. "He did not want to look like he was regal, or some fancy dignitary," legislative affairs staffer Jim Cordero said.

Governor Chiles' mangling of proper names amused reporters. Senate staffer Rick Brandon recalls the habit's early beginnings:

There was a well-known economist at the time early on in the Budget Committee, his name was Art Okun, O-K-U-N. He founded what was called Okun's law, which was the relationship of unemployment and inflation. He would come testify, and Chiles would always practice his name and have me say "Okun," and then he would say "Orkin," as in the pest control firm. He'd look at me and say, "I did it again, right?" and I said, "Yep, you did it again." It drove him crazy.

On the 1990 campaign trail, Chiles twisted "parental consent" into "perennial consent." [613] One of the Chiles administration Cabinet members, Secretary of Community Development Bill Sadowski, never heard the governor pronounce his surname correctly. Governor Chiles always mistakenly said "Sandusky." One day Sadowski told Lt. Governor Buddy MacKay, "Well, if the governor is convinced that it's Sandusky, then I guess he's right." Lieutenant Governor MacKay added, "I came to look forward to it because once he got a word in his mind wrong, it never got straightened out."[614]

Governor Chiles loved dressing up for holidays, especially Christmas, Easter, and Halloween. *Tallahassee Democrat* newsman Bill Cotterell fondly recalls introducing his son to the governor, dressed as the Easter Bunny for a 1991 party at the Mansion.[615] Mansion staffer Ann Miller, a high school classmate of the governor's, describes the first Halloween at the Mansion:

I was the wicked witch and [Governor Chiles] was the ghost. And we had a cauldron with dry ice and I had moss in my hair and face made up and the chef had put a real pumpkin on her head; she had hollowed it out and we gave out bags of candy. Well the governor sat there with these turkey legs and clanked 'em together. And it finally got to the point where we had to cool it because we were scaring the kids that were coming up the walk to the Governor's Mansion. He was sittin' in the rockin' chair in a ghost outfit!

Governor Chiles dressed up for parties, like the one he threw after the 1991 legislative session. About fifty staff and significant others attended, including Jim Cordero from legislative affairs:

And out of the Mansion comes the governor. And I don't know where he found this outfit; I can almost visualize it now. He was trying to dress up like Jimmy Buffett or something like that, and it was like a light pale aqua pair of linen pants, some horrible-looking shirt. And he had a straw hat ... maybe he even had sunglasses on. It might have been burnt orange or something, the colors were just contrasting. He may have had flip-flops on, too. He had everybody just rollin', and he had a great time. He was the clown for everybody.

Governor Chiles dressed in strange outfits for Capitol press skits, a series of sketch comedy bits traditionally performed annually by the incumbent gubernatorial administration before the press corps. In the first year skits, the governor bragged, "we got elected even though our opponent outspent us two-to-one, even though I was on Prozac and damn depressed the whole time." Then he placed a crown atop his head to mock his State of the State address: "I'm in charge. No stools needed."[616]

Governor Chiles' popular personality helped blunt political mid-year criticism at the end of the first legislative session. Gubernatorial staff and pro-Chiles reporters focused on substantive issues like his preference for office chaos. Friends wondered if the governor's interpretation of executive power called for more than decision by committee and "country Zen." They blamed his management style for the adminstration's ruinous first year—traditionally when the governor's boldest initiatives are announced and promulgated. Rhea Chiles found the governor's office shiftless, especially compared to her husband's Senate office:

> I came from eighteen years in the United States Senate and I was pretty much expecting good behavior on the part of staff and people who make things work, so I was very surprised to see the lack of organization or any machinery, organizational machinery, or intent, that had to do with the governor. It was like, "What do you wanna do, boss?"

Inspired by Alvin Toffler's book *Powershift*, Rhea tried to institute office reforms, like having senior staff share secretaries. "Why, it's like trying to get lions and tigers to perform together," she commented on the process.

Decision by committee hurt the governor's agenda, according to staffer Dean Saunders:

> In a vacuum, everybody then tries to be the leader. So you had everybody runnin' around trying to prove that they could do this and

do that. Then there were guys like me who came in from the Senate, who didn't need to establish our credibility with him.

Runaway policy fights inside the office rivaled partisan disputes in rancor, burning staff out before they even had a chance to lobby the recalcitrant legislature. Rick Farrell, Chiles' chief of staff for most of his Senate career, commented on Chiles' management method:

> One of his styles of operation is to listen to a lot of people but to keep his own council. Everybody has input, but nobody is a determinate, and I say that as someone who has tried to be a determinate.[617]

Governor Chiles acted more like a legislator and than an executive, according to Wayne Watters from legislative affairs:

> I think [Governor Chiles] really preferred working with the Senate even though you had to do more work. But I think it's that convincing, arm-twisting and debate back-and-forth—I think he really liked that.

Critics like *Miami Herald* political reporter Mark Silva hinted that chief of staff Jim Krog deserved blame for running the executive office like a campaign manager rather than a policy director:

> The reason that Lawton Chiles' launch in office was rough is that he brought the campaign into office with him. He made the basic mistake of taking the people that got you there into office. And they're two different animals: people that know how to wage campaigns and people that know how to run government.

Krog himself liked to compare Governor Chiles with former Florida Governor Bob Graham to explain his boss's style. Governor Graham typically worked all day and all night, reading technical papers and calling policy experts at late hours, whereas Chiles preferred to work fewer hours and let his subconscious process issues:

> [Governor] Chiles needed time to think. And he made time. He was somebody that if he wanted to take two hours for lunch, and you had

a meeting scheduled for one o'clock, he didn't give a damn whether he didn't show up for that meeting. He literally wasn't out because he didn't want to offend anybody; he'd make sure the meeting got covered.

At the end of its first year, however, as administration budget cuts filtered through the economy, the Chiles-MacKay staff fumed with self-doubt and self-recrimination. The famously unflappable governor even lost his temper in public. In September 1991, over 1,000 angry university students rallied in Tallahassee against education funding cuts in the administration's first budget. Governor Chiles admonished one heckler at the rally, "You get off your duff and come and help me with what we're doing."[618] Newspapers circulated the quote widely. Critics in both parties claimed that the Governor's Mansion was the only functional aspect of the administration, according to Rhea Chiles, who had begun using the facility to host lunches and other events to advance her husband's agenda:

> All of the sudden we had the lunches, and I worked with the scheduler down at the office. You let me know what the issue is and who you're inviting and I'll do the rest. We'll do them in the family dining room, and we'll put on the dog, the Mansion dog, and all that. Well that worked so well.

Miami Herald's political editor Tom Fiedler commented in December 1991: "Lawton Chiles' fall from grace may be long remembered as perhaps the fastest plunge Floridians have known since Disney opened Space Mountain."[619] A year after Chiles' election, three out of four Florida voters rated his performance as fair or poor. Ever the jester, Governor Chiles quipped to reporters: "My dog still loves me."

Gubernatorial staff, in hindsight, criticized themselves for trying to accomplish too much, too quickly in year one. Staff always deliberated at length before the regular session, Lt. Governor MacKay later recalled, and then designated every agenda item "top priority" status, ensuring chaos. Legislative affairs staffer Wayne Watters has also critiqued the agenda-setting process:

> I think that sometimes people are victims of their own image. . . . If you add a lot of legislative agenda items onto that list, you may have

had the most successful session that any governor's ever had, ever, but it may not look at way.

Krog spread blame for the situation to the governor and lieutenant governor:

> Buddy MacKay used to say, "We can only have five legislative priorities per session. We can only have five." So we put the list together and we put the list down. And I'd say, "Okay, here are the five," right, right, right—everybody agrees here are the five. Next thing you know, Buddy has sent me a note that says, "Here's three others." The governor says, "Well, we need to have these." Now I'm back at fifteen. And then the agencies are coming in screaming, "This has gotta be a priority, governor—you've gotta take this on." So the chirping little birds out here in every agency come in. And then the governor looks up and says, "I thought you were supposed to keep these priorities straight. If we are going to be successful, we'll only have five." Gotcha, boss. If you let me pick the five, we'll keep the five. And that's the problem. How do you take that enthusiasm for change and make it real and get something done at the same time?

Others on the governor's staff blamed their fellow colleagues for exploiting their boss's generosity and loyalty by treating the executive office like a social and financial status symbol. Senior staff, they claimed, hung out far too much at Clyde's—a Tallahassee watering hole popular with capital insiders—rather than doing the people's business. Chief of staff Jim Krog, himself a familiar face at Clyde's, explains the source for this fidelity:

> He was very sensitive to other people's feelings, very sensitive to old friends, and he wanted to make sure that everybody was—that because he was governor didn't mean that he wasn't the same old Lawton that they knew. That was very important to him; that was more important than anything. The title of governor only meant that he could do certain things that other people couldn't.

Former Senate staffer Dennis Beal lambasted the gubernatorial senior staff:

Those Tallahassee people treated him like a damn dog sometimes. I couldn't work for anybody and talk about him and laugh about him and do stuff like they did. There was no personal loyalty, they were just a fuckin' paycheck for some of them. . . . The only dog I had in that fight was him. . . . They did it because many of 'em thought he was just a buffoon.

Rhea Chiles believed that too many staffers and self-appointed advisers thought they could sign the governor's name, and too many actually did. Governor Chiles drew a smiley face next to his name on paperwork for fun, but it ultimately took on a practical purpose, giving his authentic imprint to a letter or note.[620]

The governor had won the first budget battle but his madhouse of executive staff had overreached and ruined his relationship with the legislature. Governor Chiles met with House Speaker T.K. Wetherell and Senate President Gwen Margolis in December 1991 to review the year and preview the next year.

The legislature had hamstrung the governor's plan to begin "reinventing government" according to his campaign promises. Governor Chiles had tried to overhaul the state bureaucracy and civil service system in December's one-week special session. During the session, Governor Chiles proposed reorganizing the Department of Health and Rehabilitative Services (HRS) and abolishing both the Department of General Services and the Department of Highway Safety and Motor Vehicles.[621] HRS, enacted into law in 1969, claimed 46,000 employees and more than a quarter of the state budget by 1990. "Everybody always wants to restructure HRS," said Budd Bell, a veteran social services advocate. "It's been Florida's second sport for years."[622]

The legislature approved the governor's civil service reform, allowing managers greater flexibility to reward job performace, but postponed most of Chiles' wish list until next year's regular session.

"Am I asking too much? Yes, I am," the governor said at the meeting with Wetherell and Margolis. "Am I asking for it to be done too fast? Yes, I am. But I don't think we can go fast enough for what the public wants us to do. We may make some mistakes, but we're going to move forward."[623] Legislators expected to vote on new taxes next year.

"I don't think we live in normal times anymore," Governor Chiles added. "I went to bed Friday night and there was a Soviet Union, and when I woke up Monday morning there was no Soviet Union."

12

I Came Here to Make A Difference

Governor Chiles announced an ambitious agenda at his 1992 State of the State address. Though his job approval ratings had tumbled, he clamored to the press that his leadership had seized "this locomotive that has been traveling down one direction for a long time, stopped it and turned it around 180 degrees."[624] He pushed Florida to reform the state tax code so that rich and poor paid their "fair share" for public investments. He also advocated a new tax for the state's service sector, which had grown substantial as a proportion of the economy since the 1970s. The governor quoted his friend LuLu Austin, the sister of the Chiles family maid Ruby Austin. LuLu, dying of cancer, refused a potentially life-saving operation, informing her doctor, "I didn't come here to stay, but I came here to make a difference." The governor likewise told the legislature:

> Now I want to know if you came here to stay or if you came to make a difference? I'm betting you came to make a difference.[625]

Governor Chiles postponed his reinventing government agenda in favor of tax reform.

The governor believed the economic recession afforded him a rare opportunity to persuade the public to accept higher taxes. State health, education, and prison costs skyrocketed, driven by high population growth. Growing Medicaid costs strained the budget more than any other single outlay. Medicaid costs grew almost ninefold over the prior decade, from $580 million

(6.7 percent of state spending) in fiscal 1981-82 to $5.1 billion (14.74 percent of state spending) in fiscal 1992-1993.[626] Florida's total bonded debt exceeded $4.4 billion, or $324 per Floridian, in 1991.[627] [figure for budget shortfall that year] Administration staffer Dean Saunders explains how these numbers built the governor's case for tax reform in spring 1992:

> We went into the whole fair share tax reform, which was essentially services tax repackaged; renamed, repackaged, with the idea that we were gonna make an investment in some areas and not in others. We tried to use the fact that the state was in a recession, the budget was hurting. And we really tried to use that as a way to get the legislature to agree to the investment in the tax side of it. Now, the difference was we were gonna phase it in over a three of four year period, as opposed to whacking everybody all at one time like the services tax. The truth of the matter is, our state's system for taxing is antiquated. We are twenty years into the information age, and we have not adjusted to the paradigm. We're still modeled on this old, manufacturing, durable goods approach to taxation. We're not gonna get a state income tax; it's not gonna happen. And so we're left with goods and services. And we're trying to tax goods and not services, but the goods are a shrinking portion of our economy. The services are burgeoning. So, intellectually, it's a debate that needs to happen. Politically, it's incredibly, incredibly difficult.

Amid the recession, Governor Chiles spoke of wanting to "call his brother." The phrase referred to one of his favorite boyhood tales, according to *Tallahassee Democrat* reporter Bill Cotterell:

> Some railroad men were havin' fun with a young employee, a new guy on the job. They said, "Suppose you're switchman and two trains are on the same track headin' straight at each other. You've got a very short time to respond. What are you gonna do?"
> The new guy said, "Well, I'd grab the big metal switch, pull it, send one of 'em off to another track."
> They said, "What if the handle comes off in your hand?"
> He said, "Well then, I'd grab my lantern, start swingin' back and forth. One lantern by itself is a sign, whatever you're doin' stop."

"Yeah, but what if it's raining and sleeting and dark at night and they can't see any lantern?"

"Well, then, I guess I'd just call my brother."

"Why? What's your brother gonna do?"

"Nothin', but my brother ain't never seen no train wreck."

Chiles, when his legislation was totally in the pits and everything was hopeless, would say, "Well, I think I'll call my brother. This is just a train wreck."

Governor Chiles ordered his senior staff to argue as long as necessary about the best size for his tax plan. "I like it better that I've got three or four rottweilers—they're all pulling at the leash—than having one whip-master that's around a bunch of lap dogs," the governor said.[628] Budget director Doug Cook wanted a $2.2 billion plan; chief of staff Jim Krog wanted what he perceived as a more realistic $1.1 billion. "The governor told Krog and me to go in a room," Cook recalls. "And he basically said, 'Jim, I want you to come out and tell me this is a number that's reasonable with the legislature, and Doug, I want you to tell me that this is a number that does right. And if you can't look me in the eye and say that, don't come out of that room.'" Cook and Krog gnashed for hours. "The difficulty of a setup like this is, we are all mature people, we have definite opinions, and we are all used to getting our way," Cook said.[629]

Governor Chiles settled on the figure announced at his State of the State address, $1.35 billion in new taxes and program cuts. Weeks later, more than 3,000 college students rallied at the Capitol to protest new cuts in education funding. After the rally, students broke up into regional clans and met with their respective state legislators. University of West Florida student David Thompson decried the state's ratio of prison funding to education funding. "I could go out and steal and get $16,000 a year, or I could pay tuition and get $5,000," Thompson said. Seventeen-year-old FSU student Joshua Utley said, "It's become a stigma to have to go to college in Florida. It seems like the only thing our schools are known for right now is their football teams—not the quality of their education."[630] David Thompson added, "Chiles came out and was welcomed with some boos. He looked very uncomfortable out there. I actually felt sorry for him. Nobody could believe he came out to talk to us. In a situation like that, you have to be firm and direct, and he wasn't."[631]

Governor Chiles began a road tour in May 1992 to publicize what they called their "Fair Share" tax plan. Donning his madras shirt, the governor warned opponents: "get a good hold—because we're coming."[632] The governor loved to take issues on the road, according to chief of staff Jim Krog:

> He loved just listening to people. Most politicians want to go out and talk to people, he wanted to go out and just listen to 'em, to what they're sayin'. What's happening here? What's happenin' with huntin'? What's your kid doin'? What are the schools like over here? He was asking a lot of questions, getting feedback all the time on what's goin' on. And everybody that talked to him, thought that no matter what they said, he was gonna do it.

For the 1992 Capitol press skits, Governor Chiles and Lt. Gov MacKay dressed up like Batman and Robin, calling themselves the "Super Reformers": "Walkin' Man" and "Buddy Wonder." The duo sang a rendition of "There's No Business Like Show Business," altering the lyrics to fit their tax reform agenda. "The Tallahassee press corps forecasts skies of gray, but we believe in another way," they chirped. "Just a small investment, just a little dough—get off your duffs and join the show!"[633]

Florida House Speaker T.K. Wetherell (D-Daytona Beach) said of expectations of budget reform for the 1992 regular session, "I think he'll get a lot of that stuff, even though he's asked for the moon and a Cadillac. He'll get a couple of stars and a Lincoln, so he'll be all right there."[634] Governor Chiles knew to ask for the impossible to ensure a fruitful compromise, Wetherell explains:

> Lawton was a smart politician and we'd sit down and we'd contrive different issues, and the idea was to form 'em in the House and ship 'em to the Senate, and they would screw 'em all up. Some, we would want them to screw up. Some, if you want a dollar, you ask for five, they'd send it back with three, and we'd bitch all the way and say we only want a dollar anyway. Lawton was pretty good about strategy in that. So we did a lot of that.

In a rare, nineteen-minute televised address to a joint session of the legislature on June 1, Governor Chiles proclaimed it was "time to get real" about tax reform. "People are tired of being patronized, lied to, misled. They want

straight talk, commitment and follow-through. People really want change."
The governor ridiculed the current tax code's loopholes for the wealthy. "The
man is insane," said Senator Fred Dudley (R-Fort Meyers). "He has placed
himself in a corner with no place to go but the ceiling," said Rep. Sandy Safley (R-Clearwater). "So now he peers down on this Legislature from an ele-
vation I don't think he should be at." Governor Chiles condemned the state's
largest business lobby, Associated Industries of Florida, for its hand in preserving the sales tax code's injustices.[635] Governor Chiles described the new
Associated Industries headquarters in Tallahassee, a 15,000-square-foot,
36-room building:

> It's got a board room table that's so long you can't see from one end
> to the other. And around it sit the high chiefs of the railroads, the
> electric and gas companies, the telephone companies, the insurance
> companies, the sugar industry, the grocery and merchandise giants
> and the road contractors—you know, all those small business guys
> toughing it out and trying to make a payroll.[636]

"I know that I have not been the delightful bearer of glad tidings," Governor Chiles said. "Any many would like to shoot the messenger. But I have
never felt as good in my life. I think it's because I'm doing exactly what I
know is right with no reservations."[637]
Governor Chiles vetoed two budgets, forcing the legislature to stay in session through June. The state lacked a budget until the governor signed one
into law on July 1, the start of the new fiscal year. Chief of Staff Jim Krog
recalls his boss's mood:

> Chiles was more—he ruminated, ruminated, and when he landed
> on it, get out of the way, he was gonna take it to the bank. And he
> could be as tough and drive that bargain all the way, and he'd play
> poker with you. You wanna play the last card? You think you got the
> best card? Then let's play. I've seen him stare down legislators to the
> point where he'd say, "Fine, you guys wanna do that, you don't think
> I'll veto it, then you need to go ahead and check your hold card.
> Check your hold card, make your play, and then I'll play my card."
> And they'd walk away and come back and they'd roll, because they
> knew. I've heard more than one legislator—Democrat mostly—come
> up and say, "Damn, he's crazy, he's nuts." And I'd say, "If he's locked

onto something, he's the governor and he's got one vote and he's gonna exercise that vote. You may not like the answer, but he does not care."

One of the few occasions the governor lost his temper happened in Bradenton at a town hall meeting with small business owners. Governor Chiles fielded a question from businessman Wes Hackett about his "Fair Share" tax plan. Hackett called state workers "parasitic leeches," and affirmed, "None of your state employees will hold themselves accountable for their incompetence."

Governor Chiles angrily retorted, "I've got people working for me that you could not hold their socks, they're so good. You make me mad when you say all these people are incompetent." Hackett countered, "Because they can't get a job elsewhere, that's why [these people work for the state]." Governor Chiles ended the conversation: "You're so far out. I'm not going to listen to you."[638]

Governor Chiles often communicated displeasure in budget negotiations through body language rather than words, according to former Senate staffer Dave Mica:

> He'd wear the thin glasses . . . he'd wear'em there [slumped down his nose], one of his kinda signature things was he'd do his thing and he'd give you one of these—kinda looking over the glasses—and it was sort of a signal to let you know he knew you were there, didn't mean you were gonna get your way! He didn't care who you were representing, what you were, he kinda knew you were there. It was his way of making a connection.

"I think sometimes," *Miami Herald* reporter Tom Fiedler commented, "[Governor Chiles] could convey more with a smile and a shrug than a lot of people could in ten minutes of straight verbiage." The governor also wrote short, funny notes to legislators, staff, and reporters. State Senator Richard Langley (R-Clermont) wrote Governor Chiles a letter dated June 10, rebuking his tax plan and accusing him of "good ole boy politics." Langley purported that the taxes would burden the middle class most of all. "You have deceived and mislead [*sic*] the people of this state more than any political figure that I have ever known." The governor replied on official stationary:

Dear Dick:

I just wanted you to know that some nut is using your stationary to send me letters. It didn't fool me for a moment though.

Your Pal,

Lawton[639]

The governor drew a smiley face beside his name.

The Florida state legislature ultimately clung to the tax code and rejected most of the governor's tax plan. Lt. Governor MacKay reflected on their failed crusade to hike taxes of one of the most ardently anti-tax states in the nation:

I think we brought it [the backlash against their 1992 tax plan] on ourselves. And Lawton and I spent a lot of time—a lot of other people have spent a lot of time trying to get people to buy into being Floridians. Policy wise, we did some things that tried to do that. We tried to shove a lot more back to local government. . . . I think people will commit to being Floridians at the local level. They'll commit to being part of saving a piece of environmentally endangered land; they'll commit to helpin' with local schools, but in terms of the state it's very difficult.

"We were not realistic when we came in and neither were many of the people around us," budget director Doug Cook said.[640]

As the Fair Share tax plan floundered, the Chiles-MacKay team resumed work on its "reinventing government" initiative to salvage the year. *Reinventing Government*, written by David Osborne and Ted Gaebler and published during Governor Chiles' second year in office, mentioned the Florida governor five times as an example of a politician putting their ideas into practice. Governor Chiles disseminated copies of the book to his senior staff. "During that period [governors] were almost desperate for new approaches," David Osborne said, "When people got wind of this book I was writing [*Reinventing Government*] . . . it was incredible, the hunger for the ideas ." Governor Chiles, like U.S. Presidents Theodore Roosevelt and Franklin Delano Roosevelt, embraced the role of intellectuals in public policy. According to Lt. Governor MacKay, "we set out to make Florida's management look less like General Motors and more like Apple Computer."

273

Governor Chiles, who called the process of reforming the state bureaucracy "rightsizing," succeeded in reshaping multiple agencies.[641]

His push for bureaucratic reform honored an American political tradition dating back to the founder fathers' outcry over King George III's administration of the colonies. The 1883 Pendleton Civil Service Reform Act provided new protections for bureaucrats from patronage and corruption. Reformer envisioned a meritocracy to replace to the old spoils system. Federal bureaucratic expansion after the New Deal and the Great Society, however, revived the popular stigma against civil servants. Conservative politicians railed against two chief perceptions: the impracticality of government rulemaking and the entrenched status of the most incompetent bureaucrats. U.S. Senator Malcolm Wallop (R-Wyoming), a colleague of Chiles in the Senate, ran for office towing a port-a-john around the Equality State to mock Occupational Safety and Health Administration regulations requiring restrooms for ranches. President Ronald Reagan won two landslide elections by inveighing passionately against bureaucratic rigidity, waste, and abuse. He classified bureaucrates into four groups: loafers, incompetent buffoons, good ole boys, and tyrants.[642] "No politician ever lost votes by denouncing the bureaucracy," said its chronicler, political scientist James Q. Wilson.[643]

Yet, *The Miami Herald*'s Tom Fiedler and other supportive reporters saw nuance, not slash-and-burn anti-government policy, in Chiles' approach:

> Government served better if it wasn't the deliverer of the big program but that what government's role ought to be is maybe be the initiator of a program, put the idea out there and then make it possible for other forces—largely the private market—to come in and to complete his metaphor, to do the rowing. And government would just take advantage of the power provided by the private marketplace and steer it toward the common good. That was his whole idea.

Chief of staff Jim Krog interpreted the rightsizing government movement:

> The one thing that these guys did not lack for was an idea for government. They didn't see the government as an enemy. They saw the government as a facilitator. But they didn't see government as the answer either. They saw government as something that could facilitate. Both of them believed that the best delivery system for a com-

munity for programs was with not-for-profits in communities because you do it at the lowest cost. You touch the most people.

The Chiles administration dismantled the mammoth Department of Health and Rehabilitative Services. Instead, he created the Department of Elder Affairs. Governor Chiles commented, "With HRS, every kind of agency just blends in. It's hard to see where one starts and the other stops. Here, this will be a candle on a hill."[644] The administration also created the Department of Juvenile Justice, replaced the Commerce Department with a public-private partnership called Enterprise Florida, and merged two environmental agencies into one.

Regardless of rightsizing, the Chiles administration's second legislative session, like its first, ended in heartache. "That was something that I still think Florida needs," Governor Chiles said of his Fair Share tax plan. "I thought it was a reasonable thing to do and got handed my head and went on to try and do something else."[645] *St. Petersburg Times* political journalist Martin Dyckman spoke for most of the press corps in his assessment:

> But when it comes to governing, the record is mixed. His agencies run well, but his relations with the Legislature—the ultimate measure of any governor's success—have gone from strained to abysmal. The six bitter months spent on the budget, netting barely a third of the new money he had wanted and precisely the sort of tax patchwork he had said he did not want, have left him with no chits to call in.[646]

Administration senior staff reshuffled after the 1992 session, despite the governor's powerful sense of personal loyalty, said Secretary of Environmental Regulation Virginia Wetherell:

> The one fault, but it's an honorable thing, was that Lawton Chiles hated to fire people, and he just couldn't hurt people. I saw this over and over again. When I would have problems with my staff and I would say I have just got to replace this person, you know and they have a family, he just had the hardest time with that and so the people who came and went in my view, with a couple of exceptions, pretty much did it on their own volition. It was just time for them to move on. I know there were a couple of exceptions. I am trying to remember the one that was maybe one of his secretaries. One of the

agency's females – I think he was involved in her leaving. And then there was an inspector general I think. But it was rare for him. There were a couple of employees that I inherited with the merger and as an example I talked to him several times about the fact that they were working against his philosophy and I really needed to let them go. He had the hardest time with that. He finally after about two years let one of them go.[647]

Communications director Mary Jane Gallagher left for other political work. "He was a bit of a father figure for me," Gallagher says of her boss in retrospect:

During the deaths of the University of Florida students, we were out in Wakulla Springs one day. It was kinda the first attempt we had at a media boondoggle. We took all the capitol press corps out on Wakulla Springs, and we're actually just enjoying the day a little bit, and we got a call that another student had been murdered. And of course we pulled back to the shore and got on the plane and went straight to Gainesville, and I walked in with him to this meeting of all these law enforcement, FBI, etc. ... and it was an amphitheatre kind of meeting and I'll never forget the room got very quiet.

[Governor Chiles] said, "What's the problem?"

[One of the law enforcement officials] said, "She can't come in here."

"What do you mean?"

"Well, you know, women, and gotta keep this all quiet."

[Governor Chiles] looked at me and said, "Either she's in here with me or I'm not here."

So he clearly understood the role women could play in government and in society at-large.

Budget director Doug Cook became Director of the Agency for Health Care Administration in August 1992. His new agency was the largest formed after the breakup of the Department of Health and Rehabilitative Services.

Most important, chief of staff Jim Krog departed the administration to return to lobbying; his legislative affairs staffers Jim Cordero and Wayne Watters followed him out the door.

Tom Herndon, a veteran state bureaucrat, replaced Krog in August 1992. Friend Duby Ausley had always posited that the chief of staff should come out of the bureaucracy, not the campaign world: "You need to save your governor from themselves and your friends." Herndon had run Governor Bob Graham's budget office from 1980 to 1985, and served as a Public Service Commission member and chief of the Department of Revenue. Capitol insiders respected his rationality, discretion, and efficiency. In accordance with the governor's wishes, Herndon would manage the executive office with unprecedented, centralized authority.

Governor Chiles never tried to reform the tax code again. In 1994, he submitted his first budget recommendation without tax hikes; the Legislature rejoiced.

But the governor's principled legacy lingered. Years after his service to the state ended, budget director Doug Cook once met a fan of Chiles in the airport.

> This guy came up to me and said, "Didn't you work for Chiles?" He didn't know my name and I didn't expect him to. I said, "I did." [Reminiscing about Chiles, the fan declared,] "I still remember what he said. I wish one politician would say, 'I didn't come here to stay, I came here to make a difference.' If they said it I wish I could believe it, but I always believed it about Lawton."

13

Hurricane Andrew

Just two weeks into his tenure as chief of staff to Governor Chiles, Tom Herndon was helping craft a media strategy to prepare Florida for one of the largest natural disasters in American history—Hurricane Andrew.

The state legislature, capitol press corps, state bureaucracy, and Florida populace had placed their faith in Herndon to return stability and efficiency to the governor's office. A former social worker and long-time state burueacrat, he had developed a reputation for rationality and cool temperament. To boot, he had served as chief of staff for former Florida Governor Bob Graham, a Democrat, when Hurricane Elena pummeled Florida's Gulf coast in 1985.

No one had higher expectations for his administration than Governor Chiles. This was a fundamental test for his populism—could he protect the Floridians whose trust he had cherished and celebrated since the Walk?

On Sunday, August 23, 1992, as weather forecasters narrowed the projected path for the storm to south Florida, the governor prepared for disaster recovery.

He declared a state of emergency, ordering a mandatory evacuation for more than a million people in south Florida. More than 700,000 residents ultimately evacuated. He issued an executive order calling up about a third of the Florida National Guard. He asked the Federal Emergency Management Agency (FEMA) to provide food, water, and medical services for the impending relief effort.

"Ready or not, I guess," the governor told the press. "I hope we're as ready as we can be. I feel like we've got everything going that our plans call for, and we've been working on our plans for a long time. But do I feel comfortable? No."[648]

The Miami Herald headlined its Sunday extra edition "The Big One" in Andrew's honor. Grocery and hardware stores depleted basic foodstuffs, plywood, and sandbags.

Herald reporter Tom Fiedler describes the widely circulated radar stillshot of the eye of Andrew before it hit shore: "It was this angry ball that almost looked like a fist with a boxing glove on it ready to just punch through."

Many south Florida residents remained in their homes despite the evacuation order. Most had never experience a hurricane; the last major hurricane to hit the area was Donna in 1964.

Roman Rosario, a twenty-five-year-old fast-food cook known to his rap fans as Mo Chill, ignored local police and planned to ride out the storm at his Miami Beach apartment. "I just chill. Why worry about it?" Rosario said. City Neon Co. in Fort Lauderdale boarded up its windows and spray painted the message: "Spare Me! Andrew Be Good to Me!" Golfers played through on the Bonaventure Resort course in sunny mid-afternoon.[649] "What are you supposed to do? It's coming no matter what," said Rick Eljaiek of Miami Lakes; he had just finished his third round of the day. "I'm prepared, I've got all the food and supplies I need, batteries and flashlights. Look at the weather today, it's perfect."[650]

Vida Pernick, a Coral Gables realtor, recalls ideal Florida weather on Saturday: "The skies were blue, not a sign of rain. I remember sitting around the pool and saying to myself that it was almost impossible to think that a hurricane is coming straight at us on such a beautiful day."

Before dawn Monday, August 24, 1992, Hurricane Andrew hit south Florida about thirty miles south of Miami.

The storm extended sixty miles across. The eye of the hurricane measured almost twenty miles across. Only the 1935 storm and 1969's Camille achieved higher sustained wind speed in the twentieth century; Hurricane Andrew landed in south Florida with winds of 138 miles per hour. Before 5:20 a.m., when the storm destroyed the instruments at the National Hurricane Center at Coral Gables, winds of 164 miles per hour were recorded.[651] The maximum storm surge recorded for the hurricane measured 16.9 feet.

At the time of the hurricane's impact, experts rated it as a Category 4 storm. Years later though, scientists at the National Oceanic and Atmospheric Administration upgraded the storm to Category 5—the highest ranking possible for a hurricane.

The entire storm lasted about seven hours for most south Florida residents. The eyewall of the storm entered Biscayne Bay at 4:28 a.m. Emergency dispatchers processed about five thousand 911 calls between 2:30 a.m. and 4:30 a.m.

Hurricane survivors said their ears popped, and sinuses and teeth ached in reaction to the low pressure in the storm's eye. Some compared the sound of the hurricane to a freight train in the living room, or a fighter jet on the roof. Others likened it to a bomb.

Karen Baldwin, an elementary school teacher who rode out the storm in south Florida with her husband and teenage son, describes the experience:

> The wind was so loud that you could not talk or hear without shouting. . . . The noise level got to be eerie. To me, it was absolutely the most horrible noise that you could imagine. Everybody says it sounds like a freight train. It was much worse than a freight train, between the howling and the whistling of the wind. It was an incredible, indescribable noise.[652]

The brunt of the storm hit at five in the morning, Baldwin maintained. "I was scared. I've never been so scared in my life. I realized I was sitting in the room shaking. At least I thought I was shaking. And then I kind of took a deep breath and realized that it wasn't me shaking, it was the wall behind me that was literally moving back and forth, almost vibrating."

"It was like being in a war," southwest Miami resident Stephen Tiger said. "It was like bullets were flying through our windows, only the bullets were tiles from the roof."

Grace Laskis, a Head Start disabilities coordinator, experienced the hurricane with her children in an upstairs hallway of their house:

> Everyone was frantic. I took each of my children piggyback, covered them with a blanket, downstairs. My daughter was frantic for her cats, but they ran away. We grabbed the dog and all went into the half bathroom downstairs; imagine it, two adults, three teenagers and another child and the dog in this two-by-two half bath. . . . We

pushed blankets under the door, but we had to keep pulling it out to get some fresh air. . . . We heard things flying around outside the door. Bombs going off, it seemed. . . . windows were exploding. . . . The girls were nervous and they got sick, vomiting, everything . . . everyone on top of each other.[653]

Tim and Veronica McGraine stayed with their daughter Kaitlin at their home in Kendall, southwest of Miami. "It was like explosion after explosion," Tim McGrane said. "A barrel tile shot through one window and tore a three-foot hole in one of our walls. It was like a cannonball."

Hurricane Andrew's monetary damage totaled $30 billion. A quarter-million were homeless.[654] More than a million south Floridians were without power. The storm ruined the region's real estate, military, and agricultural sectors. It destroyed more than 25,000 homes and damaged another 100,000. Yachts and small freighters lay beached in residential neighborhoods. More than 50,000 street signs were damaged; their replacement would cost $7.25 million.

The hurricane demolished ninety-five percent of Dade County's 840 ornamental and tropical nurseries, a total capital loss of $300 million. It killed almost 70 percent of the county's 6,500 acres of lime groves. Altogether, the storm inflicted more than $1 billion in damaged to agriculture in south Florida.

The storm ruined Miami's Metrozoo. The aviary and monorail saw heavy damage. About three hundred baboons escaped from the University of Miami Primate Center. Police advised the public to keep a distance from the animals. "If you can, just put out some water and some food or anything you can throw out for the monkeys, then call some [phone] numbers," Metro-Dade police Sgt. Ralph Fernandez said. Frank Koutnik recalls, "Senator [Bob Graham] at the time was holding a press conference down at Homestead. And in the background there was a troupe of monkeys that walked by— 'cause they had gotten loose!"

Homestead, Florida City, and Perrine were the urban jurisdictions in Dade hit hardest. The storm destroyed Homestead Air Force base and either damaged or destroyed nearly every home in Homestead. "I'd say 95 percent of our community is wiped out," City Manager Alex Muxo said.[655] The city manager estimated damage cost at more than $250 million. The storm had knocked out the city's water and electrical plants, and cut nearly all telephone service.

"The Miami-Dade building code was the strongest in the nation at the time of Andrew," Frank Koutnik explains. "By far the strictest, toughest, least enforced code in the nation."

"Florida City is destroyed, you hear me? Destroyed!" Mayor Otis Wallace said. Monday, the mayor ran communications from the single working pay phone in the city. He tried to coordinate relief despite losing his home and his law practice.

The zone of storm wreckage equaled the city of Chicago in square mileage. One *St. Petersburg Times* article said south Dade County resembled a "tropical Beirut."

"When you look out your window it looks like what you see on CNN during a hurricane," West Kendall resident Phil Kabler said at dawn. "We're wiped out. In my other life I'm vice president of Miami Coalition for the Homeless. Now I know how it feels."

Before the chainsaws and choppers fired up, an uncommon stillness and quiet characterized the disaster zone in the first hours after the hurricane passed, according to Miami television anchor Art Carlson. The storm had suspended car traffic and snuffed out natural noises like birds and crickets. "The stillness was unbelievable," said Carlson. "It sounded to me like the third battalion rolling through the neighborhood with just me walking aross through the leaves and over the branches. I was the only noise that you could hear."

Monday afternoon Governor Chiles surveyed the devastation from a military helicopter. "It was like an atom bomb went off," he said.[656] He ordered 20,000 National Guard troops into the area immediately to curb looting and distribute supplies. They also guarded grocery stores and directed traffic. Miami's wealthy Coconut Grove area needed property protection, while Florida City and Homestead were so storm-ravaged that little of value remained for thieves.

The governor nixed plans for a vacation and stayed in Miami Lakes that night at a hotel without food, electricity, or potable water. Guests lit their rooms with small votive candles issued by the management. "Right now, people have got to know somebody is going to help them," Governor Chiles said. "I thought I'd show the flag." He looked that night for Cuban food, but dined on Florida National Guard C-rations instead. "Nobody was complaining," he said.[657]

Governor Chiles insisted that his senior staff and most agency heads move to Miami. Secretary of Community Affairs Linda Shelley joined the governor and lieutenant governor at the disaster site. Former chief of staff Jim Krog returned to the governor's side as a senior advisor to aid in hurricane recovery. Herndon and the rest of the senior staff set up the emergency governor's office in an old airline building in Miami, intending to stay as long as necessary. Krog, stationed in Tallahassee, ran the executive office of the governor in their absence.

The White House also responded to the storm on Monday; President George H.W. Bush pledged disaster assistance via FEMA. Twelve hours after Hurricane Andrew struck, President Bush arrived at Opa-locka Airport for a site visit. The president declared Dade, Broward, and Monroe counties federal disaster areas, but FEMA warned that for the first few days, local first responders would be on their own.

Tuesday, Governor Chiles had informed MacNeil/Lehrer NewsHour in good faith that "we are getting good help" from Bush and FEMA. Given the enormity of the disaster, he anticipated generous federal support for the recovery. He expected substance to accompany the symbolism of declaring south Florida a federal disaster area. Meanwhile, the Florida National Guard began rescuing victims of the storm.

By Wednesday, however, the governor's mood had soured; he had visited Florida City and found survivors going hungry. Thursday, he found the same conditions in an Everglades camp.

Without electricity or air conditioning, south Florida residents barbecued outside for nearly every meal. They slept outside with the mosquitoes and rats. Many refugees moved north to Broward County in search of better living.

Governor Chiles wondered if the state should continue to rely on Dade County to provide food, water, and other supplies. During the first seventy-two hours after the storm, "nobody seemed to be in charge; nobody seemed capable of making decisions that would break up logjams and cause aid to flow," *The Miami Herald*'s Tom Fiedler reported.

Florida National Guard and the Red Cross dominated the initial relief reffort. By Monday evening, the Red Cross had served 91,000 meals. Police and firefighters worked the neighborhoods. But demand for relief far exceeded supply.

Three days after the storm, Governor Chiles asked President Bush formally for help. Thursday afternoon, in writing, he requested Army troops to deliver meals and tents en masse. In meetings with federal emergency officials, he fumed. "No one has shown me anything that says requests have to be in writing," Governor Chiles said. "And they damn sure didn't show it to me before the storm."

The White House blamed Governor Chiles for the delays in storm recovery. The Bush administration claimed to have offered Florida an Army battalion hours after the storm, only to have Governor Chiles decline. Washington said it was ready to help, but Florida had not asked for anything.

The governor denied these claims. Leaders of the Florida National Guard had requested the Army's assistance, and the governor complied. "I can't believe they said that," Lt. Governor Buddy MacKay said. "We've been telling them what we need in every way we know how." The governor's staff insisted that on Tuesday their boss had asked FEMA's on-site director to airlift in military field kitchens and medical units, but their request had gone unanswered. They also maintained that as late as Thursday morning, Dade County officials had said they did not need federal troops.

President Bush also claimed that Governor Chiles' letter formally requesting federal assistance had been improperly addressed to the commandant of the Corps of Engineers rather than the secretary of the Army—causing further delay.

The accusation angered Governor Chiles. Chuck Wolfe, an aide at the time, describes the governor's frustration:

> If you look back at news accounts of Hurricane Andrew, you'll find a really big drama that played out between the White House and the state of Florida, and the people in the federal government saying, "Well, you didn't sign the right letter and you didn't call the right person." . . . I was on the plane, using the aircraft phone connecting the governor and the White House. So I'm the one calling, leaving a message, "Call us back at this number." They'd call back, and [I'd connect] them, so I knew the call had happened. So I'm listening to this, going, "Oh, that's horse hockey." Obviously, we've made the request; they're just messed up in Washington.

Lt. Governor Buddy MacKay observed the personal tension between President Bush and Governor Chiles: "At one point during the second week, Lawton got into a shouting match with President Bush in front of a bank of television cameras as the president exited the door of Air Force One. Bush had just landed at Miami International Airport to show his concern and Lawton decided to ambush him."

Governor Chiles resented criticism from Washington and other political corners about his state's management of the disaster recovery. "I've seen more dadgum work done here than I've seen in my lifetime," the governor said Thursday on the lawn of Homestead City Hall. "I say to those naysayers, come down and help and see for yourselves."

Kate Hale, director of Dade County's Emergency Management, issued a stinging rebuke to federal and state officials for their political posturing amid the disaster cleanup. "Quit fighting like a bunch of kids and victimizing us in the process," she said at a news conference Thursday. "If we don't get more food and water down here, we're going to have more casualties. The Feds know. They've got our request. For God's sake, where are they?" Her message and others like it resounded in Washington. Her plea, "Where in the hell is the cavalry?" became a ubiquitous sound bite on the national news.

U.S. military assistance finally arrived in south Florida on Friday, August 28—a force of 3,500 dispatched by the president. "Help is on the way and it will be a major effort," President Bush said. The Army presence in Dade County eventually peaked at 23,800; it represented the largest U.S. military rescue mission in history. Mindful of the importance of battleground states in its tough reelection fight, the Bush administration had a political as well as humanitarian interest in overseeing Florida's successful recovery.

The troops performed many roles in the recovery, including reinforcing security against looters. Many storm survivors had hung signs at their homes to ward off would-be property thieves: "Looters Will Be Shot" and "Warning! Mad Dog Will Eat Looters!" South Florida resident George Brown chased away would-be looters with a shotgun. "They didn't want to talk to Mr. Twelve Gauge," Brown recalls.[658]

The Army set up field kitchens to cook and distribute food. Soldiers build tent cities for the homeless. They gave away thousands of radios with batteries.

Turf wars between FEMA, Florida state government, and local officials continued though, as political leaders competed for their share of the spotlight. Lack of land-line phone or cell phone access in the disaster zone, combined with blocked roads, exacerbated the political tensions.

President Bush "didn't know what to do about it" most of the time, claimed Chiles staffer Doug Cook. "He didn't have enough good people in FEMA because he'd had another political cleanout [removing career professionals and replacing them with loyalists]." At the time Hurricane Andrew hit, FEMA had the largest percentage of at-will employees—subject to political patronage—of any federal agency.

"FEMA was not prepared for Hurricane Andrew," argued James White, an employee of the federally funded Family Adolescent and Development Center assigned by the agency to do general counseling with hurricane victims. "They weren't prepared to work with special populations such as the migrant workers, the poor, and the elderly."

Dade County's government functioned no better than the state and federal governments, according to *The Miami Herald*'s Tom Fiedler. The county was "headed by a mayor who delights in having no authority, a county manager with no political constituency, and eight commissioners with no meaningful ties to any particular neighborhoods." Dade County mayor Steve Clark refused to help in the relief effort, adamant that disaster management was outside the scope of his office.

Without a single official entity to govern the recovery, the overall effort floundered. The homeless went sick and hungry. Supplies were wasted. Homestead and Florida City suddenly enjoyed a surplus of food, but lacked a system of distribution to ensure its delivery.

President Bush released 372 tons of food held in reserve by the U.S. Department of Agriculture. Governor Chiles worried some of it might spoil without better distribution. Some areas, he feared, might never receive food. "Well, we've got 120,000 C-ration meals that are here somewhere but we don't know where the hell they are," the governor complained. "Right now, a truckload of food gets there, 200 people show up, 50 people get food, and 150 people are angry. We've got to find a way to solve that."

"Every day things look considerably different, considerably better," Governor Chiles said. "We know we've got enough food. We know we've got enough volunteers. It's a question of communications, coordination and consistency."

The governor resolved to strengthen the hurricane recovery despite the impasse of agencies. First, he would marshall all Florida state resources available to meet the region's need independent of FEMA, Dade, and other stakeholders.

The governor established a state-run headquarters for South Florida's recovery in Palm Beach County—near enough to the disaster zone to provide quick relief but far enough away to be fully functional. The headquarters at the Palm Beach County fairgrounds boasted about 20,000 volunteer workers. It amassed goods donated from around the world, delivered by seaport, airport, train, and highway.

Second, Governor Chiles provided a constant, reassuring public face for the recovery effort, on location in south Florida. For two weeks after the storm, he spent virtually every minute in the disaster zone. Typically, he woke at six-thirty at the Biscayne Bay Marriott in Miami, donned a plaid shirt and khaki pants, and meandered to the lobby for breakfast: orange juice and a muffin. Then he would join his press secretary for a car tour around Homestead or Florida City.

"Some federal officials have implied that Governor Lawton Chiles should have called for the military sooner," wrote *St. Petersburg* Times columnist Martin Dyckman, "but at least Chiles went to Miami and stayed there, while President Bush came, saw and went."

The governor's personal charisma lifted the spirits of survivors, according to senior advisor Jim Krog:

> He was their governor and they didn't want to see him on TV. They couldn't see TV; there was no electricity. Herndon and the rest tried to get him out and about, traveling around, using the helicopter, using the Hueys that they had down there, to get him into some of these neighborhoods. For him just to get in there physically [was very important].

Governor Chiles made phone calls to state and federal emergency officials from the streets of Homestead, greasing the wheels of bureaucracy to provide supplies to the needy. "Maybe I can't do much," the governor said, "except get a phone call through that wouldn't have if it had been made by somebody two or three levels down." Relief workers would beg him for supplies and services: baby food, diapers, refrigerated trucks, trash removal, and building supplies.

The Miami Herald's Tom Fiedler witnessed Governor Chiles' visit to the devastation. "As soon as Lawton arrived, it was truly transformative," Fiedler reported later. "You could see people light up and they would surround him. It was as if suddenly there was hope, because here was Lawton, and he was in their neighborhood and he could see what they had gone through, he could understand their suffering. He represented in many ways the cavalry." The governor, Fiedler observed, "sweated, he went hungry and thirsty, he became alternately angry and sad."

Third, for optimal recovery the governor and his staff leveraged contacts in the private sector around the country. In Tallahassee, senior adviser Jim Krog led a team of staff on the phones recording requests and scavenging for equipment from generous business interests. Texaco oil called in and offered to retrofit their tanker fleet for water.

Krog, a former lobbyist, reached out to his friends at Coca-Cola in Atlanta to restore water supply in South Florida. He asked company officials to con- ver their bottling plants to water production and start shipping bottled water to every truck going South. He called friends at Anheuser-Busch in Florida and had them convert their facilities to water production for shipment to the disaster zone; the company pledged 200,000 cans of drinking water. The plant produced water-filled Busch beer containers. "We were notorious for the Busch beer water," Frank Koutnik said.

The Stroh Brewery Co. converted its breweries in Tampa and Longview- Texas to water production. It promised 7,000 cases of fresh drinking water to the Miami area.

Motorola provided 1,500 radios and Zephyrhills sent 500 cases of bottled water. Humana, an insurance company, donated $1 million to the relief effort. CSX railroad company sent a train with fifty cars of earth-moving equipment and several cars of ice.

More than two weeks after the storm, however, Florida's recovery still lagged far behind public needs and expectations. President Bush had asked Congress to approve a federal aid package worth $7.6 billion, and Governor Chiles was grateful that the federal government finally committed to absorb- ing the full cost of the storm. "I have looked into the abyss and I have seen the devils that are down there," he said, "and I am very happy we are back from the edge." But he also believed this sum to be insufficient—at least $2 billion short.

Governor Chiles decided to renew his fight for more federal commitment of resources to Hurricane Andrew recovery. This time he would target Con- gress as well as the White House.

The governor, joined by his lieutenant governor and staffers Tom Herndon and Doug Cook, traveled to Washington to lobby his old friends in the legis- lative branch for emergency relief funds. Cook, formerly the governor's bud- get director, now served as health policy director.

Herndon recalls the struggle to convey the magnitude of the storm to Washington. By this time, the Dade County medical examiner had published the official death toll from Hurricane Andrew as thirty-five; yet, federal power brokers inside the beltway balked at authorizing a gargantuan aid bill:

> I can remember being in meetings and some senior Senate Ways and Means staffers that had worked for Governor Chiles. . . . They were arguing the policy and the precedent of the federal government getting involved in a "local" problem and he was just very impassioned and frustrated and argumentative about what they were thinking and how they could characterize this as a "local" problem.

Governor Chiles showed lawmakers before-and-after satellite photos of locales in south Dade county to emphasize the urgency of the cause.

The governor addressed the Senate Democratic Caucus, lunched with former colleagues in the senators-only Capitol dining room. He met privately with House Speaker Tom Foley, Senate Majority Leader George Mitchell, House Majority Leader Richard Gephardt, and various GOP leaders.

Governor Chiles intended to leverage his U.S. Senate connections for every penny, even if it meant agitating his old rival in the upper chamber, Senator Robert Byrd.

As chair of the Senate Appropriations Committee, Senator Byrd of West Virginia, enjoyed seeing a good grudge to its conclusion. Any junior senator who crossed him would see their pet projects vanish from the federal budget.

When Governor Chiles attended a meeting of the Appropriations Committee; Senator Byrd refused to recognize him or hear his testimony. The governor persisted though. He would not be dissuaded from his mission by Senator Byrd or any other politician with a lordly air. "I never saw him impressing someone, trying to impress someone," his wife Rhea recalls. Gubernatorial staffer Doug Cook set up a private meeting between Senator Byrd and Governor Chiles to mend fences:

> It's Byrd and Chiles and me [Cook]. I'm quietly sitting in the back, acting like I'm not there, which is what staff does most of the time. . . . Chiles has this book of pictures, and he gets on his knees and walks [on his knees to Byrd's] chair, and he opens the book and goes through it. Byrd keeps him there for thirty minutes on his knees.

Then [Chiles] sits back and says, "Mr. Chairman, I don't blame you for being upset with me. And I'm not asking you to forgive me, but you're a great public servant and I know you want to help my people."

Byrd looked at him, put his arm on his shoulder, and said, "I'll reconvene the committee in an hour." And he was very nice to [Chiles] and gave him the full chance to [lobby Congress for hurricane relief funds].

The resulting emergency federal legislation, lobbying heavily by Governor Chiles, included $11.1 billion in relief funds for Florida and other distaster-stricken states. The bill, which passed September 18, was unprecedented for natural disaster recovery. Senior advisor Jim Krog called the relief sum "the first big dip ever."

Congress and the White House consented to pay all disaster relief costs and rebuild Homestead Air Force Base. The governor quipped in response to news of the dollar amount: "The moon was in a good phase."[659] He attributed the success of the bill to the pressures of presidential election season; everyone in Washington wanted to appease the electorate. Governor Chiles and other state officials hoped at least $9 billion of the relief bill would go to Florida.

Once the billions in federal money began to flow, south Florida's recovery quickened considerably.

Legislators, reporters, and Tallahassee insiders applauded the new team at the helm of the state executive—Tom Herndon as chief of staff, Ron Sachs as communications director, and David Coburn as budget director—for establishing a new, more harmonious order in the governor's office during the hurricane recovery. They especially trumpeted government veteran Tom Herndon's poise and professionalism.

Hurricane Andrew recovery had quickly bonded the governor to his new chief of staff. Herndon, who had worked six and a half years for Governor Bob Graham, did not know Governor Chiles at all before becoming his top staffer:

One of the first experiences I had with him [Governor Chiles] was in his little private office off the main suite of the governor's office, going in there one day and talking to him about something and the next thing I know he's getting up and taking off his pants. I'm trying to think, What in the hell is going on?—and he's changing into some hunting clothes. He's just taking off the pants and putting on camos and getting ready to get out to go hunt. For him it wasn't important, that was the way he was.

Yet, he found much to admire in his new boss:

> The contrast between the two governors was just remarkable. Bob Graham was young and very energetic, very studious and his approach to government was as a manager. He wanted to analyze things, he wanted all the facts; he wanted to be very analytical about his approach to issues, working relationships, and everything else. Governor Chiles was just the opposite. He'd been everywhere, done everything, met every visiting head of state in Washington for fifteen years and really wasn't particularly impressed with them or himself anymore. He didn't feel the need to impress anybody and he wasn't gonna set out to do it.

"We've become main-line, as opposed to bomb-throwers," Governor Chiles said in December 1992, remarking on the change in style in his executive office since Herndon had come aboard. "Governor Chiles was very fortunate to have a person with Tom's calmness and ability to bring order to a crisis situation," U.S. Senator Bob Graham said. "There aren't many people who could do the same." Republicans liked Herndon, too. Praising the new chief of staff's performance, Senator Richard Langley (R-Clermont) said, "I think it's probably one of the few good things that Lawton Chiles has done—and I mean one of the few things."

Governor Chiles, however, took much of the blame for governmental failures during the recovery; his public approval numbers tumbled after Hurricane Andrew. Gubernatorial staffer Doug Cook explains, "The press was—aw, they were just eating us alive, because what can you do? You're not making progress." The daily criticism of the public and the press, combined with the stresses of working in the disaster zone, took an emotional toll on senior staff. "It was one of those things where you almost have to make fun of it in some ways because otherwise it was just so overwhelmingly depressing that it got you down after a while," chief of staff Tom Herndon said.

Hurricane Andrew recovery continued to shape the governor's legislative agenda through the spring of 1993. "Andrew cast a pall over everybody and everything, no doubt about it," Tom Herndon said. "It influenced an awful lot of what took place from that point on." Senior advisor Jim Krog concurred; the storm took "all the mental energy that you had."

All state staff immersed in disaster recover had tales to share about the drama that had dominated their lives for weeks or months.

Emergency managers reflected on the daily shocks of relief work, like the abundance of chain link fence amid the debris. Normally, the fencing faded into the background of the south Florida landscape; but after Hurricane Andrew, the warped and broken metal sections were visible roadblocks everywhere. Hundreds of miles of fence lay in tatters, among the rest of the 35 million tons of debris created by Hurricane Andrew. The storm generated enough garbage in a single night to equal the normal projected landfill for Dade County for the next thirty years.[660]

Jim Cordero, a gubernatorial staffer at the time of the storm, recalls the unexpected but significant problem: "You just don't go picking them up. You can't roll 'em back up nice, they're all twisted." Fortunately for south Florida, a South Carolina debris company with hurricane relief experience addressed the issue.

Hurricane Andrew recovery provided a major field test for the first generation of cellular phones, the Motorola "brick" phone. The storm rendered these heavy, short-range devices useless. Even the governor's car phone failed routinely.

Some who experienced the hurricane, like University of Miami geology professor Harold Wanless, worried that the political class would ignore the lessons of the storm for public safety. "In a year," Wanless claimed, "people are going to start to forget everything, and people are going to let building codes slip a little bit. Every year it'll slip a little bit more. And fifteen years from now, we'll have forgotten most of the things that everybody in Dade County has learned from this storm. It's amazing how rapidly we forget."[661]

But the governor had compiled his own massive logbook of the emergency mismanagement he witness. He championed the notion that no state could marshal the resources to address a major hurricane; the federal government must lead the recovery. Further, he concluded that not all federal actors are equal in effect. "FEMA may be well-meaning," Governor Chiles said, "but they have no clout in the initial phase . . . and . . . you've got to loudly and strongly and probably with all kinds of paper tell the White House what you need." He believed the U.S. military, not the Red Cross, should take the lead in providing emergency shelter after a major hurricane.[662]

Governor Chiles tasked his administration with consolidating these lessons learned from the disaster and codifying them for use by future state governments.

The governor saw to it that "never again" would be Florida's battle cry. He envisioned his state as the most prepared in the Union for natural disaster—especially hurricanes.

Perhaps the governor's most enduring and eloquent contribution to Florida's emergency management was the Lewis Commission, a blue ribbon committee formed soon after Andrew. Governor Chiles persuaded Phil Lewis, ex-Senate president, to chair the commission.

The Lewis Commission met from November 1992 to about the first week of January 1993. The resulting report was first published that January. It issued about one hundred recommendations to secure Florida's from catastrophic harm in a future natural disaster. Several became state statutes and cornerstones of Florida's emergency management policy.

In December 1992, the Florida legislature convened for a special session dedicated to hurricane relief. The governor signed off on a state relief fund, paid for by sales taxes on select goods during the two years after the storm. The Emergency Management Assistance Trust Fund, one of the Lewis Commission's recommendations, generated about $525 million.

The storm, according to Frank Koutnik, had "caused a huge blip in the sales tax. . . . [Governor Chiles] took that increased revenue and funneled it back into the impacted states as a trust fund solely designed to fill the gaps and meet the needs that that FEMA recovery programs couldn't do."

Governor Chiles provided the template for what become known as EMAC (Emergency Management Assistance Compact), an essential partnership to share National Guard assets across state lines without constraints. EMAC, now adopted by all fifty states and territories, began as an alliance between Georgia and Florida called SREMAC (Southern Regional Emergency Management Compact). "It really started after Hugo in '89," according to Frank Koutnik, the bureau chief of operations for Florida Division of Emergency Management during Hurricane Andrew. "[Chiles, as a U.S. senator] was the one who really got that ball rolling in '89. . . . He was adamant. He wanted to be able to share resources across state lines easily."

The Chiles administration persuaded the insurance lobby to sign off on a surcharge to the annual insurance premium to fund emergency management at the county and state level. The surcharge revenue would empty into EMPATF (Emergency Management Preparedness Assistance Trust Fund).

This measure, the 94th and final recommendation of the Lewis Commission, was revolutionary according to Frank Koutnik. "No one has ever accomplished something of that magnitude in the field of emergency management before."

"He became the EM governor. . . . He was the first," said Joe Myers, Director of Florida's Emergency Management Agency during Hurricane Andrew. He and Koutnik credited Governor Chiles' reforms for the success of Florida's future responses to natural disasters.

When the 1993 storm with no name struck Florida, killing more than a dozen on the Gulf Coast, Governor Chiles reacted swifly to ensure reform. He forced Joe Friday, the National Weather Service director, to drag a weather buoy from the Bay of Campeche near Mexico's Yucatana Peninusala to the water off Keaton Beach in rural Taylor County. The storm's arrival had been a shock to the Gulf Coast; no sea bouys were close enough to Keaton to record a storm surge. The new buoy position would solve this problem.

The governor, as usual, imprinted Florida's Hurricane Andrew legacy with his unique signature. He "was just not intense like Governor Graham was. He was intense in his own way," chief of staff Tom Herndon explains. "If you could be intense and at the same time be relaxed, that's what he was."

Governor Chiles understood that he, his staff, and the survivors of the hurricane needed moments of levity amid the tragedy A modicum of gratitude was in order, too, despite the gravity of the experience; had the storm collided directly with downtown Miami, it could have cost as much as $100 billion in damages and killed thousands more residents.

A month after the hurricane, Governor Chiles made a cameo appearance at a Hurricane Andrew benefit concert in south Florida. He donned sunglasses and pretended to play the saxophone to kick off the event at the West Palm Beach Auditorium. "Eat your heart out, Bill Clinton," the governor quipped on stage before a crowd of more than five hundred.[663]

14

Healthy Start

No initiative during Chiles' first gubernatorial term enjoyed more success than Healthy Start.

The program, signed into law in 1991, provided superior prenatal care for mothers and babies. It involved three components: universal screenings for pregnant women and their babies to measure health risks; services to address those risks, and the establishment of nonprofit community coalitions, "Healthy Start Coalitions," one per county or region, to ensure local input into early childhood health policy. The coalitions included a variety of stakeholders, from doctors, hospitals, schools, charities, social services agencies, and citizens.

"These are major changes," said Patricia McGovern, director of the South Florida Perinatal Network, when Healthy Start began. "Local communities are going to make local decisions about how to improve the services. That's exciting." Florida children's advocate Jack Levine extolled the program:

> It was looking at the cycle of pregnancy and the needs of the pregnant girl or woman and then realizing that right now she was only in two systems. Either the family system or the medical system. And the brilliance of Healthy Start, and again he learned this as chairman of the National Commission on Infant Mortality, was you have many other sectors that have a stake in the health of that mother and baby. You have education, you have faith, and you have business. You have philanthropy, you have a spectrum of special services, whether it be

drug or alcohol, mental health, that could be brought to the same table and the plan could really include a wider view of the community concern for that stage of life, the pregnancy stage.

Healthy Start also expanded Medicaid membership to help thousands of low-income mothers and infants receive the care they need. It also increased Medicaid reimbursement feeds for obstetricians.

When Healthy Start began serving patients, April 1992, Florida's infant mortality rate ranked among the worst in the nation. Thousands of its babies suffered from low birth weight, placing them at risk for a host of health problems during and after childhood. With Chiles' signature initiative in place, however, results of universal health screenings—such as low birth weight— were filed with each newborn's birth certificate. Doctors and social workers then took heed of these warnings and intervened on the child's behalf.

"If you do a good job with Healthy Start," said Cathy Mellinger, a Gadsden County Health Department nurse, "you're going to have a healthy baby, a full-term baby, and a mother who understands parenting concepts, the need for immunizations, and the emphasis on reading and early brain development."[664]

Healthy Start screened 81,000 pregnant women and newborns in its first six months of operation, from April to September 1992. The program cost $41.7 million its first fiscal year, from July 1991 to July 1992. The next fiscal year Healthy Start received $67.4 million in funding. The number of Healthy Start coalitions soon grew from a dozen to nineteen. The next fiscal year the program cost $100 million. By fall of 1993, Governor Chiles sought to expand Healthy Start by allowing children up to age two to qualify for services. "We'd like to cover every child at risk," the governor said. "We're going to extend the lifeline."

During the course of the Chiles-MacKay administration, Florida's infant mortality rate dropped 26 percent—largely due to Healthy Start. The percentage of women initiating prenatal care during the first trimester increased from 75 percent in 1991 to 83 percent in 1997. The low birth weight rate among Healthy Start mothers declined substantially. In 1998, the number of Healthy Start coalitions had grown to thirty-one.

The program prospered under the governor's consistent personal supervision. Healthy Start embodied everything he had learned about early childhood development during his tenure as chairman of the National Commission to Prevent Infant Mortality. His investigation into the roots of

Florida's infant health crisis had sustained him spiritually and professionally after his departure from the U.S. Senate. Now he would ensure that Healthy Start institutionalized all the vital lessons from this experience.

The governor's family and staff could sense the depth of his devotion to early childhood health care. "There were things about himself that he discovered," Rhea Chiles said, "little keys. The arc was long but it always bent toward revelation—self-revelation." The first lady partnered with the governor in children's policy more than on any other issue. Governor Chiles likened early child development to crop management, according to Rhea:

> He was determined that this was the way to get to these intractable social conditions, that there was no other way but this was the one string to pull out of the snarl—if you got to children soon enough, early enough, and the generational thing, you could eventually improve the crop. If you prepare the seed crop, you could eventually grow a better product.[665]

In the context of early childhood, the governor talked about a "widget factory" with 60 percent of the output defective, according to younger son Ed. The smart factory operator went back to the source to fix the widget, since he would never have the resources to fix it at the back end. Likewise, in the social policy realm, no quantity of emergency rooms or jail cells could rehabilitate long-standing illnesses.

Mary Jane Gallagher, communications director during Healthy Start's inception, says of Chiles, "He believed that if we were ever going to stop the cycle of poverty, the place we needed to do it was in [the fields of] prenatal care, early infant care, and early child care."

Doug Cook, health policy director for the governor, explains his boss's ethos:

> In certain ways he was a throwback, in certain ways he was New Age, particularly in his reliance on non-traditional issues like children's health. . . . He not only wanted healthier babies, but to create better parents, because—and he would say this a hundred times— "That's the key to [reducing] child abuse. That's the key to lower crime rates," and—his words—"That's the key to a more civil society: loving parents caring for their children."

Healthy children, the governor believed, would learn better, find better jobs, and become successful adults. "These are doors that can lead to a life on the payroll, instead of being on the welfare roll," Governor Chiles said. Good health policy was also good education policy and good economic policy. Governor Chiles also asserted that dollars spent on prenatal care would save the state millions in future spending. "All of our figures," he said, "show that we save eleven dollars for each dollar spent on vaccine."

Through extensive study and conference with obstetricians and clinical researchers, Governor Chiles made himself an expert on the most technical details of early childhood development. "He and Rhea both, they really knew the issues," said Dr. Charles Mahan, state health officer at the time. "I always sorta joked, but only halfway, that he and Rhea knew more about pregnancy and [childhood from birth to age five] than most obstetricians and pediatricians I knew."

Governor Chiles liked to cite research at the University of Alabama in Birmingham by the child development experts Craig and Sharon Ramey. "At birth," the governor often proclaimed, "the brain has about 100 billion neurons. By age one, that figure explodes to 1,000 trillion. Talking to children, showing them games, even playing classical music to them during these first years can make a difference of twenty IQ points—an astounding implication for the state as it struggles to provide good childcare for mothers who are leaving welfare for work." Governor Chiles asserted to the state legislature, "Education must start at gestation."[666] He compared Florida's infant mortality rate to those of "Third World" countries to emphasis its severity.

The governor also infused the Healthy Start program with his sense of humor, Dr. Mahan recalls:

> When I came down with [Governor Chiles], I was state health officer and we kicked off a new children's immunization campaign. We'd gotten some more money from the Feds to do it. Saint Joseph's Hospital here had bought an immunization van to go around Tampa playgrounds and so on, daycare centers to help. And so we went to a daycare center, and there were mostly little black kids there, but they ranged in age from two to five or eight or something like that—preschool. So the van was there, and all these kids are lined up lookin' at the van. And Lawton gets down, he hunkers down in front of 'em and he says, "Now, in a few minutes you're going to go in that van and you're going to get a shot and it's to keep you healthy. It's going to a

hurt a little bit, but not very much. And when you come out, you can have your choice of this" (he had a t-shirt on one hand) "or this" (he had a couple balloons in the other hand). So you can see the kids looking back and forth between the two. And there's this real tall kid in the back. There is a fierce look on his face. And he pushes his way through and he gets right up in Lawton's face and he says, "We want money." Lawton just fell back on his rear end laughing.

Governor Chiles' country diction amused and sometimes confused Dr. Mahan. "You don't come into the house of a man who has been hanged and talk about rope," the governor once told him. But what mattered most to Dr. Mahan was the governor's mastery of the public policy.

The rapid achievements of Healthy Start emboldened Governor Chiles' public health agenda. His next goal would be to provide health care access to all Floridians. "Health reform with Lawton was a passion," Doug Cook said. "He hated that people could work and not have health insurance. It drove him crazy. He pounded the table."

This major move for reform would build on efforts begun in the governor's first year. Among other concerns, he feared that escalating Medicaid costs would soon leave him no choice but to reform the failed system.

In August 1991, at the National Governor's Association meeting in Seattle, Washington, Governor Chiles had asked other governors to issue a deadline for the federal government—he wanted them to demand a national plan for universal health care by 1994. The governor "made a statement then that if we could draw a line in the sand in Iraq and Kuwait, then we ought to be able to draw a line in the sand and say we ought to have universal coverage," Doug Cook recalls.

Governor Chiles failed to make a foothold due to Republican oppositon, but he could sense popular momentum for reform coalescing. "This whole thing is accelerating a lot faster than people realize," he had concluded after the event.

Governor Chiles' national media coverage at conference had raised the profile of health care as an issue in the 1992 presidential race between Bill Clinton and George H. W. Bush.

Clinton, as governor of Arkansas, was one of Governor Chiles' few allies in his bid to force the federal government to reform health care. His wife Hillary shared Governor Chiles' commitment, too. "Clinton's fire was primarily economic," Doug Cook said. "Hillary's fire was more the passion for equity."

The conference also had convinced Governor Chiles of the imperative of accomplishing health care reform in Florida without Washington's help. In March 1992, he signed the Florida Health Care Reform Act, which proclaimed that every resident of the state would be guaranteed access to health care by December 31, 1994.

By early 1993, Governor Chiles deemed it time to announce his vision for a new Florida health care system.

That year, almost all of the state's revenue growth had to be dedicated to the rising cost of Medicaid. The average yearly cost of each Florida Medicaid beneficiary had tripled in the past decade, to $3,814. The state of Florida spent $38 billion on health care in 1992, up from $9.4 billion in 1980.

In his State of the State address, the governor asked the state legislature to make universal health care a priority in its first thirty days. "Two-and-a-half million of our Floridians go to bed every night, literally afraid to get sick," he said.

Governor Chiles had reason to view the upcoming legislative session with optimism: one of his most hardened political adversaries, Associated Industries of Florida President Jon Shebel, had become an ally in the fight for universal health care in the state. Shebel had once mocked Chiles' Senate career, saying, "The guy's just a nothing. He's just kind of gone up there and sat."[667]

In January 1993, however, Shebel and Governor Chiles appeared on the cover a bestselling edition of *Florida Trend*, entitled "Strange Bedfellows." Shebel had conceded that all Americans would ultimately be covered somehow. He wanted to ensure that business and government worked together to enact reforms on a state and local level rather than suffer a Washington-mandated solution.

Governor Chiles did not begrudge Shebel for the change of heart. Gubernatorial Chief of staff Tom Herndon considered the partnership typical of Chiles' style. Herndon explains, "People would say, 'So-and-so voted against you, so we've gotta punish them.' [Governor Chiles] didn't think that way and he didn't function that way."

Besides the boon presented by this new alliance, the governor was looking forward to seeing his new executive team take charge of the first regular legislative session since Hurricane Andrew. His new trio of senior staff—health policy director Doug Cook, communications director Ron Sachs, and chief of staff Tom Herndon—had proven themselves efficient and reliable during their first major crisis. Dr. Bob Bradley, deputy budget director for Governor

Chiles' first term, commented, "Tom Herndon taught the office not to fight and to work together."

Governor Chiles proposed to reform health care in 1993 through "managed competition," whereby employers and consumers would pool purchasing power to bargain for the lowest cost health care. "The concept is simple," the governor said. "Businesses, individuals and the government pool their money and purchase the best care at the best price. You spread out the risk so that everybody in an area is covered."

The governor and Doug Cook, chief health care negotiator, met with large insurers like Blue Cross Blue Shield to talk about their plan. Success depended on the Democratic-controlled House passing an acceptable version of the legislation. "The special interests are dancing around the issue and avoiding real health care reform," Governor Chiles said. "They don't want large purchasing pools, just a bunch of puddles."

After a nine-week debate, the legislature approved the plan, to the delight of the governor. Many important lobbies ultimately offered their lukewarm support because they preferred the plan to a Washington-imposed solution. Jon Shebel, the president of Associated Industries of Florida, approved it; so did the National Federation of Independent Business.

Florida became the first state to institute managed competition's fusion of free market and government forces. Its plan would operate on a scale unimagined by leaders in other states reforming health care, like Oregon, Vermont, and Hawaii.

The plan for managed competition failed to achieve universal health coverage for Floridians though. It marginally expanded coverage through the establishment of what the governor called community health purchasing alliances, or "CHPAS." Chiles senior advisor Jim Krog explains the program's shortcomings:

> [Health policy director Doug] Cook had worked through a lot of these ideas, on Chippas, and all these delivery mechanisms to do it and how you do it. And I think honestly at the end of the day, we didn't ever hit on the right combination. Because we had to involve the federal government in doing it. It involved an entrenched hospital industry, an entrenched medical industry, an entrenched HMO industry—all of which had different styles of doing business and we [were] trying to from the top down make that thing change, by pure kind of, will.

"This is an experiment," health policy director Doug Cook said. "We're going to have to see how it works as we go along. This is the first shot across the bow, and there aren't any guarantees." Liberal Democrats in the legislature believed the program did not go far enough. "Do not think with this vote you're about to cure the problems of Florida's health care crisis," said Ken Jenne (D-Fort Lauderdale).

Expanding each year from 1993 to 1998, the Chippas ultimately covered 110,000 Floridians, but Doug Cook acknowledged the program's faults. "The Chippas became a double-edged sword for us," Cook said. "First, we had to make a huge compromise and give up negotiating for the Chippas. The exchanges under federal law have a great deal of power. The Chippas didn't have any other power."

Undaunted, Governor Chiles tried to reform health care more extensively in 1994. By then he was recognized nationally as an expert on the issue; he had successfully shepherded through the legislature an incremental improvement to the system despite opposition from the Florida Medical Association and other powerful interests. President Bill Clinton had endorsed Florida's approach to managed competition, and had modeled his own health care reform plan after Governor Chiles'. Florida's governor had sent aides to Washington to help the president and first lady devise a winning strategy. "We would like to be able to chart the way for the federal government," Governor Chiles said.

Like President Clinton, Governor Chiles wanted to make 1994 the year of health reform despite a legacy of defeats on the issue going back to President Harry Truman.

The governor proposed a new, more ambitious $1 billion plan for universal health insurance called Florida Health Security.

Under the proposed system, no new taxes would be necessary to fund the expanded health care coverage. The federal government would pay half the cost, the state would pay 32 percent, and employers and employees would each pay 9 percent.

In its first three years, the plan would cover one million of the 2.8 million Floridians still uninsured in 1994. The remaining 1.8 million would gradually attain coverage in the succeeding years.

The Florida chamber of commerce supported the reform bill; employers would not be required to provide coverage, which endeared the plan to big business. Most doctors, hospitals, and insurance companies supported the bill. Again, the governor partnered with powerful corporate lobbyist Jon Shebel, according to health policy director Doug Cook:

> Shebel had really come to admire Chiles. You talk about a long-time incumbent, the old Democratic icon, scion, and one of the leaders of the Republican Revolution—Association Industries. But they had become quite close on the health care issue. Shebel admired his courage. And Shebel had accused him of kind of being, everything to everybody, this moderate, flimsy moderate—I think he really came to like him. And Chiles really liked Shebel. And in my opinion, for lack of a better word, they saw fortitude in one another that they hadn't seen before—a willingness to take on tough issues.

Shebel credited the governor with helping to reduce the cost of health care in Florida. "We're doing very innovative things with a lot of risk," he said. "I think it's worked in an outstanding way."

The Republicans in the Florida legislature felt ambivalent about the health reform plan. Georgia Congressman Newt Gingrich's national movement to revive the Republican Party and return it to its core conservatism stoked the fires of many in the caucus. But they were reluctant to publicly attack the plan.

The GOP caucus ultimately aligned in opposition to the bill. The Senate was split evenly on the issue. The governor wanted to cut a deal but could not find the right legislator to sponsor one.

Jon Shebel offered to help break the logjam. He would use his lobbying muscle to the pass a fifty cent tax increase on tobacco to fund the Florida Health Security Act, in exchange for the governor's agreement to suspend his plans to sue the tobacco industry, according to Cook.

But Big Tobacco refused the deal and Florida Health Security failed.

The White House health care plan collapsed, too. Health care industry warnings against reform had blanketed the television airwaves across the nation, especially the effective "Harry and Louise" ads depicting a middle-aged couple struggling to understand health reform.

Republican State Senate leader Ander Crenshaw, a candidate for governor, rejoiced in the bill's death. He described it as a victory for free markets.

"They have not hurt Lawton Chiles, they've thrown me in the briar patch," the governor said of the defeat. "They've hurt themselves and the people of this state, because they've denied [the people] health coverage."

Future Florida Lt. Governor Toni Jennings, then a Republican state senator from Orlando, related that "at that point, we were, the Republicans, were
just the evil empire. We were giving him such grief about it, that it kind of
went on, and on, and on."

Health policy director Doug Cook felt the loss viscerally. He thought the
administration could revive the issue during a special session, but the effort
stalled. "He gave me the ball," he says of Florida Health Security, "and I
didn't get it across the goal line."

Governor Chiles handled the loss with humor though, allowing his staff to
forgive themselves and move on, Cook related. "He was very kind to me
when it was over with," he said. "We went out to this place and we drank rum
and Cokes out of jelly jars. He called me Sancho."

Communications director Ron Sachs explains his boss's style:

> [Governor Chiles] always had better balance than those of us work-
> ing for him. But he realized that lightening up a tough time could
> actually help you through it better. And so some of his best practical
> jokes probably happened when you would least expect them because
> he was in a tough political battle. And some people might wonder
> how he would have time for that stuff. But I think he thought it was
> important to have that kind of balance, and be well-rounded. And
> remind people that we're doing hard work; we're trying to do good
> things for our state, but let's not get so serious about it that we forget
> to have balance in our lives.

The governor had by this time developed a signature comedy routine
called "gotchas." Almost every staffer, no matter how short his or her tour of
duty, witnessed it. Bragg Crane, who served as the governor's "body man," a
sort of personal assistant responsible for luggage, call time, wake-up calls,
and many other tasks, recalled one of his favorite gotchas:

> One time we were flying in [the governor's] plane, the six-seat Mal-
> ibu. He was talking to the pilot, which kinda struck me as odd. And
> halfway through the flight, the alarms start goin' off, the plane goes
> into a dive. Chiles grabs I think it was Tim Nickens next to us, grabs
> his knee, he goes, "Tim, you know what this means?" And Tim didn't
> like to fly to begin with, that's why Chiles set this up. He goes, "This

means: Gotcha!" He'd had the pilot lower the landing gear, which, if you're going too fast, sets off alarms.

Jim Daughton, another body man for the governor, recalls that on his first day, his boss told him that "he would never tell me whether I was doing a good job or not, but somehow I would know." The gotchas often provided wordless emotional support to staff.

After the 1994 session, Governor Chiles and his staff deferred the dream of universal health insurance. The governor "had more of an inclination to tilt windmills than is probably good for any of us," added health policy director Doug Cook.

None of Governor Chiles' health policy initiatives succeeded as much as Healthy Start. He redoubled his efforts on this and other children's programs, crafting what he called a "constituency of children."

Family, friends, and staff saw the sincerity in his mission. Official events involving children always put the governor at ease, senior advisor Jim Krog later recalled: "It improved his mood completely. That's the way he recharged, because his interest was there. Florida children's advocate Jack Levine recounted the governor's affection for preschool visits:

> [Governor Chiles] had to be reminded or almost coaxed into wearing a jacket and tie. I've seen him in preschools on numerous occasions where he knew he was going to walk out dirty. There's no way to be in a preschool and walk out clean. And again there would be some who would [say], "Oh, I'm not going there." For Chiles it was part of the fun: which finger paint or which glop of glue would end up on his pants?

Rhea and Governor Chiles invited Make-A-Wish kids to the Governor's Mansion for ice cream. "She made those kids feel like they were king at the moment," Florida House Speaker Wetherell recalls. "[Governor Chiles] just never said no." Malicious lobbyists meeting with Governor Chiles sometimes tried to pawn pork projects off as child-focused projects. "He by and large had a pretty good antennae," law school classmate and attorney Dexter Douglass recalls. "You could fool him if you were prepared well enough to convince him and good enough actor that your primary interest was helping children, you might suck him in. But not many. He could tell when they were doing it."

Governor Chiles' prematurely born grandson, Lawton Chiles IV, a teenager during the governor years, continued to inspire the governor's quest to improve early childhood care in Florida. Lawton IV remembers his grandfather fondly, especially his "gotcha" sense of humor. Governor Chiles once pushed his grandson out of a park state airplane before a press pool:

> We were on the state plane, I think, and we landed in some airport in Florida, and there were a bunch of reporters outside . . . probably about thirty of them, or more. They were all in a semi-circle, looking back toward the plane, and he's like, "Well, you go out there." . . . But he pushed me out there first, and they were like, "What's your name? And how old are you?" And I didn't know what to say. So I think he just didn't want to deal with 'em. He was like, "Well, this'll buy me five or ten minutes, shove my grandson out there." But that was definitely a gotcha.

Lawton IV recalls his boyhood, when his grandfather read him stories about Br'er Rabbit, Br'er Fox, and Br'er Hen. The two enjoyed seeing movies in the theater together, like *Batman* and *Get Shorty*. Governor Chiles talked music with Lawton IV, according to the grandson:

> I remember he liked Willie Nelson and Johnny Cash, about the time when I started getting into music. He gave me some of his CDs that he had. I remember he kept them in the bathroom. He goes in the bathroom, right, and gives me this CD, and I'm like, "What's this doing in the bathroom?"

The governor would give his eldest grandchildren hundred dollar bills, inserted into perfectly sized envelopes by Rhea. Or Governor Chiles would give the kids a handful of icebox cookies and a glass bottle of Coke.

The governor would have preferred his singular strategy of children's advocacy to the pettiness of political campaigning. When well-meaning senior staffers began to discuss the exigencies of reelection with him, he chagrined.

Some close to the governor wondered if he would retire at sixty-four years of age. "Trying to get the governor focused on running for re-election was far and away the biggest problem that we had," chief of staff Tom Herndon said. "I don't want to say he didn't care. . . . He was not focused on that." He focused on public policy every day. "I don't think he cared about winning a second term, if he could get a lot done in the first term," communications director Ron Sachs added. Allies of Lt. Governor Buddy MacKay hoped the elder statesman would soon make way for the younger.

The governor's first term, moreover, had tested his faith in Floridians. The tourist murders of 1992 and 1993 in his state shocked Governor Chiles and the nation; the governor and lieutenant governor had campaigned in 1990 on the notion that the state should be a community, not a crowd. The crime wave claimed the lives of two Canadian tourists, the most common foreign tourist in Florida. Two more Canadians were shot in robbery attempts. One Argentine was shot and another accidentally ran over his wife with a car during an armed robbery. One British tourist was murdered and another wounded during a robbery attempt at a rest stop in north Florida. A Venezuelan diplomat was robbed and killed. One German tourist was murdered while driving his rental car in Miami.[668]

Communications director Ron Sachs would distinctly recall when he first heard of the crime against New York tourist Christopher Wilson on New Year's Day 1993. Three white men abducted Jamaican-born Christopher Wilson in Hillsborough County, soaked him with gasoline, ignited him with his own cigarette lighter and left him for dead. Wilson, suffering from burns on almost 40 percent of his body when the police arrived at the scene, begged a sheriff's deputy to shoot him to end the pain. Ron Sachs recalls Governor Chiles' reaction to news of the incident:

> I remember the governor doubling over, as if someone had just gut punched him, when he heard this news. And he had us call the hospital [in Tampa] immediately; he got on with the administrator of the hospital. He said, "This is Lawton Chiles, the governor of Florida. I'm calling about Mr. Wilson. I wanna know his condition. I'd like you to please call my staff with an update for me every day. And please let him know that I've called, that we're praying for his recovery, and as soon as he is able to hear me, I want to speak to the man." [They had told Chiles that Wilson was unable to speak for a while and he might not live.] . . .
>
> I was on a trip with the governor several weeks later, and I got a message through my phone that it was the hospital calling. And Mr. Wilson, whose head was still swathed in bandages, could not speak, but he could hear if the governor wanted to speak to him [the victim's mother held the receiver to his ear]. And I handed the governor his phone from

the back seat. There is no press there, it's no public there. It's just the governor, and two staff people. And he got on the phone and he cried . . . and he said, "Mr. Wilson, this is Lawton Chiles, I'm the governor of Florida. And I wanna tell you that every single day since your injury and this crime against you, I've been praying for you, and I've been following your progress medically. I'm glad you're doing better."

And then he said something that made me cry. He said, "I want you to know, this is not what the people of Florida are like, this is not what our state is about. And our entire state has been praying for your full recovery."

These moments of the governorship were also what rationalized Governor Chiles' decision to seek reelection.

The governor enjoyed better mental and physical health than ever in 1994. From time to time, he took detours from his diet but he had mostly quit red meat in favor of sushi. Governor Chiles stuck to his healthy habits even when staff ordered fast food. He exercised on the stationary bike and shot archery for target practice and hunting, among other physical activities, chief of staff Tom Herndon remembers:

[Governor Chiles] was just as strong as a bull. Even though he was slender for somebody his height, he was just as strong as he could be. I remember pulling that bow that he hunted with, and that was a lot of poundage to pull that bow. And he'd pull it without any problem whatsoever.

Governor Chiles loved the executive power of his new job, the antithesis of his U.S. Senate prerogatives. "He was the one who put the ball into play," Rhea Chiles said.

The governor believed that the Republican frontrunner Jeb Bush lacked the experience to manage a state like Florida—large, complex, and sometimes unforgiving.

He also knew that infant mortality numbers would not see a substantial decline without a longer commitment. And the health care providers across Florida who had made Healthy Start an early success needed their champion.

Once the governor settled his mind on the reasons for it, he dedicated himself to reelection.

15

The He-Coon Walks . . .

On a doldrums day during his 1994 re-election campaign, Governor Chiles, his wife and a few friends escape to the movie theater to see *Forrest Gump*. During the film, Rhea Chiles leaned over and told her husband, "Lawton, if this movie is a success, you're sure to get re-elected."[669]

Pundits liked to talk about how Lawton Chiles represented the end of an era. The small-town political pastimes of Governor Chiles' childhood survived in the 1990s, but attracted a smaller, nostalgic crowd. Munn Park rallies, once a regular attraction in Lakeland, now happened once a year in the form of a straw poll called "Politics in the Park." The fall 1994 edition of Politics in the Park pitted Governor Chiles against his Republican opponent in the general election, Jeb Bush.

Rhea Chiles also said of the 1994 re-election campaign, "The guy who beats us is gonna be another Lawton Chiles." Jeb Bush, about the same age as Governor Chiles during his 1970 Walk, exuded charisma and energy. He lacked the handshake of a natural-born populist like the governor, but compensated with a wealthy, famous last name. John Ellis Bush, born in Midland, Texas, had just turned forty a year before the Lakeland straw poll. Bush graduated Andover, then University of Texas in Austin, and subsequently moved to Florida in 1981 with his Mexican-born wife, Columba Garnica. His father, George H. W. Bush, had become vice president, and Jeb wanted to start his family and career away from Texas. The younger Bush joined a Miami commercial real estate firm, which promptly renamed itself the Codina Bush Group. One Miami developer compared Bush's hiring at the

Codina Group to "hiring General Norman Schwarzkopf. He'll command attention."[670]

Jeb Bush called himself a "head-banging conservative."[671] In December 1983, Bush won the Dade County Republican Party chairmanship.[672] Fluent in Spanish, Bush worked hard to leverage Miami's large Cuban community for his party's advantage. During the Martinez years, Bush supported the administration's service tax: "If this is a way to broaden taxation and at the same time lower the rate, I think a lot of people would really go for it."[673]

In 1987, when Bob Martinez became governor, Bush became the state's secretary of commerce. After a year and a half on the job, Jeb left and joined his father's successful 1988 presidential campaign.[674] By 1993, Jeb had amassed a fortune of $2.2 million. "I've worked real hard for what I've achieved and I'm quite proud of it," he told the *St. Petersburg Times*. "I have no sense of guilt, no sense of wrongdoing."[675] Bush sold his share of the Codina Bush Group in July 1993 and began campaigning to be Florida's governor full-time.

Bush had witnessed tax revolt sweep out Governor Martinez; it could do the same, he figured, to Governor Chiles. Chiles' Cracker roots mattered in election less than ever; like nearly two thirds of Florida in the 1990 census, Bush hailed from out of state. A poll in 1993 indicated Chiles had unfavorable ratings at 71 percent. Some Democrats wanted U.S. Senator Bob Graham to step down and run for another non-consecutive gubernatorial term. In March 1994, President Bush and Barbara raised $1.1 million for their son in three days. Jeb Bush's campaign hired fifteen staffers for the September Republican primary, ensuring their candidate won 46 percent of the vote. Like Governor Chiles, candidate Bush often conveyed anger to his aides through silence; unlike the governor, Bush demanded punctuality from his staff. Both candidates happily campaigned long hours. "I love it. I really do," Bush said of the campaign trail. "The only drawback is I don't eat and don't sleep." Bush sometimes arranged with staff to have a cheeseburger, fries, and milkshake waiting for him at his hotel room when his campaign bus arrived at day's end. "[Governor Chiles] thought he was Camelot, everybody would bow down to him," Bush said. "He tried to explain what he wanted to do, he thought everybody would march in line. I know that's not the way to make it happen." He explained his definition of leadership. "It requires humility. In a state this diverse, it requires an energy and a passion. It requires hard work. It requires sensitivity to other people's points of view. It requires an open, caring personality. I think I have these skills that are uniquely suited to this job."[676]

Governor Chiles was excited to perform in his hometown of Lakeland. The crowd of about 2,700 crowd goers, wearing t-shirts and carrying signs, exceeded expectations. Bush, eager to embarrass the governor in his hometown, took the podium first. Hearty applause followed the speech.

Governor Chiles then climbed the platform and gazed out over Munn Park, looking for familiarity. He saw many friendly faces but an altered landscape. The bandstand, however, was gone since the 1950s, fire claimed Lake Morton School in 1963, and Union Station terminal was demolished in 1961. Golf courses had replaced orange groves. The candidates spoke from a railroad car prop, since actual trains now passed Lakeland non-stop. Lawton's nephew Greg Ruthven and other Democratic activists worked the crowd, but many loud boos greeted the governor as he denigrated the Bush record. A Chiles supporter and a Bush fan got into a shoving match. "That's the Munn Park I remember!" Governor Chiles beamed.

"John Ellis has had eighteen months to call me soft on crime and ultra-liberal," the governor said. "I'm up to bat, now. It's my turn, and let me tell you what: Come the November race, we're going to beat the hell out of them."[677]

Bush won the Lakeland straw poll 1,008 to 969. Political strategists pointed to Bush's victory as a sign of changing times in Florida—especially in the pivotal central region stretching along Interstate 4 from Daytona Beach to Orlando and Lakeland to Tampa. Statewide politicians in the 1990s began scouring the booming, densely populated "I-4 Corridor" for swing voters early in the campaign season. Central Florida mixed the state's rural "Crackers" and new, cosmopolitan influences. Disney World's opening in 1971 had transformed central Florida. Between 1971 and 1994, more than a billion people visited Disney World and the greater Orlando area. Orlando's arms manufacturing and military training centers had closed. Disney planned to break ground on a new company-owned residential development near Kissimmee called Celebration. Opened in 1990, Universal Orlando Resort joined Disney World as the titans of Florida's tourist industry.

Many tourists from America and abroad settled in the state. One could exit Interstate-4 at Disney's Magic Kingdom and hear only Japanese, New York, and New Jersey accents all day. A few exits later in Polk County, one could pull into a Democratic Hispanic middle-class suburb and still find a few outliers—houses with Confederate flags and stickers on their windows that read, "Protected by Rebel [Confederate] Security Force," or metal signs on their fence that read, "Forget the Dog. Beware the Owner" and "It's 12:25, do you know where your gun is?" Highway billboards advertising fast food restaurants and hotels rendered the exits for Lakeland indistinguishable from Tampa or Orlando or Daytona Beach or any major American city. Residents started and ended their day listening to the I-4 traffic report. Before they had to chance to hire contractors to fix the roof, new residents planted "No to New Growth" signs in their yard. New central Floridians bought homes in gated communities; they eschewed civic and community organizations; they viewed Sunshine State life as a vacation and many bet that tax-cutting Republicans would guarantee a restful stay. Throughout Florida and the rest of the South, many conservative Democrats, usually middle-aged or older, re-registered as Republicans in reaction to President Bill Clinton's policies on gays in the military, NAFTA, and health care reform. State voter registration still gave Democrats a 500,000 advantage on the GOP, but the momentum favored conservatives.

When Governor Chiles kicked off his re-election campaign at the Higgenbotham Ranch in Lakeland on April 27, 1994, he sensed agitation for political change in the air. In Washington, he saw the national mood channeled by U.S. Rep. Newt Gingrich, the GOP's Southern political flamethrower. "If we are not careful, our children could inherit a dark and bloody planet in the twenty-first century," Representative Gingrich would warn rapt audiences. "I came here tonight to recruit you. To recruit you to the cause of freedom and to the cause of your country." More than three hundred GOP candidates joined Gingrich's call for a "Contract with America" in late September 1994, a platform of lower taxes, less government, balanced budgets, term limits, tort reform and other provisions. The crusader advised young conservatives on how to radicalize and ruin liberalism for good. One reporter noted, "Voters are bursting with frustration. Gingrich offers to explode on their behalf."[678] Governor Chiles likewise envisioned Jeb Bush as a likely messenger in Florida for this new conservative movement. "If I ever saw a textbook campaign, they had it," Governor Chiles said of Bush. "They polled, and they found out everything people are mad about . . . and they built Jeb."[679] Jim Krog, manager of the 1994 Chiles campaign:

> He knew that 1990 was a lay-down campaign. That was easy, sixty to forty bam each way. He knew what the political environment was in 1994. He knew from talking to everybody in Washington what was happening, and he knew the change that was getting ready to happen

there. He could feel that change in Florida when he talked to people. He knew that out of that it was gonna be a real tough race.

Governor Chiles, always attuned to timing, whether in politics or humor, saw strange changes in Florida's future. The governor "knew that his ilk would be gone and things were changing." He wondered if he could dash "under the tent."

Governor Bob Martinez's worst political wounds had been self-inflicted in the 1990 gubernatorial race. Governor Chiles, however, tried to inflict Jeb Bush's every hurt. Though initially reluctant to campaign, the governor pained at the idea of leaving Florida's future to Bush. "What I like about this race," Governor Chiles said, "is I think it will be a very clear test of philosophies. Of whether government can do something and should be doing something or whether we want to get rid of government.'"[680] The governor also mocked Bush's supposed qualifications for office. Governor Chiles said of his opponent, "They tried to put him in a grade he wasn't ready for." He railed, "The state is a 747. It does not fly by itself. Jeb needs to solo before he flies the 747."[681] Governor Chiles also declared: "I have given my life to the state of Florida. It is not a toy. It is not a toy for somebody to experiment with, with no experience."[682] Governor Chiles always called Bush campaign manager "Mac" Stipanovich "Max." Chief of staff Tom Herndon on Governor Chiles' attitude toward Jeb Bush:

> I don't think he felt like, certainly in the first term, that he was—I don't want to misuse this word—but I don't think he felt like he was qualified for the job when they first ran against each other. But he was an admirer of his intellect and his energy and his enthusiasm and liked some of his ideas.

Governor Chiles said to Jeb Bush during the campaign, "I respect very much your father and I like your mother. I just have found no reason from their past service to see where it gives them the opportunity to give one of their sons Texas and the other Florida."[683] Governor Chiles sprinkled his campaign speech with Cracker sayings, to reporter's delight and Bush's confusion. Any scribe suffering writer's block could fill a column inch just translating the governor's sayings. "We've got to go to the lick log" meant that it was time to end debate and set policy.[684] Governor Chiles once told a Bush supporter, "Cracker is the plain-spoken language of the country, spoken from the heart so anybody can understand."[685] Singer Jimmy Buffett even wrote a letter on behalf of Chiles' candidacy, praising his environmental record. The mailing, sent to targeted voters, added to the Chiles campaign's populist mystique.

The governor especially scorned Bush's approach on children's welfare issues. "I heard Jeb say he sees Florida's future through the eyes of his children," Chiles said. "That's good. I see Florida's future through the eyes of all of our children."

As Bush's poll numbers rose and the campaigns ran neck-and-neck, Governor Chiles reveled in turning his opponent's money advantage into a weakness. Per legislation enacted with Governor Chiles' sponsorship, gubernatorial candidates who restricted their campaigns to a $5 million spending cap could qualify for public campaign financing. For every dollar Bush exceeded the cap, Chiles gained a dollar in public financing. The provision channeled about $2 million in public funds to the Chiles campaign. Governor Chiles accepted public money by the truckload, but rejected donors who "double-dipped" Chiles-Bush to hedge their bets on the election outcome. "I'm not in the insurance business," the governor would say.

The Florida Republican party challenged the constitutionality of the public financing law in court, but the Florida Supreme Court ruled in favor of public money. Republican Party chairman Tom Slade claimed that the law benefited Governor Chiles specifically: "It was slipped through in the name of ethics and campaign reform, and it's a blatant special interest."

Governor Chiles campaigned extensively in the Panhandle, despite its conservative tilt. He still felt a kinship with the land, livelihood, and language of north Florida. "I wanted them [Crackers] to know I had the blood that they had. That I think like they think," the governor said.[686] He believed that his personal presence could force the Bush campaign to compete for the region's votes. Deputy chief of staff Jim Daughton recalls, "It was anathema to him to think that these [Panhandle voters] weren't his people." Governor Chiles, against his staff's wishes, ran TV ads in Panama City and Pensacola, and attended country cookouts instead of urban rallies. Gubernatorial staffer Deborah Kilmer reflected on the connection to the Panhandle:

> I traveled with him repeatedly in north Florida where I tasted moonshine for the first time. He knew where every still was. And they would come out and it was like a treasure for them to be giving

him—out of their trunk they would bring this stuff to him that literally could probably run the car. It had fumes coming off of it.

Governor Chiles attended the annual Wausau Possum festival in north Florida, a traditional political event held the first Saturday in August. Gubernatorial candidates walked in the hour-long parade, delivered two-minute stump speeches at the Possum Place, and bid on live possum for $200 and up. The festival drew about 5,000 people each year. Sharon Howell, a twenty-six-year-old Wausau native, explained the phenomenon. "If you ever see a possum dead on the road, his nose is always going to be pointed at Wausau."[687]

Staffer Dennis Beal accompanied Governor Chiles to the festival. He recalls:

> Our plane landed at this little airport, on a Saturday I guess, and the car wasn't there to meet us. And then the car that did meet us had a flat or some shit. We finally get in a car; it's one of those SUV-types. We're going down the highway, we're late, and there's a fuckin' possum dead in the middle of this highway. Chiles makes [the Florida Department of Law Enforcement driver] stop and pick it up, and this thing had been out there two or three days—really bad. And so we go on in, and Chiles says, "I'm gonna take that possum in there with me." I said, "you can't do that." He said, "Why?" I said, "You can't do that, I mean think about it. People are gonna know you're crazy!"

Ultimately, the FDLE agent and Beal persuaded Governor Chiles to discard the carcass.

The Bush campaign answered the governor's jibes with his own salvos, some of which blew back in his face. Bush proposed demolishing the State Department of Education, telling an audience, "I'm not kidding when I say that government's power needs to be controlled."[688] He declared that "government is an obsolete dinosaur. I don't consider that being from the far left or far right, or far anything."[689] Asked what he would do to help black Floridians, Jeb said, "It's time to strive for a society where there's equality of opportunity, not equality of results. So I'm going to answer your question by saying: 'Probably nothing.'"[690] The press publicized the quote widely, often out of context, damaging his support in the black community.

Bush's TV and radio ad succeeded initially, until it focused on the death penalty. The campaign's Wendy Nelson ad accused Governor Chiles of slack enforcement of the death penalty. The accusation infuriated Governor Chiles, in style and substance. Governor Chiles detested the political distortion of his death penalty position and the impersonal bitterness of TV ads. "Everything about Washington that he hated was getting ready to come to Florida," campaign manager Jim Krog said. The ad decried the supposed mishandling of a specific murder case in which the perpetrator awaited execution. *Tallahassee Democrat* reporter Bill Cotterell describes the ad:

> A guy killed some little girl . . . and Bush made a TV commercial with the child's mother, saying you know, the killer of my little girl has been sitting on death row for X number of years and Lawton Chiles won't do anything about it. As I recall, Bush then came into the shot and said, you know, when I'm your governor, people who kill little children will die themselves. Well, the very next day, the press checked on that. I think Chiles had signed a warrant and it was routinely stayed. The case was under review by the U.S. Supreme Court. Chiles said, well, what do you want me to do, execute a guy who's got a case pending before the U.S. Supreme Court? And Bush took just enormous heat.

Governor Chiles defended his conduct, claiming that the courts were still working the case and explaining his work to address the backlog of inmates on death row. His predecessor Governor Bob Martinez had signed innumerable death warrants before they worked their way through the judicial system, causing the bottleneck. Like a majority of Floridians, Governor Chiles supported the death penalty as a deterrent, but he also supported due process, and refused to campaign on the issue.

Former communications director Mary Jane Gallagher recalls the first execution under Governor Chiles. The governor, Gallagher, and deputy general counsel Bobby Brochin gathered in the executive office: "The first one was the biggest shock emotionally to all of us. He looked at us and was very quiet and he said, 'Now, let's get on our knees.' And the three of us knelt down, and he prayed out loud." Jim Krog describes the routine for executions when he served as chief of staff:

It is a very, very sobering process. When you sit down and he's on the phone to the prison, I'm on the phone to the attorney general, and J. Peterson is on the phone to the courts, to give the line, on final appeals. This is back when we had the electric chair. Then he gives the signal to do that, to execute the warrant. And it seems like an eternity, it's about five minutes before they come back on the line, after the doctor has pronounced him dead.

Eldest son Bud Chiles once joined Governor Chiles during a "death watch," the period leading up to a scheduled execution. He reflected on his father's views on the death penalty:

I think he definitely changed as governor. And I think anybody who sits through that Death Watch as governor—and I went through it one time with him and I'll never forget it—being on the end of that phone line and being able to play God and stop that, that was by far the worst part of the job for him. And signing those death warrants. Because I think he knew that as a lawyer that the system was inherently fallible. And I think he knew about the way the death penalty was done and the resources and all that, that it was the system. So I think his real gut level feeling was "the death penalty is more trouble than it's worth." So his conviction changed from the standpoint of having a deep conviction that the death penalty was gonna be deterrent to the death penalty, by the time he died, was more of a hindrance to justice than a help. During the Bush campaign when Bush made it an issue, he said "Well I'll sign the death warrants 'cause it's the law, but I'll never brag about it." [Governor Chiles] had been through it; he'd really been through it.

As assistant general counsel at the time, Mark Schlakman, helped the governor on capital cases. He recalls the Bush campaign rattling "off ten cases that were intended to show that Governor Chiles was asleep at the switch." The figure shocked Schlakman, who called the Bush campaign to verify their source. "The Bush people said, 'Let's let the people of Florida decide.'"

Governor Chiles focused on the last of the three official debates with Jeb Bush, on November 1 at the Tampa Bay Performing Arts Center, to close the gap in the polls. After the second debate, Bush had the momentum in a tight race with ten percent of voters still undecided. The final debate would be the first broadcast statewide, and the only many would see. Governor Chiles opened up to criticism, despite his distaste for Washington media strategy. The governors' younger son, Ed Chiles, led the debate prep team for the final debate. He recalls sitting in the Florida Room in the governor's office, waiting in vain for his father to come prepare with a media consultant brought in by communications director Ron Sachs. "I remember being in Tampa with [Governor Chiles]," chief of staff Tom Herndon recalls, "and going for walks around the Harbor Island area where we were staying before the debate, and him saying, 'No more fact books, leave the briefing books in the hotel room for a while. I need to get a different kind of orientation.'"

Ed Chiles said the final debate was "like watching a guy on a high wire." The first question asked by NBC moderator Tim Russert concerned the death penalty. The question made Jeb rock back on his heels. Ed Chiles nudged Lt. Governor Buddy MacKay in his chair, saying, "We're on fire." During the intermission, a heckler yelled at the governor, "Stop living in the past!" Governor Chiles responded by sticking out his tongue—to the audience's amusement.[691] Lieutenant Governor MacKay would recall the final question to Governor Chiles:

> [It] was something like this: "Governor, your opponent says you are out of ideas and energy, and need to be replaced. What is your response?"
>
> Lawton thought for a minute and then said: "The old He-Coon walks just before the light of day."
>
> Russert turned to Jeb for a rebuttal. It was apparent that Jeb, a newcomer to state politics, had no idea what Lawton was talking about. ... Coon hunters knew what Lawton meant: the younger coons, driven by hunger pangs, left the den early and were at risk when the dogs caught their scent. The old He-Coon, however, waited until dawn, after the hunter had departed, before leaving the safety of the den. Translated, this meant that Lawton knew enough about Florida politics not to allow his campaign to peak too early.[692]

Friends, strangers, and current and former staff puzzled over the "He-Coon" admonition. All parsed its meaning differently; all agreed it was vintage Lawton Chiles. Former gubernatorial staffer Dean Saunders interpreted:

Of course, Lawton knew, "I'm speaking to my people; I'm speaking to all those Crackers out there that know."And he was telling Jeb, "I'm the He-Coon, this is my time. Next two weeks, this is my time."

Fred Schultz, former Florida Speaker of the House and Chiles' rival for the 1970 Democratic U.S. Senate nomination, recalls the expression:

> What immediately popped into my head was "Lawton you're doin' to Jeb Bush what you did to me in 1970. You're pullin' that man of the people, populist, good ol' boy approach and it worked against me, and it worked against Jeb." Schultz added, "You know, I doubt that it was premeditated, but I also believe strongly that that's a remark that Lawton was waiting to use at some point in time."[693]

According to Rhea, after the final debate, Governor Chiles "knew that he had scored with the Panhandle" and "the rest would catch up later." The debate drew nearly one million viewers, beating Jeopardy, Wheel of Fortune, and Roseanne for TV ratings, and saw broad coverage in state newspapers the next day.[694] Governor Chiles himself explained the "He-Coon" comment backstage after the debate: "It's sort of like saying, 'Don't mess with the Lone Ranger.'"[695]

Governor Chiles confidently called the final debate a "turkey shoot."[696] The Saturday before Election Day, he elated to hear that forty-five-year-old George Foreman, thought to be too old for boxing, defeated the twenty-six-year-old, undefeated Michael Moorer in a tenth round knockout. Governor and Mrs. Chiles, family and staff awaited the returns on Election Night with trepidation, though, as Democratic governors in Connecticut, Texas, Alabama, and New York conceded defeat. Future President George W. Bush won the Texas governorship. Florida Republican U.S. Senator Connie Mack was easily re-elected and Newt Gingrich became Speaker of the U.S. House. Social conservative Rick Santorum won a U.S. Senate seat from Pennsylvania; GOP doctor Bill Frist defeated Chiles' friend and Democrat Jim Sasser for his Tennessee Senate seat. Ed Chiles says "every big oak in the forest fell" during the year's "Republican Revolution." As midnight drew close, Governor Chiles' staff anxiously read returns from Broward and Dade Counties.

At 11:30 p.m. Election Night, Jeb Bush called Governor Chiles to concede. Then the governor took the stage at the Wyndham Harbor Island Hotel in Tampa to speak to his supporters. Someone in the crowd gave him a coonskin cap, which he donned with a grit-eating grin. The governor danced the stage, imitating "Georgie" Foreman's one-two knockout punch the weekend prior.[697] Then he calmed the crowd down for a moment. "This campaign is different from any campaign I can ever remember," Governor Chiles said. "There is a feeling loose in the land of utter frustration, tremendous anger, and it is something that has been building."[698] Gubernatorial adviser Jack Peeples called Governor Chiles "the Dutch boy with his thumb in the dike" against a Republican "tidal wave [that] just swept over everybody."[699]

"He's always been a funny fella to me, "said Chesterfield Smith, friend and former president of the American Bar Association. "He believes in some mystical way that the people are always right, that if you can get the issues to the people, it will always turn out right. And if the people didn't elect him, he'd still feel they are right, and that he must've done something wrong."[700] Mallory Horne scratched his head: "He was the most unlikely political figure that I knew that never got beat! It was an enigma to me always, because he was naïve in a real practical sense until the very end."[701] Governor Chiles credited his victory to the Walk across Florida. "I think that walk," he said, "helped build a residual of good feelings that has stayed with me throughout the years and been there when I needed it."[702] He also believed his victory proved that "Florida has elections, not auctions." Limiting contributions to $100 per person, Governor Chiles had raised $6.23 million—including over $2 million in public money—to Bush's $8.8 million.[703]

In one of Florida's closest political contests, the governor defeated Jeb Bush by about 64,000 votes, 50 percent to 49 percent. Both candidates garnered over two million votes. Governor Chiles won in what had become the Democratic "Big Three" jurisdictions: Miami-Dade, Broward, and Palm Beach.[704] The election put conventional wisdom about the state to the ultimate test. It taught a good rule of thumb: if a Democrat can carry Dixie and Miami-Dade County, they win the state. Dixie County—a swampy jurisdiction full of snakes, bald cypress, and saw palmetto, at the mouth of Suwannee River—supported Governor Chiles. So did Miami, center of international commerce and culture. Lt. Governor MacKay told one of his favorite Dixie County stories:

It is about a hotly contested sheriff's race "in the old days." The incumbent noticed that he was trailing as the ballots were manually pulled from the box and counted. He asked for a short recess, and retired with his chief deputy to the graveyard, where he allegedly obtained the ballots of a few more faithful constituents who had failed to vote because they were deceased. It was cold and rainy, and after a while the deputy said, "Let's go, Sheriff. It's cold and besides, we've got enough names." To which the sheriff responded with indignation: "Oh no! This is America! Everybody's got the right to vote."[705]

The "Dixie-Dade Strategy" rewarded Chiles in 1990 and 1994.

To his disappointment, Governor Chiles ran worse than ever in the Panhandle and lost his beloved Polk County. Cross City native Marjorie Chewning, from the heart of Dixie County, recalls that "it broke his heart." Chewning baked pound cakes for the governor's birthday. "He didn't like to lose friends and the little counties were his friends. It was a personal thing, a personal hurt." Hal Chewning chimed, "People slept better, knowing that Lawton was there." Marjorie Chewning added, "I don't think the common folk realize what we have lost."[706]

Governor Chiles also reacted emotionally to losing the Miami Cuban vote. Joe Pena, a Cuban-born Democrat, served as policy coordinator for Governor Chiles. The most senior Latino staffer in the administration, Pena helped the governor maintain strong ties with Miami, beyond its food. Pena recalls, "Versailles [restaurant], Versailles was a hang-out for us . . . and they would treat him like a rock star. They weren't always necessarily his voters, but they would have a special appreciation that he was there. . . . One election eve, we had to ship black beans up to Tallahassee because his superstition or tradition was he needed to eat black beans the night before the election. And we did an order through Versailles and we got it up to him."

After the 1994 elections, the GOP took control of the Florida State Senate for first time in a century, but it was Bush campaign accusations of "scare tactics" in the final hours before Election Day that broke up the governor's victory party. A bloc of Chiles campaign get-out-the-vote paid phone calls had labeled Bush a tax cheat and bashed his running mate Feeney for wanting to abolish Social Security. The phone script fraudulently claimed attribution to an apocryphal "tax fairness" organization and a senior citizen advocacy group.[707]

"Although we'll never know, it's quite possible the Chiles campaign stole the election by fraud," Bush campaign manager J.M. "Mac" Stipanovich said in November 1995. Jeb Bush himself commented, "That's for others to speculate about. It's over and you can't redo it. You can't speculate on the impact of those calls on the outcome."[708]

Governor Chiles denied authorizing the approximately 70,000 calls, but apologized anyway and signed a law banning malattribution of get-out-the-vote campaign calls.[709] Campaign manager Jim Krog on the phonegate scandal:

We had a young guy, in our operation, who had put together this script and had made up a name of a group. And it was a pretty scurrilous script. But it went to maybe 85,000 calls. Even after we won, we won by 75,000 or 80,000. Those phone calls became the legend—that that's the only reason we won, because of those calls. I said, well, if we converted every one of those calls over, on that thing—obviously we didn't because some of those people were complaining. So that theory is shot. But then they had this whole Senate investigation and all that, and they subpoenaed everybody and we all did this week-long show for 'em. They carried it out for a couple months, just a day or two at a time. There was nothing illegal.

According to Krog, the governor told him, "That was pretty good, you get me re-elected, and you have all the trouble. Krog also emphasized that the message of the fraudulent phone calls was true: "The essence of what we said was true. The message was true. The screw-up was we should have put it out in the name of the campaign."

In December 1995, Governor Chiles, the first modern Florida governor to testify under oath before a legislative committee, swore that he knew nothing of the "scare calls" to the Senate Executive Business, Ethics, and Elections Committee. Before the Ethics Committee, Governor Chiles apologized: "I want to apologize to the voters who were misled by those calls and to the people of the state of Florida."[710] He added, "I've got thirty-five years or so in this, and this is as murky water as has been under my bridge."[711] The gesture slowed the momentum of the Republican media campaign on the scandal known as "phonegate," reducing it to a one-man operation led by future Florida Governor Charlie Crist, an unknown GOP State Senator at the time. The political press tired of writing on the scandal. *Tallahassee Democrat*'s Bill Cotterell on the phone calls:

If you believe that every one of those calls reached its target and that the target wouldn't have voted otherwise, but then went and voted, that could have produced maybe 85,000 votes. And we got a lot of phone calls, letters to editor, saying Chiles wouldn't have been re-elected if he hadn't cheated. Let's say there were 120,000 phone calls. I'm quite sure you know, at least half of them just hung up, never even listened to the message. And those who did probably said, well, that's ridiculous, the governor of Florida can't repeal Social Security or the lieutenant governor of Florida can't repeal Social Security.

Miami Herald's Mark Silva on phonegate: "That campaign was won before that happened. The idea that that somehow tipped the election was a canard, it wasn't true. But it was sort of, the kind of thing that came out a campaign which had a lot of money to burn." Silva added, "I'd be amazed if [Governor Chiles] knew."

Celebration resumed in the Chiles camp as phonegate faded. Jim Cordero and Wayne Watters, former legislative affairs staffers in the governor's office who had reported to Jim Krog, attended a victory party and planned to play a "gotcha" on the governor. Despite their starkly different appearances, Governor Chiles managed to always confuse their names, and now the two wanted payback, according to Watters:

We saw the governor kinda walkin'. Jim and I were standin' kind of in the middle of the place, we were havin' a drink. And we saw the governor kinda make eye contact with us, like we knew he was gonna work his way over to us. . . . So Jim and I thought it'd be funny, so we switched name tags. I've got a picture of it. And we switched name tags. And he walked up, and he starts to shake hands, and you could tell that he knew something wasn't right. Finally he realized it, and just started laughin'. And we got this great picture.

For the governor's inauguration in winter 1995, the mayor of Tallahassee had opened the streets to everyone who had "Walked a Mile for Chiles." A street festival featured a dozen music acts and food vendors serving possum, alligator, mullet, and swamp cabbage. Supporters in the 3,000-strong crowd wore t-shirts proclaiming "the He-Coon Walks . . ." chowed down on "He-Coon stew" sold by street vendors and chanted "He-Coon, He-Coon" as they followed their governor—dressed in khakis and a coonskin jacket—on his victory walk through downtown Tallahassee.

"When I went work for him," Ron Sachs recalls, "Mrs. Chiles had me over and said, 'I wanna warn you that he will put on anything anybody gives him.'" At the festival, the governor ate black beans and rice, and took the stage during the set of one of the blues bands. He borrowed a microphone and strutted and strummed an electric guitar before belting out "You Are My Sunshine" to bring the band home. Governor Chiles waved goodbye with his trademark double thumbs up.

His next trick: firing a potato gun outside the Governor's Mansion. "Oh my God, it's going out in the street," Governor Chiles said after his first shot. Lake County Democratic activist Linda Olini commented on the spectacle: "You never would have had this if you had Jeb Bush."

16

First Base Is Our Children

When Governor Chiles first told his staff that he intended to use his second inaugural address to denounce burdensome state rules and regulations, they figured their boss was playing a "gotcha" on them. "I thought he was kiddin' me," communications director Ron Sachs recalls, "'cause he had this celebrated sense of humor and I was often the butt of his jokes. I said, 'No, really, what are we talkin' about?' He says, 'Cuttin' rules and regulations by fifty percent.'"

The governor's recent renovations of his hunting cabin, Sachs discovered, had violated county building codes. Governor Chiles had worked for years building the "cook shack" of his dreams outside Tallahassee on Miccosukee Road. Miccosukee Native Americans first used their namesake road to downtown Tallahassee as a footpath. In the nineteenth century, cotton plantations used Miccosukee Road to haul thousands of bales of cotton to Tallahassee for sale. By the twentieth century's end, Florida designated the road a historic monument. Live oaks, their branches hung with Spanish moss, canopy the road. In the spring, dogwoods bloomed and webs of purple wisteria meshed the forest ceiling. Before rainshowers, breeze spread the light, sweet aroma of wisteria. Bumble bees pulsed through the vines.

Soon after taking office in 1991, Governor Chiles bought two hundred acres of forest and field on Miccosukee Road; in the meadow he positioned two nineteenth century cabins found in neighboring counties. When they heard about the structures barreling down the highway, sons Bud and Ed remarked, "Well, he's lost it this time, have you seen the pile of junk he's taking down the road?" Rhea Chiles called it a "labor of love."[712] Governor Chiles called the estate as a whole "Chemonie" or simply the "cook shack."[713]

At Chemonie, the governor would take walks, chew tobacco, fry bass, hunt turkey, and ride horses. At nearby Bradley's Country Store, a single-story house erected in 1927, Governor Chiles stocked up on fresh grits, sausage, and gossip. He invited friends to cook country sausage and talked pioneer history around the campfire, according to former chief of staff Tom Herndon:

> To hear a story from somebody meant a whole lot more to him than reading a chapter in a book, and not to say he wasn't an avid reader because he was. That was a more powerful medium to him and it meant something additionally on a personal level.

Especially in the company of old pals like Mallory Horne, Dexter Douglass and Dubose Ausley, Governor Chiles relaxed his speech and "spoke Cracker":

> It would be wrong to say I spend time thinking about them. I don't. I was raised in Central Florida at a time when everybody I was raised with were natives and were of the same kind of stock. I always liked to go hunting. I always liked to sit around the fire. It's like a vernacular or a vocabulary that you use. Wherever you came from, there are words and things you say, and people there understood what you said, while other people say, "What the hell does that mean?"

The governor added, "You never know when they will come out. You don't write these down. They come out of your skin. Like splinters."[714]

Former State Senate colleague Mallory Horne liked to see the governor outside Tallahassee:

> Coming out of places, [Governor Chiles] looked sometimes like a bum. We'd come out of hunting and we'd go to a store to get a Pepsi or something and he that old sloppy hat, and sloppy clothes, and he slouched over a little bit. But he never did this thing that politicians instinctively do, or I never saw it, and that is walk in "Hi, I'm Lawton Chiles," or "Hi, I'm Governor Chiles." But then people would say,

"Hey, I think that's the governor over there." It was very effective to be totally ineffective.

Sometimes, the governor preferred to enjoy the wild in silence. Mallory Horne: "Lawton was—I know it's probably contradictory—but he was sort of a lonely guy." Friend and former president of the American Bar Association, Chesterfield Smith:

> Lawton always takes his own counsel. He thinks if he can get five or six hours by himself out in the woods, sitting under a tree, just thinking and thinking, he'll come up with the answer. I don't want to make him sound too mystical, but that's how he works.[715]

Sometimes, Governor Chiles disappeared into himself even among friends, according to eldest daughter Tandy:

> He was like a colored stone, because you never know, there were so many colors in there, you didn't know which one was gonna surface, and sometimes it would be difficult to say what color it was at all, because he was an enigma also. You'd be talkin' to him, and he's just not there. He was just in his own place, his own zone. And a lot of people, staff people especially, made the mistake of thinking that he didn't hear them, and regretted it. But it wasn't that he didn't hear you, he did hear you. He just was not going to communicate back to you. And you'd look at him, and you'd kind of want an answer, and it wasn't gonna come.

"That was how he communed with his God," former chief of staff Tom Herndon said, "was to go to the woods."

In the cook shack, Governor Chiles had found a metaphor for what he perceived as overregulation. When he refit one of the cabins, replacing the roof and resurfacing the façade, an anonymous tip led Leon County building inspectors to the construction site in 1993, and they cited the governor for building code violations.[716] The previous owner of the Chemonie property had illegally subdivided the lot. The inspectors delayed the governor's construction on this count and for moving the cabin, replacing its roof, and digging a well without proper permits. The cook shack anecdote distinguished his second inaugural address:

I have two hundred acres of woods north of Tallahassee where I have an old log cabin. I wanted to build a cook shack out back—wood poles, tin roof, screened sides, and an old stove. I've been trying to get a permit for over a year. "You must have plans," they say. But a cook shack is unusual; there are no regulations for one. So they ask: "Does it have a stove?" Yes. "Does it have a toilet?" Yes. "Well, the closest thing we have is a single-family residence; so it needs steel tie-downs; it must withstand Andrew-type winds, etc." The cost went from $15,000 to $65,000. I've concluded the Lord gave me this problem so I could understand why people hate government so much. Mr. Speaker, Mr. President, every member of the Cabinet, I respectfully request your help in this. Let's set a goal to reduce the present rules and regulations by 50 percent within two years.

Helge Swanson, an environmental permitting director for Leon County, recalls, "The governor made an awfully big deal about having to comply with wind-resistance requirements. But the thrust of what held him up was his own failure to comply with a fairly non-complicated subdivision ordinance."[717] Community Affairs Secretary and incoming gubernatorial chief of staff Linda Shelley reacted to the speech:

It was a pretty big issue. That was awkward for me because I was secretary of the department of community affairs, which is in charge of building codes, and I had looked at the inaugural speech—the second speech—the night before and nothing about that was in there. And so I'm sittin' on the platform with the other agency heads, and he starts talkin' about these bureaucrats and his cook shack . . . and we're tryin' not to laugh, and I'm tryin' to keep a straight face, and he's just essentially callin' me out.

Three months after the inaugural address, the governor got his building permit.[718]

The conflict with county regulators reminded Governor Chiles of the near-closure of his beloved Bradley's Country Store due to regulatory issues. New Year's Eve 1993, Governor Chiles visited Bradley's, bought grits, and chatted up the ownership. Frank and Lillian Bradley told the governor how the Florida Department of Agriculture had cited the store for failure to bring their seventy-five-year-old grist mill into compliance with modern standards. At the next Cabinet meeting, Governor Chiles spoke to Agriculture Commissioner Bob Crawford, who sent inspectors to help Bradley's comply. The store flourished once more, selling cornmeal, honey, and preserves to buyers as far as Maine and California, and sponsoring an annual fall festival called Country Fun Day. Governor Chiles bought Bradley's grits for President Bill Clinton's Florida visit in March 1995. "There were no pretensions about him," said Janet Bradley Fryzel, whose grandfather founded the store. "He was just a real person who didn't try to be something other than what he was. He was just Lawton Chiles, who happened to be governor."[719]

Despite the governor's passion for the rural way of life, staff found his vendetta against regulations a dry diversion from their principal agenda. As in 1991, when David Osborne's books influenced the first policies after inauguration, in 1995 Governor Chiles found a literary script for his ideology. The governor passed out the bestselling *The Death of Common Sense: How Law is Suffocating America* by Philip K. Howard to staff at the beginning of his second term. In Howard's book, he described government's tendency to replace intuition with overdetailed rules:

> Look at what we've built: a legal colossus unprecedented in the history of civilization, with legal dictates numbering in the millions of words and growing larger every day. Our regulatory system has become an instruction manual. It tells us and bureaucrats exactly what to do and how to do it. Detailed rule after detailed rule addresses every eventuality, or at least every situation lawmakers and bureaucrats can think of. Is it a coincidence that almost every encounter with government is an exercise in frustration?[720]

Governor Chiles pointed to a stack of over 3,500 government rules, paper stacked a foot high, and proposed repealing at least half of the rules by the end of the 1996 legislative session. He could cut a few thousand via executive order, but the rest would require legislation. At the time of his inaugural pledge to cut rules by half, the state had almost 30,000 regulations. By December 1995, the Florida Administrative Code had cut almost 5,000 rules and added more than 1,000 new ones. Instead of relying on rules to clarify and detail legislative mandates, Governor Chiles envisioned the rule of "common sense." Florida Transportation Secretary Ben G. Watts, embraced the agenda, sending his boss a note:

A little over 1,000 years ago, Alexander the Great came to the city of Phyrgia and saw the impossibly complex knot tied by King Gordius. Learning of the legend that gave the rule of Asia Minor to anyone who could untie the knot, Alexander drew his sword, sliced the knot in half and went on not only to rule Asia Minor but all the known world. Hence, the classic example of proper rule reform.

Executive services director Nevin Smith likened the anti-regulation movement to the mangrove trimming movement. To protect Florida's mangrove swamps, the state issues rules prohibiting pruning and cutting; people simply stopped planting mangroves.[721] Major business leaders found they didn't want to get what they wished for. "Entire businesses are built around the expectations that are in those rules," said Jodi Chase, lobbyist for big-business powerhouse Associated Industries of Florida. "If those were to change on the whim of a regulator, it would wreak havoc on the private sector." Governor Chiles often told Linda Shelley about the rules, "you have to weed the garden every day." Shelley acknowledged that the administration probably never cut regulations by half.

Governor Chiles' agenda on children's welfare dominated his second term. The work challenged and rejuvenated him. "If you have a lifetime ambition, as I did, to go to the United States Senate," the governor confessed, "and you find out that it did not create nirvana and happiness—in fact you end up disillusioned and frustrated—then this is second life. It's a gift."[722] New chief of staff Linda Shelley later recalled, "It used to be easy to give talks about the governor's priorities because his top three priorities were kids, kids, and kids." Shelley, having worked for previous Florida Governor Bob Graham, also a Democrat, compares the two governors' agendas:

In hindsight, Graham was much less oriented to the human services end of the equation than Chiles was. All of the early childhood, prenatal, Healthy Start, Healthy Kids, healthy, healthy, healthy—that wasn't Graham, that was Chiles. Health care generally, [for] children specifically, was Chiles. Graham spent very little time or money on that; he wanted to focus on education. Chiles considered education a pit into which you could not throw enough money, so he and MacKay were not in complete sync on that. He wasn't trying to starve public education, he was a big believer in public education, but he also wasn't going to spend his last minute on it, or last dime; he would have spent it on health care.

Mrs. Chiles collaborated with her husband to advocate for children's health care. Communications director Ron Sachs commented, "I credit Rhea completely with getting the governor back on the path of what his legacy as governor has been, which is to be the children's governor." Rhea approached her role as first lady with confidence in her own values. "You have to really find your own song of yourself before you can sing to anybody else," she said.

As a first step on children's policy, Governor Chiles worked to maintain adequate funding levels for Healthy Start, despite Republican control of the state legislature starting in 1996. The governor worked successfully with new Senate President Toni Jennings (R-Orlando), who led the upper chamber from 1994 to 1998. Chiles and Jennings were aligned in rejecting "party orthodoxy," whether Democrat or Republican, according to state children's advocate Jack Levine:

> Probably the person I saw him most closely aligned with during his crusades, or cause-related activities around children, was Toni Jennings. And what Senator and then-President of the Senate Toni Jennings [could always do, as he could, was find a way] to negotiate around what would have traditionally been called "party orthodoxy." Now, I know, 'cause I was in the room, on at least a few occasions, when he pled with her to make something happen in the Senate, which he needed desperately, whether it be budgetary or statutory; he did not want to have his own people be direct interventionists. He did not seem . . . to want to go the traditional route of senator-to-senator, count your heads, count your votes, bargain and deal—especially around the issues I focused on, which were kids' policy, Healthy Start, early childhood education, and other services for kids. I saw him look across the room at [Toni Jennings] and pretty much say, "I'm gonna leave this up to you, but I'm counting on you."

In response to critics who expected the Chiles administration to flounder in the face of a Republican State Senate and a Cabinet split evenly between the two parties, Governor Chiles muttered, "I bend like a reed—like spaghetti. We bend but we don't break."[723]

The election of a new class of Republicans to the legislature, though a shock to many in the Chiles administration, offered a chance to build a rapport among lawmakers and learn from mistakes made in the first term. In meetings with his top legislative affairs staff, Governor Chiles insisted that proposed administration bills have at least one Republican cosponsor before they reached his desk for consideration and debate.

Governor Chiles took a sterner tack with the freshman class of Republicans in Washington, especially those anxious to pass health care reforms found in Newt Gingrich's "Contract with America." When in early 1995 Gingrich revolutionaries in the Republican Congress floated a plan to give states control of Medicaid, Governor Chiles traveled to Washington to mount a defense.

Congressional Republicans' planned to convert Medicaid to a block grant—a fixed one-time sum of money—and give governors greater flexibility to administer it. The formula for the grant total would change, too. It would increase by a maximum of 5 percent each year regardless of the growth in eligible citizens. In the long run, the GOP plan would profit slow-growth or no-growth states like Wisconsin, Illinois, and Michigan, and shortchange high-growth states like Florida, California, and Texas.

Confident that his beltway experience would help his message find an audience, Governor Chiles warned a House subcommittee of its error. "Shifting new responsibility without a fair, equitable shifting of resources is not any kind of New Federalism," he stated. "It is an unwise attempt to balance the federal budget on the backs of high-growth states and even worse, on the backs of children, the poor, the elderly and the sick. That's just plain wrong." Governor Chiles knew Florida's senior population was growing and would soon require greater support from Medicaid. The program was the biggest item in Florida's budget and the fastest growing. He preferred that Medicaid stay the way it was—an entitlement paid out to states based on their per capita poverty population.

Governor Chiles tried to rally Republican governors of Arizona, Texas, and California to his cause, appealing to their fiscal self-interest as leaders of high-growth regions. Arizona Governor Fife Symington concurred with Chiles and wrote a letter to Bob Dole, the Senate Republican leader. Florida's governor chastised Republican governors of low-growth states for supporting Medicaid reform in the hopes of shoring up their finances. He called them "Judas goats"—a farmer's term for an animal trained to lead others to the slaughterhouse. "It's no wonder the Governors of Wisconsin, Michigan, and Massachusetts are on this bandwagon," Governor Chiles said. According to the new proposed formula for Medicaid, "a poor child in Massachusetts would get three times as much as a poor child in Florida."

The Republicans in Congress ultimately passed Medicaid reform as part of its budget reconciliation bill, but President Bill Clinton vetoed it. Governor Chiles lauded the president's decision. "This is a watershed, this issue. It's a ball-breaker. The federal government needs to guarantee to poor children, the disabled and the elderly that there is going to be some standard of heath care." The governor's Democratic and Republican allies on Medicaid policy credited him with raising its national profile and educating the public. Chiles had the ear of the president and a detailed sense of the federal budget; both were crucial to his success on national health policy.

Governor Chiles continued to work the issue with fellow governors in succeeding months. He probably considered the country's roster of state executives to be more even-tempered and practical than federal politicians embittered by the 1994 elections. In late 1995 and early 1996, Chiles joined a task force of six governors—three Republicans and three Democrats—intent on securing Medicaid's finances for the long-term. Even if it remained an entitlement, budget experts like Governor Chiles acknowledged two truths about Medicaid: the program needed a better funding formula and any reform needed bipartisan backing.

Florida's governor worked over a hundred hours behind closed doors with the Medicaid task force and reached a compromise in February 1996 to maintain Medicaid as an entitlement with some concessions to states. Charlie Salem, Special Counsel to the Florida Governor's Office of Federal Relations in Washington, D.C., staffed the gubernatorial task force and admired Governor Chiles' negotiating style. He "knew better than anyone," Salem recalls, "when saying nothing was more powerful than saying something." The governor had a strategy to his silence. He "let other people run themselves tired, run their mouths, let 'em get all their issues out there, so he sensed what's really important, and at the end, at the right time, he would spring it on them and really drive the debate in the final, final moment when it's most critical."

The White House was overjoyed that the National Governors Associated had approved a bipartisan Medicaid reform deal and a bill was drafted in Congress to make it law.

Congressional Republicans, however, ignored the governors' deal and wrote a bill that ended Medicaid as an entitlement and broke it into block grants. They followed the letter of the Contract with America as they did the previous year. Governor Chiles and President Clinton cried foul and the bill never came to a vote.

Governor Chiles' Medicaid reform dealings in Washington may have soured his disposition toward Gingrich-worshipping Republicans in his own state. With Florida conservatives eager to make headlines by beating a veteran governor, Governor Chiles could be glib, according to health policy director Doug Cook:

> [A state legislator] came in, and he's pointin' his finger at Chiles, telling him the revolution has taken place, and he needs to get on board, "we'll bury you." And I'm sittin' in there, and Chiles is just listening and listening, doesn't say anything. . . . He could just sit forever. And the guy said, "Well, Governor." And [the Governor] said, "In the words of the late-twentieth-century philosopher Mick Jagger, 'You can't always get what you want.'" And the staff, we couldn't help it, we all started laughing. . . . He pulled it out of nowhere, just like the he-coon thing.

Communications director Ron Sachs admired the governor's intransigence in the face of GOP opposition:

> I remember once saying to him, "Governor, if you do this, the press is gonna write this in their criticisms, the Republicans are gonna say this, it might be perceived like this." I was trying to get him to take a look at what he was doin'. He said something to me that made me scratch my head. He said, "You know, Ron, I may be wrong, but I'm not in doubt." I came to understand what it meant, which is that he had a very strong sense that he woke up every morning, believing what he was doing was the right thing for the state, and if he was proved wrong eventually, it didn't matter. He believed at that moment he was doing the right thing, and he had to go by his own moral compass on policy issues.

Children's health care was an issue that state Republicans found difficult to oppose politically. Even without gubernatorial advocacy the programs were popular, and with Governor Chiles' imprint they were morally unimpeachable. Their purpose was easier to phrase for a broad audience than the rationale for tax reform or regulatory reform.

In 1996 Governor Chiles oversaw the creation of the Lawton Chiles Center for Healthy Mothers and Babies, a research and advocacy non-profit under the leadership of founding director and state health officer Dr. Charles Mahan. The governor initially disliked the notion of having a building named after him, but ultimately consented. Dr. Mahan had originally devised the idea for the center in the 1980s as a way of maintaining Chiles' momentum on children's issues after he retired from the U.S. Senate. "This center is working hard to fulfill our dad's dream—that every baby have a healthy start in life," said the governor's youngest daughter, Rhea Gay Chiles.[724] The Chiles Center ultimately moved to the College of Public Health at University of South Florida.

Though Governor Chiles quit pushing universal health insurance on the legislature, he succeeded in expanding children's access to insurance through the enactment of Healthy Kids Corporation. Dr. Steve Freedman, the founding director of the Institute for Child Health Policy at University of Florida—and a friend of the governor's since his days as a professor in Gainesville—served as vice chair of Healthy Kids Corporation. Dr. Freedman called Governor Chiles "intensely curious" about the latest children's policy breakthroughs. "I remember him lecturing me once," Dr. Freedman recalls. "We were going out, I picked him up for lunch, and I wasn't wearing my seat belt. He was unmerciful. He said, 'I don't ever wanna see you without a seat belt on.'" The comment stunned Dr. Freedman momentarily. "It was almost [a] fatherly thing, like 'Wear a damn seat belt.' So I did that." Dr. Freedmen comments on Healthy Start and Healthy Kids Corporation:

> I think those two are emblematic of the fundamental idea that . . . if you give access to quality health care at the earliest possible stage, you avoid the very expensive downstream problems you get when kids go unseen and untreated for initially minor things that turn out to interfere with their education. I think that was the other piece. He really understood the link between a good start in life and being able to take advantage of educational opportunities later on and ultimately be a good citizen because you're healthy and you got a good education. He made that link very easily; most politicians don't think that way.

Healthy Kids Corporation won the 1996 Innovations in American Government award from the Ford Foundation and the Kennedy School of Government.

By 1996, Governor Chiles' success in working with the GOP-controlled state legislature on children's welfare and other issues, coupled with a rebound in the national economy, had revived his administration's job approval ratings. Violent crime was on the downswing nationally.[725] In a mid-decade Harris Poll, Americans chose Florida as their chief preference if they could move and live anywhere.[726] A Mason-Dixon poll in October 1996 placed Governor Chiles at his highest popularity rating, 64 percent, since he'd taken office, making him the thirteenth most popular governor in the nation among his constituents.[727]

The Florida public held Governor Chiles in such esteem that President Clinton leaned on the governor to ensure his national re-election, according to chief of staff Linda Shelley:

> When Clinton was a governor of Arkansas, Chiles was a big shot in the United States Senate, plus he was a southern Democrat. . . . So Clinton called on Chiles quite a bit when Chiles was governor. Unfortunately, Clinton often called at night, when the governor would not remember, after he went to bed, that he'd even talked to him.

There were multiple parallels between the Chiles and Clinton administrations in style and substance. The pair of Southerners enjoyed a strong friendship. Lieutenant Governor MacKay recalls, "Al Gore and Bill Clinton— I didn't ever know whether they were just being polite or not—but they said publicly, over and over, 'Our relationship is based on this working relationship of Chiles and MacKay.'" Carol Browner, Governor Chiles' first Secretary of Environmental Regulation, and later EPA administrator for Bill Clinton, claims, "Clinton loved [Chiles]. And I think [Chiles] genuinely liked Clinton."

In memoriam, Clinton remembers Chiles' influence on him:

> Every one of us who knew Lawton Chiles feels blessed. If we knew him very well, we loved him. He gave something to all of us. He gave me a lot when we were serving together as Governors. I mean, I couldn't imagine—I was serving as Governor with someone who had been chairman of the Senate Budget Committee. And he made sure that I was always aware of what I should know before I voted how-

ever he wanted me to vote in the Governors conference on whatever it was.[728]

During his presidential administration, Clinton used pages from the Chiles-MacKay playbook—welfare reform, a "New Covenant" theme, reinventing government, and a "Putting People First" theme. After David Osborne, the reinventing government guru, guided the philosophies of the Chiles-MacKay team, he joined the Clinton-Gore administration as Gore's intellectual muse. Osborne and Gore went about reshaping core institutions of the federal government.

St. Petersburg Times reporter Tim Nickens compares Chiles and Clinton: "I think you can see a lot of parallels there on the policy level. . . . They would both reach across the aisle, but yes, they could also play the partisan thing, too. They both could be very partisan but they both compromised in the middle." Both leaders favored strong lieutenants. "I don't think you'd find anywhere a team like that where he trusted so much authority and responsibility in the lieutenant governor, in Buddy," Nickens says of the Chiles-MacKay partnership. Clinton invested a similar degree of trust in Al Gore.

This ideological and personal kinship between Florida's governor and America's president made the Sunshine State a major Democratic rallying point in the 1996 presidential election. Governor Chiles championed the Clinton re-election campaign with gusto. "Chiles was as nervous as he was for his own campaigns for the last Clinton presidential election," staffer Deborah Kilmer recalls. "He was so excited and pleased that Florida went for Clinton. And Clinton gave him a lot of credit."

An hour after the polls closed in Florida, President Clinton called Governor Chiles. "We can turn out the lights, we won Florida," the president said. If GOP challenger Senator Robert Dole (R-Kansas) couldn't take Florida, it was all over.[729]

The Chiles administration celebrated its success in building a constituency of children and helping re-elect an ally in this fight to the White House in its spring 1997 State of the State address. The governor, as in prior years, revised the speech up until the morning of delivery. Chaos no longer ruled his executive office though. By his second term, Governor Chiles only worked overtime on special projects; he paced himself better and watched his mental health. He trusted staff more, according to April Herrle, who replaced Ron Sachs as communications director in February 1996:

One time I was briefing him before a press conference about something, and someone made a comment about the business community, and I told him of a rumor that I had heard. Well, we walk into the press conference and at the end of the press conference he gets a question and he says, "Well, as I understand it, Associated Industries of Florida, this major business organization, has done dadadadada." It's coming from me, now, and I didn't know it to be a fact; I had just told him what I had heard.

I quickly learned that you don't do that, 'cause he trusts your judgment, he trusts what you say, and if you say it, you'd better be a hundred percent right. Fortunately, as I quickly back-pedaled and checked and checked and checked, it turned out to be correct, but it was so startling to me that he took that advice and counsel very seriously. It wasn't just another voice; it was trusted advisors telling [him] this. He didn't need to do any further checking; as far as he was concerned, it was a fact.

Governor Chiles depended most on his new chief of staff Linda Shelley, the first female gubernatorial chief of staff in Florida history. Governor Chiles called his senior staffer "chief," to which Shelley replied, "You just cannot remember my name, and so you just call me chief."

Shelley filled a power void in the governor's office that General Counsel occupied during the transition between chiefs of staff. When Shelley came aboard, Jodi Chase, a lobbyist at the Asosciated Industries Florida, commented, "It depends on whether Dexter Douglass lets her be chief of staff." Shelley ultimately helped the governor balance his working life:

[I often wondered] how do I bring somebody into the universe scheduling-wise that will put him [Governor Chiles] back in a happy equilibrium state? Because governing can be very lonely, and almost every friend—and I've told this to other chiefs as they say, "What's the secret?" I say you have to divide the friends into givers and takers. And almost every friend of a politician is a taker."

Shelley helped Rhea Chiles integrate into the governor's policy shop through "working lunches" at the Mansion. Rhea explains the operation:

I realized that when we had meetings in the garden room, they were always very productive . . . so we had to start having more and more meetings in the garden room. So the Mansion really became an adjunct to the office. And I did it in a way, or it worked out in a way that it didn't threaten anybody in the staff in the Capitol.

Governor and Mrs. Chiles raised money to renovate the Mansion, hosted lavish events for thousands of guests, and exhibited Florida artwork, leveraging it for the public interest. Federal relations director Deborah Kilmer called Governor Chiles "one of the best hosts I've ever seen . . . [he had a knack for] including everybody [at the table in a discussion], mentioning something, or remembering, 'How's your Daddy's sore back? Is it any better?'" Mrs. Chiles wrote a successful book on the history of the Governor's Mansion, entitled *700 North Adams Street*, which raised money for Mansion restoration.

In return for their service, Governor Chiles humored his staff with regular "gotchas" and other unique displays of gratitude. Communications director April Herrle enjoyed the interplay between industry and humor:

> The thing I think about all the time is how fun he was. I'm sure you've heard this from many people, but he loved to laugh, he loved to play tricks on people, he loved to pull reporters' legs. One time we had—I think it was—Mike Griffin in the car with us in Orlando, and he was spending a day with the governor, and the governor decided that he wanted to scare the reporter and pretend that there was a bomb in the car. And so we had FDLE all geared up with this, two cars with agents, staff, and so forth, and the agent pretended to get a call, and say "Everybody clear out the car." And so everybody jumps out of the car and we were all in on it of course the reporter was like, "Oh my God." That was the kind of thing that Chiles loved to do. When things got really intense—and we dealt with a lot of very difficult issues—he was the first one to crack a joke or just be very mischievous and a lot of fun. It made working there just a real joy.

Governor Chiles communicated often through small gestures and facial expressions, according to deputy chief of staff Dan Stengle:

He didn't say, "Oh my, that was a fine job!" But he would smile and say, "That's just right." We all knew when he was happy, when he was not happy, when he was pleased with what was goin' on, when he wasn't. Again, with him, a lot of words were not required to get his message across. . . . You recognized, if he was angry with you, that you had somehow failed him. And God, you didn't want to disappoint this guy.

Budget director Dr. Bob Bradley concurs:

I used to say that he had four types of silence. He was silent positive, silent negative, silent neutral, and silent what-the-hell-are-they-talking-about? So when he was sitting there, he would be listening to what people say, and he wouldn't necessarily say that much to them. He would just listen very carefully, and then he would say the right thing, because it's easy to make commitments that you can't come up with. He thought if he told somebody [he would do] something, that was it, he was gonna do that. He pretty much lived up to that.

April Herrle explains further :

He had very high expectations, and boy, when you hit the mark, you were on the moon. And if you felt like there was more on the table that you could've, should've done, it was just demoralizing. It just cut you to your core, because he inspired such loyalty. It was like, it wasn't about him, it wasn't for his personal glory.

Governor Chiles also found new social outlets beyond Chemonie, or accessed old ones more efficiently. He still stored and cooked his wild game at the Mansion, but expanded his palette, taking Italian cooking classes, according to federal relations chief Debbie Kilmer:

When he took the Italian course, we used to argue, he got a few things wrong, confused between orzo and polenta. But he had this pot. He thought he was an expert on making polenta. And he carried this pot on the state plane periodically, if he was going down to somebody's house, that he wanted to impress them with making his polenta. And I thought he had lost it then. But that whole aspect of him a lot of people never saw, that he really enjoyed food, from a social standpoint.

Governor Chiles would invite his man-friends over to watch Roy Jones box on pay-per-view. Deputy chief of staff Dan Stengle marveled at the diversity of his boss's friendships: "I think of him sort of as geologic time because he knew so many people throughout his almost forty-year public career and then he knew them from the guy who used to vacuum the carpet at J. Hardin Peterson Jr.'s Dad's law firm to President Clinton."

Above all, at this juncture in his career Governor Chiles knew precisely when he needed time outside Tallahassee to relocate his spiritual balance. "If we have him in the office too long, it shows," said communications director April Herrle.

The 1997 State of the State reflected the tone of the Chiles administration at the time: confident, studied, but still prone to the occasional goof. The governor filled the address with facts which he could have recited from memory. He stated that from birth to age one, the number of brain connections grow from about 50 trillion to 1,000 trillion; by age ten, the majority of the brain's network is built. Babies who lack a nurturing environment, moreover, develop brains that are smaller than normal. Once a child attains ten years of age, its brain is "cooked," he explained, and "you have to play catchup, and the cost of that, as we know, is very high." At one point in the address, the governor stumbled on the statistics:

> When a child is growing in its mother's womb, its brain adds twenty-five thousand [250,000] neurons per minute, per minute. At birth, a baby's brain contains one hundred thousand, no, no, one billion, one thousand billion, I'll get it right in a minute, one thousand billion [100 billion] neurons. That's about the same number of [nerve] cells that there are stars in the Milky Way.

But he had already announced his theme with eloquence:

> Today, I want to speak with you about a journey that I've been on. It started here in this House, where I served eight years. I went down the hall and served four years in the Senate. I took a little walk and that led me to the United States Senate where I spent eighteen years.

And now for the past six years I've been proud to serve as Florida's Governor.

I thought I was pretty darn good. I knew a lot of answers. I had worked on a lot of solutions. I thought I knew how to play the game. But now, thirty-six years later, I find I didn't even know where first base was.

First base is our children. The answer to all of our pressing problems begins with the child.[730]

17

The School Prayer Veto

When Florida's Christian Coalition succeeded, on their third try, in pushing a bill sanctioning prayer in public schools through the state legislature in spring 1996, everyone watching expected the governor to sign it. Lawton Chiles once responded to his Lakeland church's survey that his favorite hymn was "The King is Coming."[731] At a March 1976 campaign rally, Chiles told voters he supported law restoring prayers in schools without violating the separation of church and state.[732] In his 1982 Senate campaign, Senator Chiles vowed support for a vote on a constitutional amendment allowing voluntary school prayer.[733] Since his first inaugural address, Governor Chiles had publicized his religious fervor in public oratory. "We all just sort of looked at each other, like, I can't believe he's saying this," south Florida Democratic lawmaker Ben Graber said in reaction to Biblical references in the 1991 speech. "We felt like we were at a sermon," Graber said. "I sort of feel like I'm in Sunday school," said Rep. Sandy Safley (R-Clearwater).[734]

The governor's staff saw flashes of his spirituality, according to communications director April Herrle:

> I know he and Rhea prayed every morning and discussed that. At the end of the term, probably the last two years of the term, we actually started a Bible study. I'm a Catholic, and we don't do a whole lot of Bible study. And so I didn't quite know what to make of it at first. And then it was such a wonderful insight into Chiles as a person, as

well as into my own faith, but just the level of knowledge and perspective that he had was tremendous.

Chief of staff Linda Shelley, Presbyterian like Governor Chiles, enjoyed seeing prayer as part of her boss's daily ritual. "He loved Scripture," policy advisor Jim Towey says of his boss. "And he would read it the way one savors a fine wine or a little child's hug."[735] Chiles attended Red Masses in Washington and Tallahassee as a U.S. senator and governor, out of an intellectual interest in religion, according to Director of Federal Relations Deborah Kilmer.

The Chiles family knew the connection between the governor's spirituality and his self-worth, thanks to copious diaries. In his spiritual diaries, scribed in the Mansion bedroom, Governor Chiles called his lower nature the "Old Man." Since recovering from clinical depression, the governor had "pegged" his stressed, depressed state of mind, according to Rhea Chiles. The "pollution of conscience" that began in Washington would recur, but "it wasn't throwing him down anymore." The governor's family rejoiced in his new-found ability to rule his ego, according to eldest son Bud:

> My dad struggled with his lower nature—he fought the demons that sometimes raged inside him. This passion to become a better man was the hallmark of his greatness. He turned to God for strength, he spent hours reading and re-copying scriptures that inspired him to change. He did not conquer all his demons, but he never gave into them. He rarely talked about any of this to anyone.

The struggle opened the governor emotionally, Bud explains. "He was much more, trying to figure out what he was really like inside and being able to deal with it and give more of himself to his family, connect more." Tandy Chiles, the governor's eldest daughter, agreed. "He'd call me up and he'd say, 'I didn't tell you goodbye.' He'd catch himself. And to him, that was a huge thing. Those were things that meant something." Kitty Chiles, the governor's daughter-in-law, admired the new priorities:

> He had that Bible . . . and he was reading it. And sharing it a lot. We would talk a lot when we would be together. Rhea was huge in that. She was the leader and got him in many ways interested in plumbing those depths and trying to understand himself more and wrestling

down what he called the Old Man and just dealing with all the things that somebody who is in the limelight like he was, all those demons, people want to treat you like you're something that you're not. He always tried to fight that down and not become somebody that he wasn't. To me that was the most admirable thing about him. He did some cool stuff, but he probably became more and more humble as the years went by. He really did. And valued relationships more. And just became—simpler.

Governor Chiles not only eschewed the search for a "twenty-fifth hour" in the work day, he had found a spiritual routine just as fulfilling. According to former Senate staffer Dave Mica, "He had reached the point in life where it wasn't about changing the world that way."

School prayer had seen extensive debate; it had "cooked" enough in the legislature, in the governor's parlance. At the start of the March 1996 regular legislative session, the Florida chapter of the Christian Coalition enumerated school prayer as one clause of its "contract with the Florida family."[736] The House sponsor was Rep. Randy Mackey (D-Lake City). Senator Charles Williams (D-Live Oak) was the Senate sponsor for the measure for the last three years. "I'm not trying to impose my religion upon anyone else," said Williams. "I believe everyone has a right to express their faith."[737] Then-State Rep. Debbie Wasserman Schultz, a Jew, decried, "This amendment will impose the will of the majority on the minority in schools. It's offensive."[738] Nancy Kipnis of the National Council of Jewish Women: "Organized, meaningful prayer belongs in our homes and in our religion institutions, not in our schools."[739] "

In an impassioned speech that commanded the attention of lawmakers and a packed gallery, Senator Robert Wexler, a Jewish Democrat from Boca Raton, said no other issue in his five years in the Senate had made him so uncomfortable. His voice cracking, Wexler said the prayer proposal wouldn't solve the problems students faced, such as pregnancy and drug addiction, and would make those whose religions were in the minority feel like outcasts. "They'll be frowned upon," Wexler said. "They'll be made fun of. They'll be humiliated."[740]

"It's clear that tyranny of the majority will rule the day and schoolchildren are going to be uncomfortable, ostracized, picked on, and tormented because of their religious beliefs," said Bernie Friedman of the Florida Association of

Jewish Federations, which represents about 800,000 Jewish residents of Florida.

Senator Charles Williams, a Baptist, said in response to critics, "I believe the children of Florida will handle this a lot better than some of us do as adults. This is something that might bring our children together in a spirit of harmony and friendship."[741]

In April the House passed school prayer as an unrelated amendment, or "rider," on a larger bill designed to raise high school graduation standards, requiring high school students to graduate with a 2.0 or "C" grade point average. The rider would allow school boards to authorize student-approved, student-led "nonsectarian and nonproselytizing" prayer at secondary school graduations, football games, and other optional school events and assemblies outside the classroom. The amendment defined prayer as "an invocation or a benediction."[742] There was no time limit proscribed for the prayer. The Senate approved the amendment after the House, in late April. Democrats from north Florida sponsored both bills. In 1996, students nationwide already could pray privately as individuals, according to the U.S. Supreme Court; Florida allowed two minutes of silent meditation or prayer since 1980.[743] Governor Chiles had fifteen days—until May 31—to veto or approve the prayer bill once it arrived at his desk.

At a National Day of Prayer rally, Governor Chiles withheld comment on the bill itself but stated:

> I don't think there should be a set prayer, I don't think there should be a denominational prayer but I've always felt that a public school is no different from any other public place as far as an individual being able to exercise their right of freedom of speech and freedom of worship.[744]

Chief of staff Linda Shelley assisted Governor Chiles with assembling the necessary information for a successful deliberation on the bill:

> We had the rabbi and we had the Muslim and we had the cleric collar—people that we could reach out to quickly that would be able to come and say, "This is how it would feel to me if I was in the classroom and I had to hear something that I didn't. . . ." That was the basic message that he got, is do we have the governmental authority to impose that on somebody?

In the governor's meetings with stakeholders on issues, Governor Chiles spoke through body language as well as words, according to Florida children's advocate Jack Levine:

> He seemed to be very comfortable in all of his interactions to get to the core of who he was having this conversation with. He was never, ever above them. He seemed to always be with them. That's something that you don't see it much in that game. He always leaned forward. There was a body style, the way you hold yourself, he never seemed to want to relax back and have people come to him. He always seemed to, his posture as always leaning forward. Some people could call it poor posture, and I'd call it connecting posture. He leaned forward, he sat forward. He always made the person he was engaged with feel a little closer to him as he leaned up.

Governor Chiles met with the primary opposition to the bill, including Rev. W. Henry Green, pastor of St. Petersburg's Heritage Community Church.[745] Rabbi Stanley Garfein of Temple Israel said, "This is something that would certainly not help religion, but create one more irritant in the public-school system. It's not a Jewish-Christian issue, it's a constitutional issue." The Reverend Brant Copeland of First Presbyterian Church in Tallahassee said, "The school-prayer provisions, in our opinion, are irreligious and they violate the consciences of religious people of all ages. They won't stand constitutional scrutiny. They show no respect to people of various religious convictions." The Reverend Len Turner of East Hill Baptist Church in Tallahassee said in retrospect, "This was not a Jew versus Christian issue. My heritage as a Baptist is to say 'whoa' when I see government trying to get involved in religion. I don't want the state telling us how to conduct our religion. And no matter how non-threatening this seemed, if it was not a foot in the door, then it was a little toe.'"[746]

Governor Chiles also met personally with the bill's two sponsors, and considered an unprecedented volume of constituent correspondence on the issue. As of the afternoon of Thursday, May 30, the governor's correspondence office had recorded 11,222 calls and letters in support and 9,860 against since the bill was passed on May 4.[747] He had to decide on the bill by 11:59 p.m. Friday, May 31. On Wednesday, May 22, eight religious leaders met with Governor Chiles to discuss the bill; only one, Rabbi Stanley Garfein, predicted a veto after the meeting.[748] "I guess if he were to veto it at this point, it wouldn't surprise me," said John Dowless, executive director of the Christian Coalition of Florida (a strong supporter of school prayer), after general counsel Dexter Douglass recommended a veto to the governor.[749] "This statute puts such religious and personal psychological pressure on students," Douglass wrote in his message to the governor, "that the very essence of the solemnity, holiness, and spiritual serenity that is prayer itself would be a major harmful event to those students selecting the invocation . . . as well as to the minority which loses the vote."

Governor Chiles vetoed the school prayer bill, to the shock of many advocates and critics of the practice. Eldest son Bud Chiles spoke to his father on the phone about the issue.

> I knew he was wrestling with [the issue], mostly because people would misunderstand his position, and he hated that. He definitely had very strong convictions about not pandering on that issue. That was very fundamental. He had basic things that you just were not going to move him off of. They were real rock things with him, and that was one of them, that there was a distinct separation between church and state, and it needed to be preserved. He thought [it] gave us a lot of strength in our constitution and form of government.

Freshman GOP legislator William Andrews of Delray Beach wrote him a caustic letter, denouncing the veto; Governor Chiles responded harshly. *Tallahassee Democrat*'s Bill Cotterell remembers the governor saying that "he didn't want his granddaughter being told, 'Okay, now it's time to pray,' just like, now it's time to go out to lunch, now it's time to go to the playground, now it's time for science class, now it's time for math, now it's time to pray. He said that was something he'd leave to the family." The governor questioned "leaving his highly charged and emotional decision to a vote of secondary students."[750] Jack Levine surmised the school prayer veto in hindsight:

> What was so clear to me, and we were inside that conversation both legislatively and then in anticipation of the veto, was he created around him a vision for inclusion rather than separation or exclusion. What this man believed deeply, it appeared to me, was he never wanted anyone or any public policy to cross the line of imposition.

And he rightly believed, and I am with him every step of that way, that when the majority feels their authority to impose, that's where he felt the obligation to push back. I think he really put himself personally in the place of a parent, a grandparent, or even a child within a system that could be offensive around the majority rule, and really just had this uncanny creative ability to play that role: What if it was me?

Opposition leaders handed Governor Chiles a copy of a May 4 *Gainesville Sun* article where the bill's House sponsor, Rep. Randy Mackey (D-Lake City) said the measure "is what's going to help return Christianity to the schools."[751] The comment infuriated Governor Chiles, who had trusted Mackey's public assurances of religious tolerance in spite of public school prayer.

Representative Mackey commented on the outcome: "What we say to our children through our actions such as this, 'We will teach you about sex and alternative sex preferences, we will teach you about drug abuse, we will tell you the evils of tobacco use and alcohol use, yet when you come in great numbers to use as responsible adults and ask us to afford you your freedom of speech and your right to pray, we will not allow that." When told of the veto, anti-school prayer advocate Rabbi Garfein exclaimed, "Well, hallelujah!"[752]

Staff considered Governor Chiles' veto message one of his best. *The St. Petersburg Times* called it "the shining moment of his second term," and "vintage Chiles."[753] Democratic attorney General Bob Butterworth:

> Lawton was the most experienced. . . . He knew the legislative process. . . . He knew how to deal with it, which meant he showed up on day one, and gave his state of state speech, and then he let go of the legislature, by and large. He would occasionally kick a tire if something that he was concerned about was not going right . . . and then he'd be totally engaged at the last thirty-six hours, which is really when everything happens. So he knew the legislative process so well that he did not have to spend sixty days looking at it like other governors did. He would just look at it when he knew he had to look at it. And he did a great job on the issues that concerned the state. . . . The last thirty-six hours he was totally in control, as to the entire agenda,

as to what he wanted to get through, and it was his show completely, completely.

In a Mason-Dixon poll conducted June 21-23, 50 percent of respondent Floridians supported the bill, 39 percent supported the veto, and 11 percent were unsure. The governor's job performance rating remained within the margin of error of March's pre-veto rating.[754] Deputy chief of staff Dan Stengle collaborated with Governor Chiles on the veto message:

> [I arrived at] the Mansion, and the governor [came out] in his pajamas. ... I said, "I know you're not gonna hang around tomorrow." He was goin' fishing at six o'clock in the morning with Mallory Horne. He didn't want to become the prayer veto governor. He just thought it was the right thing to do. But that was it. He said it in the message. He didn't have any more comments about it. ... I said, "This was a really courageous decision, governor, I know this is difficult for you." He grinned and said, "That's why they pay me the big bucks." He thanked me and shuffled off to bed.

Many advocates and critics of school prayer questioned the disparity between Chiles' positions as governor and U.S. senator on the issue. The governor explained this perceived evolution in his veto message. He used his own words for several paragraphs of the message, a rare move for a Florida governor, to ensure the public would not misunderstand him.

Ambivalence, he attested, had always characterized his feelings on school prayer. As far back as his days in the state legislature, the issue pricked his conscience. He had never reached a resolution in it, even when he professed to support it as a U.S. Senate candidate.

He had never deliberated it to the degree that he did in the leadup to the 1996 veto. Previous bills on the issue had died too soon in legislature to require his lengthy consideration.

Faced with the real prospect of seeing children enter schools fearful of state-sanctioned religion, Governor Chiles resolved to make a definitive ruling this time. Every official word on the issue would enjoy his personal attention.

Thus, his veto message was a paragon of eloquence and equanimity. *The Palm Beach Post, The St. Petersburg Times, The Miami Herald*, and the

Tallahassee Democrat, aware of its status as a political milestone, printed his message in full:

> There are a number of provisions in House Bill 1041 that would benefit Florida's system of public education. Indeed, many of the provisions in the bill can be accomplished through action of the State Board of Education or by local school boards within their current authorities. Contained also within the bill embracing these provisions, however, is also a provision which would authorize school districts to adopt resolutions allowing invocations or benedictions at enumerated secondary school events. On balance, I believe that this so-called "school prayer provision" will not be beneficial to our system of public education and, for the reasons which follow, compel me to veto House Bill 1041.
>
> The issue of school prayer has been very troubling for me for many years—first as a state legislator, then as a United States Senator, and now as Governor. School prayer was an everyday occurrence for me as a student in public school, and as a member of the Christian majority. I had, and still have, feelings that this is something that we should be allowed to do. Listening and trying to place myself in the circumstance of a minority, however, gives me a different perspective. I do not believe that the right to petition the divine should be granted or withheld by majority vote.
>
> I grappled with my decision on this particular school prayer issue for many weeks. I listened to the arguments of supporters of this school prayer measure, and of its opponents. I sought the views of thoughtful and sincere clergy with opposing views on the issue of school prayer. I considered the governmental, theological, and personal aspects of my approval or disapproval of this measure. Coming to what I consider to be the right decision—even at my age, and with my lifetime of experiences—was extremely difficult, and appropriately so.
>
> I am especially mindful of the very thoughtful and sincerely held beliefs of many Floridians both for and against this legislation. While I readily admit that I do not possess any superior wisdom, judgment, or insight on this question, it falls within my duty—by virtue of this office that I hold—to render my judgment on this issue, and to the best of my ability, I hereby do so.

There are those who have urged me to allow this bill to become law, leaving to the courts the decision as to whether it is constitutional. I do not invade the province of the courts by vetoing this bill today. Instead, I exercise my authority and responsibility, as the chief executive of Florida, to give or to withhold my approval of legislation which has been presented to me. I do so not principally on the grounds of its constitutionality, but upon the appropriateness of the public policy embraced by the legislation. It is my conclusion that the school prayer provision in this legislation is not appropriate as a matter of public policy.

I believe personally that a prayerful and spiritual life is richly rewarding. I commend it, and I recommend it. But endorsing such a life is for me to do as an individual. It is different for the state.

Our Founding Fathers engrafted onto the Bill of Rights the doctrine of Separation of Church and State, forbidding any "law respecting an establishment of religion, or prohibiting the free exercise thereof." By so writing, our forefathers bound us to a twofold principle: that in the United States we shall have freedom *of* religion, as well as freedom *from* religion. By allowing us freedom from religion, the concept of freedom of religion is strengthened and purified. Our wise forebears conceived of a democracy strong enough to tolerate a broad array of personal beliefs, knowing that by our diversity, our democracy is further strengthened.

What our Founders knew is that the decision as to whether to pray, when to pray, and to whom to pray, is an intensely personal decision. It cannot be decided by majority vote.

Even so, I also believe deeply that prayer has a place in every facet of our everyday lives, including our public schools. Clearly, students who wish to engage in silent prayer are allowed to do so in our schools. There is nothing in the court cases, the statutes, or the rules which govern our educational system that prohibits students from exercising their religious freedoms in this way. There is likewise nothing in the action that I take today that will remove prayer from the public schools.

We know from experience that our school children are capable of dealing with a wide variety of decisions and choices in their lives. We appropriately give them broad opportunities for personal choice, as these opportunities can be rich and growing experiences. But to impose upon them the choices of others in so personal and subjective a matter as prayer is not of such value. As well, I question the appropriateness of leaving this highly charged and emotional decision to a vote of secondary students. It is unfair to expect such a vote to bear the hallmarks of sensitivity, to say nothing of reflecting adequately the multiple facets of this complex, important and private decision.

Further, the school prayer provision will diminish the importance of the views and beliefs of those who are not within the majority. The public schools in our pluralistic society are grounded upon the principle of inclusion. School programs which at their best bring people together in common bonds - at sporting events, school assemblies and commencement exercises - could be turned into events that tear people apart.

I am mindful, however, that worshiping together can be unifying and fulfilling experience. We gather together in churches, synagogues and mosques, in other places designated by certain societies and cultures as holy places, and at campfire services to celebrate and practice our religious beliefs with those who share our beliefs and our faiths. We do so—willingly, comfortably, trustingly—to share the common bonds of our faiths. Praying together is a devout act which is to be embraced, not an act to which one is to be subjected. One commentator wisely said that religion cannot be forced; it must be found. The very act of prayer may be trivialized by requiring it of the believers and non-believers alike, obliged to listen to rote recitations of pre-approved benedictions and invocations.

Prayer itself, personally and spiritually woven as it is into the strong fiber of our society, would not be well-served by allowing this bill to become law. The school prayer provision, as it is contained within this bill, would reduce this profound and spiritual devotion to school board and classroom debate. After full and prayerful contemplation of this measure, I reach the conclusion that it is better for us to reverently honor prayer as individuals, in our places of worship, in our homes, and in our hearts.

For these reasons, I am withholding my approval of House Bill 1041, and hereby veto the same.

Sincerely,

LAWTON CHILES

Governor

18

Taking Joe Camel to Court

Soon after the Florida legislature rejected the administration-sponsored Florida Health Security Act in spring 1994, Governor Chiles fished with Mallory Horne, a friend from their days serving together in the state legislature who on separate occasions served as both Florida's Speaker of the House and President of the Senate. They sat on opposite ends of the boat. The governor said, "I don't know what my problem is with that damn Legislature!" Horne said, "Your biggest problem is sitting on the other end of this boat." Three months later, Governor Chiles asked Horne what he meant, and Horne replied:

> You're making every decision based on whether it's good or bad and that's noble, but a sign of weakness and vulnerability in government. They know you're going to play our hand that way and not be tough in turn. Pretty soon it gets to be fun to be kicking the governor's ass.[755]

Governor Chiles embraced the executive prerogative in his second term, according to Florida children's advocate Jack Levine: "Chiles at that stage of his political and personal life was not into incrementalism any more. He was into big bites, and the biggest bite of all was the tobacco challenge."

Governor Chiles first considered suing the national tobacco industry on behalf of the state of Florida during his first year as governor. The impact of escalating Medicaid expenditures on the state budget troubled him, as did tobacco's responsibility for hundreds of millions of these health care costs. Florida Speaker of the House at the time, Democrat T.K. Wetherell, presumed Governor Chiles would tax tobacco. A proposed 25 percent tax could garner $250-to-$300 million annually. Wetherell describes the debate:

> We started talking about the tobacco deal the first year he was in . . . It was only the most private of discussions at the Mansion, but I was convinced we were gonna do something. I thought it was gonna be a tax, to be honest with you. Lawton had a bigger idea. As it began to unfold the second year, and then, when he wouldn't do it in the second year . . . he politely said, "I'll do it the next year." But he wanted Bo [Johnson, Florida's speaker-designate], I think, to do it. He wanted it out of reapportionment. He thought strategically.

National expenditures in 1993 for medical costs attributed to smoking were $50 billion. Estimates of smoking-related costs for Florida Medicaid from 1992-1993 ranged from $385 million to $517 million. Former Florida U.S. Senator and Governor Bob Graham called Medicaid "the great white shark that threatens to gobble up Florida's budget for schools and everything else."[756]

Eldest son Bud Chiles recalls, "My father was most shocked and revolted about the way tobacco companies targeted teen smokers to continue to replenish the ranks of smokers." Florida knew Mickey Mouse as well as national tobacco industry symbols Joe Camel and the Marlboro Man.

Governor Chiles decided he wanted to smash the tobacco industry's marketing machine, not simply recover revenue. He wanted to take Joe Camel to court, and began investigating the necessary legal tools:

> We started seeing that the same defense that tobacco was using against individuals, they would attempt to try to use against the state. And we thought, that is not fair, we ought to have a level playing field in which they should not be able to say to us—what they said to the smoker—the warning was on the pack in that the state did not have those kind of choices. So that is where the idea for the Medicaid [Third-Party] Liability Law came from.[757]

The Medicaid Third-Party Liability Act amendment of 1994, its writers hoped, would help the state recover Medicaid funds spent as a result of the tobacco industry's negligence. Though Florida had the original law on the books since 1978, the new, amended version would clarify and strengthen the original, allowing the governor's office to hire private lawyers on a contingency basis to file a lawsuit against tobacco. Fred Levin, eminent Pensacola attorney and Chiles law school classmate, and Harold Lewis, state inspector general and high school friend of the governor's, helped draft the Liability Act amendment and devise a legislative strategy that required absolute confidentiality. Chiles' co-conspirator State Senator W.D. Childers offered the amendment to a non-controversial Medicaid bill just before Senate recess, announcing, "This just cleans up a couple glitches in the law." The bill passed unanimously.[758] Convinced of its potential threat to Big Tobacco, Governor Chiles personally oversaw the bill's successful passage by the legislature. The Republican caucus and tobacco lobby immediately cried foul, calling the governor's strategy "secret" and "stealth." Tobacco advocates lost their jobs due to the defeat. General Counsel and long-time friend of the governor, Dexter Douglass, defended the administration maneuver:

> Well, they're lying, because they all knew that the bill was going through; they didn't recognize what was gonna happen. And they said, 'He sneaked it. Sneak attack. Lawton's a dirty guy.' I thought, there are thousands of bills that get passed that way every year. And of course you don't respond to that except to say, well, you passed it. And all the lobbyists were the ones that were caught short, they weren't paying attention. But truly I think that it germinated in the minds of Harold [Lewis] as to how to do it, and also Fred [Levin]'s understanding that in large litigation like that, you needed a statute. And I think that's how it happened. I don't care what anybody else says, I'm almost positive that's how it happened—and I think Lawton would say that, too.

Communications director April Herrle:

> [Governor Chiles] would say they were aware it was passing. They knew it and they decided it wasn't gonna be that big of a deal. . . . Yes, it was passed in the middle of the night. Yes, it was one of those little amendments that went in, but they did know that it was going in. They just didn't feel like they had the oomph, or that they would fight it another way.

Tallahassee Democrat's Bill Cotterell saw the maneuver as vintage Chiles:

> [Governor Chiles] was a very good political craftsman. ... You think he's this country lawyer—and he can follow you in a revolving door and come out first. And you don't notice it until he's done it to ya.

With the legal foundation in place, Governor Chiles directed the state of Florida to file suit against the tobacco industry in February 1995. He aimed to recover billions in Medicaid costs due to tobacco, terminate the industry's teen-targeted marketing operation, and spread the truth about tobacco's health effects.

Undefeated despite a legion of lawsuits directed at its product, the big cigarette makers, Philip Morris, RJR, Brown and Williamson and UST, viewed the Third-Party Medicaid Liability Act's 1994 amendment as a minor skirmish and Governor Chiles as a minor skirmisher. The industry and its allies in the legislature quickly organized a political rematch with Governor Chiles. In the long-term, they planned to eradicate their opposition by challenging the constitutionality of the Liability act. In the short term, they wanted to kill the lawsuit in its first weeks by repealing the Liability Act. Big Tobacco, a $45 billion a year industry, lobbied successfully for the repeal in July 1995.

Governor Chiles swiftly countered with a veto, and the 1995 legislation session ended amid rumors of a veto override. The stalemate reminded former state legislator and Chiles ally Mallory Horne of the political tale where a wary patient lying in a chair, watching his dentist prepare to drill, grabs his torturer by the balls and exclaims, "We don't want to hurt each other, do we?" The bitter tenor of the fight strengthened the governor's resolve for the next session; however, according to communications director April Herrle:

> I think that while people knew that this was important to him, I don't think they knew the degree to which he was personally, I mean laser beam, on this issue. ... And the tobacco companies basically laughed at him, when he said, we need to do something to address this. They laughed at him.

Chief of staff Linda Shelley recalls,

I always felt very clearly the governor's spiritual grounding in his service. I don't know if it was always that way. By the end, it was. It was the widows and the orphans, to the least of these. . . . He just saw that was the forces of evil against his people, it really motivated him that way.

"The Governor has made it very clear [that] if you expect access to this office to get the great favors, you're with him on this issue," General Counsel Dexter Douglass said. "We've adopted fixed bayonets, and when that order comes, that's it. It's them or you. You start using the knives when the bullets run out."[759] "He was so fired up about that," said Tandy Chiles, the governor's eldest daughter. "The tobacco thing was something that he really, he saw, it was like black and white to him. He saw the total evil of it."

Associated Industries of Florida, the state's leading corporate lobby, made permanent repeal of the Third-Party Medicaid Liability Act its number one legislative priority in 1995 and 1996. It alleged the Liability Act would lead to junk lawsuits against milk and orange juice producers. Philip Morris lobbyist John French blasted the law:

What this law says, essentially, is that if the state sues you, just get out your checkbook. It says that if you get sued by the state, you have no rights. It is the most one-sided piece of legislation passed by any legislature in the country—ever. I've had a successful career representing the tobacco industry. I'm galled at the tactics the governor and his henchmen used to get this done. Papa Joe Kennedy says forgive your enemies but remember their names. I'm remembering some names.[760]

Corporate lobbyists derided what they perceived as the Liability Act's vagueness. They claimed its broad language would expose myriads of innocent businesses to litigation. In response, Governor Chiles commented, "Heifer dust"—his expression for "bullshit."[761] Of all Bible stories, Governor Chiles loved David and Goliath best. Rhea explains, "David was a rascal, he was courageous; he was full of devotion and wanting to serve and go," yet he "kept getting himself in trouble." Bud Chiles notes that "[David's] band was the misfits." That appealed to Governor Chiles.

Governor Chiles expected a fight to sustain the veto in the 1996 legislative session and the tobacco industry delivered it. "I generally love animals,"

Governor Chiles said in an April 1996 speech in Tallahassee. "I hate Joe Camel. I want to kill Joe Camel."

To quash debate entirely on abuse of the Liability Act, Governor Chiles signed an executive order that committed his cause to tobacco, saying: "If we were going to sustain this veto, it had to be something akin to the hallmark of my administration or anybody's relationship with me as Governor for the rest of my term, so to speak."[762] Hoping to force an endgame, the tobacco industry swarmed the state legislature with lobbyists. One observer called it the "lobbyist Olympics."[763] Governor Chiles targeted the State Senate for persuasion; the House had already voted and overridden his veto. Senate President Toni Jennings (R-Orlando) supported the override, but Governor Chiles evened the odds by assigning old pal and veteran politico Mallory Horne as his chief Senate lobbyist on the issue. Lt. Governor Buddy MacKay called Horne a "genius in terms of understanding people." Horne contrasted his own political style with the governor's: "The first thing we learn to do in politics is gut our enemy—and [Governor Chiles] wouldn't play that chip. He let me play it, ultimately, but he wouldn't."[764] Horne surveyed the field and focused the fight to three swing votes. Senator Rick Dantzler (D-Winter Haven) switched to the governor's side after a weekend of negotiation with Mallory Horne, General Counsel Dexter Douglass, and Governor Chiles. The other two votes would need to come from Republican State Senator Virginia "Ginny" Brown-Waite and Democratic State Senator Pat Thomas.

When Horne heard that the governor's old friend Senator Thomas was sincerely wavering, he wrote a note for the governor to sign. Horne ran it by the governor, who was on another floor hearing clemency cases with the Cabinet, and returned to the Senate floor. In tears, Senator Thomas sided with the governor after reading the note: "I know the weight of the tobacco forces are heavy on your shoulders; I hope the weight of our forty-year friendship is heavier."[765]

As the final week of the legislation session approached, the governor was nervous. "I feel like my kids are out," Governor Chiles explained. "It's after curfew, and I don't know whether to be mad at them or scared, hoping they're safe. We've got a lot of children out there who haven't come home yet."

Ron Sachs, former gubernatorial communications director, returned to the governor's side to help coordinate press events to persuade Brown-Waite to sustain the veto. Sachs recalls a joint Senate-House hearing on the issue:

Most of the people in the room were tobacco lobbyists. And this is when they were trying to take down the third-party liability law, and we found a lady who was dying of lung cancer, and her three daughters were also addicted to tobacco products. And she consented to appearing at that legislative hearing to provide testimony. And they had all these pro-tobacco people testify. But when we wheeled her into the room on an oxygen mask—she was three weeks away from dead. ... I remember hearing one of the tobacco lobbyists utter under their breath, "oh shit," and with good reason. We wheeled her up to the podium; we bent the gooseneck microphone down. And she took the oxygen mask off, and in a matter of about two minutes, she owned that room, with the message that cut through all the bullshit.

State Senator Brown-Waite, who had lost her father, mother, and sister to smoking, eventually declared her intention to sustain the veto on the floor of the State Senate in March 1996: "I can't sit here any longer and play the tobacco game."[766] Senator W. D. Childers broke the silence in the chamber, taking the floor and shouting, "It's over. It's over! The governor wins!"[767] The Republican leadership, accepting defeat, withdrew the motion to override from the floor. There was no floor vote. Ultimately, sixteen senators, three more than necessary, backed Governor Chiles. The same morning as the governor's victory, the *Wall Street Journal* reported that Liggett Co., the country's fifth largest cigarette manufacturer, had settled a lawsuit filed by Florida and several other states. It was the first time a tobacco company had ever settled a lawsuit. For tobacco, "the dam burst," according to *Tallahassee Democrat*'s Bill Cotterell.

At the press skits that spring, Governor Chiles celebrated by dressing in a gorilla suit and dancing for reporters.[768] He savored the chance to face the tobacco industry in court with a legal weapon like the 1994 Medicaid Third-Party Liability Act:

There is a billboard in Tallahassee positioned almost so I have to look at it every day on my way home. On the billboard, Joe Camel is there throwing dice. He's rolling snake eyes on the billboard, but as far as I'm concerned, he's rolled craps. It's time he left the table, and I'm the man who's going to send him away.[769]

While its lobbyists battled Governor Chiles on the floor of the legislature over the Liability Act, the national tobacco industry had already begun battling him in the courtroom.

Florida had filed suit against the industry on February 21, 1995 in Palm Beach County with Judge Harold Cohen presiding. The state chose Palm Beach because south Florida juries generally knew Medicaid issues and tended to award large verdicts.[770] Soon after the Florida legislature passed a resolution prohibiting the state from allocating any funds to the litigation, but Governor Chiles hired private counsel, pursuant to the Third-Party Medicaid Liability Act. After the Florida legislature failed to repeal the Liability Act in March 1996 and the Supreme Court upheld the act's constitutionality in a June 1996, four-to-three decision; Governor Chiles confidently based his case on the statute.

A "dream team" of eleven law firms invited by Governor Chiles would represent the state in court. The team would work independently, report back to the governor's office regularly and enjoy the governor's encouragement. Though they worked for the first large state to file suit against Big Tobacco, and collectively brought dozens of years of legal experience to the case, the governor's team faced a peerless legal behemoth.

The tobacco industry concentrated on its first and favorite pretrial courtroom tactic—intimidation. "The industry was so used to just overwhelming their opponents and I think that part of their strategy was to overwhelm us," the governor's team lawyer David Fonvielle said, "and part of the overwhelming was, 'Look at all these lawyers. Look at all these resources. We're gonna have a fresh guy in there every day, and we're gonna wear you out.'"

A 1988 memo from an R.J. Reynolds attorney to his client indicated the industry's defense strategy: "To paraphrase General Patton, the way we won these cases was not by spending all of Reynolds' money, but by making the other son of a bitch spend all his." Tobacco retained more than 130 lawyers to appear in the Florida case, outnumbering the state's lawyers by at least five-to-one. "We had eleven firms and we had eleven lawyers, and of the eleven lawyers there were four of five us that really handled 95 percent of the litigation," added Fonvielle. By 1994, plaintiffs had litigated eight hundred cases against the tobacco industry, and every one had failed to produce even a single dollar in damages. In the 1983 *Cippolone* case, the tobacco industry had spent about $75 million and lost, but overturned the verdict for $400,000 in damages on appeal.[771] The tobacco industry had always reversed guilty verdicts in appellate courts. "That won't happen here," warned Florida team attorney Bob Montgomery. "Tobacco has never faced the resources this group can muster. And they may never have faced the enthusiasm this group has for taking them on." Fellow team member Ron Motley assessed the case: "I believe we can bankrupt the tobacco companies if we win in Florida. Faced with those kinds of judgments from each state in the nation, we can, at the very least, send them running for cover."[772] Governor's team lawyer W.C. Gentry doubted their case initially:

> When I got into it, I really, I did not think we had much more than a snowball's chance in hell to win this thing. The industry had won every case. It was like we were takin' on overwhelming odds. I just saw it as the best chance to ever do anything. Having the state of Florida as your client is a lot better than having an individual.

David Fonvielle figured his firm and every other participant firm would have to invest at least $1 million in a four-to-seven-year case, and that every participant firm would generate zero income during the litigation.[773] "I don't think any of us are intimidated by the odds," team attorney Bob Kerrigan said at the outset of the case. "One friend told me our chances were like betting on the three worst dogs at the track ... to win the trifecta. But there really is a feeling here that we're doing something special. There aren't many times in life when you can really do something special." General Counsel Dexter Douglass sounded off optimistically:

> We can win. Remember, Hitler had never been beaten until we came in and kicked his butt. Japan had walked over a few people until the United States came along. With all we've got at stake— remember, if they win, the state will collect more than $1.6 billion, really helping our financial situation—I can't imagine a group I'd rather have in the foxhole with me.[774]

Fonvielle "cautiously" believed they would ultimately prevail over Big Tobacco, given their collective financial strength as eleven firms. "Our feeling collectively was that it would be appealed forever, and maybe our grandchildren might see something from the case," Fonvielle said. "But that it was a good cause." When Florida filed suit against tobacco, only a quarter of the public supported the lawsuit.

The close proximity of the two legal teams in Palm Beach tempted the tobacco industry to intimidate its opposition. The tobacco team stayed at the Breakers hotel; Florida's team stayed at the neighboring Brazilian Court. The governor's team rented out a full wing of the hotel, took walls out and installed a library and computer system. They operated their own switchboard and hired security to protect their resources. "We would get motions for hearings slipped under our door at two in the morning, for a hearing at eight o'clock that morning," the governor's team lawyer David Fonvielle said. "We did find them wandering around our hotel. And there was a court order saying they couldn't do that," added Fonvielle. The tobacco industry believed that Florida's team could be delayed to death with motions to continue hearings, motions for continuance of the trial, and other tactics, according to Fonvielle:

> The Industry's tactics were best summed up in a reply we made to one of their many motions for continuance of a hearing. One of our team members stated in our reply memorandum, "Indeed, if the hearing were set for the Twelfth of Never, the Industry would ask for a continuance on the Eleventh."[775]

The industry served over six hundred discovery requests on the state, requiring Florida to produce 500 million pages of documents, redact confidential Medicaid information for more than a million Americans, and attend more than three hundred depositions. To speed the case toward trial, the state chose to comply with nearly every one of the requests.

The governor's legal dream team credited the Third-Party Medicaid Liability Act with kickstarting their case, according to Orlando lawyer Mike Maher, who served as a liaison between the team and the governor's office:

> It was a huge thing. And it was incredibly well-thought-out, legally. Because it prevented the case from being about something it wasn't about. It was not about the smokers. . . . I do believe people have the right to smoke. And if they choose to do it, they know what it's gonna cause, and they assume the risk of doing it, and that's that.

Governor's team lawyer Wayne Hogan:

It was important because of the feeling that it generated in two ways. One, among those who felt that and wanted to take on the industry, who felt that this would provide the avenue that had always been missing to be able to hold them responsible for what they had done. It was important also because it caused the industry itself, the cigarette industry itself, and the titans of other industry who joined together with them—associated industries and the like—to fear that they might also be held responsible for certain kinds of wrongs. So it was the atmosphere that it created.

Democratic Florida attorney general Bob Butterworth, an ally of the governor's, concurred: "It allowed us to file a lawsuit that we could eventually get through without having to worry about twenty years of discovery and a lot of other stuff."

Soon, however, the tobacco industry found a way to exploit the Liability Act to lock the governor's legal team in the appellate courts. "We really backed off the statute," said David Fonvielle of the governor's team. One Florida team member stressed to the judge and jury that the only difference between the tobacco case any another other product liability case was the "number of zeroes included in the damage figure."

The longevity of the case and legal intelligence of its adversary eventually starved even the tobacco industry of its resource advantage. "I think they pretty much gave up trying to outspend us timewise and moneywise after about two years," the governor's team lawyer David Fonvielle says of the tobacco industry, "because things didn't slacken up but we weren't running into as much resistance with the industry as far as them coming into court, trying to buy time, trying to get continuances, trying to delay things. The judges just wouldn't listen to it." Judge Harold Cohen held firm to a trial date of August 4, 1997. The Florida team's decision, 18 months into the case, to amend their suit to allege racketeering under a RICO statute reinforced their cause for the long-term by allowing the state to ascribe the wrongs of one company to an entire industry and, if their case prevailed, to ask for triple damages. "It's all of our opinions that it's the racketeering count that won the case," said Fonvielle, who attributed the idea for RICO to fellow team member W.C. Gentry. "That's what scared them to death in the long run."

Both legal teams thereafter engaged in a war of attrition. The tobacco industry depended on its revolving door of sterling attorneys; the Florida team depended on the brilliance of a few bleary-eyed lawyers. The tobacco industry sent as many as forty lawyers to a single hearing. At an average hearing, the Florida team sent three lawyers and tobacco sent sixteen to twenty. Governor's team lawyer Wayne Hogan pointed to a weakness in tobacco's strategy to stagger their opposition by sheer numbers:

> They had a lack of consistency of knowledge, institutional knowledge as to what it was that had happened and what the court had said and what was done at an earlier hearing. So somebody knew who was the next star for them would come into argue something special, but he didn't really, he might not necessarily know the other bits and pieces that had gone on. We, on the other hand, were there constantly.

Florida team lawyer David Fonvielle concurred. "We knew from past experience that the side that would maintain the most credibility with the Court was going to be the one with the best overall working knowledge of the case," Fonvielle said. "That had to be us." For the Florida team to exploit the breach, however, they had to devote their every hour to the case. Team member W.C. Gentry took responsibility for continuous knowledge of the case at every proceeding and other core members worked just as hard. "I needed two lawyers, two back-up lawyers, associates," the governor's team lawyer David Fonvielle said. "I figured I needed two paralegals. Turned out I was wrong on everything." In the last year and a half of the case, Fonvielle worked eighteen-hour days, seven days a week. "Although we anticipated that costs would exceed original estimates of $100,000 per year per firm," Fonvielle added, "we did not foresee that costs would escalate to $100,000 per *month* per firm."[776]

Egos clashed, moreover, among the governor's dream team, according to Florida team member Wayne Hogan:

> We knew of each other and we knew how hard each of these other lawyers worked on behalf of their clients, and so that gave us confidence in one another. And then we did the very best we could to hold together. It wasn't always perfect because you're talking about individual lawyers and law firms, principals in law firms, who were used to calling their own shots.

Fellow team member W.C. Gentry appointed himself as an unofficial mediator for what he called "bitter fighting." When "it came time to decide who was actually gonna try the case, who was gonna be doin' what, it got really bad," Gentry said.

Two weeks before the trial date, W.C. Gentry worried that fellow Florida team member Ron Motley would quit. "You can't imagine the names they were callin' each other," Gentry said. "I was havin' to spend several hours a day hand holding, dealin' with all these fires that kept springin' up." Florida inspector general Harold Lewis, who would appear occasionally to offer help on the case, required a special detail, according to Gentry. "The only liability, the only deficiency, that I really ever saw with Governor Chiles, if it is one, is loyalty to friends," Gentry said. "We saw that in our dealings with . . . Harold Lewis. Harold Lewis was a nice guy. Harold had lots of problems." Gentry and his team "worked around" Lewis, assigning a staffer to Lewis to walk him around away from the legal proceedings.

Cognizant of both legal team's disintegration, Governor Chiles personally controlled settlement negotiations with the tobacco industry once representatives from the industry signaled they were ready to retire Joe Camel. Since the case began, the governor "did not ever try to micromanage or dictate," Florida team member W.C. Gentry said. Governor Chiles "just wanted to know where we were, and whether we were winning." Perhaps the governor's biggest contribution to the effort was quitting chew tobacco to ward off opponents' claims of hypocrisy. The settlement talks, however, required one-on-one politics, the governor's specialty. They transpired in secret for three months in Washington, D.C., and New York City, their details known to the Florida legal team only through newspapers and television. "He was, best I can tell, intimately involved in the settlement negotiations," W.C. Gentry said. "Which is pretty unusual." Florida team lawyer Mike Maher remembers the division of responsibility:

> We had meetings that the governor is talking and he's a very persuasive guy, and very smooth and smart, and he wasn't missing any steps. And he said, "Who are you guys?" [The dream team] said, "We're the people's trial advocates! Yeah!" He says, "You're daggum right! You're the best trial group that's ever been assembled to take on big corporations. You're the best trial lawyers. That's exactly what you're gonna do. Try this case. And you don't need to worry about settlement. I'll take care of the settlement."

In negotiations, Governor Chiles demanded non-economic concessions aimed at ending the tobacco industry's teenager-targeted marketing. The industry balked at the demands, but the governor ignored his legal team's scuffling and presented a calm, resolute face to tobacco representatives, according to W.C. Gentry:

> [Governor Chiles] knew that he didn't have any hole cards. We looked good and so he knew he was under the gun to get this case settled while we looked like we were good. The chances were that once we started, had that jury picked, that by then, the wheels were gonna be off. And so he was under a lot of pressure, but by the same token, he held his cards, and made them believe that they were gonna get crushed. And eventually got out of them the concessions, and once he got that, then he settled it.

Attorney General Bob Butterworth sometimes attended settlement negotiations on Florida's behalf, including the final settlement session:

> When it came time to settle the case ... Lawton Chiles and Rhea Chiles were at the table in ... my office in West Palm Beach. There were about four of us on the side of the state, and then of course a number of lawyers on the other side. We were negotiating how we were gonna actually handle the actual negotiation. ... Literally, the governor was at the table, with Rhea Chiles, and one of the important things that the governor put in there ... even though he knew he could not direct where the money would go, was that the money should be spent on preventing smoking of teenage kids—this is for preventing smoking. ... I can recall giving the governor a call and saying, "Governor, I think we have the structure of a settlement," and I went through it, he says, "They will give more, go back and get more." And so I went back and said, "The governor is not satisfied yet, come up with something else."

Attorney General Butterworth therefore returned to negotiations; tobacco industry officials agreed to retire Joe Camel and the Marlboro Man, and tear down their billboards as part of the Florida settlement. Butterworth then reiterated, "The governor is not satisfied. He wants an anti-teen smoking campaign." The tobacco industry consented to pay a quarter billion in up-front money to fight teen smoking.

With the tobacco case days away from finishing jury selection, Governor Chiles invited every member of his legal team to dinner at the 21,000-square-foot oceanfront Palm Beach home of team member Bob Montgomery. Florida's team took their seat at the table in the ballroom reluctantly, exhausted and anxious to return to trial, according to team member David Fonvielle:

> None of us had an inkling of what was to come, and some of us, myself included, were upset that we would be pulled into what we all thought would be a "rah-rah" meeting so the governor could give us moral support.

Governor's team member W.C. Gentry's state of mind mirrored Fonvielle's: "And when we actually had the meeting at Bob's, I didn't wanna go. I was just burned out [from mediation]. I had been goin' around the clock." At a table that included Rhea Chiles and Attorney General Bob Butterworth, Governor Chiles proposed a toast—to the surprise of the audience, Fonvielle recollected:

> He started with some of the earlier events and gradually worked his way up to the fact that he had just been in North Carolina on vacation, when he got a call from the tobacco lawyers. They said they were ready to deal and wanted to settle the case and had officially retired Joe Camel as a good faith gesture. At some point in his toast, Governor Chiles began referring to the tobacco case in the past tense. He also threw in some comments about Tobacco billboards in the past tense. I turned to the team member sitting next to me and asked him if it sounded like the case was settled, and his response was, "It damn sure does!"

Governor Chiles subsequently confirmed news of a successful settlement to his legal team, a deal which included considerable non-economic concessions. When Florida team member W.C. Gentry learned the settlement details, they stunned him. Governor Chiles "could have settled the case earlier for this humongous amount of money that we ultimately got, but he was absolutely committed to getting the non-economic concessions for the kids,"

Gentry said. "I was absolutely astounded," Bob Montgomery said.[777] "We never dreamed this case would settle, going into it. It was never even considered," added David Fonvielle.

Per settlement agreement, signed on August 25, 1997, the tobacco industry agreed to terminate Joe Camel and the Marlboro Man, and dismantle all its billboards within six months, including those near public schools. The deal banned tobacco ads on public transit systems and in sports arenas. Economists computed the value of these and other non-economic concessions at more than $30 billion over fifty years. By Sept. 15, the industry would pay $750 million, including $200 million earmarked for a two-year anti-tobacco advertising pilot program targeting youth. Payments from tobacco to Florida would continue, per the formula hammered out in the agreement, as long as cigarettes were sold in the state; the first twenty-five-year bloc of payments totaled $13.5 billion. To maximize Florida's public benefit, Governor Chiles ensured that the settlement decreed that the tobacco industry pay the attorneys' fees of the governor's trial team over and above the main body of payments to the state. An arbitration panel awarded the trial team an amount equal to about 25 percent of Florida's recovery in the case, without costing the state a cent. Finally, the agreement called for the tobacco industry to release hundreds of internal documents to the public. "We've blown away the smoke screen of lies," Governor Chiles said.[778]

Perhaps only his decision in late 1997 to fire Florida inspector general Harold Lewis, a friend since their days in Boys' State together, diminished the moment of glory for Governor Chiles. The governor knew Lewis best from their college years in the ATO fraternity; he appointed him inspector general as a personal favor. Lewis, perpetually indebted, had borrowed more than $24,000 from P. Tim Howard, a Tallahassee attorney for whom he helped secure a $102,000-year contract working on the Florida tobacco case. Lewis then failed to declare the loans on his state financial disclosure forms. The revelation crushed Governor Chiles, but they remained friends, according to General Counsel Dexter Douglass:

> God, he loved Lawton. And Lawton had to let him go when he got in trouble. That was one thing that Lawton really did, was stay with his people. And whether they were pilloried by others, he'd stay with them, he didn't care. He was gonna stay with Harold—he stayed with him as long as he could.

The Florida Department of Law Enforcement had begun investigating Lewis. The crime "broke [Governor Chiles'] heart," Mallory Horne recalls. "He just didn't talk about it. It's like none of that ever existed."

Harold Lewis in July 1998 found work as an attorney in the state Division of Retirement in the Department of Management Services, a division which reported to Governor Chiles. "There were people who took that loyalty and did stuff with it, who were inappropriate," according to gubernatorial adviser Chuck Wolfe. Lewis has said of Governor Chiles, "He was one of the greatest men a person ever had the privilege of calling a friend. He was an absolute, total friend. The last fifteen months have been totally unreal for me and my family. Governor and Mrs. Chiles were there every minute giving us encouragement . . . just as friends."779

Nonetheless, after Florida's victory, every other state in the country and the federal government emulated their successful legal model, from courtroom tactics to settlement details, to Governor Chiles' unique anti-teen smoking campaign, known best by its advertising arm—the "Truth campaign." The governor wanted teens to direct the anti-tobacco campaign from the beginning, to the shock of the state legislature. "If you let the kids work it out, they'll figure it out," Governor Chiles said. Rhea Chiles helped her husband craft the message and reach out to youth; Jenny Lee, then a teen anti-tobacco activist, recalls meeting Rhea:

> I was [a senior and] president of Leon High School in Tallahassee, Florida, and I gave a speech welcoming all the freshman and their parents in orientation. And did that speech and then a couple days later got a call at the school from [the governor's office. Rhea Chiles] called me at school and said, "I saw you speak, and we're really interested in having you serve as a youth on our advertising agency selection committee for this anti-tobacco campaign that we're working on at the governor's office." . . . My father had been a smoker since he was thirteen . . . at the time he was still an avid smoker, and I had always been trying to get him to quit. And so I jumped on the opportunity.

Jared Parez, an eighteen-year-old high school student who served as executive director of Students Working Against Tobacco (SWAT), a grassroots youth advocacy program created by the governor, called Governor Chiles an "inspiration." Parez added, "You could not be around him for more than a few minutes without getting that down-home country boy feeling."[780] He had originally joined the opportunity for fun, but found a higher cause:

> I kinda got into it in the first place thinking that I'd go to this thing, I'd go to Orlando, I'd miss a few day of school, and that's all it would be. But then, after I heard some of the presentations, and talked with some of the people there, and shared my own ideas, it snowballed into this bigger participation. But it's my recollection that it was either Governor Chiles' idea or his wife's idea that if we're gonna make a teen anti-tobacco campaign aimed at young people, why don't we ask young people how do it? And as obvious as that might seem, it really hadn't been that way before.

A teen tobacco summit in March 1998 produced the idea for a "Truth Train" to travel across the state spreading an anti-tobacco message. Members of the governor's staff at first pushed back at the idea, asking if youth would accept a bus campaign instead. But Governor Chiles exploited connections with private freight company CSX to arrange for a train filled with teens to run from Pensacola to Miami on a ten-day tour from July to August. National television network CBS joined the teens for part of the ride. Governor Chiles lunched with teens on the train, and spoke at some of the train stops. The governor did his best to show his knowledge of popular culture to connect to youth, according to anti-tobacco teen activist Christina Scelsi. "One of the things that sticks out in my mind, was the song . . . "Raise the Roof" . . . really big at the time, the hip-hop song. And Lawton Chiles, on several occasions, when he was talking to youth, he would raise the roof."

The March summit also generated ideas for the first youth-driven TV commercials in Florida. An ad agency pitched the slogan "rage" as a title for the ad campaign, but the gathered youth advocated "truth" as the slogan, and the latter name prevailed. A week from airing its first commercials, the governor's staff shared the ads with television networks, until the Florida attorney general's office called to urge them to suspend the public relations campaign due to a legal issue. The Truth campaign had to change the wording of the ads from "tobacco industry" to simply "tobacco" or risk losing the entire settlement earnings. Governor Chiles pushed the Truth campaign to move forward with the "tobacco industry" verbiage, according campaign marketing director Peter Mitchell.

It could have been that, that was it. That was all the money. And for somebody like me who had worked with a lot of senators, who are very cautious, very careful, this was a very gutsy move because he was being told that the whole settlement could be put at risk.

The first ads aired in April 1998, to great acclaim; they reduced teen smoking by 50 percent, the largest decline in any state. According to a Florida State University survey published in December, the percentage of teens who agree that "smoking has nothing to do with whether or not a person is cool" rose from 35 percent in April to 58 percent in November. Nine out of ten Floridian teens surveyed were aware of the anti-tobacco ads.[781] The first four states in the Union that settled with Big Tobacco—Mississippi, Florida, Texas, and Minnesota—derived the same non-economic concessions including money for anti-teen smoking advertising. But by the time the rest of the forty-six states settled, in a multi-state settlement, the tobacco industry struck the teen anti-tobacco clause from the settlement agreement, fearful of its consequences. One Florida ad parodied the Brady Bunch TV show opener. The governor approved the ad despite his ignorance of the TV show, according to Peter Mitchell:

> We had an ad with the Brady Bunch, but they're all smoking—and one had asthma because the parents smoke—set to the Brady Bunch song, which we got rights to use in Florida for free . . . and so I sat down and gave the update to the governor. . . . [Governor Chiles] looked at April [Herrle, communications director], and April said, "It's a popular program, many people will recognize it."

During a major tobacco case in Miami, the cigarette industry even asked the court to request that the state suspend their anti-teen smoking ads during the trial. The judge refused.

In his final month in office, Governor Chiles enjoyed greater national renown than ever thanks to tobacco. "I think he saw the tobacco industry as people that had screwed with him," Truth campaign marketing director Peter Mitchell recalls, "and he would show them, 'No, don't screw with me.'" Philip Morris lobbyist John French saw something else in the governor:

> He had a vision of how he wanted things to be. He wouldn't let people shake him from that vision. When he got in trouble, it was when

he let people shake him from that vision. When he stuck to what he believed in, he was better.[782]

19

Died With His Boots On

"Somebody will decide what my legacy is, or whether there's a legacy," Governor Chiles said when asked about the Florida tobacco settlement in late 1997. "That's not something I decide." Then he added, "But it ain't half bad."[783]

Reporters nonetheless routinely hunted for ways to frame the governor's legacy. The demographic shifts in Florida alone during the governor's life inspired their stories; between Chiles' birth and his sixty-eighth birthday, his state had grown from the thirty-first largest state to the fourth largest. From his first election as governor in 1990 to the end of his term, his state had gained two million in population—mostly through emigration—for a total of fifteen million citizens.

Historians worried about how they would chronicle Chiles' forty-year public life, since their potential subject's written communication to staff was restricted to scribbles on news clippings or memos, signed with a frown or smiley face. "You'd try to get the smiley faces, you'd get the frowns every once and a while," former gubernatorial deputy chief of staff Jim Daughton recalls. Governor Chiles once forwarded a news clipping to advisor Jim Towey; the clip quoted a legislator: "Towey's reputation is less than stellar." The governor wrote two questions in the margin, "Who is stellar? Is he a fellar?"[784] Chiles never maintained a regular journal or diary except his progress reports in his 1970 campaign newsletters (since compiled as *The Walk That Inspired Florida*); he wrote no memoirs and composed few letters. He told stories aloud, with good company, like his Florida Cracker forbearers. "I know I'm a Cracker; I can't tell you what it means to be a Cracker, but I think [that it's] someone . . . that loves the land and the people and cares about the state," the governor said.[785]

Rhea Chiles, however, cautioned against this impulse to bracket her husband's public life under a solemn or grandiose theme:

> I'll never forget his calm with the Queen of England. I was a nervous wreck! And he was just chatting her up. I'm sitting right across, I'm sitting with Philip [the Queen's husband]. And I look across, and they'd be just chatting. I was trying to think of something to say. He didn't take himself too seriously and he didn't take you too seriously.

The National Institutes of Health tried to frame Governor Chiles' legacy by naming a building after him. The governor accepted the honor before an audience of scientists, doctors, reporters, and politicians. His prepared text included about twenty references to the word "organism," which Governor Chiles pronounced as "orgasm." The governor's eldest son, Bud, remembers the address:

> My mom was sitting on the podium with him and she was dying. She was convinced that he was doing it purposefully to shame and embarrass her, because she was hearing the little reactions from the audience very time he said the word. But he plowed on with the speech and continued to litter his speech with his unintended sexual context. When he finally sat down my mom was livid. "Do you realize that you said orgasm, you said orgasm about twenty times in your speech?" she railed. "You said orgasm over and over in front of God and all these people!" My dad never missed a beat as he gave her the crinkly smile, "I didn't say I was against it, did I?"

The governor moved forward without a moment for contemplation, adding to his legacy as others struggled to define it, according to deputy chief of staff Dan Stengle:

> He was letting people underestimate him because it was their fault not his. He didn't pride himself that people sometimes underestimated him. But he didn't feel it necessary to correct 'em until he had won. And then they realized "Oh, my God. He beat me. And I thought

he was no opponent at all." This was a man who never really was a lame duck, even after he got a Republican legislature.

Governor Chiles advocated a massive public investment in Florida school construction during a special legislative session in November 1997. "We made room for the criminals in our prisons. Now, I challenge you," he told the state legislature. "Make room for kids in our schools."[786] Governor Chiles thought about school policy differently than previous Florida Governor Bob Graham, examining the connections between health and education. But both Graham and Chiles led with conviction on education reform, according to Florida children's advocate Jack Levine:

> I think that Graham was more categorical and Chiles was more holistic. I think Graham saw these very, very strong powerful constituents—the public education lobby, the higher ed lobby—and saw them as important to the future of the state. But he saw both of those, the K-grad school entity as a very, very forceful constituency that needed the revenue to do their job. Chiles, in his own style, saw the relationship between health and families as the first educational opportunity. Chiles saw healthy children as more able to learn. He saw families as the first teachers. He saw the nature of what it takes to have a more successful life, not only a more successful educational career. I would never say Chiles didn't care about education, I would say he defined it more holistically than any other governor before and since. And again to his credit, it is true that when you're dealing with a one-third drop-out rate, and you're dealing with a one-third early childhood failure rate, it's the same third, and ten years hiatus. So I mean the clarity of the logic for all of us who ever studied this is you do your best [for children from birth to age five], and you're gonna have your best outcomes at [age] fifteen. I mean, it almost seemed too simple because then the question was, well, why haven't we done it before? Well, because there is no power in the [birth-to-age-five bracket], very little power. And I think that was maybe one of the core attractions for Chiles. Chiles had this magnet sense of who needed him.

Communications director April Herrle remembers Governor Chiles playing "gotchas" during the campaign for school construction, still his trademark touch to every public policy:

> We were on the school overcrowding campaign, we were doing a series of town hall meetings all over the state, and they were pretty high pressure because they were live and we had a live studio audience and of course all the TV stations would have their major executives there who wanted to have a little reception for the governor and meet and greet. So I would usually go to the station early and make sure everything was set up. In Orlando, he was supposed to be at the station at seven a.m. I got a call from the staff [saying] the governor was tired and wanted to take a nap. I said, "Well, you need to go wake him up." They said, "I don't wanna do that. I'm not gonna do that." So then they got the press secretary on the phone and I said, "Ryan, go get the governor." I'm standing in a newsroom full of people who are waiting for him to walk in the door, and [his staff is] telling me he's still in bed. Then they said, "Well, we'll call you back." Three minutes later they said, "He doesn't have a tie, so we're gonna have to stop by the mall and get a tie."
>
> This goes on for about fifteen minutes and I am getting more and more insistent although trying to be very quiet so that people don't know he really is not on his way. We're just a few minutes to showtime here. [I'm] on the phone, and [I'm] threatening my press secretary: "If you do not get him here soon, I am going to . . ."
>
> And just then the governor walks in the door with the phone in his hand. He says, "Oh you will, will you?"
>
> He liked to pull those gotchas, and that's when he'd say, "Gotcha."

After a five-day special session, the state legislature approved the governor's plan to raise $2.7 billion—mostly through bonds—for school construction. Governor Chiles was so surprised that told his chief of staff, "I'm going down to the chapel. I'm gonna take a minute and go down to the chapel."

Friends and family remember Governor Chiles in full bloom during his last months in office. Current and former staff and friends reacted. "He had this glide about him, nothing rattled him," former chief of staff Jim Krog recalls. "He was comfortable in his own skin and would glide in." Well-meaning new colleagues still mistook executive staff for the governor himself, Governor

Chiles wore his office so loosely sometimes, according to General Counsel Dexter Douglass:

> We were down there in the tobacco case, and we were having so-called mediation in this hotel and golf place. [Governor Chiles] was in his suite, and we were all going to go down and meet. So I went in and sat down and was drinking orange juice or something when this hot shot lawyer from South Carolina [he was on the team] came into the room. I was dressed and had a coat and tie on. Lawton was sitting and hadn't finished dressing. And the guy [came over to me, reached out to shake my hand, and said], "Governor, how are you?" Lawton said, "I wish you'd quit telling people you're the governor!" He handled it so well!

Former Lakeland neighbor Juanita Black recalls seeing Lawton socially as governor, "He was just like Lawton on a boat fishing in the backwoods of Florida as he was when you went to Tallahassee to visit him." Dexter Douglass recalls a Gator football game in Tennessee where he wished Governor Chiles had abused his public power:

> We went to Tennessee and two damn idiots sat in front of us and stood up the whole game . . . and wore big hats. . . . Even the police wanted to know if Lawton wanted to remove them. He said, "No, they paid for their tickets." I was saying, "Tell 'em to take them sombitches off!"

Governor Chiles enjoyed using his office to check up on friends across the state, former chief of staff Jim Krog recalls. "He'd pick up the phone, driving somewhere, and he'd say well we haven't talked to such-and-such, pick up the phone, let's get 'em on the phone, let's talk to him. Not for anything, just to let him know he was still around." Joe Pena, a former Senate aide, met with Governor Chiles in the last weeks of his term. "I took the time to thank him for the privilege. He talked about how he had seen me grow; he was almost apologetic about some of the things he asked me to do. He told me he loved me and I told him I loved him."[787] Brian Proctor, one of the governor's Tallahassee fishing and hunting buddies, talked with Governor Chiles as they returned one night from deer hunting in Madison County. "For some reason I was compelled to tell Lawton how much he meant to me," Proctor remembers, and "how much he mentored me in my faith in so many areas and how proud I was for what he had accomplished as the governor." When long-time *Tallahassee Democrat* political reporter Bill Cotterell had heart surgery, Governor Chiles contacted him at the hospital. Cotterell recalls the conversation:

> What impressed me was, he said, "Don't try to come back too fast, don't think that you have to do it all yourself." He said that when he was a United State senator in 1976 it was his re-election year, and he had a campaign run and a U.S. Senate office, and naturally he assumed that the staff couldn't be trusted; he had to do everything himself. He said, "Trust me, you don't. The world will keep turning."
>
> And then the other thing he said that really stuck with me was . . . about depression. 'Cause you know it came out there in the 1990 election, when he ran for governor, he was taking Prozac and had been treated for depression. . . . Let's see, I would have been fifty-five at the time, fifty-four actually. He said, "Particularly men start gettin' [old] in middle-age, they're slowin' down, their bodies are beginnin' to wear out a little bit. . . . It hits you mentally, you start feeling sorry for yourself, thinkin' that you know the end is near. . . . I've got some books, some information that I'd be happy to share with you about depression. And call me, anytime you want to talk about it. Call my office, let me know. If I'm not in town I've got some friends, I know some people that have dealt with depression." . . .
>
> I didn't happen to have depression after [my surgery], and I didn't go rushin' back to work. I took the full time that my doctor advised. I just thought [the governor's concern for me] was very typical of him.

Grade school friend Snow Martin Jr. reflects: "That probably was the best thing he ever did for Florida, was [being] governor. I mean, hell, anybody can be a United States senator; they don't do anything but quack."[788] High school and college classmate Bill Ellsworth:

> When you're a Senator, you've got to worry about everything! It's got to be absolutely an overpoweringly tough job and he was there 18 years. After a while, "hey, I'd rather be the King of Florida." And I think he loved being the King of Florida.[789]

Governor Chiles explained his preference for the governorship over the U.S. Senate: "If you don't like what's going on in the main ring, you can go start something in the second ring or the third ring and that's what I would do at times."[790]

Governor Chiles called the governorship "the best political job there is—better than the presidency."[791] He hoped to continue pushing his anti-tobacco agenda in a new ring after his term in office. His last year as governor, he had leveraged the tobacco case earnings for further health care form. "That was the final booster on the rocket," Tandy Chiles explains, "'cause that was after tobacco. . . . It was like somebody had just opened an aperture to him." The legislature passed the administration-sponsored Florida Kid-Care, which used tobacco case winnings to fund the expansion of low-cost health insurance coverage to a quarter million children. One of the private lawyers hired for the tobacco case, W.C. Gentry observed that the legislature "respected him [Governor Chiles] and they weren't gonna tangle with him [about tobacco money] as long as he was alive."

On December 11, 1998, Governor Chiles visited the White House to meet with Secretary of State Madeleine Albright and senior staff about the prospect of taking the open post for a Special Envoy to the Americas. As envoy, Chiles would travel abroad spreading an anti-tobacco message, according to former state health officer Dr. Charles Mahan:

> He wanted to travel . . . to other countries, where U.S. companies were dumping their tobacco—like the Philippines, for instance—and I showed him this religious poster that tobacco companies were handing out in the Philippines. It was magnetic, it was about this big, and it went on your refrigerator. And it was a calendar for the year and around the Virgin Mary were all the U.S. cigarette packages. And that just infuriated him. So he wanted to travel to other countries, meet with the leaders, and say "You don't have to put up with this. It's killing your people."

Rumor held that Governor Chiles had secured the post if he wanted it, despite the governor's tendency to call the Secretary of State "Marilyn" instead of "Madeleine." The governor's eldest son, Bud, added, "I know she was thinking who is this man, and why doesn't someone get him out of my office!"

When Governor Chiles returned home to Florida that Friday night, his family supported his bid for the envoy post. Soon their favorite politician would be a private citizen again. The governor had presided over his last Cabinet meeting and last clemency meeting. He had appointed two justices to the State Supreme Court, including the first black woman to be so honored, Peggy Ann Quince. Dee Jeffers, the first director of Florida Healthy Start Coalitions, recalls the governor's last time in front of the Healthy Start staff:

> He told 'em, "You're like my legions." Like Caesar used to have. And their job was to watch out for the mothers and babies. He started crying. We had everyone in the room that was at a table write him a note, on a little yellow piece of paper, as their farewell to him as governor.

Ann Davis, the executive director of the Capital Area Healthy Start Coalition, called Governor Chiles "our knight in shining armor."[792] Rhea Chiles shared her husband's faith in public life, and supported his continued service:

> I met Lawton and we became engaged in politics at the University of Florida together. I knew that was on the label, and he was going to be a politician and run for public office. And I loved it. I loved the campaigning; our kids cut their teeth on it. No, it's been a wonderful life. Some ups and downs, maybe, but still a wonderful life.[793]

The governor, moreover, had already practiced international affairs as part of his state's Cuba policy, and during his two official visits to Haiti. He planned a third trip to Haiti before his term expired. Sons Bud and Ed had encouraged their father to attain an ambassadorship in a country where he could hunt and fish at his leisure. Governor Chiles would always say in response, "I don't want to entertain congressmen for a living."[794] The governor did speak of visiting a fishing hole in central Florida called "glory hole," once he retired.[795] "He was concerned about getting up in the morning and not having anything to do and not having anyplace to go," confided longtime friend and former state legislator Mallory Horne.[796] Governor Chiles observed, "there is nothing that I have to do."[797]

The governor tabled the envoy negotiations for another day. He looked forward to soon joining his wife, children, and grandchildren for their last Christmas at the Mansion, which was already decorated with wreaths and a lit tree. An official thank-you party the next day for Florida Department of Law Enforcement (FDLE), the agency providing his security detail, would precede family festivities. The agents and the governor had bonded over the eight years, Federal Relations director Deborah Kilmer explains: "[Governor Chiles] so thoroughly enjoyed nauseating the members of his security team. He would take them for sushi. Some of these guys had never been out of north Florida. This one, I remember relating to me, never had even seen a raspberry before." Governor Chiles would eat eel for dessert and loved to tease others about the beast. Kilmer recalls "watching some of these great big, in-shape, healthy guys just turn green 'cause their governor was tellin' them 'You've gotta eat this.'"

The morning of Saturday, December 12, Governor Chiles rose at 7:30 a.m. to walk his new dog, Tess—a stray that had wondered onto the Mansion grounds in summer of 1997, gaunt and hungry. The state police on the grounds had failed to catch the dog for three days, until they lured her into a cage with a piece of meat. The officers planned to send her to the dog pound until the governor adopted the mutt and named her Tess. The new dog ran away constantly, but Governor Chiles doted on her. "She was a lot like him and he was a lot like her," Rhea Chiles recalls.

When Governor Chiles stopped at the FDLE duty station to pick up Tess for her walk, he chatted with agent Joe Brinson, who commented later on "how good the governor looked" at the time.[798] After the walk, the governor entered his exercise room in the Mansion. He had no appointments the rest of the day until the Mansion reception for FDLE. He had always asked Rhea and FDLE to allow him private time in certain parts of the grounds, like the cabana and workout room in the recreation building. The governor would routinely vanish there for as long as eight hours. He would read the Bible, work out, listen to music, or nap undisturbed. He instructed staff not to bother him at the cabana unless they were forwarding calls from President Bill Clinton, chief of staff Linda Shelley, or another from a predetermined "pass through" list. "I did worry sometimes when he went off alone," FDLE Commissioner Tim Moore recalls. "But he said that's how it would be, and that's how it was."[799] The cabana and workout room had no security camera, per the governor's request.

Rhea first looked for husband unsuccessfully around 10:30 a.m. She decided he must have gone hunting solo. Governor Chiles especially guarded his privacy while hunting and Rhea kept her own schedule, sometimes leaving to paint at a small home in nearby Havana, Florida. "The woods were an antidote for everything that troubled, confused or weighed heavy on my dad's heart," eldest son Bud Chiles says. "He was an escape artist when it came to hunting and spending time in the woods."

When Rhea Chiles noticed her husband's absence at the Mansion reception, she asked someone to locate him. An FDLE agent found Governor Chiles at about 4:00 p.m., and used his cell phone to call 911 and report that "the governor is down." Governor Chiles had died instantly of abnormal heartbeat on his exercise bike.[800]

JoEllyn Hill had just arrived at the reception with her husband, FDLE agent Robert Hill, and three daughters, when FDLE commissioner Tim Moore entered the room and asked that mothers and children step outside while he made an announcement. "We all surmised, we knew it had to be something terrible," JoEllyn Hill recalls.[801]

Bud Chiles recalls hearing the news while spending time with family friends in Patterson, New Jersey who needed help with their gravely ill son:

> I remember feeling very, very tired that day. As if the energy had been sucked out of me. I could barely drive home—I actually almost pulled over to rest. . . . When I got home around 7:30 p.m., there were a lot of familiar cars out front. Inside, my friends were all gathered. I was so tired I just couldn't deal with a surprise party. Someone said, "you need to talk to Kitty upstairs." I'll never forget the moment as long as I live. She put her arms around me and told me the news I never wanted to hear.

Among the first of the governor's associates to hear of his death was Ron Sachs, former communications director. The current communications director April Herrle was on vacation, and an NBC reporter called Sachs to confirm the governor's death.

> And that's the first I'd heard anything. . . . I called the Mansion. . . . I went over, and because I was not a current staff of him, I think I maybe was able to better respond by everything he taught me and allowed me to do when I had worked for him, drawn on all those

skills, but everybody was just pulled apart. Mrs. Chiles was upstairs. The FDLE people were there, and it was just turmoil. There were reporters outside the front gates of the Mansion. And I went to Linda Shelley, who was pretty broken up. And, I didn't know the facts. I got Tim Moore, and I tried to put together some basic facts as a reporter would, since you actually have to tell people it's happened officially.

After helping write an official press statement, Sachs joined his former colleagues in mourning. Former Senate staffer Bob Harris's children had played with Chiles' kids when they lived in Washington; Harris's son and daughter "cried uncontrollably" at the news. "I was just sore all over," deputy chief of staff Dan Stengle recalls. "And my wife and I spent the day out at Chemonie. Just walkin' around and crying and just trying to catch up with the grieving process."

Florida children's advocate Jack Levine and a team of workers had just finished an outdoor deck behind Levine's office, which they planned to dedicate to Governor Chiles, when Levine heard of the governor's passing. They were going to call the deck, the "Lawton Chiles Gathering Place," a meeting place for children's organizations around the capital. The construction team struck the last hammer blow, and Levine returned home and heard the news on the TV. "I will tell you that we finished that deck moments from his death," Levine claims, his voice breaking as he adds, "So the plan, of course, was remarkably changed."

Former Senate staffer and Secretary of Elder Affairs for the governor, Bentley Lipscomb: "I couldn't do anything. I cried for three days. I was just an emotional basket case." Former Secretary of Environmental Regulation Virginia Wetherell remembers her precise location and activity when she received a call indicating the governor's passing. "I was in the driveway making Christmas wreaths out of some pine boughs that I cut down on the farm," Wetherell said. "It was just so hard to believe because he was almost immortal." Former Chiles chief of staff and campaign manager Charles Canady Sr.: "He's the last of his breed, the last of the Cracker breed. I don't think we'll ever again see anyone like Lawton Chiles."[802] Florida GOP chair Tom Slade compared Chiles to an old pair of shoes: "They've been around a long time and they're comfortable. Even though they get a little mud on them, you can wash it off."[803] Florida Republican strategist J.M. "Mac" Stipanovich, former campaign manger to Jeb Bush, added, "He's probably the last guy in

Florida politics who can talk about whenever raccoons walk and not get laughed out of the state."[804]

In Washington, the House Judiciary Committee temporarily suspended impeachment hearings against President Bill Clinton to observe a moment of silence for Governor Chiles.

Lt. Governor Buddy MacKay flew down from Massachusetts with his wife Anne to be sworn in as Florida's new governor late Saturday night.

Saturday night, General Counsel Dexter Douglass visited the Governor's Mansion. Rhea Chiles was upstairs alone, talking to President Bill Clinton. When she hung up the phone, she told Douglass, "You know, Lawton is up there laughing at us."

Douglass said, "You bet he is."

Rhea said, "He always gets the last laugh." She recalled his last days, when he was "doing what he really loved to do" and was "just as happy" as he could be. "And he died."

Douglass said, "Yeah, he's gonna have the biggest funeral anybody ever could have in Tallahassee."

Rhea replied, "He probably thought of that."

At his Sunday service, Rev. Edwin Ayers, pastor of the Christ Presbyterian Church, led the congregation in mourning the governor's passing. Lawton and Rhea had joined the church in 1996.

"He attended every Sunday, very unobtrusive," church member Jack Maguire recalls. "He was just a very godly man who practiced what he preached in a very ungodly profession." Christmas 1997, the governor had worn a turban and robe to play the innkeeper in the church's nativity play. The pastor had looked forward to a greater contribution from the retired governor as a Sunday school teacher.[805]

The governor's eldest son, Bud, and the rest of the Chiles children looked for a casket for their father. "My dad always made it very clear," Bud recalls, "that he wanted to be buried in a pine box." They looked at a variety of ornate wooden caskets at the funeral home before settling on one. Kay Hagan, Governor Chiles' niece, recalls, "Finally, I think Bud said, 'Well, what do you put prisoners in? That's what we want.'" April Herrle, Chiles' communications director, describes the casket: "It's the kind of box that they put bodies in to cremate them. They are mass-produced in Batesville, Indiana."[806] The funeral home director, according to Bud, "had no idea what to charge us for this storage coffin, I think we paid about two hundred dollars. It was one of our best decisions and one that we knew he would treasure."

Bud Chiles watched his father's body as it lay in the funeral home:

> I needed to be alone with him. I needed to say goodbye. Of course, it was a great shock to see him there. It was not right for him to be so inanimate. Without the energy, the twinkle in his blue eyes, the ready grin and the warm embrace.

Debate ensued about the governor's privacy rights. Staff asked how long had the governor been dead before security arrived. Could anything else have been done?

"They love that man," FDLE commissioner Tim Moore said of his security agents. "They're being pretty hard on themselves. But they followed the procedures to a T."[807] A short inquiry by FDLE settled the matter to the family's satisfaction that security agents had followed protocol.

The Chiles family asked that, in lieu of flowers, donations be made to the Lawton and Rhea Chiles Center for Healthy Mothers and Babies at the University of South Florida.

The immediate and extended Chiles family celebrated their favorite politician's legacy.

"What we miss most in Chiles' passing is the sense of duty he brought to politics and public service," said former staffer and long-time friend Doug Cook. "The 'Walk' and his limits on campaign contributions are symbolic of this."

"At first I was mad and upset," said Mallory Horne, a longtime friend and former state legislator. "But I woke up in the middle of the night and realized it was okay. He died with his boots on, he was still governor, and now I'm sort of celebrating."[808]

Younger son Ed Chiles said, "He lived a full life and he died right. We're so joyful for him. He could not have gone out a better way. The idea of dying with his boots on was something he'd talked about. . . . Death held no fear for him."

Deputy chief of staff Dan Stengle recalled,

> I don't know that I met many people as fearless of death as he was. He was just absolutely fearless of it. We had him on some treacherous state plane rides. The day when the vice presidential debate was in St. Pete, when President Clinton was running for re-election, the pilot said, "We don't even wanna go." Well, they were going to a

senior center and Lawton Chiles was going to be shown, and Gore was gonna say in that debate, "This morning when Governor Lawton Chiles and I. . . ." It was a horrific storm we got him through. He was very circumspect about it all, if it was his time. When he was a U.S. senator his plane was shot. If he was asleep on the state plane and woke up and said, "Funny noise," you should panic.

Tandy Chiles Barrett said, "He really went out at the apex, and this was a crescendo. The one thing Dad was not going to be able to do was do nothing."[809]

Dan Stengle further recalled,

After he died, Bud and Ed thanked me for "playing with their father." Because he was so playful. He would use the fact that he was governor as just a device to play tricks on people sometimes, and it would scare the hell out of a lot of people. But he loved playing, and I had little enough sense that I would play with him, and it was a lot of fun.

Rhea Chiles reflected on her partnership with Lawton Chiles:

I think my fondest memories [are] of the times we had in the mornings. We always had a time together to read the Bible and to have a little spiritual time, setting the tone of the day. . . . I treasure those moments and I think back on them and I think [they] created very much a bridge for me now because I feel very close to Lawton.[810]

Senator Sam Nunn said, "I guess he's the closest friend I had on Earth and he's one of those rare people that is really not gone—in my mind—because I still see him every day, virtually, and remember him so well."[811]

Rhea Chiles added with emphasis:

He didn't get emotional about his life. He was movin' on. He was always goin'. He was just full of fun. . . . [He would say,]"You worry about my legacy. I'm not worried about my legacy." He just didn't take himself too seriously, ever. And sometimes I wished he'd take me a little more seriously, because he just didn't. He just didn't.

20

The Chiles Trail

Three days after the governor's death, the Chiles family and gubernatorial staff organized a funeral cortege to retrace the Walk from Century to Tallahassee, a two-hundred-mile leg. Bud and Ed Chiles rode with old campaign hands Jim Boyd and Tom Staed in a Florida Department of Law Enforcement car in the motorcade. Rhea Gay and Tandy stayed with their mother at the Capitol.

The motorcade would depart Century on Tuesday, December 15, 1998, at 8:30 a.m., slowing to twenty miles per hour through each town. Bud would record his reactions in a private journal:

> Northwest Florida was an area my father always returned to. He loved the piney woods, he loved the Cracker people, the barbecue, the dove and venison, the fried mullet dinners. I think it was the fact that the Panhandle retained its roots, which reminded him of how he grew up. A Florida focused on agriculture and the outdoors—a simpler way of life with real people, characters that he related to and loved. People like Neal Cobb, a longtime political friend who epitomized loyalty and a Cracker friendship. Neal would say, "Senator, if you feel froggy, jump!" Or he would say, "It's a poor frog that won't croak in his own pond."
>
> So, I knew he had to make one last trip across the Panhandle. I told my family and his senior staff that were planning the funeral with us—we were going to Century and we were going to take him with us

391

and he was going to make one final journey across the piney woods, the creeks, the foothills of the Appalachians, through towns like Baker, Bonifay, Chipley, Marianna, Chattahoochee, Gretna, and Quincy.

The first hour or so of the trip neither my brother nor I could even speak—we were so overcome by emotion. You see, we didn't have any idea what to expect. With only two days notice to everyone and no press conferences we just started up the trip like he did back in 1970. What we saw amazed us that day. The trip began with an elderly black woman, walking behind his funeral coach as we pulled out from the little intersection in Century. She had walked with him in 1970 and she was determined to walk with him, tears streaming [out of] her eyes—tears streaming [out of] all our eyes as we watched her halting progress.

Rhea Chiles worried that the family had erred in organizing the procession; she feared that few would show up to observe it.

Nearly thirty years after the Walk across Florida, Century had modernized little. The town's welcome sign read, "The Dawning of a New Century." The Alger-Sullivan lumber mill had closed in 1974. Plant closings in nearby Alabama towns like Flomaton, Atmore, and Brewton had hurt the town. Granny Hattie's restaurant had burned down; a Burger King was located near its foundation.[812] A state prison built in 1989, Century Correctional Institution, lifted the economy, but many residents commuted to Mobile, Alabama, and Pensacola for jobs and entertainment.[813]

Benny Barnes, mayor of Century, said Lawton Chiles had "sort of put us on the map when he started his first journey here. It looks like he's doing the same thing here on his final journey."[814]

After the official eleven-vehicle motorcade lined up, countless unofficial cars joined. About a hundred mourners assembled in the Century post office parking lot. Century and the rest of the Panhandle were decorated for Christmas.

"We in Century have always been just a drop in the bucket, the country cousins to the rest of Florida, so to speak," said seventy-year-old Lina Showalter, a forty-year resident. "But that one thing, Chiles walking down our streets, let people know that he could identify with our area, that he was a salt-of-the-earth kind of person."[815] Those gathered held campaign signs and photos of Chiles. "He loved his job and he loved the people," said Robert

Tims, a maintenance worker.[816] "When he came here to start that walk of his, it was something we'd never seen before," local Bert Carrilla, fifty-seven, recalled. "We just didn't know what to make of it. But he sure surprised a lot of folks."[817] Patty Stone, "walking with Lawton Chiles' pin" affixed to her coat, remarked, "He was so personable, so easy to talk with. There really are not many like him."[818]

"He identified with the grassroots of Florida," said John Broxson, a former Escambia County state legislator who had served with Chiles. "He was one of the people who seemed to have a feel for everyday citizens in the state like I'd never seen before or since."[819] Ruth Paige, seventy-six, sat along the highway with her eight-year-old son Cordelle, the latter covered under Chiles' Healthy Kids program. "He had more love in his heart for those of us below the poverty level than anyone in Florida," Paige said. "It really hurt me Saturday. I cried until I couldn't cry no more."[820]

Century Town Council member Marie McMurray, seventy-two, remembered walking with Lawton for his 1982 re-election campaign. Beside Lawton's hearse, she walked with him again. "He had the heart of a tiger," McMurray said. "His was a job well done." She held a worn photo of herself with the governor. "I'm so sad to see him go, but I have this picture and I'll always treasure this, even though my hair was much darker then." Chiles had written, "To Marie, with thanks for walking with me" and had drawn a smiley face on the five-by-seven photo. In 1982, they had eaten at Granny's diner. They ordered eggs and grits and "talked about serving the people." Their bond "was kind of like a teenager with a girlfriend. I had a crush on him for who he was."[821] She remarked, "I just want to be right beside the motorcade when it starts, that's all."[822]

From the intersection of U.S. highway 29 and State Road 4 in Century, the cortege eased forward.[823] The motorcade passed Century's new city hall, the Country Bumpkin Store, and the Panhandle Restaurant. Prison inmates had picked up litter along the route the day before.[824] The cortege climbed Jay Hill. Local Ruth Godwin, who walked the hill with Chiles in 1970, 1976, and 1990, joined the procession in her van. The governor had recently given Godwin three of Rhea's paintings.[825] Godwin, seventy-five, said: "That was our hill. I'm going up Jay Hill one more time with him, and I'll do it with pride." In Jay, Maxine Ivey recounted her meeting Lawton in 1970: "I thought he was a different breed. But when he stopped to talk, we knew he was our kind of person." Alton Harrison, another witness of the 1970 campaign, commented, "The type of person he was, you just don't raise them nowadays."[826] Beer cans, candy wrappers and fresh, wind-blown cotton littered the town of Jay.

In Munson, thirty state Division of Forestry workers waited with a sign that read, "Now you walk beside God, your memory will live through our children."[827]

Baker honored the procession. Someone tied a black ribbon to the city limits sign. A funeral wreath covered a stop sign in the middle of town. Past the Bent 'N' Dent Trading Post, an honor guard of high school ROTCs saluted. Resident Ralph Ellis took off his baseball cap and held it to his heart as the cortege passed. "I wanted to recognize the legend of Lawton Chiles," Ellis says, "because that's what he is in Florida."[828] *Miami Herald*'s Mark Silva rode in the funeral motorcade:

> I think the thing that really caught my attention was literally, going through these lonely stretches of forest where there would be this long dirt driveway to a home that you couldn't see, and the people had come out down to the end of the driveway and were standing there, two or three people there. These were the people who had really come out, and were spontaneously wanting to see this.

More than 1,000 turned out in Crestview, at the intersection of State Highway 4 and U.S. Highway 90.[829] The local Chevy dealership flipped on the headlights of its row of pickup trucks in memoriam.[830] Diane Wilkinson gathered with hundreds of others outside the Okaloosa County Courthouse. "He loved the school kids," Wilkinson said, "and they loved him."[831]

Crestview Resident Robert Hill recollected: "He was a man of the people, and I'm afraid he may be the last one." Ray Fox, sixty-eight, took off his cap for the procession, claimed Chiles "didn't just walk. He stopped and he talked to people and he listened. I didn't agree with him all the time, but I knew he cared about doing the right thing."[832] Pensacola resident Frances Yeo, parent-education chairwoman for the state PTA, watched. "When you've got brand-new PTA groups," she said, "and here comes the governor—saying, 'What you're doing is important'—that really makes a difference. He really rallied out troops for education all his life."[833] One woman prayed in a field; her husband waited in the car with the engine running. Elbert Davis, eighty-two, retired Crestview real estate broker and former Fort Walton Beach mayor, observed the cortege, remembering when he first met Chiles in 1970. "I thought it foolish" at first, Davis said, but he came around. "He left a tremendous legacy," Davis added, "Lawton's been a good friend of this part of the country. We all love him for it." Davis' son-in-law, Tom Barrow, a state trooper who walked with Chiles in 1970 and every other time he campaigned in the area, wished he could attend. Barrow, at home recovering from brain cancer surgery, used to cook quail and other wild game for Chiles' visits. Unable to speak well, he wrote on a note pad on Monday in reaction to the governor's death: "I will take back anything I could if it could be as it was then."[834] Ed and Bud Chiles called their mother to report the popular outpouring. "She was choked up," Ed related later. "She was really glad we called."[835] Bud added: "She has been supporting us through the last couple of days."[836]

In DeFuniak Springs, eighty-nine-year-old Oscar Harrison, self-proclaimed "Mr. Democrat" and 1970 campaign veteran, waited along U.S. 90 to pay his respects. "I've seen him, I've been with him, I've loved him and he's loved me," Harrison said. "The governor was a true Democrat, but he was not a politician. He was a statesman who could get things done." At the hearse's approach, Harrison placed his hat on his heart.

Julie Smith watched outside her floral shop. "I'm not a fan of the governor's," she said, "but I respected him. I think this procession is wonderful—that we got a chance to see somebody who's been involved in all our lives so much. It kind of makes me feel like a part of history."[837]

One DeFuniak Springs resident carried a Chiles-MacKay '94 campaign sign. J.W. Atkinson, sixty-two, owner of Thrift-Way Supermarket, called Chiles a "friend to Walton County." Henry Mooney, retired pastor of the First Presbyterian Church, recalled the governor's stop to worship with his congregation during the Walk. "I must have done a good job," Mooney recalled, "because he was always a good man."[838]

Angus Andrews, attorney and friend, dressed in khaki pants and red-orange-yellow plaid short-sleeved shirt to see the memorial procession, joining hundreds at the Walton County courthouse. "We call these our Lawton clothes," Andrews said. "This is what we wore whenever he went walking here." He and his wife Deborah shared Lawton stories, including one occasion when Chiles had to borrow a jacket and tie for a formal party; Andrews framed the tie. The motorcade passed. Andrews hugged his wife. "Boy, that was tough. I have a lump in my throat. But it was appropriate, very appropriate. I could almost see him walking by."[839]

On the road from DeFuniak Springs to Ponce de Leon, Charles Day came out in blue jeans and brown jacket, a retired military man full of affection:

"He was an excellent governor for the common man, just the common man."[840] Jim Boyd sketched the Panhandle scene, viewed from his place in the motorcade:

> That trip across Florida was really extraordinary. . . . When you drive across the roads, we drove across roads where he had walked, where we had walked . . . out in the middle of a great long field, you'd find a farmer with his truck up against the fence line, standing waiting for the procession to go by. And that happened so many times, black and white. And then to go by schools, I get emotional just thinking about it. And the whole school would be out in front of the school, black kids, white kids, the teachers, the principals would be out, watching the procession go by . . . it was such a powerful experience. A wonderful statement of what he meant to the heart and soul of the people of the state.

"He came right by my house with his coat over his shoulder," said Edsel Brooks, seventy-four, of Ponce de Leon, a two-store, one-gas station town. "I thought he was a real common person. I really liked him and I have voted for him every time since. I'm a Democrat, full-blooded, and he kept the faith with the people."[841]

Charles Looney rode his tractor to the shoulder of U.S. 90 and waited with his family. "To me, he's still our governor," Looney said, "and I guess he always will be."[842]

White signs, each marked by two black footprints, lined the highway median at the Holmes County border. The sign artwork copied Chiles' first campaign buttons. "Holmes County remembers Lawton Chiles," stated a banner among the signs. A high school ROTC color guard stood at attention in Bonifay.[843] Elementary school students held up a sign: "Thanks for walking into our lives."[844] Another sign read, "No more shoes needed, rest in peace."[845]

"It's just something you'll never see again," said M.W. Williams in Chipley. "You know you can't see him, but it's the memories of what was."[846] Jayne Peel, Chipley middle school principal, brought her 470 students to view the procession. "It was special," Peel said, "that he would walk through these small towns and meet people that way. People don't forget that."[847] John Newberry, forty, a real estate appraiser from Panama City, drove to Chipley to see the cortege go by. "I think this marks the end of an era in Florida and the nation as far as the old-schooled statesman," Newberry said.[848] "These little towns don't get to see much history," added Davie Green, a car wash owner. "It's giving the children something to tell their grandkids, that he was a good man."[849]

At Cottondale, Charles F. Bailey, sixty-five, chewed tobacco along the roadside. "He was a great person," he said, "he will be hard to replace." Wade Skipper remembered riding a school bus as a teenager when Chiles had walked by in 1970. The bus stopped and the kids onboard shook hands with "Walkin' Lawton." "He asked us to please have our mommies and daddies vote for him," Skipper said. "I always remembered that."[850]

Hundreds took to the streets in Marianna.[851] Bud Chiles recorded in his journal what he saw from his car in the funeral cortege:

> They came with their hands or their farm caps over their hearts. They lined up like soldiers along the road in the town we passed to pay their last respects. They cried, they looked sad, they hugged each other as he passed. They stopped and got out of their vehicles and took their hats off, they saluted if they had a uniform on. The construction workers stopped their work and lined up in formation, took off their hard hats in a show of respect. Whole schools and whole towns turned out – in many towns lining the road several people deep. The children lined the road by the hundreds – their hands held lettered signs that made us cry. We saw old friends of the governor. We saw people sobbing that we knew had never met him. They came out of nowhere, just pulled up from an old dirt road, stopped and waited for him. They came out of buildings, like the Northwest Water Management District and the Transportation Department – where the whole buildings emptied out onto the streets. I'll never forget the images that day – a woman waiting on the median of the highway, waiting to throw a dozen red roses at his funeral coach – she hit! The farmer with his two crew-cut tow-headed sons and all three standing stiff in attention with tears running down their faces, our friend Robert Trammell sobbing in front of his Marianna law office as we drove by.

Eighty-year-old W.W. "Coonbottom" Glenn held his hat over his heart as the procession passed. Glenn, a retired Jackson County extension agent and long-time Chiles friend, reflected on good times. "I picked him up and fed him catfish at the Red Top," he recalled. "I didn't call him Governor. I called him Lawton. But in front of a lot of people, I called him Governor." "Coon-bottom" Glenn of Marianna related how he had met Lawton:

The first time I met him was in 1970, when he stopped in Marianna. I told him, "You need to know somebody in this county." So we began at one side of the county and just started talking to people. From what I heard about him he came from good Florida stock. I understood that he really liked people and that he had a feeling for people. He wasn't devious in any way. He was just an up-front type of person. Someone who wouldn't beat around the bush. I felt like he was the best one to represent Florida. He wouldn't take but ten dollars, and he was serious about it. That made it pretty rough to raise money.

At some point I said, "I suppose you want to know what I want from you."

He said, "Well, it had crossed my mind."

I said, "I just want to be able to talk to you. If I call your office about something, I want to talk to you. I don't want to talk to somebody else."

So that's the way it was between us. He was a real friend of mine.[852]

Bill Stanton, also waiting at the town center's white gazebo, met Chiles on the 1970 campaign. "I thought," Stanton recalled, "'That man is going to go places!'" Seventy-one-year-old Willie Blossom Halbert compared the funeral cortege to the childhood spectacle of watching Franklin Delano Roosevelt's presidential train rush past her family farm. "I connect with Chiles," she added, "because he loved the country, just like I do." Her husband Lewis commented, "It's an honor for us to pay tribute. This gives us an opportunity to pay our respects. We're not able to get to Tallahassee. I think it's marvelous. They're taking him back to where he did his walking."[853]

Dozens of Mount Pleasant Elementary school kids waved at the procession; most bearing black construction paper bands stapled around their left sleeves. Gretna Elementary School students, gathered on the roadside, waved crayon-colored pictures of broken hearts. Their sign read, "Good-bye Governor Chiles. We love you. We miss you."[854]

In Quincy, Al Gunn awaited the procession outside a bank. Chiles had helped Gunn procure the $20,000 in college funding he earned through the Army. The aspiring scholar wrote to Chiles, and very soon the money arrived. "He just seemed to be a genuine good guy," Gunn remarked.[855] "He was helping the schools," said Angelica Cummings, a ten-year-old student at Stewart Street Elementary School in Quincy.[856] "He'd rather educate than incarcerate," added Bruce Ballister at the Gadsden County Planning Department. Ballister's wife, Christine Chiricos, program administrator at the Dick Howser child outreach center, wanted to take her kids out to the highway to see the cortege, but, according to Bruce, it was their naptime. Bruce spent his lunch hour on the roadside out of respect for Chiles, "one of the few genuine heroes of my recent lifetime. He treated all Floridians with respect, regardless of origin or means. . . . Did you see all of the pickup trucks pull over [U.S. highway] 90 and the groups of children? A lot of people in this state love him."[857] Gadsden County Sheriff W.A. Woodham, watching the cortege, recalled how Chiles would "show up at the hunting camp with no security. He was just a regular guy."[858]

Thirty-three-year-old Patty Gomez, a worker at the state Healthy Start program at the Gadsden County Health Department, credited Chiles with giving her daughter Marylu a chance at life, through Healthy Start's aid for premature births and infant mortality. "I had a tiny baby," Gomez explained, "and I didn't know if she was going to be surviving." Mexican-born Gomez grew up in a migrant farm workers' camp in Greensboro in Gadsden County. Through Healthy Start, Gomez got medical aid and advice on nutrition and breast-feeding for her premature, light-weight baby. When Governor Chiles gave his 1997 State of the State, happy and healthy 4-year-old Marylu held his hand. In preparation for the funeral motorcade, Patty Gomez cut out photocopies of her daughter's small footprints, colored them, and glued them to a banner. The banner read, "Farewell and Thanks for Caring for Our Children." In a thick Spanish accent, Gomez added, "People should remember that he help us in our bad sickness. He was a sweet person, a good person to talk to."[859]

In Tallahassee, at the end of the six-hour, 196-mile journey, the motorcade met mourners on Monroe Street. Mary Hardesty, eighty-two, a Republican who never voted for Chiles, proclaimed, "We were miles apart on some issues, but not when it came to helping children."[860] Army veteran Gil Leffler, thirty-five, saluted as the procession passed. "He was in jeans, boots, a flannel kind of shirt. Line us all up against the wall and you'd never be able to pick him out as the governor," Leffler said. "But that's what was special about him. He was one of us."[861] John Collins, forty-two, owner of a Tallahassee communications company, wore a coonskin cap, a gift from Chiles for his work on his gubernatorial campaigns. "He was a breed apart," Collins said. "He was a real people's governor, and I don't think you'll find that anymore."[862] Nellie Payne, fifty-six, awaited the motorcade outside the St. John's Episcopal Church. Payne's daughter joined a youth group Chiles created called American Pride. "He was a people person," Payne commented, "a very common man, yet an uncommonly kind man. He wasn't so far up that you couldn't reach him."[863]

Wilson Burton traveled from Nashville, Tennessee to see the cortege. He recalled the last time he saw the governor—a North Florida turkey hunting trip. "He had on his cowboy hat and a great big grin," Burton said. Carol Wintermute, a sixty-nine-year-old Tallahassee retired public school teacher, said Chiles "fought long fights for right things—not political things." She added, "I can only hope that there will be more like him." An air traffic controller at the Ocala airport, Diane Murphy of Belleview, brought a flower bouquet and small American flag to leave at Chiles' casket. "He used to fly in there to see Buddy MacKay," Murphy explained. She added, "What I remember most about him was his eyes. They were honest."[864] Long-time Chiles friend Dubose Ausley reflected: "There are probably 50,000 people—probably more than that—in Florida who think they're close friends with Lawton Chiles."[865] Former chief of staff Jim Krog: "If Chiles were alive today, and went to West Tampa, they could still get five hundred people for a spaghetti dinner there."

Two blocks from the Capitol, mid-afternoon Tuesday, the cortege stopped. Lawton's children and grandchildren met behind the hearse to walk the rest of the way. Bud Chiles noted in his journal: "The response of people was equally poignant as we drove into Tallahassee and we made the final turn up to the Capitol where he would lie in state for a day and a night. I got out of the car along with my family and walked the last half mile behind his car because I knew we would rather walk than ride, especially when people were gathered to see him – and they were gathered by the thousands." His brother Ed concurred. "It's touching . . . the look in their eyes. People in wheelchairs, black people, white people, old and young, the children, the salutes. [Dad] would love this." Rhea awaited them at the Governor's Mansion, last stop before the coffin's arrival at the Old Capitol. People had left pairs of running shoes, candles, stuffed animals, and flowers outside the Mansion gate. "He was an everyday guy. You didn't have to have money to talk to him," said Charles Wilson, fifty-six, a retired electrician sitting outside the Mansion. He and his wife Sharon traveled up from Inverness. Like the governor, Charles grew up in Lakeland. "We fished the same lakes. He was a good guy, a good man." Sharon added, "Anytime we'd see him out, he'd talk to us for a long time." Leroy Allen, forty-eight, also waited outside the Mansion for the hearse. "He was the governor of all the people," Allen said, "no matter who you are."[866] Marc Kane called Chiles "unpretentious, unassuming." A Florida State University student in 1990, Kane recalled bumping into Chiles on the street. Kane waved; Chiles crossed the street for a quick chat. "I wasn't crying until I walked through and saw the coffin," said Lynda Keever, publisher of *Florida Trend* magazine. Keever wore a coonskin cap, a gift from the governor. "It was very fitting. That's what you expect of a man of the public. I hope he's not the last of an era."[867]

A color guard from the Florida Army National Guard carried the pine coffin into the Old Capitol building. The American flag covered the coffin. The Chiles family bible lay on top. Rhea placed a white rose on the casket, a symbol of her husband's military service.[868]

The family opened the Old Capitol to the general public while Lawton lay in State until 11:00 a.m. the next day, followed by a 1:00 p.m. funeral service at Faith Presbyterian Church. Nick Fallier, a friend and hunting partner of Chiles, cried after he place two turkey feathers on the top of Chiles' coffin. "I've been working on getting that old gobbler for a while now," Fallier said.[869]

Blocks of mourners waited to pay their respects. "Over the next day and night," Bud Chiles recorded, "over 25,000 people came to see him in an old pine box with the family Bible on top and his old walking boots beside. They came from all over Florida, and they listened to the gospel music and they cried and they told stories about him and how they loved him dearly." Deputy chief of staff Dan Stengle:

> We had him lay in State in the old Capitol, and we had singers downstairs. He served as governor in the new Capitol, but [the old Capitol] would have been more his style. And that's where he was a House member and a state senator, was the old Capitol. So we put him up there. I can't remember what time we closed, but we extended it like three hours until we absolutely had to get the building cleaned and stuff. I walked out, I can remember, with still a

block-long line of people shivering in the cold after we'd kept it open two hours or three hours longer, and I said, "I am so sorry." I told them who I was, and [I] said, "We really don't want to turn you away, but this just can't go on all night."

They said, "We'll come back in the morning.'

The day of the service, we were opening again for maybe an hour or something. . . . I went by maybe forty-five minutes before it was supposed to open, and the line was around the block.

George Addison, sixty-nine, had grown up in Polk County, as had Chiles. Addison came to the Old Capitol to say good-bye to the politician whose campaign he'd fueled with a one-dollar contribution years ago. That dollar had earned Addison a certificate from Chiles. "He was so nice and a gentleman," Addison said. "I'd have done anything for him." Addison's deceased mother, Doratea, had walked with Chiles to the grocery store in Polk County where she'd worked, and she'd given him a Coke. "She was so proud of him," George recalled. "She really thought a lot of him."[870]

Augustin Giannillo had met Chiles when the U.S. senator had walked into his Holmes Beach pizza shop in the 1970s. Subsequently, Senator Chiles had arranged for Giannillo's sick son to receive treatment at a Washington, D.C., hospital, and for the boy to meet then-Vice President George H. W. Bush in Daytona Beach. "This guy had the biggest heart in the world," Giannillo said.[871]

At the open house at the Mansion, friends who showed up to see Rhea in mourning included Amory Underhill, eighty-eight, who had known Chiles since the governor had graduated from high school in Lakeland. "Even then, you could tell he was going somewhere," Underhill recalled. "He had the instinct of being kind of people." Although Underhill had worked with Rhea on the Florida House, a hospitality center in Washington D.C., he had a long wait in line at the Mansion's open house, but he said he was glad to be there. "I flew up from Orlando this evening," he said. "I've been around a long time, and I can tell you: There will never be another one like Lawton Chiles."[872] Robert Barkely, twenty-eight, a recent Florida A&M graduate, visited the Old Capitol. "I just felt obligated to pay my respects to him," he said. "As a member of the black community, I've got to take my hat off to him."[873] Former staffer Doug Cook recalls the visitation:

When he was buried, Rhea had us "sentinels" [as she called a few of us] stand by the casket and answer [any] questions. . . . It was not the typical funeral where all the limos drive up and all the rich guys tell a few stories, drink a few cocktails, and go home. It was days and days of people in cut-off jeans and beat-up automobiles, coming to pay respect to him. He cared more about that than anything else.

Long-time friend and legal counsel Dexter Douglass recalled the visitation:

I was even more amazed because people had to park somewhere and walk to the funeral, and there were just a lot of people. And when you walked through there, it did kinda touch you. You felt like reaching over and poking him and saying, "All right, you fooled us enough. Get your ass up! Say 'Gotcha!'" He was the kind of guy that you cry over, but you don't, because he wouldn't have cried over [his death]— certainly not publicly."

Wednesday afternoon's funeral at Faith Presbyterian Church attracted Vice President Al Gore, Cabinet officers, governors, senators, and members of Congress. Singer Jimmy Buffett filed into the church, which fit over eight hundred for the two-hour service.[874] Marcelle Potter, twenty-five, traveled with her niece, Omara Petersen, twelve, to see the funeral; they sat outdoors and watched a wide-screen TV erected for the overflow crowd of six hundred. Potter saw Chiles when he visited Shanks High School in Quincy. "He showed up in a station wagon," she recalls, "it was just like somebody's parents showed up." Omara, who missed a day of middle school to attend, said Chiles had helped a friend secure a state job.[875] Lakelander John Anthony left home at three in the morning to wait in line for a seat in the church for several hours. Anthony, one of Chiles' first law clients in the mid-1950s, explains, "I couldn't have existed with my conscience if I didn't come."[876] Twenty-year-old Daryl Levine, a sophomore at Florida State University, waited five hours for a seat in the church. "He wasn't just a politician," noted Levine, who planned to become a history teacher. At the age of thirteen, Daryl had approached Chiles onstage at a Broward County Democratic rally. When a security agent had tried to break up their conversation, the governor had looked at him and said, "We're talking, please let him through." The two had gone backstage and talked for about fifteen minutes, Levine said.[877]

403

Lawton Chiles IV, sixteen, delivered a musical tribute at the funeral service, singing and playing guitar for a tune called "Walkin' Man": "Walkin' man, he always wanted to hold somebody's hand." Lawton IV and David Lareau wrote the song.

From church the honor guard from the National Guard led the coffin to the black hearse that took him to Roselawn Cemetery. Chiles was buried under a moss-covered live oak tree with his favorite wild turkey callers. They included a walnut and poplar caller, a small rectangle with a paddle, crafted by a friend in North Carolina.[878]

Wednesday evening, the Governor's Mansion received public condolences by the hundreds. Daisies and red carnations cluttered the Mansion gate; a card on one bouquet read, "Dear Governor: May you walk your greatest walk among angels. Love, the Children of Florida."[879] Leon County Commission Chairman Cliff Thaell announced to the line of mourners, "His family was remarkable. . . . It's a private time, but they're still giving to the public." Outside, a video played images of the governor: Chiles wearing a hippie wig, a cowboy hat, a turban, a coonskin cap, a fur vest, and other costumes.

Inside the Garden Room, Rhea Chiles greeted visitors. "She has shaken the hands of 2,000 people," observed Mansion volunteer Mary Bryant. "She's much braver than I am." Hours later, the Florida Department of Law Enforcement stopped the line of mourners to allow the family some time to grieve in private.[880] Lydia Harris, director of administration of Florida House, explained that Chiles tradition decreed "not to close the door until the last person is in the door." Katie Nall, executive director of the Indian River Healthy Start Coalition, and Marie Marshall, executive director of the Bay/Franklin/Gulf County Healthy Start, shook hands with Rhea. Mrs. Chiles said, "Oh, it's the Rangers," when she met them, as in the Lone Rangers—referring to their heroic efforts on behalf of children's welfare. Richard Wittenberg, president of the American Association for World Health, which had given Chiles an award in April, decided last-minute to travel from Washington to Tallahassee. "I flew in to pay my respects to someone who is a true statesmen model," Wittenberg said. Mansion doors closed at seven-thirty in the evening, too late for Sharisse Turner and her three children to offer their condolences. "I want my children to come and see a part of history," Turner explained. "I admired Governor Chiles' work, especially with children."[881]

Thursday morning, more than three hundred children from all over the state gave tribute to Lawton Chiles at the park in front of the Governor's Mansion. Governor Buddy MacKay hosted; ten students delivered short speeches. Jack Levine, executive director of the Center for Florida's Children, organized the children's tribute; legions of organizations co-sponsored it.

"He gave me a challenge and the tools to meet that challenge," said Chrissie Scelsi, a seventeen-year-old Port Charlotte High School junior who led Chiles' statewide Students Working Against Tobacco campaign. "He gave me the chance to make a difference. He lives in my generation. He lives in our battle against tobacco and our feelings about ourselves."[882] Scelsi began crying as she spoke. "He believed we could make a difference." She explained that every day 3,000 kids start smoking and 1,000 of them will ultimately die from it. "Governor Chiles gave us a chance to save those lives. I can't imagine a more powerful gift or a more important challenge for a governor to offer."[883] Mary Katherine Grimsley, a nine-year-old fourth grader, commented, "He pushed me on the swing and made me feel special. I will always remember him as a special friend." Her mother, Susan Grimsley, a frequent Republican voter, called her daughter's role in the ceremony "such an honor." Despite politics, "Governor Chiles appealed to everybody. He had something to offer everybody and we certainly supported him."[884] Seven of the governor's ten grandchildren attended the tribute. Ten-year-old Christin Chiles, played guitar and sang Shania Twain's "You're Still the One." "His walk has ended, ours has just begun," said Ashley Chiles, daughter of Ed Chiles.[885] Three-year-old Darrel'Lisha Denmark barely reached the microphone, announcing, "Thank you, Governor Chiles, for all you did for children and the state of Florida." Ashley Blakely, an eighth-grader from Griffin Middle School and anti-tobacco campaigner, called Chiles a "father to the fatherless, a friend to the friendless." Samantha Sachs, fifteen, the daughter of Chiles' former communications director Ron Sachs, remembered the annual staff Christmas parties where Chiles played the role of Santa Claus. "Even though we knew that Santa was really the governor, we didn't tell him. He loved doing it, and we loved letting him."[886] Katie Chiles pushed the kids onward."He did his job," she said. "Now you have to go and do your part and make a difference." After Florida A&M University freshman Wendell Holden sang "Thank You" and "Amazing Grace," the Chiles grandchildren led the other kids across the street to the Mansion gate so they could leave flowers. One child left a two-by-four sign that read, "Hecoon! Hecoon! Hecoon!"[887]

Questions lingered in the minds of the mourners. Who would guard the Chiles Tobacco Endowment? Would any politician again limit campaign donations to $10 a head? Would anyone begin a campaign in Century, Florida? Would anyone walk the "Chiles Trail" again? Bud Chiles commented to the press, "I think there always will be a mystique [about Dad]," he said. "There's a side nobody quite figures out."[888]

At the Tallahassee memorial service, Governor Chiles' eldest son had shared his father's unspoken last words. Bud felt his father's powerful presence in the days since his death and channeled it into a farewell address to Florida. "This is the letter that he wanted to write," Bud told the audience, "but that I had to write for him":

> Insert your name for "Bud." Dear Bud, I'm kinda sorry for pulling this all as a big surprise without speaking to you first. Some things can't be helped. My personal feeling after the last couple days is it ain't half bad. I noticed also that you and your brother couldn't organize a two-car funeral between you, so I'm thankful to Tandy and Rhea Gay, Kitty and Anne, and especially to my wonderful staff, who loved me so much and gave so many happy times to me. And you know the pine box is just about perfect. Thanks for picking up on my need to make the final funeral trip, the final Panhandle trip. And please tell Buddy, I wish he could see and feel what I did from all those children along the way. Tell Buddy and Anne that I love them and I'm proud of them that they could be my governor. Buddy, if the election were today, we'd be pretty strong out there in the Panhandle.
>
> The next governor, Jeb Bush, he's my friend, too.
>
> I am glad that you are seeing what I have known about your mother all along. You always appreciated her creative energy, you know with Florida House, with the walking idea, all the policy things that came through her, the children's issues, the Mansion book, her wonderful wit, and her style. But now you see how strong she is and how much she supported me in everything I did. She is a great woman and I love her forever.
>
> I couldn't tell Wilbur or Burke or Sam or any of my old friends about the fact that the Walk was Rhea's idea. I had 'em convinced that I was the crazy one. But that all worked out okay.
>
> What's the lesson from the Walk? Don't hold back on life. You grab it, you believe, and you continue to believe—even when no one else does.
>
> But I know that you didn't understand what came over me on Election night, that night. Why I was so burdened. And it's because the

faces of the average man and woman that I looked into across this great state, they sort of haunted me because I know they believed me and they kinda expected I'd be different. The same way those faces haunted me yesterday in the Panhandle.

You know how I feel about the people. Don't forget to take time to give yourself to people. And always look for the best in them.

Now, it's time to close, 'cause I'm startin' to ramble. You always told me to close rather than to ramble on. I didn't always do what you thought I should do. So I'm gonna ease along this creek for a bit, and then I'm gonna cross over into the cypress hammock where I saw that big tom scratchin'—saw him last night. I'm gonna lay down my walkin' pack there. And I might rest my eyes for a few minutes. Tell Wilbur to meet me there later. I'll see ya—your Mom, your brothers and sisters, and the rest of the Florida Crackers I love so much—a piece down the road.

Appendix A

Table of Contents

Appendix A
The Walk That Inspired Florida

Progress Reports from the Historic Walk of Gov. Lawton Chiles
from Century to Key Largo, Spring – Summer 1970
Lawton Chiles Foundation
Lawton Chiles Walks—and Talks—Through Florida

Progress Report #1: Century to Jay—8 miles

Well, we started off yesterday morning at 8:30 at Century, Florida. Century is a town that is primarily a sawmill town, and it's on the Florida–Alabama line.

The first fellow that I saw I had to lure down off a power pole. He kept trying to get a word in and I kept talking to him about my running for the United States Senate and finally he got an opportunity to break in and tell me he was from Alabama. I just told him I sure hoped he had some Florida friends to pass the word on to.

We talked with a number of people in Century and had breakfast there. At first they wanted to talk only about the 800-mile plus walk before me, but then everybody started telling me about the Jay hill which lay ahead of me on the way to Jay.

I don't believe it was more than three or four miles but it looked like eight miles when I started up. The word was that if I could make it up the Jay hill, the trip would be coasting the rest of the way to the Keys. I thought I had made it up and stopped to rest. About that time Officer Wood, a highway patrolman who used to be stationed in Lakeland, came by and stopped to see what I was doing there. He broke it to me that I was only halfway up the hill. It was kind of a blow cause I hadn't realized that when the road curved ahead, I'd have another half of the hill to traverse.

They're breaking ground for their crops up here and the wind is blowing good and hard so everything is red sand and red dust. By the time I walked into Jay I looked like a red man. I met John Pittman at the electric co-op here and I think he felt so sorry for me—my hair looking so bad and I had so much dust on my face—he decided to take me home to dinner. I went to his house and we had collard greens and fried chicken and dressing and rice and apple popovers for dessert. I can tell you one thing: I haven't had an appetite like that in a long time. I had all that dinner and then finished up with another piece of chicken for dessert.

I reached Jay about noon and after I had lunch it looked like it was starting to rain, so I went to the livestock auction. That worked out real well because there were some 200 farmers there. By the time I got there, the bottom had fallen out—a real cloudburst. It would have been impossible to walk the streets of Jay and visit with the people.

There was a break in the auction and I was able to get on the microphone and give them a little talk about my campaign, to tell them why I was walking and talking through the state of Florida. And I had a good opportunity not only to talk but to do some listening. I found out a lot about the problems of the row farmer.

The people are trying to raise wheat and soy beans up here and one of them was telling me that of a loaf of bread, the farmer himself gets about two and a half cents; and with their costs for fertilizer, help and tractors and everything going up continually, they're really caught in a squeeze. They're particularly hurt by the high interest rates, having to borrow a lot of money every year to make their crops. They're very disturbed with the government buying wheat and corn in other parts of the country and holding it till they're ready to put theirs on the market. Then the government starts to sell their holdings and that breaks the market. It keeps them from being able to make a profit. They don't want to see government controls and yet they feel that is the way they're heading unless they can get together in some kind of co-op and do more to see that the farmer gets a decent price for his goods and that all the profits aren't taken up by the middleman and the people handling the end product.

They had a lot of good looking livestock—hogs and cattle. Prices for them seemed to be pretty good. The row farmer is the one who's really having a tough time of it. It's great to have my feet on the ground and to be with good Florida people, to learn from them and to tell them of my ideas. This day has certainly confirmed my belief that there is a crying need to bring more of our government back closer to home and to the people it is intended to serve.

Progress Report #2: Jay to Munson—18 Miles

We left this morning from Jay about 8 o'clock. I knew we had a long day today to try to go to Munson. The first people that I saw on the road—a car stopped and out jumped J. Kirby Smith from Bagdad. I had met him at the

Milton Kiwanis Club earlier and had also seen him at Milton at a dinner Dick Stone had. He heard at the Gopher Club at Pensacola this morning that I was out on the road so he came out to see me and brought the Chairman of County Commission of Santa Rosa, W. O. Kelly, with him and Clifford Wilson, also one of the commissioners from Santa Rosa County. So we had a nice visit out on the road. Then they took leave and I started on down the road.

The first place that we came to on the road this morning was a place called Crossroads. That's the local name for it. I think it's where the road goes south to Milton and north goes up to Alabama. I met a couple of mechanics there. Had an interesting visit with them. One of them told me—a hard-working young man—that this year he was paying $3,000 in income taxes, Daniel Sims was his name, and he had the feeling that the money he was paying, that much of it was being used to give people. He didn't mind helping anybody who couldn't help themselves, but he thought a lot of people were getting his money that weren't working and didn't want to work. He felt there were people that had made more money than he that wouldn't be paying as much taxes on a pro rata share of taxes as he was paying, that there were too many people that just didn't want to work today. He was also real concerned about the general permissiveness of our society. He said he was concerned about a bus driver who had almost lost his job because he had tried to stop the kids from throwing screws with a sling-shot. This general permissiveness of our society certainly concerned him. Both of these fellows felt that they had never gotten a chance to see anybody that went to Washington before and they both said they were going to help me and they wanted me to remember them when I got up there.

Then I went on down the road and came to Jay prison. This is actually one of the Dept. of Transportation road camps. This is where 30-something prisoners lost their lives when the fire swept through that building in about a minute. In the Senate we tried to outlaw the use of temporary barracks and also dealt with claim bills in connection with this fire. It was very real, seeing what had happened there as a result of the fire in Jay prison. I had a chance to talk with some people there today—a couple of them were there when the fire occurred.

Again today 3 or 4 people stopped and offered to give me a ride. I had one fellow—Dewell Adams was his name and he heard that I was out on the road—he went to a store and bought a coke and brought it out to me. He stopped and said he knew I wouldn't take a ride but he wanted me to have a coke.

Then I had one of the fellows stop from Independent Life Insurance. He told me that he had seen Rosemary Emmett, who said in Century she was going to sell me a walking policy. So I'm still looking for Rosemary; she's supposed to be getting me an application form. She's got a policy that's going to cost me 50 cents a week, but it's going to insure me as I walk so I think she'll be bringing an application out as I walk here.

Then as I walked up towards Pittman's Grocery which is getting close to the tail-end of my walk for today, two young ladies, Brenda Ellis and Alicia Simmons—these young ladies were 14 years old—had seen on television last night that I was walking and they told one of the daddies, Mr. Simmons, that they'd like to come out and walk with me a while. So he brought them out to the road and they walked down the road with me a while. Mr. Simmons was in the car along with their sister who was sick and we had a nice visit. I walked into the Pittman's Grocery store and I got to meet Hank Locklin's mother. Hank Locklin is a country music star and has a home in Milton. His mother lives with him at the home. We had a visit about Hank, who is now in Scotland. His mother is keeping his home while he's gone. Then I visited in Pittman's store and talked with people there. Munson is a couple more miles down the road. I'm going to make Munson before the end of the evening. I'm a good bit sore today. When I stopped for lunch or a little break, I notice that my legs get kinda stove up like the old race horse and it takes a while before I get loosened up again. At one stretch yesterday I timed myself; and I was walking as much as 4 miles an hour. Today I was timing it and this morning I think I was making 3 miles an hour. I stopped for lunch and doctored by feet since I have two blisters on both feet, and after lunch I was walking at a rate down to 2 miles an hour. It's going to take more hours right now until I get into a little better shape in the legs and get these blisters taken care of.

Progress Report #3: Munson to Baker—13 miles

We made camp after dark last night because I was a little bit slow getting into Munson and had to walk a little by moonlight. The camper had already gone ahead and they'd located the camp and we camped out by a pool in the Blackwater Forest. I couldn't see it very good that night and we stayed in the camper. We got up this morning about 6 o'clock and found that we were by a beautiful pool. They dammed up the stream there and have a beautiful swimming place. It's among some real big pine trees and there were big docks going out. It was nice weather so we decided to take a dip this morning about 6 o'clock. It was awfully brisk when we got into the water. We had the camp completely to ourselves so we had sort of a swim in the altogether. That really loosened up my legs a little bit this morning. The sunrise was beautiful at that time.

Then I got out on the road this morning about 7 o'clock. One of my first calls was to the state forest nursery at Munson. They raise 30 million pine seedlings there a year and they sell them at a very low cost, $6 a thousand I think, to people who'll plant trees. They also raise cypress and cedar trees.

The nursery has overhead sprinklers and a cold storage room and a belt— they're very automated. They work about 40 women when they're packing the pine seedlings, and they can keep them 4 or 5 weeks by just sprinkling them down and shipping them.

Then I got out on the road and I noticed that we have a pretty good head-wind today. You usually think about headwinds when you're flying in an air-plane, but I was facing a headwind walking on the ground today. I found that the wind was so brisk that it cut 10 steps a minute off my pace. I usually was stepping off at about 120 steps a minute; it cut my pace down to 110. That doesn't seem like too much but the way I was figuring, it was going to add about an hour to my day, so I was a little disgusted with the headwind.

The soil was still damp enough that the dust hadn't started blowing yet, and I was real thankful for that.

I was walking today in some service boots that I haven't worn since I was in Korea. I started thinking back and remembering that it was during the "cease-fire" and we had a Colonel that wanted to keep the troops occupied so that they wouldn't get bored so he had us go on forced marches. I used to lead the column on a 20 mile forced march wearing these boots. At that time I was a first lieutenant and could step out ahead of the column and slip back to the back and pick up stragglers and see how they were getting along and dog-trot back up to the head of the column and march at a clip that would make 20 miles in a day. I was kinda wondering what was wrong with these boots today 'cause I wasn't making quite that kind of time. Maybe it's the 18 years in between and not the boots. Lt. Chiles was still at the head of the col-umn today, but he was having a lot of trouble with Senator Chiles who was a straggler. Senator Chiles kept looking for a corpsman, and I think he was looking for a stretcher to ride on.

I met two very fine ladies on the road today, Miss Lilian Killam from Bag-dad and Mrs. Abbie Carr from Crestview. They said they'd been reading about me in the paper and were delighted to see me. They stopped and we chatted for a long time. They laughed and said I'd made their day 'cause they were hoping they'd get to see me on the road. I really had a great visit with them.

One of the most pleasant surprises I had today was when I met Mr. Nixon on the road. Mr. Nixon stopped and introduced himself to me and I told him I was running for the U.S. Senate and Mr. Nixon pledged his support. It turned out that this was Mr. Perry Nixon, Route 2, Baker, and not Mr. Richard Nixon, but I was delighted to meet Mr. Nixon and get his support.

Baker certainly is a welcome sight!

Progress Report #4: Baker to Crestview—10 miles

49 down, 151 to go to Tallahassee!

Yesterday, my third day of walking and talking in the Panhandle, was the tough one. Every stop twinged sore muscles; I think even my bones ached. But today was a new day. When I started off this morning, the spring was back in my legs, and I found I was walking a good bit faster between visits with people. I left Baker this morning around 8 o'clock with only nine miles to Crestview and a goal of getting there by noon. It was raining a little bit this morning—one good shower got me wringing wet and I had to change clothes. After a four-mile stroll, I came off State Road 4 and onto U.S. 90 at Milligan and headed toward Crestview, the largest town on my route to date. It had been on the radio quite a bit around here—and in the newspapers—that I was due in Crestview today. It was interesting, and exciting, that at almost every crossroad—or where there was a dirt side road—there were people waiting in cars and pickup trucks. These people had heard that I was coming and that I wanted to talk with people and listen to them, and they all had something they wanted to tell me. About Interstate 10, for example. They have the feeling out here that they're being shortchanged on I-10 and I agree with them. Originally, the designated interstates were to be built before any extensions would be considered. Well, most of them have been built except I-95 where we have some missing links. Yet, I-10 has not been completed. Many people feel, and I think there's legitimate reason for it, that there's been some finagling in the funds and that this money is being held for extensions or perhaps other interstates, and the original commitment to build the designated interstates has not gone forward.

This road is needed. Not just for up here, but this road would be the gateway into South Florida from the entire midwest. There's been way too much foot-dragging, and I told these people I would do everything I possibly could to see that I-10 is completed as it should have been a long time ago. Another favorite topic of discussion today was conservation. Up here you find more ardent fishermen and hunters than most anywhere. Many people live in this area because the fishing and hunting has been so good. A number of them are air force or army employees or were servicemen who've chosen to retire here for the outdoor sports. Now, they're really concerned with the pollution problem and what's happening to much of the hunting land up here—that this beautiful country is going to go by the wayside unless something is done to protect it.

The bays and rivers—and some of the streams and lakes—are tremendously polluted. I explained to many people my feeling that we can't continue to deal with this problem piece-meal but must attack it with a major task force assignment. I told of my desire to see a NASA-type team with management skills, technological know-how, venturesome spirit and sufficient funds set up to find new and improved methods for dealing with this critical problem. Again today, everyone has been most kind to me. Many came out beside the road apparently because they'd heard I was coming by, wanted to see me and wanted a chance to shake hands. They certainly encouraged me in my race. A lot of people had heard that I had blisters on my feet and that I was sore, so I naturally got a number of home remedies about what to do to toughen my feet. One fellow said soak them in clorox, another gave me a special foot powder to use. We talked about different kinds of boots and how to wear my socks and I got all kinds of remedies. I have been looking in Crestview for some boots; I had a pair that were light and I really liked, but they turned out to be the wrong size.

I got a pleasant surprise when I ran into a Mr. Lance Richbourg waiting on the road for me. He tells me his family has been settlers around Crestview for over a hundred years. He was the school superintendent for a number of years before he retired and now raises cattle. Mr. Richbourg is the father of Nancy Dewey of Lakeland, a good friend, and it was a delightful visit. He told me of his long-time friendship with Senator Holland. They went to the University of Florida together and were fraternity brothers in the same fraternity I was a member of at the university some years later. I mentioned how close Senator Holland had been over the years with my family, and we agreed the Senator has been a fine public servant for Florida. When I got into Crestview, I was surprised to find that a group of businessmen there had arranged a luncheon for me. There were about 25 people—community and county officials and leading businessmen—and I had a chance to talk to them about my Senate campaign. They responded enthusiastically. And I was pleased with Senator Wig Barrow's public expression of support for me. Mr. James Lee, who is a former road board member for this area through a couple of governors, was very kind to me and had me to dinner at his home. It gave me a chance to prop my tired feet up and watch Jacksonville University be victorious over St. Bonaventure in the national basketball championship tournament. This walking-talking effort may be the hardest way to campaign, but I'm convinced it is the best way for me to get to know the people and their problems and for them to get to know me. When I complete this walk, I will have gut-knowledge about this state that no other candidate for any office can possibly have.

Progress Report #5: Crestview to Mossy Head—14 miles

63 down, 137 to go to Tallahassee!

Newspapers, radio stations and television stations have so thoroughly spread the word through the Panhandle about what I am doing that each day seems to bring another pleasant surprise. Today was no exception. After spending the night in Crestview, I moved out toward Mossy Head about 7:30 this morning. It's 15 miles away, but every day I'm getting into better shape. Between visits with people along the road, I step off a brisk pace.

Today, for the first time, I had company all the way. Cecil Anchors, Clerk of the Circuit Court in Okaloosa County, decided he'd walk along with me to keep me company. There have been some lonesome moments and I greatly appreciated his interest and company. He's an old quail hunter and has a pace that's really something. His hunter's pace is a little longer than mine, so I played keep-up most of the way. Certainly welcomed chances to stop and visit with people by the road and catch my breath. But we made real fine time!

Then came the big surprise of the day! Along about noontime we walked up on a picnic beside the road. Cecil's wife and four other couples from Crestview had erected a shelter and had spread a picnic lunch of fried chicken, potato salad, baked beans, French fries, angel food cake and refreshing iced tea. We had a real feast, but it sure was rough carrying all I ate on down the road. Still, we made it to Mossy Head about 2 o'clock.

Traffic sure moves faster on U.S. 90 than it did on State Hwy. 4. A lot is through traffic on U.S. 90 and it zooms by fast. I can vouch for the fact that a lot of cattle and hogs are shipped through here. I don't know how many of these vans went by, but every time one did, it would blow my hat off and I could always tell by the smell that it contained livestock and had come from a good distance.

The walking continues to put me in contact with people I enjoy meeting and talking to. One young man who has just finished his work for graduation from the University of West Florida stopped and said he'd heard I was on the road so he was looking for me. He went by, stopped, then turned around and came back to talk with me. His name was Charles Barefield and he lives at DeFuniak Springs. Charles said he had heard what I was doing and he just wanted to tell me that everybody at the University was talking about it. He wished me every success and said he was going to try and see me when I got to DeFuniak. That will be next Monday.

I also walked into a school teacher, Bill Griffin, who lives further down the rood. He is a rank 5 teacher, but he's going to Troy Stare now to get his degree. Started back to college at age 30 and his wife is also going to college even though they have four children, all young. They're deeply interested in education. They're also interested in what I'm doing and made a special effort to find me so we could have a talk. It's this kind of contact that makes my effort here worthwhile.

The weather was overcast and drizzly today—two of the three times it rained pretty hard. I got wet and changed shirts a couple of times. But getting to know people like these still makes the day seem bright. Besides, I was thinking to myself that the time is going to come along about July or August when I'm going to wish I had a cool and kinda wet day like today.

Progress Report #6: Mossy Head to DeFuniak Springs—14 miles

77 down, 123 to go to Tallahassee!

The kindness and generosity of the people in this part of Florida has completely overwhelmed me. I went to church yesterday in DeFuniak Springs at the First Presbyterian Church. When the service was over, I think just about everyone there came over and spoke to me. It was one of the most friendly groups of people I have ever seen.

Then, this morning, we parked our camper in downtown DeFuniak, and Mrs. R.D. Claussen, who runs a restaurant, came up and said she'd been following my walk since it first started and she would like very much to have me be her guest for lunch.

Gosh, what a wonderful lunch it was—fried chicken, turnip greens, black-eyed peas, rice and gravy and cornbread and chocolate cake. People keep asking me if I'm losing any weight, but with all the food everybody is giving me, there's no way in the world that I can lose weight, even with all this walking and talking.

Senator Wilbur Boyd from Manatee County, with whom I have served some 12 years in the legislature, came up last night and is going to stay with me through Tuesday night. I'm delighted to have his company and have him walk along with me and have the opportunity to meet some of these fine people.

Walking along as I am, you really get a chance to look at the shoulders of the roads end highways. I'm really distressed by the amount of trash and debris that people have thrown out of cars. The aluminum can looks like it's going to be with us forever; there are more cans littering up the highway than you'd believe.

And some of the roadside parks that I have gone by have been great sites, beautiful places, but about all of them have been hit by vandalism. The lights have been broken off, the barbecue grills have been taken, faucets have been wrenched off. Isn't it terrible that we have a few people who spoil what so many would like to use?

I intend to take a strong look at our state laws to research what the penalties are. Apparently they aren't severe enough. It's awfully hard to catch this kind of people, but I'm sure going to work to see that the penalties are made more severe—for littering as well as vandalism.

The more I walk along U.S. 90 and see the tremendous amount of through traffic and truck traffic, the more I realize that it's essential to all of Florida that Interstate 10 be completed and that it be completed as soon as possible. It's ridiculous that I-10 has been allowed to drag on as long as it has. Obviously, someone has been dragging their feet and some of the money that should be used for I-10 has been placed elsewhere. I'm certainly going to check this out when I get to Tallahassee to see what I can do about speeding up this project.

A group of people I've met on the walk are going to put on a fish fry for me tomorrow at Ponce De Leon, some 10 miles out of DeFuniak Springs. I'm very pleased and look forward to visiting with the people there. Frankly, I'm learning more each day and believe I'll be better informed about the people and problems of Florida going into this legislative session than ever before.

Progress Report #7: DeFuniak Springs to Ponce de Leon—11 miles

88 down, 112 to go to Tallahassee! One thing I found out up here is that you sure can depend on what people tell you. I was in a conversation about dogs with a couple of fellows from DeFuniak Springs. I related to them some of the incidents which happened when my wife, Rhea and I were knocking on doors in 1956 in my first campaign for State Representative. We campaigned for weeks without any bad trouble from dogs even though we saw a number of them. Then, one day, a little dog bit Rhea and within the next week four more dogs either bit her or tried to. Obviously, she became afraid, they sensed it and started attacking her. So we swapped stories. One fellow said that if a dog came after you and if you pointed your finger at him, many times he wouldn't attack you. Which prompted the other follow to suggest this just might be a good way to lose a finger. Then this man said someone had told him that if a dog really charged at you, you should pull your pants pockets out and then kinda bow over and make a loud noise. This would present a picture so different from a man that it would thoroughly confuse the dog. So, we all laughed about this and I went on walking and talking. Well, this morning as I was walking out of DeFuniak, a dog—looked like he had a lot of hound in him and maybe some mastiff or pit bull—started for me, barked some, then went back. I quit paying attention to him and kept walking. But I heard or sensed something and looked around. Here he came, really bearing town on me. His head was all in a ruff and he was charging. I started to point my finger at him when I realized that that wasn't going to stop him. I somehow thought about what the man had said and I turned my pockets out, bowed over and bellowed. Well, that mutt just veered off and went yelping away. I just had to sit down—though I was still a little scared—and laugh about the picture I must have made to that dog (and any nearby voters). Thank goodness I had seen that fellow the day before.

The legs are getting stronger, and the new boots are getting pretty well broken in. I stepped off 12 miles in a little over three hours, arriving in Ponce de Leon around noon. I was met by Mayor Martin of Ponce de Leon just out of town. With him was one of the councilmen, Mr. Johnson, their wives and Mr. Bill Ralson. After the men walked me into town, they told me that Mr. Ralson is a Republican, and we had a lot of fun out of that. Senator Wilbur Boyd was walking with me, so we took Mr. Ralson's hat off, walked around him and examined him. We told him we'd heard there were some Republicans up here but that we hadn't seen one and were glad to get a good, close look. Some people from Crestview had come over and we had a real fine time with a noontime fish fry at a little wayside park at Ponce de Leon. There was a good group of people and it was another memorable experience proving how much better it is to be down-to-earth with people than up in the air. The springs here at Ponce de Leon are the oldest known springs in the state of Florida. They were incorporated in the Congressional Record back in the 1920s. They're not operating now, but some of the citizens here have been working hard to put together land for a state park and the springs would be an integral part. Senator Boyd and I looked over the proposed park site and the springs. The springs and 50-plus acres that go along with them can be bought very reasonably, and the whole park would consist of about 1,600 acres. The land would be split by Interstate 10, but there would be an exit that would go right into the park. Imagine how many people making a trip to Florida, maybe for the first time, would stop at a state-sponsored, historic park such as this. It would be a tremendous attraction and would be preserving some natural beauty in the public domain. I'm certainly inclined to support this project wholeheartedly.

Senator Wilbur Boyd of Manatee County Walks and Talks, Becomes a Believer

"When Lawton first started on this walk, I was, I must admit, a little leery, a little dubious of this undertaking. First of all, the great physical effort concerned me. Second, Lawton's got a tremendous background in government—he serves now as chairman of the Ways and Means Committee of the Senate; he's had 12 distinguished years in state government and I look at him as one of the outstanding members of the Florida legislature; and I was concerned that people might think Lawton Chiles is maybe a little bit off his rocker or something. But I decided last Sunday morning to drive to North Florida and meet Lawton and see for myself how things were going. Now, I have to admit that my feelings of fear were not well founded. The couple of days I have been with him have been very exciting. I only wish many more people all over Florida could see the reactions of the people here as Lawton walks through and visits with them. I spent all day yesterday in DeFuniak Springs with him, and the thing that just amazed me and excited me was the look in people's eyes which said they really just wanted to talk with Senator Lawton Chiles. They had heard and read about him coming; they knew why he had undertaken this grueling task. The thing that I sensed most in these people was that they feel like they are part of his, they agree with Lawton's mission and they think what he is doing is great. I, of course, have changed my thinking completely after watching him now for two days."

Progress Report #8: Ponce de Leon to Bonifay—17 miles

105 down, 95 to go to Tallahassee!

Spring gobbler season sort of disrupted the early part of today's schedule. I had planned to walk into Bonifay for an early morning radio program, but Ed Hammond of Ponce de Leon said he'd heard a couple of turkeys the day before and offered to take me hunting, So, it was up at 4:20 in the morning. We didn't hear any gobblers, unfortunately, and it put me on the road a little late so I didn't get into Bonifay until noon.

Then, too, it took me longer than usual to go that distance because more and more people are looking for me along the road and stopping to talk.

One man wanted to talk about the busing situation. I told him that I had explained my thinking on the subject last January 12, before the governor or anyone else spoke out on the issue. I told him I felt the purpose of the educational system is to educate children, not to achieve a mathematical formula for mixing of races, and that I was concerned that compulsory busing would hurt the school system.

I pointed out it was wrong over the years that black children were bused to maintain segregation and it is wrong now to bus black and white children against their will and disrupt the entire school system. We need to get back to the school system being to teach children rather than an instrument of social change. I told this man that as a member of the U.S. Senate, I would support freedom of choice even if it took a constitutional amendment. People are still very much concerned about my feet. They stop me along the way and ask me how my blisters are doing. Well, they're certainly better. My new boots are working better even though they are hot and heavy and get damp inside. I have to stop and change now and then. I bought some new shoes in Bonifay, not as high-topped and I hope cooler, but it means some new blisters breaking them in.

I was really hoofing it between Ponce de Leon and Westville yesterday to get to some people who wanted to meet me in Westville and I was trying to get there before dark. Well, a man stopped me, and he was a shoe salesman. He'd heard I was having problems with my feet and came out with his catalog to show me these special shoes with padding between the soles and bottom of the shoe where it meets the foot. I was in a hurry so pretty quick I decided to buy some, but he had a spiel he wanted to give. He wouldn't let me interrupt and got wound up for about 30 minutes. They were mail order and when I asked if I needed to give him any money now, he said, "No, I'll find you," and added, "In fact, what I'd like to have is a letter from the walking Senator about how good my shoes are." I told him I'd be happy to give him the letter if the shoes worked out as well as he claimed they would. I may be a walking advertisement yet.

Walking into Bonifay today, I had a chance to go into the forestry department facility here. They have a four-county program going with which wasn't acquainted. In this RFD—rural fire department—program they take surplus army and air force trucks and make fire engines out of them for small communities, both incorporated and unincorporated. They put pumps and other firefighting equipment—most of it surplus—on the trucks. I saw one truck just completed and two in the process and was very impressed with this low-cost operation. It's an excellent program with the forestry department and communities working together.

Today was a special day. I walked past the halfway mark between Century and Tallahassee. It's a great feeling, and I only hope the next half brings as many interesting, worthwhile experiences and surprises.

Progress Report #9: Bonifay to Chipley—8 miles

113 down, 87 to go to Tallahassee!

I was delighted today, as I was walking down the road, to look up and see Senator Dempsey Barron. He came riding up on a horse, leading another horse. He was really trying to tempt me, I think. He kept handing me the reins of that horse and telling me that I needed to get up on there and travel a little by horseback. I resisted, but he's still around and still persisting. Dempsey, I want you to tell them about that horse.

Senator Dempsey Barron

Well, we were having a conference down at my law office in Panama City today and it was voted by the members of my firm that we probably should establish a Pony Express to move Senator Chiles along a little faster. So I brought the horses up and thought I'd tempt Lawton to join me in a ride, but as always he was a man of his word and continued to hoof it across Florida. If Lawton shows the same perseverance in his walk across Florida that he shows in the Florida Senate, I'm sure that he will make it all the way through Florida and eventually walk into Washington, and when he does, we will all be better off for his being there. One thing for sure, he'll know all about the primary road system of Florida, foot by foot.

Gosh, I certainly was pleasantly surprised today. As I was walking into Chipley, a car drove up and out of the car hopped Tom Bailey, the former superintendent of public instruction for the state of Florida. He said that he'd heard about my walk to Tallahassee and he'd driven over from Tallahassee to walk with me a while. This is his former home country over here. Tom was a school principal in this area at one time and has a lot of people around here that he thought I ought to meet. He came out and walked with me the rest of the way into Chipley. I was so delighted to see him. I later asked him if he would accept an honorary chairmanship for my campaign for the United States Senate and he said he certainly would. I am delighted. Tom, I want to tell you how much I appreciate your coming out and walking with me and agreeing to serve as honorary chairman for me.

Tom (Thomas D.) Bailey

Thank you very much Lawton. I'm very pleased to serve in this capacity if I can be of any service to you in your campaign for the Senate. I had the pleasure of working with you when I was a member of the cabinet and state superintendent of education and you were in the Senate. You were always very courteous and very understanding of our educational problems. I know of your service in the state legislature as senator, I know of your integrity as a man and I am very pleased to offer any service I can to assist you in winning not only this nomination but election to the U.S. Senate. I think you will be a great credit to the state of Florida.

Progress Report #10: Chipley to Marianna—18 miles

131 down, 69 to go to Tallahassee

We got away from Chipley about 7:30 this morning. It was a really beautiful morning—cool enough that you almost needed a sweater but warming later—and a truly beautiful day.

I guess I've become a pretty familiar figure out here. It's interesting that even the bus drivers recognize me now. Every bus that comes by, the driver always blows the horn and waves at me. I told Tandy, my daughter who's out of school for the holidays and is walking with me, about the buses and it became quite a game for her to watch for them and see if they would show recognition.

In addition to Tandy my oldest boy, Bud, and Chris Hanahan, also from Lakeland, are walking with me today. Each day it seems like I have more company than before and bigger welcomes as I walk from community to community.

Yesterday, a delegation from the Florida Library Association met me outside Chipley and walked in with me. Bet I'm the only state office-holder who has ever been lobbied while walking down U.S. 90. Well, we walked, they talked and I listened. They talked about a bill that has been prefiled for the session which would increase state contribution to library services. For example, the county we were in, Holmes County, would be increased from the $3,000 it is now receiving to $6,000. The library services program is a good one and in many counties, particularly small ones, is the difference in whether people have library services or not. They use bookmobiles very effectively. I listened closely to their plea that the program's funding be increased from $250,000 to about $500,000.

I think I can fully appreciate what this library program means to people. I haven't seen a library yet on my walk, but I was able to check a book out of the bookmobile—something to relax with at night when I prop my weary feet up for a little.

A couple of books I was interested in couldn't be found on the bookmobile, but today a man from library services dropped by with one of them. It was "The Peter Principle," which I understand is a takeoff on politicians which says that everyone eventually finds his level of incompetency. I'm looking forward to reading it.

There's a division headquarters for the old State Road Department, now the Department of Transportation, just outside Chipley on the way to Cottondale. I walked in there this morning and met a number of the employees and the chief planning engineer.

Now that I've walked the highway as much as I have, especially U.S. 90, I guess I'm sort of a self-appointed expert, particularly on road shoulders. So I gave them the benefit of my ideas on what to do about protecting the shoulders and the road base so that they don't wash out.

Also, I tried probing for information about the Interstate 10 problem, but it looks like I'll have to find out in Tallahassee why it's been delayed as long as it has.

Progress Report #11: Marianna to Chattahoochee—23 miles

154 down, 46 to go to Tallahassee!

Saturday night we doubled back from Marianna and went back over to Chipley to go to a wild game dinner. This is put on by the Sportsman Club at Chipley. The menu was possum and sweet potatoes, my first experience eating possum, but when I was with those good people from Chipley I sure tried some possum. In addition to that they had raccoon, rabbit, duck and turkey, deer and moose.

Congressman Bob Sikes made the address and they had people from all over Washington County and I really enjoyed it very much being there. Sam Mitchell, who's the school principal in Washington County and a former football coach that I served with in the first session of the legislature, was there and introduced Bob Sikes. He made an interesting comment. He was talking about hard times and he said he remembered well in the depression days how hard the times were and how hard it was to get something to eat. He said one time his dad carried him out and showed him a track where the animal had left his footprint and he said, "Son, on the other end of that track is your next meal. You'd better get going." I was thinking about that as I was walking along the road today and it occurred to me that when I get to the end of the road in the Keys, that's when I am going to get my next political job in the United States Senate.

I visited the Marianna School for Boys in Marianna and I really enjoyed that visit. The last time that I went to a correctional school for boys was in Okeechobee a little over a year ago and that time I came away tremendously depressed. The boys all had very vacant looks, a complete lack of hope, a frustration on their faces and even the staff people did not seem to have any enthusiasm for the program.

But all that is changed, I think, in our whole system and I know it has in Marianna. Lennox Williams, who's the director of the school, is doing an excellent job as is Ollie Keller, the director of the Division of Youth Services.

They have put in group sessions. They have the boys in cottages and in those cottages they have several groups. The boys get together with anything that's bothering them or any problems that they're having between each other. It gives them an identity, it really gives them something that they can attach to and it makes them realize, I think, that someone does care. They get to caring about each other in that group and helping each other.

I talked to a number of the boys that had been to Marianna 2 or 3 times before this group program went in. All of them felt that they had a better chance of helping themselves and being able to get back into society than they'd ever had before. Now there is an air of hope about these boys. They're all enthused about the program. So I came away from there with a feeling that Florida is really on the track in this correctional institution for our boys.

Yesterday, as I was walking, I looked down and found an arrowhead, and when I found that arrowhead, I knew that I had to be on the right track. After all, if the Indians have come along here, then I must be on the right track. I also found 2 horseshoes and then came to Victory Bridge just outside Chattahoochee. So I know we are getting closer to victory.

Even though it was raining this morning, 4 or 5 people stopped in their cars and wanted to talk. One fellow wanted to talk to me about the census report. He was upset about it. His wife had received the application that comes out prior to the census report. He felt that the government was doing a lot of prying—that the purpose of the census report should never be to ask him how many toilets he had in his house, what entrance he used to get into his house, how much he would sell his house for, what the payments were on his house. He felt like a lot of money is being squandered. I want to see one of these applications because I think he's got some pretty good points. It certainly shouldn't be doing anything to pry into your personal life.

Another fellow stopped me today and asked me about Judge Carswell's nomination. I'm getting this question a lot. I told him I feel that Judge Carswell will be confirmed. I noticed that 79 Tallahassee lawyers that have practiced before Judge Carswell sent a letter saying that they thought he could make a qualified U. S. Supreme Court Justice. These are the men who practiced before the judge and they should know what kind of a jurist he'd be.

Progress Report #12: Chattahoochee to Mt. Pleasant—10 miles

164 down, 36 to go to Tallahassee!

While in Chattahoochee, I spent several hours at the Florida State Hospital for mental patients. There's been some controversy in the newspapers lately regarding patient care here. I spot checked some of the files, some of the death certificates and the newspaper reports. In the files I checked there was no evidence of negligent treatment on the part of hospital.

While some of the people did have malnutrition as the secondary cause of death, in the case I checked the man had come into the hospital suffering from acute malnutrition and was a confirmed alcoholic, was in the hospital only six days before he died.

What I did find that concerned me, though, was that the patient to doctor ratio is way, way too high. There's nowhere near enough doctors in the hospital nor are there enough nurses, aides or attendants. Of the four state hospitals that handle mental patients, this one is in by far the worst condition in regard to the ratio of staff to patients. Yet, it's the largest hospital. There are over 5,000 patients. Something is definitely going to have to be done to increase personnel.

They also need equipment. Over half of the hospital is not air conditioned. The administration has been applying for air conditioning for some time, and I think the legislature must provide the capital outlay so that much of the hospital can be air conditioned.

The thing about the hospital that alarmed me more than anything else is that over 10 percent of the patients—584 of them—have criminal charges pending against them, yet there are only 20 beds under security. So there are all kinds of patients in here charged with rape, murder, assault with intent to commit murder and other serious offenses without proper security measures.

This is very dangerous for the other patients and for the people in the surrounding community. The legislature is definitely going to have to address itself to this problem. These people are either going to have to be held in prison and the doctors brought to them, or we are going to have to make additional security provisions in the hospital. The present situation cannot be allowed to continue.

Progress Report #13: Mt. Pleasant to Quincy—10 miles

174 down, 26 to go to Tallahassee!

I passed thru Gretna last night, which was just on the other side of Mt. Pleasant, and then we spent the night in the camper pretty close to Quincy. Today is the first day that I can say summer has arrived in North Florida. It was hotter today than any day on the trip so far, and I really noticed it. I know I didn't do anything but lose weight today because it sure was hot.

I got an opportunity to visit city hall in Quincy and they were having a city commission meeting to canvass votes from the city election. None of the candidates were opposed so it was kind of a happy meeting. I did get a chance to meet the city commissioners and have a picture taken with them.

I talked with a number of business people here today and their concern is how to attract industry. Actually, this has been a concern all across West Florida. One man, a Mr. Davis, had what I think could be an excellent idea. He suggested enabling legislation which would let counties own a tract of land and use it for an industrial site. He said that one of the problems is when an industrial prospect does come by, he wants to be able to look at and make a decision on a piece of land, to know what it would sell for and know the facilities are there for the water, the power and the transportation or siding that he'll need. He said many times they're put in the position of saying "Well, I think Mr. So-and-So will sell this." But he says the prospect is just going to go on and make a decision somewhere else. I promised him that I would look into this. When I get to Tallahassee, I'm going to see if such legislation is feasible. I don't believe we should put the counties in the business of competing with private industry but in some of these counties it can't be done any other way. It would really be an aid to the county and to private industry. So many of these counties are losing their young people because there are no jobs available even though many of them would like very much to stay.

Quincy is in the shade tobacco belt. As I began to walk south from Gretna, I saw the first shade tobacco and tobacco farms. I talked with some farmers last night and learned something about shade tobacco. There are no quotas or allotments as there are on regular tobacco. The only allotment is that the tobacco company tells you how much of your tobacco they will buy. They make a contract with you and then from this contract they finance anywhere from 2/3 to 3/4 of the cost of planting shade tobacco. Now, shade tobacco costs more to make a crop than about anything you can raise—around $3,000 an acre. So of course it's every risky business, but the returns can be high. One of their fears is too much water, and they're very concerned this year with all of the water that they have. Also, they're concerned because there was generally a cut by the tobacco companies, about 40 percent across the board, on their contracts. This has kind of depressed the area. I asked them if the new requirements in regard to television advertising of cigarettes and the warnings that have to be applied on the package have affected them, and they told me that it wouldn't affect them at all. Actually, there may be more shade tobacco needed because this is the outside leaf used in rolling the cigar. So they won't be affected by any cutback in cigarettes.

I ran into a young man today who attended Boys' State. As a matter of fact, across the panhandle I've run into a number of young men that were at Boys'

State and some of them I counseled while working with Boys' State the last 12 years. It's good to see these young men. They're always very involved in their high school activities, or out of high school and involved in civic activities.

It's great to be in Quincy, looking downhill to Tallahassee!

Progress Report #14: Quincy to Tallahassee!!!

200 down! 650 to the Keys!

Tom Cumbie, a druggist here in Quincy, offered to take me turkey hunting this morning, so we got up about 5:30 to go out and see if we could hear a gobbler. There was a lot of wind which caused Tom to say he thought the trip was going to be in vain, but we hadn't been in the woods 15 minutes when we heard the gobbler gobble and within another 15 minutes I had bagged a 15-pounder.

It got me to shaking so bad that Tom wanted to know what made me so nervous. But it was a real experience hearing that fellow rattling the woods. Tom had rattled his yelper and a hen had come up close and that brought the gobbler. It was quite a sight to see him stalking through the woods, and the experience was a thrill for me.

Later, in downtown Quincy, I was telling Sheriff Bob Martin and County Judge H.Y. Reynolds about getting the gobbler. Well, they kind of pulled a little joke on me. They said that since I was from out of county, they just might arrest me and hold me for a few days so I wouldn't even make Tallahassee. I finally made amends by telling them I would leave the turkey there and come back to eat it. They bought that idea.

Word came that a lot of people were looking for me to come to Havana, so even though it wasn't on my schedule, I made a side trip over there. It's just outside Quincy. One fellow invited me to his house for catfish stew for lunch—it sounded good—but the day was slipping away and I had to get back over to U.S. 90.

A lot of rain and a cold front came through Thursday morning, but it had cleared pretty well by that afternoon. It was really nice for walking, fortunately. I had 11 or 12 miles to make to Midway, from which I would start out for Tallahassee on Friday.

A real nice guy stopped in his pickup truck this afternoon to talk to me. He told me right away that he is from Georgia and won't be able to vote for me; but he said he lived just across the state line, had been following the walk and wanted me to know he thought it was great. He said his wife works in

431

Florida and they shop in the state. He assured me they have a lot of friends in Florida and he was going to talk to everybody he knew here about me. He asked for some of my folders so that he could help me out all he could. This is the kind of response I've found all across the panhandle, and it's really given me strength for this task I've undertaken.

Friday, April 3rd, my birthday! None of my people mentioned it and I sure didn't, it being my fortieth. But it was a beautiful day—clear and cool and a good day for walking and talking. We were sure pleased because we had some people coming up from home to walk into Tallahassee with me, and there'd been so many wet days.

Mike Wright, a reporter for the *Tallahassee Democrat* , met me at Midway bright and early to walk all the way with me. About a mile from where we started, we came to construction of a big overpass for Interstate 10 to go over 90. There were a lot of men working there so I promptly mounted a ladder and went up to see them. I remembered after I got up there that I've never been very partial to heights, plus the wind was right stiff. After talking to everybody, I began wondering about getting back on that ladder and getting down.

I was sorta looking around for some help when suddenly a newspaper photographer appeared. Well, I'd have to say that convinced me to get with it and get down posthaste. So I did. But I think I'll be a little more careful what I climb in the future.

Right after leaving the construction site, several TV men from the capitol news corps met me to do some walking interviews. We had about six different sequences shot. One man told me he was shooting some film for a Mobile, Alabama, station. I was a little surprised until he told me the channel is watched through much of the panhandle and had covered the beginning of my walk at Century. He said the station particularly wanted film of my entry into Tallahassee.

Maybe it's the close quarters or something, but the crew with me seemed to get a little rebellious at the end of the Century to Tallahassee leg. Jim Boyd, a campaign worker who has been with me all the way, got to issuing a lot of directions all of a sudden. Guess he knew it was too late to make him get out of the camper and walk with me. Too, Jack Pollock and Wayne Meade, a couple of volunteer helpers from Manatee County who spent most of the last week with me, started showing considerable signs of independence. As a matter of fact, Wayne has been making noises all week about getting us straightened out and shaped up. Well, I decided there was nothing to do but take firm action, so right after we walked up to the capitol building, I suspended them all for 60 days. Naturally, I'll look for them back on the trail soon as the session is over.

As I approached Tallahassee, which is more urban and cosmopolitan than anywhere I'd been on my walk, I was wondering what the reaction would be there. The response had been great across the panhandle, but I must admit I was a little concerned about the people in Tallahassee. Well, I quickly found there was no cause for concern.

I went into the Volkswagen agency on the outskirts of the city. As I went through the showroom and into the garage, at least half the people recognized me and said things like, "You must be the walking senator," and "How are your feet?" and "How's the trip been?" and "How do you feel now?" Then, I got to the shopping center where the Varsity Theater is and went into the supermarket, beauty shop and other stores. Again, I was delighted to find people knew of the walk and asked me questions just as it had been before Tallahassee. It certainly was a wonderful feeling.

Then, about 1:30, a busload of supporters from Lakeland drove up. Gosh, it was great to see that door open and Rhea, my wife, and my mother and an aunt and a lot of good friends from Lakeland. Then we all walked the last three miles to the capitol together. Mother, who's about 70 but doesn't know it, was doing real well, even with those Tallahassee hills, but I wouldn't let her walk all the way. Asked by a newsman how she thought the campaign was going, she replied, "We're gaining ground every day." Also, when someone urged her to ride, she said, "I walked him when he was a baby. I can walk him now."

When we got to Gray Park next to the capitol building, there were more people, including reporters, waiting. Before I knew it, three or four cakes were produced and everybody was singing "Happy Birthday." I guess I really realized for the first time that it was number 40, but I felt so good that it certainly didn't bother me.

Now that the first phase of my walk through Florida is over, everybody wants to know what the schedule is from Tallahassee to the Keys. Well, I guess I'm kind of a single-minded person. About all I've had on my mind was to get to Tallahassee and to get there before the session. At the time I started walking I didn't know how many miles a day I could walk, there was weather to consider, etc. Now, I've made it and I want to use the experience I've had in planning for the future. But I haven't even looked at a map yet. I do know that I want to get on the east coast and the west coast, as well as Central Florida, so I'll probably criss-cross the state some. We will be planning further shortly.

Yes, I do feel great and have a confidence that I didn't have before I started this effort. The contact with people has really been valuable; I truly feel like I know much better now what people are thinking. I have learned so much from the walk that I can better represent them—in Tallahassee and in Washington.

For example, I have learned an awful lot about farm matters—soybeans, livestock, cotton, corn, peanuts and shade tobacco. I've learned more about parity prices and marketing aids and I know the effects of the high interest rates on farmers and businessmen. I understand the need for industry to locate in North Florida and I saw the housing need. And the growing concern about over-centralization of our government and the inability to reach public officials any more was made crystal clear.

I've certainly learned something about listening. I know now that no matter how much money you can spend on television and even if you reach a million people at once that way, you can only listen to one person at a time. So I'm more satisfied, happy and confident with what I'm doing, knowing that when I complete my walk from one end of Florida to the other, I'll better understand the state and the people and be better able to serve as U.S. Senator. I believe the people will know this, too.

Progress Report #15: Tallahassee to Monticello—27 miles

254 down, 963 to go to the Keys!

(Actual road mileage from Century to Tallahassee was 227 . . . estimated mileage for zigzag route from Tallahassee to John Pennecamp Coral Reef State Park at Key Largo is 790 miles)

Back on the road at last! For the last two weeks it seemed like the session was never going to get over, but it finally did. The last morning a breakfast was sponsored by a number of my friends to start me on my way down the road. They planned for about 100 people and ended up with over 200 attending. I'd have to say I was real delighted; we had a crosssection of Tallahassee folks and a number of people came by my office later to tell me that after looking over the breakfast attendance, anybody else was going to have an awful hard time trying to best me or even come close to me in Tallahassee.

The last day of the session was hectic as always. Even though I've been frustrated, wanting the session to end, when the handkerchief dropped and we sang Auld Lang Syne, it hit me a lot harder than ever before because with it came the realization that this could be the last day I would be in the Florida Senate. Of course, if Governor Kirk vetoes the appropriations bill, I'll be back but just briefly, I'm sure. I've spent 12 years in the legislature, some of the most enjoyable times of my life, and made so many friends and it really got to me, seeing it end.

The nostalgia didn't last long, though. Twenty-two senators had volunteered to walk with me, and we went straight from the senate chamber down the stairs and out the front steps of the Capitol, down Monroe Street. A number of Tallahassee policemen had come to my breakfast and surprised me with an escort down Monroe.

Ken Plants, a Republican senator, had presented me with a surprise gift just before the session ended. It was a "slow moving vehicle" sign to wear on my back as I walked through the state.

We went out Monroe to U.S. 90 and turned toward Monticello. Before long my compatriots began straggling, then turned back to pack and head for home.

I walked by Leon High School and thought of the quiet, lonesome mornings I'd spent there over the past 60 days. When I got to Tallahassee for the session, I was determined to stay in good shape so it wouldn't be so painful when I started to walk again. I lived about a half mile from the high school track, so every morning I walked there and ran a mile and a half. This time, I was pretty happy to walk right by the track and keep on going.

There was a good story in the *Tallahassee Democrat* about the breakfast and that I [was] going to walk out of town about 5 o'clock down U.S. 90. Almost more than before, people were standing along the road waiting. They came out of their houses to see me. It was a great feeling.

We have a different camper now, a big red one with a loudspeaker on it. Harp Robson, who helped start me off on this journey at Century, came up from Lakeland to drive the camper and start me off right again. He was on the loud speaker, inviting people to come out and visit "the walking senator," and it really got results. I walked from 5 o'clock till about 10 p.m. in order to make the 15 miles I needed that day.

Pete Rich and his wife drove out to meet me. Pete has a beautiful, beautiful farm on 90. I was delighted to see them, and they had me stop at their peach stand where they gave me some of the most succulent peaches I've ever eaten.

435

By 10 o'clock, when we stopped to eat and spend the night, I knew that running hadn't fully done the trick cause my legs got a little stove up.

Saturday, June 7

Started off bright and early this morning for Monticello. Walking into Jefferson County, it struck me the name is certainly appropriate. This country is beautiful, very much like Virginia. Walking into Monticello made me think of Jefferson's home at Monticello that I had visited with my family some time ago.

Mayor Ike Anderson was on hand to meet me as I got to the Ford place along with Bill Scruggs. Bill is an old friend of Senator Holland. I had met him at a Senator Holland appreciation night in Panama City, and he'd told me that when I came to Monticello, he sure wanted to see me. He's putting me up at his house tonight and walked around town with me. Bill's up in his 70's but he sure walks well and I can tell he's done a lot of it in his time.

Wilton Sheppard and Mason Revels came out to meet me and Dexter Douglass had come over from Tallahassee. Dexter ran for Congress in this district and while he wasn't elected, he carried a tremendous vote in Jefferson County. I appreciated his coming over to talk to his friends about my candidacy. I also enjoyed seeing Marvin Bishop, who is with the power company here, and his wife.

I got into Monticello just before noon, in time to visit in the bank before it closed. Tom Clarke runs the bank and I had an enjoyable visit with him. His son, Buddy, is an attorney in my hometown of Lakeland.

My legs have performed pretty well today, but I've accumulated a few blisters—one real big one on my heel that I know is going to give me some trouble. Had another little problem, too. I had on boxer undershorts and they were kind of what you would call Indian underwear. They kept creeping up on me all day. I'd walk a couple of steps and tug them down, walk a couple of steps and tug them down. So I switched to jockey shorts and walked so fast and long that they chaffed me pretty bad. Now, I'm sort of like the bra-less generation. I'm shorts-less because there just wasn't anything I could stand to wear today.

I visited the dog track this afternoon since they told me more people would be there than any place in the county. The track management was very kind and said if I wanted, they would put my name over the loudspeaker. I figure I have to get the name out all I can, so they announced that "the walking senator" had visited Monticello that day, had visited the track to inspect it and was on my way to the Keys. They wished me good luck. So I got good exposure although I think half of the people there were from Georgia.

I met an interesting fellow this morning named Frank Mosely. He is a black man who runs a little grocery store at Lloyds Crossroads. He told me he was born around there but had lived in New York a while and had a ship sunk under him in the Merchant Marines during the war. He said he's seen a lot of life and been a lot of places and he has come to the realization that you aren't going to get anything out of this life that you don't work for. A number of white people stopped to trade with him while I was there; he obviously had their respect and he gained mine also. I really feel our time and efforts should be spent seeing that everybody has an opportunity to get to the point that they can do for themselves. We simply can't do everything for everybody. We should provide basic education and opportunities. Frank Mosely told me his wife is the agency manager in Tallahassee for the Central Life Insurance Agency and has been with the company since 1934. It did my heart good to talk to this man, to see the kind of business he's doing there and to listen to his philosophy.

Progress Report #16: Monticello to Live Oak—62 miles

316 down, 901 to go to the Keys!

Putting on my walking shoes, I headed out of Monticello early this Sunday morning. Then, about 10:30 we went back to Monticello, where I went to the First Baptist Church with Bill Scruggs and then had lunch. Back on the road in the afternoon, I walked into Greenville to spend the night. During the afternoon Sam Black and his wife, from Mulberry, stopped by the road and visited for a while. It was mighty good to see some Polk County folks. They had just taken their daughter to school at FSU.

And who should come down the road again but James Lee and some other friends from Crestview. With Bill Dempsey and Nate Sharron from Tallahassee, they were returning from Jacksonville. I guess I see James Lee on 90 more than anybody. He seems to be a constant rider on 90 and he always stops when he comes by. If I ever need anyone to testify that I walked all the way, he would be the man. I'll always remember his kindness when I walked in Crestview, awfully tired and kind of low, and the great dinner his wife cooked for me.

This afternoon I came to a house where there were lots of cars in the yard and some people on the front porch. I waved and approached the house, and they all started laughing and saying "You must be the walking senator." I told them I was and found this was the Kinsey family—Jeff W. Kinsey, several of his sons, also his father who is 84 and came walking down the road using a cane. I enjoyed sitting on the front porch and visiting with the Kinsey Clan which had gathered for Sunday dinner.

We talked about Cambodia, about the war in Viet Nam. One of the grandsons had been to Viet Nam. We talked about government in general and again got from these people the strong impression that they are out of touch with government officials and have no real chance to express themselves about government. They said the visit with me was an experience they hadn't had in a long, long time.

One thing for sure, you never know who you are going to run into along the road. C.R. Cason of Jacksonville stopped to talk to me. He's with the Division of Corrections and I had met him when he was at Bartow. At the time they were experimenting with an early release program for prisoners which has turned out to be very successful. Under this program, six months before the prisoner is to be released he is allowed to take a job on the outside during the day and return to the institution at night.

One of our great problems has been that when a prisoner finished his term, he was given a $10 bill, a prison-made suit, a bus ticket home and was thrown into the outside world from which he'd been cut off for years. No time for adjustment, no job. In a large percentage of cases the guy would wind up right back in prison.

The work program helps them adjust. It also proves an inducement to good conduct which will get them into the program, and at night they return and talk about their experiences and this encourages other prisoners to work to get into the program.

Mr. Cason was elated that a half-way house is being started in Jacksonville. This allows prison inmates a place of confinement away from the atmosphere of the prison. It will be tied into the work release program and should be great for rehabilitating prisoners. I think it's an important step forward.

We must do everything we can to make productive citizens of these people and keep them out of our prisons. We must work to protect society, protect the individual. This will also help control the costs to us taxpayers for keeping people in prison.

Had a few distractions today. First, there was a close call when a car passing another one almost clipped me and a boy walking with me. I was telling Mrs. Yarborough, who runs a store about midway between Greenville and

438

Madison about how difficult it was walking in the grass after we decided to get further from the road. It had been raining, the grass was tall.

She told me that in the last few days four rattlesnakes had been seen right by her place and suggested that out in the grass wasn't too good a place to be walking. I told her I'd seen a few snake skins but no live snakes, and I'd kept telling myself that people must be throwing snake skins out of their car windows. Well, I'm afraid I hadn't convinced myself and after talking with Mrs. Yarborough, I hunted snakes the rest of the way into Madison. The choices are kind of tough: getting hit by a car or bit by a snake!

Well, I heard that Farris Bryant had finally announced for the U.S. Senate. It really comes as a relief to get him in the race. I've had the strong feeling for a number of months that he was going to run, but he's been like a phantom because he was not announced. Some of his people have been saying that as soon as Farris gets in the race, Lawton Chiles is going to drop out.

Well, as long as he wasn't in, they could say this and it would alarm my supporters. I would get calls asking "Are you really going to run if Farris Bryant gets in?" and there was really no good answer to satisfy them until he became a candidate. Now that he is announced, I'm sure that people will know that my still walking and talking, still going as hard as I can, proves that Lawton Chiles is not going to get out. I'm running just like I was five months ago when I was convinced he was going to be a candidate.

I supported Farris Bryant actively for governor. I was his floor leader in the House of Representatives. Certainly, I'm disappointed he decided to run against me; if I had my druthers, I'd druther he hadn't. But if I were a quitter, I would have quit months ago. The confidence that I've gained from my walking-talking campaign is solid and I'm going all the way.

Farris Bryant is a fine man but he's of another era. I think that his era is now past and people are looking for something different. His was the era in which he fathered the Cross Florida Barge Canal without too much worry about the rape and destruction of the Oklawaha River and in which he was so proud of luring an Aerojet facility to Florida that he didn't worry about the fact that he put it adjacent to Everglades National Park. He didn't worry very much that some of the off-shore lands that we sold and the dredge-and-fill permits that were made during his time as governor were going to give us a great deal of consternation now. That was another era before we became concerned with conservation and with the quality of living. It was instead, quantity. Get industry at any price, but it's a different time now.

439

Someone said to me that Farris Bryant is strong but is going to have difficulty with certain groups of people. He said Bryant is going to have difficulty with the working people, relating to young people, with teachers, with conservation-minded people, with people from South Florida because they didn't build any roads down there during his administration. Other than that, the fellow said, Farris Bryant is going to be kind of strong. I just chuckled at that because he'd just named off a healthy portion of what makes up our voters today.

Progress Report #17: Live Oak to Lake Butler—50 miles

366 down, 651 to go to the Keys!

I met a fine gentleman, Mr. O.T. Watley, in Live Oak. He was cutting the grass of a business establishment and when I shook hands with him, I noticed his hands were gnarled. He told me that he had been hit with 7,500 volts of electricity and that it had literally blown up his hands and feet. The doctor told him he would never be able to work again and that he was 100 percent disabled. Mr. Watley decided he didn't want to spend the rest of his life lying around feeling sorry for himself, and now he has a lawn care service. What a wonderful example this man is and what a contrast he is with the people who refuse to even try to get a job but rather want someone to hand it all to them on a platter.

Then I moved on to the Occidental plant nearby. It's a phosphate operation, and I talked with many of the workers. I had an opportunity for them to ask me questions and one fellow asked what I could suggest to help the small farmers today. He pointed out that the farmer is getting $1.10 to $1.20 a bushel for wheat, exactly the price he was getting 10 to 15 years ago, yet the price of bread has gone sky-high during that time. I certainly had to agree with him that farmers have really had to improve efficiency and work doubly hard to stay alive with the price levels staying the same. The markup has been with the broker, the stores and others in the chain from grower to consumer. This, of course, is why the farmer is gradually disappearing and this is a critical problem. I told this worker about a bill we'd just passed which allows soybean producers to get together and work together to promote the use of soybeans and get better prices. To me this is a much better answer than government controls. I think the small farmer is an essential part of this country, and to save him we must give him help and encouragement in every way we can—AND freedom to do anything he can for himself.

Another question I've run into quite a bit lately is, "What are your views on Viet Nam?" Well, I point out that I had always considered myself a hawk before, but I have now reached the position that I believe we ought to pull out of Viet Nam as soon as possible. President Nixon has now said we are not seeking a military victory. If we are not going to seek to win, then I think we should get our troops out as soon as possible. The danger is that Viet Nam will drain us economically, is dividing the country and is costing the lives of our fine young men. We cannot afford any of this. The greatest strength we have is our economic strength, being able to prove we've got a better system than Russia or Communist China. We cannot continue to produce more and do more for people if we allow this war to drain us, and to push us into the trap that the Russians have set for us. I don't know how soon we can pull out. We must prepare the Vietnamese people; I hope that this is already well along. But we must be firmly committed to getting out, and I don't think we should get involved in any more land wars in Asia.

The remark I made about my undershorts the other day brought many reactions. Senator Beaufort from Jacksonville and his daughter, Mike, took pity on me. They came to walk with me Saturday and they left me two pairs of silk shorts, one pair bright orange and one bright green. I want to thank them. I wore the green pair and they cured all my troubles. I got in on the tail end of a meeting at Madison High School the other night. The men there were making plans for the integration that their schools have to go through in September. I thought it was interesting because these men had gotten together and decided that, since they were under court order and there was nothing they could do, they were going to see that merging the black and white schools went as peacefully and as orderly as it possibly could. They had arranged to have the athletes from both schools have spring training together and the black coach had come over as the assistant coach in the white high school. They had brought a number of parents and students in from both schools, and all of them were really proud that they had decided to see that this thing worked smoothly.

As I went through Live Oak, I had a tour of the Boys Ranch with Jim Strayer, his wife Betty and their 5 year old son. Betty (Skipper) Strayer was a classmate of mine at Lakeland High School, and their son is a real pistol. It was after dark, but I could see what outstanding facilities they have there. They have several thousand acres with two-and-a-half miles of frontage on the Suwannee River itself. They have beautiful, cottage-type red brick homes with a couple living in with the boys. There is a gymnasium and stables, and some volunteers had flown in to build a ham radio station. There are over 100 boys here. These are dependent boys, not boys in trouble. They are either from broken homes or families where something has happened to the parents. They can really grow up here as boys. They have dogs to play with, they have family life, and many of the boys have gone on to the service or college. The ranch has been operating now for over 10 years. It is sponsored by the Sheriff's Association, and they've done an outstanding job here for the boys.

Progress Report #18: Lake Butler to Ocala—76 miles

442 down, 575 to go to the Keys!

Going out of Lake Butler this morning, I was happy to see George Harmon of the *Jacksonville Journal,* who walked with me and talked with me. While he was with me, we ran into Sgt. Collins, head of the Florida Highway Patrol division around here. He had some thoughts about taxes he wanted to talk about; and I told him he sure wasn't the first person I'd seen who wanted to talk about that subject. He had worked out some equations which kind of indicated taxes should remain constant with services, that new people in a community would pay taxes that would pay for expanded services to meet their needs.

I pointed out that Florida is a growth state, and the rate of growth is not constant. We get new people all the time and have to build new schools, sewers, prisons, libraries, and other things and these have to be built out of current dollars. It's capital expenditures that are always making us have to look for new money. This is the problem at the local and state level particularly. I suggested that places like Florida with an accelerated growth rate could be helped if the national government would allow tax credit against income tax, thereby allowing us to keep part of the money at home and use it more effectively than they do in Washington.

Sgt. Collins also expressed a concern I've heard over and over since I left Century that we have too many bureaus and too many government programs. He said with government it is kind of like we're going to help the old lady across the street whether she wants to be helped or not.

He's an interesting fellow, showed me a cut on his right wrist he got putting a tear gas grenade through a window at the MacClenny hospital to flush the man who shotgunned and killed the head psychiatrist there.

I'm certainly learning a lot about North Florida farming. The first day I started this campaign, I walked from Century to Jay in the dust storm caused by them breaking the ground, readying the soil. A little further along they were waiting for rain so they could plant seeds. As I came across through Bonifay and DeFuniak and on to Quincy, they were transplanting the young tobacco plants under the shade. Then I stayed in Tallahassee for 60 days and as I came out into Madison and Monticello, still shade tobacco country, it has grown all the way up through the shade and is being harvested. Corn is coming in, and peas and squash and other fresh vegetables. It's great. For example, I stayed with Senator Bishop a night in Lake City and he had what they called leftovers—conch peas, corn bread, country fried ham, fresh roasted corn ears.

I was thinking back to the fine time I had in Lake City. The word was that it was Bryant country, but the reception I got there sure didn't convince me I was wasting my time. They put on a real good public affair for me, well attended and the people were enthusiastic. I spoke to the Kiwanis Club and the Lions and got a very favorable reaction. I came away with pledges of active support from some outstanding men and a strong feeling of confidence. Kinda keeps spring in your legs even in this summer weather.

As I walked from Starke to Waldo, I was met at the Alachua County line by a group of people from Gainesville, the county seat, and the University of Florida. There was Clyde Martin, banker who was formerly from Lakeland, Senator Bob Saunders, Bill Cross from the University and faculty advisor to Blue Key, John Dotson who is treasurer of the student body this year and other students and people from Gainesville.

Senator Saunders walked with me most of the day, and he's a pretty good walker. We made it almost to Waldo, then jumped back to Starke as guests at Rotary, and returned to walk into Waldo. We covered the downtown area, accompanied by Police Chief J.B. Huckeba and the ex-mayor, Mr. Prevatt.

Waldo took me back a few years. I had to think back to when I was a student at the University of Florida and I was campus chairman for Billy Mathews running for Congress. There were rallies being held all over the congressional district and he couldn't make them all, so I was allowed to substitute for him and spoke from the stump for the first time one night in Waldo.

Early the next morning, I headed toward Gainesville. It's interesting how these newspaper, radio and TV people like to test themselves by getting out on the road with me. Gregory Favre, editor of the Palm Beach Post, drove all the way from West Palm Beach to get on the road with me and see what's happening in my campaign. I'm all for that because I've found that it really gives them the fever.

Well, I got into Gainesville and really got put through the paces. I began to think maybe it was a contest to see who would give out first, me or Bob Saunders. We covered the Sperry plant, county courthouse, city hall, banks, drug stores, service stations and just about everything else where people moved. Then there were parties, breakfasts and two nearby watermelon festivals. I had the pleasure of speaking at a Jaycee-Jaycee wives dinner and was asked my views regarding a volunteer army. I told them I'm scared to death of a volunteer army. I know a lot of people would like to get rid of the draft, but having a volunteer army means having a professional army. And anybody who is worried about a military-industrial complex or military establishment would really need to be worried with a professional army. It would be the largest lobbying force we could have. It would be a tremendous political force, something we should not have. People who are drafted and serve 24 months are just looking forward to getting out, and we need this civilian-oriented element in our military. I'd rather stick with the draft and see that we get it working fairly than to develop a volunteer army.

Like Waldo, Gainesville brought back many memories. Seems like I spent about half of my life at the university there. Two of my children were born there and another while I was in the army in the middle of going to school. We lived in Flavet 3, temporary buildings they've been talking about tearing down since before I was there. Well, I went by and they are still there. And the yard's still full of children. I just hope the students are enjoying it as much as Rhea and I did.

Friday afternoon I walked out of Gainesville on Highway 441 and out onto Payne's Prairie. A fellow stopped, chatted and said, "Do you know it is 100 degrees out here? Aren't you mighty hot?" Well, I thought he was kidding, but it's amazing how much hotter it felt after he told me that. In fact I got so hot that when a thunder storm came up when I was almost to the other side I stayed out of the camper and without a raincoat so that the rain could cool me off. Crossing the prairie, I counted 42 dead snakes or snake skins so I guess I've proved I can stand the elements better than they can.

I had a great evening with L.K. and Marge Edwards at Irvine. They have a wonderful white-frame house that Senator Edwards was born in, and the land has been in the family for over 100 years. I had a home-cooked, home-grown meal—country ham, creamed corn, English peas, deviled eggs, home-made butter so rich it was actually orange in color, beef. This was topped off with a brimming dish of ice cream with chocolate and nuts and cocoanut and lemon cake that Marge had baked that day. Marge had had 22 people for lunch, then we dropped in on them for dinner and she still was able to throw together this little snack.

Had an entertaining and worthwhile visit with L.K. after dinner. The young men with me sat somewhat in awe, listening to "The Sage of Irvine," and he was in great form. He played a record about a former distinguished senator from Kentucky, Marcus Cassius Clay, who was a third cousin of Henry Clay. Cassius Clay was against slavery and was a Republican in Kentucky when it wasn't really a safe thing to be. He fought many fights and killed five or six men. Once, running for the U.S. Senate, he was told that if he went to a particular town, they would kill him. He walked into the town, ascended the platform and said something like this: "For those of you who believe in the law of God, I brought this," and he placed a Bible on the stand; "and for those of you who believe in the law of man, I brought this," and he placed the U.S. Constitution there; "and for those of you who don't believe in either one of those laws, I brought these," and he pulled out two Colt dragoons and his Bowie knife. He then spoke unmolested and left town with no problem at all. With Farris Bryant's hometown, Ocala, just ahead, I made some mental notes.

It turned out my apprehensiveness about Ocala was wasted. I walked past the city limits early Monday morning, was greeted by supporters and well-wishers and walked into a half-hour live radio talk show, followed by a really full day they had planned for me. I was delighted with my reception as I visited four shopping centers, made a speech to the Kiwanis club, went through the city hall complex and the county commission building, had a meeting and chicken dinner with a real good turnout of supporters, then spoke to the Young Democrats in the evening. I'm convinced Marion County is wide open and that Bryant, having left here for Jacksonville after being governor and paying few visits prior to becoming interested in the U.S. Senate race, may be surprised here.

Progress Report #19: Ocala to Sanford—49 miles

491 down, 526 to go the Keys!

Leaving Ocala, I walked toward Silver Springs and a trip we've planned on the Oklawaha River. Buck Ray, whose family owned Silver Springs for many years and who's still affiliated with the attraction, walked with me part of the way.

445

Some evenings, after I've finished my walking and talking schedule for the day, I've taken side trips to nearby communities. For instance, I got into Pasco County, visiting Zephyrhills, had a reception in Dade City and then spoke at the big retirement community in New Port Richey.

Another evening I visited Leesburg to be with a group of supporters and took a boat trip on Lake Harris. The people around there are greatly concerned about pollution of the chain of lakes—Lake Harris, Lake Eustis, Lake Griffin, Lake Dora. High concentration of nutrients is causing green algae and they've had several bad fish kills in Lake Griffin. Lake Harris is probably in the best shape but the pollution is even accumulating there. Sources of the pollution seem to be sewage disposal, fertilizer from groves, from peoples' yards and street drainage. It's been going on for years but now it's developing into a major problem. The cities are trying to help solve the problem but they're in a bind needing money for sewage treatment plant improvements. They need tertiary rather than secondary treatment plants to do the job.

All of this convinces me more and more that we desperately need a technological break-through in the area of dealing with pollution problems. We really should be attacking this the same way we attacked the project of going to the moon—an advanced team made up of people from universities, government and industry.

The morning after arriving at Silver Springs, we were up early for the boat trip. It felt pretty good, realizing that instead of pounding the pavement between and in cities all day, I would be sitting and riding on the water. I saw some mighty secluded areas during the day but I wasn't lonesome. With me were Ross Allen of Silver Springs, Oscar Rawls of the Corps of Engineers, and reporters from the *Lakeland Ledger, Palm Beach Post-Times,* and Channel 2 TV. We went down the Silver River into the Oklawaha and from there up to Eureka Dam; then on through the Rodman Reservoir and Dam, completing the trip at the St. Johns Locks. It seems like I've been reading tons of material about the Cross-Florida Barge Canal but this was my first opportunity to see it for myself.

When you go down the beautiful Silver River and Oklawaha, the idea that anything should change is certainly upsetting and I think we have to be most careful that Silver River and Springs be protected from damage. I was surprised that the damage further up the river was not really as great as I had imagined it would be. Certain stretches of the river that don't have so much water impounded look like the natural state. I was amazed at the magnitude of the locks that have been completed. The project is about 31 percent completed now; some $65 million have been expended. The question now, I think, is what they can do to minimize damage as they continue the project and how they can make sure they are doing everything possible to protect the ecology of the area.

I saw the tree crusher they call "the monster" which was developed under Corps of Engineers contract to clear out the logs where the Rodman Dam was built. This is a tremendous machine that rolls over the trees and supposedly crushes them into the mud to get rid of them. The contract was for $4.5 million, and it's been a colossal failure. The crusher knocked down the trees and put them in the mud, but for the last year and a half they've been popping up like corks and the corps is now having to spend tremendous sums of money keeping a dredge out picking up the logs, piling them on the banks for burning. The corps people kind of indicated that as they continue their work further south, they're not planning to use the crusher anymore. They're going to use the conventional means of cutting the trees and burning them. I'm afraid this is another case like you see in government too often where somebody's grandiose idea just didn't pan out, and the taxpayer pays.

On the trip I met a young ecologist who is working for the Corps of Engineers, Dave Bowman. He graduated from the University of Florida with a degree in wild life and ecology and told me there were three or four others in his class graduating with the same degree. All but Dave had to go into military service. He had his behind him. He said his job offers were scarcer then bald eagles, and this disturbs me. When you think of how important ecology is to our very existence, it's kind of surprising that there is such little demand for a young man with such expertise. I sure hope the trend is changing. I believe that everyone—certainly government agencies that are putting in projects where it's possible to destroy some of our natural resources—should have ecologists working with them to see that we keep nature's life balance as constant as we possibly can.

Next day I took a short boat trip down the St. Johns with John Mattingly and Clyde Lankford of DeLand and some other friends to Crows Bluff landing. From the landing I walked into DeLand, about seven miles away. After being on the water for a long day, it wasn't so bad being back on my feet. I spent the rest of the day visiting the courthouse, banks and the downtown area going through the hospital (just visiting) and a couple of shopping centers, walking and talking with the people of DeLand.

In the evening I took a quick trip to Inverness, where they had chicken barbecue, pork barbecue and a bunch of people. Bob Gilstrap and Colonel Buckley really put together a great event. I got to dish up the barbecue and meet everyone as they came through the line. There were well over 250 people from all over Citrus County.

It was good to see former Senator Nick Conner, who is now a judge there, and mayors of all the towns. I made a little speech with a downpour threatening to break loose at any moment, but it waited until we were through to start raining. It was a pleasure spending the night with Johnny and Betty Eden. He's been working on a history of the Second Seminole War for a number of years and my visit was very interesting.

We've been telling tourists for many years that no trip through Florida is complete without walking on the sands of world famous Daytona Beach. Well, I'm not a tourist, but I want to make sure my trip is complete, too, so last Friday I made a little side visit to Daytona. It's pretty tough to try to walk and talk with people who are there to sun-bathe and swim, but we stirred quite a bit of interest with our camper and enjoyed a considerable amount of conversation. It suddenly occurred to me that this was as close to a vacation as I would get this summer.

On Saturday I walked in New Smyrna Beach, through the business district and on the beautiful, wide beach. Vic Vandergrifft hosted a coffee reception for me and I enjoyed meeting a number of people from that end of Volusia County, including some of the city officials.

As I approach the half-way mark in my 1,000-mile walk through our state, I get more and more excited about the reaction I'm getting. I'm getting the kind of enthusiasm that usually leads to success at the polls and I'm getting the kind of knowledge that will help me do a better job after election.

Progress Report #20: Sanford to Orlando—22 miles

513 down, 504 to go to the Keys!

Shortly after walking into Sanford Sunday I had the opportunity to attend the ground-breaking of the Good Samaritan Rest Home. This home for the aged is a bi-racial project, and the ceremony was outstanding. It certainly was a tribute to Mother Ruby Wilson, a black lady who has been an inspiration to the community of Sanford. She has been caring for other people since she was nine years old, and has been primarily responsible for building a church and a rest home. Then the state board of health told them they were going to have to close the rest home because of inadequate fire protection.

But Mother Wilson would not be discouraged and has started this building project involving a cost of over $50,000. During the ceremony they sang a spiritual that kind of got home to me. It went something like this: "When I have done the best I can and then when some of my friends don't understand, stand by me, Lord." It struck me that this could be a politician's hymn, because I know I've been in that position and needed that help many times. The community really turned out for the ground-breaking, and I thought once again that I wished everyone could be with me to be inspired the way I am almost every day by the wonderful things happening in our state. It seems a shame that Mother Ruby Wilson's life should be hidden in Sanford rather than being an influence all over the state.

At a coffee given for me in Sanford Monday, I met and talked with a teacher named Dorothy Bethel. She teaches a remedial reading course that has been sponsored by the federal government for four or five years but now the funds have been cut off. She called this a communications course for the young people and it was taught at the tenth grade level. They found that many of the boys in this course, both black and white, had reading ability of about the fifth grade. They kept the classes small, about 12 in each, and gave individual attention. She said it was amazing to see the improvement in their communications and reading, how it completely changed their attitudes and personalities. She said they no longer wanted to drop out, but wanted to stay in school and learn, to participate in activities they previously would have no part of. They developed great pride. It really frustrated me to see an important program like this—one that helps people help themselves—curtailed while at the same time millions and millions of dollars are wasted by the federal government. This is one of the reasons I'm in this race.

Sunday afternoon, I went on a boat tour of Lake Monroe and up the St. Johns River to Blue Springs with Howard McNulty and Don Rathel. Again, there's a steadily developing pollution problem here. I saw the construction for a new barge port just in the mouth of the St. Johns from Lake Monroe. It was a tremendous project. Howard McNulty hosted a fish fry for me and invited about 250 couples. There was a huge crowd from all over Seminole County and even some from Orange County, including State Senator Bill Gunter and State Rep. Bill Fulford. I was enjoying meeting and visiting with all these people. Then, I looked up and saw Jay and Nancy Peterson and George and Susie Carr from Lakeland. They came up for the fish fry and to bring wife Rhea to remind me I still have a home back in Lakeland.

Starting from Sanford at 7 a.m. Tuesday, I walked to Maitland by lunchtime. I looked up and saw a fellow walking toward me from about a quarter of a mile away and I could tell he had something in his hand. Well, it turned out to be Martin Peden and he's a Borden's milkman who lives in Orlando. He saw me walking and thought I might be hot and thirsty, so he stopped his truck, crossed over the highway and brought me a cold carton of milk. I enjoyed it almost as much as I did discussing with him different current events as we walked along back toward his truck. He said he'd been following my walking campaign through the press and TV but had never really expected to get to see me.

At the shopping center in Casselberry Councilman Bill Brier was waiting for me and kind of introduced me to his town. I had a pleasant visit there. At Fern Park I met Richard L. Evans who has just opened an exhibit on Lincoln. He asked me to come in and be his guest. It's a very good exhibit and has been open about 30 days. Mr. Evans collected mementos of President Lincoln as a hobby for some 10 years before deciding to open up the exhibit. It's very educational and I hope he does well. In the early stages of this walking-talking and listening campaign a lot of people commented (some predicted) that I'd get a real good reception in north and west Florida because people there are more grass-roots oriented in their politics but that in the central and southern part of the state I wouldn't get the same reaction. I'm really finding out that that's wrong. People are people everywhere. They like to talk politics, they like a politician who will listen to their ideas and concerns. They like the walk.

Progress Report #21: Orlando to St. Petersburg—118 miles

631 down, 386 to go to the Keys!

People all along my walk have expressed concern about the gross waste of taxpayers' money by the bureaucrats in Washington. I found a classic example of this. HEW's Office of Economic Opportunity made a $58,000 grant to Seminole Community Action, Inc., in Seminole County to study the need for a food stamp program for the poverty-stricken.

The ironic thing, though, is the grant came after the legislature had adopted a statewide food stamp program and after Seminole County Commissioners had entered into a similar program with the U.S. Department of Agriculture. Still, OEO made the grant, an absolute waste of tax money. If these agencies would quit ignoring local elected officials and would work with them, [waste] such as this could be greatly curtailed.

Our visit in Orlando was just great. Rob Lyons and his group did an outstanding job of planning and execution. Television, radio and newspaper people met me at the city limits and walked with me. They had a big pan of water and put dry ice in it to make it bubble and smoke. They had me sit down and stick my feet in it, assuring me there was a brick in there to protect my feet from the dry ice. But the first thing I hit was the ice. It stuck to my foot and I was really scrambling to get it off. It turned out OK.

My time in Orlando was organized to the minute. I toured various buildings, institutions and city hall, and visited some retirement homes. There were coffees, a cocktail party, a breakfast, and many other activities. The TV, radio and newspaper coverage was excellent and many people commented on the coverage in the Orlando area. Also, George Saunders accompanied me on a tour of Winter Park, along with Nan Geary. The people of Winter Park and Orlando seemed very receptive to our campaign.

After walking out of Orlando I stopped at Gatorland and visited with owner Owen Godwin. Though this is a very good tourist attraction with over 300,000 visitors a year, it is more than just a tourist attraction. Mr. Godwin has probably accomplished more with alligator breeding than anyone and says he's still working and learning about propagation. With our problems of declining gator population, what he's learning becomes more and more valuable.

I walked into Kissimmee Saturday morning and right on into the Silver Spurs Rodeo parade. For the most part it was just me and the horses walking in that parade. Unfortunately, there were a bunch of horses ahead of me and I would have to say it caused a bit of a problem for me. But it being July 4th and my first taste of getting home—Osceola County is in my senatorial district—no problem could keep it from being a great day. The crowd was tremendous and reacted warmly to my walking while the other officeholders and office seekers rode in cars. They talked to me and applauded enthusiastically and about had me floating over the problem the horses were leaving in the road ahead of me.

In the afternoon I went to the rodeo and stood inside the gate meeting people for so long that my face and nose sunburned even after all the days I've been on the road. Then I had a chance to watch some of the rodeo and it looked to me like the horses and bulls were winning most of the events. It was a real show and as I watched the cowboys performing it occurred to me that this represented a down-to-earth part of America that has strong meaning for many of us.

I've been reading where one of the Nixon administration officials stated that unemployment has climbed to 4.7 percent but that this shouldn't be considered alarming, that after all it had been higher one time during the

Kennedy administration. This made me think of Frances Kershlis, a lady who's a skilled tool and die worker at the Martin Co. Her husband also works there. She told me of the large number of workers that have been laid off by Martin, highly skilled workers who haven't been able to find anything to do but simple labor like picking fruit.

It certainly gives a statistic new meaning when you personalize it this way. Mrs. Kershlis was very interesting. She was one of 10 children raised on relief and in a housing project, but through hard work with her husband she now enjoys her own home and even a swimming pool. She expressed a lot of interest in social programs and said in her opinion we haven't assigned the proper priorities to these federal programs and that she feels a lot of money is being wasted.

From Kissimmee I headed for Polk County. It was a long, 18-mile day, but the group of supporters which met me at the county line removed any feeling of weariness. For some eight miles into Davenport, I had folks walking and talking with me. It was great to be back home but there was one anxious moment. A little dog slipped up behind me shortly after passing the county line and snapped at my heels, just missing me when I jumped. I thought wouldn't it be a heckuva note if I got bit by a dog in my own county after walking 550 miles through Florida undamaged?

Getting in home territory started me thinking about that 1958 door-to-door campaign again. Rhea was really afraid of the dogs so she carried dog biscuits in her pocketbook. I always kidded her about being afraid and told her that if a dog can't smell fear on you, he won't bother you. Well, came the day in Lake Wales when I got backed down by a German shepherd and a pointer and no matter how I turned, one of them was always at my back. Finally, I had to holler across the street to Rhea, "Dog biscuit!" Wifelike, she's never let me forget that.

And it was hot that campaign, too. But it was before Gatorade and I used a lot of salt tablets, and at the end of the day I could take off my shirt, throw it in the corner and it would stand up. Well, I'm getting another feeling I had in 1958. The time came when I knew from the way people were responding that our campaign was working. No one else really seemed to realize it, but Rhea and I would go home at night, look at each other and say, "It's there. We're going to win." I have that feeling now, just like in 1958.

Our first planned activities in Polk were in Haines City. Well, Red Phillips and the crew there did an outstanding job. They met me on the outskirts of town, Mayor Courtland Witcher was there to greet me. Some of the young people had a tub of water for me to soak my feet in. We walked into town for a coffee reception, then had a luncheon with 60 to 70 local businessmen. I walked and talked in the downtown area and that evening spoke to a rally at the football field.

Also in the afternoon I visited with the city commission and city manager of Lake Alfred. Early the next morning I made it to Winter Haven where Jack Rynerson had handled scheduling of the day's activities. It included walking and talking in shopping centers and the downtown area, speaking to a luncheon meeting of the realtors, visiting at the State Farm Mutual offices, newspaper, TV and radio interviews and a free public supper. In addition I attended a hearing at the chamber building held by the Department of Transportation concerning widening of a highway into Winter Haven to relieve traffic problems and also give a route from I-4 into the city.

The DOT people told about the detailed steps they would have to go through to get federal funds. In answer to my question they said the law passed by Congress to do with states getting matching federal funds was about two paragraphs long, after which the Bureau of Roads had written 29 pages of regulations which turns out to be the real law governing the hearing. Proof again that the agencies are writing more laws than Congress is by over-interpreting it and extending it far beyond the original intent.

Example: it is required that if any person is displaced by a highway, before construction can start on the road you must prove by affidavit that the person has been placed in another residence. It is not enough that you pay him for his property, but you must actually prove he is established in another residence. This can be kinda tough if he decided to leave the area. The DOT personnel said they are frustrated with this sort of thing, yet the pages of regulations increase almost daily. All of this just so we can have some of our tax money back.

After returning to Tallahassee for a one-day session, I left Winter Haven early for Auburndale and finally Lakeland in the late afternoon. Almost every car would blow at me, and I could get spoiled by this kind of recognition. Stopped off in Auburndale long enough to visit the mayor, city manager and tour Adams Packing Plant, Minute Maid, the downtown area and a shopping center.

Then, after lunch, I left for Lakeland, Lonnie Brown of the *Lakeland Ledger,* who has been almost a constant companion since I hit the county line, walking with me. It was real hot in the early afternoon sun, and pretty soon up drove a fellow named Ray Justice, a young soldier from Lakeland, with a

Coke for each of us. He said he was returning soon to army camp, then on to Viet Nam. I asked him what he thought about the war and he said he just wasn't sure whether we ought to pull out or not, but he had his orders and he was certainly willing to go. Though I think we should get out of Viet Nam just as soon as possible, I appreciate his attitude and commend him for it. He said he'd been reading about my walking-talking campaign and came looking because he wanted a chance to talk with me.

Before we got into Lakeland a big thunder storm came up. The rain was cool and refreshing, but the thunder and lightning convinced me to get in the camper quick. You can dry off from the rain but that lightning has a lasting effect.

As we approached Lakeland, traffic on U.S. 92 picked up and more and more people were blowing their horns at me. Ten or fifteen more people joined the walk, and when we got to Sertoma Park on Lake Parker, several hundred people, including Mayor Marvin Henderson, met us and most of them continued the couple of miles with us to Lodwick Hangar for chicken perlieu. Even with the heavy rain we had had and the weather still threatening, more than 2,000 people were on hand at the hangar.

Ben Hill Griffin, who had met and walked with me some, made a good talk and I was presented some funny gifts for the rest of the walk. Ben Hill gave me some orange seeds to plant along the road, and I got a small umbrella, a portable toilet, a bathing suit for walking in the rain, some shoes, a pair of crutches with a horn on one, and a giant ball of twine to unwind as I go along so I would be able to find my way back home. When I stood up to speak, the crowd response was so great and so warm that it really got to me and I could hardly talk. I told them of my experiences walking through Florida, of what I had learned, of how people in other parts of the state shared their same concerns, and of how the reaction I was getting convinced me I was on the road to victory in the U.S. Senate race.

Morning brought an early start for Plant City. I had a chance to visit Plant City Steel and got a scare there that I won't soon forget. I jumped off of a beam and immediately a pain shot through my right foot. The foot got sore and I was afraid I had sprained the arch. I visited a doctor and it turned out to be just a bruised tendon and with a little extra caution I was able to keep walking. I could see myself having to use that pair of crutches that were given to me at Lodwick to complete the walk.

I was a little surprised that recognition of me and knowledge of my campaign seemed to continue as strong in Hillsborough County as it was in Polk

County. While most everyone responds to the walk and talk campaign, working people are the ones who really get a kick out of it. They always like to talk about the weather, and how hot it has been and how much hotter it's going to get as if they don't believe I can keep it up. Well, a team of plow mules couldn't get me to stop.

I was met at the Hillsborough County line by Senator Louis de la Parte and Senator Ray Knopke and they walked on into Plant City with me. The active support of fellow senators has been very helpful in my campaign and I kinda have an idea the walking does them some good, too — physically and politically. On the outskirts of Plant City we were met by Channel 8 and Channel 13 television, radio station and newsmen and the publisher of the *Plant City Courier*. Through the efforts of Albert Miles and John Cone, we had a worthwhile schedule in Plant City.

Topping it off was a big dinner meeting with many community leaders and public officials. On Saturday I walked 18 miles to the outskirts of Tampa. My staff told me that if I walked all the way from Plant City to Tampa on Saturday that I could have all day Sunday off to rest. Sounded pretty good to me.

Going toward Tampa, I met an interesting lady, Mrs. E.L. Stoodum of Dover. She was in her front yard picking up beer cans, so I stopped and asked her if she had to do that often. Well, she almost cried. She said her husband tells her that their yard must be exactly one beer away from a stop down the road, and every morning she has to go out and pick them up. It's a shame that so many have little respect for other people's desires. Mrs. Stoodum obviously was proud of her home and worked hard to keep up the appearance of her yard, but she said it gets mighty discouraging.

As a car approached me from the rear I happened to glance over my shoulder and saw in it an elderly gentleman with white hair. Just as he got to me, he waved his hand and called out, "Bravo!" That sure tickled me because that was my first "Bravo" and it was his way of saying that what I'm doing has meaning for people. I just read where the bill calling for a "volunteer army" has been introduced in the Senate under joint sponsorship of doves and hawks—Church and McGovern as well as Barry Goldwater. Personally, I think the bill is misnamed because what it will wind up producing is a professional army—a giant lobbying force—and we don't need that. I think we will be doing much better with a fair and reasonable draft where most young men will serve and get out, offering a balance with the career force.

I'm delighted to announce that Ben Hill Griffin has accepted the job as campaign finance chairman. I told Ben Hill that I don't expect him to have to raise the kind of money that the other candidates are spending in this race. I set out on my walk of over 1,000 miles so that I wouldn't have to spend $1 million and be beholden to the kind of special interests that give it. He has agreed to help me organize my finance committee and it's difficult to express my appreciation fully because I know how tough it is for a man with demands on his time like Ben Hill has to take on more responsibility.

Senators Knopke and de la Parte joined me again bright and early Monday morning. We visited with employees at American Can Co. and then headed into Ybor City. With some supporters we walked from the Spanish Park Restaurant to the Columbia. As we walked along, a fellow named Bill Hyder stuck his head out of a door and said, "I think your walking campaign is great and I want to participate," and he handed me a check. I'd never seen him before but it was for $100. It sure gave me a lift. A crowd was waiting at the Columbia, and they had Cuban coffee and hot Cuban bread with butter on it. I learned the way to do it is dunk the bread in the coffee. I'd never had it this way before but like I say, you're always learning something in this kind of campaign.

We moved on to Cuervos, a real coffee house, and had a long discussion with people there. Then Louis de la Parte's dad escorted me through downtown Ybor and now I know how Louis gets his vote. His dad has had a store there for years and everyone knows him and holds him in the highest esteem. He carried me through some cigar factories and again everyone knew him. He's the one who really gets the vote! Sure makes it easy on Louis.

I went through the Health Center, toured city hall with mayor Dick Greco, went through the University Club with Senator Truett Ott and on to Kiwanis Club for lunch. Visited with Roland Monteigo of *La Gaceta*. Everybody likes to read Roland's political column because his man "No Sabe" seems to always have a line on interesting political information. In the afternoon I visited the Model Cities office and this is one of the best federal programs I've seen.

The final decisions are made by local officials who understand local needs and this is what I've said over and over in my campaign that this country needs more of. I was very impressed with the personnel. Some are black and all seem highly qualified and dedicated. They're organizing block clubs in the neighborhoods to get people to have pride in their neighborhoods, to develop community spirit and to help them learn to communicate what they think their needs, interests and frustrations are. To me this is important to helping people in ghetto-type situations.

They tell me the two things that have great impact on people in these neighborhoods are jobs and scholarships. These are tangibles they can really understand as ways of helping them and their children. Many, many scholarships have been granted, not just to colleges but to trade schools, junior college, a vocational program, beauty school, barber school, etc. Whatever seems to best suit a person who wants to improve himself is what they're trying to provide.

Tampa's Model Cities program also puts information on computer to evaluate the police department, recreation department and other such local government agencies. They are working out a traffic plan whereby all traffic lights would be controlled by traffic flow itself feeding information into a master computer. Sounds like magic to me, but I'm sure this is the sort of thing we'll see more of in the future. Monday evening over 300 people attended a dinner for me in Tampa. They were responsive to what I had to tell them and many of them were enthusiastic to help in the campaign. Hillsborough is our country and we're going to tear those other guys up there.

After dinner we went to the fights and along with it was Sonny Frazier's song and dance act. Somebody asked me how I liked it, and I answered that big as he is, when he sings, I smile! I was introduced from the ring as "the walking senator," and sure enough, somebody suggested I get in the ring and show 'em my fancy footwork. I decided to save it for the road.

Tuesday was another busy day walking about town, visiting the University of South Florida, attending a breakfast in northwest Tampa where Dick Sale had a great group of people and visiting the newspaper offices.

The next morning, at 6:30 we headed out Bayshore Boulevard toward Gandy Bridge. I had an enjoyable chat with two young men, Ron Black and Bob Lastra, students at Tampa University who have chartered a pollution and environment club. We discussed pollution problems, then got on the subject of the volunteer army which one of them was for as a great way to eliminate the draft. However, after I explained my idea of how this could result in a professional army, he said he'd never really thought of it that way before and seemed to change his mind. Bob commented that his brother is a career army man with 18 years in service and is very distressed about the professional army prospect. He feels it will lessen the stature of the career soldier, that people will look at them as hired hessians.

At the Pinellas line I was met by a group of supporters, including county coordinators Glenn and Cindy Moon, and some newspaper and television reporters. As we walked into St. Petersburg, we passed Goodwill Industries and I enjoyed visiting with the handicapped people working there, seeing the fine job they are doing.

I had another walking challenger today in Mike Richardson of the *St. Pete Times*. He stayed with me all day, about 20 miles, and by the end of the day he looked like a pretty tired young man. It was an extremely busy time, visiting the mayor, the new state office building and the courthouse, and in this so-called Republican territory the response was outstanding. I can't tell the difference from Polk and Hillsborough counties. In fact I had more people come out from filling stations and stores and stand by the road to talk and cheer me on.

Folks are sure kind to us. Gordon Mather and his wife had us to their house for a nice, hot shower and tremendous dinner. They even had a cake baked with my name on it and a big, soft chair tagged with a sign, "This chair reserved for the next U.S. Senator, Lawton Chiles." While in Pinellas County, I also visited Pinellas Park, Clearwater, Tarpon Springs and the Largo-Seminole area. The Moons really put together a hard[-]hitting schedule for me as we blanketed the county, and I congratulate and thank them. It's this kind of leadership that has given the campaign great impetus across Florida. I also congratulate them for their staying power on the road.

Progress Report #22: St. Petersburg to Ft. Myers—87 miles

718 down, 299 to go to the Keys!

After I left Pinellas County, where we had saturation exposure, I wondered how it would be in Manatee County. Well, we arrived in Bradenton by boat and met with about 150 people, and again had tremendous coverage. Wilbur Boyd, the senator there, had things well organized and has a great committee working for us there. Ed Price helped out too, and it was great to have him introduce me around.

We had a sit-down dinner for over 400 people at Pete Reynard's restaurant. I got an opportunity to speak there, and after seeing the response I got from the cross-section of people attending, I'm convinced that Manatee County is going to be in our corner.

Tuesday we went into Sarasota and were met at the Ringling Art museum by Mayor Jack Betz and a delegation from the city. We had a busy day touring downtown Sarasota and visited the newspaper offices there. That night we capped it off with a reception at Sam Dee's house where I had a chance to talk with 125 to 150 people.

Wednesday we went from Sarasota to Venice, around 18 miles. We ran into Buddy Cummings who used to work for my brother-in-law, Joe Ruthven, in Lakeland. He now has the O.K. Tire Store in Venice, and it was great to have him introduce us in his city. I also got a chance to see Dan Boone, an ATO brother from the University of Florida.

We then headed toward Port Charlotte and Punta Gorda with a side trip to Englewood, where I spoke on the radio for the second time that day. I had had an opportunity to be on the radio in Venice that morning.

Punta Gorda and Port Charlotte have joined forces and are working together to improve their area. I had a chance to speak to a meeting of their joint Kiwanis Club. I talked to them about the big issue here, U.S. 41, a subject I really have firsthand knowledge of now. I always thought S.R. 90 in northwest Florida was the worst road that I had walked on, but now I'm not sure. Around Venice U.S. 41 is a nice four-lane road where industry thrives but as it goes south, it narrows into a two-lane road where the bottleneck of traffic is dangerous.

The politicians have been giving these people the run-around about the 4-laning of this road for years. I mentioned to the club that I thought one of the best ways of getting this problem solved would be to get all of the candidates for Governor and U.S. Senator to walk the route. Then they'll all be advocates for 4-laning U.S. 41. But flying over it won't make them understand the need.

I understand that Governor Kirk has said that the four-laning of U.S. 41 through Punta Gorda is some six years away. There was a recent public hearing on the issue of roads, and although Kirk was staying in a local motel at the time, he was too busy getting ready to leave town even to speak with reporters concerning the problem, much less attend the hearing.

The population here has gone from 12,000 to 36,000 in the last 10 years, so you can get some idea of what is going on down here. One strong asset this area has is its retired citizens. They have brought their brain power into the area, and with their added purchasing power, you can really feel the new breath of growth and life in the area.

I had occasion to see a real "Good Samaritan of the Road." A load of bricks had fallen on the highways and Jim Chappell, a Manatee County deputy from Sarasota had parked his car with the blinker lights flashing so that oncoming cars would be warned. Then he had gone to a filling station for a big push broom. As I approached, he pushed the bricks to the side of the road so that cars would not hit them. He pointed out that these bricks could cause an accident, or could even be knocked by one car into another car (or a pedestrian). Many times you hear about people that pass right by a situation like this, but not Jim Chappell.

Webster Chapman of Osprey insisted on taking me to breakfast while I was in his town. He is retired and drives a big Cadillac car with New York license plates, and after we ate, he went up and down the road ahead of me, stopping at almost every house and business to alert the people that "the walking senator" was coming. He was a great help. I usually don't get someone driving a Cadillac that goes as my advance man heralding everyone out to the road. A motel owner outside of Venice came to the side of the road and invited me to be a guest of the motel. This was a direct result of Chapman's introduction.

I ran into a lineman from General Telephone, Bill Vasbinder from Englewood. He was working up the pole, and when I told him I was running for U.S. Senate, he said he might vote for me if I would throw up a piece of equipment that he had dropped on the ground. I threw it up all right. I threw it so hard I almost knocked him off the pole. After that I wasn't sure if I had his vote, but he got me a little eager when he said he might vote for me if I threw the equipment up to him.

I met Mrs. Godown and her daughter, Jan, on the road, and they told me that they had been looking forward to seeing me. They had been following my progress and plotting it on a map since I had left Century, Florida. This made me feel good, of course, but the thing that really made me feel good was that they said each night before they went to bed, they said a prayer that I would be safe on the highway. Lots of people have asked me if I feel alone out on the highway and I say I don't. There is always something to think about and plan. But now I really know why I haven't felt alone; I have people like the Godowns looking after me like that.

I walked past one of Farris Bryant's billboards today and I thought the artist did a tremendous job on the likeness of Farris. He looked as young as he did in 1960 when he first ran for governor.

I understand that Fred Schultz has just started his commercials on television. Although I haven't had a chance to see one yet, it seems a little late to start. My commercial starts every morning about 7:00 and it goes on till about dark. People can see it any time they come by the section of the road that we are walking on, and I think we're getting excellent coverage.

I read some further comments on President Nixon's Welfare Reform Bill, and in a Senate hearing, it came out that a mother of three earning $7,000 a year and paying taxes would actually be making less money than a mother of three who was not working at all and was collecting benefits under this Welfare Reform Bill. That's ridiculous! The public is not going to put up with a federal program that pays a person not to work!

I ran into Bob Wolff, a contractor from Ft. Myers who fabricates aluminum and builds screen porches and rooms and he really knows the meaning of inflation. He served in Viet Nam for one-and-a-half years. When he left, the price of a window was $12, and when he returned one-and-a-half years later, the same window cost $24. He says he pays a salary to three employees, has one partner, and tries to hold $100 a week out of the business for himself, and he winds up having to borrow money every three months to pay his employee withholding tax. He believes government agencies are only interested in large business, because when he asked the Small Business Administration for assistance, they wanted to talk about million-dollar loans and up—not what he needed at all.

We're concerned about our orange pickers but many of them make more money than this fellow who is trying to establish his own business and can't even take out $100 a week. The only way he can cope with inflation is to work longer hours and take more jobs to make as much money as he used to make working reasonable hours. I asked him what he would do about inflation. He said first he would find out what's causing it, then pull out the cause by the roots like a poison plant, not merely chop away at the stalk.

He really made an impression on me. I think that is our problem. We're not dealing with inflation at the roots. We're just dealing with it at the top of the stalk, and it keeps growing faster than we can chop it out.

Tuesday we'll start the long trek from Ft. Myers to Palm Beach on SR 80. It's a long, hot stretch, about 140 miles, through such communities as La Belle, Clewiston and Belle Glade, and I think it will be a great time for looking at nature and reflecting on my walk and the things I have learned about our state and its people. I've invited a lot of people to come walk part of the way with me. The sun will be hot, but at the end of this stretch lies the east coast. I'm looking forward to walking down the famous Gold Coast through mighty Dade, and on to Key Largo—the end of the walk.

Progress Report #23: From Ft. Myers to West Palm Beach - 142 miles

860 down, 157 to go to the Keys!

A great delegation was waiting for us at the Lee County line. There was Hugh Starnes, my county campaign chairman, and the members of the campaign committee, and there was Kenneth Daniels, chairman of the county commission, Sheriff Snag Thompson and Fort Myers Mayor Oscar Corbin Jr. I've been on a lot of picnics in my life, but the one we had right there wasn't like any other I'd been on. We had Spanish bean soup and fresh boiled shrimp and you have to admit that's unusual picnic fare. I ate too much and we still had 11 to 12 miles to go into Fort Myers.

After all these weeks I got my worst sunburn that day and I felt like I was on fire by the time we got to town. That afternoon I went to Bonita Beach where the Young Democrats were having an anti-pollution rally. As soon as I arrived, they put me on the program and I emphasized my concept of how pollution, conservation and other problems of how man is to live in his own environment should be attacked as a whole rather than piecemeal.

I told them of my idea that NASA itself or a NASA-like team should be used to harness the best available talent from the country's government, universities and industry to make the technological breakthrough that is needed if man is to be able to live within his own environment in the years ahead. I pointed out again that if our scientists could find the ways to handle man's waste on a trip to the moon, then we certainly should be able to devise revolutionary means of effectively handling our garbage and wastes in the cities.

After my speech an interesting fellow named Newt Harrington, who lives in Pine Island, visited with me. He's vitally concerned about pollution and conservation and told me that in Pine Island they're working on a new sewer system which is the result of some of the space exploration. They plan to use radiation to kill the bacteria and rather than throw the water into the bays or rivers or lakes like we're presently doing, it will be recirculated on land and give us use of the water again. This sounds great to me because it would cut down pollution and would help conserve our water supply. This is the sort of thing we can accomplish in many problem areas with an all-out attack in the '70s through research, hard work and proper utilization of our tax funds.

I was delighted with my visit in Fort Myers. On Sunday night we had a covered dish supper with 60 or 70 people present and some of the finest food I've ever eaten. It was a good cross-section of people and representative of Fort Myers leadership. My supporters set a schedule that really put me through the paces. As a matter of fact, there were some pretty good walkers among them.

The people around Fort Myers were very friendly to the campaign and media coverage was quite good. I sometimes get the feeling that the news reporters get as much fun out of covering this kind of campaign as I get out of doing it.

Had a big country breakfast this morning at the home of Floyd Ellis, a cousin. It was made by Alan Ellis, another cousin. They gave me some Dismal Key Fish Chowder and told me it was named that way because it is usually prepared in a cabin located on Dismal Key, an island about halfway between Marco Island and Everglades City. The recipe has never been recorded but was passed down through word of mouth from several generations of the Ellis family. I tried to get the recipe out of them but I couldn't. It was really delicious.

This reminded me of a story I picked up while walking in Columbia County a few weeks ago. Years ago, the cracker families would gather on the banks of the Suwannee River for a good, ole-time get-together. Some of the men would take to the small wooden boats with dynamite with a half-inch fuse to obtain the fish for fish chowder, which in those days was called "wash pot chowder" because that was what it was prepared in. Well, it's said Columbia County had more one-armed men than any other county in the state.

As I walked along outside Fort Myers, I had a chance to meet a real old walker, James W. Wightman. He told me that he once walked behind six mules for about 17 miles a day harrowing wheat in Washington State. This was over 50 years ago. He said he once broke the state record by harrowing a quarter section in three days where the previous record was half a day more, and he said he was able to do this with four horses and two mules because he could harrow such a straight line. Mr. Wightman thought what government needs today is just a little common sense and someone who has guts enough to say what is right and what is wrong. He looked 50 but is 72, and he is still running 65 cows on 75 acres and working mighty hard!

On a side trip to Arcadia some of the folks there started likening me to the legendary "Acre-foot" Johnson who carried the mail back in the 1800s between Fort Meade and Fort Myers—on foot. He's supposed to have been a giant of a man with about a size 20 foot and that's where he got his nickname. They tell tales about how he would get out of a buggy and walk off and leave it because he could move faster than the horse. Another tale had him sitting on his porch one afternoon and someone asked him to call a square dance in Arcadia that night. He said he'd love to but he'd have to have a pair of shoes, and he bolted off the porch, walked down to Fort Myers, got the shoes and was back in time to call the square dance. It's said he quit carrying the mail because he wanted to strap a chair on his back and carry a passenger along for company, but the post office wouldn't let him. I'm sure glad I'm not walking against him for the U.S. Senate.

We had a great time in La Belle. Parked the camper there well in advance of my getting there, and people were really looking for me. It was a lot of fun. While there, I found another situation which shows why government is often ineffective today. Dr. Elizabeth Baldwin of the public health clinic said the federal people just won't listen and it's hurting her operation there. They've required her to set up a night clinic for migrants to come in at night for medical treatment. But she says the migrants won't come in at night.

Still, she had to take half her staff off day shift to set the night shift and this has left her short-handed in the daytime when the migrants actually do come for services. The doctor says she can't get the federal people to listen. Somebody at the top seems to know it all though they've not been there to see what is really going on. The day I was there the clinic was full of workers, mostly Mexican-American and blacks. But I was happy to find they are giving birth control advice and dispensing contraceptives in order to help them control the size of their families.

Wednesday I got into Sebring and Avon Park for quick visits. Took in the courthouse in Sebring and the city hall and spent some time in the downtown area. That afternoon wife Rhea and little Rhea Gay came down with some fresh clothes and supplies and we had lunch together.

Thursday was the longest walk so far—31 miles from La Belle to Clewiston. Along the way I stopped at Goodno where I met Mr. and Mrs. Ralph McGill. They run a little store and had been looking for me for a day and a half, with cold limeade fixed all the time. Both the limeade and my visit with them was refreshing.

Friday was a very full day in Ft. Pierce. Tom Driscoll is heading up my campaign there and he's representative of the kind of man I like best to get involved. He's very active in the community, runs First Federal there, and has never been involved in politics before. He's energetic and enthusiastic, and he's really doing a job. At a Dutch-treat luncheon I spoke to a good group of people from various walks of life. Then we stayed on the go, visiting the newspapers, television stations, key members of the community, and then we invaded most of the shopping centers in the late afternoon.

The migrant worker situation in Florida has certainly been in the news a lot lately, and I took advantage of the opportunity while in Belle Glade to try to learn everything I could about the problem. In Belle Glade there seems to be a tremendous housing shortage. There are two public housing projects that will handle about 3,200 people, and there is another one in Pahokee nearby. The government has just made some $4 million in loans to housing projects, and they're completing a number of new units, but there will still be a shortage.

I talked with Harvey Poole, a black man in charge of one of the Belle Glade projects, with Dr. John Grady, mayor of Belle Glade and a medical practitioner, a representative of one of the sugar companies and a man with the State Health Department. The problem is tremendously complex and anyone who seeks to oversimplify it does a disservice to the situation and the people involved. I think everyone has spent too much time worrying about who is to blame for inadequacies and too little time finding solutions. For instance, Senator McGovern came to Florida, had a big expose with the publicity that goes along with it, but his recommendations are yet to come. He was down over a year ago.

Certain things are apparent. One is that there is a great need for vocational education in this area. There is some, but not enough. They need the opportunity to develop skills rather than continuing through life as common laborers. Another thing is education regarding self care. The legislature doubled funds for county health units and this will help. Provisions are being made for food stamp programs, but in addition most of these people must learn about proper diets and how to prepare the foods for those diets.

Another thing is that many of the migrant workers appear satisfied with the way they are living. I talked to a number of the workers and they don't want to work regularly, don't want a residence to be responsible for, don't want to be tied down to any place. They are resistant to anyone who wants to change all this.

Another thing is that the growers are right when they say that the whole story is not being told by the TV people. The growers are not required to provide housing, but over the years many have. For example, much has been said about the place called Big House, which is owned by grower George Wedgeworth. It will house 120 people and is better than much of the private housing around there. The owner provides it rent free, and right now some 70 to 80 people are living there. Joe Collins, the black man who manages the house, said only about 12 or 15 of them are actually working for the grower. Wedgeworth pays for all the lights, water, and electricity and that alone costs over $14,000 a year. Maintenance costs are high, too.

I have always felt that the answer to such problems as this is to work with the young, to provide the educational opportunities which will help them

465

break the cycle. I couldn't help thinking back to my walk in Tampa when I observed the Model Cities Program in operation. The same thing would do wonders in this area of Florida. The people of Belle Glade are tremendously upset over the television documentary's representation that nothing has been done over the past 10 years. Yet, there have been improvements. Free public health units, even portable units that go out to provide medical treatment for the workers. Federal migrant education funds, paying up to $35 a week to migrants going to school at night. Additional federal housing.

There's a great deal that needs to be done, more than the talking, the pat answers that too many politicians and others are giving. It needs a sincere, major cooperative effort between the federal and state governments and the patience to work for years to bring about a lasting solution.

Saturday was a heavy walking day, taking me to within a few miles of West Palm Beach and the Gold Coast. This is an experience I've been waiting for.

Progress Report #24: West Palm Beach to Key Largo—157 miles

1,000 down, 000000 to go—we're there!

We got to the outskirts of Palm Beach on Sunday afternoon and after a short walk Monday morning, and we were met by John Moyle and some supporters at Publix just on the edge of Palm Beach. The long trek from Ft. Myers to the sea is now ended, and I realize that I will be knee-deep in people down the east coast walking through Palm Beach, Broward and Dade Counties.

We twice visited the RCA plant where they have approximately 2,000 employees on one shift. Most of them were doing bench work — skilled labor working on computer components. There are great employee-employer relations here, and we were allowed to go down the lines and talk to the people. They were working hard, but stopped to talk to us when we came up to them. Many of the employees were women. They make good money and have excellent working conditions.

I spoke to the Palm Beach Kiwanis Club one day. The next day I went to the West Palm Beach Kiwanis Club where they had another speaker; however, they have a provision which allows 10 minutes for any political candidates that come to the meeting. Since I was the only one there that day, I got the full 10 minutes. I think that's an excellent provision. Candidates will be coming through town; if they can't make an actual speaking date with a club, the members still have an opportunity to hear them.

Bill Walton, an ATO fraternity brother, put together a great barbecue in West Palm Beach. There were over 100 people there, and I really enjoyed being with them and speaking to them.

In Boca Raton I visited Florida Atlantic University. It was registration time so I got a chance to visit with a number of the students there. I met many of the faculty members at a reception later that day.

Boca Raton is really growing. There are a tremendous number of condominiums, apartments and housing developments being built in the area.

We went all the way from Boca Raton to Pompano Beach and spent a busy half day visiting with the people at the Pompano mall. This is a tremendous new shopping center and mall and has all of the major stores- Sears, Penneys, Riches, Burdines together with about 106 little stores. Lots of people to see.

I was met at the Broward County line by A.J. Ryan, a former fellow legislator, Emmet McTigue, who I knew at the University of Florida, and a group of supporters. They walked with me into Pompano Beach.

The people in Broward County are more frustrated and hostile than about any place I've been. I can remember about 10 years ago when people were saying, "Why would anyone live in Dade County when they could just move across the line and live in Broward?" Well, it looks like too many did move. The county has had a tremendous impact of people, and they are still coming; however the facilities in the area are not adequate. Subdividers came into Broward County and incorporated many little towns, thereby setting up their own zoning requirements and building codes. When the developer left, the people had to take over the city government and cope with the problems of inadequate sewage, schools and other problems.

I talked to one man who told me he spends an hour and a half a day on the road trying to get home. When he gets there and takes out his boat to relax, he can't even fish where he used to fish. He says he can buy less with his paycheck, and he's paying more taxes. "I don't know who the hell is supposed to be representing me in government, but whoever it is has sure not done anything for me." This seems to be the complaint of many other people in this area, too.

Going from Pompano Beach to Ft. Lauderdale, I became very much aware of the serious traffic conditions on U.S. 1. Cars were bumper to bumper. It rained some that day, and due to the added hazards of wet, slick pavement I saw six traffic accidents along that stretch of road. I think part of the problem is the missing link in I-95. All the traffic in this area is detoured over to

U.S. 1. I wonder if this missing link is due to an agreement that was made when the turnpike was refinanced. Part of the refinancing deal, as I understood it, was that the road department would not 4-lane a parallel road or it might be in competition with the turnpike, thus interfering with the turnpike bonds. This would directly affect I-95 as well as 27, both parallel routes.

Going into Lake Worth, we were met by a group of ladies from the Zonta Club. This is a women's civic organization that sponsors a walk every year to provide money for the junior college there. We exchanged walking tips and they invited me to join them during the latter part of September. They walked with me a while, and we were joined along the way by the Lake Worth Chamber president, Wally Ferguson, who runs a laundry and dry cleaning establishment in town.

We spent a busy day Monday in Ft. Lauderdale. In the morning we visited Florida Power and Light and a number of industrial plants in the area. That afternoon we walked toward Dania.

Tuesday we arrived in Hollywood. That afternoon I broke from the walk and went ahead for the first time into Miami where we appeared with other candidates in a program at the Tiger Bay Club. This is a very active organization in Miami. They had an interesting panel, and I thought everyone did well, but in the brief time, it was hard to feel that you were really able to show your stuff. I did note that Farris Bryant spent more time talking about his past and very little telling about what he expected to do in the Senate in the future.

We went from there to a taping at Channel 7 for an hour television program. We had a little more time for questions, and a better opportunity to express ourselves. I wish we had more shows of this type, where the voters have an opportunity to compare the differences in the candidates.

Early the next morning we went back to Broward County and walked into Dade County where we were met by a number of our Dade County supporters and members of the press. Sylvan Meyer, editor of the *Miami News,* came out and walked with me some five miles into North Miami Beach. Four of the papers, the *Miami News,* the *West Palm Beach Post,* the *Daytona Beach News-Journal,* and the Cowles papers have agreed to pool their reporters to cover the Senate and Governor races. They are doing in-depth profiles of the candidates, and Sylvan Meyer is doing his profile on me, so he has spent considerable time with me finding out what makes me tick.

My Miami visit was really organized, and I was busy walking in all the different sections of the city. We visited in the North Dade and North Miami

Beach areas, meeting people in the city halls and along the streets. That afternoon, I went to the Systems Club for a fund raising event, and that evening I was on the Larry King Show, an hour long talk show hosted by a very sharp guy, Larry King.

The following morning, we visited with aircraft employees during a shift change at the airport, then went to Hialeah, Miami Springs and Palm Springs Mile Shopping Center. We then jumped over to Miami Beach, where I made an appearance at the Vocational Teacher convention which was being held at the Fontainbleu Hotel, then back to the airport for a shift change at Pan American.

Senator Lee Weissenborn had set up a meeting with the board of directors of the association representing the condominium owners. The condominium owners made it clear that they may be retired, but they are not old. They're very active and interested, protecting their rights. After my discussion with them, they voted to endorse my candidacy. The board represents some 80 different condominiums that have at least 250 units, and this could be a tremendous help to us in Dade County.

We spent three hours that night on the Allen Courtney Show. The first hour was spent in an interview, and the last two hours were a telephone marathon. I enjoyed this show, and both the Allen Courtney and the Larry King shows have tremendous listening audiences. People mentioned my appearances on both during the rest of my visit in Dade County.

We've had excellent television coverage on all Dade County channels. They've come out and covered parts of the walk.

Friday morning we met some more airline personnel during shift changes, and went through the Justice Building where there are a couple thousand employees. That afternoon we went to Miami Beach and visited the Lincoln Mall, then went to the *Miami Beach Daily Sun*. An interesting fellow was waiting for me there. His name was Harry Reichenthal. He had cut out letters and prepared a sign which he had hung around his neck. It said, "Welcome to Miami Beach, Lawton Chiles, the walking senator, the man that will represent the people and is campaigning without spending money." He had a wonderful accent which Myron Cohen would have admired, and he preceded me from the *Sun* office down Lincoln mall saying "He's coming, he's coming! The walking senator is coming! Come out and see the walking senator." He said that if he wasn't out campaigning for me, he would have nothing important to do at all. We need something meaningful for these retired people to do. They have much to contribute and they want to play a valuable part in society, so we must help them find a way to put their experience to work.

I walked in Liberty City on Saturday. There had been several severe riots there and a store had been burned. There was open hostility here. This is a black neighborhood, and it was obvious that the same zoning codes and road repairs were not used here that were applied to other portions of the city. I talked to one young man, 24 years old, who had two years of college working on a sociology degree. He has now dropped out of school and is doing nothing. He had been drinking beer all morning, and he poured out his frustrations to me. He wondered why we can't have human rights where people want to help each other rather than just civil rights, where someone was made to do something by the law. He said many politicians came there promising many things, but nothing was ever improved. When I left, the people seemed a little more friendly toward me, and thanked me for bothering to visit their neighborhood and listen to them.

That afternoon I walked in Little Cuba and the contrast was apparent. The Cubans have taken over an area and fixed it up. They have little coffee shops about every three or four stores, and they sit and discuss politics. They want to know definitely what our position is regarding Cuba and Castro's government. They realize now that we are not going to give them arms aid, but they want to know if we are going to recognize Castro and trade with his country. They are frustrated by not knowing, and I feel that they are entitled to answers to their questions. I have the strongest feeling that the clock is running on us in Latin America, and Latin America is more important than Europe to us. We've got to keep Latin America from becoming Communistic. I hope to become an expert on Latin American affairs for two reasons: 1) because I think Florida is the Gateway to there; and 2) because the United States Senate has no real expert on this vital problem.

Saturday night I went to the Dolphin game where I stood outside the gates and handed out literature. I was amazed at the recognition that I had there. During the half somebody recognized me and started talking about the walk. Before I knew it, I had people three rows up and three rows down talking to me, and took about 15 minutes to get back to my seat. People in Dade County really like the walk. The media coverage has really brought it to their attention. I think there's a hatful of votes here, all available. I am really going to work hard here and hope to do well.

Well, it's over! There were times when I dreamed I was an old man and I was still walking, like maybe this was going to go on forever. But surprisingly, the several days since Miami went extra fast and when the finish line slipped up on me, I wasn't really ready. I certainly faced the end of the road with mixed emotions. But it was a fine feeling to have a number of friends and supporters with me for that last mile—newsmen, too (would you believe John McDermott, *Miami Herald* political writer, walking? It sure looked good on him, too). Key Largo (John Pennekamp State Park) was absolutely beautiful; it was a great place to wind up.

What has the walk accomplished? Unquestionably, it has given media exposure I could never have had otherwise. It helped me prove my concern about overspending in political campaigns. And I have to admit that I may never be as healthy physically again . . . unless I decide to go another 1,000 miles another day!

I'm delighted I've been able to meet and talk with over 40,000 people all over the state. I have first-hand knowledge of the problems of our state, better than anyone else in the race. Now, I'm looking forward to the rest of the campaign, and I'm counting on all the friends I've made to go to work these last few days before the election September 8th. Whewwwwww . . . can it really be over? With kind regards, I am

Sincerely,

Lawton Chiles

Appendix B
Chiles Family Recipes, as Related by Ed Chiles

Turkey pilau (pronounced "purloo")

Wild turkey is excellent table fare. We were fortunate to have it often. The way Dad loved to do it was to strip fry the breast and thighs and then make turkey pilau out of everything else.

Once the turkey breast and thighs are strip fried, debone them. Cut the turkey across the grain in one-inch by half-inch strips. Salt and pepper the meat. Crush 2 or 3 cloves of garlic per half pound of meat and place the turkey and garlic in a zip lock bag for 20 minutes or so to marry up the flavors.

Dust the turkey in flour and fry in canola oil. When the turkey gets a little golden color, it should be ready. Don't overcook it.

Take the residue in the bottom of the pan and pour off as much oil as possible. In a hot skillet, deglaze the pan and add stock or water and allow to reduce to make a nice gravy for the fried turkey. Salt and pepper to taste.

After taking the fillets and thighs off, Dad would put the rest of the carcass including the giblets, minus the liver, into a large stock pot that would hold the bird. Rough chop onions, celery, and carrots and add that to the pot along with salt and pepper. Bring to a boil and then reduce to a medium simmer for an hour or until the remaining meat falls off the bones. Let it cool and strain off the stock and reserve it. Take all of the meat off of the bones and add that to the stock. Lightly sauté a fresh batch of chopped onions, celery, and carrots, medium diced, and add that into the stock as well. Place the stock pot back on the stove with all of the ingredients and bring to a boil. Add the appropriate amount of long grained rice, a cup or two, and reduce the heat and cover. The rice will absorb all of the stock.

Fried Corn

This was a recipe passed down from Dad's parents. We made it when Zellwood or Silver Queen corn was in season, and we often did it when we cooked fried turkey or fried chicken. We would serve beautiful sliced vine ripe tomatoes on the side.

Serving Guidelines:
2 ears per person
I slice of bacon per 2 ears of corn.

Directions:
Cook the bacon, reserving the bacon and about a third of the bacon grease. Shuck the corn, and, taking a very sharp knife, cut just the tips off the kernels. With a butter knife, gently scrape the remaining meat and milk from the ears of corn into a bowl. Just the tips are cut, and the corn is scraped gently so as not to get the tougher husk of the kernels. Add a splash of milk or cream and salt and pepper. Heat the bacon grease back up in the same pan that the bacon was cooked in. The corn mixture should sizzle as it goes in. Lower the heat and sauté the corn mixture for 8 or 10 minutes, adding more milk or cream if needed. Crumble the bacon over the top and serve.

Venison fillets

Take venison back strap or other deboned venison muscle pieces. Slice across the grain at least a half inch thick. Salt and pepper the medallions and rub them with fresh crushed garlic and a little olive oil. Let them sit for 10 minutes and cook in a hot skillet with a touch of canola oil, which holds up well to a higher heat. The secret is to get a nice color on both sides while keeping the venison on the rare side of medium rare. Let the meat rest for 5 minutes. Deglaze the pan with a little red wine and add some stock and reduce for a nice pan sauce. If you would prefer to grill the venison medallions, add a bit of balsamic vinegar and Dijon mustard to the olive oil and garlic, and let it marinade for a bit before you cook it on a hot grill, making sure to keep it on the rare side.

Notes

1.   The newsletters were later collected and edited as *The Walk That Inspired Florida,* a single document published online by the Lawton Chiles Foundation and printed in the Appendix of this volume. The online publication can be accessed at the Lawton Chiles Foundation website, http://chilesfoundation.org/lawton-chiles/the_walk/.

2.   Lawton Chiles, Progress Report 4, in *The Walk That Inspired Florida* (see the Appendix in this volume).

3.   Peter Wallsten, Diane Rado, and Julie Hauserman, "Overflow crowd bids farewell to man they admired," *St. Petersburg Times,* December 17, 1998.

4.   William J. Clinton, "Remarks at a Memorial Service for Lawton Chiles," January 28, 1999, *Public Papers of the Presidents of the United States: William J. Clinton,* Book I (Washington, DC: U.S. Government Printing Office, 1999), 116-117, http://www.gpo.gov/fdsys/pkg/PPP-1999-book1/html/PPP-1999-book1-doc-pg116.htm

5.   Bill Rufty, "Politics in the Park—A Polk Tradition," *Lakeland Ledger*, September 26, 2002.

6.   "A Statesman Speaks," Editorial, *Lakeland Ledger*, April 26, 1940; Mary M. Flekke and Randall M. MacDonald, *Lakeland* (Charleston: Arcadia Publishing, 2005), 35.

7.   "A Statesman Speaks"; Flekke and MacDonald, *Lakeland*, 35.

8.   "Lakeland welcomes Holland," Editorial, *Lakeland Ledger*, April 25, 1940.

9.   "Bartow looks into career of native son," *Polk County Record*, March 1, 1940.

10.   "Spessard L. Holland's Experience and Valor as World War Flier Typical of His Character and Spirit as Public Official Today," *Polk County Record*, January 16, 1940.

11.   "Spessard Holland announces for governor," Editorial, *Polk County Record*, January 2, 1940.

12.   Flekke and MacDonald, *Lakeland,* 16.

13.   "Launches campaign in county," *Polk County Record*, March 5, 1940.

14.   "Off to enthusiastic start, stands on his many years of service," *Polk County Record,* March 5, 1940.

15.   "Sen. Holland defends his record here," *Lakeland News,* April 26, 1940.

16.   "A Statesman Speaks," Editorial, *Lakeland Ledger*, April 26, 1940.

17.   "Holland cheered by 3,500 as he talks labor and citrus," *Lakeland Ledger,* April 26, 1940.

18.   Ibid.

19.   "Spessard Holland announces for governor," Editorial, *Polk County Record*, January 2, 1940.

20.   "Off to enthusiastic start, stands on his many years of service," *Polk County Record,* March 5, 1940.

21. Martin Dyckman, *Floridian of His Century: The Courage of LeRoy Collins* (University Press of Florida, 2006), 27.

22. "Holland cheered by 3,500 as he talks labor and citrus," *Lakeland Ledger,* April 26, 1940.

23. Bill Rufty, "Lakeland's Own Governor," *Lakeland Ledger,* December 13, 1998.

24. Canter Brown Jr., *In the Midst of All That Makes Life Worth Living: Polk County, Florida, to 1940* (Tallahassee: Sentry Press, 2001), 322.

25. Ibid., 323.

26. Canter Brown Jr., *None Can Have Richer Memories: Polk County, Florida 1940-2000* (Tampa: University of Tampa Press, 2005), 17.

27. Canter Brown, *In the Midst of All That Makes Life Worth Living*, 322; Canter Brown, *None Can Have Richer Memories*, 18.

28. Canter Brown, *In the Midst of All That Makes Life Worth Living,* 306, 324.

29. Ibid., 318.

30. Ibid., 317.

31. Ibid., 318.

32. Canter Brown, *None Can Have Richer Memories*, 15.

33. Charleston (S.C.) *News and Courier*, July 23, 1894, quoted in Cal Logue, *The Oratory of Southern Demagogues* (Baton Rouge: LSU Press, 1981), 48.

34. Chicago *Tribune*, November 28, 1906, quoted in Logue, *The Oratory of Southern Demagogues,* 62.

35. Omaha *World-Herald,* May 15, 1907, quoted in Logue, *The Oratory of Southern Demagogues,* 62.

36. Waterloo (Iowa) *Daily Courier*, September 8, 1906, quoted in Logue, *The Oratory of Southern Demagogues,* 63.

37. Harry S. Ashmore, *An Epitaph for Dixie* (New York: W.W. Norton, 1957), 99.

38. Shreveport (La.) *Journal*, December 12, 1904, and New Orleans *Daily Picayune*, January 23, 1905, quoted in Logue, *The Oratory of Southern Demagogues,* 132.

39. New Orleans *Daily Picayune*, December 13, 1904, quoted in Logue, *The Oratory of Southern Demagogues,* 133.

40. New Orleans *Daily Picayune*, January 27, 1905, quoted in Logue, *The Oratory of Southern Demagogues,* 134.

41. Confidential interview, THW Papers, Mss. 2489, LSU LLMVC; T. Harry Williams, *Huey Long* (New York: Alfred A. Knopf, 1969), 3.

42. "Jacob Summerlin: The cowman who was king of crackers," *Tampa Bay News Weekly,* August 22, 2007; Bill Whitehead, "'Cracker King' Built Florida's Cattle Industry," *Lakeland Ledger,* October 26, 1958.

43. Dana Ste. Claire, *Cracker: The Cracker Culture in Florida History* (Gainesville: University Press of Florida, 2006), 29-30; Bill Whitehead, "'Cracker King' Built Florida's Cattle Industry," *Lake-*

land Ledger, October 26, 1958.

44.   Canter Brown, *None Can Have Richer Memories*, 4; Canter Brown, *In the Midst of All That Makes Life Worth Living,* 54-55.

45.   "Jacob Summerlin: The cowman who was king of crackers," *Tampa Bay News Weekly,* August 22, 2007.

46.   Canter Brown, *In the Midst of All That Makes Life Worth Living,* 103.

47.   Ibid.

48.   Bill Whitehead, "'Cracker King' Built Florida's Cattle Industry," *Lakeland Ledger,* October 26, 1958.

49.   Cinnamon Bair, "Crackers: Straight to the Point," *Lakeland Ledger,* February 3, 2003.

50.   Lloyd Dunkelberger, "Sayings from a Cracker," *Lakeland Ledger,* December 13, 1998.

51.   Tom Fiedler, "Chiles reflected: 'there is nothing that I have to do,'" *Miami Herald,* December 13, 1998.

52.   Ste. Claire, *Cracker,* 82.

53.   Ibid., 94.

54.   Joe W. Chiles Sr., "Our Family History," October 25, 2000, personal papers of Joe W. Chiles Jr.

55.   Ibid.

56.   Clark Hoyt, "Will Chiles Walk in Middle of Road?" *Miami Herald,* November 15, 1970.

57.   Bill Rufty, "Lakeland's Own Governor," *Lakeland Ledger,* December 13, 1998.

58.   "Lawton Chiles: A Florida Giant," Editorial, *Lakeland Ledger,* December 13, 1998.

59.   Canter Brown, *In the Midst of All That Makes Life Worth Living,* 22.

60.   Canter Brown, *None Can Have Richer Memories,* 6.

61.   "Wanted: 5 Colored Women," Want ad, *Lakeland Ledger,* September 10, 1944.

62.   Canter Brown, *None Can Have Richer Memories,* 7.

63.   Mike Denham interviews Bill Ellsworth 2-27-04, Dr. Mike Denham Interviews.

64.   Ibid.

65.   Canter Brown, *In the Midst of All That Makes Life Worth Living,* 141.

66.   Ibid., 248.

67.   Canter Brown, *None Can Have Richer Memories,* 6.

68.   Canter Brown, *In the Midst of All That Makes Life Worth Living,* 248.

69.   Ibid., 93.

70.   Ibid., 199.

71.   Canter Brown, *None Can Have Richer Memories,* 9.

72.   Paul Ortiz, *Emancipation Betrayed: The Hidden History of Black Organizing and White Violence in Florida from Reconstruction to the Bloody Election of 1920* (Berkeley: University of California

Press, 2005), 151-152.

73. Canter Brown, *None Can Have Richer Memories*, 7.

74. Ibid.

75. Canter Brown, *In the Midst of All That Makes Life Worth Living*, 203-204.

76. Ibid., 204.

77. Ibid., 268.

78. Michael Newton, *The Invisible Empire: The Ku Klux Klan in Florida* (Gainesville: UP of Florida, 2001), 43; Canter Brown, *In the Midst of All That Makes Life Worth Living,* 269.

79. Ibid., 269.

80. Newton, *The Invisible Empire,* 78-79.

81. Canter Brown, *In the Midst of All That Makes Life Worth Living*, 321-322.

82. Ortiz, *Emancipation Betrayed,* 114.

83. Mike Denham interviews Joe P. Ruthven 1-06-04, Dr. Mike Denham Interviews.

84. Ellen Debenport, "The world of politics isn't so bad after all," *St. Petersburg Times,* November 11, 1990.

85. Mike Denham interviews Joe P. Ruthven 1-06-04, Dr. Mike Denham Interviews.

86. Bill Rufty, "Lakeland's Own Governor," *Lakeland Ledger,* December 13, 1998.

87. Ben Funk, "Walking Lawton: Opponents Laughed At Him, But He Grinned At Finish.' *Lakeland Ledger,* January 3, 1971.

88. Mike Denham interviews Bill Ellsworth 2-27-04, Dr. Mike Denham Interviews.

89. Bill Rufty, "Lakeland's Own Governor," *Lakeland Ledger,* December 13, 1998.

90. Mike Denham interviews Bill Ellsworth 2-27-04, Dr. Mike Denham Interviews.

91. Mike Denham interviews Snow Martin Jr. 4-16-04, Dr. Mike Denham Interviews.

92. Bill Rufty, "Has Lawton Chiles' Legacy Faded?" *Lakeland Ledger,* January 17, 2005.

93. Mike Denham interviews Bill Ellsworth 2-27-04, Dr. Mike Denham Interviews.

94. Ibid.

95. Clark Hoyt, "Will Chiles Walk in Middle of Road?" *Miami Herald,* November 15, 1970.

96. Mike Denham interviews Bill Ellsworth 2-27-04, Dr. Mike Denham Interviews.

97. Canter Brown, *None Can Have Richer Memories*, 67.

98. Mike Denham interviews Bill Ellsworth 2-27-04, Dr. Mike Denham Interviews.

99. Canter Brown, *None Can Have Richer Memories*, 20.

100. Ibid.

101. Ibid., 27.

102. Ibid., 31.

103. Ibid., 32.

104. Ibid., 29.

105. Ibid., 36.

106. Ibid., 40.

107. "Buy your invasion bonds today!" War bond ad. *Lakeland Ledger,* September 10, 1944.

108. Mike Denham interviews Bill Ellsworth 2-27-04, Dr. Mike Denham Interviews.

109. Ibid.

110. Mike Denham interviews Snow Martin Jr. 4-16-04, Dr. Mike Denham Interviews.

111. Philip Longman, "Who Can Get To Chiles," *Florida Trend,* January 1991.

112. Mike Denham interviews Jack Pridgen, March 5, 2004, Dr. Mike Denham Interviews.

113. Mike Denham interviews Bill Ellsworth 2-27-04, Dr. Mike Denham Interviews.

114. Ibid.

115. Ibid.

116. Ibid.

117. Bill Rufty, "Lakeland's Own Governor," *Lakeland Ledger,* December 13, 1998.

118. Canter Brown, *None Can Have Richer Memories*, 101.

119. Mike Denham interviews Bill Ellsworth 2-27-04, Dr. Mike Denham Interviews.

120. Ibid.

121. Ben Funk, "Walking Lawton: Opponents Laughed At Him, But He Grinned At Finish.' *Lakeland Ledger,* January 3, 1971.

122. Bill Rufty, "Lakeland's Own Governor," *Lakeland Ledger,* December 13, 1998; Canter Brown, *None Can Have Richer Memories*, 101.

123. Anthony Schiappa, "Holland Maintains Long Victory String," *Lakeland Ledger,* September 10, 1958.

124. Bob Arndorfer, "Chiles made his mark early at UF," *Gainesville Sun,* December 17, 1998.

125. V. O. Key Jr., *Southern Politics in State and Nation* (Knoxville: University of Tennessee Press, 1949), 605; Newton, *The Invisible Empire,* 101.

126. "Bartow looks into career of native son," *Polk County Record*, March 1, 1940.

127. Canter Brown, *In the Midst of All That Makes Life Worth Living*, 319.

128. Bill Rufty, "Lakeland's Own Governor," *Lakeland Ledger,* December 13, 1998.

129. Jac Wilder Versteeg, "Still Walkin' The Walk," *Palm Beach Post,* October 30, 1994.

130. Canter Brown, *None Can Have Richer Memories*, 67.

131. Mike Denham interviews Bill Ellsworth 3-5-04, Dr. Mike Denham Interviews.

132. Ibid.

133. Bob Arndorfer, "Chiles made his mark early at UF," *Gainesville Sun,* December 17, 1998.

134. Lawton Chiles, Progress Report 18.

135. Bob Arndorfer, "Chiles made his mark early at UF," *Gainesville Sun,* December 17, 1998.

136. Guy McCarthy, "News of Chiles' Death Stuns Hometown Friends," *Lakeland Ledger,* December 13, 1998.

137. Bob Arndorfer, "Chiles made his mark early at UF," *Gainesville Sun,* December 17, 1998.

138. Ellen Debenport and Lucy Morgan, "No office but a lot of chairs," *St. Petersburg Times,* January 7, 1991.

139. Bob Arndorfer, "Chiles made his mark early at UF," *Gainesville Sun,* December 17, 1998.

140. Ibid.

141. Mike Denham interviews Snow Martin Jr. 4-16-04, Dr. Mike Denham Interviews.

142. Ibid.

143. Ibid.

144. Guy McCarthy, "News of Chiles' Death Stuns Hometown Friends," *Lakeland Ledger,* December 13, 1998.

145. Bob Arndorfer, "Chiles made his mark early at UF," *Gainesville Sun,* December 17, 1998.

146. Ibid.

147. Mike Denham interviews Bill Ellsworth 3-5-04, Dr. Mike Denham Interviews.

148. Ibid.

149. Ibid.

150. Mike Denham interviews Snow Martin Jr. 4-16-04, Dr. Mike Denham Interviews.

151. Clark Hoyt, "Will Chiles Walk in Middle of Road?" *Miami Herald,* November 15, 1970.

152. David Royse, "Colleagues prize what little Chiles put to paper," *News Chief,* December 12, 1999.

153. Mike Denham interviews Jack Pridgen, March 5, 2004, Dr. Mike Denham Interviews.

154. James Denham (J. Mike Denham) interviews Bill Ellsworth 3-5-04, Dr. Mike Denham Interviews.

155. Mike Denham interviews Snow Martin Jr. 4-16-04, Dr. Mike Denham Interviews.

156. Mike Denham interviews Reubin Askew. 10-19-06, Dr. Mike Denham Interviews.

157. Mike Denham interviews Joe P. Ruthven 1-06-04, Dr. Mike Denham Interviews.

158. Ibid.

159. Mike Denham interviews Snow Martin Jr. 4-16-04, Dr. Mike Denham Interviews.

160. Bill Rufty, "Lakeland's Own Governor," *Lakeland Ledger,* December 13, 1998.

161. Mike Denham interviews Bill Ellsworth 3-5-04, Dr. Mike Denham Interviews.

162. Mike Denham interviews Bill Ellsworth 2-25-05, Dr. Mike Denham Interviews.

163. Ibid.

164. Charles T. Thrift Jr. *Of Fact and Fancy...at Florida Southern College* (Lakeland: Florida Southern College Press, 1979), 111.

165. Mike Denham interviews Bill Ellsworth 3-5-04, Dr. Mike Denham Interviews.

166. Mike Denham interviews Burke Kibler 3-24-03, Dr. Mike Denham Interviews.

167. Mike Denham interview Mr. and Mrs. Robert Waters 1-19-04, Dr. Mike Denham Interviews.

168. T. Harry Williams, *Huey Long*, 200.

169. Paul Reid, "Our governor . . . their dad," *Palm Beach Post,* December 16, 1998.

170. Buddy MacKay with Rick Edmonds, *How Florida Happened: The Political Education of Buddy MacKay* (Gainesville: UP of Florida, 2010), 11.

171. Mike Denham interviews Joe P. Ruthven 1-06-04, Dr. Mike Denham Interviews.

172. Mike Denham interviews Jack Pridgen, March 5, 2004, Dr. Mike Denham Interviews.

173. Ibid.

174. Mike Denham interviews Bill Ellsworth 2-25-05, Dr. Mike Denham Interviews.

175. Mike Denham interviews Snow Martin Jr. 4-16-04, Dr. Mike Denham Interviews.

176. Dyckman, *Floridian of His Century,* 9.

177. Ibid., 10.

178. "Polk Back-Country," Editorial, *Lakeland Ledger,* July 8, 1958.

179. Newton, *The Invisible Empire,* 150.

180. Nancy Jarrett, "Lakeland Negro School for Retarded Children in Dire Need of Many Items," *Lakeland Ledger,* May 11, 1958.

181. Anthony Schiappa, "Holland Says Secret Bombshell To Blast Pepper's Senate Hope," *Lakeland Ledger,* July 25, 1958.

182. Cortland Anderson, "Circuit Judge Candidates Tangle as Polk Democratic Rallies Open at Kathleen," *Lakeland Ledger,* August 15, 1958.

183. Cortland Anderson, "Bartowans Hear Candidates Bid for Support," *Lakeland Ledger,* September 5, 1958.

184. Cortland Anderson, "Successful Candidate's Wife Recounts Campaign Adventures," *Lakeland Ledger,* September 16, 1958; Lawton Chiles, Progress Report #21.

185. Ben Funk, "Walking Lawton: Opponents Laughed At Him, But He Grinned At Finish.' *Lakeland Ledger,* January 3, 1971; Cortland Anderson, "Successful Candidate's Wife Recounts Campaign Adventures," *Lakeland Ledger,* September 16, 1958.

186. Lawton Chiles, Progress Report #21.

187. Clark Hoyt, "Will Chiles Walk in Middle of Road?" *Miami Herald,* November 15, 1970.

188. Art Carlson interviews Rhea Chiles, September to November 2003, Art Carlson Interviews.

189. Garth Germond, "Polk-A-Dots." *Tampa Tribune,* March 23, 1970.

John Dos Passos Coggin

190. JudyDoyle and Gary Fineout, "Chiles remembered for courage, vision," *Tallahassee Democrat,* December 13, 1998.

191. Cortland Anderson, "Successful Candidate's Wife Recounts Campaign Adventures," *Lakeland Ledger,* September 16, 1958.

192. Canter Brown, *None Can Have Richer Memories,* 101-102.

193. Mike Denham interviews Jack Pridgen, March 5, 2004, Dr. Mike Denham Interviews.

194. Jac Wilder Versteeg, "Still Walkin' The Walk," *Palm Beach Post,* October 30, 1994.

195. Mike Denham interviews Bill Ellsworth 2-25-05, Dr. Mike Denham Interviews.

196. Mike Denham interviews Joe P. Ruthven 1-06-04, Dr. Mike Denham Interviews.

197. Mike Denham interviews Bill Ellsworth 2-25-05, Dr. Mike Denham Interviews.

198. Tim Nickens, "Chiles leaves footprints in many parts of Florida," *St. Petersburg Times,* December 13, 1998.

199. Randolph Pendleton, "Through long career Chiles was always 'one of the guys,'" *Florida Times-Union,* December 13, 1998.

200. "Surles upset by Chiles for Polk house seat," *Tampa Tribune,* September 10, 1958.

201. Ibid.

202. "The People Have Spoken," Editorial, *Lakeland Ledger,* September 10, 1958.

203. Mike Denham interviews Snow Martin Jr. 4-16-04, Dr. Mike Denham Interviews.

204. Art Carlson interviews Rhea Chiles, September to November 2003, Art Carlson Interviews.

205. Mike Denham interviews Reubin Askew. 10-19-06, Dr. Mike Denham Interviews.

206. Mike Denham interviews Ed Price 8-13-03, Dr. Mike Denham Interviews.

207. Mike Denham interviews Ed Chiles 6-22-2004, Dr. Mike Denham Interviews.

208. Mike Denham interviews Ed Price 8-13-03, Dr. Mike Denham Interviews.

209. Canter Brown, *None Can Have Richer Memories,* 147.

210. Longman, "Who Can Get To Chiles."

211. Jac Wilder Versteeg, "Still Walkin' The Walk," *Palm Beach Post,* October 30, 1994.

212. D.G. Lawrence, "Chiles Set to Go If Holland Retires," *Orlando Sentinel,* October 19, 1969.

213. Mike Denham interviews Homer Hooks 7-29-03, Dr. Mike Denham Interviews.

214. Bill Rufty, "Has Lawton Chiles' Legacy Faded?" *Lakeland Ledger,* January 17, 2005.

215. Mike Denham interviews Reubin Askew. 10-19-06, Dr. Mike Denham Interviews.

216. Randolph Pendleton, "Through long career Chiles was always 'one of the guys,'" *Florida Times-Union,* December 13, 1998.

217. Mike Denham interviews Snow Martin Jr. 4-16-04, Dr. Mike Denham Interviews.

218. Bill Rufty, "Lakeland's Own Governor," *Lakeland Ledger,* December 13, 1998.

219. Mike Denham interviews Snow Martin Jr. 4-16-04, Dr. Mike Denham Interviews.

220. John Kennedy, "Chiles' Wealth Came from Success in Real Estate," *Orlando Sentinel,* October 21, 1994.

221. Philip Carter, "Florida: Reporting Law Helps," *Washington Post,* November 22, 1970.

222. Clark Hoyt, "Will Chiles Walk in Middle of Road?" *Miami Herald,* November 15, 1970.

223. James Malone, "Chiles Finds Even Walking Takes Money," *St. Petersburg Times,* October 19, 1970.

224. Michael Griffin, "2 partners, incredible legacy," *Orlando Sentinel,* December 20, 1998.

225. James Malone, "Chiles Finds Even Walking Takes Money," *St. Petersburg Times,* October 19, 1970.

226. Ibid.

227. Margaret Talev and David Cox, "More to legacy than just politics," *Tampa Tribune,* December 13, 1998.

228. Dr. Mike Denham interviews Homer Hooks 7-29-03, Dr. Mike Denham Interviews.

229. Art Carlson interviews Dexter Douglass, 2003, Art Carlson Interviews.

230. Ben Funk, "Walking Lawton: Opponents Laughed At Him, But He Grinned At Finish.' *Lakeland Ledger,* January 3, 1971.

231. Brian Crowley, "Remembering Walkin' Lawton's 92-day trek across Florida," *Palm Beach Post,* August 19, 1995.

232. Malcom Johnson, "Stunts Don't Often Work," *Milton Press Gazette,* April 2, 1970.

233. Key, *Southern Politics in State and Nation,* 83.

234. Ibid., 84.

235. David Colburn and Lance deHaven-Smith, *Florida's Megatrends: Critical Issues in Florida* (Gainesville: University Press of Florida, 2002), 4.

236. Mike Denham interviews Burke Kibler 4-7-03, Dr. Mike Denham Interviews.

237. Brian Crowley, "Remembering Walkin' Lawton's 92-day trek across Florida," *Palm Beach Post,* August 19, 1995.

238. Art Carlson interviews Bob Graham, 2003, Art Carlson Interviews.

239. Mike Denham interviews Reubin Askew 10-19-06, Dr. Mike Denham Interviews.

240. Lonnie Brown, "Chiles' integrity left own footprint," *Lakeland Ledger,* December 16, 1998.

241. Otis Wragg, "Chiles Starts Voter Walk," *Lakeland Ledger,* March 17, 1970.

242. "Bound for Florida Keys," *Deland Sun News,* March 18, 1970.

243. Lonnie Brown, "Walk Now a Commitment for Lawton Chiles," *Lakeland Ledger,* July 12, 1970.

244. Lonnie Brown, "Chiles' Campaign: 'Crazy,'" *Lakeland Ledger,* September 30, 1970; Bud Chiles, personal papers in his private collection; Otis Wragg, "Chiles Starts Voter Walk," *Lakeland Ledger,* March 17, 1970.

245. Troy Moon, "Down but not out yet, Century dreams of a kinder life in 21st century," *Pensacola News-Journal,* December 30, 1999.

246. Ibid.

247. Cindy George, "More than a Century of history," *Pensacola News-Journal,* March 10, 2002.

248. Ibid.

249. "Demos Hold 3-1 Registration Edge," *Miami Herald,* August 21, 1970.

250. Bill Cotterell, "Cortege will retrace steps of Walkin' Lawton," *Tallahassee Democrat,* December 14, 1998; "Chiles' walk 'invigorating.'" *Lakeland Ledger,* March 18, 1970.

251. Lonnie Brown, "Chiles' Campaign: 'Crazy,'" *Lakeland Ledger,* September 30, 1970.

252. Lonnie Brown, "Walk Now a Commitment for Lawton Chiles," *Lakeland Ledger,* July 12, 1970.

253. "Bound for Florida Keys," *Deland Sun News,* March 18, 1970.

254. John Van Gieson, "That Speck on the Horizon: It's Walkin' Lawton Chiles," *Lakeland Ledger,* March 25, 1970.

255. Thomas Pfankuch, "Chiles back in Century," *Florida Times-Union,* December 15, 1998.

256. Lawton Chiles, Progress Report 1.

257. "Chiles' walk 'invigorating.'" *Lakeland Ledger,* March 18, 1970.

258. "Bound for Florida Keys," *Deland Sun News,* March 18, 1970.

259. Lawton Chiles, Progress Report 1.

260. "Bound for Florida Keys," *Deland Sun News,* March 18, 1970.

261. Linda Kleindienst and Michael Griffin, "Today is 'Walkin' Lawton's' last trek," *Orlando Sentinel,* December 15, 1998.

262. "Chiles' walk 'invigorating.'" *Lakeland Ledger,* March 18, 1970.

263. "Chiles' last trip closing a circle," *Palm Beach Post,* December 15, 1998.

264. "Bound for Florida Keys," *Deland Sun News,* March 18, 1970.

265. "Chiles' last trip closing a circle," *Palm Beach Post,* December 15, 1998.

266. John Van Gieson, "That Speck on the Horizon: It's Walkin' Lawton Chiles," *Lakeland Ledger,* March 25, 1970.

267. Bill Cotterell, "Cortege will retrace steps of Walkin' Lawton," *Tallahassee Democrat,* December 14, 1998.

268. Julian Clarkson, "Stand Up and March," June 1971, private collection of Bud Chiles.

269. Lawton Chiles, Progress Report 1.

270. Ibid., Report 2.

271. "Walkie-Talkie Candidate," Editorial, *Tampa Tribune,* March 19, 1970.

272. Charlie Robins, "Walk on, Lawton," *Tampa Times,* March 19, 1970.

273. Douglas Waitley, *Best Backroads of Florida* (Sarasota: Pineapple Press, 2003), 155.

274. *Baker Block Museum Journal.* North Okaloosa Historical Association. http://www.rootsweb.com/~flbbm/baker.htm. 2007.

275. Waitley, *Best Backroads of Florida,* 152.

276. Ibid., 131.

277. Lawton Chiles, Progress Report 4.

278. Gary Mormino, *Land of Sunshine, State of Dreams* (Gainesville: UP of Florida, 2005), 159.

279. Lawton Chiles, Progress Report 4.

280. Margaret Talev and David Cox, "More to legacy than just politics," *Tampa Tribune,* December 13, 1998.

281. Lawton Chiles, Progress Report 4.

282. Martin Dyckman, "A man of and for the people," *St. Petersburg Times,* December 14, 1998.

283. Lawton Chiles, Progress Report 5.

284. Waitley, *Best Backroads of Florida,* 148.

285. Ibid., 150.

286. Visitor's Brochure, Town of DeFuniak Springs Visitors Bureau.

287. Bud Chiles, personal papers in his private collection.

288. Lawton Chiles, Progress Report 7.

289. Mike Wright, "Walking Lawton Chiles Makes It to Tallahassee," *Tallahassee Democrat,* April 4, 1970.

290. Kathy Wolf and Sandra Friend, *An Explorer's Guide: North Florida & the Florida Panhandle* (Woodstock: Countryman Press, 2007), 309.

291. John Van Gieson, "That Speck on the Horizon: It's Walkin' Lawton Chiles," *Lakeland Ledger,* .March 25, 1970.

292. Ibid.

293. Michal Strutin, *Florida State Parks,* (Seattle: Mountaineers Books, 2000), 38.

294. Lawton Chiles, Progress Report 7.

295. Dick Bothwell, "Out Walking Florida For Some Votes," *Lakeland Ledger,* March 25, 1970.

296. Lawton Chiles, Progress Report 8.

297. Lonnie Brown, "Senate Race A Fast Walk," *Lakeland Ledger,* March 29, 1970.

298. Lonnie Brown, "Walk Now a Commitment for Lawton Chiles," *Lakeland Ledger,* July 12, 1970.

299. Lawton Chiles, Progress Report 8.

300. Ibid.

301. Waitley, *Best Backroads of Florida,* 123.

302. Lawton Chiles, Progress Report 9.

303. Alan Judd, "Touring Familiar Roads," *Lakeland Ledger,* December 16, 1998.

304. Bill Cotterell, "Grown children fondly remember father," *Tallahassee Democrat,* December 16, 1998.

305. Lawton Chiles, Progress Report 11.

306. Waitley, *Best Backroads of Florida,* 135.

307. Lawton Chiles, Progress Report 11.

308. Gil Nelson, *Exploring Wild Northwest Florida: A Guide to Finding the Natural Areas and Wildlife of the Panhandle* (Sarasota: Pineapple Press, 1995), 182, 186.

309. Ibid., 186.

310. Tom Henderson, "Walk Provides Time To Listen, Think," *Lakeland Ledger,* April 5, 1970.

311. Waitley, *Best Backroads of Florida,* 132.

312. Lawton Chiles, Progress Report 12.

313. Waitley, *Best Backroads of Florida,* 130.

314. Ibid.

315. Mormino, *Land of Sunshine, State of Dreams,* 17.

316. "NAACP Chief: Black Voters 'Striking Out,'" *Miami Herald,* August 23, 1970.

317. Lawton Chiles, Progress Report 13.

318. Wolf and Friend, *An Explorer's Guide,* 227.

319. Malcom Johnson, "Stunts Don't Often Work," *Milton Press Gazette,* April 2, 1970.

320. Waitley, *Best Backroads of Florida,* 103.

321. Mike Wright, "Walking Lawton Chiles Makes It to Tallahassee," *Tallahassee Democrat,* April 4, 1970.

322. Lawton Chiles, Progress Report 14.

323. Tom Henderson, "Walk Provides Time To Listen, Think," *Lakeland Ledger,* April 5, 1970.

324. Ibid.

325. Ibid.

326. "In Florida Candidates Face 3 Types of Voters," *New York Times*, March 12, 1972.

327. Mike Wright, "Walking Lawton Chiles Makes It to Tallahassee," *Tallahassee Democrat,* April 4, 1970.

328. Julian Clarkson, "Stand Up and March," June 1971, private collection of Bud Chiles.

329. Gary Fineout, "Chiles to make final journey," *Tallahassee Democrat,* December 15, 1998.

330. Mike Wright, "Walking Lawton Chiles Makes It to Tallahassee," *Tallahassee Democrat,* April 4, 1970.

331. Duane Bradford, "Turning 40 Victory For 'Walkin' Lawton,'" *Lakeland Ledger,* April 14, 1970.

332. Lawton Chiles, Progress Report 16.

333. Ibid.

334. Lonnie Brown, "Walk Now a Commitment for Lawton Chiles," *Lakeland Ledger,* July 12, 1970.

335. Julian Clarkson, "Stand Up and March," June 1971, private collection of Bud Chiles.

336. Ben Funk, "Walking Lawton: Opponents Laughed At Him, But He Grinned At Finish.' *Lakeland Ledger,* January 3, 1971.

337. Waitley, *Best Backroads of Florida,* 112.

338. Mormino, *Land of Sunshine, State of Dreams,,* 187.

339. Waitley, *Best Backroads of Florida,* 112.

340. Lawton Chiles, Progress Report 15.

341. Ibid., Report 15.

342. Art Carlson interviews Dexter Douglass, 2003, Art Carlson Interviews.

343. Lawton Chiles, Progress Report 15.

344. Ibid., Report 16.

345. Ibid., Report 17.

346. Ibid., Report 23.

347. Ibid., Report 17.

348. Waitley, *Best Backroads of Florida,* 84.

349. Lawton Chiles, Progress Report 18.

350. Ibid., Report 18.

351. "Chiles Opposes Volunteer Army," *Lakeland Ledger,* June 20, 1970.

352. Lawton Chiles, Progress Report 18.

353. Ibid., Report 18.

354. Jim Dawkins, "Chiles Eyes Barge Canal," *Lakeland Ledger,* June 25, 1970.

355. Ibid.

356. Ibid.

357. Lawton Chiles, Progress Report 19.

358. Ibid.

359. Julian Clarkson, "Stand Up and March," June 1971, private collection of Bud Chiles.

360. Lawton Chiles, Progress Report 19.

361. Ibid.

362. Lawton Chiles, Progress Report 20.

363. Ibid.

364. Ibid.

365. Lawton Chiles, Progress Report 21.

366. Mormino, *Land of Sunshine, State of Dreams,* 167.

367. Lawton Chiles, Progress Report 21.

368. Lonnie Brown, "Chiles Walks Home on Campaign Trail," *Lakeland Ledger,* July 6, 1970.

369. Lonnie Brown, "Walk Now a Commitment for Lawton Chiles," *Lakeland Ledger,* July 12, 1970.

370. Ibid.

371. Lonnie Brown, "Chiles' integrity left own footprint," *Lakeland Ledger,* December 16, 1998.

372. Lonnie Brown, "Walk Now a Commitment for Lawton Chiles," *Lakeland Ledger,* July 12, 1970; Lawton Chiles, Progress Report 21.

373. Lonnie Brown, "Walk Now a Commitment for Lawton Chiles," *Lakeland Ledger,* July 12, 1970.

374. Ibid.

375. Ibid.

376. Lonnie Brown, "Chiles' integrity left own footprint," *Lakeland Ledger,* December 16, 1998.

377. Lonnie Brown, "Walk Now a Commitment for Lawton Chiles," *Lakeland Ledger,* July 12, 1970.

378. Lawton Chiles, Progress Report 21.

379. Ibid., Report 22.

380. Ibid., Report 23; Julian Clarkson, "Stand Up and March," June 1971, private collection of Bud Chiles.

381. Julian Clarkson, "Stand Up and March."

382. Ibid.; Garth Germond, "Polk-A-Dots." *Tampa Tribune,* March 23, 1970.

383. Lawton Chiles, Progress Report 23.

384. Bruce Hunt, *Visiting Small-Town Florida* (Sarasota: Pineapple Press, 2003), 152.

385. Lawton Chiles, Progress Report 23.

386. Art Carlson interviews Rhea Chiles, 2003, Art Carlson Interviews.

387. Hunt, *Visiting Small-Town Florida,* 153.

388. Ste. Claire, *Cracker,* 95.

389. Mormino, *Land of Sunshine, State of Dreams,* 221.

390. Ibid., 213.

391. Lawton Chiles, Progress Report 24.

392. Ibid.

393. Brian Crowley, "Remembering Walkin' Lawton's 92-day trek across Florida," *Palm Beach Post,* August 19, 1995.

394. Lawton Chiles, Progress Report 24.

395. Margaret Talev and David Cox, "More to legacy than just politics," *Tampa Tribune,* December 13, 1998; Julian Clarkson, "Stand Up and March," June 1971, private collection of Bud Chiles.

396. Bill Foley, "Chiles kept path set in '59," *Florida Times-Union,* December 20, 1998.

397. Julian Clarkson, "Stand Up and March," June 1971, private collection of Bud Chiles.

398. "Chiles Ends State Walk; Gurney Admits Violation," *Miami Herald,* August 20, 1970.

399. Julian Clarkson, "Stand Up and March," June 1971, private collection of Bud Chiles.

400. Mike Denham interviews Fred Schultz 7-09-04, Dr. Mike Denham Interviews.

401. Julian Clarkson, "Stand Up and March," June 1971, private collection of Bud Chiles.

402. "1970 Endorsements: For U.S. Senator," *Miami Herald,* August 25, 1970.

403. "$500 or More Contributors To U.S. Senate Candidates," *Miami Herald,* August 23, 1970.

404. William Amlong, "Schultz Outspends the Salary of U.S. Senate Seat He Seeks," *Miami Herald,* August 23, 1970.

405. Julian Clarkson, "Stand Up and March," June 1971, private collection of Bud Chiles.

406. Mike Denham interviews Fred Schultz 7-09-04, Dr. Mike Denham Interviews

407. Julian Clarkson, "Stand Up and March," June 1971, private collection of Bud Chiles.

408. Bill Foley, "Chiles kept path set in '59," *Florida Times-Union,* December 20, 1998.

409. "Walkin' Lawton Wins In Stride," *Lakeland Ledger,* September 30, 1970.

410. Charles Stafford, "Post Office Sends Bogus Newsletters 'Back' to Cramer." *Miami Herald,* October 11, 1970.

411. Lonnie Brown, "Chiles' Campaign: 'Crazy,'" *Lakeland Ledger,* September 30, 1970.

412. Julian Clarkson, "Stand Up and March," June 1971, private collection of Bud Chiles.

413. Lonnie Brown, "Chiles' Campaign: 'Crazy,'" *Lakeland Ledger,* September 30, 1970.

414. Julian Clarkson, "Stand Up and March," June 1971, private collection of Bud Chiles.

415. Richard Harwood, "Florida Electorate Remains Apathetic," *Washington Post,* September 6, 1970.

416. David R. Colburn, *From Yellow Dog Democrats to Red State Republicans: Florida and Its Politics since 1940* (Gainesville: UP of Florida, 2007), 67.

417. Ibid.

418. Ibid., 68.

419. "Demos Hold 3-1 Registration Edge," *Miami Herald,* August 21, 1970.

420. "NAACP Chief: Black Voters 'Striking Out,'" *Miami Herald,* August 23, 1970.

421. Robert P. Steed and Laurence W. Moreland, eds., *Writing Southern Politics: Contemporary Interpretations and Future Directions* (UP of Kentucky, 2006), x-xi.

422. Ibid., xi.

423. "Walkin' Lawton Wins In Stride," *Lakeland Ledger,* September 30, 1970.

424. Charles Stafford, "Post Office Sends Bogus Newsletters 'Back' to Cramer." *Miami Herald,* October 11, 1970.

425. Lonnie Brown, "Chiles Plans Tough Battle," *Lakeland Ledger,* October 1, 1970.

426. Julian Clarkson, "Stand Up and March," June 1971, private collection of Bud Chiles.

427. Roland Evans and Robert Novak, "Florida: A Battle of Styles," *Washington Post,* October 19, 1970.

428. Julian Clarkson, "Stand Up and March," June 1971, private collection of Bud Chiles.

429. "$1,000 Cocktail Party vs. $1 Chicken Picnic," *St. Petersburg Times,* October 15, 1970.

430. Janet Chusmir, "Martha Mitchell Really 'Liberated,'" *Miami Herald,* October 14, 1970.

431. Julian Clarkson, "Stand Up and March," June 1971, private collection of Bud Chiles.

432. "Mitchell Boosts Cramer," *St. Petersburg Times,* October 14, 1970.

433. Robert Shaw, "300 Chiles supporters eat $1-a-box chicken." *Miami Herald,* October 28, 1982.

434. Bill Rufty and Carl Hulse, "The Walking Senator," *Lakeland Ledger,* December 13, 1998.

435. Robert Shaw, "300 Chiles supporters eat $1-a-box chicken." *Miami Herald,* October 28, 1982.

436. Bill Purvis, "Cramer Charges Chiles 'Soft' On Radicals." *Tampa Tribune,* October 30, 1970.

437. Charles Hendrick, "Boosts From Holland Repaid Chiles For Walk In 1940 Governor Race," *Tampa Tribune,* November 8, 1970.

438. Office of Senator Lawton Chiles, "A Walk Through The Record of Lawton Chiles, U.S. Senator, Florida," 1976, University of Florida Archive, Series 2a, Box 1.

439. Bill Purvis, "Cramer to Print 'Truth Tabloid' In 9 Papers," *Tampa Tribune,* October 27, 1970.

440. Julian Clarkson, "Stand Up and March," June 1971, private collection of Bud Chiles.

441. "Chiles for Integrity," Editorial, *St. Petersburg Times,* October 25, 1970.

442. "Mr. Nixon's Always Welcome, But Floridians Can Decide," Editorial, *Miami Herald,* October 28, 1970.

443. Philip Carter, "It Really IS a Footrace in Florida," *Washington Post,* October 25, 1970.

444. David Watson and Bill Purvis, "Nixon Boosts Kirk, Cramer," *Tampa Tribune,* October 28, 1970.

445. Charles Hendrick, "Chiles Would 'Probably' Not Continue Private Law Work," *Tampa Tribune,* October 30, 1970.

446. "Police Clear Path." *Tampa Tribune,* October 30, 1970.

447. Bill Purvis, "Cramer Charges Chiles 'Soft' On Radicals." *Tampa Tribune,* October 30, 1970.

448. Michael Richardson, "Numb Chiles 'Aware of Responsibility,'" *St. Petersburg Times,* November 4, 1970.

449. Ibid.

450. Charles Hendrick, "Chiles Claims Senate Victory," *Tampa Tribune,* November 4, 1970.

451. Michael Richardson, "Numb Chiles 'Aware of Responsibility,'" *St. Petersburg Times,* November 4, 1970.

452. Jill Young Miller, "Rhea Chiles 'I Call My Own Shots'; Governor Discusses His 'Conscience,'" *Sun-Sentinel,* January 13, 1991.

453. Michael Richardson, "Chiles' Cadre: Who Will Be In It?" *St. Petersburg Times,* November 9,

1970.

454. Letter to Lawton Chiles from George McGovern, November 5, 1970, University of Florida Archive, Series 2b, Box 1.

455. Letter to Lawton Chiles from Edward Kennedy, November 5, 1970, University of Florida Archive, Series 2b, Box 1.

456. Jim Dawkins, "Chiles: A Legend Is Born," *Lakeland Ledger,* November 10, 1970.

457. JudyDoyle and Gary Fineout, "Chiles remembered for courage, vision," *Tallahassee Democrat,* December 13, 1998; Michael Richardson, "Chiles Looks Cautiously at His Future in U.S. Senate," *St. Petersburg Times,* November 5, 1970.

458. Philip Carter, "Florida: Reporting Law Helps," *Washington Post,* November 22, 1970.

459. "Chiles Tells City: 'Thanks,'" *St. Petersburg Times,* November 7, 1970.

460. John Harwood, "The quest for a different role," *St. Petersburg Times,* October 14, 1990.

461. Robert A. Caro, *The Years of Lyndon Johnson: Master of the Senate* (New York: Vintage Books, 2003), 23.

462. Bernard Nossiter, "Sen. Holland Won't Run Again," *Washington Post,* November 13, 1969.

463. Barbara Frye, "Running Easy to Holland But Not to His Successor," *Tallahassee Democrat,* November 16, 1969.

464. Clark Hoyt, "Will Chiles Walk in Middle of Road?" *Miami Herald,* November 15, 1970.

465. Caro, *The Years of Lyndon Johnson,* 81.

466. Ibid., 79-84.

467. Clark Hoyt, "Will Chiles Walk in Middle of Road?" *Miami Herald,* November 15, 1970.

468. Michael Richardson, "Chiles' Cadre: Who Will Be In It?" *St. Petersburg Times,* November 9, 1970.

469. Clark Hoyt, "Will Chiles Walk in Middle of Road?" *Miami Herald,* November 15, 1970.

470. Lonnie Brown, "Polk Honors Senator-Elect Lawton Chiles," *Lakeland Ledger,* December 18, 1970.

471. Michael Barone, Grant Ujifusa, and Douglas Matthews, *The Almanac of American Politics* (Boston: Gambit Publisher, 1972), 139; Morris Harth, ed. *The New York Times Encyclopedic Almanac, 1972* (New York: New York Times, 1971), 157.

472. Lonnie Brown, "Polk Honors Senator-Elect Lawton Chiles," *Lakeland Ledger,* December 18, 1970.

473. Jim Dawkins, "Chiles: A Legend Is Born," *Lakeland Ledger,* November 10, 1970.

474. Colburn and deHaven-Smith, *Florida's Megatrends,* 40.

475. David Colburn and Lance deHaven-Smith, *Government in the Sunshine State: Florida Since Statehood* (Gainesville: University Press of Florida, 1999), 32.

476. Ibid., 33-34.

477. Margaret Talev and David Cox, "More to legacy than just politics," *Tampa Tribune,* December

13, 1998.

478. Jack Anderson, "Air Guard Uses Birch Film on Vietnam," *Washington Post,* May 10, 1971.

479. Mike Denham interviews Reubin Askew. 10-19-06, Dr. Mike Denham Interviews; Art Carlson interviews Reubin Askew, September to November 2003, Art Carlson Interviews.

480. Art Carlson interviews Senator Sam Nunn, September – November 2003, Art Carlson Interviews.

481. Hilda Maness Lynch, "Lawton Chiles: Democratic Senator from Florida," *Ralph Nader Congress Project: Citizens Look at Congress* (Grossman Publishers, 1972), 10.

482. "Chiles Political Career," *Palm Beach Post,* December 13, 1998.

483. Ellen Debenport, "Plaid-clad Chiles shows his colors." *St. Petersburg Times,* August 29, 1990.

484. Office of Senator Lawton Chiles, "A Walk Through The Record of Lawton Chiles."

485. Ibid.

486. Caro, *The Years of Lyndon Johnson,* xiv.

487. Earl Black, *Southern Governors and Civil Rights: Racial Segregation as a Campaign Issue in the Second Reconstruction* (Cambridge: Harvard University Press, 1976), 82.

488. Art Carlson interviews Senator Sam Nunn, September – November 2003, Art Carlson Interviews.

489. Art Carlson interviews Rhea Chiles, September to November 2003, Art Carlson Interviews.

490. Art Carlson interviews Senator Sam Nunn, September – November 2003, Art Carlson Interviews.

491. Brendan Farrington, "Florida House a Haven in Washington," *Lakeland Ledger,* November 22, 2003.

492. Jill Young Miller, "Rhea Chiles 'I Call My Own Shots'; Governor Discusses His 'Conscience,'" *Sun-Sentinel,* January 13, 1991.

493. Mike Denham interviews Burke Kibler 4-13-03, Dr. Mike Denham Interviews.

494. Longman, "Who Can Get To Chiles."

495. Mike Denham interviews Mr. and Mrs. Robert Waters 1-19-04, Dr. Mike Denham Interviews.

496. Ibid.

497. The Associated Press, "Children say Chiles always there for them," *Tampa Tribune,* December 21, 1998.

498. Brian Crowley, "Remembering Walkin' Lawton's 92-day trek across Florida," *Palm Beach Post,* August 19, 1995.

499. Former U.S. Senator Sam Nunn, The Economic Club of Florida, A Tribute to Rhea Grafton Chiles, Thursday, February 12, 2009, transcript electronically provided by Sam Nunn to author.

500. Beth McLeod, "The Women Beside the Candidates," *Palm Beach Post,* November 4, 1990.

501. "For the Record: Trading Public Trust For Secret Meetings," *Washington Post,* March 9, 1973.

502. Tom Fiedler, "Chiles reflected: 'there is nothing that I have to do,'" *Miami Herald,* December 13, 1998.

503. Art Carlson interviews Bob Graham, September to November 2003, Art Carlson Interviews.

504. Art Carlson interviews Rhea Chiles, September to November 2003, Art Carlson Interviews.

505. Martha Angle, "Chiles Sets Limit For Gifts at $10," *Washington Star*, June 16, 1975.

506. Lynch, "Lawton Chiles," *Ralph Nader Congress Project*, 8.

507. Mike Denham interviews Burke Kibler 4-7-03, Dr. Mike Denham Interviews.

508. Mike Denham interview Mr. and Mrs. Robert Waters 1-19-04, Dr. Mike Denham Interviews.

509. Art Carlson interviews Senator Sam Nunn, September – November 2003, Art Carlson Interviews.

510. Bud Chiles, personal papers in his private collection.

511. Compiled by Jill A. Elish, "In Their Own Words," *Florida Living*, April 1999.

512. Everette Williard, "Chiles Sees Florida in Demo Fold," *Florida Times-Union*, July 7, 1976.

513. "Chiles thanks voters from roadside; Grady blames media for loss," *St. Petersburg Times*, November 4, 1976.

514. Kathleen Laufenberg, "Healthy Start: Chiles' legacy." *Tallahassee Democrat*, December 20, 1998.

515. Morris Udall, interview by Hedrick Smith, January 23, 1986, quoted in Hedrick Smith, *The Power Game: How Washington Works* (New York: Random House, 1988), 27-28.

516. Hedrick Smith, *The Power Game*, 26.

517. Kathleen Laufenberg, "Healthy Start: Chiles' legacy." *Tallahassee Democrat*, December 20, 1998.

518. Art Carlson interviews Senator Sam Nunn, September – November 2003, Art Carlson Interviews.

519. William Safire, *Lend Me Your Ears: Great Speeches in History* (New York: W. W. Norton, 2004), 954-955.

520. Ibid., 955.

521. "Walkin' Lawton Fusses Over Budgets," *The South*, October 1978, 17.

522. Al Burt, *The Tropic of Cracker* (Gainesville: University Press of Florida, 1999), 19-20.

523. Robert Shaw, "GOP had golden chance in Florida: dogged by problems, 'they blew it,'"*Miami Herald*, November 7, 1982.

524. Sam Nunn, Lawton Chiles Eulogy, December 16, 1998, Tallahassee, Florida, transcript electronically provided by Sam Nunn to author.

525. JudyDoyle and Gary Fineout, "Chiles remembered for courage, vision," *Tallahassee Democrat*, December 13, 1998.

526. Robert Shaw, "300 Chiles supporters eat $1-a-box chicken." *Miami Herald*, October 28, 1982.

527. Robert Shaw and Paul Anderson, "Chiles, Poole Begin Sparring for 'Tough' Senate Campaign," *Miami Herald*, October 7, 1982.

528. "Mrs. Ruthven, Senator Chiles' Sister." *Miami Herald*, August 22, 1982.

529. Lloyd Dunkelberger and Alan Judd, "Gov. Lawton Chiles Dies of Heart Attack at 68," *Lakeland Ledger*, December 13, 1998; Joe W. Chiles Sr., "Chiles Family Tree," October 22, 2000, personal papers of Joe W. Chiles Jr.

530. Paul Anderson, "Chiles, opponent dispute why he won," *Miami Herald,* November 4, 1982.

531. Tom Fiedler, "Chiles describes battle to ward off depression," *Miami Herald,* April 17, 1990.

532. Robert Shaw, "Chiles welcomes new challenge as top Democrat on budget panel," *Miami Herald,* December 2, 1982.

533. Bill Rufty and Carl Hulse, "The Walking Senator," *Lakeland Ledger,* December 13, 1998.

534. Paul Anderson, "Senator Chiles: From dead last to the fore," *Miami Herald,* November 25, 1984.

535. David Durenburger, interview by Hedrick Smith, May 9, 1986, quoted in Smith, *The Power Game,* 109.

536. MacKay, *How Florida Happened,* 71-72.

537. Paul Anderson, "Senator Chiles: From dead last to the fore," *Miami Herald,* November 25, 1984.

538. Jonathan Peterson and R.A. Zaldivar, "Chiles seeks to lead party in U.S. Senate, wants Democrats to unseat Byrd," *Miami Herald,* December 7, 1984.

539. Helen Dewar, "Byrd Reelected Minority Leader of the Senate," *Washington Post,* December 13, 1984.

540. Mary Ellen Klas, "Chiles' depression surfaced in '86; signs emerged after heart bypass surgery," *Palm Beach Post,* August 21, 1990.

541. Mike Denham interviews Burke Kibler 4-13-03, Dr. Mike Denham Interviews.

542. Craig Pittman, "Chiles' health an issue for years," *St. Petersburg Times,* December 13, 1998.

543. Bill Rufty, "Chiles Was a Political Reporter's Dream: Colorful, but Sharp," *Lakeland Ledger,* December 14, 1998.

544. Candace Samolinski, "Polk residents proudly remember their native son," *Tampa Tribune,* December 13, 1998.

545. Art Carlson interviews Senator Sam Nunn, September – November 2003, Art Carlson Interviews.

546. John Harwood, "The quest for a different role," *St. Petersburg Times,* October 14, 1990.

547. Laura Parker, "Lawton Chiles, firing up after 'burnout,'" *Washington Post,* July 2, 1990.

548. JudyDoyle and Gary Fineout, "Chiles remembered for courage, vision," *Tallahassee Democrat,* December 13, 1998.

549. Laura Parker, "Lawton Chiles, firing up after 'burnout,'" *Washington Post,* July 2, 1990.

550. Tom Fiedler, "Chiles describes battle to ward off depression," *Miami Herald,* April 17, 1990.

551. Laura Parker, "Lawton Chiles, firing up after 'burnout,'" *Washington Post,* July 2, 1990.

552. Martin Merzer, "He kept it real by holding fast to his beliefs, ideals," *Tallahassee Democrat,* December 13, 1998.

553. Mike Williams, "Florida's governor is wounded—but still walkin'—after the most bruising campaign of his long political life," *Atlanta Journal-Constitution*, November 13, 1994.

554. JudyDoyle and Gary Fineout, "Chiles remembered for courage, vision," *Tallahassee Democrat,* December 13, 1998.

555. Bill Rufty and Carl Hulse, "The Walking Senator," *Lakeland Ledger,* December 13, 1998.

556. Mike Denham interviews Burke Kibler 4-13-03, Dr. Mike Denham Interviews.

557. Tom Fiedler, "Chiles describes battle to ward off depression," *Miami Herald,* April 17, 1990.

558. Mary Ellen Klas, "'I was locked in,' Chiles says of days on Capitol Hill," *Palm Beach Post,* May 13, 1990.

559. Tom Fiedler, "Listening to that inner voice," *Miami Herald,* April 15, 1990.

560. Art Carlson interviews Rhea Chiles, September to November 2003, Art Carlson Interviews.

561. Art Carlson interviews Reubin Askew, September to November 2003, Art Carlson Interviews.

562. Mike Denham interviews Joe P. Ruthven, 1-06-04, Dr. Mike Denham Interviews.

563. Mary Ellen Klas, "'I was locked in,' Chiles says of days on Capitol Hill," *Palm Beach Post,* May 13, 1990.

564. Mike Denham interviews Burke Kibler 4-13-03. , Dr. Mike Denham Interviews

565. Laura Parker, "Lawton Chiles, firing up after 'burnout,'" *Washington Post,* July 2, 1990.

566. Ken Cummins, "Chiles aims to kindle reformist spirit," *Sun-Sentinel,* April 14, 1990.

567. Beth McLeod, "The Women Beside the Candidates," *Palm Beach Post,* November 4, 1990.

568. Ellen Debenport, "The easy part is over for Chiles and MacKay," *St. Petersburg Times,* November 8, 1990.

569. Ellen Debenport and Lucy Morgan, "No office but a lot of chairs," *St. Petersburg Times,* January 7, 1991.

570. Mickey Higginbotham, "Florida's best-loved 'Cracker' to be sworn in a final time." *Tallahassee Democrat,* January 3, 1995.

571. Tim Nickens and Tom Fiedler, "Chiles says he's being treated for depression," *Miami Herald,* April 14, 1990.

572. Ken Cummins, "Chiles aims to kindle reformist spirit," *Sun-Sentinel,* April 14, 1990.

573. Tom Fiedler, "Chiles describes battle to ward off depression," *Miami Herald,* April 17, 1990.

574. John C. Van Gieson, "Chiles says slip in pep got him back on Prozac," *Orlando Sentinel,* August 8, 1990.

575. Ellen Debenport, "Chiles, Nelson load their guns," *St. Petersburg Times,* September 2, 1990.

576. Lucy Morgan, "Georgia's Senator Nunn joins Chiles," *St. Petersburg Times,* October 26, 1990.

577. Lucy Morgan, Bill Moss, and Charlotte Sutton, "Prize-winning author assails 'stigma' of depression." *St. Petersburg Times,* April 29, 1990.

578. Mike Denham interviews Burke Kibler 4-13-03, Dr. Mike Denham Interviews.

579. MacKay, *How Florida Happened*, 124.

580. Ibid., 124.

581. Mike Denham interviews Burke Kibler 4-13-03, Dr. Mike Denham Interviews.

582. Ellen Debenport, "Plaid-clad Chiles shows his colors." *St. Petersburg Times,* August 29, 1990.

John Dos Passos Coggin

583. Longman, "Who Can Get To Chiles."

584. Bill Moss, "Budget forecasts are gloomy; Chiles seeks cuts," *St. Petersburg Times,* December 5, 1990.

585. Ellen Debenport, "Chiles lets inner voice call his spots," *St. Petersburg Times,* October 21, 1990.

586. MacKay, *How Florida Happened,* 132.

587. JudyDoyle and Gary Fineout, "Chiles remembered for courage, vision," *Tallahassee Democrat,* December 13, 1998.

588. Charlotte Sutton, "Chiles inauguration plans open, free, but not simple," *St. Petersburg Times,* December 6, 1990.

589. John McKinnon, "Chiles is planning a people's inaugural," *St. Petersburg Times,* November 23, 1990.

590. Mary Ellen Klas, "'I was locked in,' Chiles says of days on Capitol Hill," *Palm Beach Post,* May 13, 1990.

591. Linda Kleindienst, "Children at heart of governor's legacy," *Sun-Sentinel,* December 13, 1998.

592. Lucy Morgan, "Chiles undaunted by pessimistic outlook," *St. Petersburg Times,* January 6, 1991.

593. John McKinnon, "Chiles chooses top campaign aide for chief of staff," *St. Petersburg Times,* November 18, 1990.

594. Jill Young Miller, "Rhea Chiles 'I Call My Own Shots'; Governor Discusses His 'Conscience,'" *Sun-Sentinel,* January 13, 1991.

595. Longman, "Who Can Get To Chiles."

596. Bill Cotterell, "Gov. Chiles Dead," *Tallahassee Democrat,* December 13, 1998; David Colburn, "Chiles' death may close chapter on progressive Democrats." *Gainesville Sun,* December 13, 1998.

597. Bill Moss, "Down home at the mansion," *St. Petersburg Times,* March 14, 1991.

598. Dave Bruns, "Governor tries to calm state fears," *Tallahassee Democrat,* March 6, 1991.

599. Dave Bruns, "Rating the governor," *Tallahassee Democrat,* April 1, 1991.

600. Lucy Morgan, "No free trips?" *St. Petersburg Times,* November 18, 1990.

601. Mark Silva, "Governor's Top Staffers are often a scrappy, bruising bunch," *Miami Herald,* January 19, 1992.

602. "Chiles says budget mess dire," *St. Petersburg Times,* December 6, 1990.

603. John Harwood, "It's the toughest political job in America," *St. Petersburg Times,* November 18, 1990.

604. Robert E. Crew Jr., "Florida: Lawton M. Chiles, Jr., Reinventing State Government," in *Governors and Hard Times,* edited by Thad Beyle (Washington: Congressional Quarterly, 1992), 102.

605. MacKay, *How Florida Happened,* 140-141.

606. John Kennedy and Aaron Deslatte, "Crist channels optimistic Chiles in plan to soothe nerves on TV," *Orlando Sentinel,* February 24, 2008.

607. Philip Longman, "It Gets Worse," *Florida Trend,* September 1992.

608. "Time for a turkey hunt," Editorial, *St. Petersburg Times,* December 11, 1990.

609. Bob McNally, "Turkey hunting a unifying force for political rivals," *Florida Times-Union,* March 31, 2012.

610. Tyler Bridges, "Chiles demanded privacy and often spent long hours alone," *Tallahassee Democrat,* December 15, 1998.

611. Art Carlson interviews Dubose Ausley – September to November 2003, Art Carlson Interviews.

612. Mike Denham interviews Virginia Wetherell. 9-24-04, Dr. Mike Denham Interviews.

613. Randolph Pendleton and Jim Saunders, "Voice of the 'little guy,'" *Florida Times-Union,* December 17, 1998.

614. Jackie Halifax, "Chiles honored as man of great devotion, faith," *Atlanta Journal-Constitution,* December 17, 1998.

615. Bill Cotterell, "For Gov. Chiles: a fine memorial, a fond memory," *Tallahassee Democrat,* December 14, 1998.

616. Adam Yeomans, "A good ol' boy with an offbeat sense of humor," *Tallahassee Democrat,* December 17, 1998.

617. Longman, "Who Can Get To Chiles."

618. JudyDoyle and Gary Fineout, "Chiles remembered for courage, vision," *Tallahassee Democrat,* December 13, 1998.

619. Tom Fiedler, "Chiles' Fall From Grace," *Miami Herald,* December 22, 1991.

620. Steve Bousquet, "Forgotten Lawton," *St. Petersburg Times,* April 3, 2005.

621. Crew, "Florida: Lawton M. Chiles, Jr.," in *Governors and Hard Times,* 84

622. Charlotte Sutton, "Troubled HRS to get a new look," *St. Petersburg Times,* November 27, 1990.

623. Bill Moss and Charlotte Sutton, "Session plods on cautiously," *St. Petersburg Times,* December 12, 1991.

624. Lucy Morgan, "Critics walk all over Lawton's year," *St. Petersburg Times,* January 5, 1992.

625. "Topics for the State of the State" 1992, *Office of the Florida Governor,* Florida State Archives, Series 1467, Carton 2.

626. Longman, "It Gets Worse."

627. Ibid.

628. Mark Silva, "Governor's Top Staffers are often a scrappy, bruising bunch," *Miami Herald,* January 19, 1992.

629. Ibid.

630. Cynthia Barnett, "Students jam Capitol to protest latest cuts," *Gainesville Sun,* February 5, 1992.

631. David Sheets, "Students demand end to education cuts," *Pensacola News Journal,* February 5, 1992.

632. Tom Fiedler, "For Chiles, return of the plaid shirt may not be enough," *Miami Herald,* May 17, 1992.

633. Adam Yeomans, "A good ol' boy with an offbeat sense of humor," *Tallahassee Democrat,* December 17, 1998.

634. John C. Van Gieson, "Housebreaking legislature, dog among Chiles' first-year woes," *Orlando Sentinel,* December 23, 1991.

635. Bill Moss, Charlotte Sutton, and Lucy Morgan, "Chiles tells state: 'It's time we get real,'" *St. Petersburg Times,* June 2, 1992.

636. Philip Longman, "A Mansion Unfit For The Governor," *Florida Trend,* August 1992.

637. Bill Moss, Charlotte Sutton, and Lucy Morgan, "Chiles tells state: 'It's time we get real,'" *St. Petersburg Times,* June 2, 1992.

638. Bill Moss and Kim Norris, "Governor's hot seat gets warm," *St. Petersburg Times,* May 21, 1992.

639. David Royse, "Chiles: man of colorful quips, but few letters." *Tampa Tribune,* December 12, 1999.

640. Tim Nickens, "Chiles leaves footprints in many parts of Florida," *St. Petersburg Times,* December 13, 1998.

641. MacKay, *How Florida Happened,* 144-146.

642. Larry Hubbell, "Ronald Reagan as Presidential Symbol Maker: The Federal Bureaucrat as Loafer, Incompetent Buffoon, Good Ole Boy, and Tyrant," *American Review of Public Administration* 21 (3) [1999]: 237-53.

643. James Q. Wilson, *Bureaucracy: What Agencies Do and Why They Do It* (New York: Basic Books, 1989), 235.

644. Bill Cotterell, "In a state with 3 million retirees, a special agency for the elderly," *Tallahassee Democrat,* October 1, 1991.

645. Lloyd Dunkelberger, "Last Cracker Governor," *Lakeland Ledger,* December 13, 1998.

646. Martin Dyckman, "Someone to fix Chiles' shop," *St. Petersburg Times,* July 19, 1992.

647. Mike Denham interviews Virginia Wetherell. 9-24-04, Dr. Mike Denham Interviews.

648. Michael Young, "Batten down! S. Florida scrambles as Andrew closes in," *Sun-Sentinel,* August 24, 1992.

649. David Barstow, "1-million flee as Florida braces for worst hurricane," *St. Petersburg Times,* August 24, 1992.

650. Craig Dezem, "Hurricane Andrew zeroes in on Miami hundreds of thousands ordered to leave south Florida—emergency declared governor calls out guard units," *Orlando Sentinel,* August 24, 1992.

651. Arnold Markowitz, "An awful howl: Andrew hits hardest in south Dade; at least two dead," *Miami Herald,* August 24, 1992.

652. Karen Baldwin, interview by Eugene F. Provenzo Jr., Miami, FL, September 1, 1992, quoted in Eugene F. Provenzo and Asterie Baker Provenzo, *In the Eye of Hurricane Andrew* (Gainesville: University Press of Florida, 2002), 18.

653. Ibid.

654. Craig Pittman, "Storm's howl fills the ears of survivors," *St. Petersburg Times,* August 18, 2002.

655. Louis Lavelle, "Governor tours hurricane-ravaged South Florida." *Tampa Tribune,* August 26, 1992.

656. Louis Lavelle, "Bush, Chiles find atom bomb-like destruction," *Tampa Tribune,* August 25, 1992.

657. Mark Silva, "Chiles wades into the thick of suffering," *Miami Herald,* August 30, 1992.

658. Richard Coletti, "Swift Recovery, Stronger Economy," *Florida Trend,* October 1992.

659. David Olinger, "Chiles in the eye of the storm," *St. Petersburg Times,* September 20, 1992.

660. Grace Laskis, interview by Lynne Katz, Miami FL, October 17, 1992, quoted in Provenzo and Provenzo, *In the Eye of Hurricane Andrew,* 3.

661. Provenzo and Provenzo, *In the Eye of Hurricane Andrew,* 107

662. David Olinger, "Chiles in the eye of the storm," *St. Petersburg Times,* September 20, 1992.

663. Bill Moss, "Who's that cool sax player? It's Lawton Chiles and storm relief," *St. Petersburg Times,* September 27, 1992; Susannah A. Nesmith, "Chiles joins performers, 'rocks' 500 at grief relief," *Palm Beach Post,* September 27, 1992.

664. Kathleen Laufenberg, "Healthy Start: Chiles' legacy." *Tallahassee Democrat,* December 20, 1998.

665. Art Carlson interviews Rhea Chiles, September to November 2003, Art Carlson Interviews.

666. Bailey Thomson, "Others knew it, too: Lawton Chiles was an advocate for children," *Tallahassee Democrat,* December 16, 1998.

667. Robert Shaw, "In politics, Chiles walks middle road," *Miami Herald,* October 31, 1982.

668. Sue Carlton, "Wilson begged to be shot to end pain," *St. Petersburg Times,* February 5, 1993; Judy Plunkett, "2 Men who set tourist afire get life sentences," *Miami Herald,* October 23, 1993; Margaret Talev and David Cox, "More to legacy than just politics," *Tampa Tribune,* December 13, 1998.; Susan Benesch, "German tourist slain in rental car in Miami," *St. Petersburg Times,* September 9, 1993.

669. Michael Griffin, "2 partners, incredible legacy," *Orlando Sentinel,* December 20, 1998.

670. Colburn, *From Yellow Dog Democrats to Red State Republicans,* 158.

671. S. V. Date, *Jeb: America's next Bush* (New York: Penguin Books, 2007), 8.

672. Ibid., 78.

673. Ibid., 78-79.

674. Ibid., 10.

675. Ibid., 80-81.

676. Ron Thompson, "For candidate Bush, humility's the thing," *St. Petersburg Times,* November 4, 1994.

677. Bill Rufty, "Lakeland's Own Governor," *Lakeland Ledger,* December 13, 1998; Ursula Wiljanen and Doug Nurse, "Chiles receives mixed welcome," *Tampa Tribune,* October 24, 1994.

678. Richard Lacayo, "Bringing Down the House G.O.P. Guerrilla," *Time,* November 7, 1994.

679. Tim Nickens, Terry Neal, and Mark Silva, "Bush, Chiles Draw Viewers As Campaign Trail Nears End," *Miami Herald,* November 3, 1994.

680. Jac Wilder Versteeg, "Still Walkin' The Walk," *Palm Beach Post,* October 30, 1994.

681. "The 'He-Coon' speaks," *St. Petersburg Times,* December 14, 1998.

682. Martin Merzer, "Governor Chiles dies: An enduring legacy of service," *Miami Herald,* December 13, 1998.

683. Date, *Jeb: America's next Bush,* 44.

684. Lloyd Dunkelberger, "Sayings from a Cracker," *Lakeland Ledger,* December 13, 1998.

685. Cinnamon Bair, "Origin of Crackers Is Still Debate," *Lakeland Ledger,* July 22, 2002.

686. Tim Nickens, "Chiles leaves footprints in many parts of Florida," *St. Petersburg Times,* December 13, 1998.

687. Bill Moss, "Possums bring out politicians," *St. Petersburg Times,* August 7, 1994.

688. Colburn, *From Yellow Dog Democrats to Red State Republicans,* 146.

689. Date, *Jeb: America's next Bush,* 154, 177.

690. Colburn, *From Yellow Dog Democrats to Red State Republicans,* 160.

691. Tom Fiedler, Tim Nickens, and Terry Neal, "Chiles-Bush in fierce finale both are forced to defend their attack ads." *Miami Herald,* November 2, 1994.

692. MacKay, *How Florida Happened* 166-168.

693. Mike Denham interviews Fred Schultz 7-09-04, Dr. Mike Denham Interviews.

694. Tim Nickens, Terry Neal, and Mark Silva, "Bush, Chiles Draw Viewers As Campaign Trail Nears End," *Miami Herald,* November 3, 1994.

695. "The 'He-Coon' speaks," *St. Petersburg Times,* December 14, 1998.

696. Brian Crowley and Larry Kaplow, "Fired-up Chiles rips Bush: Challenger struggles to score debate points." *Palm Beach Post,* November 2, 1994.

697. Mike Williams, "Florida's governor is wounded—but still walkin'—after the most bruising campaign of his long political life," *Atlanta Journal-Constitution*, November 13, 1994.

698. Ellen Debenport, "It's Lawton by a little, but Republicans romp," *St. Petersburg Times,* November 9, 1994.

699. Steve Bousquet, "Forgotten Lawton," *St. Petersburg Times,* April 3, 2005.

700. Mike Williams, "Florida's governor is wounded—but still walkin'—after the most bruising campaign of his long political life," *Atlanta Journal-Constitution*, November 13, 1994.

701. Art Carlson interviews Mallory Horne, September to November 2003, Art Carlson Interviews.

702. Brian Crowley, "Remembering Walkin' Lawton's 92-day trek across Florida," *Palm Beach Post,* August 19, 1995.

703. Phil Willon, "Voters pick Chiles: Heavy Democratic turnout in Tampa Bay and South Florida offsets strong conservative GOP support," *Tampa Tribune,* November 9, 1994.

704. Colburn, *From Yellow Dog Democrats to Red State Republicans,* 148.

705. MacKay, *How Florida Happened,* 45.

706. Ron Matus, "Area friends recall Chiles' gentle touch," *Gainesville Sun,* December 13, 1998.

707. Bill Cotterell, "Gov. Chiles Dead," *Tallahassee Democrat,* December 13, 1998.

708. Brent Kallestad, "GOP adviser: Chiles stole election," *Lakeland Ledger,* November 7, 1995.

709. Kevin Metz, "Chiles decries deception," *Tampa Tribune,* December 20, 1995; Bill Cotterell, "Gov. Chiles Dead," *Tallahassee Democrat,* December 13, 1998.

710. Kevin Metz, "Chiles decries deception," *Tampa Tribune,* December 20, 1995.

711. Martin Merzer, "Governor Chiles dies: An enduring legacy of service," *Miami Herald,* December 13, 1998.

712. Art Carlson interviews Rhea Chiles, September to November 2003, Art Carlson Interviews.

713. Gerald Ensley, "Tallahassee mourns its neighbor," *Tallahassee Democrat,* December 17, 1998.

714. Tim Nickens, "The wit and wisdom of a he-coon," *Miami Herald,* December 18, 1994.

715. Mike Williams, "Florida's governor is wounded—but still walkin'—after the most bruising campaign of his long political life," *Atlanta Journal-Constitution,* November 13, 1994.

716. Tim Nickens, "Code 'Crazy,'" *Miami Herald,* January 6, 1995.

717. Mark Hollis, "Regulations dogged 'Chief Coon's house,'" *Lakeland Ledger,* January 4, 1996.

718. Mark Hollis, "Chiles' ambitions mired in red tape." *Lakeland Ledger,* January 4, 1996.

719. Gerald Ensley, "Tallahassee mourns its neighbor," *Tallahassee Democrat,* December 17, 1998.

720. Philip K. Howard, *The Death of Common Sense* (New York: Warner Books, 1994), 10-11.

721. William Booth, "Florida Seeks End to Rule By the Book," *Washington Post,* March 14, 1995.

722. Jac Wilder Versteeg, "Still Walkin' The Walk," *Palm Beach Post,* October 30, 1994.

723. Mickey Higginbotham, "Florida's best-loved 'Cracker' to be sworn in a final time." *Tallahassee Democrat,* January 3, 1995.

724. Jackie Hallifax, "Center Carries on Governor's Passion," *Lakeland Ledger,* December 16, 1998.

725. Charlton Tebeau and William Marina, *A History of Florida* (Coral Gables: University of Miami Press, 1999), 523.

726. Ibid., 524.

727. "Chiles soars to unprecedented popularity," *Tampa Tribune,* October 8, 1996.

728. William J. Clinton, "Remarks at a Memorial Service for Lawton Chiles," January 28, 1999, *Public Papers of the Presidents of the United States: William J. Clinton,* Book I (Washington, DC: U.S. Government Printing Office, 1999), 116-117, http://www.gpo.gov/fdsys/pkg/PPP-1999-book1/html/PPP-1999-book1-doc-pg116.htm

729. William Booth, "From Fla. Voters, a Mixed Verdict," *Washington Post,* November 7, 1996.

730. 1997 State of the State Address, Florida State Archives.

731. David Royse, "Chiles: man of colorful quips, but few letters." *Tampa Tribune,* December 12,

1999.

732. Robert Clendening, "Chiles talks campaign issues at Pinellas fund-raising rally," *St. Petersburg Times,* March 15, 1976.

733. Paul Anderson, "Graham, Chiles score easy wins, senator outpaces Van Poole, 'Walkin Lawton' gets a third term," *Miami Herald,* November 3, 1982.

734. Diane Rado, "Lawmakers split on Chiles' religion," *St. Petersbug Times,* June 18, 1992.

735. Compiled by Jill A. Elish, "In Their Own Words."

736. Mary Ellen Klas, Scott Shifrel, and Meg James, "Session opens to live TV, tardy Chiles." *Palm Beach Post,* March 6, 1996.

737. Gary Fineout, "Williams' bill has more than a prayer in Senate/The Senate Education Committee passed a measure already approved by the House," *Tallahassee Democrat,* April 24, 1996.

738. "Bill targets smaller classes, prayer," *Bradenton Herald,* April 18, 1996.

739. Diane Rado, "Senate committee passes bill to allow school prayer," *St. Petersburg Times,* April 24, 1996.

740. Rob Chepak, "Senate OKs limited school prayer," *Tampa Tribune,* May 3, 1996.

741. Meg James, "Senate OKs oral prayer in schools: Measure covers only noncompulsory events." *Palm Beach Post,* May 3, 1996.

742. "Prayer goes to school," Editorial, *Miami Herald,* April 23, 1996.

743. Viola Gienger, "School Prayer Rides Election Year Wave," *Palm Beach Post,* March 16, 1994.

744. Meg James, "Senate OKs oral prayer in schools: Measure covers only noncompulsory events." *Palm Beach Post,* May 3, 1996.

745. Diane Rado, "Chiles prays over school-prayer bill," *St. Petersburg Times,* May 22, 1996.

746. Meg James, "Keep prayers in hearts, not in schools, Chiles says in veto." *Palm Beach Post,* June 1, 1996.

747. Randolph Pendleton, "School prayer bill veto likely," *Florida Times-Union,* May 31, 1996.

748. Bill Cotterell, "One religious leader sees veto in prayer bill's future: Rabbi Stanley Garfein was one of eight religious leaders who met privately with Governor Chiles," *Tallahassee Democrat,* May 23, 1996.

749. Diane Rado, "Chiles advised to veto school prayer," *St. Petersburg Times,* May 30, 1996.

750. Meg James, "Keep prayers in hearts, not in schools, Chiles says in veto." *Palm Beach Post,* June 1, 1996.

751. Steve Bousquet, "Jewish leaders urge prayer-bill veto," *Miami Herald,* May 22, 1996.

752. Bill Cotterell, "Chiles vetoes school prayer: Government, he says, has no business intruding in the very personal matters of prayer and religion," *Tallahassee Democrat,* June 1, 1996.

753. "Chiles at his best," Editorial, *St. Petersburg Times,* June 4, 1996.

754. Michael Griffin, "Poll: Prayer veto fails to diminish Chiles' job rating." *Orlando Sentinel,* June 29, 1996.

755. Margaret Talev and David Cox, "More to legacy than just politics," *Tampa Tribune,* December 13, 1998.

756. Tebeau and Marina, *A History of Florida,* 524.

757. Colburn, *From Yellow Dog Democrats to Red State Republicans*, 152.

758. MacKay, *How Florida Happened*, 189-199.

759. Elizabeth Gleick, "Tobacco Blues," *Time,* March 11, 1996, http://www.time.com/time/subscriber/article/0,33009,984241-1,00.html.

760. Don Yaeger, "Where There's Smoke . . ." *Florida Trend,* October 1996.

761. "The 'He-Coon' speaks," *St. Petersburg Times,* December 14, 1998.

762. Colburn, *From Yellow Dog Democrats to Red State Republicans,* 153.

763. MacKay, *How Florida Happened*, 189-199.

764. Art Carlson interviews Mallory Horne, September to November 2003, Art Carlson Interviews.

765. Lucy Morgan, "Tobacco law nearly went up in smoke," *St. Petersburg Times,* March 15, 1996.

766. Tyler Bridges, "Chiles triumphs over big tobacco," *Miami Herald,* May 5, 1996.

767. MacKay, *How Florida Happened,* 197.

768. Adam Yeomans, "A good ol' boy with an offbeat sense of humor," *Tallahassee Democrat,* December 17, 1998.

769. Yaeger, "Where There's Smoke . . ."

770. David Fonvielle, "Making Big Tobacco Pay The Damages," *Law Talk, A Quarterly Publication of Fonvielle Hinkle & Lewis,* Special Edition, July 2001.

771. Ibid.

772. Yaeger, "Where There's Smoke . . ."

773. Fonvielle, "Making Big Tobacco Pay The Damages."

774. Yaeger, "Where There's Smoke . . ."

775. Fonvielle, "Making Big Tobacco Pay The Damages."

776. Ibid.

777. John Schwartz, "A Fee Fight Worth $2.8 Billion," *Washington Post,* December 2, 1997.

778. John Schwartz, "Cigarette Makers Settle Florida Suit For $11.3 Billion," *Washington Post,* August 26, 1997.

779. JudyDoyle and Gary Fineout, "Chiles remembered for courage, vision," *Tallahassee Democrat,* December 13, 1998.

780. Compiled by Jill A. Elish, "In Their Own Words."

781. Mark Silva, "Uninsured children to win big in tobacco settlement," *Tallahassee Democrat,* December 12, 1998.

782. JudyDoyle and Gary Fineout, "Chiles remembered for courage, vision," *Tallahassee Democrat,* December 13, 1998.

783. Martin Merzer, "Governor Chiles dies: An enduring legacy of service," *Miami Herald,* December 13, 1998.

784. David Royse, "Chiles: man of colorful quips, but few letters." *Tampa Tribune,* December 12, 1999.

785. Bill Cotterell, "Gov. Chiles Dead," *Tallahassee Democrat,* December 13, 1998.

786. Martin Merzer, "Governor Chiles dies: An enduring legacy of service," *Miami Herald,* December 13, 1998.

787. Meg James and Karen Branch, "Many express warm tributes," *Miami Herald,* December 13, 1998.

788. Mike Denham interviews Snow Martin Jr. 4-16-04, Dr. Mike Denham Interviews.

789. Mike Denham interviews Bill Ellsworth 2-25-05, Dr. Mike Denham Interviews.

790. Mary Ellen Klas interview with Governor Lawton Chiles, November 1998, personal papers of April Salter.

791. Tom Fiedler, "Chiles reflected: 'there is nothing that I have to do,'" *Miami Herald,* December 13, 1998.

792. Kathleen Laufenberg, "Healthy Start: Chiles' legacy." *Tallahassee Democrat,* December 20, 1998.

793. Norman Morgan, "Recalling 40 Years of Public Life," *Lakeland Ledger,* December 24, 1997.

794. Bill Cotterell, "Grown children fondly remember father," *Tallahassee Democrat,* December 16, 1998.

795. "The 'He-Coon' speaks," *St. Petersburg Times,* December 14, 1998.

796. Charles Elmore, "'Old he-coon' never lost a vote in 40 years," *Palm Beach Post,* December 13, 1998.

797. Tom Fiedler, "Chiles reflected: 'there is nothing that I have to do,'" *Miami Herald,* December 13, 1998.

798. Alan Judd, "Chiles was found eight hours after death," *Lakeland Ledger,* December 14, 1998.

799. Tyler Bridges, "Chiles demanded privacy and often spent long hours alone," *Tallahassee Democrat,* December 15, 1998.

800. Bill Cotterell, "Inquiry firms up details of Chiles' last day," *Tallahassee Democrat,* December 30, 1998.

801. Martin Merzer, "Governor Chiles dies: An enduring legacy of service," *Miami Herald,* December 13, 1998.

802. Canter Brown, *None Can Have Richer Memories,* 281.

803. Randolph Pendleton, "Through long career Chiles was always 'one of the guys,'" *Florida Times-Union,* December 13, 1998.

804. Lloyd Dunkelberger, "Last Cracker Governor," *Lakeland Ledger,* December 13, 1998.

805. David Cox and Michelle Pellemans, "Chiles' faith 'was core of who he was,'" *Tampa Tribune,* December 14, 1998.

806. Catherine McNaught, "Pine coffin is just what the governor wanted," *Tallahassee Democrat*, December 16, 1998.

807. Alan Judd, "Chiles was found eight hours after death," *Lakeland Ledger*, December 14, 1998.

808. Lucy Morgan, "Chiles' last journey to recall his famous first," *St. Petersburg Times*, December 14, 1998.

809. Bill Cotterell, "Grown children fondly remember father," *Tallahassee Democrat*, December 16, 1998.

810. Art Carlson interviews Rhea Chiles, September to November 2003, Art Carlson Interviews.

811. Art Carlson interviews Senator Sam Nunn, September – November 2003, Art Carlson Interviews.

812. Margaret Talev and David Cox, "State salutes favorite son," *Tampa Tribune*, December 16, 1998.

813. Troy Moon, "Down but not out yet, Century dreams of a kinder life in 21st century," *Pensacola News-Journal*, December 30, 1999.

814. Mark Silva and Tina Cummings, "'Goodbye, He-Coon': Chiles' Last Ride Follows Familiar Route," *Miami Herald* December 16, 1998.

815. Thomas Pfankuch, "Chiles back in Century," *Florida Times-Union*, December 15, 1998.

816. Mark Silva and Tina Cummings, "'Goodbye, He-Coon': Chiles' Last Ride Follows Familiar Route," *Miami Herald* December 16, 1998.

817. Brian Crowley, "Panhandle remembers Gov. Chiles." *Palm Beach Post*, December 16, 1998.

818. Tim Nickens, "Hundreds line roads for Governor Chiles." *St. Petersburg Times*, December 16, 1998.

819. Lloyd Dunkelberger, Mark Hollis, and Alan Judd, "No cynicism toward death of Gov. Chiles," *Gainesville Sun*, December 20, 1998.

820. Thomas Pfankuch and Randolph Pendleton, "Thousands line route of Chiles' hearse," *Florida Times-Union*, December 16, 1998.

821. Mark Silva and Tina Cummings, "'Goodbye, He-Coon': Chiles' Last Ride Follows Familiar Route," *Miami Herald* December 16, 1998; Michael Griffin, and Linda Kleindienst, "People of Florida mourn 1 of their own," *Orlando Sentinel*, December 16, 1998.

822. Bill Cotterell, "From Century one last time," *Tallahassee Democrat*, December 16, 1998.

823. Alan Judd, "Touring Familiar Roads," *Lakeland Ledger*, December 16, 1998.

824. "Chiles' last trip closing a circle," *Palm Beach Post*, December 15, 1998.

825. Thomas Pfankuch, "Chiles back in Century," *Florida Times-Union*, December 15, 1998.

826. Alan Judd, "Touring Familiar Roads," *Lakeland Ledger*, December 16, 1998.

827. Mark Silva and Tina Cummings, "'Goodbye, He-Coon': Chiles' Last Ride Follows Familiar Route," *Miami Herald* December 16, 1998.

828. Thomas Pfankuch and Randolph Pendleton, "Thousands line route of Chiles' hearse," *Florida Times-Union*, December 16, 1998; Mark Silva and Tina Cummings, "'Goodbye, He-Coon': Chiles' Last Ride Follows Familiar Route," *Miami Herald* December 16, 1998.

829. Bill Cotterell, "From Century one last time," *Tallahassee Democrat*, December 16, 1998.

830. Tim Nickens, "Hundreds line roads for Governor Chiles." *St. Petersburg Times,* December 16, 1998.

831. Ibid.

832. Brian Crowley, "Panhandle remembers Gov. Chiles." *Palm Beach Post,* December 16, 1998.

833. Bill Cotterell, "From Century one last time," *Tallahassee Democrat,* December 16, 1998.

834. "Chiles' last trip closing a circle," *Palm Beach Post,* December 15, 1998.

835. Margaret Talev and David Cox, "State salutes favorite son," *Tampa Tribune,* December 16, 1998.

836. Mark Silva and Tina Cummings, "'Goodbye, He-Coon': Chiles' Last Ride Follows Familiar Route," *Miami Herald* December 16, 1998.

837. Alan Judd, "Touring Familiar Roads," *Lakeland Ledger,* December 16, 1998.

838. Wayne Linke, "Gov. Chiles takes sentimental journey," *Defuniak Herald,* December 17, 1998.

839. Curtis Morgan, "Small Towns Suited Chiles: 'He Talked to Everyone,'" *Miami Herald,* December 16, 1998.

840. Mark Silva and Tina Cummings, "'Goodbye, He-Coon': Chiles' Last Ride Follows Familiar Route," *Miami Herald* December 16, 1998.

841. Brian Crowley, "Panhandle remembers Gov. Chiles." *Palm Beach Post,* December 16, 1998.

842. Thomas Pfankuch and Randolph Pendleton, "Thousands line route of Chiles' hearse," *Florida Times-Union,* December 16, 1998.

843. Bill Cotterell, "From Century one last time," *Tallahassee Democrat,* December 16, 1998.

844. Mark Silva and Tina Cummings, "'Goodbye, He-Coon': Chiles' Last Ride Follows Familiar Route," *Miami Herald* December 16, 1998.

845. Margaret Talev and David Cox, "State salutes favorite son," *Tampa Tribune,* December 16, 1998.

846. Lloyd Dunkelberger, Mark Hollis, and Alan Judd, "No cynicism toward death of Gov. Chiles," *Gainesville Sun,* December 20, 1998.

847. Alan Judd, "Touring Familiar Roads," *Lakeland Ledger,* December 16, 1998.

848. Margaret Talev and David Cox, "State salutes favorite son," *Tampa Tribune,* December 16, 1998.

849. Alan Judd, "Touring Familiar Roads," *Lakeland Ledger,* December 16, 1998.

850. Tim Nickens, "Hundreds line roads for Governor Chiles." *St. Petersburg Times,* December 16, 1998.

851. Mark Silva and Tina Cummings, "'Goodbye, He-Coon': Chiles' Last Ride Follows Familiar Route," *Miami Herald* December 16, 1998.

852. Compiled by Jill A. Elish, "In Their Own Words."

853. Jan Pudlow, "Small-town Floridians line up to pay big-time respect to Chiles," *Tallahassee Democrat,* December 16, 1998.

854. Bill Cotterell, "From Century one last time," *Tallahassee Democrat,* December 16, 1998; Alan Judd, "Touring Familiar Roads," *Lakeland Ledger,* December 16, 1998.

855. Thomas Pfankuch and Randolph Pendleton, "Thousands line route of Chiles' hearse," *Florida*

Times-Union, December 16, 1998.

856. Ibid.

857. Jan Pudlow, "Small-town Floridians line up to pay big-time respect to Chiles," *Tallahassee Democrat,* December 16, 1998.

858. Ibid.

859. Julie Hauserman, "Mother prays for girl's savior," *St. Petersburg Times,* December 16, 1998.

860. Thomas Pfankuch, "Visitors pay respects to family at mansion," *Florida Times-Union,* December 17, 1998.

861. Ibid.

862. Thomas Pfankuch and Randolph Pendleton, "Thousands line route of Chiles' hearse," *Florida Times-Union,* December 16, 1998; Bill Cotterell, "From Century one last time," *Tallahassee Democrat,* December 16, 1998.

863. Thomas Pfankuch and Randolph Pendleton, "Thousands line route of Chiles' hearse," *Florida Times-Union,* December 16, 1998.

864. Hollis, Mark. "Floridians pay tribute to Chiles, 'a man of the people.'" *Gainesville Sun.* December 16, 1998.

865. Art Carlson interviews Dubose Ausley, September to November 2003, Art Carlson Interviews.

866. Mark Silva and Tina Cummings, "'Goodbye, He-Coon': Chiles' Last Ride Follows Familiar Route," *Miami Herald* December 16, 1998; Bill Cotterell, "From Century one last time," *Tallahassee Democrat,* December 16, 1998.

867. Melanie Yeager, "All walks came out to say goodbye to Walkin' Lawton," *Tallahassee Democrat,* December 16, 1998.

868. Alan Judd, "Touring Familiar Roads," *Lakeland Ledger,* December 16, 1998.

869. Bill Cotterell, "From Century one last time," *Tallahassee Democrat,* December 16, 1998.

870. Melanie Yeager, "Vignettes," *Tallahassee Democrat,* December 17, 1998.

871. Gary Haber and Kevin Horan, "Friends recall Chiles' human touch," *Bradenton Herald,* December 13, 1998.

872. Julie Hauserman "Mansion opens its doors, heart for one last goodbye," *St. Petersburg Times,* December 17, 1998.

873. Shirish Date, "Mourners pack Old Capitol to bid Gov. Chiles farewell," *Palm Beach Post,* December 16, 1998.

874. Randolph Pendleton and Jim Saunders, "Voice of the 'little guy,'" *Florida Times-Union,* December 17, 1998.

875. Bill Varian, vignette, in Melanie Yeager, "Vignettes," *Tallahassee Democrat,* December 17, 1998.

876. Tim Nickens, "Florida salutes Chiles on his final walk," *St. Petersburg Times,* December 17, 1998.

877. Jackie Hallifax, "Chiles' place in Florida history assured," *Tampa Tribune,* December 20, 1998.

878. Tim Nickens, "Florida salutes Chiles on his final walk," *St. Petersburg Times,* December 17, 1998.

879. Jan Pudlow, "Rhea Chiles bravely greeted visitors for more than two hours," *Tallahassee Democrat,* December 17, 1998; David Nitkin, "Florida's youth honor Chiles' legacy," *Orlando Sentinel,* December 18, 1998.

880. Julie Hauserman, "Mansion opens its doors, heart for one last goodbye," *St. Petersburg Times,* December 17, 1998.

881. Jan Pudlow, "Rhea Chiles bravely greeted visitors for more than two hours," *Tallahassee Democrat,* December 17, 1998.

882. Margaret Talev, "State's children say goodbye." *Tampa Tribune,* December 18, 1998.

883. Randolph Pendleton, "Children say goodbye to Chiles," *Florida Times-Union,* December 18, 1998.

884. Margaret Talev, "State's children say goodbye." *Tampa Tribune,* December 18, 1998.

885. Tina Cummings, "Students statewide pay tribute to Chiles," *Miami Herald,* December 18, 1998.

886. The Associated Press, "Children recall Chiles with their words, silence," *Gainesville Sun,* December 18, 1998.

887. Sharon Rauch, "Children remember Lawton Chiles," *Tallahassee Democrat,* December 18, 1998.

888. John Wark, "A man (of Florida) in full," *Tampa Tribune,* December 19, 1998.

Bibliography

Because sources for this book are predominantly oral interviews and newspaper articles, archived interviews follow the general listings and are followed by a list of newspapers and dates of issues.

General

Ashmore, Harry S. *An Epitaph for Dixie.* New York: W.W. Norton, 1957.

Baker Block Museum Journal. North Okaloosa Historical Association. http://www.rootsweb.com/~flbbm/baker.htm. 2007.

Barone, Michael, Grant Ujifusa, Douglas Matthews. *The Almanac of American Politics.* Boston: Gambit Publisher, 1972.

Black, Earle. *Southern Governors and Civil Rights: Racial Segregation as a Campaign Issue in the Second Reconstruction.* Cambridge: Harvard University Press, 1976.

Brown, Canter, Jr. *In the Midst of All That Makes Life Worth Living: Polk County, Florida, to 1940.* Tallahassee: Sentry Press, 2001.

Brown, Canter, Jr. *None Can Have Richer Memories: Polk County, Florida 1940-2000.* Tampa: University of Tampa Press, 2005.

Burt, Al. *The Tropic of Cracker.* Gainesville: University Press of Florida, 1999.

Caro, Robert A. *The Years of Lyndon Johnson: Master of the Senate.* New York: Vintage Books, 2003.

Chiles, Lawton. Progress Reports #1 – #24 in *The Walk That Inspired Florida: Progress Reports from the Historic Walk of Gov. Lawton Chiles from Century to Key Largo, Spring – Summer 1970.* Lawton Chiles Foundation. http://chilesfoundation.org/lawton-chiles/the_walk/. Printed as Appendix A in this volume.

Chiles, Office of Senator Lawton. "A Walk through the Record of Lawton Chiles, U.S. Senator, Florida." 1976. University of Florida Archive, Series 2a, Box 1.

Clinton, William J. "Remarks at a Memorial Service for Lawton Chiles." January 28, 1999. *Public Papers of the Presidents of the United States: William J. Clinton.* Book I. Washington, DC: U.S. Government Printing Office, 1999. http://www.gpo.gov/fdsys/pkg/PPP-1999-book1/html/PPP-1999-book1-doc-pg116.htm

Colburn, David R. *From Yellow Dog Democrats to Red State Republicans: Florida and Its Politics since 1940*. Gainesville: University Press of Florida, 2007.

Colburn, David and Lance DeHaven-Smith. *Government in the Sunshine State: Florida Since Statehood*. Gainesville: University Press of Florida, 1999.

_____. *Florida's Megatrends: Critical Issues in Florida*. Gainesville: University Press of Florida, 2002.

Crew, Robert E., Jr. "Florida: Lawton M. Chiles, Jr., Reinventing State Government." In *Governors and Hard Times*, edited by Thad Beyle. Washington, DC: Congressional Quarterly, 1992.

Date, Jeb S. V.: *America's Next Bush*. New York: Penguin Books, 2007.

Dyckman, Martin. *Floridian of His Century: The Courage of LeRoy Collins*. Gainesville: University Press of Florida, 2006.

Elish, Jill A., compiler. "In Their Own Words." *Florida Living*, April 1999.

Flekke, Mary M., and Randall M. MacDonald. *Lakeland*. Charleston: Arcadia Publishing, 2005.

Fonvielle, David. "Making Big Tobacco Pay the Damages." *Law Talk: A Quarterly Publication of Fonvielle Hinkle & Lewis*. Special Edition, July 2001.

Gleick, Elizabeth. "Tobacco Blues." *Time*, March 11, 1996.

Harth, Morris, ed. *The New York Times Encyclopedic Almanac, 1972*. New York: New York Times, 1971.

Howard, Philip K. *The Death of Common Sense*. New York: Warner Books, 1994.

Hubbell, Larry. "Ronald Reagan as Presidential Symbol Maker: The Federal Bureaucrat as Loafer, Incompetent Buffoon, Good Ole Boy, and Tyrant." *American Review of Public Administration* 21 (3) [1999]: 237-53.

Hunt, Bruce. *Visiting Small-Town Florida*. Sarasota: Pineapple Press, 2003.

Key, V. O., Jr. *Southern Politics in State and Nation*. Knoxville: University of Tennessee Press, 1949.

Logue, Cal. *The Oratory of Southern Demagogues*. Baton Rouge: LSU Press, 1981.

Longman, Philip. "It Gets Worse." *Florida Trend*, September 1992.

_____. "Who Can Get To Chiles." *Florida Trend*, January 1991.

Lynch, Hilda Maness. "Lawton Chiles: Democratic Senator from Florida." *Ralph Nader Congress Project: Citizens Look at Congress*. New York: Grossman Publishers, 1972.

MacKay, Buddy, with Rick Edmonds. *How Florida Happened: The Political Education of Buddy MacKay*. Gainesville: University Press of Florida, 2010.

Mormino, Gary. *Land of Sunshine, State of Dreams*. Gainesville: University Press of Florida, 2005.

Nelson, Gil. *Exploring Wild Northwest Florida: A Guide to Finding the Natural Areas and Wildlife of the Panhandle*. Sarasota: Pineapple Press, 1995.

Newton, Michael. *The Invisible Empire: The Ku Klux Klan in Florida*. Gainesville: University Press of Florida, 2001.

Ortiz, Paul. *Emancipation Betrayed: The Hidden History of Black Organizing and White Violence in Florida from Reconstruction to the Bloody Election of 1920*. Berkeley: University of California Press, 2005.

Provenzo, Eugene F., and Asterie Baker Provenzo. *In the Eye of Hurricane Andrew*. Gainesville: University Press of Florida, 2002.

Rosenthal, Alan. *The Third House: Lobbyists and Lobbying in the States*. 2nd ed. Washington, DC: CQ Press, 2001.

Safire, William. *Lend Me Your Ears: Great Speeches in History*. New York: W. W. Norton, 2004.

Smith, Hedrick. *The Power Game: How Washington Works*. New York: Random House, 1988.

Ste. Claire, Dana. *Cracker: The Cracker Culture in Florida History*. Gainesville: University Press of Florida, 2006.

Steed, Robert P., and Laurence W. Moreland, eds. *Writing Southern Politics: Contemporary Interpretations and Future Directions*. Lexington: University Press of Kentucky, 2006.

Strutin, Michal. *Florida State Parks*. Seattle: Mountaineers Books, 2000.

Tebeau, Charlton, and William Marina. *A History of Florida*. Coral Gables: University of Miami Press, 1999.

Thrift, Charles T., Jr. *Of Fact and Fancy . . . at Florida Southern College*. Lakeland: Florida Southern College Press, 1979.

Waitley, Douglas. *Best Backroads of Florida*. Sarasota: Pineapple Press, 2003.

"Walkin' Lawton Fusses Over Budgets." *The South,* October 1978.

Williams, T. Harry. *Huey Long*. New York: Alfred A. Knopf, 1969.

Wilson, James Q. *Bureaucracy: What Agencies Do and Why They Do It*. New York: Basic Books, 1989.

Wolf, Kathy, and Sandra Friend. *An Explorer's Guide: North Florida & the Florida Panhandle.* Woodstock: Countryman Press, 2007.

Yaeger, Don. "Where There's Smoke . . ." *Florida Trend,* October 1996.

Archived Interviews

Art Carlson Interviews. Corporation collection of Ron Sachs Communications. Tallahassee, FL.

Dr. Mike Denham Interviews. Florida Southern College's Center for Florida History. Lakeland, FL.

Newspapers

Atlanta Journal-Constitution, November 13, 1994. December 17, 1998.

Bradenton Herald, April 18, 1996. December 13, 1998.

DeFuniak Herald, December 17, 1998.

Deland Sun News, March 18, 1970.

Florida Times-Union, July 7, 1976. May 31, 1996. December 13, 15-18, 20, 1998. March 31, 2012.

Gainesville Sun, February 5, 1992. December 13, 16-18, 20, 1998.

Lakeland Ledger, April 25-26, 1940. September 10, 1944. May 11; July 8-25; August 15; September 5, 10, 16; October 26, 1958. March 17, 18, 25, 29; April 5, 14; June 20, 25; July 6, 12; September 30; October 1; November 10; December 18, 1970. January 3, 1971. November 7, 1995. January 4, 1996. December 24, 1997. December 13, 14, 16, 20, 1998. July 22; September 26, 2002. February 3; November 22, 2003. January 17, 2005.

Lakeland News, April 26, 1940.

Miami Herald, August 20, 21, 23, 25; October 11, 14, 28; November 15, 1970. August 22; October 7, 28, 31; November 3, 4, 7; December 2, 1982. November 25; December 7, 1984. April 14, 15, 17, 1990. December 22, 1991. January 19; May 17; August 24, 30, 1992. October 23, 1993. November 2, 3, 18, 1994. January 6, 1995. April 23; May 5, 22, 1996. December 13, 16, 18, 1998.

Milton Press Gazette, April 2, 1970.

New York Times, March 12, 1972.

News Chief, December 12, 1999.

Orlando Sentinel, October 19, 1969. August 8, 1990. December 23, 1991. August 24, 1992. October 21, 1994. June 29, 1996. December 15, 16, 18, 20, 1998. February 24, 2008.

Palm Beach Post, May 13; August 21; November 4, 1990. September 27, 1992. March 16; October 30; November 2, 1994. August 19, 1995. March 6; May 3; June 1, 1996. December 13, 15, 16, 1998.

Pensacola News Journal, February 5, 1992. December 16, 30, 1999. March 10, 2002.

Polk County Record, January 2, 16; March 1, 5, 1940.

St. Petersburg Times, October 14, 15, 19, 25; November 4, 5, 7, 9, 1970. March 15; November 4, 1976. April 29; August 29; September 2; October 14, 21, 26; November 8, 11, 18, 23, 27; December 5, 6, 11, 1990. January 6, 7; March 14; December 12, 1991. January 5; May 21; June 2, 18; July 19; August 24; September 20, 27, 1992. February 5; September 9, 1993. August 7; November 4, 9, 1994. March 15; April 24; May 22, 30, June 4, 1996. December 13, 14, 16, 17, 1998. August 18, 2002. April 3, 2005.

Sun-Sentinel, April 14, 1990. January 13, 1991. August 24, 1992. December 13, 1998.

Tallahassee Democrat, November 16, 1969. April 4, 1970. March 6; April 1; October 1, 1991. January 3, 1995. April 24; May 23; June 1, 1996. December 12-18, 20, 30, 1998.

Tampa Bay News Weekly, August 22, 2007.

Tampa Times, March 19, 1970.

Tampa Tribune, September 10, 1958. March 19, 23; October 27, 28, 30; November 4, 8, 1970. August 25, 26, 1992. October 24; November 9, 1994. December 20, 1995. May 3; October 8, 1996. December 13, 14, 16, 18, 19, 21, 1998. December 12, 1999.

Washington Post, November 13, 1969. September 6; October 19, 25; November 22, 1970. May 10, 1971. March 9, 1973. December 13, 1984. July 2, 1990. March 14, 1995. November 7, 1996. August 26; December 2, 1997.

Washington Star, June 16, 1975.